# ·HISTORIOGRAPHY·

# H·I·S·T·O·R·I·O·G·R·A·P·H·Y

*Ancient, Medieval,*
*&*
*Modern*

## ·ERNST BREISACH·

Third Edition

THE UNIVERSITY OF CHICAGO PRESS

*Chicago & London*

The University of Chicago Press, Chicago 60637
The University of Chicago Press, Ltd., London
© 1983, 1994, 2007 by The University of Chicago
All rights reserved. First edition published 1983.
Second edition published 1994. Third edition published 2007.
Printed in the United States of America
16  15  14  13  12  11  10  09      2  3  4  5

ISBN-13: 978-0-226-07282-1 (cloth)
ISBN-13: 978-0-226-07283-8 (paper)
ISBN-10: 0-226-07282-7 (cloth)
ISBN-10: 0-226-07283-5 (paper)

Library of Congress Cataloging-in-Publication Data
Breisach, Ernst.
   Historiography : ancient, medieval, and modern / Ernst Breisach.—3rd ed.
      p. cm.
   Includes bibliographical references and index.
   ISBN-13: 978-0-226-07282-1 (cloth : alk. paper)
   ISBN-10: 0-226-07282-7 (cloth : alk. paper)
   ISBN-13: 978-0-226-07283-8 (pbk. : alk. paper)
   ISBN-10: 0-226-07283-5 (pbk. : alk. paper)   1. Historiography.   I. Title.
   D13.B686  2007
   907.2—dc22
                                                        2007010112

♾ The paper used in this publication meets the minimum requirements
of the American National Standard for Information Sciences—
Permanence of Paper for Printed Library Materials, ANSI Z39.48-1992.

Ad Hermam
uxorem et sociam

# ·CONTENTS·

## ·6·

## ·7·

## ·8·

## ·9·

## ·10·

## ·11·

## ·12·

## ·13·

Contents

# ·23·

# ·24·

# ·25·

# ·26·

# ·27·

# ·28·

# ·29·

Contents

# ·PREFACE·

This book is not the result of a spur-of-the-moment decision or of its author's wish to ride a wave of fashion. Rather it grew over many years together with my fascination with historiographical problems. Again and again I confronted the question, Why has Western culture so persistently exhibited a concern for the past and produced so great a variety of historiographical interpretations? The expectation I held as a youthful historian, that I could find clear and ready answers, has long since yielded to a sense of awe for the complexity of the problem and the perplexing if not embarrassing realization that history, the discipline identified with reflection on the past, has no satisfactory account of its own career in English or any other language. In tranquil times that might not matter, although it seems hardly proper even then. But in the late twentieth century, when there is much talk about a crisis of historiography and when historians attempt to construct theories of history in order to justify the discipline and defend its territory, the lack of a comprehensive survey of historiography is more than an annoyance. It leads even historians to make ad hoc judgments on the nature and theory of history which—irony of ironies—fail to understand the problems of historiography historically.

There exist excellent monographs on aspects and periods of historiography. They are most valuable but cannot substitute for a continuous account. Only in the context of the whole of Western historiography's development can we truly fathom the role and nature of history as a human endeavor. The desire to demonstrate that whole made me stubbornly stress the main lines of development and reject the temptation to write a handbook or encyclopedia with the obligation inherent in such works to mention as many worthy historians and their works as possible. Neither did I, nor could I, trace all the influences and cross-influences exhaustively; a work of many volumes would have resulted and, in Sir Walter Raleigh's words, I fear that "the darkness of age and death would have covered it and me, long before the performance."

The present work, which shows the role history and historians have played in the various societies and phases of Western culture, proved substantially more difficult to write than a "Who wrote what, when" book. The latter would demand much time and patience but little sense of development or interpretation. Readers who fail to find expected names and works here should remember that this book is designed to narrate and interpret, not to recite lists. Omission signifies not a lack of distinction but only that the historian or the work was not needed to illustrate a development or the thought of a school. Readers will also notice that I have avoided judgments on historians and schools of thought. I entrust these judgments to the readers and to life. The former will wish for that freedom and the latter has its own ways of judging—harsh, relentless, and final. And if some modern historians have entered the story of historiography through achievements of a lesser magnitude than those of Thucydides, Tacitus, or Gibbon it is precisely because life's judgment on their worthiness is still outstanding. Finally, those who would have preferred a topical to a narrative account will find sufficient guidance in the detailed Table of Contents and the Index. As for dates, I have included many but relied in other instances on the context of narration to fix the time of a historiographical development. In addition, the life spans of the authors discussed are given in the Index.

My own expectations for this book are well measured. If the work will make discussions on the nature of history a bit more informed, help define the dimensions of the so-called crisis of history in a more realistic manner, kindle enthusiasm or simply respect for the discipline, and even lead some to read more in the works of past historians, its purpose will have been fulfilled and the many years of labor on it well spent.

At the beginning of all acknowledgments must stand the general and sincere one to the dozens of scholars who have written monographs on special periods and without whose labor my own would have been prolonged by many years. The select bibliography is in this sense also part of the acknowledgments. There were others who assisted me more directly in various ways: Eric Cochrane of the University of Chicago and Richard Mitchell of the University of Illinois, who critically reviewed some sections; colleagues at Western Michigan University, particularly Alan Brown, Albert Castel, Edward O. Elsasser, Robert Hahn, Paul Maier, Howard Mowen, and Dale Pattison, who helped me in many ways; Elizabeth White, who rendered editorial help; officials of Western Michigan University, who granted me two professional leaves; Opal Ellis and Becky Ryder, who patiently typed and retyped. My expression of gratefulness to them is no mere formality but the result of sincere appreciation.

# ·INTRODUCTION·

During the nineteenth century—often called the Golden Age of History—historians counseled kings, were leaders in the unification of Germany and Italy, gave a prime minister and a president to France, provided identities to new and old nations, inspired the young American nation in its mastery of a continent, endowed revolutions with the authority of the past, and ascended to the rank of scientists. Above all, they convinced most scholars that everything must be understood in terms of development; in short, historically. No wonder that Thomas Carlyle proclaimed history to be immortal: "Some nations have prophecy, some have not: but of all mankind, there is no tribe so rude that it has not attempted History."[1]

Today many smile not just about Carlyle's quaint language, but also about his cocksure confidence. Living in this skeptical age they miss in the passage a proper measure of doubt and caution, if not a share of their suspicion that history has become a bit old-fashioned. Had not the historians of the nineteenth century proclaimed that everybody and everything changes and that there are no timeless concepts? Could it be then that history's days have faded with those of the nineteenth century? Our age, these skeptics argue, may simply require new methods for and new approaches to the "final" explanation of human life or, as some would put it, new intellectual instruments for mastering the world; a world in which it no longer suffices to observe "how things had gradually come to be," as traditional historians have been doing, but one in which historians have to be content with unearthing the raw materials for the social scientists who alone explain, maybe even reorder, human life in a "scientific manner." More recently, others have exhorted historians to realize that the aim to reconstruct the past in its actuality—even imperfectly—was an illusion altogether. History was a special type of literature. Hence literary criticism and theory were the proper models of explanation.

Historians have reacted to such skepticism with bewilderment and, sometimes, with indignation. But in a world fond of new theories of history with either scientific or literary preferences, they have been increasingly drawn into theoretical discussions. When pressed to answer the query "Why history?" historians have fallen back on the long-standing defenses of history as a teacher of moral or practical lessons, an object of nostalgia, a justification for either old or new regimes, a gratification of human curiosity, a witness to God's power, and, of course, a science of its own kind. The history of historiography has shown the role these uses of history have played, mostly in combinations. Yet their pragmatic functions have pointed to a more basic insight. The claim of history to be perennial cannot be based on a limited list of functions; it can only be sustained by demonstrating the existence of a necessary link between history, as reflection on the past, and human life.

An examination of the list of functions history has performed over the centuries reveals that these functions stem from the central fact that human life is subject to the dictates of time. At this point it is best to refrain from asking what time is unless one wishes to share in the exasperation of an ancient questioner: "What, then, is time? If no one asks me, I know: if I wish to explain it to one that asketh, I know not" (St. Augustine). Psychologists, whose love for experiments and expressing results in numbers provides them with proper contemporary credentials, have in their way reaffirmed that the dimension of time is central to all of human existence. They have found that the span of time which we actually experience as "now," the "mental" present, is only a fraction of a second long. It does not matter that in everyday life we mean a longer time span when we refer to the present, the conclusion is inescapable that human life is never simply lived in the present alone but rather in three worlds: one that is, one that was, and one that will be (or better, that people envisioned to be). In theory we know these three worlds as separate concepts but we experience them as inextricably linked and as influencing each other in many ways. Every important new discovery about the past changes how we think about the present and what we expect of the future; on the other hand every change in the conditions of the present and in the expectations for the future revises our perception of the past. That linkage constitutes a nexus in life and hence in the historical study of life. One that is best called the historical nexus. Historians of historiography have discerned the historical nexuses people of the past have shaped in their lives as they have tried to make sense of the human condition—a condition marked by the full dimension of time, that is, change and continuity alike. The nexuses, with their concrete manifestations of change and continuity, have always testified to the unbreakable connection between life and historical thought.

Some readers may well consider such pondering on history to be one of those strange flowers from the philosopher's garden. Not at all; the existence of an inescapable link between past, present, and future, which destroys history's image as an activity resembling idle rummaging in a bag of dry leaves and makes it into an activity necessary for human life, is experienced in daily life by everybody. There we observe how expectations for the future turn first into the realities of the present and then become the memories of the past—whether it be the fading of day into night, the change of seasons, the rise and fall of governments and states, or our own maturing and aging. They all testify to the continuous "flow" of time, although at a first look they accentuate the phenomenon of change. However, if we were to conclude that change is the only fundamental aspect of human life we would err seriously. Histories of seemingly unconnected changes, even if they were brilliantly written, would affect the reader like a thousand-hour-long look through a kaleidoscope; at first the observer is gripped by a fascination with the ever-changing patterns, then by increasing boredom, and finally by a deep sense of futility. History cannot for long remain the record of changes alone because that would deny the true nature of human life in which the experience of change is counterbalanced by that of continuity. Individuals and groups have long since discovered that even in the aftermath of the most radical revolutions the "new age" still carries many marks of the past. This continuity displeases advocates of sudden and complete change but contributes to human life a sense of stability, security, and even comfort. Once we accept that human life is marked both by change as that which makes past, present, and future different from each other and continuity as that which links them together, we begin to understand why historians have played so central a role in Western civilization. They have designed the great reconciliations between past, present, and future, always cognizant of both change and continuity. In other words, they have made sense of or, as some would put it, have given meaning to human life without denying its development throughout time. This link between life and historiography also explains why in generation after generation and in society after society historians have created ever new interpretations of the past. Those who use these changing views of the past for proving that historical truth is unreliable ignore the fact that it is life which goes on creating the ever different worlds—not quite new, but also not quite the same—to which historians must respond. All other branches of scholarship dealing with human life have so far shared in this failure to bring forth the unchanging truth, although many of them have claimed timelessness for their theories and insights.

The task of historians of historiography then does not seem too difficult to describe; it is to trace the ways in which people in Western culture have reflected on the past and what these reflections have told them about human life as it passes continuously from past to present to future. But time is not a type of space in which things happen, but it rather is interwoven into all aspects of life at any given moment. It introduces a tension into human existence between inescapable change and the human need for continuity. All of that happens in awareness of the unalterable linearity of individual and collective lives.

Historical accounts tell of the events and thoughts of people in the past—all of them marked by the historical nexuses that guided these people. Historians of historiography record how life tested and modified these nexuses often in dramatic fashions. But how should historians of historiography relate that seemingly wave-like development, ever rising and falling? They could simply compile an inventory of past historical views, perhaps even produce an encyclopedia of historiography. But that would deny the assertion by historians that chronological sequence is crucially important. Yet it would settle little if one arranged narrative portraits of historians and their views chronologically, as pictures are arranged in a gallery along a corridor. It still would leave unresolved the all-important question whether there is more to historiographical development than a record of historiographical views that reflect merely the idiosyncratic attitudes of period after period. The life experiences and insights gained in these periods would become invalid outside of their settings. Even modern historical science would be peculiar just to our period and have no special claim to universal validity. These arrangers have discerned no inherent direction in historiography or indeed in life itself.

In contrast, other historians of historiography have given preference to those historians whose views have presumably helped guide historiographical development toward a clear and known goal. By far the best known and presently most influential version of this view has equated the story of historiography with the emergence of the modern historical science. In their accounts these historians of historiography sort the wheat from the chaff, that is, they separate in all of past historiography those views which have contributed to the forming of the modern science of history from those which were based on "wrong" perceptions; the former earn praise, the latter reproach.

No simple technical trick enables us to make an easy choice between these two views or others. Once the link between history writing and the human condition is grasped in all its complexity, simple solutions vanish. Aware of that, I have endeavored to trace the complex story of history writing in a manner that will enlighten readers but will not satisfy the lovers of simplifications. Just as history as a human endeavor has persisted and will persist, despite contemporary doubts and criticisms, because it has rejected arid theoretical schemes and has remained sensitive to the complexity and the creativity of life, so the study of historiography is most fascinating and worthwhile if it is not reduced to catchwords and formulas but is studied in its fullness. Only then can it inform us about the career of history throughout Western history and its service to human life.

# ·1·

# The Emergence of Greek Historiography

## The Timeless Past of Gods and Heroes

*We and the bards.* The Homeric epics, now innocuously enshrined in the treasure house we call Great Literature, were in centuries past sources of inspiration and pride. The ancient Greeks found them endlessly fascinating, edifying, and particularly useful for the education of the young. The Romans traced their origin to the Trojans, and so did other people in their quest for prestige. As late as four hundred years ago, some English and French scholars pointed with pride to their peoples' Trojan lineage.

Yet for us today Homer's magnificent Troy (most likely Troy VIIa, destroyed around 1240 or 1230 B.C.) was just a town favorably situated at the entrance to the Hellespont (the modern Dardanelles) whose inhabitants had become moderately prosperous through trade, levying tolls, textile manufacturing, and horse breeding. Its conquerors were a motley lot of Mycenaean nobles bent on destroying and looting. The Trojan campaign may have been the "last hurrah" of the Mycenaeans (or Achaeans) who, between 1600 and 1200 B.C., had dominated the Aegean area as sharp traders and even keener warriors. Soon after the Trojan War the Dorians moved into the Aegean area, shattered the Achaean world and ushered in the Greek Dark Age.

Four to five hundred years after Troy had been laid waste, Homer (or, as some scholars would have it, a number of *rhapsodes* or bards) "composed" the *Iliad* and the *Odyssey,* either by creating through artistic imagination new epics from traditional material or by simply coordinating a few existing epics. More troubling to the historian is the fact that the surviving versions of the two epics which so greatly influenced Western civilization were, of course, those versions somebody wrote down. Yet, the first of these appeared only during the sixth century B.C. in Athens, about two centuries after the emergence of the epics. The most influential version was that by Aristarchus of Samothrace from the second century B.C., in which the Mycenaean or Achaean, the Dorian

5

Homeric, and the post-Homeric elements were already intermingled. Gradually and still dimly, the modern image of the Mycenaean period and the Greek Dark Age is taking shape. Its elements are trade relationships, empires, expeditions of plunder and destruction, strategies of war and trade, and intricate social hierarchies: conceptual schemes which would puzzle the bards of the Homeric period. These differences between the early Greek and the modern views of the past are not the result of mere communication problems. The bards and we do not agree on such fundamental issues as how one knows about the past, which forces shape events, and what is the purpose of historical accounts. Two different experiences of the world confront each other.

*Language, gods, and heroes.* As bards sang of gods, heroes, deeds, suffering, and glories, they created a characteristic appreciation of the past: the heroic epic. It could contain humor or stories about mundane life, even some irreverent passages, but in essence it spoke of life in the grand and noble manner and of gods. Hence the language of the epics was not that of the daily routine or of the marketplace. The bards recited the tales of the past in a lofty manner using a rhythmic speech, which alternated long and short syllables according to strict patterns. In the case of the Homeric epics, which were the heirs of many song traditions, the hexameter added to the solemnity with which heroic history was recited and listened to. It all enhanced the reverence in which listeners held the epics as the records of the distant past and the respect they gave the bards as the teachers about the past. The latter were able to maintain a seemingly unbroken epic tradition by the process of adaptation. In the absence of an "authoritative" written text, the bards could adjust their messages to the changing preferences and realities of collective life.

The *Iliad* is aristocratic history. Merchants, craftsmen, and peasants play little part in the actions. It fitted aristocratic tastes that there was not a chronological narrative of a war lasting ten years but a dramatic account of a few weeks; by implication the rest of the siege was uninteresting, dull, and of no importance, and it appears only in some explanatory flashbacks. The campaign which moved men and ships in great numbers became the background for the actions of gods and the deeds, passions, glories, and defeats of a few heroes. "Sing, goddess, the anger of Peleus' son Achilleus and its devastation...," begins the *Iliad*, and it keeps to that theme.[1] Exceptions are few, the foremost being the undramatic catalogue of Achaean allies and ships. While that list delights the modern historians, since it describes the Mycenaean coalition which waged the war against Troy, it retards the action and lessens the excitement. Those who loved to listen to the *Iliad* were much more enamored by the dramatic core of the epic, the story of Achilles—his courage, strength, moral code, excessive passion, and doom; the related deeds of other heroes; the sufferings of noble women; and the machinations of gods and goddesses.

Does Homer in his *Iliad* ever venture beyond the aristocratic world and refer to the broader human life and its order? On occasions he says "the will of Zeus was accomplished."[2] But Zeus was far from being the author of all human events, and he was not even the initiator of the Trojan War; it had what must appear to moderns a frivolous base: the vengeance taken by Athena and Hera on the Troy of Paris, who had judged their beauty to be less than Aphrodite's. In return, Aphrodite had seen to it that Paris could carry off the most beautiful woman in the world, Helen. Menelaus, Helen's husband, became the instrument of vengeance. Other gods and goddesses interfered in the war according to their preferences by participating actively in battles, directing and deflecting weapons, scheming against others, persuading Zeus, influencing mortals, or quarreling among themselves. The gods shared influence with the heroes whose fighting, winning, wounding, and dying fill epic history. Indeed, heroic history shrank the world and time to the world of the hero who struggled, inspired by an unchanging code of honor, guided by often excessive passions, hindered and helped by gods and goddesses, and finally met death as the noble end to a triumphant life.

*Disdain for the unheroic.* Heroic history paid little heed to the collective human fate. The *Iliad* remained silent on the siege, even on the destruction of Troy and was followed by a personal adventure story, the *Odyssey*, as if the fate of the Achaeans did not matter. Only that part of the Achaean past was important which was ennobled by the presence of extraordinary persons, the heroes who still mingled with the gods. Since epic history clearly wished to inspire rather than to inform, events could remain timeless. What did it matter to those who imitated or admired the heroes when exactly the Trojan War had occurred?

Only the unheroic, the stuff of everyday life, is under the yoke of continuous time. Homer knew of the flow of unheroic life: the sun rises and sets; people are born, grow up, age, and die; and winter yields to spring and summer. He was aware of the fate of the many—their joys and sorrows, their institutions and possessions—but he rarely recorded it. No bard would recite to aristocratic audiences events lacking heroism, or tell the people at religious festivals and public gatherings about things which reminded them of their own daily toil. The audiences came to be inspired, excited, and in the best sense entertained. Neither they nor the bards had any notion that events, big and small, when told in proper time sequence, would result in an explanatory narrative. The past showed only heroic deeds performed in connection with isolated great events, and the future could be foretold only by oracles and portents. The idea that the events of the past could influence those of the present was far from the minds of the bards and their audiences. They recognized only the continuity of timeless ideals and virtues which the heroes of the past taught to the people of the present. Hence the persistence of heroic history throughout centuries when life no longer resembled that in archaic Greece. In the fourth century Homer's influence was still so strong that Plato regretted the poet's hold on Hellenic education and his power over individuals.

The didactic use of the *Iliad* was not defeated—even if the stunning dramatic unity of the work was weakened—when its story was spun out into a quasi-continuous account, which elaborated on and added stories to the Homeric epics. The authors of the subsidiary epics "filled in" what they considered to be missing links in the *Iliad*: an elaborate story centering around the rape of Helen, the tale of the Trojan horse, the Laocoön story, and the return of the heroes from Troy.

### Discovering a Past of Human Dimensions

*Hesiod and the collective human fate.* Notwithstanding the enduring enthusiasm for Homer, the dominance of heroic history could not last. An approximate contemporary of Homer, Hesiod of Ascra, already suggested a different view of the past. His *Theogony* (700s B.C.) showed a greater sense of abstract order as the cosmos emerged from chaos and sketchy genealogies of gods and goddesses were established. Most remarkably, Hesiod affirmed a collective human past and divided it into five ages ("races"): the Golden Age, in which people lived like gods, without care, suffering, and chores, and in which they died peacefully without aging; the Silver Age, when life was marked by utmost cruelty and unbridled love of war, and people revolted against all things divine and met an early death; the Age of Bronze, which was peopled by a race of extraordinary physical strength and vigor that destroyed itself by incessant warfare; the Age of Heroes (not identified with any metal), filled with noble humans and half-gods, who, unfortunately, also destroyed themselves in wars, one of them being Homer's Trojan War; and the Iron Age, the time of Hesiod and common man, which offered little but misery, injustice, a general lack of benevolence, aging, and death.

The past had acquired not only something akin to continuity but also a direction. The assertion that human history is the story of a decline from a Golden Age would reverberate throughout Western historiography, although other forces would be blamed for it than the will of Zeus.

*New views on the world and time.* After 800 B.C. the Greek world changed remarkably with the emergence of the *polis*, that is the city-state with an urban center and a contiguous rural district. These states, of widely varying sizes, types of government, and degrees of cultural development, were closely knit, self-governing communities marked by a keen and creative tension between their assertion of the individual's autonomy and their demand for conformity to the order of law and custom. During its best years the *polis* provided a context for

Greek life that released a wave of human energy. One of its significant manifestations was the colonization movement, and soon the Greeks sat on the coasts
of the Mediterranean Sea "like frogs around a pond." When these Greek colonists,
particularly those on the coast of Asia Minor, confronted other cultures with
different sets of customs and beliefs, they were reminded of their identity as
Hellenes. Although the Greek sense of superiority limited cultural assimilation,
the awareness of a wider and diverse world did affect Greek thought. It assisted
substantially in bringing about changes in poetry, art, and thought, with philosophy receiving most attention.

The intellectual revolution began in the sixth century B.C. with Thales of
Miletus and was continued by other philosophers. Under its impact the cosmos
lost its anthropomorphic structure. Instead, philosophers searched for the basic
substances from which all known objects were made up and for the processes
which transformed these substances into the great variety of things. Yet all of
these early philosophers explored the mystery of the cosmos rather than the
problems of human existence. Only in the fourth century did the Sophists
turn their attention to the phenomena connected with human life. But the
changes in Greek life, of which the intellectual revolution was an important
aspect, soon affected Greek views on the past.

As the Greeks, especially the Ionians, grew more confident in the practical
and intellectual mastery of the world, they launched a broad inquiry into the
geography and the peoples of the *oikoumenē*. Those who engaged in such an
inquiry (a ἱστορία or *historia*), altered Greek views on the two basic dimensions
of all of life, space, and time. From Greek explorations of the coastal areas of the
Mediterranean and the Black Sea, the Middle East, and even a bit of the Atlantic
coast, came new descriptions of wide parts of the contemporary world, particularly Hecataeus of Miletus's *Periegesis* (meaning approximately "journey round
the world"). His work and that of other pioneers made known, described, and
rationally organized the terrestrial space known to the Greeks.

The same zeal for exploration and rational organization soon transformed
the Greek view of the dimension of time. The world of geographers and the
cosmos of philosophers were continuous, while heroic history was by its nature
discontinuous. Homer's heroes had "lived" at an indeterminate point in the past
and were connected with the present solely through the inspirations and lessons
derived from the heroes and their deeds. There were no dates in the *Iliad*.
Homer neither had a time frame available in which to place the Trojan War, nor
would it have mattered to him to "know the dates." Since the heroic epic had
no use for the continuity of time, it made little difference to Homer that year
followed year. Glaucus mirrored the Homeric attitude when he told Diomedes:
"As is the generation of leaves, so is that of humanity. The wind scatters the
leaves on the ground, but the live timber burgeons with leaves again when the
season of spring is returning. So one generation of men will grow while another
dies."[3]

Eventually some Greeks would use the very concept of generations, those layers of human life, as a first step towards building a continuous account of the past. But in the *Iliad* the passage of generations merely points out the unimportance, even futility of routine human life.

Around 500 B.C., the Greeks began to grope towards the concept of continuous time and with it a history in which an unbroken line of years filled with events would stretch from the present into the most distant past. The timeless gods did not decree that view nor did the heroes need it, whose deeds surpassed all time, but the dwellers of the *polis* had use for it as they began to shape their lives. Life in the *polis* consisted not of isolated episodes in heroic lives but relied on the continuity of institutions, rules, laws, contracts, and expectations.

*The chronological control of the past.* Hecataeus of Miletus, who strained so hard to shape the geography of his world according to rational concepts, also dealt with the problem of time in his *Genealogies.* Fragmentary remains indicate that he attempted to link the age of humans with the so far timeless mythical age by constructing an unbroken sequence of identified generations for that long interval. The habit of looking for illustrious ancestors of cities, peoples, or families in the dim period of heroes and gods had established that link to the distant past which Hecataeus now wished to organize in human terms.

In the fifth century B.C. the Lydian Xanthus recorded the past of his people up to the downfall of their King Croesus. It is remarkable that he already attempted to relate the human events of the past, mythical and otherwise, to memorable and potentially datable natural events such as earthquakes and droughts. Later in the century, Hellanicus of Lesbos used a generation count as a chronological tool in his *Troica* and, based on it, placed the fall of Troy in the year equivalent to about 1240 B.C. In his *Attic History* Hellanicus proceeded beyond a mere generation count and, Thucydides' subsequent criticism notwithstanding, proposed a new tool for dating events: lists of officeholders kept by cities and temples. He himself used the list of the priestesses of Hera at Argos and in another work the list of winners of the Carnean games. Using the Argos list, Hellanicus tried valiantly to sort into chronological order a multitude of events—Greek, Sicilian, Roman (including the founding of Rome).

Hellanicus's idea led to other lists: those of Olympic victors (Hippias of Elis), of the ephors in Sparta (beginning with 755 B.C.), and of archons in Athens (since 683/82 B.C.). But how could one fit together all these separate records of ephors, archons, priests, priestesses, and games so that they formed one time frame? This question was not answered for a long time. When it was, the answers originated less in intellectual contemplation than in practical needs. A uniform time-scale for all Greeks was not yet a practical necessity for the fragmented world of city-states. Hence even Hellanicus's two famous contemporaries, Herodotus of Halicarnassus and Thucydides, remained traditional in chronology.

Herodotus, whose wide-ranging account would have had the greater need for a chronology, simply improvised. Perceiving no unifying tie between the histories of the Lydians, Persians, Egyptians, and Greeks, he gave them no proper chronological cohesion. Each segment had its own chronological structure. His occasional attempts to coordinate Greek and oriental time schemes failed, most notably his experiment with the Egyptian dynastic lists. The stretches of plotless ethnographic and geographic descriptions in his *Histories* called for no consistent time frame, and in the narrative sections he let the logic of stories suggest the sequence in time. Only from the Ionian revolt on did Herodotus's chronology become more systematic.

In this as in most respects, Thucydides was more systematic. He displayed both the achievements and limitations of contemporary Greek chronology when he dated the beginning of the Peloponnesian War:

> For fourteen years, the thirty years' peace which was concluded after the recovery of Euboea remained unbroken. But in the fifteenth year, when Chrysis the high priestess of Argos was in the forty-eighth year of her priesthood, Zenesias was ephor of Sparta, and Pythodorus had four months of his archonship to run at Athens, in the tenth month after the engagement at Potidaea at the beginning of spring, about the first watch of the night, an armed force of somewhat more than three hundred Thebans entered Plataea, a city of Boeotia, which was an ally of Athens.[4]

Yet, after he had located the start of the war in time, Thucydides had no more recourse to the lists of officeholders. From then on he simply counted the summers and winters which had elapsed. The story of the war built its own time frame.

# ·2·

# The Era of the *Polis* and Its Historians

### The New History of the *Polis*

The old ἱστορία faded slowly. While in Herodotus's *Histories* the accent eventually came to rest on the Great Persian War, ethnographic and geographic elements were still prominent. Herodotus delighted in telling about the origins and customs of people, towns, regions, constitutions, politics, and about curiosa in Egypt, Arabia and India, Scythia, Libya, and Thrace. These descriptive parts of his work were no mere digressions, satisfying human curiosity about strange people and places, but substantial inquiries, constituting a wide-ranging cultural history. Scholars have argued heatedly over whether Herodotus's *Histories* could be considered a unitary work. However, for demonstrating the eventual claim the *polis* laid on Greek historiography, it suffices that the Great Persian War established a unity between the books on the Persians and Greeks. Subsequently, Greek reflection on the past would focus on the fate of states and thus narrow the scope of the old ἱστορία considerably. Thucydides' work was to be the most significant result of that trend.

*War as the critical collective experience.* The Trojan War had been the grand stage of life for heroic history. Within its framework the heroes lived and died and, to a lesser extent, the Achaeans as a people showed their brilliance and failings. In the works of Herodotus and Thucydides the Trojan War was ousted from its preeminent place by two more recent momentous wars. Herodotus became the historian of the period of Greek victory and glory when he narrated the Great Persian War while Thucydides was the historian of the period of Greek self-destruction, through his narration and analysis of the Peloponnesian War.

In these accounts, much more changed than the names of battles and heroes. Unlike Homer's Trojan War, which had been the business of noble heroes, the wars reported on by Herodotus and Thucydides were collective experiences of commoners. Their description was less well served by poetic

12

genius and inspiration than by prose skills and analysis. After all, the Trojan War had occurred in the distant and misty age of gods and heroes while the Persian and Peloponnesian Wars were recent experiences involving people whom one could still meet in the marketplace or at the court of Persia. About a war seen as a general human experience one also could ask questions of Why? What? When? and Where? and expect answers primarily in terms of human motives and actions. Also, with the reflection on the past so clearly focused, the study of the past was no longer submerged in a broadly conceived inquiry, the old ἱστορία, but acquired a clear and separate identity: the study of human experience through the analysis of the past.

Herodotus and Thucydides differed not only in the wars they dealt with but also in their approaches. Herodotus, who developed elements of the old ἱστορία to perfection, concluded his account with the story of the Great Persian War (in 490 and 480/79). Thus his broad cultural history ended with a celebration of the Greek city-states, especially Athens. Not so Thucydides, whose aim in writing history differed radically from that of Herodotus although much else about him and his work is not clear: why he described the Peloponnesian War only up to 411 B.C., well before it ended; when he wrote his history; when he died; and whether or not he really understood that the series of campaigns he described constituted just one Peloponnesian War. Whatever definitive answers scholars will eventually give to these questions, nobody can doubt the unitary character of Thucydides's history, which set a dramatic account against the broad Herodotean cultural history. Only five segments seem to digress from the main story of the war and even they function as further explanation of the war or of Thucydides' method of work. Throughout his work Thucydides relentlessly pursued contemporary history; that meant the exposition and exploration of the Peloponnesian War. Why should one bother with anything prior to it, since "former ages were not great either in their wars nor in anything else?"[1]

Both historians wrote about war not in order to glorify it but because they perceived it as an essential force in the shaping of Greek destiny. Herodotus viewed the Great Persian Wars as the grand battle between the forces of despotism and freedom, between Orient and Occident, and between a despotic monarchy and city-states governed by their citizens. Lest anybody equate that battle with a simple struggle between good and evil, Herodotus pointedly reminded his readers or listeners of the many admirable customs of the Persians, the fickleness of the masses in a democracy, and the contrast between the serene unity of the Persian Empire and the strident discord among Greek city-states. Such understanding for the "barbarians," that is, non-Greek-speaking people, testified to a remarkable cosmopolitanism, which many Greeks found unacceptable and forgave only because Herodotus glorified the Greek cause in the Persian War.

Thucydides wrote about the Peloponnesian War as one who saw the power and glory of Athens first reduced and then subjected to the misery of defeat; a development so grand that it spurred him on to lay bare the forces, stresses, decisions, strategies, policies, and passions involved in war. The Peloponnesian War thus deserved a record not only because it was a crucial event in Greek experience but also because as a great war it revealed most clearly the essential and unalterable patterns which structure political events. Searching for these patterns, Thucydides found wars to be only partially controlled by human will. When Sparta and Athens collided it seemed to be solely the result of conscious decisions made freely by the two parties, but actually strong impulses toward war originated in the very structure of the political situation: Sparta and Athens had a basic conflict of interests. These interests in turn originated in the relentless human drive for power which is the central force in human events.

*The gods fall silent.* In Homer's epics gods and goddesses participated lustily in the affairs of mortals. Hecataeus and other early historians did not dispute these tales in their search for the genealogies of gods and heroes. But the spirit in which they approached the traditional stories was already less one of reverence and more one of detached observation. These men did not doubt the gods and heroes but they trimmed the mythical and epic traditions to the dimensions of human life. Hecataeus expressed the spirit well in his *Genealogies*: "I wrote about that in the way it seems to me to be true; because what the Greeks tell about it [the mythological tradition] varies quite a bit and is, it appears to me, laughable."[2]

Gods and goddesses retained a prominent position in Herodotus's work, but he spoke of the still important intervention of gods and goddesses on fewer occasions and in subtler ways. Arrogance, excessive pride, blind enjoyment of riches, seemingly endless successes—they all evoked the angry jealousy of the gods. "My lord," replied Solon to a question posed by Croesus, "I know God is envious of human prosperity and likes to trouble us; and you question me about the lot of man!"[3] In a similar vein Artanabus warns Xerxes not to wage war: "You know, my lord, that amongst living creatures it is the great ones that God smites with his thunder, out of envy of their pride. The little ones do not vex him. It is always the great buildings and the tall trees which are struck by lightning. It is God's way to bring the lofty low."[4] Aside from such occasional episodes of wrath, the gods fell silent in Herodotus's account. This ambiguity expressed Herodotus's puzzlement about the exact linkage between human decision, human fate, and divine verdicts. He ended up seeing human beings as shaping their lives, with human weaknesses now causing the doom which gods formerly pronounced and human greatness yielding the triumphs which gods used to grant. Only if human beings were relatively free of divine influence could history become the history of persons and their deeds which Herodotus tried to write.

According to Thucydides the gods never directly influenced the course of human events. He granted that those persons who shape human destinies are often guided by a belief in gods, oracles, or divinations, although he did not approve of such guidance. On occasion, however, even Thucydides appeared to waver. When at the outset of his account he pronounced the Peloponnesian War to be one of the great wars, he cited severe earthquakes, droughts causing famines, the plague, and eclipses of the sun as its portents. Yet, in his further analysis he had no use for such phenomena. His interpretation of war and empire relied on forces which originated in the structure of human life. Passions, miscalculations, and overreaching ambitions doom humans and their accomplishments. Of gods, Thucydides felt, he need not speak.

*Forces and causes.* Changing perceptions of the past are particularly apparent in the causes Homer, Herodotus, and Thucydides gave for the wars they described. According to Homer, the Trojan War stemmed from Paris's foolish judgment and Hera's and Athena's desires for vengeance. In Herodotus's account of the Persian Wars the forces pushing toward war were an odd lot: mischief-making exiles at the Persian court who urged Xerxes to wage war against the Greeks; fraudulent oracles; a peculiar sense of duty which told Xerxes that he must add to Persia's power; the hope for booty and for control of "Greek wealth"; and, of course, revenge for Athens' support of the Ionian revolt against Persian rule. But above all there was in Xerxes that burning if somewhat vague ambition "that the sun will not look down upon any land beyond the boundaries of what is ours."[5] In the end that grandiose ambition also provoked the Persian catastrophe by arousing the gods, who frowned upon excessive power. Essentially, Herodotus's list of reasons for the war is a list of human motives.

Thucydides found Herodotus's explanation insufficient. He introduced the remarkable distinction between the triggering incident, in this case the intervention of Sparta and Athens in the quarrel between Corinth and Corcyra over Epidamnus, and the underlying cause which, "though it was least avowed, I believe to have been the growth of the Athenian power, which terrified the Lacadaemonians and put them under the necessity of fighting."[6] The Peloponnesian War resulted not from the capricious wishes of gods or kings, or from misguided human passions, but from the ceaseless human quest for power. Thus, when Athens gradually transformed the once voluntary alliance of city-states against Persia into an Athenian empire, she harvested the enmity of some of those subjugated and of her competitor, Sparta. The Athenians, on their part, were driven to imperialism by the basic human obsession with dominating others and were encouraged in it by the inertia of her allies, who preferred paying tribute to the rigors of preparing for and going to war.

Once the wars were underway, Homer and Herodotus treated them as dramas of colliding passions. Thucydides, however, pointed out the links between wars and the forces structuring collective human life, in his analysis of how power, once gained, influenced the destiny of a state. Although the Athenians, who had chosen the strenuous life, deserved to rule others, they soon discovered that an established empire cannot be abandoned at will since, if they were to do so, they would destroy their new way of life. Therefore, as time went on, the empire changed its immediate motive for existence: it dominated others first out of fear, then for honor, and lastly for profit. In such a process, justice, which can only exist between equals, is lost when "the powerful exact what they can and the weak grant what they must."[7]

The Athenian hegemony collapsed when the weaknesses of the Athenian state, which in times of peace had only been irksome, became fatal under the stress of war. Early in the war the plague, a chance misfortune, hit Athens and caused many Athenians to lose all hope for the future. As people began to live strictly for the present, the hold of tradition weakened. Norms, restraints, and moderation, all of which presuppose confidence in the continuity of life, lost their shaping power, and the social fabric began to tear in places. As social cohesion loosened, the stresses of war became even more burdensome. The war, which was begun to solve Athens' problems, showed a tendency to amplify risks, breed misfortune, punish miscalculations, evoke acts of violence against internal opponents, and erode the basis of the very society which was to profit from it. Brutal oppression of people, such as the massacre of the Melians, evoked fierce counterforces. Reverses in battles prepared the political arena for the entrance of the demagogue, particularly Thucydides' bête noire, Cleon. Thucydides, distrusting the clever oratory in the popular assembly, saw a frustrated populace gullibly following those orators who promised solutions which at first sight were pleasant but eventually disastrous. Both the lessons of the past and long-range projection into the future were sacrificed for the quick alleviation of what was felt to be burdensome. Such action proved easy, since neither the populace nor the demagogues ever needed to take responsibility for consequences that were unwanted.

Thucydides traced the fate of the Athenian state in a splendid narrative that at the same time was analytical history. He saw no contradiction between the two. After all, life itself demonstrated the coexistence of the particular event (the subject of the narrative) and the general patterns (the focus of analysis). Thucydides explored the complex interrelationship between these two aspects of life when he described the role of the individual. He stressed the destructive influence of the demagogue and placed an even stronger emphasis on the positive role of the statesman. The latter's hold on the masses endowed his wise counsel with effectiveness, and he could thereby maintain the always precarious proper order in the state and, thus, secure its existence. But Thucydides did not answer the intriguing question whether Athens would have suffered utter defeat had the plague not taken Pericles away. Could a brilliant statesman enable a state to defy the larger forces at work in politics? Thucydides gave no clear answer as to the relative strength of the individual and these larger forces structuring human life. For him the tension between the two simply formed a constituent part of human life.

*New style and old purpose.* The Homeric epics and to a lesser extent Hesiod's work could be recited and listened to with pleasure. But Hecataeus and other early "historians" already conveyed their messages in Greek prose. Interestingly, the change from poetry to prose occurred together with the change in the attitude toward the past. Prose would not have served the heroic history of Homer and the bards but it did work in the undramatic sorting and cataloguing of gods and heroes and in the construction of genealogies.

Freed from the restraint of meter but also lacking the power which rhyme had given to language, Herodotus had to rely on human curiosity and on the internal tensions of stories for captivating his audiences. Nevertheless his prose was pleasing enough to be recited successfully, a feature of great value in a period with a still strong oral tradition. Curiously, it was Thucydides, disclaiming any concern with pleasing the audience and wishing his work to reflect "a lack of romance," who developed the most expressive and precise prose style. His relentless search for the essence of history, rather than for the merely interesting detail, found its stylistic counterpart in a sparse, rhythmic prose which had an impact on his audience like that of poetry. This magnificent unity of style and content captivated listeners and readers—the criticism and disdain of later rhetoricians notwithstanding.

Modern praise of Thucydides' work, however, has never included his use of thirty to forty speeches in the *History of the Peloponnesian War*. Homer and Herodotus had used speeches in their works, but Thucydides had labeled the first an unreliable poet and rejected the type of history the second had produced. How then did he justify the use of speeches which obviously were not accurate records of what was said?

> As for the speeches made on the eve of the war or during the course, it was hard for me, when I heard them myself, and for any others who reported them to me to recollect exactly what had been said. I have therefore put into the mouth of each speaker the views that, in my opinion, they would have been most likely to express, as the particular occasions demanded, while keeping as nearly as I could to the general purport of what was actually said.[8]

He also could have stated that speeches set the stage, described situations, and told about motivations without recourse to long enumerations and the use of abstractions. They read well and sounded even better in recitations. They also came closer to the ideal of truth whenever they contained parts of actual speeches, as in the case of Pericles' so-called Funeral Oration. In other words, the speeches of Thucydides contained what was said, could have been said, or should have been said. Indeed, speeches became so useful a narrative device that historians abandoned their use only a few centuries ago.

Writing in a manner that would produce the desired effect on the public mattered greatly to Greek historians, who, beginning with Homer, never lost sight of the public purpose of historical knowledge: history as the story of the past must above all inspire and teach (occasionally, it may entertain). The *Iliad* told people about the heroic age, its gods and heroes, extolling the worthiness of noble and proper conduct. Those early historians who practiced ἰστορία as a general inquiry, research, fact gathering, and reconnaissance, also had their public purpose: to build a new tradition free of "fictional" parts and to link the heroic age with the contemporary period.

Herodotus proclaimed the public purpose of his *Histories* at the very outset. He hoped "to preserve the memory of the past by putting on record the astonishing achievements both of our own and of the Asiatic peoples."[9] Then he proceeded to inspire, inform and—incidentally—entertain. Herodotus fulfilled his intentions by relating stories which taught the proper moderation, by telling of the many ways of human life, and by directing the attention of individuals to the great issues of the past. For his broad approach to recounting the past Herodotus has not only been called the "father of history" by later generations but has also been credited with the creation of a specific type of history: cultural history.

Thucydides taught the Greeks, at the same time, less and more. He led Greek history away from the broad inquiry into earlier times and the lives of other peoples to a concentration on the much smaller world of the *polis* and the contemporary period. Having limited his field of study in terms of periods and areas covered, Thucydides analyzed and described the field thoroughly in his search for those general forces which shaped the fate of states. In its analysis and purpose Thucydides' *History of the Peloponnesian War* resembles his report on the plague epidemic in Athens, in which he carefully described all symptoms of the disease in order to enable medical experts to cope with future outbreaks of the plague. Those in public office were offered a clinical study of the politics of war, democracy, and empire and had pointed out to them the lessons to be heeded. With all his passion for accurate reconstruction, Thucydides had no use for history as the object of intellectual contemplation. With all his passion for accuracy, he never aimed at a simple reconstruction of what actually happened but joined the other ancient historians in holding fast to a public purpose for the study of the past.

By a supreme irony, Thucydides himself unintentionally limited the public usefulness of history he so ardently advocated. His "new" history, precious to those who searched for sophisticated and complex answers, became slowly separated from the consciousness of the broad masses. Most Greeks, while they may have respected and listened to Thucydides' history, found the traditional narrative accounts of the past sufficient, even more congenial. Thucydidean history, like much of the new Greek cosmology and philosophy, became the special concern of a segment of the populace; it acquired what might be called an elitist character.

*The new problems: truth and methods.* For centuries the story of the *Iliad* exerted a powerful influence. Recited by bards in its rhythmic cadences, it entered into the hearts and minds of listeners. But something beyond poetic beauty and appeal to contemporary ideals enhanced the *Iliad*'s influence; for a long time it had no real competitors in shaping the image of the past. It had mattered little that Homer's century also saw the rediscovery of writing, since few people could read. Also, what at first was written down, such as the lists of officeholders, priests, priestesses, and winners of athletic games, as well as records of official actions, did not challenge the primacy of the heroic vision of the past. Oral traditions carried authority and evoked few doubts in their listeners, partly because they always fitted so well to the perceptions and ideals of the audience. Segments of the story which no longer "fitted" gradually fell into disuse and, being no longer recited, disappeared, while more suitable versions replaced them. Once written down, however, narratives lost that elasticity and frequently confronted other, competitive accounts of the past. Thus, during the fifth century B.C., Homer's version of the past stood next to those of Herodotus and Thucydides. Although Homer's account did not overlap much in subject matter with those later ones, the two views of the past, expressive of two ages centuries apart, confronted each other. At that point Greek historians began to grasp—in a rudimentary manner and occasionally—the need for proper methods. This awareness never involved more than trying to ascertain the accuracy of some features of the narratives.

Herodotus, dealing with different traditions, mentioned the problem of accuracy and evidence on a number of occasions: "So far the Egyptians themselves have been my authority; but in what follows I shall relate what other people, too, are willing to accept in the history of this country, with a few points, added from my own observation."[10] Herodotus even pointed to physical remains such as art objects and to language itself as evidence. Nevertheless, he could be gullible. He believed the accounts of past battles when they estimated Xerxes' army in 480 B.C. to have numbered 5,283,320 men.[11] More often, however, he showed good judgment: "At this point I find myself compelled to express an opinion which I know most people will object to: nevertheless, as I believe it to be true, I will not suppress it."[12]

Thucydides did not contribute much to the cause of documentation. As a writer of contemporary history he argued for the value of eyewitness accounts. He attacked fiercely all accounts of the early Greek past as being based on poor evidence. A person interested in the past

> must not put more reliance in the exaggerated embellishments of the poets, or in the tales of chroniclers who composed their works to please the ear rather than to speak the truth. Their accounts cannot be tested; the lapse of ages has made them in general unreliable, and they have passed into the region of romance.[13]

Only a few sections of the *Iliad* appeared of value, such as the Catalogue of Ships. Thucydides counted the ships, established their carrying capacity, and found the expeditionary army to have been a rather small force. Since a part of the army had to search constantly for provisions, the ready fighting force was even smaller.

When Thucydides sorted out what he considered to be facts from fiction he demonstrated how rationalistic the view of the past had become. Hecataeus of Miletus had still tried to separate the "historical" Heracles from the "legendary" one. Hellanicus of Lesbos rewrote Homer's story of Achilles fighting the River Scamander so as to adapt the story to the standards of credibility of his time rather than to repudiate it. With Thucydides history had assumed a purely human scope. He considered most of the still revered *Iliad* a poetic extravaganza, containing little useful information. He thought equally little of parts of Hellanicus's *Attic History*, which he considered inaccurate in its chronology. That negative assessment of other historians foreshadowed a characteristic trait of subsequent Greek historiography. Too often, however, legitimate criticism changed into criticism prompted more by the critic's vanity or contentiousness rather than by scholarly integrity.

Once historians dropped heroes and gods from the center of their accounts they encountered another problem: which of the many human events should historians select for their narratives of the past? In Herodotus's work one encounters two principles of selection. As heir to the ἱστορία tradition he collected a vast amount of geographical and ethnographical information which he then joined to the story of the Persian Wars with its different focus. His ethnographic and geographic accounts suggested that all kinds of human experiences should fill the pages of historical accounts; his dramatic stories of individuals, such as those about Croesus and Polycrates, emulated the epic tradition, and his story of the Great Persian War proclaimed the value of contemporary and political history.

> In this book, the result of my inquiries into history, I hope to do two things: to preserve the memory of the past by putting on record the astonishing achievements both of our own and of the Asiatic peoples; secondly, and more particularly, to show how the two races came into conflict.[14]

Thucydides rejected the broad cultural approach. The historian must relate the essence of past human life, no more and no less. It alone is of use and hence worthy of recording.

> But if anyone desires to examine the clear truth about the events that have taken place, and about those which are likely to take place in the future—in the order of human things, they will resemble what has occurred—and pronounce what I have written to be useful, I shall be content.[15]

He eventually paid a price for stripping his history of everything he considered nonessential. Later scholars have deplored his exclusive political and military emphasis which cost them the broad picture of the period a Herodotean historian could have delivered to them.

What about partisanship in the works of the two historians, each of whom experienced political exile? Both Herodotus and Thucydides knew that truth seen as conformity with the events in the past was a sine qua non of history; it alone separated them from the poets. While their sympathy for Athens was obvious, it never turned into petty bias. Herodotus deliberated in a judicious way on the best form of government without automatically awarding the prize to Athens. Thucydides, who wished to understand the very structure of events, could not afford blind partisanship. Indeed a commitment to public affairs, if not experience in it, became well-nigh the common background of most ancient historians, especially those who lived in republics. Thucydides would have hardly understood the modern controversy over his objectivity in which some have praised him as the ancestor of modern objective historians, because he wanted to tell things "as they had occurred," while others have condemned him for single-mindedly selecting "facts" which fit his concept of history. Thucydides could have pointed out that neither his zealous defenders nor his ardent detractors quite understood his reason for writing history.

## The Decline of the *Polis*
## The Loss of Focus

After 479 B.C., when the immediate Persian threat ended, the Greek world became a relatively self-contained system of city-states, dominated by the Athenian empire and its Spartan counterweight. When seventy-five years later Athenian power was shattered, Sparta and then Thebes tried to build systems of domination, succeeded temporarily, exhausted their slim resources in doing so, and suffered defeat. Athens participated in the struggle off and on. Other city-states never aspired to great-power status but they, too, were often drawn into wars. By 350 B.C. a general weariness had spread through the world of the Greek city-states. Memories of past glory, delight in a relatively stable and prosperous period, and social tensions marked Greek life until in 338 B.C., at Chaeronea, the Greeks paid the price for their failure to create a political structure beyond the *polis*. When King Philip of Macedonia brought the era of independent city-states to an end, the *polis* remained as the unit of life but the center of power had shifted to the Macedonian court.

*Political history without drama.* How did the Greeks of that period see their past? They had available Homer's epics, Herodotus's *Histories*, and Thucydides' work. Modern historians, convinced of the cumulative and advancing nature of knowledge, would proceed immediately to combine the three accounts into a composite whole, but the Greeks of the fourth century let the three stories of the past stand separately, each as an authority in its own right. This was possible because the subjects of the accounts did not really overlap much. It also was inevitable because the Greek historians lacked a concept for unifying the accounts beyond the, in this case, useless sense of cultural unity of all Hellenes and because the sources they employed left them no other choice. The more distant the past the less possible it was to rewrite the account. Contemporary history, a combination of the more immediate past and the present, appealed to Greek historians because the sources for it were available and fit better their use of sources. In addition they not only failed to re-search the past but they lacked expectations for a different future. The years to come would bring merely new variations of the old human drama whose script was written by a timeless human nature. Even those who looked to Panhellenism, the only broad Greek vision of the future, were convinced that it would not supersede the *polis* as the basic unit of life.

The writing of contemporary history encountered its own peculiar problems. Thucydides had been able to shape the multitude of past events into a unitary account because his narration and his analysis focused on one great war. But now historians had to describe the many events between 400 and 338 B.C., all of them lacking grandeur, long-lasting influences, and above all any clear unity. In the parts of his work on the non-Greek world Herodotus had offered descriptive cultural history as a possible approach to the past, but such a history found little acceptance because of the strong admiration for Thucydides' political and contemporary history. What came now was a series of Greek contemporary histories each referred to as *Hellenica* (Histories of Greece) and each in a sense continuing Thucydides' account—Cratippus to 394, Theopompus to 394 or 387, and Xenophon to 362. They dealt largely with a period in which the crisis of the *polis* was still approaching and the world of Greek city-states seemed secure enough to go on forever.

Without the drama of a great struggle, Xenophon was left to describe the steady flow of routine human life, sometimes turbulent, sometimes quiet. Instead of Thucydidean reflections on the dynamics of politics, his *Hellenica* taught simpler, more conventional lessons: that the cultivation of tradition, with its gods, rules, and values, was a good thing; that the gods were helping those who had self-discipline, exerted themselves, and brought sacrifices; and that loyalty was praiseworthy.

*A muted Panhellenic manifesto.* In their days of glory the Greek city-states had brought forth citizens of a magnificent willingness to devote their lives to public affairs. Yet the same devotion to one's own *polis* had also rigidly separated city-state from city-state. Hegemonies by some powerful city-states had brought about some entities larger than the *polis* but they were built on force and did not last. All along there had been, however, a keen awareness of the cultural unity among Hellenes. Could that spirit of commonality not also be infused into Greek political life, thereby endowing that life with a sense of development toward Greek integration? The famous fourth-century rhetorician Isocrates realized that at one time the fight against Persia had given a sense of commonality and continuity to Greek political life, and he favored a new Greek war on Persia as a means to achieve political panhellenism. Two historians who probably had some direct connections with Isocrates wrote works which reflected the contemporary concerns: Ephorus of Cyme and Theopompus of Chios.

The fragments remaining of Ephorus's *Histories* tell us that he wrote Greek history in the broad Herodotean manner, reaching out beyond the limits of the Greek world and dealing with "barbarians" whose past he considered venerable and important. Nevertheless, Ephorus concerned himself above all with the Greek world, which he consistently treated as a whole. Yet Ephorus's Panhellenism seems to have been without a political connotation. Without a dynamic, unifying concept, he seems to have painted a portrait of human, although primarily Greek, life. Characteristically, his dedication to the wider Greek world did not diminish his intense dedication to his native *polis*, demonstrated in his history of Cyme.

When modern scholars ask how original Ephorus's *Histories* were, they put a question Greek historians would not have understood. Ephorus had, like most ancient historians, no taste for making his own inquiries into so distant a past. He merely wished to demonstrate a different viewpoint, write in a better style, or teach a new lesson rather than unearth new material.

*Calls for a conservative Greece.* In the fourth century a rich body of literature dealt with the ideal form of government. Athens' defeat in the Peloponnesian War lay as a heavy burden on democracy, and the instability of the Greek world of states spurred talk of panehellenism. The historian Theopompus of Chios suggested a solution to both problems in his *Philippica*, a history in quasi-biographical form of which only fragments are left. It demonstrated the political importance of Philip II of Macedonia (359–336 B.C.) whom Theopompus considered the greatest man of the age. From a panhellenism under Macedonian leadership, he hoped, would come a conservative reconstruction of Greek society. Theopompus, twice an exile from democratic Chios, mustered little enthusiasm for democracy.

Yet Theopompus had no weakness for uncritical adulation. Contemporaries called him quarrelsome, and he loved to expose the weaknesses of the famous, deny their achievements, and attribute shady motives to them. Theopompus promptly criticized Philip for his drinking parties, sexual debauchery, and lack of self-restraint. Such weaknesses destroyed a potentially great leader of Greeks —a cost too high for forgiveness.

But, like Ephorus, Theopompus spurned Thucydides' single-mindedness. He loved digressions. They prove that the broad curiosity about the world which had inspired the old ἱστορία had never ceased to exist side by side with the

Thucydidean type of history. Still, on the whole, the *Philippica* stuck to its main purpose—to tell about and even celebrate the monarch whose soldiers, in 338 B.C., destroyed the Greek city-state system.

Macedonian rule ushered in a panhellenism condemned to be superficial because few Greeks were willing to bridge the gap between the Macedonians, perceived forever as barbarians, and themselves. Despite a general fading of civic consciousness, the city-states remained the immediate life-context of individual Greeks. Even those whose lives now centered on their individual pleasures felt some pride and sense of belonging as members of the *polis*. The distinctive traditions of each city were cultivated, and in that endeavor state, local, and regional histories proved to be pillars of support.

Local history had been one of the earliest results of the Greek's search for their past, as Hellanicus's *Attic History* shows so well. Ever since, pride in one's *polis* and availability of sources had fostered that type of history. Now another motive entered.

When the tugs of rationalism and of a strong individualism began to pull the web of tradition apart, the cities experienced the growth of a conscious traditionalism as a counterforce. Local histories were used to reenforce those features of the contemporary collective life which linked the present to a past now perceived as having been sound and pure. The so-called attidographers, an awkward name for Attic historians who wrote in the manner of Hellanicus's *Attic History*, were such traditionalists. In their works they inquired after the exact histories of local festivals, temples, and rites, putting to work the contemporary passion for accuracy, which actually was a part of the corrosive rationalism, in the cause of traditionalism. Thus, traditionalist historians busied themselves, for example, with finding the version of the Theseus legend most acceptable to a rationalist age, thereby hoping to safeguard tradition from radical doubts.

The traditionalists represent the first antiquarians who unearthed and preserved much valuable information in their search for new insights into the distant past. Tedious as their works may be, they actually manifested a greater determination to go beyond the generally accepted knowledge of the past than did the works of contemporary historians. Their goal also forced them to abandon the typical preoccupation of ancient historians with the motives and actions of individuals and the timeless lessons gained from those sources for present and future individuals. Instead they dealt with features of the anonymous collective life. But the traditionalist historians failed in their primary aim of strengthening the collective spirit by preserving tradition. By their passionate search for the accurate corroboration of communal traditions, the attidographers made these traditions slightly more acceptable to people who were already tinged by skepticism; but they did so at the cost of introducing scholarly controversies into tradition which needed simple acceptance more than accuracy. History, used as a buttress for tradition, did not blunt the thrust of skepticism but forced traditionalists to accept at least partially the method of systematic doubt.

*History writing without a clear public purpose.* Far from the subject matter of other Greek historical works, Xenophon's *Anabasis* (The march up-country) traced not the fate of states or heroes but that of a group of mere mercenaries and their leaders, among them Xenophon. They had been hired by the Persian prince Cyrus to help him overthrow his ruling brother, Artaxerxes. The motives of the Greek mercenaries really amounted to the search for adventure, booty, and glory. Cyrus's defeat at Cunaxa in 401 B.C. dashed these hopes, and the arduous struggle to leave Persia began, the struggle which is described in the *Anabasis*.

The antagonists in the struggle were the Greeks on the one hand and the elements, the barren land, the wild tribes, and the Persian satrap Tissaphernes on the other. When Tissaphernes trapped and murdered the Greek generals, Xenophon, seemingly an experienced soldier, led the Greeks past many a danger. All of it was accomplished not for the glory of any state or cause but for a simpler reason: "Now for it, men, think that the race is for Hellas—now or never—to find your boys, your wives."[16] Fulfillment did not come with winning a decisive battle but with the shouts from the advance guard: "Thalassa! Thalassa!" ("The sea! The sea!"). They had survived. It all had been a magnificent adventure but no more than a historical sideshow.

In both, Xenophon did not identify himself as the author of either the *Anabasis* or the *Hellenica*, despite the highly individualistic tenor of his work. In it individuals make history as they rise to power and prominence by their actions and excellence and then fail through accidental circumstances or the machinations of conspiring opponents. Xenophon never searched for or understood those relentless forces which, according to Thucydides, shaped the fate of social and political institutions. Hence it was fitting that Xenophon became one of the early writers of Greek biography.

*Biography as an account of the past.* Homer's *Iliad* had been unabashedly individualistic. However, its figures were not those one could meet in the public square; they were exemplary figures of a glorious and distant age, whose conduct could inspire human beings to transcend their ordinary lives. Scholars who have searched for the early traces of biography as the life stories of famous mortals have spoken vaguely of a biography of the tyrant Heraclides of Mylasa, written in all likelihood by Scylax of Caryanda, the explorer. Some indications point to biographical works by Xanthus the Lydian and Ion of Chios. Since all of these authors lived in Asia Minor or areas close to it, scholars have suspected an oriental impulse to biographical writing. That may well be, with Near Eastern biography an established fact and, one must add, with significantly different interests prevailing for a long time on the Greek mainland.

In fifth-century Greece interest focused on the state, on power, and on hegemony. But the histories of Herodotus narrated stories about individuals whose lives could teach a lesson, and Thucydides acknowledged the important role of individuals when he spoke of statesmen and demagogues. Then, in the fourth century, the gradual loosening of communal ties and the corresponding increase in the weight given to individuals favored the growth of biography. Xenophon's *Anabasis* could be seen as a collective biography of people whose fate made no difference to the course of history. The same venture provided the incentive for Xenophon's *Cyropaedia* that told the story of Cyrus the Great. With its emphasis on the moral and political growth of the king, it represented the peculiar "education of..." genre within biography, quite favored in the ancient period and revived in the Renaissance. That the term "biography" itself was not used until centuries later, and that the Greeks for a long time simply used the term *bios* (life), is merely an issue of terminology.

Later, in his encomium for the Spartan king Agesilaus, Xenophon moved biographical writing away from the historical genre in the direction of the philosophical contemplation of life. The encomium had been a poem of praise, particularly for the winners of athletic games, when the orators of the fourth century discovered it for their purposes and Isocrates set a standard with his encomium for Evagoras of Cyprus, wherein he praised the king and used Evagoras's life as an example of a wise ruler. Xenophon retained some historical elements in his encomium to Agesilaus, the Spartan king whom he had served, when he dealt with the actual events of Agesilaus's life, but he gave most attention to Agesilaus's virtues: piety, justice, self-control, courage, wisdom, rationality, and urbanity.

# ·3·

# Reaching the Limits of Greek Historiography

### The History of a Special Decade

Suddenly, exciting contemporary events began to overshadow all political maneuvering and the Macedonian conquest. Philip's twenty-two-year-old son, Alexander of Macedonia, set out to march eastward and crown the long Greek struggle against the Persians with total victory and conquest. He won his victory, inspired many Greeks, founded cities, explored hitherto untouched areas, and performed outstanding feats of courage as well as misdeeds against old associates. Even his original rather simple motive for the campaign was adjusted to the grandeur of the venture when it was changed from defeating the Persian Empire to unifying the Greek and Persian cultures. But when Alexander died suddenly he did not leave the Macedonians or Greeks in control of a united state but rather bequeathed to them exciting memories, an incipient cultural fusion, and much political instability.

At first glance it is perplexing that among those who wrote about Alexander the Great's amazing life, with its breathtaking events and grandiose endeavors, there was no Herodotus or Thucydides, not even a Xenophon. It is unlikely that among the great number of writings on Alexander, of which only a few incomplete works remain, there was such a grand account. What remains is not overly impressive. The ancient geographer Strabo had already criticized those who followed Alexander and then became his historians, charging that they "preferred to accept the marvelous rather than the true."[1] Their accounts lacked vision, depth, and creativity. Such small results were a poor reward for Alexander's solicitude for historians, some of whom he had encouraged to accompany him on his expedition. But not all of the blame must be attributed to the lack of talent or skills on the part of historians. Alexander's campaign and its achievements and aftermath, proved difficult to treat in the context of Greek history. The reason why will be more readily apparent after a look at the Alexander historians.

*The hero, the exotic, and some gossip.* Alexander himself loved the Homeric epics, a copy of which had been prepared for him by Aristotle and, possibly, Aristotle's relative the historian Callisthenes of Olynth. What Callisthenes, who accompanied Alexander, actually reported we know only sketchily. But he seems not to have hesitated to depict Alexander as the hero favored by the gods: one whose ancestry even may lead back to Zeus and Achilles. Others added a line of descent from Priam and the noble Trojans, which gave Alexander a claim to the Trojan heritage now represented by the Persian Empire. Those who knew no such genealogical lines simply discerned a resemblance between the Greeks and Macedonians attacking the Persian Empire and the Achaeans assaulting Troy. As for Callisthenes he never had a chance to complete Alexander's history; he lost his life as a suspect in the conspiracy of the pages against Alexander. To Greeks and later historians he left a *Hellenica* for the period between 387 and 357 B.C..

Onesicritus of Astypalaea perceived Alexander as an entirely different hero, when he portrayed the mature Alexander as a "philosopher in arms," specifically a Cynic philosopher in the manner of Diogenes of Sinope. The reader may well wonder what Alexander, who loved life, adventure, and eventually the wealth, pomp, and power of a Persian king, had in common with the ascetic Diogenes, except possibly some cosmopolitanism. In any case Onesicritus neglected Alexander the philosopher when he told interesting stories such as the one about Alexander's turning away from further eastward progress after meeting the Amazon queen at the river Jaxartes, and when he described the customs of strange people, exotic plants and animals, Indian holy men, and the legendary peaceful kingdom of Musicanus. There also were accurate observations on the monsoon rains and on the sea journey through the Persian Gulf that Onesicritus had gathered as the chief steersman of Admiral Nearchus. However, Strabo could not forget what he considered the fantastic element in Onesicritus's work and called him for it "chief steersman of fantasy." As for Nearchus of Crete, who guided Alexander's fleet that carried part of the army from India to Mesopotamia, he was an observer in the manner of Herodotus. Lacking any specific purpose or theme, Nearchus recorded whatever intrigued him, be it rivers, tigers, monkeys, or parrots. His judgments about other people were measured, as when he considered the Indians different but nevertheless brave and civilized. Unfortunately, in all of that Nearchus had little to say about Alexander, except on one occasion when he put forth the interesting opinion that Alexander began his great venture moved by *pathos*, meaning a vague and powerful longing in his nature to do something not yet attained, but that, in the process of conquering, Alexander unwittingly brought Greek civilization to the East.

Another group of historians concentrated on "human-interest stories" or, one could say, high-class gossip. Chares of Mytilene served Alexander in one of those offices which the Persian influence had brought about, a position combining the duties of a chamberlain, appointment secretary, and chief of protocol. His *Stories of Alexander* betrayed the frame of mind which that position required and fostered. Alexander appears as fond of eating, of drinking parties—although not actually drinking himself—and of apples. The *Stories* also told much about feasts, fabulous clothing, the pleasant life of Alexander, the persons surrounding Alexander, and the king's tent and furniture but nothing at all about the purpose and grandeur of the expedition. Little remains of what a few others, apparently writing in the same vein, had to say (for example, Alexander's secretary, Eumenes of Cardia).

Alexander histories improved with the passage of time. Aristobulus of Cassandrea started writing his history at the age of eighty-four and gave a good account of Alexander's reign, one marked by restraint in the stories of the battles, the king's drinking, and natural phenomena. And while Aristobulus also painted picturesque scenes of the cutting of the Gordian knot, of the sailor's reward and punishment for recovering the king's diadem, and of the courteous treatment of the Babylonian priest who foretold the imminent death of Alexander, he related a large body of sober information and avoided much that was fanciful. When he thought it proper, he even criticized Alexander, particularly his insatiable desire for conquest. Aristobulus earned no accolades for his restraint or style. He was only copied widely.

Ptolemy was equally unappreciated, except much later by Arrian who trusted him as "a king for whom it would have been specially disgraceful to lie."[2] Ptolemy, one of Alexander's favorite generals, did not bother much with geography, overall historical development, or local customs. Battles were his favorite subject and he described them well and soberly. He saw no need for embellishment since he did not wish to entertain his readers.

That leaves Cleitarchus, whose now lost history of Alexander was read and listened to by many although he himself most likely had not participated in Alexander's campaign. Through Diodorus Siculus he influenced later generations. What is known of his history inspires little confidence although it explains his onetime popularity.

*The problem.* What then made for the glaring discrepancy between Alexander's genius and accomplishments and the poor quality of the histories about him? Historians simply had trouble fitting Alexander into their narratives of the past. His grand endeavor could be seen as one of many campaigns designed to crush Persian power and, interpreted in this manner, it inspired some Greeks. But Alexander was a Macedonian, a barbarian, whose destruction of rebellious Thebes had chilled Greek enthusiasm for him. Hence some historians, such as Ephippus of Olynth, reported in a hostile manner how Alexander the Great drank too much unmixed wine too often and how he wore sacred ritual clothing for everyday wear. Some were not even happy when victory after victory shattered the Persian Empire because that doomed the Greek states to continue as dependencies of Macedonia. Other Greeks lost their pride in Alexander's grand victory when the expedition turned into a civilizing mission aiming at one empire and one culture. Because of Alexander's sudden death this idea of a fusion of Greek and Persian cultures had only enough time to provoke and offend but not to convince. All of that contributed to the fundamental problem: Alexander's grand deeds and short-lived empire, involving so many barbarian areas and peoples, could not be located in the Greek view of the past which remained stubbornly centered in the *polis*. Hence, historians transformed the history of Alexander's life and deeds into stories about a hero, satisfied the Greek curiosity about the peoples and places of the *oikoumenē* in the manner of the old ἱστορία or of Herodotus, or lapsed into gossip. The implications were even wider for Greek historiography at large. It was left in search of the proper theme of history beyond heroes, *polis*, and failure of empire.

## Hellenistic Historiography
## Beyond the Confines of the *Polis*

When Alexander died, his empire died with him. The grand vision dissolved into a power struggle between the commanders, who eventually received provinces they were to govern—nominally—as satrapies. Two decades of warfare produced a state system dominated by the Diadochi (Successors); one in which unity had become a fiction but a tolerable stability was reality. Antigonid Macedonia, Ptolemaic Egypt, and the Seleucid Empire encompassing Persia, Mesopotamia, Syria, and Palestine emerged as the three great powers in the Eastern Mediterranean area. The Greek city-states maintained a precarious existence under Macedonian domination, becoming sometimes more, sometimes less, autonomous. Eventually, the forming of federations of cities—particularly the forming of the Aetolian and Achaean Leagues—gave the city-states some influence. The areas of the monarchies and of city-states differed in many ways, not the least in their historiographies. The Seleucid and Ptolemaic kingdoms had special difficulties in developing an appropriate reflection on the past. In each of them a small Greek ruling group and a larger group of merchants lived among great numbers of people with venerable cultures and traditions of their own. Grecization never became more than partial. The Greek city-states on the mainland, even with their autonomy clearly delimited, could still use the old historiographical models, except the Thucydidean analysis of the structure of hegemony.

*Historiography as scholarship.* In Ptolemaic Egypt scholars were a part of the Greek elite and a favored part at that. Royal patronage ensured the existence of the famous Alexandrian Museum, an institution given to pure learning. In splendid isolation a group of scholars worked on many problems. When it came to history they chose to focus primarily on the distant past: a choice not illogical for people whose states knew no true continuity except the elite's link to Greek culture. To secure that heritage through scholarly efforts and to record it in writing seemed a proper task. Hellenistic scholars collected, stored, and preserved the old texts, particularly Homer's works. In the course of doing so they engaged in textual criticism, that is they tried to expunge later additions and mistakes, improve understanding by punctuation and accents marking pitch variations, and published dictionaries of words and names. It all showed sophisticated learning but was hardly the stuff many people read. Other scholars, particularly those of later generations, furnished the audience. Such isolation from life had its price. Relatively few copies were made of many works and the copies were easily lost. And although Timon was too harsh in referring to the Museum as a "hen coop" in which scholars were expected to produce works routinely, the creative work of the scholars, with all their sophistication, lacked spontaneity and a genuine connection with the life surrounding them.

Did this scholarly literary criticism bring forth work on historical theory? Only to a minor degree. Questions of historical truth stayed reduced to the demand for narrative accuracy. Greek historians had generally understood the concern with the truth of their accounts in that sense. At question was the proper portrayal of individual past phenomena and—with the exception of Thucydides—not the forces shaping these phenomena and certainly not whether one could find the truth at all. Truth depended solely on the historian's skills, available material, and will to be truthful. Hence one discussed the wisdom of relying on eyewitness accounts, documents, one's own experience, reliable reporters, and other sources. With the sifting of mythical accounts by Hecataeus of Miletus had begun the trend to accept only accounts of the past which human reason could approve of. Decades later, Antiochus of Syracuse had searched for the "clearest and most convincing elements" in the Greek mythical tradition. In the fourth century Ephorus had simply ignored that tradition as unreliable. A similar process had gradually phased out the interference of gods in human affairs. Accurate history became defined as an account of the past with purely human dimensions, based on reliable reports, and referring to an order of things that was timeless and accessible to reason.

Temptations to leave the scholar's study and once again write history with a public purpose were few for Greek historians in the states of the Diadochi because they no longer participated as active citizens in the affairs of a *polis*. Like all other people, they lived as subjects without opportunities for discussing public affairs and influencing the decision-making. Gone was the passionate concern that had made Thucydides, for example, analyze the fratricidal war between Greeks and to search for the forces tearing apart the Athenian Empire. Hence, while biased in favor of a patron, a region, and all things Greek, Hellenistic historians had no trouble in mustering detachment.

The Hellenistic philosophers were of no help in defining the historical endeavor. They neglected discussions of the state and the cosmos and instead designed proper ways to live for individuals who had lost their moorings in tradition. But then historians and philosophers had never cooperated. Aristotle's famous dictum on history's position vis-à-vis poetry and, by implication, philosophy had only formulated a long-standing view on the nature of history.

> Hence also poetry is a more philosophical and serious business than history; for poetry speaks more of universals, history of particulars. "Universal" in this case is what kind of person is likely to do or say certain kinds of things, according to probability or necessity; that is what poetry aims at, although it gives its persons particular names afterward; while the "particular" is what Alcibiades did or what happened to him.[3]

History, telling only about such transitory phenonema as individual events, persons, and institutions, did not commend itself to the philosophers, who searched for the timeless truth and wished to state that truth in systems of general propositions. Historians themselves were in tune with that attitude only when they looked in events and deeds for timeless human motives and lessons, and that activity was insufficient to satisfy philosophers. Banned from the field of philosophy, history writing found itself associated with rhetoric, which had begun as the skillful use of language—the art of persuasion—but in Hellenistic times had become a vast, sophisticated enterprise including literary theory and criticism. In the realm of rhetoric historical writing became one of the narrative forms. All Hellenistic systems of education and of scholarly disciplines reaffirmed that placement, and the prestige of Aristotle made sure that history remained a part of rhetoric for centuries to come.

When democratic government was reduced to insignificant proportions in the Hellenistic period, rhetoric, like history, lost its public, specifically political, function. In turn the rhetorical enterprise became a central part of the pedagogical system, where generations of scholars and schoolmasters kept it alive as training in style and argumentation as well as a science of language. It developed into a highly technical affair with elaborate textbooks, invented debates, and practice speeches. The great historical texts became favorites for teaching proper grammar and style and for teaching moral philosophy through exemplary lives.

*History and the old city-states.* The Greek past now had four distinct segments: the era of the gods and heroes, the period of the Greek city-states, Alexander the Great's time, and the time of the recent successor states. Historians in the states of the Diadochi had no incentive to write a history encompassing all of them. Doing so would have only emphasized the great break between the age of the *polis* and the world of the Diadochi. Historians on the Greek mainland had only a slightly stronger incentive to accomplish such a quasi-universal history. Recent Greek and Macedonian events captured their attention. This was especially so since the *polis* had found both a modus vivendi with Macedonia and a form of political organization—the league or federation—which kept the *polis* autonomous but reached beyond its borders. The surviving fragments of the works on the recent period of Greek history by Diyllus of Athens, Nymphis of Heracleia Pontica, and Hieronymus of Cardia indicate that these works, as valuable as they were, brought no new interpretations or concepts to historiography. Most historians of the Greek heartland stayed with local and regional history.

*History as artful narration.* History as scholarship was known to few people. History as political narrative or local story had a somewhat greater public appeal. History as dramatic account—serious or frivolous—received the major share of attention. That aspect of history had been present in the stories of heroic deeds in Homer's *Iliad*, the anecdotes that Herodotus relished, the tales of adventure in Xenophon's *Anabasis*, and even occasional passages in Thucydides' austere account. But now the wish to catch the public's attention became a major feature of some historical works. Life in the Greek world after Alexander the Great favored such a development. At least in the urban areas, a large segment of the population enjoyed peace, leisure, and relative comfort. These people craved excitement and entertainment, and historians simply took account of that.

Duris of Samos and Phylarchus (early second century B.C.) captured a wide audience not by the importance of their subject matter but by the manner of their writing. More than a century later that manner evoked the wrath of Polybius, who condemned the whole class of historians to which Duris belonged:

> Though their subjects are simple and without complications, they seek the name and reputation of historians not from the truth of their facts, but the number of their books, and accordingly they are obliged to give petty affairs an air of importance, and fill out and give rhetorical flourishes to what was originally expressed briefly; dress up actions and achievements which were originally quite secondary; expatiate on struggles; and describe pitched battles in which sometimes ten or a few more infantry fell, and still fewer cavalry.... Such historians as I refer to, when they are describing in the course of their work the siege ... are forced to display all the contrivances, bold strokes, and other features of a siege ... they must draw on their own resources to prolong the agony and heighten the picture, and are not at all satisfied with me for giving a more truthful relation of such events as they really occurred.[4]
>
> ... And being eager to stir the hearts of his readers to pity, and to enlist their sympathies by his story, he talks of women embracing, tearing their hair, and exposing their breasts; and again of the tears and lamentations of men and women, led off into captivity along with their children and aged parents. And this he does again and again throughout his whole history, by way of bringing the terrible scene vividly before his readers.[5]

The historians who dramatized their accounts, told anecdotes, and did not shy away from trivia to enhance the human interest wanted history to offer its listeners and readers *mimesis*, an imitation of reality which, like drama, "involved" them by stirring up their emotions, even passions. History was to be relived rather than merely heard or read. Phylarchus and others could have pleaded that in this way history teaches its lessons most effectively except that they had no particular lessons in mind. Polybius's criticism notwithstanding, dramatic history as a purely narrative art fit the Hellenistic age quite well: decisive political events were absent, active citizenship had withered away, theories on individual morality occupied the minds of the elite, and the need for entertainment grew. Long prevented from joining philosophy in interpreting human life, and never perceiving history as the attempt to reconstruct the past for the love of truth alone, historians utilized the techniques of drama in order to evoke emotions, convey a lesson or two, and above all entertain.

### The Problem of New Regions and People

Alexander's campaign had brought Greeks into permanent contact with diverse cultures which stimulated the old Greek curiosity and produced much ethnographic and geographical material. While most of it did not directly deal with the past of the people described, the historical dimension was rarely ignored. Quite often a practical motive joined that of simple curiosity. For example, since the Seleucid monarchy bordered in the East on the subcontinent of India, it became a political necessity for Seleucid kings to keep on good terms with the strong northern Indian kingdom of Chandragupta. A Greek, Megasthenes, stayed at its court in the years around 300 B.C. He recorded his experiences and observations in his *Indica*, which described the territories and people around the Ganges and Indus rivers. Unfortunately, little remains of his work beyond a few puzzling figures, among them the assertion that the area had 153 kings in 6,042 years, which would result in an average tenure of 39.5 years. Less puzzling was Megasthenes' attempt to show traces of activities by the god Dionysius in that area. Alexander's historians had also "found" such traces, particularly some "left" by Heracles. Such quasi-history was a simple way, indeed, for integrating the newly found area into the Greek cosmos.

*Babylonian and Egyptian histories*. The Greeks of the East could have learned interesting lessons from the non-Greeks, many of whom prided themselves on having a more illustrious past and older records than their conquerors. Two works wished to impress this fact on the new rulers while attempting to court their favor. Between 280 and 270 B.C. Berossus, a priest of Bel in Babylon, demonstrated in his three-part *Babyloniaca* the venerable age and achievements of the Mesopotamian peoples. He figured that the world was about 468,215 years old and that the history of Babylon and Chaldea reached back 435,600 years. After 432,000 of these years went by, the Great Flood occurred, the event which is the turning point in the *Babyloniaca*. After the flood, another

3,600 years elapsed until Alexander burst into the Middle East. How did Berossus know all this? Up to the time of the Assyrian Empire he relies on myths and other traditions, but from then on he consults extensive temple archives.

An Egyptian priest at Heliopolis, Manetho of Sebennythus, also could use temple archives for his *Aegyptiaca* (ca. 280 B.C.), in which he, too, stressed the illustrious career of his native area before the arrival of the new masters. The work, dedicated to Ptolemy II, was chronologically well organized, using as principle of organization the Egyptian royal dynasties.

The works of Berossus and Manetho shared two other features besides chronological finesse: they were written in Greek and they were virtually ignored for generations. Manetho's sober history yielded in popularity to an earlier Greek history of Egypt by Hecataeus of Abdera; a fanciful, impressionistic, and often unreliable work which intended to let the world know about the greatness of the territories ruled by the Ptolemies. But Berossus's and Manetho's histories were eventually appreciated. By 70 B.C. Alexander Polyhistor's digest of Berossus's *Babyloniaca* began to interest the Jews, who found in it much material concerning their early history. The Jewish historian Flavius Josephus used the *Babyloniaca* and the histories of Egypt by Hecataeus and Manetho for reconstructing Jewish history. Early Christian scholars, particularly Eusebius, scrutinized the *Babyloniaca* in their attempts to date the creation of the world and of Adam.

*History and chronology.* As culture met culture in the new political units, a long-neglected task needed to be taken up again: the construction of a uniform calendar. Only such a calendar could help historians in coordinating the records left by the many different peoples who inhabited the immense area now penetrated by Greek civilization. When they wrote their works, they could hardly use phrases like "when Pythodorus had four months of his archonship to run at Athens," which had already meant little to a Spartan and now meant even less to inhabitants of Ptolemaic Egypt or Seleucid Babylonia.

The new attempts to sort out the many different calendars were by no means solely prompted by scholarly interests. Seleucus had gathered into his monarchy a multitude of Middle Eastern regions and people. For administrative reasons Seleucus gave his kingdom a new and uniform calendar, one that began with his conquest of Babylon in October, 312 B.C. With so recent a beginning date, the calendar solved few of the problems of historical scholars but provided a useful chronological standard for the region, so much so that many Jews figured years according to the Seleucid era until the eleventh century A.D. and Syrian Christians still do. Berossus had offered another potentially universal time-scale in his *Babyloniaca*. He had used as his basic unit the Saros period, which represented the time from a certain constellation of sun, earth, and moon to its exact duplication 6,585 and 1/3 days later. When the *Babyloniaca* was ignored, the Saros periodization suffered the same fate.

Greek historians eventually found a Greek solution to the synchronization problem, and Timaeus of Tauromenium has been credited with it. The credit is deserved, if given in proper measure. In the third century B.C. he "drew out a comparative list of the ephors and the kings of Sparta from the earliest times; as well as one comparing the archons at Athens and priestesses in Argos with the list of Olympic victors."[6] In short, Timaeus continued the line of those who had studied existing local time-frames in order to bring them into proper relation to each other. He most likely had access to earlier work done on the issue, including the improvements made by Aristotle in the figuring of the Olympiad and the dated list of victors in the Pythian games by Aristotle's nephew Callisthenes. It remained for Timaeus, first, to improve upon the work of his predecessors by his own *Olympionicae* and, then, to use the Olympiad scale consistently in his work.

The usefulness of Timaeus's Olympiad calendar is attested to by Eratosthenes. That famous geographer, mathematician, astronomer, and poet also wrote an erudite work, *On Chronology*. But when he needed a chronology for his own history of Greek comedy, Eratosthenes accepted Timaeus's system, thereby giving it his sanction. Yet neither he nor Timaeus seem to have extended the Olympic scale backwards beyond the first Olympic Games (776 B.C.).

After Timaeus, Greek historians finally had available a common calendar with which they could synchronize past events. But the lack of political unity of the Greek areas of the Mediterranean world prevented the uniform use of the Olympiad calendar. People still lived their lives in local and regional contexts. They felt no urgent need to accept the uniform Olympiad time-scale as long as local and regional calendars sufficed for their daily life.

*The Greeks meet their future: Rome.* The people who eventually changed Greek politics decisively lived to the West, untouched by Alexander and the Diadochi. Life in the Hellenistic East went its course while on the Italian peninsula the city of Rome was extending its dominion over the Etruscans, Latins, Samnites, and, by 275 B.C., the Greeks of Magna Graecia (Greater Greece in southern Italy). After Rome had consolidated its hold on central and southern Italy, she eyed Sicily where she would confront her most important opponent: Carthage.

The Greeks of the West were shadowy figures to historians of the Greek heartland, appearing only intermittently in the well-known histories. Only historians in and from Sicily, an island with frequent cultural and military collisions, wrote extensively on the history of the Greek West. Antiochus of Syracuse, a contemporary of Herodotus and Thucydides, described the history of Western Greeks from the mythical age to the Peace of Gela in 424 B.C. In the process he recorded the momentous fact that in 480 B.C., when the Greeks in the East won their famous victory over the Persians at Salamis, the Greeks on

Sicily achieved a similar triumph. The tyrant Gelon of Syracuse defeated the Carthaginians at Himera, thereby rescuing the Greek settlements on Sicily from Carthage's grasp. The next decisive event in the West was the destruction of the Athenian expeditionary corps by the Syracusans; in the fourth century the Sicilian Philistus told about it. Philistus's *Sicelica* also contains some hints on why Sicilian history was not easy to write. The extensive role tyrants played points to the lack of internal stability in many of the city-states, which in turn severely impeded the forming of a stable tradition and the development of a sense of continuity.

Political problems also shaped the life of the third and most important of the Sicilian historians, Timaeus of Tauromenium, who spent fifty years as an exile in Athens. His *Olympionicae*, already discussed, was a chronological study of Olympic victors. Of his main work, his *History* (possibly called *Sicelica*), only 386 fragments remain. We owe much of what we know about it to Timaeus's relentless critic Polybius, who tells us that Timaeus treated the past of Italy, Sicily, and North Africa. Even fewer fragments are left of a supplementary work, the *History of the Pyrrhic Wars*.

Timaeus apparently wrote history in the broad manner of Herodotus and seems to have enjoyed an excellent reputation in the ancient world, Polybius's objections to such a rambling history notwithstanding. It helped that Timaeus wrote about Rome at the historical moment when that city had started its steep ascendancy to dominance. As for the origin of Rome, he mentioned briefly the story of Heracles' crossing of the Tiber River at Rome, the warm hospitality Heracles received on that occasion, and the promise of a good future contained in the episode. He also knew the stories about Aeneas as the Trojan ancestor of Rome and about the Roman tradition of Romulus and Remus. But Timaeus did not ascribe the founding of Rome to gods, heroes, or Trojans. He linked Rome's origin with that of Carthage, which, he maintained, was founded by fugitives from the Phoenician city of Tyre. He calculated 814/13 B.C. as the founding year of Carthage on the basis of data he had found in the Tyrian annals. For unknown reasons he then simply stipulated the same date as the founding year of Rome. Timaeus must have known full well what such a comparatively recent date—over 400 years after Troy's fall—did to the by then well-known affirmation of Rome's Trojan origin. He granted that a Trojan settlement might have preceded Latin Rome. What other reason could Romans have had for the annual killing of a warhorse on the Campus Martius than to express their anger over the ruse of the Trojan horse which had cost their ancestors so dearly?

Timaeus's work was typical for the best that Hellenistic historiography could deliver: a sophisticated treatment of the past which, however, stayed within long-established limits of perception and interpretation. In form and content Greek historiography had exhausted its possibilities. Its next stimulus would come from outside the Greek world—from Rome. About half a century after Timaeus's death, Greek historiography began its role as mentor to Roman historians; it had much to offer its tutees.

The Greeks had created the very concept of history itself when, with Herodotus, ἱστορία had changed from a general inquiry about the world into inquiry about past events. Unlike the Near Eastern records of the past—lists of kings and dynasties—Greek history became the story of the human world; a world contingent and far from the eternal, changeless essences of philosophers. Accordingly, as the Greek world changed, Greek historiography changed with it. With the triumph of the *polis*, the epic heroes and deeds were pushed out of the center of attention by the citizens, leaders, and affairs of the city-states. Thucydidean political history remained prominent for centuries, although the basis for its prominence had disintegrated with the Macedonian hegemony and its Hellenistic aftermath. However, life in the Hellenistic world gave strength to other aspects of Greek historiography: biography, molded for historical uses by Xenophon, stilled curiosity and provided examples of excellence; ethnographic descriptions, present in political narratives as digressions, became popular in their own right; history as drama and entertainment found favor with people who lacked strong collective allegiances; chronology advanced in sophistication and in the Olympiad scheme created a symbolic Greek unity.

That splendid record had one weak spot. When Greeks attempted to reconcile the past, present, and future they were successful within short ranges in time and small regions of space. But the past found an impenetrable border in the epic period, and the expected future never varied much from the present—from the *polis* and, later, the monarchies of the Diadochi. The lack of a sense of overall development deprived Greek historiography of a strong dynamism. Not surprisingly, Greek historiography never found an effective approach to writing a universal history of the known world. Ephorus tried to transcend the *polis*-oriented political history but could not manage more than a quasi-Panhellenistic Greek history with accompanying sections on the barbarians. Only Rome would bring a new and wider concept of unity, one reluctantly accepted by the Greeks.

In turn, the Romans were offered substantial information and fully developed historiographical forms: the hard-won results of the Greek developments, from epic to prose history. While Roman historians adapted these forms for their use, they simply copied the Greek ideas on the theory of history. The Greeks themselves had not given too much thought to methodology. At an early stage they had replaced the authority of myth and epic by that of reason and, to a lesser extent, experience. Failing to develop any proper means for finding out about the distant past, Greek historians preferred contemporary history, which could be built on the testimony of eyewitness accounts. For the rest of the past a mildly critical reliance on authoritative authors had to do. Since Greek historians never thought of historiography as primarily a reconstruction of the past for the sake of truth or intellectual curiosity but always as an endeavor with a purpose—ranging from the preservation of noble memories to the education of active citizens to the gratification of desires for entertainment or even gossip—the simple methodology posed no problem. None of these purposes required the type of methodology that eventually would become a necessity when historians set out to reconstruct the past, piece by little piece. Antiquarian and local historiography, with their greater interest in sources, were insufficiently prominent to change matters.

# ·4·

## Early Roman Historiography
## Myths, Greeks, and the Republic

### An Early Past Dimly Perceived

*Of founders and of kings.* In history textbooks the Roman state rushed from obscurity unerringly to greatness, while in actuality the Roman state took a tortuous road to imperial power. The Romans, an ethnically complex people who gradually had settled on seven hills near the Tiber, were not really masters of their fate until well after 509 B.C. Prior to that time they were just another part of the Latins, who were blessed with excellent soil for their livelihood and with the presence of two highly developed neighboring civilizations; one to their north, the Etruscans, and another to their south, the Western Greeks. For centuries, however, the Etruscan influence must have impressed Romans as more dominant than beneficial. The Etruscans, most of whom were united in a federation of city-states, pursued a vigorous cultural and political expansionism, one Rome could not escape. Only with the emergence of the Roman Republic around 509 B.C. and with the Syracusan defeat of the Etruscan naval power at Cumae (474 B.C.) did Etruscan hegemony subside. By then, however, Etruscan culture had left its indelible imprint on Roman culture.

The influence of the Western Greeks was less intense. They had reached the Italian peninsula first in the Mycenaean (or Achaean) period. Then, in the eighth century, the Greeks again moved westward in an extensive colonization movement, which transformed wide areas of southern Italy into a Greater Greece *(Magna Graecia)* and made much of Sicily Greek. The settlers brought along, of course, their myths, including those telling about Greek and Trojan heroes who had sailed west; among them Aeneas, Odysseus, and Diomedes.

Among the neighbors whom the Greeks acquired were the Latins, who at that time deserved no special notice. Only after 600 B.C. and still under Etruscan influence did Rome take shape, when the hill dwellers established a common marketplace, the *Forum Romanum*, a paved area on drained marshy

40

lowland. That *Forum*, together with the *Forum Boarium* (the cattle market close to the Tiber) eventually developed into the municipal core of Rome.

During the early sixth century Romans must have become acquainted with elements of the Greek mythological past, judging from the fact that in those years pottery adorned with pictures of Aeneas carrying his father, Anchises, from burning Troy was used in Etruria and Rome. Such filial concern must have appealed to the always strong Roman sense of family solidarity. We may assume that Romans by then also were aware of the Greek tradition telling about Aeneas's flight to the West. Like other people of the area the Romans eventually accepted the view that Aeneas was one of their ancestors, although we do not know for certain when that acceptance occurred. It is easier to ascertain when the Greeks claimed that Rome had been founded by Aeneas or his descendants. Hellanicus of Lesbos did so in the fifth century when he told how Aeneas came to Italy, after or with Odysseus, and founded Rome.

It was one more example of the characteristic Greek reaction to the intrusion of a new people into the Greek field of vision. The new people were hellenized by having their early past integrated into the by then elaborately worked-out Greek mythological past. Nobody was allowed to exist outside that orbit and few people resisted being drawn into it. It mattered little that the accounts of what happened differed as long as the differing versions stayed within the proper perimeter. Thus in one version Aeneas was forced to stay in Italy by a Trojan woman named Rhome who burned the Trojan ships, while in another Aeneas became the husband of Rhome. In either case Aeneas was the common ancestor of the Romans.

But Romans also had a Roman story on Rome's origin. In the centuries preceding 509 B.C.—a common although by no means firm date for the beginning of the Roman Republic—kings governed Rome. Seven of them, or eight if one counted Romulus's coruler Titus Tatius, were recognized later by Roman historians, although modern scholars have not been so sure about any of them. The first of these kings, Romulus, became the core of another tradition concerning the founding of Rome. The name itself contains the Etruscan suffix *-ulus*, which seems to stand for "a founder of." In the prevalent version of the story, which took centuries to develop fully, Romulus was the twin brother of Remus. The boys resulted from the rape of the vestal virgin Rhea Silvia by the god Mars. Rhea Silvia's uncle, the king of Alba Longa, ordered the boys slain but the man charged with the deed only abandoned them. A she-wolf nursed them and a herdsman and his wife eventually raised the boys. After killing Remus, Romulus founded Rome and became its first king. When exactly Romans accepted Romulus as founder of their city and how widespread that acceptance was at a given time also remain obscure. However, by 296 B.C., the story of the two young men must have been well known since in that year a statue was erected and a coin struck both depicting Romulus, Remus, and the she-wolf.

The first Greek mention of Romulus and Remus appeared in the work of the Sicilian historian Alcimus (ca. 300 B.C.), although in that version Romulus and Remus belonged to different generations. Some scholars have maintained that Eratosthenes was the first Greek to credit Romulus with founding Rome.

*Traces of the past beyond the legends.* The Roman Republic came about, so tradition has it, when the series of seven kings ended with the fall from power of Tarquinius Superbus (the Proud). The event, usually dated as happening in 509 B.C., was the subject of an early historiographical reference to Roman history. A historian, some have suggested Hyperochus, wrote about the life of Aristodemus the Effeminate who, as a ruler of the city of Cumae (ca. 504-480), wished to diminish Etruscan influence and to that end interfered in the struggle of Rome against the Tarquinii—a fact mentioned in Hyperochus's record.

The Roman sense for history, the strong Greek influence notwithstanding, was rooted in the basic social units, the *gens* and the *familia*. The *gens* consisted of kinspeople who claimed to descend from a common prehistoric ancestor, were tightly bound together by common rituals, and even had their own burial rites and cemeteries. The family *(familia)* centered around a similar ancestral cult although it did not reach so far back in time. Waxen masks of ancestors and inscriptions listing honors and offices of the ancestors were displayed at a prominent place in the Roman home. As a part of the funeral rites, speeches praising the deceased's merits were delivered *(laudationes funebres)* and copies eventually were preserved next to the pictures of the ancestors. These biographies, flawed by flattery, formed a loose record of past generations and became a rudimentary source for later writers. For the individual Roman the past and the present were joined through the memories and records of the *gens* and of the family, sources that inspired piety and offered historical *exempla* as standards for current conduct.

The Greeks had used the sequence of generations as a means of creating a rudimentary chronology, but the Romans did not do so. For centuries Romans were content with a record of the past whose segments were uncoordinated. They did develop a calendar, which according to tradition received its lasting shape through the reforming work of the second king, Numa Pompilius. It was essentially a lunar calendar with solar rectifications. Romans used it to make sure that sacrifices, religious rituals, the gathering of assemblies, and other activities were all executed at the proper time. But the early Romans, who tried to be accurate about measuring time within the year, have left us few traces of their systems for the counting of years. We only know of the pounding of nails into the *cella* wall of the Capitoline Temple (Minerva's room), presumably for counting the years, and of a method to reckon years according to the year of the *rex sacrorum*.

The keepers and compilers of past records were the Roman priests, all of whom belonged to specific priestly groups, one each for the sacred dimensions of agriculture, processions, ceremonial public meals, and *auspices*. The *pontifices* who supervised these groups of priests were subject to the *pontifex maximus*. That supreme priest compiled a master list of those days on which sacred law permitted business and court transactions to take place (the *dies fasti*), implying of course, the forbidden days (the *dies nefasti*). How far back these records went we do not know. By 304 B.C. the records, written on wooden tablets, were exhibited in the *regia*, once supposedly the palace of King Numa Pompilius, later the residence of the *pontifex maximus*. The *Annales Maximi* gradually began to include also the names of high officials, proper dates for religious functions, the death of priests and the names of their successors, and notes on fires, floods, famines, battles, laws, and treaties. It is not too farfetched to assume that the habit of recording year by year the events in the collective life of the state shaped the historiographical genre of annals, which became characteristic of much of Roman historiography. Annals stood in stark contrast to the Greek love for freer literary forms and testified to the intimate and lasting connection between Roman public life and Roman historiography. A number of other records in annalistic form, which also began early in the Republic's life, testified to that link. The *fasti consulares* recorded the highest officials for each year. Lists of magistrates were kept in the temple of Juno Moneta (until ca. 50 B.C.), of treaties in the Capitoline Temple (destroyed by fire at the time of Sulla), of statutes in the temple of Saturn (until Julius Caesar), and of Senate acts in the temple of Ceres (until Augustus).

## The Roman Past and Greek Learning

The near extinction of the Roman state by the Gauls under Brennus in about 390 B.C. was so dramatic an episode that the stories of the terrible defeat at the Allia, the heroic defense of the Capitol by Marcus Manlius, and the help the defenders received from the Capitoline geese would be reported over and over again in Roman history. Even Theopompus and Aristotle were fascinated, and their narrations were the first to place a Roman historical event in a Greek context. But the linkage between Greek and Roman historiographies came later and only gradually. With the exception of Timaeus of Tauromenium, Greek historians paid no attention to the subsequent Roman drive for dominance over the Latin League and the Roman subjugation of the Hernici, Volsci, Aequii, Sabines, and the city of Veii. However, Rome's war against the Greek Tarentum (282-275 B.C.) changed things. In it the ally of Tarentum, King Pyrrhus of Epirus, even used Greek epic history to give the struggle a higher meaning. Claiming ancestry from Achilles, Pyrrhus saw himself as an avenger of the Achaeans on Rome, a city supposedly founded by the Trojan Aeneas. After Rome won and became master of Magna Graecia, Greek historians became somewhat more interested in Rome. Timaeus of Tauromenium had already for some time inquired more closely into the past of that newcomer to the

Mediterranean system of powers and in doing so permanently linked Greek and Roman historiographies. Now in 273 B.C. Ptolemy sent an embassy to Rome to assess the new power, and one of the Alexandrian librarians and historians, Lycophron, spoke of the steady rise of Rome to hegemony over the Western Mediterranean.

*Synchronizing the oldest Roman traditions.* The meeting of Roman and Greek historiographical traditions initiated a process as inevitable as it was slow. No scientific urge for compatibility worked toward properly combining the traditions; nevertheless the need for a reconciliation grew from generation to generation as the fates of the two cultures and peoples intertwined. At issue was the fact that the various accounts of the Roman origin soon betrayed grave inconsistencies in chronology. Aeneas, a survivor of the Trojan War, obviously lived during and shortly after it. When Timaeus placed the fall of Troy at about 1193 B.C. (Eratosthenes thought 1184/83 B.C. to be proper) and then insisted that Rome was founded only in 814/13 B.C., a gap of nearly four hundred years opened up. The Romans, who by 300 B.C. had come to regard their own Romulus story at least as highly as the story that told about Aeneas, eventually needed to reconcile the two traditions. Clearly, the relationship between Aeneas and Romulus could not forever remain the widely accepted one of father and son or grandfather and grandson, although even some early Roman historians still maintained the latter relationship. In the end, other Latin traditions, particularly those of Lavinium and Alba Longa, helped out. Alba Longa won its long-standing competition for prestige with Lavinium when a series of Alba Longa kings was used to fill the gap between Aeneas and Romulus.

*Two early Roman histories—in Greek.* The second historiographical consequence of Rome's encounter with the Greek world was the emergence of narrative histories done by Romans. It took the Romans incredibly long to look reflectively at their past and celebrate the dramatic success of so small a group of people who conquered and subjugated so many in so short a time. By 272 B.C., Rome had become the mistress of central and southern Italy. Then she collided with powerful Carthage in the monumental First and Second Punic Wars. These jarring collective experiences finally produced some Roman historians: a poet from Campania, Gnaeus Naevius, and two Roman senators, Quintus Fabius Pictor and Lucius Cincius Alimentus.

They wrote their works, of which little remains, on behalf of Rome. Naevius called his work the *Bellum Poenicum*. Although the title indicated a Roman version of the First Punic War, the work was really a Roman national epic with a lengthy account of Rome's mythological past and a deliberate preference for the old Roman Saturnian verse pattern over a Greek one.

Both Fabius Pictor and Cincius Alimentus participated in what later on would be considered the greatest Roman war, the Second Punic War. The catastrophic defeat at Cannae in 216 B.C. made Cincius a prisoner of war and sent Fabius Pictor, on behalf of the senate, to the oracle of Delphi for advice on what Rome should do. On that trip Fabius undoubtedly experienced the cross-currents in Greek public opinion on Rome and Carthage and also the role of historiography in shaping that opinion. The Carthaginians had found historians defending their case, such as Philinus of Acragas, who had pointed out the general lack of justice in the Roman cause. Had the Romans not broken a treaty with Carthage when they had crossed over to Sicily in the first place? On the other hand the highly respected and widely known Timaeus of Tauromenium had been more sympathetic to the Roman side. The wish to gain sympathy for Rome in the Hellenistic world certainly was one of the motives that led Fabius Pictor and Cincius Alimentus to write their Roman histories in Greek. That Roman prose lingered at too undeveloped a stage—as some have argued—may have made the decision to write in Greek easier but could hardly have been the main motive. Enough samples of old Roman oratory survive to show that Roman prose was not altogether that primitive.

Only fragments, not even the title, remain of Fabius Pictor's work, which by all indications was superior to that of his fellow senator. He wrote about the past in a year-by-year account—annalistically—which explains Cicero's reference to it as the Greek Annals (Graeci Annales). They, it may be safely stated, gave a continuous account from mythological time to the present. The work also seems to have carried other marks of future Roman historiography. Reflection on the past was linked to moral judgments, a keen interest in the early Roman past, an emphasis on the senate as the central institution for the destiny of Rome, and the tendency to enhance the status of one's family. Most important, by the early second century B.C. Romans had available, albeit only in Greek, a unified view of their past.

### Greco-Roman History Writing
### Triumph and a Latin Response

When the pioneers, Fabius Pictor and Cincius Alimentus, wrote their works in Greek they acknowledged the power of Greek culture; so great was that power that much of early Roman historiography could be more accurately called Greco-Roman. In historiography the Greek influence flowed easily through the conduits of Timaeus and Philinus of Agrigentum, both of whom had written about the past of the Mediterranean area and therefore held a special interest for Romans. The Greco-Roman historians in the narrow sense of the term, namely those who wrote Roman history in Greek, were of second rank compared to Fabius Pictor and Cincius Alimentus.

The exception was Polybius, a native of Megalopolis, who became the greatest of the Greco-Roman historians. His lifetime, from ca. 200 B.C. to ca. 118 B.C., spanned the period in which Rome reduced her strongest competitor in the Western Mediterranean, Carthage, to insignificance and turned East to conquer large segments of the Hellenistic world in wars against Philip V of Macedonia, Antiochus III of Pergamum, the Seleucid Empire, and Perseus of Macedonia. After Perseus's defeat at Pydna (168 B.C.) one thousand prominent men of the Achaean League, among them Polybius, were brought as hostages to Italy. Until 150 B.C., when the hostages were released (safe enough by then, as Cato the Elder quipped, to be entrusted to the Greek undertakers), most of them wasted away in provincial Italy. Polybius escaped that fate because Lucius Aemilius Paullus, the victor of Pydna, made it possible for Polybius to stay in Rome, first as tutor and then as friend of Publius Cornelius Scipio Aemilianus. Although he was legally bound to remain under praetorial supervision in Rome, nobody prevented him from traveling widely, sometimes as an observer of Roman campaigns. As Scipio's confidant Polybius also could watch the ultimate destruction of Carthage in 146 B.C. Therefore his *Histories* represent a report on Rome's recent past by an outsider who could observe Roman government, military arts, and diplomacy from an extremely favorable position. During the composition of his account of the Roman expansion between 220 and 167 B.C., Polybius's admiration for the Romans exceeded that of most Greeks, but eventually, in his account of the years from 167 to 146 B.C., he was more critical of Rome and less sure of her lasting success.

*Polybius on order and forces in history.* The *Histories* were tightly constructed around the theme of Rome's rise to the status of a great power. Although Polybius, in a manner reminiscent of Thucydides, kept a tight rein on digressions, such digressions were acceptable in ancient historiography as resting points in the flow of the narrative and he did include some, on the Roman constitution, on Timaeus of Tauromenium, on geography (one book each), and on some minor items such as his own contribution to fire signaling, a technique of communication.

Polybius, never content with mere description, asked why the Romans succeeded where the Greeks had not and gave a threefold answer. First, there was a set of proper attitudes. The Roman character featured the traits of statesmanship, perseverance, and steadiness of purpose; Roman public figures showed an intense and selfless dedication to the state; and Roman policy towards the defeated avoided brutality and vindictiveness and emphasized moderation and humanity. All of these attitudes and policies combined to make the Roman state more stable and Roman imperialism more moderate and enlightened than anything that Athens and Sparta had produced. Later in his life Polybius was no longer so sure about Roman benevolence.

Second, Roman political institutions were better suited to insure the necessary social stability than those of democratic Athens had been. At issue was the cycle of birth, rise, acme, and decay discussed by the early philosophers, mentioned even by the unphilosophical Thucydides, and turned into a theory of successive government forms by Plato and other philosophers (see figure 4.1).

For some years Polybius seems to have thought that Rome would be exempt from the cycle of government forms, and thus from decay, by virtue of her mixed constitution. In it the government forms which usually succeeded each other were coexisting (see figure 4.2). As Polybius saw it, Lycurgus legislated such a mixed constitution for Sparta, but the Romans developed their remarkable constitution by trial and error.

Figure 4.1

Polybius's Regular Cycle of Constitutional Revolutions

"Precivilization": People herd together, prompted by weakness as individuals; the strongest and bravest one leads. Result: *Despotism*. As family ties and other social relations are established, concepts of duty and justice appear; they lead to

1st form: *Monarchy*

King instead of despot, after notions of goodness and justice have been formed.

King has courage; offers protection; acceptance of his rule is by reason; lives much like subjects.

return to:                                          corrupted to:

*Tyranny*

Unprincipled leaders use the mob, which has become accustomed to have its greed fed constantly; corruption and demagoguery rampant; violence is used. Now the despot returns to establish order.

Comes about when king's descendants imagine themselves to be "superior persons"; indulge in violence; evoke opposition to their luxury, greed, arrogance.

*Mob Rule*

changed to:

corrupted to:

2d form: *Aristocracy*

Those who have the public interest in mind take over and govern. But eventually those who never experienced the oligarchy no longer value equality/freedom.

Those who revolt are accepted as leaders out of gratitude for deposing tyrant. They first have the common interest as their guide. After a few generations

3d form: *Democracy*

corrupted to:

changed to:

*Oligarchy*

Aristocrats treat their power and positions as rights; exploit them; avarice, debauchery . . .

Source: Compiled from Polybius *The Histories* 6.6–9

Figure 4.2

The Roman Mixed Constitution

| General forms: | Monarchy | Aristocracy | Democracy |
|---|---|---|---|
| | ↓ | ↓ | ↓ |
| Embodied in: | power of consuls | senate | popular assemblies |

Eventually, Polybius began to doubt Rome's immunity to the cycle, and he indicated that Rome, too, would suffer the usual consequences of being a great power and of the prosperity connected with it. When the sympathies of the masses spoiled by extravagance could be bought by demagogues, the corruption of leaders could hardly be avoided. At that stage the old virtues will have vanished, together with the fear of the gods, freeing people to do as they please. The three forms mixed in the Roman constitution will then have reached their corrupted stages together.

Third, there was *Tyche* (Fate or Fortune). Since 217/6 B.C. it had guided events towards the merging of the many Mediterranean peoples into one state system under Rome's leadership; a great compliment, indeed, since Polybius viewed Fortune not as a capricious or neutral force but as the upholder of the moral law. He argued with his contemporaries that "if a man were disposed to find fault with Fortune for her administration of human affairs, he might fairly become reconciled to her in this case; for she brought upon those monarchs the punishment they so well deserved, and by the signal example she made of them taught posterity a lesson in righteousness."[1] On a few occasions Polybius spoke directly of *Tyche* as an overall providence whose designs the historian must trace. "Just as Fortune made almost all the affairs of the world incline in one direction, and forced them to converge upon one and the same point; so it is my task as an historian to put before my readers a compendious view of the part played by Fortune."[2] Still, the power conceded to *Tyche* knew one definite limit. Polybius, like Thucydides before him, wanted to view history as an orderly process but not to diminish more than was necessary the human role in it; this was a dilemma which caused Polybius to leave the nature of *Tyche* and the relationship between human actions and Fortune's power without exact definition or resolution.

*Unity of period, chronology, and sources.* Polybius lauded Ephorus for guiding Greek history beyond narrow regional limits. He himself stressed that in the year of the 140th Olympiad (217/16 B.C.) Italy, the Hellenic world, and North Africa were for the first time parts of the same history. From that point on, the writing of histories of individual localities and regions must yield to the concern with the wider Mediterranean area. But with regard to the time span to be covered, Polybius did not require comprehensiveness. He, who had no use for stories about the early past, began where Aratus's *Memoirs* had ended (220 B.C.) and told primarily the story of the recent period, specifically from 217/16 to 144 B.C. That gave his narrative a sense of unity, as it reached from one of Rome's lowest points to her unification of large parts of the Mediterranean area. He further enhanced the unity of his narrative when he used consistently the chronological system of Olympiad years, following in this case Timaeus's lead.

Polybius acknowledged, sometimes grudgingly, that historians of some stature had preceded him. He read their works, learned from them, and criticized them severely. Polybius did not care for Theopompus's moralizing and philosophizing, Phylarchus's and other dramatic historians' emotionalism and sensationalism, Philinus of Agrigentum's Carthaginian partisanship, and Fabius Pictor's Roman bias. Minor historians such as Chaereas and Sosilus earned merely derision since their works were more "the gossip of the barber's shop and the pavement than history."[3] The famous historian Timaeus of Tauromenium became the target of an especially fierce criticism—one whole book (Book 12). Polybius accused Timaeus of misstatements, ignorance of warfare and politics, mistakes, poor observations, insufficient inquiry, lying, errors in chronology, and telling only the bad things about Agathocles. One senses in his harsh criticism something beyond professional purism, namely, jealousy of Timaeus's fame.

At issue was accuracy. Even ancient historians who wrote contemporary history often covered periods longer than their lifespans and an area wider than their own; so they encountered the issue of sources. Polybius thought that the most reliable accounts came from eyewitnesses or at least from those with appropriate personal experiences. One cannot tell whether he used documentary sources at all. As an exile he lacked for many years access to Greek depositories, and one doubts that, as a man who wrote in Greek and knew even contemporary Latin poorly, he mastered the Roman records written in old Latin. His knowledge probably came from his personal contacts in the worlds of Greece and Rome. In addition, he also inspected the locations of some historical events. In one instance he attempted to retrace Hannibal's crossing of the Alps. All in all, Polybius held to a number of well-considered methodological principles, although he wrote no books on methods.

*On the purpose of history.* Polybius angrily rejected history written for entertainment, in the manner of Duris of Samos and Phylarchus, or for the satisfaction of antiquarian or local curiosity. History must teach about life. On occasion, that might mean to console individuals whom fate has struck a blow, since "the most instructive, or rather the only, method of learning to bear with dignity the vicissitudes of fortune is to recall the catastrophes of others."[4] However, history must above all teach lessons to those active in public life, who can then apply the lessons to the present.

Proper history was pragmatic history which had a political and military focus, tried to demonstrate causes, and concerned itself with the state and its welfare. Ironically, in this regard Polybius had most likely no direct effect on his contemporaries. We have to assume that few Romans were reached by a work written in Greek and few Greeks really cared enough for Roman history to read Polybius's work. Those who did were surely hesitant to accept their compatriot's urgings to submit to Rome because *Tyche* herself had chosen Rome to rule. The *Histories* impressed above all a small intellectual elite in Rome and the historians of subsequent generations, particularly Livy.

*Roman history in Latin.* Between 200 and 146 B.C. a fundamental transformation changed the whole context of Roman life as the Romans moved relentlessly toward the domination of large areas of the Mediterranean world. Power and wealth accrued to the Romans with grave consequences for their society. Of most immediate import was the encounter with Greek culture, which in most aspects, including literature, philosophy, and historiography, proved to be more sophisticated than Roman culture. But the influx of Greek goods, ideas, and attitudes also produced a greater awareness of the distinctive Roman culture. For quite a few Romans, pride in things Roman turned the encounter with Greek culture into a confrontation, one not systematic or altogether hostile but nevertheless competitive and evoking passions. As a result Roman traditionalists could soon turn to the works of Roman historians who emerged from the generation of the Second Punic War and shared an immense pride in everything Roman. One was a poet, Quintus Ennius of Rudiae, and another a public figure, Marcus Porcius Cato.

Ennius came from Rudiae in Calabria, an area steeped in Greek culture, and for it he himself was called a "half-Greek." But Ennius used his Greek learning to shape Roman history into a Latin epic. His two spiritual homes showed in the verse form he used, hexameters, and the title he gave his work, *Annals*. And in telling about the Roman past from the origin to 171 B.C. Ennius affirmed all things Roman without rejecting all things Greek.

Marcus Portius Cato's *Origins* were written in prose and lacked any dramatic unity, dealing as they did with a disparate set of topics such as statesmanship, wars, political events, the fat Cisalpine sows, and horse breeding. It had nevertheless a central theme, namely, the gradual building of the Roman tradition and state, which Cato viewed in a perspective reaching beyond the city of Rome.

Prominent among Cato's motives for writing the *Origins* was his wish to buttress the proper, that is, traditional Roman way of life. In a rich and colorful prose he exhorted Romans to be proud of their past, particularly in the face of the increasing hellenization of Rome, which for Cato and for many other Romans was no mere matter of private taste but a public issue. Cato pointed out how Roman soldiers had defeated all opposition in Magna Graecia, Sicily, and Greece proper but had imported Rome's own conqueror, Greek culture, when they brought back Greek books, scholars, tutors for their children, slaves, furniture, and clothing. Domination of so wide an area also increased Rome's wealth, and Roman life changed visibly in the direction of comfort, leisure, ease, and individualism. The price paid was a weakening of the collective spirit and of tradition. It is not surprising that hellenization shared in the blame for the vanishing of the Old Rome. In 161 B.C., Greek philosophers and rhetors were driven from Rome and in 155 B.C. an Athenian delegation was forced to cut short its stay in Rome because its members, three philosophers, offended many Romans by their attitudes and ideas. Cato was the ablest spokesman for those who sensed a danger to Rome's traditions, particularly to the Roman sense of civic duty and to the military spirit, from excessive wealth and from an overly eager acceptance of Greek models in life and thought; an attitude which came easily to Cato, the provincial from Tusculum, who throughout his life maintained a simple traditional outlook and an austere way of life.

Accordingly, as senator he tried to curb Rome's involvement in the East because of its tendency to increase Greek influence on Rome even further. He urged Romans, instead, to finish the old war against Carthage. Cato had been a member of a mission to Carthage and had been shocked to see the extent of that city's recovery.

Still, Cato never rejected simply and indiscriminately everything Greek. He even willingly acknowledged elements of the Greek mythological tradition as part of Rome's past. And while he cared little for Athens, the Sparta of Lycurgus and Leonidas bore a kinship to what Cato wished the Rome of the future to be: austere, proud, moderate in wealth, and with a ruling elite that would avoid tastes and standards harmful to the Roman state. But contemporary Greece must be rejected for its excessive concern with overly theoretical thought, wealth, luxury, and the individual, all of which seriously weakened the public spirit without which Rome could not remain great. In a special rebuke to excessive individualism, Cato stressed that Rome's rise was a collective achievement.

# ·5·

# Historians and the Republic's Crisis

### History as Inspiration and Structural Analysis

By 146 B.C., centuries of struggles were over and Rome was secure in her domination of the greater part of the Mediterranean area. Wars continued to be waged but they were no more than the martial routine of hegemony. Yet, the Romans discovered that as their old problems faded they faced new ones, which unfortunately could not be attacked simply by sending legions into the field.

The troubling and unresolved problems were many. Unjust distribution of the vast public land acquired by conquest led to bitterly contested reform attempts, mainly those by the Gracchi brothers. The vanishing of the family farm made many rootless people crowd into the slums of Rome, where they became a volatile element in Roman politics. A new class of men, called the *equites*, had wealth but in general lacked the power and influence of the senatorial aristocracy. Many Roman allies wanted citizenship but received no satisfaction from the aristocratic senate or even from the urban poor, both groups that feared for their quite uneven privileges. Then the war against the desert king Jugurtha of Numidia, in itself a minor event, demonstrated the damage that luxury and wealth had done to Roman society, particularly its elite. There showed poor discipline and a lack of endurance in the military, corruption in high places, and overreaching ambition in prominent individuals. After the Jugurthine War Romans resumed internal strife like that in the time of the Gracchi. In the civil war between the *populares* under Marius and the *optimates* under Sulla (88-82 B.C.) Romans killed and exiled Romans on a large scale. The Republic lived on as a mere shell in which the ambitions of men like Sulla, Pompey, and eventually Caesar governed events, often to the detriment of the Republic. For the first time Romans became aware that their life differed greatly from that of their ancestors and that the continuity of Roman tradition had been broken. That experience proved extremely disturbing. How did the past, seen as glorious and ideal, fit with the troubled present? Historical and quasi-historical works were written under the spell of this question.

*Old Rome as refuge and inspiration.* In ages of political and social strife, the past perceived as a tranquil, good, and purposeful world has often become a source of pride, consolation, and guidance. It had happened in Greece and now it happened in Rome. In his time, Cato had defended the Rome of traditional virtues which, if it ever existed, was by now only a memory. Some Romans, who looked fondly back to the Old Rome, found their nostalgia somewhat assuaged by a new antiquarianism. The contemporary of Cato and sponsor of Ennius of Rudiae, M. Fulvius Nobilior had published a collection of *fasti.* After 130 B.C. somebody, most likely the *pontifex maximus* Publius Mucius Scaevola, compiled a collection of the *Annales Maximi.* Had Roman historians cared more for documentation they could have found in these annals a rich source.

The peculiar traditionalism which aimed at extolling Old Rome found its historiographical expression in the detailed study of Roman antiquity—often with fanciful results—persisted throughout the troubled age. L. Aelius Praeconinus Stilo's studies gave him a considerable reputation and greatly influenced Cicero. A student of Stilo, Marcus Terentius Varro, became the greatest of these antiquarian scholars. In his old age he had the satisfaction of seeing the Augustan stabilization of contemporary Roman society in the image of Old Rome. Varro, a conservative landowner of the senatorial class, loved Roman antiquity and wrote between thirty-nine and seventy-four works on it. So brilliant was Varro's inventory of Roman culture that his interpretation of the Roman mythical age as well as his date for the founding of Rome, 753 B.C., became canonical. Unfortunately only a minor portion of his *Roman Antiquities,* which was the most historical work of them all, is known to us.

Aside from the antiquarian writings, historical works held to a less clear direction. The evocation of a greater civic consciousness may well have been the only unifying bond. Some historians yielded without objection to Greek influences. Gaius Fannius produced a somber account of strife-filled Rome, enhanced by Greek stylistic devices. His younger contemporary, Sempronius Asellio, a onetime military tribune, followed Polybius in going beyond the joys of pure narration to a search for motives and causes. In a sparse style and with stern admonitions he tried—and failed—to influence his fellow citizens.

Others, possibly influenced by the Hellenistic dramatic historians, wished to invoke in their audience an admiration for Old Rome by means of dramatic exposition. Characteristically, one of the best known of them, Coelius Antipater, was not only a legal expert but also a rhetorical mentor for public figures. When he restricted his history to an account of the second Punic War, he virtually assured his story of both dramatic quality and unity, and he proceeded to exploit that opportunity. Horrendous earthquakes, destroying whole cities, occurred as *omina* of terrible things to come. A huge storm accompanied the transfer of Scipio's army to Africa. And he insisted that Scipio's army was so large that it virtually depopulated both Italy and Sicily and that when the soldiers shouted the birds fell dead to the ground. Later, L. Cornelius Sisenna who also dramatized his history, albeit in a more restrained manner, skillfully painted mood pictures. He particularly loved to describe the shouts of fighting soldiers, the clash of shields, and the massacre of victims. The reader was to re-experience fear, panic, mistrust, and ecstasy.

Then there were the annalistic writers, often called "Sullan Annalists," grouped together according to the format of their writings. Gnaeus Gellius's tale of the Roman past was thirty or so books long, full of details on early life, much of it unreliable. Some of the Annalists tried to maintain the continuity between their age and Old Rome without following the antiquarians into Rome's mythological past. Q. Claudius Quadrigarius, finding the oldest account unreliable and less readable than he desired, reached back only to the invasion by the Gauls. L. Cornelius Sisenna wrote only contemporary history (for the period from 90 to 82 B.C., and primarily about the Italian or Social War). Both men linked up with Old Rome by their use of archaic Latin words and phrases.

Two annalistic accounts *ab urbe condita* came from C. Licinius Macer and Valerius Antias. Macer, who ended up a suicide after being successfully prosecuted by the praetor Cicero, wrote an unusually democratic account and has to be given credit for discovering a new source in the *libri lintei* (the linen books, with lists of magistrates). In comparison Valerius Antias's work impresses as quasi-fictional although it became quite popular.

*Sallust's analytical historiography.* The gap between the Roman past, perceived as an ideal period, and the trouble-filled present bothered many Romans and their historians. Yet explanations for it remained rare and shallow. Then in the first century B.C. Romans could learn about the systematic analysis of political affairs from Thucydides, whose work became fashionable, although he was studied much more for his style than for his substance. Polybius's and Posidonius of Apamea's reflections on the decay of states did not find acceptance either. A partial change of attitude came with the works on recent Rome by Sallust (C. Sallustius Crispus), who had been forced out of public life by allegations that he had excessively enriched himself at the public's expense. Not having Cicero's ability to find consolation in philosophy, he seized on history writing as a substitute for his aborted public career.

Coelius Antipater had introduced the Romans to the historical monograph. Now Sallust perfected that form with *The War with Catiline* and *The War with Jugurtha,* while his *Histories,* which continued Lucius Cornelius Sisenna's narrative beyond 78 to 67 B.C., followed the traditional continuous narrative pattern.

Sallust's two monographs carried his central message: internal forces were destroying the Roman Republic. In the debate preceding the last war against Carthage Scipio Nasica had warned that without a credible outside threat Roman society would lose its tough fiber. Now Sallust elaborated on that thesis.

And when Carthage, Rome's rival in her quest for empire, had been annihilated, every land and sea lay open to her. It was then that fortune turned unkind and confounded all her enterprises. To the man who had so easily endured toil and peril, anxiety and adversity, the leisure and riches which are generally regarded as so desirable proved a burden and a curse. Growing love of money, and the lust for power which followed it, engendered every kind of evil. Avarice destroyed honour, integrity, and every other virtue, and instead taught men to be proud and cruel, to neglect religion, and to hold nothing too sacred to sell. Ambition tempted many to be false, to have one thought hidden in their hearts, another ready on their tongues, to become a man's friend or enemy not because they judged him worthy or unworthy but because they thought it would pay them, and to put on the semblance of virtues that they had not. At first these vices grew slowly and sometimes met with punishment; later on, when the disease had spread like a plague, Rome changed....[1]

The *War with Catiline,* containing the story of the years from 66 to 63 B.C., demonstrated the harmful changes in the Roman elite's mentality. L. Sergius Catiline, brutal, ambitious, and totally corrupt, would have remained a footnote to history had it not been for Cicero's opposition and for Sallust's wish to demonstrate the corruption of the Roman collective fabric.

The *War against Jugurtha* chronicled the same decay of the elite, that is, mostly the senatorial class and, within it, mainly the consular families. The Jugurthine War itself was a minor war of a mighty empire against a wily desert prince, and its strange turns could only be explained by what Jugurtha had said after his visit to Rome: Rome's elite was corrupt, money could buy it and the arrogance of power could sway it. As for Sulla's state, it simply stabilized oligarchic rule. The masses, the plebs, could not turn the tide and in Sallust's view they deserved even less trust.

Sallust disagreed with his fellow citizens, who for a long time to come remained convinced that corruption was remediable by appealing to the moral sense of people and that historians should issue such appeals. Sallust, possibly influenced by Thucydides and Polybius, searched for the causes of decadence and at least tentatively entered into the area of systematic analysis, when he spoke briefly on the general fate of empires as that was mirrored in the fate of Rome.

The process begins with the irresistible urge to make war and dominate. For the successful state the reward of victory is hegemony. Yet to gain an empire means also to acquire wealth, which immediately begins to corrupt the state and its citizens. Rome had reached her turning point with the destruction of Carthage. Since then Romans have been left without a clear purpose and "no man really lives or gets any satisfaction out of life, unless he devotes all his energies to some task and seeks fame by some notable achievement or by the cultivation of some admirable gift."[2] Luxury and wealth promptly corroded the Roman virtues.

Sallust seemed to be left only with the melancholy task of describing how Rome became corrupt without Romans being able to stop it. Yet Sallust issued admonitions against letting melancholy prevail. Romans must not despair, complaining "that they are naturally feeble and short-lived, or that it is chance and not merit that decides their destiny."[3] Despite Sallust's own diagnosis of Rome's seemingly irremediable corruption through luxury and wealth he appealed as a historian to his fellow citizens for proper actions. In all of this Sallust refused, as other Roman historians would do, to expand the "decadence through wealth" pattern into a wider theory on the development of states. Even for him, Rome was destined to be everlasting.

In the end no single aspect of Sallust's work secured his place among historians. That was accomplished by the fact that his work supported the bridge of reflective and critical history writing which spanned a sea of annalists and narrators and reached from Cato to Tacitus.

### History Divorced from Rome's Fate

*Biography as history.* Cato had warned Romans to no avail against the harm done to a republic by a cult of personalities. Individualism of a different kind had all along been deeply embedded in Roman life. From early times, Romans had praised the merits of members of their *gentes* and families and celebrated the deeds of those who had served the Republic. In each case the individual's achievements were used as examples for a proper life, and the practice continued. But now, with the cohesion of Roman society diminished, the desire for individual recognition became, to a higher degree, a function of ambition, lust for power, craving for fame. These traits marked especially the more and more numerous memoirs and autobiographies. The writing of biographies had by then reached a sophisticated level. In the Hellenistic East the practice was supported by the rhetoricians, who cherished biographical writings as opportunities for the expression of joy, tragedy, praise, and condemnation, and by philosophers, who loved to use biographies as collections of examples for problems in proper conduct.

In Rome, the time of strife, with its own cult of personalities, created a most favorable climate for biographical writing. It thus is not surprising that the Greek biographical tradition found in the first century B.C. its first Latin representative, Cornelius Nepos. He knew that the reputation of biography was not that high. "I do not doubt that there will be many, Atticus, who will think this kind of writing trifling in its nature, and not sufficiently adapted to the characters of eminent men."[4]    And he worried about transgressing the line between history and biography and indicated where it was drawn: "for I fear that, if I begin to give a full account of his actions, I may seem, not to be relating his life, but to be writing a history."[5] But Nepos's simple style and his looking at the past through individual lives proved to be popular with his contemporaries and with language students of future centuries.

Autobiographical works became fashionable in the age of strife when persons felt it necessary to show that their lives had been well-spent, or wanted to justify their actions, and when a sense of personal fulfillment was no longer the matter-of-course result of a public career. Such was the case with the autobiographical works of Q. Lutatius Catulus and P. Rutilius Rufus. More substantial were Sulla's *Commentaries* wherein he justified his actions. When he proclaimed that the gods and Fortune had selected him to carry out their mandates, he foretold something about future attitudes. As for C. Julius Caesar, he wrote his *Commentaries* not in retrospect but on his way to the top. At that point he could hardly proclaim his designation for leadership by Fortune. Indeed, in his *Commentaries* he even avoided the word "I" and referred to himself in the third person, by name. Actually, the *Commentaries* were not even a true autobiography; they aimed to inform those who mattered in Rome about Caesar's campaigns, particularly his successes and brilliance. Caesar, well trained in rhetoric, accomplished this aim splendidly. In direct and simple language he gave an account of his wars in Gaul and his excursions into England and the German area. Given the propagandistic purpose of this first extant Latin history, its accuracy is astounding. Much later, at the peak of his career, Caesar already depicted himself, in his *Civil War,* as never having made a mistake and as favored by Fortune.

*History as scholarly enterprise.* Rome had bestowed on the learned historians of the Greek East a world of peace in which scholarship continued to prosper, particularly in Alexandria. In that area historians were more often than not grammarians and rhetors, many of whom studied critically the traditional texts. In that context they addressed a few methodological issues, mostly concerning the question of accuracy. Exemplary results were the elaborate if not pedantic studies of the Homeric epics, such as the sophisticated analysis of the *Iliad's* Catalogue of Ships by Apollodorus of Athens. Among the Hellenistic scholars such scholarly attention to the epics also passed as the appropriate expression of reverence.

Despite a growing influx of Greek intellectual and artistic works, Rome remained a poor soil for cultivating the theoretical and speculative attitudes and interests which Greeks cherished. In the whole period from 150 B.C. to Augustus there occurred only one noteworthy discussion of a few theoretical issues of historiography. Characteristically, the discussant, Marcus Tullius Cicero, was a master of Greek rhetoric who also was deeply engaged in public affairs.

Cicero urged his fellow Romans to study and emulate the Greek achievements in history writing and praised those Roman historians who paid proper attention to *veritas,* good descriptions, motives, deeds, causes, and sequence in time. His was to be a last valiant call for histories which instructed people on how they could be better citizens of the Republic and lead a more constructive life. But in order to be effective these histories had to be truthful. For "Who does not know history's first law to be that an author must not dare to tell anything but the truth? And the second that he must make bold to tell the whole truth?... That there must be no suggestion of partiality anywhere in his writings? Nor of malice?"[6] On occasion this Ciceronian concept of truth was even too stringent for Cicero himself. At one time he exhorted another writer (Lucceius): "So I frankly ask you again and again to eulogize my actions with even more warmth than perhaps you feel, and in that respect to disregard the canons of history ... bestow on our love even a little more than may be allowed by truth."[7]

Cicero was diverted here from his demand for unadorned truth by a second ideal, the effectiveness of history as teacher, which required that historians must create artistic compositions and not dull annals. In doing so historians could, just as other writers, arrange and select their material in a manner which would produce a useful memory of the past and lead readers to act properly. Cicero's history still remained at a safe distance from fictional tales or falsifications. The ideal remained a history which is true, "bears witness to the passing of the ages, sheds light upon reality, gives life to recollection and guidance to human existence, and bears tidings of ancient days."[8] There the reflection on history writing ended. Both the Roman temper and the limits of rhetoric confined the range of theoretical discussions. Cicero's reflections were as theoretical as ancient historians could muster. A people whose state dominated most of the *oikoumenē* and for whom history was the story of the climb to that hegemony produced historical works of greater or lesser accuracy but much certainty of purpose. Historical truth as pure reconstruction removed from pragmatic aims and resulting from dispassionate study was foreign to all Roman historians.

*The past as viewed from the Greek East.* The Greek East had been conquered but the Greeks were not touched greatly by the Roman internal turmoil. And because Greek historians were not captivated by the Roman civil war and discord, their interests led them in many directions. They generated an amorphous body of historical works ranging from antiquarian compilations to nostalgic evocations, to school texts for grammar and rhetoric students, to moral-lesson pieces, to high-class gossip, and, finally, to new reconstructions of the past.

There was the question of why Greeks now lived under the umbrella of a Panhellenism imposed by the Romans. The exile Polybius had credited constitutional arrangements, *Tyche,* and a superb civic spirit with Rome's success. Most Greeks spoke simply in terms of a drop-off from former glory since the conclusion of the Peloponnesian War in 404 B.C., for which they variously blamed the unwise treatment of allies and noncitizens, envy, greed, corruption, and divisiveness. But even in their period of discontent, Greek scholars—prominent among them were Aelius Aristeides, Dio of Prusa, and Philostratus—found their views on Panhellenism and the *polis* at odds. On the one hand they praised past attempts at unity and harmony among Greeks and on the other they celebrated the "Old Greece" of the separate city-states, particularly Athens and Sparta, because it had the greatness which the present sadly lacked. In Athens and other

Attican cities the long-ago victories over the Persians at Marathon, Salamis, and Plataea were celebrated annually, while in Sparta the battles of Thermopylae and of Plataea were commemorated at their anniversaries.

Despite all local and regional preferences, it became obvious to thoughtful observers that Roman rule was making one world out of what had been merely a geographical unit. Now historians had an opportunity to weld the historical accounts of diverse Mediterranean peoples into a unit, if they found the proper interpretation. Polybius had succeeded because he had accepted Roman hegemony as the common goal of the events of the last few centuries, something most Greeks were loathe to do. But his *Histories* were not truly comprehensive either in the sense of dealing with the earlier past of peoples or in the sense of dealing with areas not directly linked with the Roman story. Polybius's work was universal only to the degree the Roman state itself had grown to be universal by 140 B.C. His subject matter, Rome's creation of an *oikoumenè* by force, led Polybius to emphasize campaigns, battles, treaties, constitutional arrangements, and political maneuvers.

Could there be a unified account of the Mediterranean past without the "unity through Rome" theme which Greeks disliked? Apollodorus of Athens tried to write one and failed. His *Chronica,* telling of the past of various Mediterranean peoples from the fall of Troy to about 120 B.C., had iambic meter, some scholarly standards, but no unitary concept. It turned into a panoramic view of explorations, migrations of peoples, states, wars, artistic creations, intellectual events, and became a handbook for scholars.

Three-quarters of a century later Posidonius of Apamea brought forth a history of the Mediterranean area between 143 B.C. and Sulla which encompassed all the peoples who mattered and dealt with the realms of intellect and art. His Stoic cosmopolitanism broadened his perspective and enabled him to discuss with detachment the rise and fall of empires. In the end, the rhetor Castor of Rhodes had the most influence, with his *Chronicle* of events from the Assyrians to 60 B.C., a chronicle which was based on Apollodorus and took the form of chronological tables. There, lined up side by side and synchronized by years, were lists of the kings of Assyria, Media, Lydia, Persia, and Macedonia, kings and priests of Sicyon, and archons of Athens. The work hardly made for good reading but its encyclopedic and quasi-textbook qualities assured the *Chronicle* a strong influence on such diverse writers as Varro, Sextus Julius Africanus, and Eusebius. The latter used Castor's table-type comprehensive history when he created his Christian world chronicle and with it helped shape the world chronicles of the late ancient and medieval periods.

# ·6·

# Perceptions of the Past in Augustan and Imperial Rome

### History Writing in the "New Rome" of Augustus

In 20 B.C., for the first time since the close of the First Punic War, the doors of the Janus temple in Rome stayed closed, signaling to the Romans that no major wars were being waged and, above all, that Rome and Italy were free of civil strife. Octavian had won out over Mark Antony, returned in triumph to Rome, and began to recreate the Republic. But that refurbished Republic was no true republic at all. Octavian accumulated honorific titles as well as offices and their incumbent powers: *princeps civitatis* (first citizen of the state), imperator, Caesar, and finally Augustus. In addition he kept some significant powers, such as the prerogatives of a popular tribune and censor. To a populace yearning for stability, it mattered little. They welcomed the new state with its orderly government; where the army was, for a while at least, under firm control; where the prosperous middle class found outlets for its ambitions; where the senate was purged three times of political foes but also of its least worthy members; and where the traditional religion and *mores* found official sponsorship. Only the old senatorial families were ambiguous in their attitudes. But under Augustus they accepted the trappings of power in lieu of its substance.

The new situation in the Roman state exerted a decisive influence on the cultural climate. The Roman peace enabled a secure exchange of goods and persons between the regions. Inevitably the culturally sophisticated East reasserted its influence.

*Once more: Rome and the Greek East.* In the first century B.C. four Greeks tried again to resolve the problem of how to demonstrate a link between diverse collective pasts and the Roman-dominated present. Three of them attempted histories stretching in time and space beyond the Roman Empire while avoiding the "unity through Rome" theme. One, Dionysius of Halicarnassus, took up the narrower problem of finding a historical link between the Greek and Roman traditions.

60

The historian Timagenes, a freed prisoner of war, took the most negative stance on Rome's historical claims. Protected by his sponsor, Asinius Pollio, he compiled a quasi-universal history, reaching from the Ancient Near East to the Roman and Parthian empires. In it Timagenes made Macedonia, not Rome, the central feature.

No such anti-Roman sentiment inspired Nicolaus of Damascus, who had served Cleopatra and had found his main sponsor in Herod I, but ended up in Rome. To judge from the remaining fragments, he compiled a huge universal history from earlier accounts. It contained stories, moral lessons, explanations of dreams, descriptions of battles, sibyllic prophecies, dramatic episodes, teachings of Zoroaster, and, as a belated focus, a narrative about the rise of Rome. The *History* represented a masterpiece in the Hellenistic genre of historical compendia—a profusion of subject matter without overall theme or themes.

Diodorus Siculus (the Sicilian) based his *Library of History* on what he had learned from travels and other historians, whom he honestly quoted as his sources. He was later on taken to task for having traveled less than he claimed and borrowed more than he stated. But his vision of the role of universal history transcended clearly that of a scissors-and-paste historian. "It is fitting that all men should ever accord great gratitude to those writers who have composed universal histories, since they have aspired to help by their individual labours human society as a whole."[1] Although he acknowledged Rome as the central feature of the more recent history, he demonstrated that universal history did not begin with or have its ultimate aim in the Roman world. Instead, Diodorus, for the first time since the mythologists, put human history into a cosmological context when he traced the past back to the point "when in the beginning... the universe was being formed, both heaven and earth were indistinguishable in appearance, since their elements were intermingled."[2] Later, human beings appeared and Diodorus ventured some views on early human life:

> But the first men to be born, they say, led an undisciplined and bestial life, setting out one by one to secure their sustenance and taking for their food both the tenderest herbs and the fruits of wild trees. Then, since they were attacked by the wild beasts, they came to each other's aid, being instructed by expediency, and when gathering together in this way by reason of their fear, they gradually came to recognize their mutual characteristics.[3]

Subsequently he traced the emergence and development of civilization in the histories of Egyptians, Assyrians, Indians, Scythians, Arabs, Ethiopians, Amazons, people of Atlantis, Greeks, and Romans (to 60 B.C.). It may be too much to credit him with a clear recognition of the unity of humanity, but Diodorus certainly came closer to that than any other contemporary historian.

Dionysius of Halicarnassus's aspirations were more modest. He came to Rome in 30 B.C. and justified his writing on Roman history, first, with a well-known argument adapted from rhetoric, namely, that "those who write his-

tories...ought, first of all, to make choice of noble and lofty subjects."[4]
And he considered it beyond doubt that he had chosen a worthy subject:

> if anyone turns his attention to the successive supremacies both of cities and
> of nations,... and then, surveying them severally and comparing them to-
> gether, wishes to determine which of them obtained the widest dominion
> and both in peace and war performed the most brilliant achievement, he will
> find that the supremacy of the Romans has far surpassed all those that are
> recorded from earlier times, not only in the extent of its dominion and in
> the splendour of its achievements but also in the length during which it has
> endured down to our day.[5]

But for Dionysius there was a second reason. He wished to bridge the cultural
gap between Romans and Greeks, particularly to exhort the Greeks to acknowledge Rome and learn about her.

> For to this day almost all the Greeks are ignorant of the early history of
> Rome and the great majority of them have been imposed upon by sundry
> false opinions grounded upon stories which chance has brought to their ears
> and led to believe that, having come upon various vagabonds without house
> or home and barbarians, and even those not free men, as her founders, she
> in the course of time arrived at world domination, and this not through
> reverence for the gods and justice and every other virtue, but through some
> chance and the injustice of Fortune, which inconsiderately showers her
> greatest favours upon the most undeserving.[6]

Such was the tenor of Dionysius's *Roman Antiquities,* a work on the formative
period of Rome. But would or should such praise of Rome have offended Greek
pride? Not at all, since Dionysius started from the conviction that Romans and
Greeks had a common origin. "By this means I engage to prove that they [the
founders of Rome] were Greeks."[7] But why were the "Roman Greeks" then so
much more successful than the "Greek Greeks"? Because the Romans, as Polybius had already argued, were more skilled in building their state and maintaining it.

None of the works by the four Greek authors gained a wide readership,
partly because their prose ranged from unexciting to dull. Not even Dionysius of
Halicarnassus achieved popularity, although his concern with style reflected the
fact that he, like Timagenes, headed a rhetorical school. But he aspired to revive
the outdated classical Attic idiom, which had a revival after the rediscovery of
Thucydides' work, and he rejected the flowery and popular Asianic idiom. In his
fervor for Atticism, Dionysius had composed a critical work on Thucydides
*(De Thucydide),* rewriting whole passages of the *History of the Peloponnesian
War* according to his tastes and omitting others altogether. These works did not
arouse the interest of the wider Roman public, whose members remained fascinated mainly by Rome's own past which was equated with the definitive story
of the *oikoumenē.*

Dionysius and the three other historians influenced mostly other scholars. Among them seems to have been their contemporary, the Celt Trogus Pompeius, whose work has come to us through an abridgment by a certain Justin. Trogus, like Timagenes, wrote a history focusing on the Macedonian Empire *(Historiae Philippicae)* but he cast his net so wide that it became a quasi-universal history. Christians used Justin's digest widely and found in it a shifting of imperial rule from Assyria to Media to Persia to Macedonia and, by implication, to Rome. That, together with Daniel's prophecy and Orosius's pronouncements, reenforced the concept of the *translatio imperii* as a mold for later universal histories.

*Roman history between pride and melancholy.* Roman historians, who preferred less universal matters, discovered a peculiar problem. The Augustan state harbored a contradiction between the official affirmation that the Republic simply was continuing and the profound and ongoing structural changes which aimed at an imperial state. Could Roman historians simply go on affirming a continuity of development or did they want—later on even dare—to admit that a break had occurred with Augustus?

The contradiction between the republican form and the quasi-imperial structure of the Augustan state began to mark Latin historiography. The inordinate power of one individual in a republic made especially difficult the discussion of the immediate past, the period of civil strife. Titus Labienus Rabienus ("the wild one") wrote an account with a radically republican message. It was burnt by official order in 12 B.C. However, under Augustus histories with a fair appraisal of all contesting parties could still be written.

The Augustan age found its most characteristic and prolific historian in a man from provincial and conservative Padua, Livy (Titus Livius), who spent most of his life in Rome. When about thirty-two years old, Livy began his extensive history of Rome *ab urbe condita* to the death of Drusus, the brother of Tiberius. He used, of course, many sources. Among those that have been confirmed are Polybius, Valerius Antias, Claudius Quadrigarius, Coelius Antipater, Licinius Macer, Aelius Tubero, and L. Calpurnius Piso, but their respective influences are still debated. In any case Livy's work surpassed those of his predecessors and brought him instant fame, although many who praised him had read mainly the sections on Rome's rise to power and on the Second Punic War. Nobody noticed that Livy's history of Rome was the first major account written by a Roman scholar who never had occupied a public office.

The many books were held together by the unfolding story of Rome, with only occasional hints at a general design or statements on the forces which determined the rise of Rome: the sense of mission embedded in the Roman people's will and purpose; the will of the gods; and even Fortune, which kept Rome moving forward when her leaders failed.

More visible is another theme, that of the transition from Old Rome to New Rome. Why this transition occurred interested Romans more than abstract concepts of a world plan and Fortune. Old Rome with its sense of propriety, courage, self-restraint, discipline, resilience, frugality, and a natural respect for the *pater,* magistrates, and law stood as the embodiment of the best in Romans. Only people with these traits made for superior soldiers, were able to negotiate the tortuous road to an empire, and could achieve what the quarrelsome Greeks, with their government influenced by oratory, could not: a strong, unified state. Old Rome also knew *pietas,* the devout and punctilious fulfillment of sacred duties. Clearly, for Livy the rise of a state to greatness was based on its people possessing a number of proper character traits *(virtutes)* and not, as for Polybius, on a proper constitutional arrangement. Throughout the early republican years the public virtues were carefully cultivated. But as the domination of ever wider areas increased both Rome's wealth and the comfort of her citizens, Livy, as had others before him, saw the once virtuous Romans fall victim to greed, indulgence in luxury, and softness. Every new conquest, bringing new influences from other cultures, further weakened the Roman virtues and tradition, unraveling the social fabric until civil strife resulted.

At times Livy saw Augustus as the restorer of Old Rome. But there are also signs of nagging doubt and of an awareness that the problem reached deeper. Livy, looking into himself, must have found that even he had been infected by that skepticism towards the gods and auspices which he found so corrosive for the Roman spirit. He knew, as did so many other classical scholars, about the social role of religion. "In these novel circumstances there was an obvious danger of a general relaxation of the nation's moral fibre, so to prevent its occurrence Numa [Pompilius] decided upon a step which he felt would prove more effective than anything else with a mob as rough and ignorant as the Romans were in those days. This was to inspire them with the fear of the gods."[8] How then could Livy justify his own coolness to the religious tradition which together with law formed two of the foundations of a strong society?

Livy experienced the same tug of war in himself concerning *prodigia* (ominous occurrences). His intellect negated partially what as a historian he knew must be preserved. His cautious and traditional ways made Livy work methodically without formulating a methodology. For him, like other ancient historians, truth was safeguarded simply by not filling in gaps with fiction, inventing glamorous family records, or flattering those in power. He praised Augustus, whom he knew personally, in moderation and according to merit. But Livy did not tailor his description of the civil war according to the going fashion, even though that led him to a more favorable assessment of the republican leaders than seemed prudent. Perhaps his lack of enthusiasm for the broad populace, which he viewed as violence-prone, unstable, even frenzied, helped counterbalance his sympathetic portrayal of republicans.

Livy's narrative moved smoothly along in a language that stayed at an equal distance from elegance and daily speech. When he needed to, he yielded to the rhetorical demand for *delectatio,* that is, catching the readers' attention by pleasing them. There were many dialogues designed to explain issues, there were sudden turns of events, and there was even the yielding to dramatic history with heartbroken men and sobbing women at the defeat of Alba Longa and with the gruesome description of the dead littering the battlefield at Cannae.

But what was the purpose of it all? Livy really could not hope, as earlier historians had, to educate good citizens or to help shape leaders and statesmen. And while he may have hoped at times that his *History* could help restore the qualities of Old Rome, a look into himself, at his rationalist doubts about tradition and at his acquiescence in the existing situation, must have told him how futile such hope was. The continuity he restored in his history between present and past turned out to be as tenuous as the Augustan compromise itself. Like Sallust, who had seen the socially destructive traits irrevocably receiving free play once the fear of Carthage was removed, Livy did not draw the consequences from his perception of Roman decadence which the works of Polybius and Poseidonius could have suggested. Livy, as had Sallust before him, wrote in the spirit of the *Roma aeterna* so beautifully proclaimed in Vergil's *Aeneid*. That contemporary evocation of the Homeric epic was to celebrate Rome's glorious destiny as foreshadowed by the ancestral Aeneas's fate. There Jupiter declared what Romans knew was their destiny: "for them [the Romans] I set no bounds in place or time."[9] Therefore both Sallust and Livy saw Rome's decay only in terms of the regrettable transformation of Old Rome into New Rome and kept it apart from the cyclical patterns of Polybius and Poseidonius. New Rome, inferior as it was to Old Rome, was nevertheless a stable state and not a stage in an ongoing process of decadence.

### Historians and the Empire

The principate had carefully guarded its republican facade but it faded relentlessly into the empire. The impact of these developments on history writing was not only, as has often been maintained, that historians had to take into account the sensitivities or even caprices of the emperors. A more fundamental problem was the clear and wide rift between the republican past and the imperial present, a rift that could no longer be glossed over by historians. Even worse, the new political situation made some features of the Roman past outright suspect. Roman officials understood clearly that the historians, by describing the past, commented on the present and, implicitly, defined their expectations for the future. In A.D. 12 a book by Titus Labienus Rabienus had been burnt because of his "wrong" sympathies. Thirteen years later the risks had escalated.

In the year of the consulship of Cornelius Cossus and Asinius Agrippa, Cremutius Cordus was arraigned on a new charge, now for the first time heard. He had published a history in which he had praised Marcus Brutus and called Caius Cassius the last of the Romans. His accusers were Satrius

Secundus and Pinarius Natta, creatures of Sejanus. This was enough to ruin the accused.[10]

Words were now as dangerous as deeds, although the risks varied from period to period. Nero and Domitian found few historians brave enough to make works public during their despotic periods, while the Flavian emperors, except Domitian, were tolerant.

In addition, the gathering of material for historical works became considerably more difficult as the senate lost its importance and the news from the imperial palace consisted of either official pronouncements or rumors. The two sources matched each other in their unreliability. Only later historians were helped by the better record-keeping in the empire. At the other end, the readers were no longer the educated citizens but the educated subjects. With no real participation in government, they, more often than not, wanted merely to be informed or entertained. For history as a civic lesson they had lost both taste and use.

A few emperors wrote history. Claudius, a scholar whom soldiers lifted on their shoulders and proclaimed emperor after he had protested his preference for the historian's study, had been influenced by Livy. Unfortunately, we do not have Claudius's *vita*, his history of Rome since Caesar, or his histories of the Etruscans and Carthaginians. Vespasian produced respectable memoirs, Trajan described his campaign in Dacia, and Hadrian wrote an introspective biography or, better, had it written for him.

*The theme of decadence.* The sense of foreboding had set in with Cato's worries, had intensified in Sallust's depiction and analysis of corruption, and had been once more expressed in Livy's regrets about the vanishing of Old Rome. But how many people shared those misgivings? Perhaps the Roman history written about A.D. 30 by Velleius Paterculus helps to answer the question. In one of its reflective passages Velleius, a talented dilettante, betrayed that an awareness of the transitoriness of human achievements had pervaded more minds than merely those of a few farsighted historians. He raised the issue when he puzzled over why geniuses seemed to cluster in certain periods and observed what happened to a culture once it had advanced to a peak of creativity. "It is difficult to continue at the point of perfection, and naturally that which cannot advance must recede. And as in the beginning we are fired with the ambition to overtake those whom we regard as leaders, so when we have despaired of being able either to surpass or even to equal them, our zeal wanes with our hope."[11]

It is important to note, however, that the misgivings about the direction of Rome's development never brought forth in Rome a systematic exploration of the growth and decay of empires or of cultures. Roman historiography remained consistently focused on the story of Rome, a city and state more and more viewed as eternal. Romans were unable to concede that so eminent a state could be subject to the same cyclical pattern which had governed the fate of previous empires. They considered Rome unique and viewed her problems as those of a unique internal decline. Thus the theme familiar from Sallust and Livy remained the favorite one; vigorous and exemplary Old Rome was juxtaposed with the troubled New Rome. Even Tacitus, a *novus homo* from Gallia Narbonensis with no deep roots in the city of Rome, found no new vistas, although he added new depth and subtlety to the old theme.

Tacitus professed to approach his work with an attitude of *sine ira et studio,* that is, without hatred and partisan purpose. But his motto pledged a truthfulness free of prejudical partisanship rather than one unaffected by his own experience. It could hardly be otherwise. Much of the past which Tacitus described in the *Histories* (A.D. 69 to the death of Domitian), the *Annals* (A.D. 14 to 68) and *Agricola,* a biography of his father-in-law, Gnaeus Julius Agricola, had engaged him personally. The turmoil and brutality of the four-emperor year (A.D. 69) had remained as a trauma which was reenforced by the terror under Domitian when once more Romans had turned against Romans. Tacitus, moved by concern and some guilt feelings for having been in public service under Domitian, asked why the Nero and Domitian episodes could happen.

He knew the Roman malaise since he himself was gripped by it. For Tacitus, an exconsul and a senator, Rome under wise senate guidance had been an outstanding state. In Old Rome the citizens had lived harmoniously under the law and had cherished their liberty. But why then had so substantial a decay of the state occurred?

Old Rome, a state marked by individual excellence and social harmony, had decayed because of a deterioration in public morality and civic spirit. Tacitus did not agree with Polybius's assertion that its peculiar mixed form of government had helped Rome achieve long-lasting stability. Polybius's view was too theoretical for Tacitus, who maintained that excellence of leadership, dutiful service by the mass of the citizens, and a generally austere life-style rather than any particular form of government had lifted Rome to greatness. When the power of Rome brought the curse of wealth, it destroyed the civic virtues, and then rampant luxury, greed, and ambition corrupted leaders and transformed citizens into subjects who could bear neither full servitude nor freedom. The principate concluded the process of destruction by lulling the masses into apathy and by controlling the now powerless and subservient senate. "Augustus won over the soldiers with gifts, the populace with cheap corn, and all men with the sweets of repose, and so grew greater by degrees, while he concentrated in himself the functions of the Senate, the magistrates, and the laws."[12] Although as a historian Tacitus recognized as irreversible the shift in Rome's power structure, as a citizen he never reconciled himself to it. He knew that a restoration of senatorial rule would simply return the state of strife, not the ideal republic, and that the Roman people would never exchange the present semblance of order and security for "the dangerous past." All that could be done was to prevent absolute power from becoming despotic. From that insight sprang the deep pessimism which pervaded Tacitus's work.

*Tacitus: causes, style, and purpose.* Reflecting on his subject matter, essentially Roman history since Augustus's death, Tacitus found it wanting:

> Much of what I have related and shall have to relate may perhaps, I am aware, seem petty trifles to record. But no one must compare my annals with the writings of those who have described Rome in old days. They told of great wars, of the storming of cities, of the defeat and capture of kings, or whenever they turned by preference to home affairs, they related, with a free scope for digression, the strifes of consuls with tribunes, land and corn laws, and the struggles between the commons and the aristocracy.[13]

Now the only proper foci left for the multitude of minor events were the emperors. Their characters were the driving forces and needed a thorough analysis. For Tacitus, as for the other ancients, character was a fixed, innate quality which revealed itself trait by trait in a series of situations but never changed. Thus Tiberius's character became fully known only after he gained power and after a conspiracy was directed against him. Nero's position enabled him to command an audience and to indulge his vanity in showmanship. The stimuli present in a given situation activated latent psychological forces in individuals, bringing forth actions and thus shaping events.

Tacitus's firm ideas on psychology and politics stood in contrast to his lack of clarity on the agencies of control to which he referred intermittently: gods, fortune, and fate. He formulated strictly impromptu explanations of their workings. Gods entered human events with "no thought for our happiness, but only for our punishment" and they warned humans of their anger or displeasure through *omina* and portents, which Tacitus listed in the yearly summaries of the *Annals.*[14] He doubted the validity of some of them.

> There occurred too a thick succession of portents, which meant nothing. A woman gave birth to a snake, and another was killed by a thunderbolt in her husband's embrace. Then the sun was suddenly darkened and the fourteen districts of the city were struck by lightning. All of this happened quite without any providential design; so much so, that for many subsequent years Nero prolonged his reign and his crimes.[15]

Did such a partial doubt indicate Tacitus's acceptance of other *omina*? We do not know. His thoughts on fortune and fate are even less discernible.

Tacitus's traditionalism in politics was matched by one in style and approach. What he reported on he knew from his own experience and from the works of earlier historians (such as Aufidius Bassus, Pliny the Elder, and Cluvius Rufus). Like other ancient historians he did not routinely frequent depositories of records. But he should be credited with obtaining a good deal of information and using it with critical sense, although much of the process of government and the center of power had moved into the opaque context of the court.

He unabashedly wrote "year after year" accounts, even calling one of his works *Annals.* Year-end summaries listed embassies, election of officials, changes in sacred rituals, deaths of prominent people, natural catastrophes, illness, crimes, and trials. Only his genius and the overall theme of assessing the historical role of imperial Rome made much of his work more than a calendar-type history. On occasion, like Sallust and Livy before him, he did bow to the dramatic Hellenistic historians and embellish his stories with details about the capture of cities, raging battles, and the miserable lot of the defeated. And, of course, he used the stock-in-trade of classical historians, the speeches.

In a dialogue on style Tacitus put forth the startling insight that style was not an independent entity but was subject to the overall changes in a culture. Therefore there was a connection between the decline of the Roman state and the contemporary shallow, manneristic style. Yet, Tacitus probably did not notice that he often used conditional sentences and indirect questions while Sallust had still used, even more frequently, causal statements and those indicating order in time. Between Sallust and Tacitus Romans seemed to have lost much confidence in their ability to explain events.

Did Tacitus write history in order to restore Old Rome? Some have thought that the *Agricola* was meant to show an exemplary virtuous Roman and the *Germania* the good German, with both works calling on Romans to return to the traditional virtues. Tacitus's message was more subtle. Agricola fulfilled his duty and stayed virtuous even under a terrible emperor. He did not conspire against Tiberius; he did not even refuse to serve. A decadent state was no excuse for lack of public dedication in a citizen. The *Germania* demonstrated the similarity in piety, sturdiness, and readiness to sacrifice between the contemporary Germans and the Romans of the early republic. But the Germans had stayed vigorous and now their strength threatened Rome.

Tacitus shared in the inability of other Roman historians to say much on the prospects for the future, because he, too, did not pursue the decadence argument into the available cyclical theories. Writing history without acknowledging any overall pattern that shaped human events, and writing contemporary history without an opening to the future, Tacitus was led to assume the attitude of the Stoics, for whom he really had no sympathy. Romans must bear all adversity with determination and show an imperturbable devotion to duty.

*Two narrative historians.* Non-Roman imperial historians did not share Tacitus's melancholy over the vanishing of Old Rome. They looked at the Roman Empire and found it still capable of maintaining stability and peace. Flavius Josephus, an upper-class Jew visiting Rome, returned to Palestine to fight against Rome in the Jewish War waged by Vespasian and Titus but eventually returned to live in Rome. Fame came quickly after he published his *History of the Jewish War,* which described the recent Jewish experience from Antiochus Epiphanes (ca. 170 B.C.) through the Jewish War. Writing in Greek but standing in the Jewish tradition, Josephus praised the bravery, persistence, and skills of the Jews while he also lauded the restraint and leniency of the Romans. Quite a few Jews resented Josephus's impartiality, which they attributed to his excessive Romanization.

The Jewish context was much clearer in Josephus's *Jewish Antiquities*, a quasi-universal history with the Jews at its center and in which the meaning of history stood aloof from Rome's destiny. It reached back to the origins of the world. "In the beginning God created the heaven and the earth. The earth had not come into sight, but was hidden in thick darkness, and a breath from above sped it, when God commanded that there should be light."[16] A history of such vast scope gave the Jews an excellent position in the ancient contest over collective status among Mediterranean people for whom age supplied the criterion. Thus, the Jews could easily escape the Greek "mythological imperialism" because they were older than the Achaeans. Moses preceded Homer. Later on, some of the church fathers would also consider that aspect as important in their coping with Greek philosophy. They would also, of course, accept Josephus's affirmation that God guided all of history systematically and directly and "That the main lesson to be learnt from this history by any who care to peruse it is that men who conform to the will of God, and do not venture to transgress laws that have been excellently laid down, prosper in all things beyond belief, and for their reward are offered by God felicity."[17]

Another Easterner of the second century A.D., Appian of Alexandria, produced a *Roman History* (down to Emperor Trajan) that reached back to Aeneas and then zigzagged from people to people as they, through wars and other events, came in contact with Rome. He admonished those who preferred the Macedonian Empire, saying that "the empire of Alexander was splendid in its magnitude, in its armies, in the success and rapidity of its conquests, and it wanted little of being boundless and unexampled, yet in its shortness of duration it was like a brilliant flash of lightning."[18] Appian was equally impressed by the restraint which Romans showed in extending their empire. "Possessing the best part of the earth and sea they have, on the whole, aimed to preserve their empire by the exercise of prudence, rather than to extend their sway indefinitely over poverty-stricken and profitless tribes of barbarians."[19]

*The new strength of biography.* Now that the Roman state, too, had assumed monarchical character and Roman citizens had become subjects, the biographical genre found the same favorable conditions in Rome that had prevailed in the Hellenistic East. Literary scholars found that biographies furnished the opportunity to demonstrate rhetorical skills, philosophers used such works as collections of *exempla* for ethics, and readers simply indulged in the age-old curiosity about the lives of other people. In the Roman world of the first and second centuries such focusing of attention on individuals was even justified, since individuals did play an important and visible role in society and politics. One could well point to the overpowering status of the emperor as an important stimulus.

A Greek from provincial Chaeronea, Plutarch, wrote the work which shaped contemporary Greco-Roman tastes in the field of biography: the *Parallel Lives*. He always chose two life stories, a Greek and a Roman, that had some traits or experiences in common, put them side by side, and in most cases compared them. Plutarch's judgment did not necessarily favor Greeks, since for him greatness and failings had no ethnic identity. His only bias concerned his readers; he wrote only for those who reflected seriously on the issues of life.

Even more than Nepos, Plutarch was aware of the difference between the work of a historian and that of a biographer. He pleaded:

> If I do not record all their most celebrated achievements or describe any of them [the famous persons] exhaustively, but merely summarize for the most part what they accomplished, I ask my readers not to regard this as a fault. For I am writing biography not history, and the truth is that the most brilliant exploits often tell us nothing of the virtues or vices of the men who performed them, while on the other hand a chance remark or a joke may reveal far more of a man's character than the mere feat of winning battles in which thousands fall or marshalling great armies, or laying siege to cities.[20]

The historian and the biographer complemented each other as they presented two perspectives on the same reality. The historian narrated the lives of persons in the context of events, and the biographer analyzed the personalities who brought forth the events.

What cause was to the world of the historian, character was to that of the biographer—the key for explanation. For Plutarch, as for all ancients, character was a fixed system of personal traits with which humans were born. Life did not change that character, it only made visible a person's traits. But that did not excuse or doom human beings, since Plutarch suggested that, while people could not change their characters, they could control inherent weaknesses by the force of their virtues. Nobody, for example, needed to be a tyrant because of some character flaw and a given opportunity. One could resist temptations and do so perhaps even more easily if inspired by the model of a proper life. Indeed, in the biographical perspective, all of world history shrank to a series of great lives and the moral struggles in them.

One of Plutarch's contemporaries, Suetonius, demonstrated in his *The Twelve Caesars* how Romans and Greeks still differed in their views on events and people. In contrast to Plutarch, Suetonius, who had been chief secretary to Emperor Hadrian, with access to the imperial depositories, linked individual lives and collective destinies closely together when in the first part of every biography he described an emperor's administrative activities and outstanding deeds, while he dealt in the second part with an emperor's personal life and character. Suetonius, the Roman, simply could not conceive of rulers as mere examples for moral treatises and as a result he related the genre of biography much more closely to that of history than Plutarch did. Even in episodes which could be written off as too dramatic or merely entertaining, even in scandal-mongering, the impact on public affairs of an emperor's character or state of mind was at least implied. What kind of emperor could Caligula be, who whenever he kissed his wife's neck whispered to her that he could have it cut anytime he wanted to? Or Domitian, who sat forlorn in his palace room catching flies and stabbing them with a stylus?

The biographer following both Plutarch and Suetonius, Flavius Arrianus (Arrian), could match neither of the two men nor did he choose them as his models. He preferred Xenophon as the model for his *Anabasis of Alexander,* in which he described the king who performed "such wondrous deeds, whether in numbers or greatness."[21]

Arrian's account was built on many sources, but he trusted two writers most. "Wherever Ptolemy, son of Lagus, and Aristobulus, son of Aristobulus, have agreed in their histories of Alexander, son of Philip, I record their story as quite accurate; where they disagree I have chosen what I feel to be more likely and also better worth the narrating."[22] On the whole Arrian aimed at a narrative with an even flow and a concentration on the military deeds of Alexander, not at analysis. Because of that emphasis, Arrian's *Anabasis of Alexander* became a favorite of medieval writers. The hero, Alexander, who had the "desire to emulate Achilles, with whom he had a rivalry from boyhood," could be easily transformed into the knight-like figure of the medieval Alexander romances.[23]

*A solitary work on methodology.* Ancient historians, whose main methodological concern was simply accuracy of reporting, stated their limited views on historiography usually in prefaces or in remarks intermixed with the text. After Cicero's comments on history, there were, in the second century A.D., only the remarks on history in the *Attic Nights* by Aulus Gellius and the work *How to Write History* by Lucian(us) of Samosata. The main problems for a historian, Lucian thought, were "how to begin, how to arrange his material, the proper proportions for each part, what to leave out, what to develop, what it is better to handle cursorily, and how to put the facts into words and fit them together";[24] all of this is not so different for modern historiography, except that Lucian did not proceed to the further question of how the historian knows about reality in the first place, since that question belonged not to the province of the rhetor but to that of the philosopher. But Lucian, like other ancient historians, was keenly concerned with accuracy and truthfulness, putting to shame those who have naively assumed that the mere association of history with rhetoric turned history into fiction. He exhorted historians who served rulers and other benefactors to realize that "the dividing line and frontier between history and panegyric is not a narrow isthmus but rather a mighty wall."[25] Only a true history could be a useful one. Otherwise history became just one of the many entertainments for the curious or the bored.

Lucian frowned at those who dabbled in history writing because they "think it is perfectly simple and easy to write history and that anyone can do it if only he can put what comes to him into words."[26] True historians were rare since they had to possess both political understanding and the power of expression. The first quality required an innate gift enhanced by insights from life experience and the second could be developed through training in composition and style. There one learned that good histories, although they might well have a touch of poetry, must "not resemble highly seasoned sauces" and must stay aloof from the vulgar language of the marketplace.

*Chronology.* Work in chronology languished since the dominant Romans had settled on their own *ab urbe condita* scheme for counting years and were not interested in anything else. In the East chronology continued to rest on the achievements of Timaeus and Eratosthenes. In the second century A.D. Claudius Ptolemaeus, made the only substantial contribution to that field with his chronological tables, including the *kanón basiléon* that presented lists of Ancient Near Eastern kings, Macedonian kings, and Roman rulers beginning with Augustus. The work never became popular, but in a revised edition it helped shape the chronological framework of Eusebius and other Christian chroniclers.

*Historians in the shadow of greatness.* The *Pax Romana* assured the Roman Empire of widespread support. But this satisfaction, even gratefulness, stimulated in the broad public no great pride or curiosity in the Roman past. Shortly after A.D. 200, the last comprehensive Roman history was written and it provided an ironic twist: it, like the first Roman history by Fabius Pictor, was written in Greek. But Dio Cassius needed no longer to defend Rome in a hostile Greek world because, as Dio showed in his own life, even a Greek-speaking man from Bithynia could be staunchly loyal to Rome by then. However, republican Old Rome meant nothing to him and he declared without hesitation that monarchies by their nature excelled all republics. Such an attitude also made it impossible for him to discern a decline of Rome.

After Dio, historical works became fewer and fewer. A lack of preserved manuscripts may explain part of the dwindling richness but a growing lack of empathy for the whole range of Roman history by the many diverse peoples who now inhabited the empire accounted for a greater part. The link of the imperial present with the Roman republican past had become tenuous indeed. And as for the future, historians, although troubled by doubts, expected simply a continuation of the present. In that situation some historical works, such as Sextus Aurelius Victor's *Caesars* (ca. 360) were marked by moral admonitions and biographical features. Other histories still tried to encompass the whole Roman past as, for example, that by Lucius Aennaeus Florus; a second-century epitome of earlier histories (certainly of Livy's), it showed few new insights. In the fourth century such epitomes were more numerous. Both Rufius Festus and Eutropius produced a *Brief History (Breviarium),* and for a time both held the office of *magister memoriae* under Emperor Valens (365–78). One senses the increasing need to abbreviate Roman history that had not only become voluminous but also, particularly in its earlier parts, well-nigh incomprehensible to some of the Roman Empire's inhabitants (including, it seems, the emperors). Eutropius's work exerted its greatest influence on Christian historians of the early Middle Ages, who consulted it frequently. As late as the eighth century, Paulus Diaconus continued the *Brief History* to the year 553.

The most gifted of the fourth-century historians stood apart from it all. Ammianus Marcellinus continued Tacitus's work to A.D. 378 with a rambling account, the *Res gestae,* a title best rendered in this case as "events." It was a respectable work by a man from an affluent family who had traveled widely and who had experienced the hazards of war as an officer. He knew the theme of decadence well from Tacitus. Yet, as a fourth-century Syrian from Antioch, he simply could not muster the comparable empathy for the lost senatorial republic, by then a faint memory for most people. For Ammianus the late empire was not in the process of declining but in that of maturing. In fact "declining into old age, and often owing victory to its name alone, Rome has come to a quieter period of life."[27] He did not, however, pursue that quasi-organic analogy to its logical conclusion, the eventual death of the empire; such a conclusion may have been unthinkable even for Ammianus. Or he may not have reached that conclusion because he, like so many ancient historians, did not ascribe the problems of states to structural changes but only to individual persons who failed.

As for the historians, it behooved them as good subjects to support the key institutions of the state that constituted the elements of stability. Ammianus particularly castigated those who weakened the imperial office. Even Emperor Julian, whom Ammianus admired for his military skills, asceticism, learning, and restoration of the Roman religion, received sharp criticism for his harshness to opponents and for his tendency to impulsive actions unbecoming the imperial office. And Ammianus Marcellinus praised the senate, a body with a much diminished role, while he reprimanded individual senators for debauchery, status-seeking, and a lack of proper education. If the imperial office and the senate were to lose their prestige and power, the Roman state would be at the mercy of the masses, who have never contributed to the stability of any state. Ammianus had absorbed thoroughly the lessons of the Roman historians he had read so assiduously; what mattered most in the world were the actions of leading individuals. The historian must aim, when recording the past, to influence the present, if not the future, by teaching moral, political, and military lessons. This was a difficult task, considering the limitations placed on the freedom of creative persons in the late empire at a time when it was hard "to avoid the dangers which are often connected with the truth."[28]

Ammianus Marcellinus concluded the long series of great Roman historians. He wrote when Christianity, except during Emperor Julian's rule, had become allied with the Roman state; when the early Christian world-chronicles of Sextus Julius Africanus and Eusebius were available and foretold an entirely different view of the human past; and when the Roman Empire, in its western half, had barely a century of existence left. But Roman historiography left the future one other legacy: an enigma. The mysterious *Historia Augusta* was discovered in a medieval codex named *Palatinus Latinus 899*. The *Historia* purports to have been written by six authors: Aelius Lampridius, Aelius Spartianus, Julius Capitolinus, Flavius Vopiscus, Trebellius Pollio, and Vulcacius Gallicanus *(vir clarissimus)*. They all have one feature in common: we know virtually nothing about them. The *Historia Augusta* itself also was never mentioned by any contemporary.

The work itself is a collection of some thirty biographies of emperors and Caesars from Hadrian to Diocletian (A.D. 117-284). The structure is loose, with letters, speeches, and decrees interspersed in the narrative. Unfortunately only a few of these documents are anything else than outright fabrications. Were it not for the dire scarcity of sources for that period, the *Historia Augusta* would have been shelved except by those who like historical detective work. As it is, scholars have been grateful for whatever minor insights can be gleaned from the *Historia Augusta*, while engaging in fervent controversies concerning the work, particularly about the date and method of its creation.

*Roman historiography in retrospect.* Roman historians freely adapted Greek historiographical forms but put the stamp of *romanitas* on them in a process full of friction. The contradictions between the Greek and Roman origin-stories, between respect for and differences with Polybius's account of Rome's march to greatness, between Cato's embrace and rejection of elements of Greek culture, and between the influence and impotence of successive waves of Hellenistic historiographical ideas testified to the complex process of adaptation. In turn, the annalistic tradition manifested a distinctly Roman spirit as it superbly reflected the unfolding of Rome's destiny to engulf the inhabited world. Christians would later discover the suitability of a year-by-year account for a teleological view of history. As for the Greek forms for narrating the past, they each received their own stamp of *romanitas:* biography never quite lost its link to the public life, avoiding the pure testimonial to individual virtues; monographs always were more or less moral and political treatises; summary histories (epitomes) as initiated by Theopompus's Herodotus summary, helped to master the long stretch of the Roman past but also became briefings for public officials on a Roman past largely unknown to them; and chronology was left to be pursued by Greeks because Romans found the *ab urbe condita* scheme best suited to their purposes.

The Greeks triumphed completely in theoretical matters; Roman historians rarely bothered with such matters. The clear public purpose of history put definite and narrow limits on theoretical discussion, limits which were identical to those prevailing in Greek historiography. Lacking the intent to reconstruct the past in detail and affirming history's practical purpose, ancient historians found the ideals of accuracy of reporting and reliance on "good" authorities sufficient to maintain historiography's standing in rhetoric as the nonfiction category of narration. Truth for Cicero and Lucian, the only Roman writers to make more than casual remarks on historiography, was simply needed to give power to persuasion. As for *delectatio* and drama, they were condoned in some measure while eloquence and the absence of deliberate partisan purpose were desired. The writers on Roman "antiquities" (Varro and Dionysius of Halicarnassus), could have provided a widening of the methodological repertoire but their works were not considered history.

The "noble" subject was never in doubt. For centuries the Roman state gave a clear focus to Roman history; Greeks had enjoyed such a clarity only briefly in the period of the *polis* and then only for the restricted area of a small state. Yet Roman historians encountered their own problems in the reconciliation of past, present, and future. Beginning with Augustus they perceived an Old and a New Rome, the one an ideal and the other a deviation into imperfection. But they refused to view Roman history cyclically, since they perceived Rome to be eternal, an impression fostered by the Roman Empire's staying power. External expansion continued even as the Old Rome of virtue faded, endowing even New Rome with hope. Thus, the present was viewed negatively in comparison to the past (although Romans never saw a complete break between Old and New Rome) and the expected future was thought to resemble the present or, perhaps, to be even more glorious. Roman historians could never resolve these contradictions because they refused to subject Rome to a comparative analysis with other empires. Decay was a Roman, not a general societal, phenomenon; it was a deterioration of the inner quality of Romans and hence a moral not an institutional problem. There was no incentive to transcend the Roman world. A corresponding lack of interest in the past of other peoples, including the Greeks, stood in the way of breaking through to a universal history. Those non-Romans who tried it found that once Rome was missing as the unifier, they could only produce parallel histories of nations, cultural panoramas, or convenient table histories. The historical work of Posidonius, who apparently thought in terms of imperial cycles, has been lost. Christians could make good use of the information and the table form because they knew a unity transcending regions.

Not surprisingly, Roman historiography's vitality faded away with the Roman state. Vigor came to reside in Christian historiography with its new, much wider vision of human destiny and the ability to cope with subsequent conditions: Germanic migrations and invasions, impoverishment, and the collapse of the support structure for the *Pax Romana;* in short, the vanishing of the true Roman world. In the midst of radical and seemingly endless change Christians would have to formulate histories in order to preserve the continuity of past, present, and future.

# ·7·

# The Christian Historiographical Revolution

### The Formulation of Early Christian Historiography

At first Christians baffled the adherents of the Roman tradition. Bafflement grew into irritation and finally outright hostility as the distance between Roman tradition and Christian faith and practice became ever more visible. In the second century, Celsus, a Platonist and Roman traditionalist, condemned the Christians' refusal to participate in official religious rites and their disinterest in the pagan Roman past. Such behavior, he thought, was detrimental to the Roman state because it deprived Roman citizens of the necessary sense of continuity. As proof, Celsus pointed to the plainly visible troubles of the Roman state. It was symbolic that in 247 Christians remained aloof from the "one-thousand-years-of-Rome" celebrations. At that point, *Roma aeterna* simply did not interest Christians.

The pagan and Christian inhabitants of the Roman Empire lived in two radically different mental worlds. When it came to history, the former identified the world of the past, present, and future with the Roman state; their historians spoke of the glory of the Roman Republic, great battles, and heroic deeds. These matters were of little concern to Christians. However, a distinctly Christian view of history evolved in the discussions among the church fathers, through interpretations of the Christian texts and under the impact of events. Much more was involved than the often cited change from a cyclical to a linear pattern of development, a distinction which holds true only in the widest sense. The Great Cosmic Cycle of Plato and other philosophers, which repeated itself after thousands of years, did indeed yield to a world created *ex nihilo* and running its course only once. But within that course Christians acknowledged cyclical configurations, particularly the cycle of sin (or apostasy)—judgment—retribution—restoration, affecting individuals and groups.

The basic change came in asserting the Old Testament view that God worked his ways in history. The Old Testament witnessed to the special relationship between the Jews and God, established by the Covenant in the patriarchal period when God singled out the Jews to be his chosen people, promising them land to settle on and growth as a people. That promise held hope for the future as well as the threat of severe punishment whenever the Jews deviated from God's will or from proper worship. In short, the story of the Jewish tribes—a historical phenomenon—showed a divine design behind the observable events. God, who governed all the world and its events, did not, like the gods of the Greeks and Romans, act arbitrarily or share power with Fate or Fortune but guided things directly and wisely. In the process he revealed himself.

Christians enhanced the connection of God and world when they told of the Incarnation: God had lived on earth as Jesus, the Christ. That event, central in the flow of events from the creation of the world to the eventual Second Coming of Christ (the *Parousia*), made it impossible for Christians to view human history in the Greek and Roman manner as infinite variations on the theme of a constant human nature. Instead, history showed a development with a unique beginning, central event, and ultimate goal, told by Scripture. Such a radically different understanding of human affairs would in time become difficult to contain in classical historiographical forms.

*The Bible: source and authority.* Like Christian faith itself, Christian interpretations of history have centered on the Bible with its two canons—the Old and New Testaments—as the most essential historical record. Hence, Christian historical interpretations were linked from their very beginning to the quest for the "pure" text and its proper interpretation. Which of the many extant writings were trustworthy records of God's will and his works in history? When translating the Hebrew texts how were Christians to render the important terms into other languages? Finally, which interpretation of the text followed its spirit most closely? Perhaps it was this respect for the text which already had made Flavius Josephus enrich his works on Jewish history with documents and prompted Eusebius to do the same for the story of the Christian church in his *Ecclesiastical History*. Mistakes in the sacred tradition were too costly; they distorted divine revelation and corrupted the apostolic tradition. Part of the text criticism of the later Western world had its origin in the Jewish and Christian concern for the "pure" tradition.

But pagans, who did not readily accept divine inspiration as the basis for Christian claims, needed different proofs of authority. Christians soon advanced the argument of age. Because ancients had readily used the duration of a people's history as the yardstick of collective status, Jews and Christians claimed Moses' priority in time over Homer, with Justin Martyr even suspecting that Homer had borrowed from Moses. The desire to prove the great age of the Judeo-Christian tradition eventually enhanced the Christian concern with chronology. But, more important, the concerns with the text tradition and unbroken authority were but part of a much wider concern, that with continuity.

*Continuity and discontinuity.* The chiliasts among the early Christians stressed the imminent end of human history to be brought about by the Second Coming of Christ. While Christians were undoubtedly influenced here by the apocalyptic and messianic vision among the postexilic Jews, in a period of intermittent persecution and small hope for a Christianized world an imminent end seemed a more logical—or at least preferable—expectation than that of a prolonged future. Scriptural indications for it could easily be found in the Books of Daniel and Isaiah, the Gospel of Matthew, and the Book of Revelation. Justin Martyr, Tertullian, and Hippolytus of Rome expected a thousand-year rule of Christ on earth—an age of hope, peace, and plenty—to precede the Last Judgment. But the chiliasts and millenarians would hardly have produced a Christian historiography, because their truncated future supplied little incentive for striving after a reconciliation between past, present, and future. A similar impedance to historiography would have resulted from an exclusive emphasis on the discontinuity brought about by Christ, which shortened not the future but the past. The Marcionites did that when they rejected the Old Testament as invalid for Christians. And the Gnostics denied Christianity's historical nature when they considered the apostles as only partially knowledgeable and moved the discussion about Christ from the historical to the philosophical arena. But these views did not prevail.

Christianity remained a religion of the two Testaments. While the Old Testament had only imperfect knowledge of Christ, it nevertheless prophesied his coming and his work. The New Testament, in turn, told of the fulfillment of these prophecies and thus explained the Old Testament. Yet, the events described in the two Testaments were not linked together in an unbroken cause-and-effect chain. Their connection was established by the will of God and could therefore only be apprehended in the light of faith. The characteristic methods for the harmonization of past, present, and future events were allegory, prefiguration, and typology. All three of the methods maintained that an event or a saying in the Old Testament had immediate relevance or explanatory value for a specific feature of the New Testament—a means of linkage later on applied also to the postbiblical world. Irenaeus, for example, spoke of Adam as "foreshadowing" Christ and saw in history a recapitulation of earlier events on a higher level. His view and the interpretation of the Old Testament as the preparation for the New suggested an overall "upward" development. The progress from the Old to the New Testament demonstrated a divine education of mankind—from the period of infancy in which Adam failed and elicited God's discipline to that of Christ (the new Adam), who made possible a greater maturity for all. In that sense Irenaeus spoke of revelation, up to the Incarnation, as a gradual process.

The "education of mankind" idea proved particularly useful to the church fathers when they wrestled with Greek philosophy. This philosophy paradoxically supplied not only the most formidable intellectual opposition to Christianity but also the most useful concepts for the translation of the transcendent into human language during the early theological discussions. With neither outright rejection nor full acceptance appearing proper, Christians took a historical view of Greek philosophy: it represented a stage in the growth of truth towards fullness in the revelation through Christ. Christ was "known in part even by Socrates," Justin Martyr declared.[1] Clement of Alexandria spoke of God planting the seeds early on. Plato and Aristotle were thus not completely wrong but only incompletely enlightened. Ages and individuals alike varied in their understanding of revelation, depending on their developed capacities to grasp the truth. Christ alone offered the possibility of grasping the full truth.

As every passing year weakened the expectation of the imminent *Parousia* (the Second Coming), the Christian view on the passage of time eventually was shaped less by the finality of the Last Day and more and more by the promise of the universality of redemption. The delay of the *Parousia* was due to God's compassion. For before the end "the good news must be preached to all the heathen."[2] The earliest manifestation of that mission came in the transformation of Palestinian Jewish Christianity into Gentile Christianity with its universal scope. Time was the space provided by God for accomplishing the great work of the mission to mankind. With the "fulfillment of time" now expected at the end of a long span of time, it was necessary that Christian views on the world and its past conform to that expectation. And the drama of the mission of converting mankind in the interest of universal redemption would bring about a constant shaping and reshaping of these views, including those on history. In both interpretations of mankind's course, the "education of mankind" and the universal redemption, patristic Christianity had available a dynamic principle of increasing human potential that could tie past, present, and future together. Yet, as will be seen, that principle did not become the dominant theme of Christian medieval historiography.

*The Roman Empire and Christian historiography.* Christians could not escape the influence of the Roman Empire. At first Christian life and tradition took shape in opposition to Rome, pitting the small "community of saints" against the vast empire. On their part, Romans quite often accused Christians of having brought about Rome's decline. Christians fought back, not primarily as one might expect, by pointing out how irrelevant to sacred history the fate of Rome was, but by marshalling from the Old Testament and from the armory of their accusers' charges the argument that proper religious faith and rites fortified the welfare of a state. Origen maintained that if Romans had had the truth faith they would have subdued "many more pursuing enemies than those that were destroyed by the prayer of Moses."[3] Another church father, Tertullian, doubted that Roman greatness could ever have been the aim of God's will because Romans worshiped false gods. Even the *Pax Romana*, which many attributed to Rome, came about in the age of Augustus only because of Christ's birth. But negative attitudes toward Rome became inappropriate when, after 313, Christianity became first a tolerated and finally a mandated faith. Already in the second century, Melito of Sardis had suggested that God had created the empire for Christianity's support. After Constantine the Great's conversion it was even easier to consider the *Pax Romana* as God's instrument for the dissemination of the Gospel over open roads and secure seas. When universal Rome acquired a role in the universal sacred history, the historiographical gap between Christianity and the pagan world began to close.

Already half a century before 313, Christians strove to give the human past a Christian framework—a difficult task indeed. Hellenistic attempts to write universal histories had usually ended up in mere compilations—a narrative one by Diodorus Siculus and chronological tables by Castor of Rhodes. In any case, Christian chronology was more directly linked to some Jewish attempts to trace the Jewish tradition in the course of time. The Old Testament represented an intricate historical record, but it contained no dates. Succession in time was indicated by temporal words ("then," "after," "soon") and by the passage of generations. A narrative which stayed primarily within one culture needed no more. Of course, in daily life the Jews figured time more closely, but for a long period they cared little for attaching dates to past events. After Alexander the Great, the Jews used the Seleucid era for dating their years until the destruction of the Temple in A.D. 70 (the Seleucid year 381) offered a beginning point for a genuinely Jewish era. Sometime, we know not when, the Jews, proud of their long tradition, attempted to date their beginning with the Creation. These year numbers would eventually be designated as A.M. *(anno ab origine mundi)*. The Babylonian Talmud included references to the oldest Jewish chronicle, the *Seder Olam Rabbah (Book of the Order of the World)*, which used the Creation as the reference point for dating events. However, that chronicle followed by decades Flavius Josephus's works, which already knew of such an era. All of that interested Jews less than it would Christians in their search for a chronological scheme.

Late in the third century, Sextus Julius Africanus's *Chronography* began the series of early Christian histories, which ordered persons and events from Near Eastern, Greek, and Roman myths and histories into a Judeo-Christian time frame. Adding the life years of the biblical personages and using the chronologies of other cultures, Africanus concluded that 5,500 years had elapsed between Adam and Jesus Christ's birth. A contemporary of Africanus, Hippolytus of Rome, most likely knew the *Chronography* and used it, except that his main aim was the computation of correct Easter dates.

The great achievement of patristic chronology came from Eusebius, bishop of Caesarea. He lived during the propitious early decades of the fourth century when Emperor Constantine, whose close advisor Eusebius became, made Christianity a tolerated if not a preferred faith and even assisted in establishing an agreed upon canon of faith through the Council of Nicaea (325). The Roman

Empire and Christianity became intricately linked, so much so that the theology from that period has often been called "imperial theology." Eusebius pronounced its historiographical implications in his *Chronicle* and *Ecclesiastical History*. The *Chronicle* signaled that in historiography, too, Christianity had triumphed. The core of this historiography was the chronological canons, for which Eusebius borrowed material from Hellenistic historians, especially from Castor of Rhodes. A typical page of the *Chronicle* dealing with the earliest period listed side by side personages, rulers, and dynasties of the Assyrians, Sicyonians, and Egyptians as well as the main figures and events of the Old Testament. More and more time-tables and years were included as other nations became prominent. Then with the unification of the Mediterranean world by Rome, the Roman and Judeo-Christian time-series sufficed, with the Olympiad scheme acting as a convenient control device.

As for the date of Jesus Christ's birth, Eusebius placed it in the year 5198 from Adam or 2015 from Abraham, a considerable distance away from Sextus Julius Africanus's A.M. 5500. The gap, due to the use of different versions of the Old Testament, assumed importance when Eastern historians came to rely primarily on the scheme of Africanus, who wrote in Latin, whereas those in the West came to prefer that of Eusebius, who wrote in Greek. Jerome's translation of Eusebius's *Chronicle* made Eusebius the basis for many Latin world chronicles until Bede suggested a different time-scale. Indeed, for many years after Eusebius the world chronicle as a type of history changed little. Those who tried their hands at chronicling, among them Prosper Tiro, produced minor works. Chronological works were pushing against a clear limit. As long as narratives and interpretations were eschewed, little was left but to refine the world chronicle's time schemes.

Eusebius was no panegyrist of the Roman Empire. He and other Christians knew that the Christian church and the empire were not identical. The proper Christian history was the sacred story, as demonstrated by Eusebius's pioneering *Ecclesiastical History*. Written in the years of triumph, to give an account of the lives of Jesus Christ and the apostles, it told about the people of faith—teachers, writers, martyrs, and bishops—and about persecutions as well as the final victory. To ensure a proper record and to inspire his readers, Eusebius included many documents and texts that otherwise would have been lost. It is possible but unlikely that some impetus for the inclusion came from Eusebius's distinction between facts and interpretations, although later scholars have read too much into that distinction.

As the church continued its institutional life, Eusebius's history was amplified and continued: by Socrates and two legal experts for 306–439, by Sozomen for 323–425, and by Theodoretus for 325–428. The original text was shaped into an abbreviated Latin version by Rufinus, who continued it to 410, while its continuations were put into Latin by Epiphanius. Eventually a condensation of the total work, reaching to 518, was carried out under the general editorship of Cassiodorus, bearing the title of *Historia Tripartita*.

Against such competition Sulpicius Severus's Sacred History could not prevail, although it was written in a much more pleasing style, provided a well-ordered narrative, integrated sacred and profane history more fully, and was briefer. About a thousand years later the Renaissance humanists rediscovered its value. But they liked it for its style, not for its contents, which actually relied a good deal on Eusebius.

*The Christian organization of time.* Christians agreed that mankind's development proceeded on a time-line from the Creation to the Last Judgment with Christ's work and death as the central event on it. But how many years would that history encompass? And with God's providence guiding the world's destiny, what were the special providential acts that could help structure the long stretch of years?

The duration of the world had been of burning interest to the chiliasts and remained a concern even after chiliasm had faded. The second-century Epistle of Barnabas testified to the early beliefs in a world lasting six thousand years. Eventually widely accepted, the number 6,000 was derived from the interpretation of biblical passages. First, the Book of Genesis told of the Creation of the world in six days and of one day of rest. Then, there was the passage in Psalm 90:4: "For a thousand years in thy sight, are but as yesterday when it is past." 2 Peter 3:8 sounds a similar note when it says that "with the Lord one day is like a thousand years and a thousand years is like one day." If one equated each of the six days of Creation with a thousand years, the result was six thousand years.

A sequence of stages was the Christian answer to the quest for historical periodization. That quest led inevitably to the prophecies in the Bible as opportunities for comprehending God's intentions for the future. Postexilic Judaism supplied a scheme through the visions, dreams, and prophecies of the Book of Daniel. One story tells of how Nebuchadnezzar, king of Babylon, dreamed of a statue: "its head was of fine gold, its breast and arms were of silver, its belly and thighs of bronze, its legs of iron, its feet partly of iron, and partly clay."[4] A boulder smashed the statue, and

> the iron, the clay, the bronze, the silver, and the gold were broken in pieces together, and became like chaff from summer threshing floors, and were carried away by the wind, so that no trace of them could be found; while the stone that smote the image became a great mountain, filling all the earth.[5]

Daniel's interpretation of that dream reverberated through Western historiography well into the seventeenth century: God's will made Nebuchadnezzar king and his kingdom corresponded to the head of gold. After the Babylonian kingdom there "shall arise another kingdom inferior to you; then a third kingdom, of bronze, which shall rule over all the earth. And the fourth kingdom shall be as strong as iron."[6] As Christians saw it, Daniel prophesied a sequence of four kingdoms or empires throughout history, which would end in a noble, eternal kingdom, just as the boulder had grown into a great mountain. A similar message came from Daniel's visions of the four beasts rising one after the other from the sea. The New Testament offered the dramatic sequential opening of the seven seals in the Book of Revelation as a prophetic scheme for structuring time.

Even more frequent were schemes of world ages or eras *(aetates mundi)*. In one such early scheme, Origen interpreted the parable of the vineyard (Matt. 20:1-16) as foreshadowing five periods of world history. Later, schemes with six or seven periods were more numerous, all of them based on the biblical record of God creating the world in six days and resting on the seventh. In Jerome's version of Eusebius's *Chronicle*, no distinct periods can be discerned, but the chronological "markers" (Adam, Abraham, Moses, the building of the Temple, the restoration of the Temple, Christ's birth) suggested six ages. Variations of that scheme eventually pervaded medieval historiography.

*Augustine's reassessment: a cosmic interpretation of history*. Beginning with Constantine the Great, Christians accepted the Roman Empire as the divinely willed framework for their lives, and their positive attitude toward the empire showed in the works of Eusebius, Jerome, Ambrose, and Lactantius. Then, a catastrophe ended the comfortable accommodation. The Visigoths, who were Christians themselves, albeit of Arian persuasion, had for some time roamed through the empire, looting, burning, and destroying. In 410 they captured and sacked Rome. The physical suffering was enormous, but the psychological shock was even more severe. After nearly eight hundred years Eternal Rome had turned out to be vulnerable, if not finite, after all. The event also released a flood of refugees and recriminations. It revived old pagan accusations which blamed the Christians for Rome's decay and put into doubt the Christian assertion that the Roman Empire had a supportive role in the sacred story of the world.

An answer came from Aurelius Augustinus, the bishop of Hippo Regius in North Africa, better known as St. Augustine, who encountered the Roman refugees and heard their tales of pillage, rape, and deprivation. He realized the error in linking Christian faith and Roman Empire too closely. The church, a universal institution, must not remain tied to any particular state.

Accordingly, in his *City of God*, Augustine redefined the relationship between the sacred and profane throughout time. He stipulated the presence of two great force fields in the cosmos: the City of God and the Earthly City. The two cities or communities differed sharply from each other:

> [they] have been formed by two loves; the earthly by the love of self, even to the contempt of God; the heavenly by the love of God, even to the contempt of self.... In the one, the princes and the nations it subdues are ruled by the love of ruling; in the other, the princes and the subjects serve one another in love, the latter obeying, while the former take thought for all....

But in the other city [the City of God] there is no human wisdom, but only godliness, which offers due worship to the true God, and looks for its reward in the society of the saints, of holy angels as well as holy men, that God may be all in all.[7]

The world knew the two communities only in their intermixed state, not in their pure forms. Even the chiliastic expectations of a kingdom of God on earth would, according to Augustine, involve a fusing of the mundane and the sacred. The City of God could not exist in pure form in the *saeculum*. Because of this intermixture, Christians, who studied the past, must always sort out and try to understand those events which had a direct bearing on the status of the City of God. The struggle for power between Sulla and Marius, for example, was empty of meaning to Christians, whereas the fight between Emperor Constantine and his opponents, with Christianity's recognition at stake, was vital to the advancement of the City of God in the world. Neither meaning nor stability could be found in the Earthly City, a sphere of incessant change. Every state or empire had vanished forever after it had fulfilled its historical role. The Roman Empire, although it might have had the mission to unify all people for the spreading of the Gospel, could not escape decline either. Just like individuals, states earned no merit in the eyes of God. A Christian could expect stability and order in history only from the City of God. It followed that Christian historians must use schemes of periodization based on sacred traditions.

Augustine did not use Daniel's vision of the four world empires, although it could have supported his views on the coming and going of empires in the Earthly City. But it also equated the end of the world with the end of the Roman Empire, which Augustine merely mentioned. He found three other schemes of order more congenial. In his *De Trinitate*, he mentioned a tripartite scheme that consisted of periods before the law, under the law, and under God's glory. The scheme, often referred to as the *vaticinium Eliae*, could be found in the Babylonian Talmud. "The world is to exist six thousand years; The first two thousand years are to be void; the next two thousand years are the period of the Torah, and the following two thousand years are the period of the Messiah."[8] In another scheme Augustine divided all of human history into world ages, as other church fathers before him had done. Revelation 5:1 suggested six periods between the opening of the first and the seventh seal and so did the week which God took to create the world—six days of events and one of rest. Such a division put all of human history since the Incarnation into the sixth age. Augustine, who opposed all attempts to compute the end of the world, refused to accept the stipulation that each of the six world ages would last a thousand years. More surprising are Augustine's occasional references to the human life-ages as a principle for the periodization of world history. The scheme was a pagan one, reaching back to Cicero, Livy, and Seneca, although Origen, too, had taken it up. Later Lactantius had fashioned it into an instrument for showing that all human creations, including "eternal Rome," were bound to decay and that only the spiritual was exempt from the aging process. Augustine simply made the life ages correspond to the six world ages (see fig. 7.1).

It is significant that after all the efforts at periodization Augustine did not subject the *City of God* to any particular scheme of order. He must have found it difficult to contain the dynamic relationship between the City of God and the Earthly City within the limits of such a scheme. Nevertheless, the fact that he elaborated on these schemes gave them considerable status in the eyes of later Christian historians.

*Rome and Christ: a link renewed.* Augustine's denial of the identity between the City of God and any earthly institution convinced few. Even Orosius, a confidante of Augustine, deserted him with his *Seven Books of Histories against the Pagans*. Augustine had urged Orosius to show through historical examples that Christians had not caused the hardships which of late had befallen the Roman Empire. Orosius did so with a vengeance; he described how there had been, even before Christ, "the burdens of war or ravages of disease or sorrows of famine or horrors of earthquakes or of unusual floods, of dreadful outbreaks of fire or cruel strokes of lightning and storms of hail or even the miseries caused by parricides and shameful deeds."[9] And he "found the days of the past not only equally oppressive as these [present days], but also the more wretched the more distant they are from the solace of true religion."[10] Most important, however, Orosius returned to the assertions of the "imperial theologians" that God's design linked Augustus and Christ and that the acceptance of Christianity sanctified the Roman Empire. Christian historians had a reason to take an interest in Roman history, and since medieval chroniclers generally preferred Orosius's *Histories* to Augustine's *City of God*, the link between Rome and Christianity was bequeathed to them. Those chroniclers also took note of Orosius's use of typological interpretations for the postbiblical world. The biblical past shed light on events of the present and the future. Thus the ten plagues of Egypt foretold of the ten Roman persecutions of Christians.

Finally, it mattered that Orosius emphasized Daniel's scheme of four monarchies or empires rather than Augustine's six ages. While prior versions of the scheme had proposed a sequence of Babylonians, Medes, Persians, and Macedonians, and later versions—in order to accommodate Rome—had changed it to Babylonians, Medes and Persians, Macedonians, and Romans, Orosius stipulated a sequence of Babylonian, Macedonian, African (that is, Carthaginian), and Roman empires. Although Orosius never endeavored to group his rather topsy-turvy account according to the four empires, his and Jerome's earlier acknowledgment of the four empires set an important pattern for medieval historians. To all of them the limit of four implied that from now on to the Last Judgment world history would be Roman history in its Christian version. Despite Augustine's vigorous dissent, Orosius's most important legacy was the

Figure 7.1

Augustine's Schemes of Order

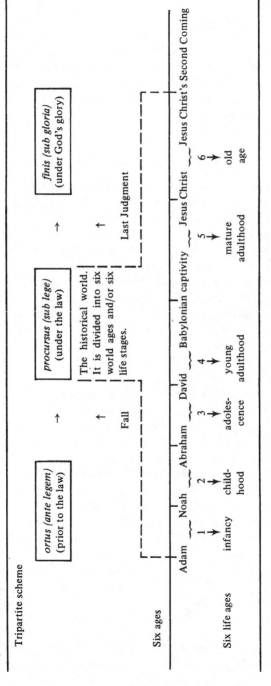

Tripartite scheme

| ortus (ante legem) (prior to the law) | procursus (sub lege) (under the law) | finis (sub gloria) (under God's glory) |
|---|---|---|

The historical world. It is divided into six world ages and/or six life stages.

Fall

Last Judgment

Six ages

| Adam | Noah | Abraham | David | Babylonian captivity | Jesus Christ | Jesus Christ's Second Coming |

Six life ages

| 1 infancy | 2 child-hood | 3 adoles-cence | 4 young adulthood | 5 mature adulthood | 6 old age |

concept of a Christian Roman Empire: somehow Rome was essential to the continuity of the sacred story.

From the fifth century on, when the Germanic migrations began to destroy much of the Roman imperial reality and to put the idea of an eternal Christian Roman Empire to a severe test, Christian historians confronted new tasks. Not the least of these would be to cope with the realization that the relationship between the sacred and mundane was not identical with the issue of reconciling Christ and Rome.

## The Problem of Continuity in an Age of Upheaval

By 500 the Roman Empire in the West had faded into the emerging world of German successor states, and Christians found not only their lives changed but also the accustomed matrix of their faith. Jesus had lived, taught, and died; the apostles had preached the faith; and the church had grown in the Roman Empire. Since Constantine the Great the empire had even assumed in the minds of many a central and permanent role in the providential plan. Now the divorce from the empire, spelled out by Augustine in theory, had become a reality and Christians had to redefine the relationship of sacred and profane history. This major redefinition started in the 500s and deeply influenced what commonly is known as medieval historiography. At its core stood the reaffirmation of the universality of sacred history in the once more obvious diversity of the temporal world; a world not of one empire but of many kingdoms.

*The integration of the Germans.* In the early 400s Augustine and Orosius had come to terms with the German problem by concluding, with some reservations, that the mission of the church to carry the Gospel to all people must be God's reason for the intrusion of the Germans into Roman history. Salvian even saw the Germans as God's instrument of punishment for a corrupt Roman world. Such views facilitated the fusion of German and Latin cultures.

In historiography, the Germans paid a heavy price for their integration into the Latin cultural world. They sang in epics and tales about warrior heroes and kings of their past, a world vastly different from the Latin one. It proved difficult to account for the continuity of past, present, and future as long as the past remained twofold: Germanic-pagan and classical-Christian. The historians of the period, the clergy, were members of the educated elite of the new kingdoms. That group, steeped in the Latin tradition, linked the German past to the redemptive history of mankind, including the Roman chapter of that history. Even those historians who wrote sympathetic accounts of various German tribes accepted only those parts of the German tradition "useful" for linking that tradition to the well-established historical framework of the Christian Latin world. The linkage, detrimental as it proved to the old oral and pagan German traditions, filled the need for continuity, stability, and legitimacy felt by conquerors and conquered alike. The epic traditions of the various Germanic people, now without official purpose, remained largely unrecorded in writing but continued to be transmitted orally. They eventually found their literary expressions in the medieval romances and were occasionally mentioned in histories. But in historiography as in other fields, the process of fusion and its results still carried the marks of ethnic and regional diversity, necessitating the constant reaffirmation of the Christian concept of human universality.

In 489 the Ostrogoths migrated into Italy, established their own kingdom, and promptly pursued a policy of reconciliation with the Roman world. The designer of that policy, King Theodoric, encouraged his administrative official, Flavius Marcus Aurelius Cassiodorus Senator, to write a history of the Goths. We possess of it only what a later historian, Jordanes, incorporated into his work, *The Origin and Deeds of the Goths*. Both men aimed at demonstrating the nobility of the Goths and their link to the Roman Empire.

> Not satisfied with extolling living kings, from whom he [Cassiodorus] might hope for a reward, he drew forth the kings of the Goths from the dust of Ages, showing that the Amal family had been royal for seventeen generations and proved that the origin of the Gothic people belonged to Roman history, adorning the whole subject with the flowers of his learning gathered from wide fields of literature.[11]

The Goths were also associated with the Scythians, those mysterious but well-known people of Greek and Roman accounts. The same desire to link Gothic and Roman traditions showed in Cassiodorus's *Chronicle*, with its message that the eternal Rome was now carried on by Germans. As for the Visigoths, who had built their kingdom in Spain, Isidore, bishop of Seville, agreed in his History of The Goths, Vandals, and Suevi with Cassiodorus's and Jordanes's early history of the Goths. He reinforced the nobility of the Gothic origin, stating that the "Goths are descended from Magog, the son of Japhet [one of Noah's sons], and shown to have sprung from the same origin as the Scythians, from whom they do not differ greatly in name. For when one letter is altered and another is removed, the Getae are almost named like the Scythians."[12]

Yet Isidore had no intention to link the Visigoths with the Roman Empire in order to improve their status. They had dignity and worth of their own. Gregory of Tours' *History of the Franks* aimed not at ennoblement but at a sober assessment of the early Franks. When "this particular people" emerged from Pannonia, they were good warriors but brutal and ignorant idol worshipers, not at all an exceptional people in ancestry or traits. It was left to the seventh-century *Chronicle of Fredegar*—probably the work of three authors—to find a lofty origin for the Franks: a Trojan ancestry. The *Chronicle* revived a tradition that had Aeneas lead one contingent of Trojans across the sea to Italy. This tradition also had Priam's group move into Macedonia, where some became the ancestors of Philip and Alexander, while others went farther west and became the ancestors of the Franks.

The Anglo-Saxons had to wait for the consolidation of their rule before they found an advocate, the monk Bede. In the sixth century the Celtic monk Gildas saw them only as destroyers, although he regarded them as God's instrument for punishing the sinful Britons. In his *Ruin of Britain* he traced the decline of Roman England after A.D. 400. "No sooner were they [the Romans] gone, than the Picts and Scots, like worms which in the heat of mid-day came forth from their holes, hastily land again from their canoes."[13] The hard-pressed Britons sealed their doom by inviting help from the fierce and impious Saxons, a race "hated by man," who then became the Britons' fierce rivals and, later, conquerors. Bede, who finished his *Ecclesiastical History of the English People* in 731 as a resident of the powerful Germanic kingdom of Northumbria, had a calmer view of the Anglo-Saxons. Fierce, even brutal though they were as pagans, they were also the instrument of the "just Judge" for punishing the sinful Britons, who had failed to convert the Saxons. Once Christianized, the Angles, Saxons, and Jutes unified the various people on English soil in the proper faith.

*The quest for universality.* The integration of the Germans into the Roman cultural world represented a step in the gradual recapture of a sense of continuity by means of the universality of the Christian faith. Yet, even in the face of the dissolution of the Roman Empire the hope of preserving continuity through Rome did not vanish quickly.

The argument for a continuation of Rome was made most strongly by Cassiodorus, who for many years traversed a sort of Roman *cursus honorum* in Ostrogoth service. His *Chronica* traced an unbroken line from early Rome to the Goth Eutharic's consulship (5,721 years). Jordanes, using the four-empire scheme, still considered the Roman Empire to be the final one, although he qualified that by a "may seem to." Both men perceived a continuity through Rome, safeguarded in their time by the Goths and the Eastern Empire.

When Gregory of Tours spoke of the empire, he referred to the Eastern Empire. Its relations with the Franks were tenuous at best, as demonstrated by the strange spectacle in which Clovis was made a consul. Indeed the Frankish story seemed to offer no more than the record of disjointed cycles of raw and brutal passions, except that the early events could be seen as steps leading to the unification of the Franks under Clovis. But in his own way Gregory did link Frankish destiny with sacred history, for example, through his profession of faith. "As I am about to describe the struggles of kings with the heathen enemy, of martyrs with pagans, of churches with heretics, I desire first of all to declare my faith so that my reader may have no doubt that I am Catholic."[14] But Gregory did not weld together sacred and profane history systematically. He simply implied that all events of this world happened in the space that God had provided—in time. Understood in that manner, the chronological order of narration turned from a mere compositional device into the reflection of how time rushed towards fulfillment. His work foreshadowed the medieval chronicle with its seemingly tedious and unimaginative account of the events of year after year—the *temporum series*.

Isidore of Seville not only ignored, he opposed outright, the idea of an ongoing Roman Empire. He identified the empire with Justinian's Empire, whose invasion of Southern Spain had threatened Isidore's family and Visigoth Spain alike. For him the end of Rome was not the end of everything. The venerated empires of Rome and Babylon were mere temporary phenomena whereas the Incarnation instituted the *imperium Christi* in which every nation could have its *regnum*. The role of being God's steward on earth devolved from the emperor to the kings. In Gregory's account the king must build churches, succor the poor, and serve the needs of all people. Isidore and other Visigoth historians, such as John of Biclaro and Julian of Toledo, spoke of the king as the "most holy king," "the apostolic king," *sacratissimus princeps, orthodoxus imperator*, or "the prince of the people." To them it was clear that such a man had no need for an earthly imperial overlord.

*The true continuity: Divine Providence*. The integration of the Germans into the classical world and the acceptance of the new states as the new context of life were steps toward a new stability. Yet, in the absence of "eternal Rome," only the Christian faith could supply a viable concept of continuity between past, present, and future. Such a concept was Divine Providence, the force behind all events in the *saeculum* and thus the key to understanding them. Providence had never been denied or forgotten but seemed simply to have chosen the Roman Empire as its instrument, becoming much easier to grasp. Now, in the absence of the Roman Empire, Christians were forced to ask once more the fundamental questions of how, when, and where God revealed his plan for the course of human events. They found answers difficult to obtain because their era, the sixth age, by definition had no clear signposts comparable to those of the biblical period. In their search for answers they studied chronology, attempted universal histories, examined prophecies, used the cycle of sin and punishment, interpreted miracles, and told of portents.

*Chronology: testimony to universality and order*. The events of the past had been given their accepted order by Eusebius. Between 400 and 650 all historians accepted this order (in Jerome's version); only Jordanes, who lived in the East, chose the system of Sextus Julius Africanus. Historians were of a mind with Gregory of Tours, who, speaking of Eusebius, Jerome, and Orosius, said:

> The chronicles of Eusebius, bishop of Caesarea, and of the priest Jerome... explain clearly how the age of the world is computed, and set out in systematic form the entire sequence of the years.... I will follow the example of these writers whom I have mentioned and in my turn reckon the entire series of years from the very first creation of man down to our own time.[15]

Isidore thought much about time and its nature but stayed with Eusebius. Yet, all contemporary historians demonstrated the influence of competing chronological schemes when they had recourse to either old Roman imperial and new regional methods for counting years. The use of the *fasti consulares, ab urbe condita* dates, imperial years, Spanish and Frankish regnal years, testified to the presence of concepts of time contradicting the Christian *anni mundi* scheme with its affirmation of the universality of the human experience. In his major chronological works *On Time* and *On the Reckoning of Time* Bede suggested how Christian chronology could be strengthened, but one of his innovations also showed how tenuous the Eusebian chronological scheme was.

Centuries of poor communications between regions had made for considerable differences in liturgical practices, including Easter celebrations. Bede's interest in chronology resulted to a high degree from controversies between the Celtic and Roman rites concerning the proper calculation of Easter dates. For Bede this was no mere question of outward uniformity but part of the wider issue of the unity of faith and truth so central to his whole work. He favored the Roman method, which in the early 500s had found its chronological genius in Dionysius Exiguus. It placed Easter on the first Sunday after the first full moon following the vernal equinox. Bede described how in England the Synod of Whitby (664) began the unification process on the basis of the Dionysian scheme.

The same scheme substituted the year of the Incarnation for the widely used accession date of that persecutor of Christians, Diocletian, as the pivotal event from which to count all years and in doing so gave the proper recognition to that event. Bede used the *Anno Domini* count of years but also, on occasion, the "before the Incarnation" (B.C.) count. But while A.D. years gradually became the norm, the B.C. counting of years found new advocates only from the 1400s on. For the period prior to the Incarnation, the world era and Roman counting schemes continued.

Bede was not much more successful with his recalculation of the age of the world. Combining St. Jerome's *Vulgate*, the Jewish tradition, and the *Vetus latina* (another Latin translation of the Septuagint) he arrived at 3,952 years from the beginning of the world as the time of Jesus' birth, rather than Africanus's 5,500 or Eusebius's and Jerome's 5,198/99. So large a discrepancy proved an obstacle for easy acceptance and only from the eleventh century on did Bede's computation begin to make an impact. As for organizing these thousands of years into periods, delimited by events serving as insignificant markers of God's design, none of the historians of the period had anything novel to say. Augustine's series of ages remained the model for those who studied the problem, particularly Isidore of Seville and Bede. With every decade it became clearer that the scheme of ages was helpful in the interpretation of history for the pre-Incarnation period but not for the years after Christ's Resurrection. The sixth age lacked figures and events equal in significance to those in the Bible for the demarcation of periods—that is, time spans in which God worked a special purpose. Gregory of Tours betrayed the resulting confusion when he put the death of St. Martin on the same level as the Resurrection, as a time marker, although he did not pretend to present a scheme of ages. Isidore drew back from the problem with the remark: "As for the rest of the sixth age only God knows that."[16]

*Prophecies, miracles, and portents.* For Christian historians, who equated historical explanation with ascertaining the designs of Divine Providence, prophecies were important as instances in which selected persons gained a glimpse of some features of God's plan. Thus Christians maintained that many prophecies of the Old Testament foretold the central event of the New Testament—the coming of Christ. But already the church fathers and early Christian historians used biblical prophecies to shed light on events in the postbiblical period. Thus Isidore of Seville linked the childless marriage of the Visigoth king Artaulf to Galla Placidia with Daniel's prophecy that no child would result from the marriage of the King of the South's daughter to the King of the North. He quoted Daniel once more as foretelling a later event: King Geiseric's persecution of Catholics. For Christians the accuracy of such prophetic history depended entirely on the appropriateness of the linkage, and Augustine had already worried about possible problems. The dangers were ever-present of sliding either into timeless and thus ahistorical allegories or into trivialization. Thus Gregory of Tours related the story of the retinue of a princess despoiling the land it traversed and then turned Joel 1:4 into a prophecy of that event. He also told stories of Frankish contemporary prophets enunciating ad hoc prophecies—the type Augustine had cautioned about—concerning the imminent death of a king or the outcome of some minor political struggle, without ever reflecting seriously on the difference between biblical and postbiblical prophecies and on the role of the prophetic in the explanation of events.

Miracles, those divinely caused temporary suspensions of the routine order of life, were rarely linked to significant historical explanations. For Gregory of Tours, who related many of them, they were more the witness of the ever-present power of God than points of decision in the flow of events. They usually saved the health, life, or possessions of an individual. Even less significant as historical explanations were the numerous portents reported by the early Christian historians, who were as uncertain about the precise role of portents for the course of events as their ancient predecessors had been. Both groups mainly listed them and at best implied their role. Portents such as lights in the sky, landslides, balls of fire, comets, wolves in the city, or cocks crowing in the evening inspired awe with no discernible link to subsequent events; they were warnings from God of things to come (see Isidore of Seville's list of portents prior to the decisive defeat of the Huns on the Catalaunian fields); or they confirmed the importance of an event. All of them needed more explanation than they offered.

*A causal scheme: sin and punishment.* The absence of a discernible large-scale design for the sixth of the world ages enhanced the significance of the causal cycle of sin followed by punishment as a means of interpreting events. Central to the Biblical view of the human condition, the cycle had been used abundantly in the works of Augustine and Orosius. Now contemporary historians did the same. Emperor Valens perished for making the Goths Arians (according to Jordanes) and so did the Visigoth King Euric for persecuting Catholic Christians. A bishop died for being evil, and the Frank Flaochad for burning a city in a campaign (Gregory of Tours). But the cycle assumed a much larger scope when historians saw the destinies of whole peoples at stake. Isidore of Seville saw the Huns as the instrument of punishment for straying nations, and Gildas made collective punishment the central theme of his *Ruin of Britain.* He reminded the Britons how God had punished even the Israelites, his chosen people, for their transgressions, and he warned the Britons that God would not spare them. Indeed, the events of recent British history could be explained only in terms of the sins of the Britons and the retribution of subsequent punishment. Insofar as Gildas wrote history it was to be an explanation of why Britons should repent: the cycle of sin and punishment could be broken. In a decisive difference from the ancient patterns prescribed by fate, human beings could sway the mind of God. Gregory of Tours reports, for example, how the prayers of a queen prevented a major battle and the fast of a people terminated an epidemic.

*The visible unity: the church.* The historians, who saw Divine Providence as the true tie of continuity between the worlds of the past, present, and future had before them the visible sign of that continuity in the church. Its actions in guarding the faith, in converting non-Christians, and in making the faith present in all of life provided a dynamic element. Yet, that type of dynamism was well removed from the apocalyptic expectation inherent in the Christian faith. And despite all the turmoil of the times, historians, who were usually "long-range thinkers," did not anticipate the imminent end of the world. Gregory of Tours, as was seen, reassured his readers: "For the sake of those who are losing hope as they see the end of the world come nearer and nearer," he wished to "explain how many years have passed since the world began" and by implication would continue to pass.[17] Isidore, without showing any apocalyptic expectations, simply claimed ignorance about the remainder of the time allotted to this world. Both historians were more interested in the developments brought about by the struggles to convert the pagans and Arians, which seemed to link the contemporary church clearly with the *historia sacra.* But only in one case was the work of the contemporary church directly linked to the biblical history: that of the conversion of the Jews. The interpretations showed the traditional puzzlement over the Jews' reluctance to convert and the expectation by some that that conversion would only happen at the Last Judgment.

The church also was involved in another process. As, in the words of Isidore of Seville, more and more states seceded from the Roman Empire, the church had to construct relationships with each of the new states in greatly different situations. That involved not only defining the king's proper personal stewardship but the whole relationship between two institutions, the church and the state. Contemporary clerical historians, who reported on that complex endeavor, always upheld the exalted role of the church yet in their accounts bore out the Augustinian view of the church in the *saeculum* as a mixed institution with features of both the City of God and the Earthly City. Gregory of Tours bewailed the ambition, jealousy, drinking, avarice, and negligence of some of the clergy but never doubted that the church represented the universal aspect of human life vis-à-vis the purely temporal structures of lay power. Yet, significantly, contemporary historians reported the events connected with the adjustment process without ever grasping the process as a whole. This view was in line with the one prevailing throughout the medieval period that transformed the historical friction between the church and lay institutions into a static problem of adjustments and readjustments best grasped by philosophers and theologians, who were to resolve it by means of logic and dialectic. Historians would act as illustrators and narrators but not as explainers of the problem.

The same static approach showed in regard to the old problem of social justice. Augustine and Orosius had not seen the problem in terms of a development, except that the coming of Christ had made possible greater benevolence in all societies through the healing power of charity. This power was a matter of assistance to individuals, not the wellspring of systematic change, a concept utterly foreign to all contemporaries. Thus Isidore opposed any alteration in the status of serfs and Gregory traced the rise of the church from austere circumstances to a much more affluent institution without connecting that development with the issue of social justice.

*Purpose, truth, and style.* By 750 a historiography had been worked out that could cope with the new situation: a world of diverse kingdoms with which the universality of the Christian faith and its institutions—the church—had to be reconciled. It had been done in histories but with little conscious effort at reflecting on the historical endeavor. Isidore of Seville came closest to such a reflection in the historical portions of his *Etymologies*. There he revived the late classical categorization of writings on the past: histories—full and somewhat artful narrations of more recent events; chronicles—brief accounts centering on dates proposed by Eusebius and Jerome; annals—year-by-year accounts of long periods; *calendaria*—month-by-month accounts; and *ephemerida*—day-by-day accounts. But Isidore did not accept the distinction between histories as interpretive accounts and annals as factual records, since he viewed both as "factual." There was no room for purely human interpretations because "events were historical facts, but as to meaning they point out the mysteries of the Church."[18] Interpretations could be derived only from the Bible. Such a view was firmly linked to the generally accepted purpose of historiography, from which in turn flowed crucial consequences related to historical truth, sources, style, and composition.

The integration of the Germans into the now Christian Roman world served historians only briefly as a purpose for their work. Even the old Cassiodorus had perceived it differently. What does a historian do? "Christian studies also possess narrators of history, who, calm in their ecclesiastical gravity, recount the shifting movements of events and the unstable history of kingdoms with eloquent but very cautious splendor."[19] Gregory of Tours added the more specific wish "to keep alive the memory of those dead and gone" in order to give encouragement to believers. Bede spelled out most precisely the purpose as one of instructing and edifying: "For if history records good things of good men, the thoughtful hearer is encouraged to imitate what is good; if it records evil things of wicked men, the good religious listener or reader is encouraged to avoid all that is sinful and perverse, and to follow what he knows to be good and pleasing to God."[20]

Such purposes were perceived not as endangering but as enhancing historical truth. While its criterion remained the ancient one of accuracy, the touchstone now was not sensory experience but reference to the sacred tradition. Thus written sources played an important role and with this role came a devotion to the correct text. Cassiodorus called for "faultless books ... for fear lest the mistakes of scribes become fixed in unpolished minds; since that which is manifestly planted and rooted in the recesses of the memory cannot easily be torn out."[21] One and a half centuries later Bede's attention to sources expressed well the concern for their reliability and orthodoxy. "But in order to avoid any doubts as to the accuracy of what I have written in the minds of yourself or of any who may listen to or read this history, allow me briefly to state the authorities upon whom I chiefly depend."[22] Indeed, so "modern" was Bede that scholars have praised him for his diligent use of sources, for his keen appreciation of documents and letters (which he often laboriously solicited and then included in his work), and for giving an unusually clear designation of author and work whenever he quoted from his sources. But Bede, of course, was not moved by "scientific" motives but by his respect for the authority of the source and the awareness that not to match account and source or to distort a document would damage the truthfulness expected of a writer on sacred subjects.

The religious purpose of the contemporary histories also governed their style and composition. Cassiodorus still was imbued with the ancient rhetoric's ideals of elegance, but to Gregory of Tours the disclaimer of stylistic excellence meant more than the ancient *topos* of routinely professing modesty about one's style. After him, one of the authors of the *Chronicle of Fredegar* professed that

"Thus I am compelled, so far as my rusticity and ignorance permit, to hand on as briefly as possible whatever I have learned."[23] The widespread lack of learning could excuse a style lacking polish, but men of faith went further and endorsed such a style as reflecting Christian humility and facilitating the instruction of the masses. Gregory of Tours proved that such a style need not be dull when he described the world and events in vivid passages like the following:

> In the year the winter was a grievous one and more severe than usual, so that the streams were held in the chains of frost, and furnished a path for the people like dry ground. Birds, too, were affected by the cold and hunger, and were caught in the hand without any snare when the snow was deep.[24]

In their often fumbling way the Christian historians of the 500s and 600s had transformed historiography in the image of the Christian faith and into a form fitting the new world of kingdoms. Occupied with this transformation, they were content to drop the ancient fascination with eloquence and to mention eschatological matters rarely. Their historiographical views would prove compatible with the world of the three centuries after the mid-700s, but also flexible enough to accommodate a profusion of historiographical forms. The latter sufficed for discussion of continuity through Rome and chronology, for integrating new people into the Latin world, and for establishing the authority of new dynasties.

### The Carolingian and Anglo-Saxon Consolidation in Historiography

In the period between 750 and 900 the writing of history flourished beyond all expectations in the Carolingian Empire and in Alfred the Great's Kingdom of Wessex. It did so in the context of a general revival of classical learning, and stimulated exciting events, two outstanding men, and the needs of two strong states. Yet, while one of the states was a kingdom, the other one cast some histories once more under the spell of empire.

*The revival of empire.* During the eighth century the Frankish state had recovered its vigor under its new Carolingian dynasty. The coronation, in 800, of Charlemagne as emperor epitomized the Carolingian accomplishments although neither contemporaries nor later scholars have agreed on the exact meaning of the coronation beyond its being a testimony to a remarkable fusion of the Roman imperial idea, Christian faith, and Frankish kingship.

Contemporary historians did not escape the spell of developments that for the first time since the fall of the Roman Empire created a quasi-universal political entity. The reality of this entity, however, never matched the universal claim implied by the title "emperor." Nevertheless, the idea of a Christian Roman Empire found once more a partial actualization and its spell would last throughout the medieval period, at least as a hope. Some elements of medieval life gave substance to the concept of such a Christian commonwealth: the shared faith and its institution, the church; the common stock of learning; and the longing for the Roman Peace. But the influence of those elements was countered by powerful regional, tribal, and strictly local forces, which favored numerous and separate units of life of less than imperial scope. This tension between universalism and localism, which became a characteristic of medieval life and thought, affected the historiography of the period. In the Carolingian state the biblical and spiritual interpretation of history was being tempted again by the lure of a congenial secular order. This temptation represented just one more variation of the wider dilemma of how to reconcile the universal sacred order with a specific mundane context. Contemporary historians succeeded in bridging the gap but, as always, only temporarily and incompletely. But it would have been difficult to discover in the histories of the Carolingian heyday the problematics of the fusion. To the contrary, historiography received a substantial infusion of vigor through the revival of classical learning. In the characteristic Carolingian manner, this revival blended renovation and innovation.

*Biography and hagiography.* The veritable renaissance of biography writing during the eighth and ninth centuries should surprise no one. Society was a network of individual relationships, and contemporaries had no doubts that the deeds of nobles and pious persons shaped the world. Outstanding leaders won battles, ruled, converted whole tribes, founded monasteries, and offered to their contemporaries ideals and standards of conduct. What better mirror of the past could there be than accounts of how monarchs, abbots, bishops, and saints had spent their lives? Models for biography writing were available from the ancients, particularly through Plutarch and Suetonius, and from the rich store of hagiography, the descriptions of saintly lives.

The Christian church had always cherished the inspiration and emulation evoked by the saint. The Bible told of such heroes of faith and so did the stories about the martyrs of the early church. The faithful narrated the lives and deeds of saintly persons over and over again and eventually wrote them down, as in the famous and pattern-setting *Life of St. Martin* (ca. 400) by Sulpicius Severus. From the sixth and seventh centuries on, hagiography flourished. The stories of the saints, who as heroes of the Christian faith gradually became patrons of days, parishes, regions, families, and professions, appeared in a variety of hagiographical material including inscriptions, liturgical texts, calendars, legends, and martyrologies. As their number increased, the stories of saints acquired some standard features. The saint's youth was either precociously pious or flawed until a conversion experience changed everything; miracles were performed and hardships endured; and after death the body might remain incorrupt. The similarities did not matter, since these biographies wished to present not innovative stories but the typical manifestations of the holy in this world. They aimed at spiritual edification, to the dismay of modern historians, who, equipped with present-day concepts of verification, have searched for but often have been unable to discern "the actual events." The *vitae* of saints persisted so well because as living documents their texts and presentation changed in accord with views and preferences of the changing periods. Already in the early medieval period most of the saints were no longer hermits but persons who acted in the world on behalf of the church. Hence the description of their deeds began to resemble much more closely historical accounts, as, for example, the lives of the great missionaries: Bede's *Life of St. Cuthbert,* Alcuin's *Life of Willibrord,* and Willibald's *Life of Boniface.* The more the Church linked up with secular society the less the lives of its heroes were given exclusively to contemplation and the smaller the distance became between saints' lives and biographies of secular persons.

Finally, Einhard created a model for the biography of a prominent Christian layman with his *Life of Charlemagne.* He, however, owed a greater debt to Suetonius than to the hagiographers, a fact apparent in the very structure of his work. Charlemagne's deeds were covered in the first part and his character portrait was given in the second. But Einhard did not share Suetonius's skeptical attitude toward his subject. On the contrary, he, who had known the elderly Charlemagne well, admired the ruler's majestic appearance, "always stately and dignified, whether he was standing or sitting," and Charlemagne's "dignity, magnanimity, discernment, and constancy."[25] One could attribute such praise to flattery by a fawning courtier, but it would be better to view it as the application of the hagiographical catalogue of virtues to the model of the ideal king. The latter also carried some Germanic marks when Einhard praised Charlemagne's martial deeds, called him king rather than emperor, recorded proudly that Charlemagne "used to wear the national, that is to say, the Frankish, dress"[26] and acknowledged benevolently Charlemagne's concubines.

Einhard exerted a strong influence on subsequent biographies, specifically on Bishop Asser's *Life of Alfred the Great* (893). That work's synthesis of personality, faith, and deeds emphasized the pious King Alfred over Alfred the Anglo-Saxon warrior-king. Alfred was like Solomon, "who, despising all the glory and riches of this world, sought first wisdom from God, and so found both"; and the work told how "the poor had no helpers, or but very few, save him alone."[27] Of course, Asser also narrated Alfred's victories over the pagans. The warrior and the pious man also coexisted in the anonymous *Life of Edward* (the Confessor). Many of Edward's features described in the first part, such as his fondness for the hunt and his great skills as a warrior, fit ill with the image of Edward the Saint, who was chaste and worked miracles, unless one remembers and accepts the contemporary Anglo-Saxon ideal of kingship with its mixture of Germanic and Christian traits in which one person could be warrior, ruler, and saint.

That unity between secular deeds and sanctity remained precarious. It burst asunder in Bishop Thegan's biography of Charlemagne's son Louis the Pious.

Thegan praised the strong sanctity of Louis, "who had learned from childhood on, to fear and love God, distributed, for God's sake, whatever property he possessed among the poor."[28] When the pope came to crown Louis, they "talked each day about the loftiest topics of the Holy Church."[29] But Thegan approvingly reported that "the pagan narratives or songs, which he had learned when young, Louis despised and would not suffer to read, or listen to, or have them taught."[30] Thus ended an endeavor which could have incorporated the Germanic epics into the body of Frankish historical writings. Charlemagne used to listen at the dinner table to music and to the stories and deeds of the ancient kings written out for posterity. But his son found them too rude and lacking in edification.

In 883, Notker Balbulus, a monk of St. Gall, wrote a biography of Charlemagne that piled story upon story to· form a treasury of anecdotes. Little as Notker's work mattered as history, it signaled a remarkable development; as the years passed, Charlemagne's biography was turning into legend.

*A distant cousin of biography: the* gesta. The Carolingian period also sponsored a peculiar form of history called the *gesta*. The name resulted from a rather arbitrary treatment of the Latin phrase *res gestae* (things which happened). Medieval scholars, who never clearly delimited the genres of history writing from each other, left the *gesta*, too, without a proper definition. The *gesta* can best be characterized as a variation of the biographical genre. It described the lives and deeds of the holders of certain offices—abbots or bishops, for example—and in the process it delivered biographies of institutions. The admirable continuity of ecclesiastical institutions made them the preferred subjects of *gesta*. When secular personages were at the center of a work, the English translation of *gesta* as "deeds" describes well the increased emphasis on actions and the more precarious link to the institution.

The *Book of the Popes*, begun sometime in the sixth or seventh century and containing an annotated list of the popes since St. Peter, could be considered the *gesta*'s archetypical ancestor. It documented the unbroken apostolic succession at the same time as it recorded pontificates, papal actions, and gifts to the church from secular rulers.

The *Book of the Popes* and his wish to please the Carolingian family inspired Paulus Diaconus to write a *gesta* of the bishops of Metz, which demonstrated how useful the *gesta* in a freer, less tablelike form could be for recording the past of institutions. Another testimony to the value of the *gesta* as institutional history came with the *Gesta Abbatum Fontanellensium*, honoring the abbots of the Norman monastery of St. Wandrille. Much like other histories the *gesta* also could serve secondary purposes. It could be useful for documenting certain rights and privileges of a monastery, whether by showing its age, mentioning its founding documents, or pleading its cause.

During the eleventh and twelfth centuries the *gesta* form remained popular for histories of bishops and their bishoprics and of abbots and their monasteries. The genre also was eventually used simply for recording deeds and events detached from a clear institutional setting and even of a secular nature. There were works entitled *gesta* that dealt with the stories of Emperor Frederick Barbarossa, Norman dukes, English kings, and the Crusades. In most of these works the genre came close to losing its distinct identity and to fusing with other forms.

*Annals: from lists to narrative histories.* Annals began to abound in the Carolingian period. Much like the *Annales Maximi* of ancient Rome the Christian annals had a religious origin. While the *Annales Maximi* told the proper days for certain rituals, the early medieval annals developed from Easter tables. And just as Romans had added more and more notes to the *Annales Maximi* and the *fasti consulares* and thus created the pattern for year-by-year—that is annalistic— treatments of the past, so medieval monks added more and more information to the Easter tables. As for the influences from the fully-developed late Roman annalistic tradition, they were probably slight. Now in the Carolingian period annals became a favorite way to record the past, particularly in monasteries. Monks, mostly anonymous, noted items of interest and importance for each year and thus created an institutionally useful ongoing history. In their fully developed form annals would closely resemble chronicles and serve a variety of aims.

When in 752, Pippin, the father of Charlemagne, wrested the kingship away from the Merovingians, his uncle Childebrand initiated a quasi-official Carolingian history, the *History or Deeds of the Franks*. It was an updated version of the *Chronicle of "Fredegar"* and was soon overshadowed by another work. For the period from 741 to 829 the Frankish kingdom possessed a kind of official history in the *Royal Frankish Annals*. The number of titles under which this work is known reminds us that medieval historians named their works with great nonchalance, if at all. The author often did not even give his own name; indeed for most annals there was more than one author. Thus, scholars have frequently named annals simply after the place where they were written or where they were found. The *Royal Frankish Annals* once were called the *Annales Laurissenses majores* after the monastery at Lorsch where their oldest version was discovered.

The compiling of the *Royal Frankish Annals* began in the 790s and ended abruptly in 829, when the annalist may have died or simply given up. However, there was rhyme and reason to the first entry, a laconic sentence: "741. Charles, majordomo of the palace, died."[31] A point in history had been reached where the Carolingian family's importance overshadowed that of the royal Merovingians. The Carolingian coup d'etat of 752 was blessed by the annalist: "Childerich, who was falsely called king, was tonsured and sent into a monastery."[32] Somehow it all seemed God's will, just as when "by God's help and the intercession of

the blessed apostle Peter, Pippin with his Franks had the victory" or when in the
Saxon campaign of 772 the whole Frankish army was saved, through God's
grace, by a sudden rainfall.[33] And while the description of the coronation in
800 was short of explanations it could have done well as an official view:

> On the most holy day of Christmas, when the king rose from prayer in front
> of the shrine of the blessed apostle Peter, to take part in the Mass, Pope Leo
> placed a crown on his head, and he was hailed by the whole Roman people:
> "To the august Charles crowned by God, the great and peaceful emperor of
> the Romans, life and victory." After the acclamations the pope addressed
> him in the manner of the old emperors. The name of Patricius was now
> abandoned and he was called Emperor and Augustus.[34]

With so close a connection between annals and ruling family it does not
surprise that the *Royal Frankish Annals* end in 829, a time of disintegration for
the Carolingian realm. Afterwards, Carolingian affairs were recorded by annals of
regional scope which quite often reflected the specific perspectives of the new
emerging kingdoms: Western, Eastern, and Central; with the latter retaining the
imperial title.

Modern readers have often been puzzled, even annoyed, by what they have
considered the haphazard mixture of the trivial and the important in annals.
Even the quasi-official *Royal Frankish Annals* spoke not only of campaigns,
assemblies, and embassies but also of the rhythm of the seasons and of the
calamities caused by their deviations from their normal course; of the deeds of
nobles; of the life of the imperial court; and of signs of divine power such as
earthquakes, strange lights, and miraculous healings and rescues. Actually such
annals provided the medieval counterpart to classical cultural history. They
reflected the Christian image of the cosmos with its spiritual unity and hierarchy
of all things and events. Annalists were well content simply to portray that world
and would have rejected the idea that mundane phenomena could by themselves, if only carefully selected and arranged, yield meaning, explanation, or a
sense of development. God's decree governed all and it was for the most part
mysterious. In such a world the records of events, besides telling of what happened, contained divine messages for human beings. An earthquake or a swarm
of locusts warned people, a vision evoked hope, and the fate of an individual
provided a lesson.

*History in the classical mode.* The historiography of the Carolingian period
included one unusually stylish narrative by an unusual man. Nithard, whose
birth resulted from a misalliance between a daughter of Charlemagne and a court
poet, was a learned man and an accomplished soldier. His *Histories* told the
story of the disintegration of the Carolingian Empire in the struggle between
Louis the Pious's sons: Lothair, Charles, and Louis. But rather than write annals,
Nithard created a quasi-classical monograph with a central theme: the decline

of a once powerful state. Nithard must have known that the division of that
state was all but final. As for the feeling of despair provoked by that insight,
Nithard was better off than the ancient historians, particularly Sallust. They
could find no hope in their human frame of reference while Nithard could at
least explain things by putting them in cosmic terms:

> From their [the Franks'] history, everyone may gather how mad it is to
> neglect the common good and to follow only private and selfish desires,
> since both sins insult the Creator so much, in fact, that He turns even the
> elements against the madness of the sinner.... About this time, on March 20,
> there occurred an eclipse of the moon. Besides, a great deal of snow fell in
> the same night and the just judgment of God, as I said before, filled every
> heart with sorrow. I mention this because rapine and wrongs of every sort
> were rampant on all sides, and now the unseasonable weather killed the last
> hope of any good to come.[35]

*The Carolingian era and the universal chronicle.* In essence the Christian
chronicle was universal history. The term "chronicle" stems from the Greek
word *chronikos* meaning "belonging to time" or "concerning time," and chronicles aimed at describing how God worked his will in time. They became by far
the most popular medieval historiographical genre, encompassing the wide
spectrum of historical works from Eusebius's pioneering codification of dates
and facts to the comprehensive and narrative portraits of the past and finally to
histories limited to regions or states during the centuries in which the universal
scope of life was merely referred to or hinted at. Not only the content varied.
No clear definition delimited the chronicle from other historiographical forms,
particularly the extensive annals of the later period. Medieval historians were not
as genre-conscious as modern scholars are. Actually the chronicle's history constitutes its best definition.

The Carolingian Empire, particularly in its declining phase, produced its
own incentives for the writing of world histories. With the role of the Carolingian
Empire in God's plan at stake, some Carolingian historians were fascinated by
the concept of the sequence of empires, the *translatio imperii*, which they could
easily learn about from Orosius and Justin's second-century epitome of Pompey
Trogus. In his digest of universal history Justin explained how the imperial
power had been "carried forward" *(translatum est)* from the Assyrians to the
Medes and so on. Later, Jordanes' *Universal History* drew a line from the Assyrians to the Medes to the Persians to the Macedonians to the Romans and even to
the Goths on Roman soil. Other Christian historians had agreed with Augustine,
who had objected to the close ties between mundane power and divine plan
implied in the *translatio* concept, or found the universal church a sufficient
universal tie.

The specific question discussed by chroniclers of the ninth and early tenth
centuries was whether the Carolingian Empire constituted a continuation of the

Roman Empire *(translatio)* or was a novel state entirely. With the post-Charlemagne Carolingian Empire beset by troubles, contemporaries hoped that the proper answer would not only yield a better understanding of their past and present but also give an indication as to their fate in the future.

Notker of St. Gall reached back to the Daniel vision and spoke convincingly of Charlemagne's Empire as the direct successor to the Roman Empire. In his universal chronicle, Ado of Vienne also reaffirmed a continuous line of emperors from Augustus to Byzantium to Charlemagne, who was the "emperor of Frankish origin." On the basis of remarks in devotional and literary works we may assume that Ado's simple trust in continuity was shared by many of those who thought about such matters. Continuity was a reassuring concept to people who saw the key institution of their political order steadily disintegrating.

Others flatly denied any link between Rome and Charlemagne. Paulus Diaconus, that supporter of the Carolingians who did not live long enough to know about Charlemagne's coronation, saw no connection of the Carolingian state with Rome. In his *Roman History*, a continuation of Eutropius's *Brief History* to 553, he concluded that the Roman Empire had ended in 476 and therefore he ended the numbering according to *ab urbe condita* (since the founding of Rome) at that date. Afterwards he used Incarnation years. Ever since 476 a new ingathering of nations had been going on, until under Charlemagne the West experienced a new integration.

The ninth-century bishop of Lisieux, Freculph, wrote his *Histories* a decade or so after Charlemagne's death, but his narrative ended two centuries short of his own lifetime. Critical of traditions in general, Freculph rejected any interpretation of the Carolingian Empire in terms of a *translatio imperii*. In the late 500s, with Pope Gregory the Great, a new age had begun and Freculph ended his chronicle at that point. For those who found both a sharp break in the past and an imperial continuity unsatisfactory, there remained—in Isidorian fashion—the unity and continuity of past, present, and future through "Christ's Empire."

Equally hostile to the *translatio imperii* concept was Abbot Regino of Prüm, who experienced some of the tribulations that the West underwent between 850 and 950 through the Viking, Saracen, and Magyar invasions; his own monastery of Prüm was devastated by the Vikings. He rejected the idea of a historical continuity through a sequence of empires. The collapse of the once great Carolingian state rather testified to Divine Providence and the transitoriness of all worldly power. Every empire so far had exhausted itself by the efforts it put into its own expansion; that pattern of self-destruction alone linked empires to each other. As for the Roman Empire, it had ended when the Lombards had occupied much of Italy, and despite dire prophecies its fall had not led to the end of the world. The only true and everlasting empire was Christ's church, whose fate was not dependent on the fortunes of any specific empire. At one point God had selected the Franks to carry out his plan. Now that the Frankish Empire had ended, nobody knew who would be chosen next. Augustine, no favorite of medieval chroniclers, would have found comfort in the works of Paulus Diaconus, Freculph, and Regino. In a sense these three historians paralleled in their rejection of the nexus between empire and Christian history the steps taken by the sixth- and seventh-century historians to dissociate Christian history from Rome.

*Alfred the Great and Anglo-Saxon history writing.* England continued on its separate historiographical path, uninfluenced by New Rome theories. Actually, the Carolingian Empire was already disintegrating when Alfred the Great, king of Wessex (871–99), built a stable and powerful political entity. In its context Anglo-Saxon historiography brought forth a remarkable work, the Anglo-Saxon Chronicle. It was written in the vernacular, an unusual practice in a time when Latin was the proper language of learned discourse. The choice of language can be explained by Alfred's deliberate Anglo-Saxonism. That outstanding king himself translated Orosius's work into the vernacular and sponsored the translations of other late ancient works. Such feats made him worthy of the first biography of an Anglo-Saxon king—the *Life of Alfred* by the Welsh bishop Asser.

The sacred history segment of the Chronicle that preceded the Anglo-Saxon history proper began with the Incarnation and in its brevity did little more than remind the reader that England was only one part of God's world. The Chronicle's major topic was the Anglo-Saxon past with a distinctly positive accent on the Wessex royal dynasty, whose founders were identified as Cerdic and his son Cynric. Was the Chronicle then an official creation? A royal commission has never been proven but the original version was sent out with official support so that it could be copied in other monasteries, as if the creation of an "official past" had indeed been desired.

While its Alfredian segment ended in 891, the Anglo-Saxon Chronicle went on in many versions and respectable continuations. Two of the long versions reached up to and slightly beyond the Anglo-Saxon catastrophe of 1066 at Hastings. That momentous event received, understandably, a reluctant recognition—exactly five sentences in the "D" version of the Chronicle. Anglo-Saxons found a better explanation for the catastrophe in a biography, *The Life of King Edward*. It told that, in late 1065, the king neglected to quell the feud between Harold and Tostig, the sons of the earl of Wessex, and that, when Edward died in January 1066, the feud went on to ruin England. As for the Anglo-Saxon Chronicle, it fared better than the Anglo-Saxons. In an ultimate compliment, the Chronicle was translated into Latin, and in that version survived the Anglo-Saxon debacle although with steadily lessening vigor and not for long.

*Two histories as monuments.* In his old age and in the seclusion of a monastery, Paulus Wanefridus, better known as Paulus Diaconus, the author of a *gesta* of the bishops of Metz and of a *Roman History*, wrote the *History of the Lom-*

*bards* as a monument to his people. In earlier years he had served a Lombard king, traveled widely, and spent an active period at the court of Charlemagne. Paulus drew for his sympathetic account on the Lombard epic tales and an earlier Lombard history, *The Origin of the Lombard People* (ca. 670). He spoke of the old Lombard home on the island of Scandia and gave a genealogy of Lombard kings as well as a brief account of the Lombard invasion of Italy in 568. He praised the Lombard invaders, contrasting them with the "unworthy" Byzantines who tried to hold on to their Italian possessions. In a surprisingly naturalistic fashion Paulus credited climate for the Lombard superiority in vigor. "The further removed the northern region is from the heat of the sun and the more it is cooled by ice and snow, the healthier it is for the human body and the more it favors the increase in population; just as in reverse all the land to the South, the closer it is to the heat of the Sun, is always full of diseases and less suited to human propagation."[36] Climate and its changes, Paulus indicated, did not only explain Germanic superiority but also the waves of Germanic migrations. Paulus' account reached only to 744, sparing him much embarrassment. After all, he himself had for years had the Carolingians as patrons—the very dynasty which finally vanquished the Lombard kingdom in 774.

Sometime around A.D. 900, the Celtic view of the past, the very antithesis of the Anglo-Saxon view, was revived in the so-called *History of the Britons*, authored by a group of compilers, among whom the Celtic monk Nennius was most important. The work offered an encyclopedic collection of Britannica: a description of the island, the history of Britons until 687, seven genealogies of people and kings, the story of a hero called Arthur, an account of St. Patrick's life, and memorable things about the land of the Britons. All of that was wrapped into a sketchy universal framework with no less than twenty-eight chronological systems.

The *History of the Britons* really wished to stimulate British pride and even hopes of a British recovery; hence the stories of origins or collective genealogies, of which no less than four dealt with the Britons, giving them a combined Roman, Greek, and Trojan origin. According to one account the Latin Lavinia married the Trojan Aeneas. Among their grandsons was Brutus (Britto) who, after having killed his father accidentally, became a wandering exile and eventually founded Britannia. In another version Brutus, as a "Roman consul," conquered Britain and his descendants populated the isle. For centuries thereafter the Brutus story, as a guarantor of the highly regarded Trojan ancestry, would form a part of early British history. As further assurance that the Britons could still have hope, there were the memories of great deeds by British heroes, especially the story of Arthur. In his twelfth victory "there fell together in one day nine hundred and sixty men in one onset of Arthur, and no one laid them low save his self alone. And in all the battles he remained victor."[37] Arthur, too, would not be forgotten in English historiography.

# ·8·

# The Historiographical Mastery
# of New Peoples, States,
# and Dynasties

The dream of continuing the Roman Empire through Frankish rule had not been shared by many, not even by all the Carolingian universal chroniclers who should have been most susceptible to it. In any case the audacious aspiration faded rapidly in the bitter Carolingian dynastic struggles of the ninth century. The imperial collapse only increased the turmoil caused by the invasions of the European heartland by Vikings, Magyars, and Saracens. When in the early 900s the political situation stabilized, the imperial idea was revived, this time in the German area, but the true reality belonged to a new world of states whose only sense of unity came through the church, the institutional representation of the spiritual bond of the Christian faith. Much of historiography reflected that reality when it dealt with the continuity of past, present, and future in terms of the integration of new peoples into the Latin West, the reaffirmation of the identity of other peoples, and the consolidation of new states and dynasties. Chroniclers found that they could master these challenges with the historiographical means and views of the previous centuries.

## Integrating Peoples into Latin Historiography

*The Normans become part of the West.* A particularly strong regional historiographical tradition emerged in Normandy, where Vikings and Franks had most recently collided. In the eleventh century, Dudo, a Frank and the dean of St. Quentin, created the first written Norman history. Although by Dudo's time Normandy had already had Norman dukes for three generations, the Franks still remembered the Norman raids and the terrible sufferings they caused. The chronicler Richer, Dudo's contemporary, expressed a widespread attitude when he still called Richard I the "duke of pirates" *(dux pyratorum)*. Dudo intended to "establish" the Normans as a respectable group so that the investiture of Rollo with Normandy in 912 would no longer appear as a concession granted to successful evildoers.

107

In the time-honored way Dudo found a Trojan origin for the Normans. He traced the Normans as Danes to the Dacians *(Daci)* and then in turn to the *Danaoi*, whom he linked to King Antenor, a refugee from Troy. Since "Fredegar" also had traced the Franks to Antenor, the Normans were now the equals of the Franks.

But why did so noble a people rob, loot, and murder? Because, Dudo explained, the Normans had been in a stage of decay ever since they had accepted polygamy, which had produced an excess population and in turn forced the younger sons to migrate in search of land and fortune. However, Dudo granted that the Normans were also driven by the wanderlust which others had criticized in them.

In his life stories of the first three Norman dukes, Dudo praised the Normans as responsible state-builders. In doing so he deemphasized their less attractive features: excessive ambition, unsteadiness, slyness, pride, and often uncontrolled tempers. On occasion Dudo showed genuine insight, as when he explained Rollo's stubborn refusal at his investiture to kiss the French king's feet. What seemed offensive behavior to the Franks only witnessed to the fact that "the people [the Normans] have a different custom from the Franks."[1]

*The strength of Saxon history.* The Saxons offered an excellent illustration of the fact that in the Christian commonwealth contemporary life remained basically local, regional, or tribal. Having been subdued by Charlemagne, they triumphed when their duke became emperor in 962. Yet, even then, the Saxons' own past stayed an object of at least equal concern and pride to them. Widukind of Corvei demonstrated in his *Saxon History* that the Saxons needed no Rome-oriented empire to lift them into historical prominence; he then told with relish the story of that "remarkable people," the Saxons, from circa 568 to 973. Charlemagne's great wars against the Saxons were mentioned in a passage four words long and only in connection with the conversion of the Saxons which, Widukind thought, made Franks and Saxons "brothers" and "one people by virtue of one faith."[2] And when in 836 and 923 relics of St. Vitus and St. Denis were transferred from Frankish to Saxon sacred places, Widukind equated the move with the transfer of the imperial power from Franks to Saxons.

Widukind proudly used the early Saxon traditions and the songs of the *mimi* (the traveling entertainers) for his account of the distant period "where all certainty is dimmed."[3] As for their origins, "it was certain that the Saxons were an old and noble people"[4] who needed no new Roman Empire to give them prestige. Widukind studiously avoided mentioning the coronation of Otto I in Rome (962) as well as Otto's ecclesiastical and missionary policies. He also could not understand why anybody would want to make the Slavs Christians and thus equals of the Germans. Saxon interests were as little served by such a conversion as by the constant imperial engagements in Italy.

Later, in the investiture controversy, imperial and Saxon interests collided once more. This time Henry IV's campaign against the Saxons called forth partisan histories: the anonymous *Song about the Saxon War* for the Saxons and Bruno's *Book on the Saxon War* for the emperor. These would have been strictly regional works had Henry IV's fate not helped shape the subsequent constitutional order of the German area. In that sense these historical works unintentionally depict the beginning of the turn away from the empire and toward the German territorial state.

*The Slavs, Danes, and Baltics join Western history.* In 950 the Latin world did not extend very far eastward in Central Europe. Beyond the Elbe River there stretched the area of the Slavs. Long and bitter struggles had been fought along a zone of interpenetration between Germanic and Slavic peoples. In the Czech area the expansion occurred relatively peacefully and gradually, beginning with the Carolingian period. Then in the tenth century the great German push eastward started in the northern plain of Central Europe. Those who moved eastward were prompted not just by the wish to save souls but also by the hope for new and rich land, by the desire to dominate and benefit from it, and by a lust for adventure. Still, the nobles, warriors, peasants, and clergymen engaged in the enterprise fought under the sign of the cross, which made the series of campaigns a worthy subject for clerical chroniclers.

Large portions of the chronicles of expansion consisted of campaign reports, and their bias was clear. Nevertheless the histories revealed how precariously balanced the eastward push was between sanctity and base motives. In his chronicle, Thietmar, bishop of Merseburg, exhibited one important German attitude: a sense of cultural superiority. Thietmar wanted to teach something "to all ignorant people and especially the Slavs."[5] Helmold, priest of Bosau, attributed characteristics more equitably in his *Chronicle of the Slavs* (c. 1170). The Saxons were praised for the military prowess but chastised over and over for their avarice, while the Slavs received mild praise for their hospitality along with sharp rebukes for their relapses into paganism and their lawlessness. None of that kept Helmold from wholeheartedly assenting to the expulsion of the Slavs from much of the land, an expulsion in the interest of Saxon settlers and nobles but definitely not of Christ. Another of these chroniclers, Adam of Bremen, demonstrated the role of ambitious men in the eastward movement. Parts of his *History of the Archbishops of Hamburg-Bremen* (late 1000s) were quite dramatic, with Adalbert, archbishop of Hamburg and sponsor of Adam, being the tragic hero, "a man of the noblest stock ... keen and well trained of mind ... a lover of chastity ... [but also with] one contravening fault ... vainglory."[6] Adalbert's drive for the conversion of the Scandinavians, for a Christian Slavic area, and for a patriarchate involved him eventually in imperial politics and "from that day, therefore, our good fortune changed to ruin."[7] Haunted by impoverishment and a host of foes, Adalbert lost his power. His work in the Slavic area collapsed.

Only the Christian virtue of compassion that was extended to the Slavs prevented these works on the eastward expansion from becoming mere campaign reports. Thietmar wrote his *Chronicle* from the viewpoint of the victors but mustered enough compassion to at least describe the sorrows and deprivations of these missionary wars. Helmold, on his part, chastised the Saxons for their rapacity. Such moderation mattered in a time when the Saxons called the Slavs "dogs" and the Slavs thought of their opponents as perfidious and avaricious.

One group of expansion histories went well beyond war reporting. The *Chronicle of Livonia* (second quarter, thirteenth century) described the conquest and conversion of Latvia and Estonia. Written by a priest, Henry of Livonia, it told on the surface mainly of battles, bravery, cruelty, sieges, and conversions, but actually it gave a shrewd analysis of the cultural collision involved in the conquest. In the first phase bishops and missionaries were the key figures; many of them were captured and tortured but the conversion proceeded. Episodes illustrated how little invaders and converted natives understood each other, as, for example, when the Livonians "thought that since they had been baptized with water, they could remove their baptism by washing themselves in the Dvina [River] and thus send it [Christianity] back to Germany."[8] Henry saw clearly that permanent success came only after a series of forts was established, cities were founded (Riga in 1202), and a military order was created (the Order of the Sword-Bearers or Livonian Brothers of the Sword). In short, only total cultural conquest could secure the area of Latvia and Estonia for Latin Christianity.

Conversion brought literacy and Latin culture to the Slavic and the Scandinavian areas, and with them came the desire to write, preferably in Latin, a record of the past of one's own people. Early in the twelfth century Cosmas, a deacon at Prague, fused Czech oral traditions with the typical features of Western historiography in his *Chronicle of the Bohemians*. A contemporary of Cosmas, an anonymous Frenchman or Walloon usually referred to as Gallus Anonymous, wrote the first chronicle of the Poles, in Latin and in verse. Both men had heard the ancient stories and used them as sources, particularly for fanciful origin explanations. Their works were succeeded in their two countries by numerous chronicles resembling closely in their form, type of data, and purpose their models in Central and Western Europe. In Bohemia a bishop of Prague, John of Drasiče, celebrated his beloved Bohemia by compiling the *Chronicle of Prague* as a composite of excerpts from chronicles since Cosmas. His chronicle was then continued a number of times. Around 1200, the Poles produced an influential historian in Vincent Kadlubek, who at one time had been bishop of Cracow. His *History of Poland,* a mixture of narration, discussion, and allegory, aimed to tell Poles of their past in order to instruct them on proper conduct in politics and life, and the work even tried to show the place of Poland in God's design. However most of Polish historiography consisted of the usual annals and chronicles, among them the *Great Polish Chronicle* (to 1271) and the Silesian *Chronicle of Poles*. Outside the Latin culture a Russian-written history first appeared where the Russians came in contact with the West. In the trading center of Novgorod, which for a long time was an international rather than a truly Russian city, clergymen compiled the *Chronicle of Novgorod* (from the

900s to the 1400s). The first indigenous history came from an old center of power, culture, and trade: Kiev. There, in a monastery, the *Nestor Chronicle* was written, and told the history of Kiev from Rurik on to 1110.

For over two centuries the Northmen had intruded into the Western world, first as plunderers and destroyers then as state-builders. To those Northmen who had remained in the ancestral area of Scandinavia the period of adventure had left a rich storehouse of sagas which told of great deeds, hardships, success, and tragedy. Then, from the eleventh century on, the message and ideals of Christianity began to overlay and slowly suppress the native traditions. In the process, Scandinavians also changed the way in which they recalled their past. Adam of Bremen and others told about that past as outsiders. In the twelfth century, a learned Dane with an excellent Latin style, Saxo Grammaticus, wrote a marvelous account of the Danish past at the point when "the holy ritual brought also the command of the Latin tongue"[9] and a rich oral Norse tradition was extant. In his *Danish History* he showed pride in that oral tradition and also in the runic records; he wrote that the Danes reported their past

> not only by relating in a choice kind of composition which might be called a poetical work, the roll of their lordly deeds; but also by having graven upon rocks and cliffs, in the characters of their own language, the works of their forefathers, which were commonly known in poems in the mother-tongue. In the footsteps of these poems, being as it were classic books of antiquity, I have trod; and keeping true step with them as translated, in the endeavor to preserve their drift, I have taken care to render verses by verses; so that the chronicle of what I shall have to write, being founded upon these, may thus be known, not for a modern fabrication, but for the utterance of antiquity; since this present work promises not a trumpery dazzle of language, but faithful information concerning time past.[10]

*A Celtic protest.* In his *History of the Kings of Britain,* Geoffrey of Monmouth simply ignored the Anglo-Norman world around him and told the story of the Britons from the dawn of history to the late seventh century A.D. How could Geoffrey know anything about that time? Through oral Welsh traditions, Gildas, and the circumstances that

> Walter, Archdeacon of Oxford, a man learned not only to the art of eloquence, but in the histories of foreign lands, offered me a certain most ancient book in the British language, that did set forth the doings of them all in due succession and order from Brute, the first King of the Britons, onward to Cadwallader, the Son of Cadwallo, all told in stories of exceeding beauty.[11]

Geoffrey, in sole possession of "that book," even warned all others not to meddle in the history of early Britain. Many modern scholars have doubted the tale of Walter's book, although it is possible that Geoffrey had access to some composite of Celtic folklore and epics; we most likely shall never know. Geoffrey's contemporaries, however, had no doubts; they loved his *History,* which, brilliantly written and full of fascinating stories, gave the British and indirectly the English a glorious past and ancestry. Enormously popular and available in many copies, it deeply influenced the writing of English history well into the sixteenth century. It seemed not to matter that Geoffrey's *History* dealt with the pagan British past and therefore had martial heroes and not saints as its central figures. The greatness of heroes produced glory and victory, and their weaknesses led to hardship, turmoil, and ruin. When Geoffrey had to account for the decline in British power he understandably blunted Gildas's theme of British sinfulness by implying that all nations rise, find glory, and decline.

Geoffrey learned from Nennius about the Trojan origin of Britons and the story of Arthur. When the Trojan Brutus landed, "the name of the island was Albion, and of none was it inhabited save only of a few giants." After Brutus had conquered the island, he named it "Britain, and his companions Britons, after his own name, for he was minded that his memory should be perpetuated in the derivation of the name."[12] In the line of British kings descending from Brutus, Geoffrey found his great hero in Arthur, who now was called a king. Arthur, the ideal monarch and soldier, had subjugated France (a fact pleasing even to Norman kings), had defeated the Picts, Scots, Norwegians, and Danes, and finally had "set his desire upon subduing the whole of Europe unto himself."[13] Geoffrey's readers, besides having their ancestral pride aroused, were entertained with stories full of magicians, monsters, giants, and witches. Against this double attraction of flattery and entertainment those who questioned Geoffrey's credibility fought for a long time a losing cause. It also helped Geoffrey's influence that his work appeared just when the fashion of chivalric romance had penetrated historiography.

## Legitimizing New States and Dynasties

*West Francia and its new dynasty.* The vision of a permanent, universal Carolingian monarchy ended with Charlemagne's grandsons. The ensuing division had its roots not only in the personal ambitions of the sons of Louis the Pious but also in the differences between the regions of the empire, differences that acted as centrifugal forces and gathered more and more strength during the turbulent 800s and 900s. Historiography promptly mirrored these changes by producing an abundance of regional annals and chronicles.

In 987 the western branch of the Carolingians lost its power to Hugh Capet. This seemed to be merely a dynastic change, but it actually was a major step toward the consolidation of what would become the kingdom of France. To the degree that historians used their talents in the service of the new Capetian rulers, they helped define the new state. They were mostly clergymen who lived and worked in monasteries or as members of cathedral chapters and often hoped to establish significant connections between their institutions and the new dynasty.

Particularly successful in that endeavor were the cathedral chapter of Reims and the monks of St. Denis. Reims was chosen as the location for royal coronations and St. Denis as the burial place of kings and the depository for the royal insignia and the *oriflamme* (the war banner).

Already in the ninth century Archbishop Hincmar of Reims had written a history of the West Frankish region. Nearly a century later, Flodoard, a clergyman of the cathedral chapter of Reims, wrote an annalistic account of the years from 919 to 966. He, together with the clerical hierarchy at Reims, clearly favored the cause of Hugh Capet. Subsequently a learned archbishop of Reims, Gerbert, encouraged the cleric Richer to tell the story of France. Richer's enthusiasm for the Romans was less important than that his narration of the recent past (up to 995) consistently stressed that the Capetians succeeded the Carolingians quite legally, and hence were the true guarantors of continuity.

*The story of the new Anglo-Norman Kingdom.* After 1066, the voice of the victors was the loudest. The *Song of the Battle of Hastings,* which some have ascribed to Guy, bishop of Amiens, and others to William of Jumièges, set the tone for how the Norman victors would justify the event which once more shattered continuity for the peoples of the British Isles. William was the "blessed king, supporter of justice and peace of the homeland, a foe to foemen, and protector of the church!"; the defeated King Harold was a perjuror and a murderer of his own brother—a total villain.[14]

William of Jumièges's *Deeds of the Dukes of Normandy* was less florid in its praise of Duke William, who nevertheless remained an ideal figure, wise as Solomon and great in battle. Above all Duke William was not a usurper. At one time Harold, after having been shipwrecked and then rescued by the Normans, had sworn that after Edward the Confessor's death he would acknowledge Duke William as king. The lesson was simply that the Norman dukes were legally the rulers of England and that God had punished those who had done "evil."

The same lofty view of the invasion and of King William could be found in *The Deeds of William, Duke of the Normans, and King of the English* by William of Poitiers, who flattered Norman pride by proclaiming that old justification of invasion: the Anglo-Saxon themselves had desired it. Nevertheless, whenever William was not pleading the Norman cause, his *Deeds* were remarkably accurate. He had, after all, one advantage over Abbot William of Jumièges; he was at court, had seen and heard what was discussed there, and had access to documents.

There also was the sad story of the losers. When evening fell over the battle-field of Hastings, more than a battle, many Anglo-Saxon warriors, and a king had been lost. A profound cultural change had begun, with the victorious Normans trying to reshape English life, including the English past. Anglo-Saxon saint stories and biographies, many of them admittedly full of inventions, were purged from the sacred history of England—not in the interest of ecclesiastical purity or historical accuracy but of Norman hagiography and historiography. At stake was the Anglo-Saxon cultural heritage.

For a while the great Anglo-Saxon historical enterprise, the Anglo-Saxon Chronicle, continued in some monasteries, particularly at Peterborough, and a few of its versions reached well beyond 1100. Alas, the record became thin, at times recording mainly events at the monastery at Peterborough. In the end, the Anglo-Saxon Chronicle faded away, despite all efforts and dedication. The ruling class now spoke Norman French and the ecclesiastical elite used Latin. Deprived of its cultural matrix, the Chronicle, with its Anglo-Saxon text and point of view, became an anachronism kept alive only in a few Latin versions which were not as harshly affected by the eclipse of the Anglo-Saxons.

As the bitter memories of 1066 weakened and the cultural collision lost some of its fury, a new breed of chroniclers, the Anglo-Norman historians, began to shape the image of the past. In their histories Norman England itself was no longer an issue; they already wished to demonstrate continuity in English history by fusing the English and the Norman components without harm to either. They were preceded by Eadmer, a clergyman at Christ Church, Canterbury, who witnessed the fierce clash between his hero, St. Anselm, the archbishop of Canterbury, and William II and wrote about it in his *Historia Novorum in Anglia*, which complemented his *Life of St. Anselm*. Eadmer, a man close to St. Anselm, produced remarkable works because he knew the persons who mattered, heard their discussions, could copy correspondence, and understood the issues. He even reproduced letters and official documents. In referring to one letter, he explained its inclusion: "In the future it [the letter in the text] may be of use to someone in dealing with like matter."[15]

Eadmer was dwarfed by two historians who became the main shapers of the new Anglo-Norman view of the past: Orderic Vitalis and William of Malmesbury, both of whom came from a mixed Norman and Anglo-Saxon family and died in the 1140s. Orderic had the broader vision. His *Ecclesiastical History of England and Normandy* turned into a universal history with a proper sacred core which began with a life of Christ, giving "devout praises to Him who is the Alpha and Omega."[16]

Orderic offers a glimpse at how medieval chroniclers struggled with the task of compiling their material. He properly consulted the authorities—Eusebius, Jerome, Orosius, and Bede for the early period—but once their accounts ended he mournfully conceded that "henceforth I shall be forced to make laborious researches through the writings of other fathers of the Church, while I endeavor to bring my history of past events down to the present day."[17] Orderic did his work well and produced a wide-ranging history up to 1141 that demonstrated the sacred dimension of the many diverse events it covered. As for the invasion of 1066, Orderic maintained that "England, desecrated by the cruelty and perfidy of Harold, was on her way to ruin."[18] The Normans, although they may have been warlike, troublemaking, ambitious, and deceitful, reformed the English monasteries and upgraded the church on the isle; such sacred and moral considerations must prevail in the judgment of past events.

William of Malmesbury's *The Deeds of the Kings of the English,* an English history from the Saxon invasion to 1120, and the *Deeds of the Archbishops and Bishops of the English,* from the conversion of the Anglo-Saxons to 1125, showed a brash young man with vigor and gusto who wished to display his learning. The second work, particularly, turned into an encyclopedic survey of English sees by a man who loved to travel and foreshadowed the antiquarian interests of later centuries when he described in great detail locations, buildings, and monuments. He also knew how to reconstruct the past from documents, although he had no way to distinguish the genuine from the forged document. The *Recent History,* which added the story of the years from 1128 to 1142, betrayed a more cautious and chastened man, a change befitting in a way the period of troubles under King Stephen.

William's works were read widely, since the Roman historians, particularly Suetonius, had taught him how to write well, characterize persons vividly, and use plenty of anecdotes and stories. His overall aims of edifying people and celebrating England proved no barrier to entertaining stories, even questionable ones.

While William's works reached a literary level superior to that of preceding chronicles, he remained a careful, accurate, and conscientious writer. That impression was not marred by his frank adulation of his patron, Robert, earl of Gloucester, and of his own Malmesbury monastery; few chroniclers resisted such obvious obligations. As for the invasion of 1066—that touchstone of historians—the Normans came out of it as brave soldiers, proud people, and sponsors of outstanding church architecture, while the Anglo-Saxons were viewed as inferior soldiers and as people given to the vices of drunkeness, gluttony, and lust. In view of these differences, God's judgment at the battlefield of Hastings could not surprise anyone.

Another twelfth-century chronicler, William of the Augustinian Priory at Newburgh, has impressed modern historians by his accurate observations and scruples over the reliability of testimony. He tried valiantly to counteract Geoffrey of Monmouth's influence. Nevertheless William was no forerunner of modern critical historians, as the nineteenth-century historian E. Freeman proclaimed. In William's impressive *History of English Affairs* (to 1198) the world was still a unity in which the natural and the spiritual were fused together. William simply applied rational analysis to all of it. Kings were evaluated with the habits of a skeptical mind rather than those of a pious admirer: still, the lengthy dissertations on demonology, including discussions of vampires and incubi, presupposed a belief in demons. It also may well have been that William criticized Geoffrey not only for reaching out into the fantastic but because William had no love for the Welsh and Scots.

*Italy and the Normans.* A poverty of records persists concerning the area which had exported its culture for centuries and in which the great Christian Rome was located. The area was now as unimportant in historiography as it was in politics. The collapse of Carolingian power in the ninth century brought turmoil to imperial Italy, in the north. The *Gesta Berengarii* reported one attempt made on behalf of stability by Berengarius, a great-grandson of Louis the Pious, who according to his partisans "ruled" from 888 to 924. The type of politics which prevailed and the historiography it fostered was well demonstrated by Liudprand, a Lombard who became bishop of Cremona and set out to write a grand history of much of Europe and ended up producing the *Antapodosis* (usually rendered in English as a *Book of Vengeance*): "this Berengar, who now is not king but rather despot of Italy, and ... his wife Willa, who because of her boundless tyranny is rightly called a second Jezebel, and because of her insatiate greed for plunder a Lamia vampire."[19] Actually, in trying to tell about those "misdeeds," Liudprand painted a picture of Italian political life in the tenth century replete with brutally fought wars, massacres, and courts with intrigues, concubines, and debauchery. He also left his *Embassy to Emperor Nicephores Phocas in Constantinople,* whose chief value is its disclosure of the hostility and lack of understanding between the Latin and Greek World.

In the eleventh century the Northmen, feared and hated as the invaders and destroyers of the 800s and early 900s, became the great state-builders. They had already shaped a political structure among the Russians and in 912 had become vassals of the French king. Then, in 1066, they conquered England and at about the same time created a Norman state in Southern Italy. On the latter event we have a well-informed report from a monk called Amatus. In his *History of the Normans* only concern for his Monte Cassino monastery's relations with the Byzantines kept his sympathies for the Normans in check. Most other historians, among them Gaufred Malaterra and William of Apulia, wrote on behalf of the new Norman rulers. William even put his *Sicilian History* into the form of a verse epic because the Normans were still reciting their epic stories of the past.

These histories felt a strong obligation to justify the blatant Norman grab for power and territory. Why did Normans travel so far afield and what right did they have to a kingdom in Southern Italy? The historians knew that landless Normans had fought as mercenaries of Byzantium in the Byzantine attempt to conquer Sicily. Then, deprived of their share of loot and left unpaid, they went to Italy and began the campaign which ended in 1071 with the ouster of the Byzantines from the peninsula. However, such an accidental satisfaction of land hunger did not make for legitimacy. Therefore Amatus interpreted the Norman conquest as a fight against schismatics and oppressors. Leo of Ostia, in his *Chronicle of Montecassino,* portrayed the Normans as helpers of the Apulians, who "could no longer endure the arrogance and insolence of the Greeks" and hence rebelled.[20] William of Apulia even considered the Normans to have been God's instrument for expelling the Greeks from Apulian soil. Historians outside

Italy dropped all noble pretenses and attributed the Norman Italian venture to quarrels in Normandy that sent some Norman nobles to Rome, where the pope diverted them to the South.

Norman legitimacy also was supported by demonstrating the brilliance of Norman dukes and kings, who were compared not to the rulers considered wise by medieval historians, such as David, Augustus, or Constantine, but to martial heroes, such as Charlemagne, Caesar, Alexander the Great, or Achilles. Against all that praise stood, without negating it, the frank recognition of brutality, cruelty, and an excessive lust to dominate. For contemporary historians such flaws were well compensated for by the earnestness with which the Normans reorganized, reformed, and supported the church in the conquered territories. Impressed by their piety, Amatus even considered the Normans akin to messengers of God, and Malaterra told of St. George himself heading the Norman host and speculated that the royal ancestral village was named Hauteville, the "High Village," not because of its location but as a sign from God that great things would come from some of its inhabitants. Amatus had an even grander vision showing Robert Guiscard conquering Apulia, Sicily, and finally—with divine assistance—Constantinople. The Normans as new lords of the world became a recurrent theme. They, at one time the scourge of the West, had indeed come a long way in life as well as in historiography.

*The glory of mundane power—histories of kings and nobles.* Matters concerning dynasties, states, and regions constantly competed with lessons of the universal Christian faith for the chronicler's attention, creating the chronicler's version of an old Christian dilemma: finding the proper resolution of the dualism between the mundane and the sacred, matter and spirit, and body and soul. The clerical chroniclers had made a clear choice for their own lives (most of them were monks) but faced the need for a resolution of the dilemma when reporting on the high and mighty of this world, whose hierarchical positions endowed them with fame, splendor, and power while their souls needed the restraints of Christian humility. What then was the proper image to be drawn in chronicles of the renowned French and English kings? Was it that of a lofty ruler performing admirable and useful deeds, or that of just another sinner who was temporarily elevated over others by God? In the main, chroniclers answered the question by supporting the legitimacy of ruling dynasties, praising the piety of rulers, and from time to time reminding readers of the proper contempt of the world.

The legitimacy of the dynastic change from Carolingians to Capetians in 987 remained an issue in French history for many years. Those opposed to the Capetians found the *History of the Franks from Sens* (to 1015) useful; it was one filled with distortions, name-calling, and accusations of usurpation against Hugh Capet. Despite or because of that the *History* found plenty of copyists and users, including such well-known historians of the twelfth century as Sigebert of Gembloux and Hugh of Fleury.

During the eleventh and twelfth centuries the Capetian kings, in turn, were well served by historians willing to present the Capetian cause in royal biographies. Capetian rulers were still gathering strength when Helgald, a monk of Fleury-sur-Loire, wrote the life of Robert the Pious. In it Robert emerged as a saintly figure. Apparently at that time humility and a strong faith served Capetian kings better than armed strength, of which they had little. In the twelfth century Suger, the abbot of St. Denis, wanted in his *Life of King Louis VI* (the Fat), "to raise him a monument more durable than bronze, whose memory no vicissitudes of time can erase."[21] The young Louis was portrayed as a benefactor of churches and orphans while the older Louis appeared as a military hero. In any case the king was God's steward on earth. Suger's fame and royal service—he administered the realm while Louis VII participated in the Second Crusade—made St. Denis more than ever the center of historiographical support for Capetian kings. But even for Suger there were limits to the king's service in the cause of faith. After the Second Crusade had failed, Suger called for a new crusade, but this time neither the king nor the French high nobility must participate, since they must attend to the business of the French kingdom.

In the twelfth and thirteenth centuries the writing of royal biographies was stimulated by a growing fashion for romance histories which, as it happened, coincided with the reigns of a few energetic kings who transformed the royal court into a true center of power. Typical royal biographies at the border of historiography and literature came from Rigord, a monk of St. Denis, who celebrated the life of Philip Augustus in hexameters, and from William the Breton, who continued the biography in his *Philippidor*.

The new power and complexity of the French monarchy found a better mirror in the *History of St. Louis* by John of Joinville. John was over eighty when he wrote his work (in the early 1300s) and Louis IX, the saint, had been dead for over thirty-five years. Since flattery would accomplish little in such a case, one can believe John when he speaks "of a king who governed himself, at all times, according to the will of God and the Church and for the good of his kingdom," when he calls the royal endeavor to make North Africa Christian again a great illusion, and when, himself a noble, he disapproves of the loss of traditional rights suffered by the nobles through the continuous extension of royal power.[22]

With all their faults as histories, the royal biographies inspired admiration for France's rulers and provided lessons for future kings. They certainly had a broader impact on contemporaries than the *Grandes Chroniques de France,* a quasi-official history of France from 371 to 1381. From the time of Abbot Suger, one of the original compilers, the monks of St. Denis were the authors and keepers of these chronicles. As time went on the chronicles would eventually overtake the royal biographies in influence.

The grandeur of kings and powerful nobles had always fascinated English chroniclers. Now, in the twelfth century, that fascination found a new stimulus when the fashionable French literary genre of the *chanson de geste* made its way into English historiography. In these *chansons* less was said about the piety of nobles than about their deeds, characters, motives, and loves, and truth was not what actually happened but a mixture of the actual, the ideal, and the imagined. Typically, a real figure of history was transformed into a heroic figure by the addition of fictitious elements, for example, El Cid or Roland. In that genre elements of the old epic, oral traditions resurfaced and were welcomed, this time not only to inspire but also to entertain. Although in England an early work in that vein had already appeared in the middle of King Stephen's turbulent reign— Gaimar's vernacular and versified *History of the English*—it was the brilliant kingship of Henry II which brought to a peak romance historiography. It helped that the king's marital connection with Anjou was one more bridge to France. Henry II himself encouraged Wace, a clergyman of Caen, to write the *Roman de Rou* with its story of Norman dukes and Anglo-Norman kings. Although Wace never finished that work, he completed his *Roman de Brut,* a romanticized version of Geoffrey of Monmouth's *History of Britain.* With its fortuitous combination of exciting tales and literary skills it became a popular favorite in England for centuries to come. Another author, Jordan Fantosme, recited in a verse chronicle the deeds of less renowned nobles. In his work, heroic and Christian ideals were linked once more in earnest; nobles fought well and gallantly, failed to live up to Christian commandments, were punished by God, and were finally forgiven as penitent sinners and blessed by God's grace.

Henry II's successor, Richard I, the Lionheart, provided an ideal subject for a heroic history and not only because of his adventures during the Third Crusade. In his *Chronicle of the Time of Richard I,* Richard of Devizes turned all of Richard's rule into a sort of *chanson de geste.* The king was a shining hero, while his opponents, especially Philip Augustus, were villains with souls darker than a moonless night. When the forces of darkness and of light confronted each other, dramatic battles were fought with lances and arrows traversing the sky, shields clashing, and swords whistling through the air. Women, occasionally celebrated as warriors, usually were beautiful, virtuous, and much courted. Richard of Devizes succeeded in making all this palatable because he had learned about good style from his "tutors"—Vergil, Ovid, and Horace. From the ancients he also accepted his decidedly unheroic love for satire, which acted as a counterpoint to exaggerated tales of the praise and glory.

With the attention of historians focused on the motives and deeds of kings, great heroes, and powerful nobles, the crucial development which saw English royal government acquire much institutional stability and sophistication remained in the shadow. The process proceeded slowly, quietly, and against much resistance, but with few incidents as dramatic as Henry II's conflict with Thomas Becket.

Only a handful of works, written mostly by clergymen who knew the court or served as public officials, described elements of that development: an anonymous *Chronicle,* often ascribed without proof to Benedict, abbot of Peterborough; Roger of Howden's *Chronicle;* and Ralph of Diceto's *Images of History,* which was the contemporary sequel to his *Epitome of Chronicles.* While these works forsook entertaining stories for dry records, such as royal itineraries, they offered insights into how the English state, with its rulers, its administration, and its judicial system, achieved a much clearer identity. They celebrated the state that in the end would become a more enduring object of historiography than all the glorious and romanticized kings.

# ·9·

# Historians and the Ideal of the Christian Commonwealth

## The Last Synthesis of Empire and Christianity

When in 962 Otto I was crowned emperor in Rome his claim to true imperial status was doomed from the beginning. In a Europe with a great diversity of languages, customs, laws, and of social and political institutions, and with poor communications from region to region, the idea of a Christian commonwealth in the image of the Roman Empire, revived by a German duke, had little chance of becoming a reality. Nevertheless, until 1250, the Holy Roman Empire of the German Nation provided the context of life in Central Europe. Its glory and its vision of universality evoked an enthusiasm which can be discerned in a number of annals and world chronicles. In most cases biography, too, supported the imperial cause by celebrating the very heart of the empire, the emperors. The forces antithetical to imperial power spoke out in regional histories.

*The Saxon and Franconian world chronicles: imperial or universal?* Otto I's brilliant rule (936-73) and the accompanying cultural renewal stimulated the writing of new histories. Many of these histories aspired to be world chronicles, as did even some peculiar annals written in a few Saxon monasteries with close links to the imperial family. While it is correct to speak of a brief revival of annalistic writing, these Saxon annals (primarily those of Hildesheim, Hersfeld, and Quedlinburg) were barely distinguishable from chronicles except in their names. In any case they provided the core of the new world-history writing in the empire.

All of these chronicles had trouble staying on course. In their narrative parts they had the usual biblical and early church history of a derivative nature and vast panoramas of God's world with reports on eclipses, weather, harvests, disease, Eastern and Christmas celebrations, military and political maneuvers, birth of malformed children, obituaries, and omens, as well as moral and spiritual lessons—all marks of universal chronicles. Yet, a look at the *Quedlin-*

*burg Annals,* the most characteristic and interesting work, demonstrates how the contemporary component—which was extensive, focused on the German area, and pervaded by an immense Saxonian pride—eroded the universal format. In many of their parts these annals served as quasi-official history of the Saxon dynasty. An opposing pope has "really become a representative of Antichrist" while other opponents of the emperor are the "deceptive originators of shamelessness and inventors of trickery."[1] As for God, he "forced them [the enemies of the emperor] to retreat by holding the shield of divine love in front of [the emperor], preventing his being injured."[2] That the German epics were still popular and were used to support Otto I's status is indicated by the inclusion of portions of the saga of Dietrich of Bern in the *Quedlinburg Annals.* It was the first time that the German oral tradition had resurfaced in written form since the short-lived Carolingian attempt to record the Germanic epics. At that time two monks at Fulda had recorded the Hildebrand epic, in which Dietrich of Bern is one of the heroes.

In 1024 the Salian (or Franconian) line of emperors began, and it was more than symbolic that the outstanding world chronicle of that dynasty's period came from the southwest German area. It was written by a monk called Hermann of the Abbey of Reichenau who could not walk, even had trouble sitting up, and suffered from a severe speech defect but overcame his handicaps and became a priest and learned man. His *Chronicle* began not with Adam but with the statement that "in the forty-second year of Emperor Octavianus Augustus...our Lord Jesus Christ was born in Bethlehem in Judea."[3] Soon sacred history turned into the history of the church as an institution of the Latin West and then gradually faded into an account of the Franconian region, an account whose scope was expanded only when describing the intricacies of imperial politics. The last entry of the chronicle stands in significant contrast to the first. After a description of where Emperor Henry II spent Christmas, Lent, and Easter and of the death of Pope Leo IX, it told of Duke Godfrey of Lorraine revolting against the emperor. After all, there was no secular counterpart to Christ's birth.

Hermann's was the last great German world chronicle before the turmoil of the Investiture controversy. Those who continued his chronicle or wrote their own could not escape the controversy which eroded the very basis of imperial universal chronicles: the necessary cooperation between the supreme lay and spiritual leaders of the Christian commonwealth. Hermann stood at the end of an age of innocence.

*The investiture conflict as a historiographical problem.* On the surface the investiture controversy was no more than a controversy over the seemingly administrative problem of who could invest bishops: the pope or the emperor. In reality the issue was much more profound and involved a movement promoting the church's autonomy in spiritual and administrative matters. Cluniac monastic reformers and canon lawyers supplied its inspiration. The struggle involved no less than the abandonment of the not so pure but workable intermingling of lay and ecclesiastical authorities, and, thus, it brought about a profound change in the institutional structure of the empire. It was commensurately bitter and inevitably involved historians, too. Indeed both sides regarded history writing as an important weapon. Lampert of Hersfeld mentioned casually in his *Annals* that both Henry IV and V had in their chanceries court historians who wrote historical tracts to buttress the imperial position in the struggle with the pope.

The stress of the controversy showed immediately in the continuations of Hermann's *Chronicle*. In the southwest of the empire the Cluniac and anti-imperial forces were strong. The trusted student of Hermann, Barthold of Constance, and the chronicler Bernold of St. Blasien displayed their dislike, even hatred, of Henry IV, the emperor who opposed Gregory VII on the issue of investiture. When dealing with the incident at Canossa (1077), Bernold accused the emperor of having simply tricked the pope into lifting his excommunication by an "unheard of simulation of humility."

Although their status as a world chronicle was questionable, Lampert of Hersfeld's *Annals* belong in this group because they were marked by the investiture controversy. While they began with creation, the period from about 1040 to 1077 occupied most of the chronicle. The reader learned little about the traditional sacred story but much about the eleventh-century world of warrior-nobles, peasants, and—significantly—a new group, the burghers of the towns. In his narrative on the investiture conflict Lampert sided with the pro-papal forces, although he did not favor the Cluniac reforms. Henry IV's wrongdoing included a lack of generosity to Lampert's monastery. Lampert gave a dramatic description of Emperor Henry IV, clad in a hair shirt, standing for days in the cold as a repentant sinner outside the castle at Canossa where Pope Gregory VII was staying at that time. While Lampert still thought such behavior to be proper for any Christian seeking absolution, nineteenth-century German nationalists would not.

Those who searched in the works of Frutolf of Michelsberg and Ekkehard of Aura for a passionately pro-imperial answer to the partisan, pro-papal chronicles did so in vain. Frutolf and Ekkehard wrote in the early 1100s when the most ardent passions had cooled and the First Crusade had refocused attention. Frutolf earnestly strove to write a genuine world chronicle, with meticulous attention to chronology. But Frutolf could not bring himself to take sides in the investiture conflict. Thus he was delighted when he could shift his narrative to a great event which reaffirmed the Christian world's unity—the First Crusade. He wrote about it with much enthusiasm and no firsthand knowledge.

Ekkehard, the abbot of a new monastery at Aura, who continued Frutolf's chronicle, supported the imperial side, although not in a strongly partisan fashion. He, like Frutolf before him, turned enthusiastically to the Crusades as the central event of his time and to contemporary sacred history as a relief from times so troubled that Ekkehard saw them in apocalyptic terms:

> At the time of Emperor Henry IV, and of Alexius, emperor of Constantinople, there rose according to the Scriptures people against people, realm against realm; severe earthquakes occurred at different places, and also epidemics, famine, and terrible things and signs in the heavens; and as the trumpet according to the Scriptures sounded the arrival of the justest of all justices, behold....[4]

In the monastery of Gembloux, another center of imperial sympathies in the West, Sigebert wrote in defense of the imperial cause. But, when late in his life, he wrote a world chronicle, he made learning triumph over bias. For his extensive *Chronographia* (c. 1100), Sigebert used a large number of world chronicles, documents, annals, *gesta,* and even some Byzantine histories and also reaffirmed the four-empire scheme of history. He wished his work to be no less than the continuation of Jerome's version of Eusebius's chronicle. While he missed that mark, his achievement was nevertheless considerable, judging from the great number of copies and continuations of his work.

*Emperors in the mirror of biography.* The empire had few visible institutions; its most important representation came through the emperors themselves. Therefore their lives mattered to people, and fascinated them. It was only a question of time until an emperor found his Einhard. In the mid-eleventh century the first of the Salian emperors, Conrad II, received a personal memorial of considerable renown, *The Deeds of Emperor Conrad.* However, its author, the imperial chaplain, Wipo, agonized over whether it was proper for a Christian to write biography at all, even of an important Christian ruler. The ancients, who as pagans had had no clear concept of immortality,

> Thought that the accomplishments of the commonwealth would die simultaneously with its rulers unless what had happened were noted and that a very great disaster would ensue from slothful silence, if the thing that any man now dead pursued during this lifetime should not be apparent from surviving writing.[5]

But must not God's reward be enough for a virtuous Christian monarch? On the other hand, "why should we suffer that to be denied to Christian princes and to champions of the Gospel Faith which pagans on their part offered to theirs?"[6] Also what could teach more effectively the proper life than the example of a pious Christian prince? Wipo also found comfort in Macrobius's justification for biography, namely, that long stretches of the Old Testament were biographical, telling us about Abraham, Noah, David, and others. He tried to live up to his high ideals by meticulously reporting what he had seen and heard, by using only what he considered trustworthy accounts, and by going beyond repeating some old *topoi* (commonplaces). Another man who was a poet would write that Conrad's successor, Henry III, achieved an empire in which "war did not disturb the peace; trumpet calls did not break the quiet; rapine was not rampant, fidelity did not speak falsely."[7] The anonymous author of the *Life of Henry IV* was not bothered by the contradiction between secular fame and Christian humility. He was determined above all to remove the stigma of excommunication and political failure from Henry IV. The author transformed Henry IV's life into a drama in which Fortune—a strange agent in a Christian work—used German nobles and even Henry's son for turning the emperor's life into one of utter failure. In all of this Henry IV played an uncertain role, vacillating between being pious and politically clever.

Biography intersected with the *gesta* in Otto von Freising's *Deeds of Frederick I.* Otto had finished "in much bitterness of spirit" his main work, the *History of the Two Cities,* when his nephew Frederick Barbarossa became emperor. Frederick's chancellor, Rainald of Dassel, thought it only proper that so talented a relative as Otto should lend his gifts to the imperial cause.

The *History of the Welfs,* a different type of biographical work, highlighted not an individual but a dynasty. Written about 1170, after the Welf family had suffered a disastrous defeat in its power struggle with the Hohenstaufen, the work clearly strove to restore prominence to the Saxonian Welfs (Guelphs), to the point of tracing their genealogy back to the Trojans. But its remaining narrative was less fanciful and, in deference to the Saxon spirit, alternated between Latin and the Saxon vernacular.

In 1254, when the last Hohenstaufen had lost his claim and life, effective imperial power vanished for over two decades, and all types of imperial historiography atrophied. In life and in historiography the focus became one's monastery, village, family, ruling dynasty, region, or, increasingly, town. Emperors and empire would never again become to the same degree the topic of German historiography. Dynastic histories, those of the Habsburgs, Luxemburgs, and Wittelsbachs, acquired more prominence and formed the core of the ever more prominent German regional history. The mounting strength of *Landesgeschichte* or *Territorialgeschichte,* as the genre came to be called, was a historiographical manifestation of the decline of the imperial idea in the late medieval German period.

### The Persistence of Christian Themes

Much had changed since the early medieval historians from Cassiodorus to Isidore of Seville had struggled as Christians to make sense of the new world of kingdoms built on the ruins of the Western Roman Empire. Their central instrument had been the reaffirmation of Divine Providence, now unencumbered by ties to a supposedly perennial Roman Empire. That and their use of prophecies, miracles, and the cycle of sin and punishment made it possible for subsequent medieval historians to cope with the events, problems, and shifts in the medieval world of kingdoms as well as with the recurrent temptations and failures of the imperial idea. As the chroniclers saw it, all these changes were noteworthy but fundamental change occurred only in sacred history and in human events related to it. Medieval historians did not grant primary importance to secular changes. The true history was the story of human redemption through Christ in time. And if we study these accounts of the integration of people into the Latin world, accounts of new kingdoms and dynasties, the rise and fall of kings and emperors, and great battles, we must not "read over" the many passages that testify to the chronicler's basic view of the world, even though such passages may have no "factual" value for one who gathers data. When we ignore that view, the medieval version of the Christian faith, then medieval historiography is left without true continuity, spark of life, drama, and, worst of all, almost all meaning.

*The monastic chronicle: imperfect mirror of sacred history.* Between 800 and 1200 most chroniclers were clerics; indeed the majority of chronicles were produced in the contemporary centers of Latin-Christian culture, the monasteries. There monks compiled, wrote, collected, and copied chronicles. They wrote "for the glory of God" and in the spirit of humility often remained anonymous. No royalties or other profits were paid and not only was there no kind of copyright but copying was even encouraged by loaning one's work to other monasteries for that purpose. Actually, the fame of a chronicle could be measured by the number of copies made. For a long time, the monasteries as historiographical centers had little competition, in any case never from universities because history was not a distinct part of the academic curriculum, neither of the *trivium* nor the *quadrivium*. Students learned about the past in grammar and rhetoric when they read or memorized texts with a historical content. History remained firmly what Aristotle had defined it to be, a form of rhetorical exposition (the factual form of prose narration as opposed to the inventive form). But while classical historical works were occasionally read at the universities, history was not written there.

Chronicles bewilder the casual reader with their range of subject matter and variations according to circumstances. But closer to their core there is also an impressive bond of unity tying not only chronicle to chronicle but also the contemporary chronicle to the much earlier Christian histories. That bond shows clearly in the answers to the question of why monks were so intent on writing history. It has been said that they loved learning and they certainly did. However, monastic chroniclers did not attempt an accurate reconstruction of the past for truth's sake. Whenever they professed their selfless service to the truth, they understood truth in a twofold way. First, they saw it in the way the ancients did, as reporting things that really happened *(res gestae)* and not fictional events *(res ficta)*. Second, they referred to the truth revealed in Scripture, not to the truth in the manner of moderns, which was as yet unknown and needed to be uncovered step by step by the historian. The historian's task was not to find the truth but to show how God works his will throughout time. The truth, as far as human beings can grasp it, is revealed in the Bible. History in that vein had "a single purpose: to relate noteworthy matters, so that the invisible things of God may be clearly seen by the things that are done, and men may by example of reward and punishment be made more zealous in the fear of God and pursuit of justice."[8] Perceived that way, history was essential, because "nothing after grace and divine law, instructs more clearly than past facts."[9] History could console the sad, admonish the sinner, and above all glorify God. And, while chroniclers were concerned with the accuracy of their accounts, they worried even more about being truthful in the sense of avoiding evil and choosing good. Truth sprang not from a detached establishing of neutral facts but from a devout look at the past in the interest of faith. Such service to God and his truth made many of the monastic historians also write liturgical texts, devotional tracts, and saints' lives.

The same purpose influenced the chroniclers' style and composition. Gregory of Tours had confessed—without much regret—to his "rustic style" devoid of rhetorical sophistication. Classical rhetoricians would have made that complaint about the style of many chronicles. It often fit the lowest speech pattern, the *sermo humilis,* which for rhetoricians had been fit only for expressing common occurrences. While some Christian chroniclers could do no better, others deliberately adhered to it in order to express their affinity for everything humble and common. Even those chroniclers who had a fine command of eloquence did—at least in parts of their work—not neglect that "common speech."

Also persistent was another feature modern historians, who have mined the chroniclers for information, have complained about: the seemingly haphazard selection of data and the lack of a scheme of order in the presentation. Most often the sequence of years alone guided the narrative, and within each year events and states of affairs were simply "lined up." Sentences were connected by the noncommital "and" or not at all. The language rarely indicated causal or subordinating relations, an arrangement called *parataxis* by Greek rhetors. Why did the chronicler not write more hypotactically, using "but" or "because," thereby showing interrelationships between the reported items? In their own defense chroniclers could have pointed to the Bible's love for paratactical passages, to the lack of enough information for a truly continuous account, or to the fact that the lining up of short episodes, unconnected with each other, served monks well when the chronicles were read aloud during meals in the monastery's refectory. For explaining the absence of a truly continuous account with causal explanations it was, however, altogether more pertinent that the chroniclers knew no world of second causes with its own order, one marked by cause-and-effect chains and by developments propelled by powerful mundane forces. God's will, not human will, governed human events, and hence every event was the result of divine planning and not simply the effect of preceding conditions or human actions. The modern concept of history as a chain of causes and effects, where a given state of affairs results necessarily from its antecedents, was in general foreign to medieval historiography. Its rare use came mainly in the works of authors who found their models among classical historians or rhetors. Chronicles usually reported events, item by isolated item, and their reason for recording an event was not its effect on the subsequent course of events but its being norteworthy in its own right or for instructing human beings about the spiritual cosmos in which they lived. In a chronicle the conversion of one person could outweigh whole battles; the deeds of a humble woman could outrank the deeds of kings; and miracles, omens, visions, prophecies, and especially elaborate Easter ceremonies could hold their own among the most impressive secular events. The world of the chronicle had only one causal sequence, the sequence that had pervaded every Christian historical account since the Bible—sin followed by punishment.

Much like human life, monastic chronicles did not always remain on so lofty a level. Monasteries as institutions of great influence strove to maintain or increase their privileges or possessions, and chroniclers often became their advocates. And there was the wide world of the laity into which chroniclers were drawn, not the least out of consideration for patrons. To the monastery it was, for example, no small matter that a highly regarded or popular chronicle, besides inspiring and justifying faith, could also bring wide recognition to the monastery, thereby stimulating institutional pride as well as visits by pilgrims. These pilgrims, together with other outsiders, whether merchants, travelers, nobles, or even kings, often brought economic benefits; the chroniclers themselves heard tales from the travelers about the outside world, material that was sometimes substantial and sometimes no more than gossip. It also was quite common for chronicles to support or put in doubt the right to rule of a monarch or a dynasty. In other cases chronicles demonstrated the continuity of customary rights or delivered proofs of legitimacy that in a traditional society were strong bulwarks for one's position.

*The chronicle and its precarious universality.* The proper Christian chronicle was always the universal chronicle, spanning all of time and all peoples. Of course, life put limits on so grand an endeavor since no medieval chronicler ever had access to sufficient knowledge about the past of the entire realm of Latin Christendom, not to speak of the areas and peoples beyond it. But threats to the universality of the medieval chronicle did not arise just from the insufficiency of data. Extensive medieval chronicles can be schematized as having three basic parts (see fig. 9.1).

The three segments stood in a fluid relationship to each other. A fundamental cleavage separated the first segment from the second and third. The biblical-patristic segment told most clearly of the human encounter with the divine, containing God's unique revelation in Christ. How to link that segment to the

Figure 9.1

Major Parts of the Medieval Chronicle

|  | Biblical-Patristic History Segment | Intermediate Segment | Contemporary Segment |
|---|---|---|---|
| Scope | potentially from creation to the early church | local or regional history from earliest time up to contemporary segment | the author's time and that immediately preceding it |
| Typical sources of knowledge | "authorities": Bible, works of church fathers, early Christian chronicles | earlier annals, chronicles | experience of author and that of author's generation |
| Basic character | strictly derivative | mostly derivative | relatively innovative |

other two, filled with mundane events, had all along been a problem escaping an entirely satisfactory solution. It could not be otherwise because the problem was not a mere technical one but another aspect of the central and perennial problem of how to relate the sacred to the profane. The chroniclers also found that although the biblical-patristic segment varied from chronicle to chronicle in length and completeness, its story remained of course the same, except for occasional chronological adjustments. Eventually, some chroniclers abbreviated the segment, for example, beginning their accounts only with the life of Christ, while others even made the sacred story an implicit statement that the reader could be assumed to know and that therefore could be omitted. The temptation to do so became stronger as more chroniclers were fascinated by contemporary affairs or by the histories of their monasteries, regions, or ruling dynasties. The gradual reduction in chronicles of the biblical-patristic segment with a commensurate gain of volume for secular affairs mirrored the changes in the political structure of the West, where the ascendancy of increasingly stable separate entities slowly dimmed all visions of universality and steadily increased the importance of the mundane.

The beneficiary of the shift in emphasis was the contemporary segment. Over the centuries that segment's narrative received more space and greater emphasis. At the same time, and more important, the hypotactical construction became more frequent, hinting of future developments: the granting of ever greater autonomy of structure to secular affairs. And while the perception of a divine order and the moral structure of the human world was still secure, the new accent on the writing of history closer to the contemporary period stimulated a few methodological considerations. The truth of historical accounts posed no real problem as long as the chronicler remained within the powerful, widely shared tradition based on Scripture, church teaching, and respected chronicles.

Only when dealing with some contemporary matters did chroniclers struggle in a small way with ascertaining truth. The problem of selection still was delimited by history's clear purpose: to teach lessons, ennoble the spirit, and stimulate proper action. As long as the traditional base of knowledge remained firm and the purpose stayed unchanged, methodology was in small demand.

*History as a lesson in contemptus mundi.* Even those medieval narratives that glorified kings, nobles, and heroic deeds never quite forgot the spiritual core of human life. Devout invocations, examples of God's grace and wrath, lengthy descriptions of ecclesiastical affairs, and stories of saintly persons reminded the reader of how fragile and transitory human power and glory were. As year followed year, even the greatest achievements were undone. In that sequence of years one year offered a special occasion for reflection on the human condition. Those who figured time in A.D. years—and that method was not yet being used exclusively—looked with awe at the year 1000. The Burgundian monk, Rudolf Glaber, writing a few decades later, decided to search for "the most important events and prodigies which occurred in or about the year 1000."[10] He noted an unusual number of famines, fires in cities, storms, and an eruption of Mount Vesuvius. Afterward the world quieted down and a revival of the church occurred.

Anglo-Norman historians demonstrated more starkly and directly the transitoriness of all mundane things. They did so while describing the reigns and praising the glory of kings, according to the motto that "there is nothing more excellent than accurately to investigate and trace out the course of worldly affairs."[11] But Orderic Vitalis's description of the brilliant career of William the Conqueror ended with reflections on the dead king's body, naked and rotting away, abandoned by the once fawning courtiers. "O wordly pomp, how despicable you are, how utterly vain and fleeting! It is right to compare you to watery bubbles, one moment all swollen up, then suddenly reduced to nothing."[12] History offered abundant "material for any writer to record of the condition and fall of man, of the chances and changes of the fleeting world, of the vicissitudes of our prelates and princes, of peace and war, and of the varying fortunes that continually befall mankind!"[13]

Henry of Huntingdon was no less ardent but a bit more subtle in his warnings about the fatal lure of the mundane. In his *History of the English* he praised much that was of the world, including his benefactors, the bishops of Lincoln. However he reminded his readers that all people, except saints, were sinners, and he promptly included critical comments about his benefactors. Even when he praised historiography, qualified approval of the world showed. In his *History of the English,* with its three added contemplative epistles, he asserted, in a quasi-classical manner, that

> precedence must be assigned to history, as both the most delightful of
> studies and the one which is invested with the noblest and brightest pre-

rogatives. Indeed, there is nothing in this world more excellent than accurately to investigate and trace out the course of worldly affairs. For where is exhibited in a more lively manner the grandeur of heroic men, the wisdom of the prudent, the uprightness of the just, and the moderation of the temperate, than in the series of actions which history records.[14]

And when history brought the past into view as if it were the present, it enabled us to fathom the future. So important was the knowledge of past events that it constituted a main distinction between brutes and rational creatures. "For brutes, whether they be men or beasts, neither know nor wish to know, whence they come, nor their own origin, nor the annals and revolutions of the country they inhabit."[15] But the recording of past secular events was ultimately useless if it did not concentrate above all on demonstrating God's grace and will, which alone are not transitory. Roman emperors and English kings alike held power and enjoyed glory for a few years, only to end up as forgotten figures. For those who did not understand such abstract statements Henry offered the story of how King Canute learned about the limits of his power when he commanded the sea "not to flow over my land, nor presume to wet the feet and the robe of your lord." The tide refused to obey, leading the king to explain, "Let all men know how empty and worthless is the power of kings, for there is none worthy of the name, but He whom heaven, earth, and sea obey by eternal laws."[16]

### Updating the sacred tradition.

In the year 5198 since Creation, 751 since the founding of Rome, in the 194th Olympiad, in the 42nd year of Augustus, in the 31st year of Herod's rule there was announced by an angel at Nazareth in the district of Galilee the coming of the Lord Jesus Christ...."[17]

That complex dating was the work of a monk at Luxeuil who in the 1030s mused about chronology. By then chronological matters had come to too grave a state for so casual an interest. Ever since Africanus and Eusebius, Christian chronology had offered the ordering scheme for the past and had served as a crucial witness to the unity of the human race and the universality of the Christian faith. But no one had done any innovative work, with the exception of Bede, in refiguring the age of the world. Now the increase in learning brought up problems with serious implications. Thus, judging from the Gospels, Jesus had his Last Supper with the apostles on 15 Nisan, which is the eve before the first spring full moon. That put his trial and crucifixion on 15 Nisan. The church fathers had stipulated Friday, March 25, as the crucifixion date, and the calendar reformer Dionysius Exiguus had placed the event in A.D. 34. For centuries these three traditions, which had been formulated independently from each other, were affirmed in combination without difficulty. But as chronology became increasingly sophisticated, scholars soon found out that the three sets of data simply did not fit together.

Marianus Scotus—who was actually an Irishman—won fame for having himself walled in twice. During those periods as an incluse he worked on his *Chronicle,* which hardly made for good reading with its annalistic notes, tables of consuls, popes, Easter dates, and a mixture of good data and trivia, including the name of Charlemagne's elephant. Eloquence meant little to Marianus, who wished to solve the bothersome chronological problems. As one would expect, he found it easier to doubt Dionysius than to dispute the Gospels or the church fathers. He ignored Dionysius's A.D. 34 as the crucifixion year after he found that the proper moon phase, weekday, and date coincided in A.D. 12. Assuming that to be the year of the crucifixion and accepting the traditional thirty-three-year life span for Jesus, he was forced to place Christ's Incarnation in 22 B.C. Marianus's adjustment thus made it necessary to increase every established A.D. year number by twenty-two.

Next Marianus "solved" another problem. The church fathers had thought that the Creation occurred on Sunday, March 18, but if one were to accept Bede's 3,986 years from Creation to the crucifixion, there would have been no full moon on 15 Nisan. So Marianus lengthened the time between Creation and Christ's birth (now placed at 22 B.C.) by 230 years, to 4,216 years. After both adjustments were made, Easter dates, world-era dates, and the Incarnation date finally fit the astronomical data. They now were consistent, we would say; they were true, Marianus would have countered. All was well, except that few historians were willing to accept the new scheme or, for that matter, Marianus's B.C. dating, glimpsed from Bede. A group of scholarly clergymen from Bamberg, among them the monk Heimo, tackled the same problem with the same lack of general acceptance of their results.

### Histories of a Grand and Holy Venture: The Crusades

In 1095 Pope Urban II told the primarily French audience at the Council of Clermont that the Turk "has invaded Christian territory, and has devasted this territory with pillage, fire, and the sword." The Turks had enslaved Christians, tortured them, destroyed churches, and threatened the Byzantine state. "Who is to revenge all this, who is to repair the damage, if you do not do it?"[18] As those who heard it shouted "God wills it!" an enthusiasm was ignited which made thousands of people march or sail toward the Middle East during the next 180 years in order to secure the Holy Land for Christendom. Few doubted that

It was the Lord's doing, a wonder unknown to preceding ages and reserved for our days, that such different nations, so many noble warriors, should leave their splendid possessions, their wives and children, and that all with one accord should, in contempt of death, direct their steps to regions almost unknown.[19]

Others said it less luminously but conveyed the same enthusiasm.

The Welshman left his hunting; the Scot his fellowship with lice; the Dane his drinking party; the Norwegian his raw fish. Lands were deserted of their husbandmen; houses of their inhabitants; even whole cities migrated. There was no regard to relationship; affection for their country was held in little esteem; God alone was placed before their eyes. Whatever was stored in granaries, or horded in chambers, to answer the hopes of the avaricious husbandman, or the covetousness of the miser, all, all was deserted; they hungered and thirsted after Jerusalem alone.[20]

At least initially, all would have agreed that "Never, I believe, has a more glorious subject been given to historians of warfare."[21]

*The First Crusade—endeavor of enthusiasm.* The participants in the First Crusade were mostly French and Norman nobles, and therefore French and Norman writers monopolized the telling of the story of that crusade. Raimond d'Aguilers, author of the *History of the Franks Who Conquered Jerusalem,* and the anonymous author of the popular *Deeds of the Franks* were both participants in the campaign and their histories told of Christian militancy, of the deep distrust between Eastern and Western Christians (who were officially cooperating), of brave knights, and above all of an ecstatic enthusiasm for the sacred cause. Doubts were rare, and the good and evil sides clearly known. Thus, when narrating the conquest of Jerusalem, the *Deeds* stressed the religious fervor of the crusaders, some of whose activities were hardly edifying. After the capture,

Our men rushed around the whole city, seizing gold and silver, horses and mules, and houses full of all sorts of goods, and they all came rejoicing and weeping from excess of gladness to worship at the Sepulchre of our Saviour Jesus, and there they fulfilled their vows to him. Next morning they went cautiously up on to the Temple roof and attacked the Saracens, both men and women, cutting off their heads with drawn swords. Some of the Saracens, threw themselves down headlong from the Temple. Tancred was extremely angry when he saw this.[22]

A first change away from enthusiastic reporting came with Fulcher of Chartres and his *History of the Expedition to Jerusalem, 1095-1127.* He, who had let twenty years lapse before writing down his experiences, painted a realistic picture of pious pilgrims, of miserable conditions which killed many crusaders, of greedy and riotous soldiers, and of a not always nobly behaving nobility.

Such realism was not the tenor of the popular works about the First Crusade. Guibert of Nogent was proud of the French nobles' role and showed it in his account. Albert of Aachen wrote at length and in a devotional manner about the crusading endeavor which he himself knew only from hearsay. Even more popular and even less concerned with accurate reporting were the crusading accounts in the manner of *chansons de geste,* those fashionable romantic narratives of heroes and their deeds. Even when the nonparticipant historians of the Crusades became aware of the less than pure motivations and actions of some crusaders, they kept their enthusiasm for and trust in the grand endeavor. Ekkehard of Aura who, full of excitement, had at one time connected miraculous portents with the beginning of the Crusades—marks in the sun, a sword-shaped comet, blood-red clouds, two riders colliding in the sky, a city floating in the air, and animals born with two heads—insisted that even if a few "naive brothers, who did not penetrate to the essence of matters, prematurely condemned the whole crusading enterprise, calling it vain and arrogant, one must trust in God to sort the wheat from the chaff" and bring the great endeavor to a fitting conclusion.[23]

The First Crusade spelled out one unexpected lesson: the Byzantines were unworthy brethren. When the crusaders had traveled to faraway areas, they had done so, at least partly, in order to help the Eastern *conchristiani,* and they had expected in return full cooperation from the Byzantines. Instead, the Byzantines seemed to justify all those old feelings of distrust toward the East. On their part, the chroniclers ignored the brutish behavior of many crusaders, lacked all understanding for the *raison d'état* of the Byzantine Empire, which could hardly consider such an occasional crusade as the major buttress for its existence, and failed to understand the precarious situation of Byzantium after the catastrophic defeat by the Turks at Manzikert in 1071. When the emperor moved cautiously, chroniclers of the Crusades saw that as an attempt to entrap the Christian knights by fraud and cunning. Greeks in general were seen in no better light. The antagonism was genuine, although one must remember that the Southern Italian, that is, the Norman, connection of some of the chroniclers of the Crusades tended to fuel anti-Byzantine partisanship.

After the conquest of Jerusalem, five hundred Christian knights and two thousand foot soldiers, engulfed by a sea of opponents, built the Latin Kingdom of Jerusalem, a federation of Christian states. That feudal state, with its grand vision and an equal measure of petty quarrels and brave deeds, found a fitting historical memorial in the *History of Deeds Done Beyond the Sea* (to 1184) by William, archbishop of Tyre. William was born in the East, received an outstanding education in the West, and had a brilliant career as chancellor of the Kingdom of Jerusalem and archbishop of Tyre. His friend King Amalric urged him to write the *History.* Another motive was added when after Amalric's death William's wish to become patriarch of Jerusalem was frustrated by court intrigue. William was back at his see of Tyre, banished from power by Amalric's successors, when he decided to finish his *History.* Ambitions that fall short of their aim have all along helped produce excellent histories.

William's *History* told much about the attitudes of the Latin nobles towards the Moslems. He, a native of the area, knew that a minority of outsiders could never keep its dominant position merely through military power but must use diplomacy and accede to a good measure of accommodation with the local culture. Even when William needed to assemble material for the Crusades from "accounts of others who still preserved a faithful recollection of earlier time," he modified these accounts from the "Eastern" perspective. He purged pronouncements of triumph from the descriptions of the massacre of Moslems and spoke of horror, carnage, and greed for booty. In the same conciliatory spirit he reported with approval the rescue of King Baldwin by a friendly Arab "chief" who put gratitude above religious differences. Such careful accommodations and gestures of conciliation gave some hope for peace but did not relieve William's pessimism for the future. He described without illusion those terrible moments when the weakness of the crusader state was obvious to all and "the realm was almost demoralized, the courage of all gave way, and the hearts of the wisest melted within them."[24]

*The stories of the Crusades as rescue missions.* In 1144 Edessa, one of the pillars of the Latin Kingdom, fell to the Moslems, and the weakness of the Latin Kingdom showed glaringly. Eventually Emperor Conrad III and King Louis VII went East to help out and failed utterly to accomplish anything. Chroniclers puzzled over how that could happen to so pious an endeavor.

Some, like Odo of Deuil, the chaplain of Louis VII, affirmed the worth of the Second Crusade in the face of failure. Of course his connections with the king and Abbot Suger made him suspect, although he observed accurately events and their settings. Odo even contributed some reasonable explanations for the antagonism between crusaders and Byzantines. He pointed out the difficult problem of provisions:

> for other countries, which sold us supplies properly, found us entirely peaceful. The Greeks, however, closed their cities and fortresses and offered their wares by letting them down from the walls on ropes. But food furnished in such measure did not suffice our throng. Therefore, the pilgrims, unwilling to endure want in the midst of plenty, procured supplies for themselves by plunder and pillage.[25]

Total misunderstanding, even ignorance of each other's life style, added conflicts, "for, when one person accuses another in a very loud voice without understanding him, there is a brawl."[26] But Odo, too, found Greek politics at best suspect, more often simply treacherous.

Few joined Odo in his positive judgment on the Second Crusade. An anonymous Würzburg chronicler ascribed the failure to the lack of proper motives among crusaders. Those who preached the Crusade were "pseudoprophets" who "urged on all sorts of men ... some, in fact, lusted after novelties ..., others were ... in bad straits at home ... others were oppressed by debts, and finally there were those who sought to escape the service due to their lords."[27] Even criminals went. Such simulated fervor God punished by failure.

Contemporaries did not understand that the Western world lacked the will and capacity to sustain the faraway Christian Holy Land. When in the late twelfth century a young Moslem warrior, Saladin, built an empire surrounding the Latin Kingdom, William of Tyre contrasted the unified Saracen empire with the Kingdom of Jerusalem, where "in the acts of princes there is nothing which seems to a wise man worthy of being committed to the treasure house of the memory, nothing which can contribute refreshment to the reader or confer honor upon the writer."[28] His *History* ended with an appeal but little hope: "It is therefore time to hold our peace; for it seems more fitting to draw the shades of night over our failures than to turn the light of the sun upon our disgrace."[29]

In 1187, after William's death, Sultan Saladin conquered Jerusalem. The enormity of the shock produced a seemingly fitting response. Emperor Frederick Barbarossa, King Philip Augustus of France, and King Richard (the Lionheart) of England went East to avenge Saladin's "misdeed" and to free Jerusalem. But the German effort ended when the emperor drowned on the way. The two kings conquered Acre and then, after endless squabbles, returned to their kingdoms. The small result was matched by an equally small historiographical achievement. By now the deeds of kings overshadowed the cause itself, and the results were primarily biographical writings of a kind which fitted well into the era of heroic romance and the *chanson de geste.*

The French story was told in the biographies of Philip Augustus by Rigord and William the Breton, while the English side found its spokesmen in Ambroise *(History of the Holy War)* and particularly in Richard of Devizes. The English histories of the Third Crusade kept a better distance from the genre of panegyrics. In the *Itinerarium of King Richard,* the king had all the noble attributes of Hercules, Ulysses, and Alexander the Great but was faulted for ill temper, stubbornness, and vanity.

In 1198, when the Latin Kingdom had been reduced to a few coastal towns, the pope called for another crusade. When after a long delay the crusaders finally gathered for the Fourth Crusade, no king and no emperor were among the participants. It even proved difficult to collect the crusade tax on the clergy, a signaling of the withering away of the spirit in an outwardly still resplendent institution. Paradoxically, this Crusade, which turned out to be the least worthy of them all, found a most able historian in Geoffrey of Villehardouin. However, Geoffrey did not understand or did not want to acknowledge the questionable aspects of the Crusade; such an admission would have been embarrassing to the man who became marshall of the Latin Empire that resulted from the Fourth Crusade. Less suspect is the account by Robert of Clari, a simple knight from Picardy, who experienced the political maneuvers from the outside and understood them more clearly.

Why did the crusaders eventually conquer Constantinople, the Christian bulwark in the East? Geoffrey attributed the crusading army's conquest of Constantinople not to Venice's self-interest and the crusaders' greed but to a duty to restore the rightful Prince Alexius to the throne in Constantinople. Robert, too, devoted pages to the same official reasons. Did Robert believe them? One doubts it, since the doge is made to say bluntly: "Lords,...now we have a good excuse for going to Constantinople."[30] Both historians would have done better had they referred back to the longstanding Western distrust, if not outright hatred, of Greeks, which previous chroniclers had made so plain.

*The epilogue to a grand story.* In the era of Innocent III and the Fourth Lateran Council the church enjoyed immense power and prestige, to which the Crusades had contributed mightily. In order to rekindle the old crusading spirit the council increased the privileges for crusaders. From the discussions, an observer could easily have drawn the conclusion that the glorious times of the First Crusade would return again, particularly since a Crusade had just been successfully concluded—this time one in Europe, against the Albigensian heresy in southern France.

In the campaigns and in the accounts of that crusade the Albigensians received little compassion and even less understanding than the Moslems of the Levant had.

Shortly after the Council of 1215, a few crusades were undertaken. Feeble efforts, they engendered little noteworthy historiography. Oliver of Paderborn reported how the Crusade of 1217 against Egypt was defeated by the Moslems as well as by the wet land, the heat, the many branches of the Nile delta, and the lack of provisions. Roger of Wendower had kind words for Emperor Frederick II's "crusade," which was really a diplomatic venture. The only noteworthy crusading record of the early 1200s, John of Joinville's *Chronicle of the Crusade of St. Louis,* formed part of a royal biography and described the futile attempt by the saintly King Louis of France to carry on in the crusading tradition. The author loved warfare, and the report is filled with battles, brave deeds, defeat, stories of captivity, and ultimate delivery. But in one section, Joinville showed how his previously mentioned wish for a strong monarchy limited even his crusading spirit.

> I considered that all those who had advised the king to go on this expedition committed mortal sin. For at that time the state of the country was such that there was perfect peace, throughout the kingdom, and between France and her neighbours, while ever since King Louis went away the state of the kingdom has done nothing but go from bad to worse.[31]

# ·10·

## Historiography's Adjustment to Accelerating Change

### The Search for Developmental Patterns

Many basic features of medieval life changed little between 1050 and 1300. Most people continued to live in villages, working hard at simply surviving. Society remained a layered arrangement of ranks with only its urban segment showing an appreciable social mobility. The empire survived, even experiencing periods of glory, until by 1300 the imperial vision outshone imperial reality by far. The church still provided a sense of unity through the shared Christian faith and its contemporary matrix, Latin culture.

Nevertheless fundamental changes were underway and already visible, although their radical impact manifested itself only gradually. Well-established trends toward clearly defined and strong kingdoms ran their course in France, England, and Iberia, spelling doom for visions of unity. Towns grew both in number and size and harbored people whose ways of life did not fit into an economy of self-sufficiency or into feudal society. Within their walls the commercial revolution not only changed the ways in which people earned a living but also how they thought about the world, as the values of rationality, efficiency, and individual material well-being came to be emphasized. These towns were made possible by a steep rise in population and in turn furthered greater population growth. In that new world of relative stability and prosperity, learning flourished, particularly at the new universities. So impressive were the intellectual and artistic achievements of the period that modern scholars have spoken of a twelfth-century renaissance. But accomplishment was joined by paradox. As learning flourished, scholarly conflicts intensified and spread. Most of them can be traced to the accelerating recovery of classical works, particularly those of Aristotle. Just as in the patristic period, the collision of Christian faith with the world views of the ancients triggered profound reassessments in the spiritual sphere.

In the 1100s and 1200s theology flourished as the discipline that by the use of logic and dialectic could express the mysteries of Christian faith in rational systems, and thereby could resolve troublesome problems. Theologians aspired to reconcile what they had learned from the sophisticated pagan philosophers, particularly from Aristotle, with Christian faith. The triumph of these attempts came with the grand systems of theology, called *summae*. But these timeless systems offered no real explanation for what puzzled contemporaries most: change. Looking at the suddenly fluid world that was engulfing even monasticism, as the end of the Benedictine age was signaled in a lessening vigor and the Dominicans and Franciscans created a new mode of the ascetic life for an urban society, Anselm of Havelberg expressed well the uneasiness of contemporaries when he asked, although only rhetorically:

> Why are there so many novelties in God's church? Why are there so many new monastic orders in it? ... Why does the Christian church make itself contemptible by accepting so many varieties, by being subject to so many new laws and customs and disturbed by too many new rules and practices which are almost annually revised?[1]

The historian's help was needed more than ever, but it proved difficult to come by.

*Traces of development in sacred history.* For centuries Christians had spoken of the flow of time from Creation to the Parousia and had organized that vast time-span into world ages, world empires, life ages, and ages of law and grace. In none of these schemes was there any notion of development, since God established the periods and ended them. But as historians and historically-minded theologians coped with the accelerating pace of change, they were affected by a subtle contemporary shift in the perceived relationship between God and human beings. So far believers had seen God primarily as a stern judge, to be approached by penitent and awestruck sinners in fear and trembling; presently human beings sought to bridge the hierarchical gap between them and God through such human emotions as love and affection. That view tended to elevate human affairs to a new importance and to transform Christ's entrance into the world from a unique atonement for human sins into a challenge to have human nature resemble more closely God's image. The possibility of substantial change entered sacred history. A group of scholars began speaking in terms of a development in time, either by simply accenting the ultimate aim of the sequence of years, the end of this world, or by insisting that the succession of ages signaled substantial changes in the human situation. The idea of history as the education of mankind, suggested long ago by some church fathers, was reborn. Prophetic history, which had become restricted in use to relatively small-scale situations, reacquired its large sweep. Finally, it was reassuring to those puzzled by the many changes around them to find that, despite its impressive continuity, Christian faith itself contained elements of discontinuity: Creation, Incarnation, and Last Judgment.

In that context, some twelfth-century theologians used old but neglected interpretations of the world's history that pointed at a development in human destiny and even in faith. Rupert von Deutz interpreted the Trinity not in terms of logical categories but in a dynamic sense (see fig. 10.1).

Figure 10.1
The Trinity and the Organization of Time

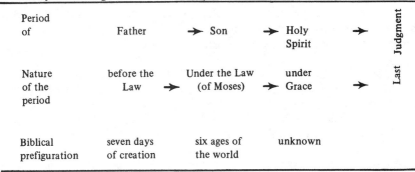

| Period of | Father | → Son | → Holy Spirit | → | Last Judgment |
|---|---|---|---|---|---|
| Nature of the period | before the Law → | Under the Law (of Moses) → | under Grace | → | |
| Biblical prefiguration | seven days of creation | six ages of the world | unknown | | |

In the early 1100s, Hugh of the Abbey of St. Victor took the clearest historical stance when he gave flux and development a positive connotation. In his central work *On Sacraments* Hugh dealt with questions contemporary scholastic theologians did not ask and could not have answered because for them theology had become an exercise in dialectic and logic, dealing only with timeless entities. For example, why did previous ages not have all of the sacraments? Why did some earlier people worship God by sacrificing animals? Hugh reminded his contemporaries that time was God's gift to mankind so that God's intended order could be fully accomplished and could become known to all. The ancient pagans had worshiped God in a different way because they had lived earlier and their relationship to God had been less well-informed. History demonstrated the change in that relationship and acted thus as God's school for mankind, teaching especially the clergy that even the sacred aspect of human life changed with time. Having acknowledged change as a genuine feature of life, Hugh proceeded to "organize" it. At first glance his tripartite scheme (see fig. 10.2) resembles earlier arrangements, until one grasps that Hugh meant to show a quasi-progress within the three periods and from period to period. Actually, the term "progress" is out of place since, for Hugh, what was being accomplished was a restoration *(opus restaurationis)* of mankind to that goodness which Adam had lost in the Fall. The sacramental improvement was therefore not akin to what moderns call progress (an ascending to unprecedented heights of human existence) but really a "turning backward."

Figure 10.2
Hugh of St. Victor's Three Ages

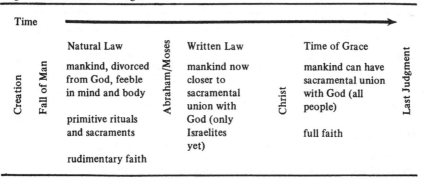

Compared with such audacious propositions, Hugh's *Concerning the Three Great Circumstances of Events—People, Places, and Time* offered little that was new. The three factors shaped the world of necessity in which human beings live and on which sacred history leaves its mark. The work itself gave little more than lists of data, which were meant to be helpful in the study of the Bible and other works.

Hugh's contemporary, Anselm of Havelberg, saw new monastic orders pour forth in profusion—Cistercians, Augustinians, Premonstratensians—and heard condemnations of these and other changes as aberrations from the unchanging divine order. God could not wish for change "for they say, what is so changeable, so variable, so unstable, how can it be worthy of allegiance by the wise?"[2] Anselm answered that God did not change at all; human beings caused all changes due to their imperfect human nature. God only saw to it that "in the progression of time the signs of spiritual grace must increase, telling more and more of the truth itself, so that together with faith in salvation the knowledge of truth might increase with the passing time."[3] Chroniclers could trace that spiritual progress in the past from idol worship to moral law and then to the Gospel. God had given change an aim and purpose.

*Sacred History with a radical promise.* The resemblance of Joachim of Fiore's tripartite order of history (see fig. 10.3) to other schemes patterned after the Trinity is superficial. Like others, he prophesied on the basis of Scripture; unlike others, Joachim spoke of radical changes in human life from age to age. "Then I saw another angel flying in mid-heaven, with an eternal gospel to proclaim to those who dwell on earth."[4] To Joachim this meant that a third age of an entirely different character was about to begin. The past, of course, would not be rejected by it since the ages of the Father and the Son prefigured in many ways the final state, that of the Holy Spirit.

Figure 10.3
Joachim of Fiore's Tripartite Scheme of History

|  | Father | Age of Son | Holy Spirit |
|---|---|---|---|
| Basic text | Old Testament | New Testament | Eternal Gospel? |
| Typical activity | labor | learning | contemplation |
| Learning | knowledge | partial wisdom | full wisdom |
| Key (typical) figure | married man | clergy | monk |
| Prevailing experience | fear of law | faith through grace | love and spiritual life |
|  | 40 genera- tions | 40 genera- tions | 40 generations? |
|  | ↑ Creation | ↑ Christ | ↑ Radical turn |

Joachim's views did not remain mere theological opinions. After his death in 1202 the wave of millenarianism reached new heights, particularly among mendicants, one of whom, the friar Gerardo of Borgo San Donnino, even predicted the "radical turn" to the third age for 1260. And the Spiritual Franciscans used Joachim's view of history as inspiration and action program long after that year had passed.

But all of these advocates of a developmental view of the Christian faith failed to shape later medieval historiography. That failure would have fateful consequences because centuries later theories of historical change with a strong developmental tendency would originate with historians less devoted to Christianity.

*Toward the end as fulfillment.* The developmental views failed to influence late medieval historiography because they were seemingly too far removed from the general framework of contemporary thought. In contrast twelfth-century historians with apocalyptic expectations could rely on a basic tenet of the Christian faith. The German theologian Gerhoch von Reichersberg thought that the story of the four horsemen of the Apocalypse prefigured four successive historical periods. His own period was under the aegis of the pale horse which foretold of Death and Hell, witnessed to in Gerhoch's time by the profusion of heretics.

*Two different views.* Shortly after Hugh of St. Victor had tried to lay bare the sacred design for the web of human events, Bishop Otto of Freising made a similar attempt. The commonly accepted title for Otto's work, *History of the Two Cities,* announces his main guide, Augustine.

However, Otto, a member of the imperial Hohenstaufen family, was much more beholden to a secular institution than Augustine had been. For him the Holy Roman Empire of the German nation was not just another state but a key feature of sacred history. While Augustine had shied away from identifying the City of God with any institution of this world, Otto maintained that the City of God had been hidden in the City of the World only prior to Christ's birth. Since then the City of God had become visible in the church, which, in turn, created the "Roman Empire of Christians" when the Roman emperors converted to the faith. In that empire, now ruled by German emperors, the Two Cities had remained interwined until the investiture conflict had ended the *civitas permixta.* Since then the *civitas Christi* (the church) and the *civitas perversa* (the corrupt City of the World), once more proceeded along separate lines, one towards perfection, the other towards doom—a separation which signaled that the end was not far off. Otto's sorrowful concern, of course, was no mere *fin de siècle* mood because "by pondering upon such [wretched] events we may be led to pass by the eye of reason to the peace of Christ's kingdom and the joy that abides without end."[5]

Otto's interpretation of history relied, again in an un-Augustinian manner, on the Four Empire scheme with its *translatio imperii.* The fourth, the Roman Empire, would last until the end of the world by means of the transfer of the imperial rule from the Romans to the Byzantines and then to the Franks and other Germans. But as the Roman Empire had handed on its power to the Byzantines and Germans, "that empire not only became decrepit and senile through lapse of time, but also, like a once smooth pebble that has been rolled this way and that by the waters, contracted many a stain and developed many a defect."[6] In Otto of Freising's time, the weakness of that empire had become fatal, foreshadowing the end of all things, although Otto granted that some features of the Western world did not conform to the pattern of decline. Learning certainly gave no signs of decaying as it was being transferred from the Greeks to the Romans and then to the Franks, and the church was charged with new energy. Otto even speculated that the sanctity expressed in the new religious orders might delay the end of the world.

Otto's emphasis on the sacred and cosmic dimension, especially in his eighth segment, dealing with apocalyptic matters, has tempted modern critics to write him off as a "speculative philosopher of history." Such a judgment overlooks the fact that he paid careful attention to secular history and did so with a remarkably critical mind. He voiced, for example, doubts about the credibility of the venerable Donation of Constantine, after a careful weighing of the available circumstantial evidence.

*A neutral attitude toward change.* Neither the end of the world nor visions of a new age figured in the *Memoirs of the Papal Court* ("Historia Pontificalis") of Otto's contemporary, John of Salisbury. He simply lived in and accepted the new world. Schemes for deciphering God's will were not for John, who willingly acknowledged that God's plan for this world was a mystery and left it at that. As he saw it, history was more closely connected with the practical problems of living, and in formulating the purpose of history he felt free to draw on the storehouses of classical and Christian concepts. History was

> to relate noteworthy matters, so that the invisible things of God may be
> clearly seen by the things that are done, and men may by example of reward
> or punishment be made more zealous in the fear of God and pursuit of jus-
> tice.... Besides, the records of the chronicles are valuable for establishing or
> abolishing customs, for strengthening or destroying privileges; and nothing,
> after knowledge of the grace and law of God, teaches the living more surely
> and soundly than the knowledge of the deeds of the departed.[7]

John himself accomplished a feat of blending. In the manner of chroniclers he set out to contribute his share of labor to a continuous account of the past by carrying Sigebert of Gembloux's highly regarded *Chronicle* forward to 1152. But he also was an outstanding representative of the twelfth-century renaissance with its appreciation of classical learning and literature. By virtue of his good judgment in using sources and by his excellence of style John wrote a lucid narrative that stood in sharp contrast to the shapeless compendia of his contemporaries. The Latin classics, which he knew so well, not only refined his style and taught him classical wisdom but also reinforced his interest in the affairs of this world, although without weakening his dedication to the Christian faith and church. He, who had been exiled from England by Henry II and was for years a member of the Roman Curia, saw in the church the true carrier of continuity, accomplishing a task which no secular state could perform.

## The Transformations of the Chronicle

A great number of late medieval chronicles still rest unedited in depositories, forcing the historian of historiography to generalize from a slimmer base than is desirable. The major development, however, can be discerned with fair accuracy. Around 1300 the monastic chronicle lost its longstanding dominance, finally overwhelmed by developments which had sapped its strength for nearly two centuries. At a time when the vigor of the old monastic orders was flagging, they ex-

perienced the vigorous competition of the mendicant orders that were more attuned to the urban environment. While the prominence of the monasteries as
centers of learning faded, that of universities and town schools increased. In general the towns and the way of life they fostered were not beneficial to the monastic life, the matrix of the medieval chronicle. Although the traditional ways of
medieval Christian historiography were not quickly abandoned, it was apparent
that chroniclers were straining hard to accommodate the information and ideas
produced by the knowledge explosion of the twelfth and thirteenth centuries.
Chroniclers coped in one of four ways with the problem: they simply continued
in their customary ways as best as they could; they managed skillful compilations; they chose an encyclopedic format; or they tried to find a new scheme to
master their material. In the end, no adaptation of the chronicle was able to save
that historiographical genre.

A case study: the late medieval English chronicle. In the late 1100s, when
monastic chronicles still flourished, the monks of the abbeys of Bury St.
Edmunds and St. Albans began to write history. They first memorialized their
abbots and then proceeded to record the past of the wider world. From monks
at Bury St. Edmunds came a world chronicle, the Annals of St. Edmunds, and
the more important Chronicle of Bury St. Edmunds, which began with the Incarnation and from 1212 told an original story.

At St. Albans, Roger of Wendower and Matthew Paris wrote chronicles. The
former left us his Flowers of History, which first covered substantial portions of
the ancient and the early Christian periods and then gave a close account of
English history up to 1234. Everything is richer and fuller in that last section,
but also more English and hence less aware of the rest of the Christian commonwealth. Roger's "successor" and fellow monk, Matthew Paris, simply used the
whole of Roger's work as the first part of his own Greater Chronicle ("Chronica
majora"). Then he completely abandoned himself to the world surrounding him,
producing a vast panorama that encompassed trivia as well as substantial
accounts of the Spain of the Reconquista; the empire with its bitter controversies
between popes and Frederick II; the Holy Land; the substance of the Moham-
medan religion, in which Mohammed was seen to have proclaimed polygamy in
order to cover up an affair with the wife of a servant; the Tartars, who were
"monsters ... thirsting and drinking blood, and tearing and devouring the flesh
of dogs and human beings";[8] the Jews, whom he alternately pitied and condemned; and, above all, English affairs. These sections of his work demonstrate
how the increasingly abundant information magnified the chronicle's shapeless-
ness, although Paris introduced some consistent themes: the complaints against
King Henry III, the pope, the friars, and foreigners—all of whom endangered, as
Paris saw it, either his monastery or the Benedictine order in England. Then, in
an unusual and most significant step for a monastic chronicler, Paris helped the
Greater Chronicle's popularity by producing abbreviated versions that concen-

trated on English affairs—the *History of the English* (1066–1253) and the *Flowers of History*. In doing so Matthew Paris acknowledged the significant widening of the audience beyond the confines of the monastery.

After 1300 the tradition of Latin chronicle-writing weakened considerably. Shortly after that year a poem, followed by a few random entries, ended *The Chronicle of Bury St. Edmunds*. At St. Albans chronicle writing continued until 1400 but lapsed into an unexciting routine, with the exception of the works by the late chronicler Thomas Walsingham. As well as can be judged, monastic chronicles diminished in number, quality, and scope on the Continent, too. Even works meant to be world chronicles did not meet the limited contemporary standards of universality, a fact visible in the popular works of Peter of Tours and Richard of Cluny.

One French monastic chronicle tradition continued on its course. While English monastic chroniclers had shown, by and large, a persistent independence from royalty, the *Grandes Chroniques de France* were a conscious effort at establishing a Capetian version of the French past. The monastic historians at St. Denis had at their disposal a rich store of Latin historical works including Abbot Suger's biography of Louis the Fat and the works by Rigord, Primat, Guillaume de Nangis, and Jean Chartier. The St. Denis chroniclers bridged the gaps between these accounts and also produced a Latin version of the vernacular chronicles up to 1450. So close was the connection between crown and monastery that by mid-fifteenth century the official St. Denis historian received payments from the king. Many copies of the *Grandes Chroniques* circulated throughout France, and printing had hardly arrived in France when a printed version appeared (1493). France had a ready-made national history with Trojan origin, heroic French kings, and a French view of events. In this case the monastic historiographical traditions survived by the grace of a secular power.

Little help came to the embattled monastic chronicle from the friars. They were innovators in contemporary religious life but not in chronicle writing. Although each Franciscan and Dominican had his "home base," much of a friar's life was spent away from it in active participation in the world. Franciscans did not share the monks' deep attachment to their monasteries and, emulating St. Francis, who had frowned on learning for learning's sake, they gave no priority to scholarship. When Franciscans eventually wrote histories, they did so primarily to edify, to educate lay people, to supply collections of *exempla* for preaching, or, as Thomas Eccleston did at about 1258 with his *On the Coming of the Friars Minor to England*, to tell friars about their own past and inspire them by examples.

The Dominicans had fewer reservations about the value of learning, but they were more often found working in theology than in historiography. Nicholas Trevet's *Annals of Six Kings of England* (ca. 1320) were a political history focusing on Edward I, who had generally supported the Dominicans.

*Chroniclers and the knowledge explosion.* Confronted by a mass of knowledge full of internal tensions, theologians produced the great syntheses that combined Greek philosophy and biblical faith. However, chroniclers with wider local and regional aspirations, who were left without such schemata as world ages or empires for structuring the post-Incarnation period, simply stuffed their works with the now abundant material. The resulting confusion of riches was well demonstrated by Matthew Paris, who reported for A.D. 1246 on the pope's annoyance with the English, Henry III's anger at the countess of Provence, dispensations by the archbishop of Canterbury, a fine levied against Londoners, the activities of preachers (friars), births and deaths of princes and princesses, Hospitalers and Templars, assemblies of nobles, events in the Holy Land, Frederick II's troubles with heresy charges and German nobles, a French royal marriage, Tartar campaigns, appointments of royal officials, taxation, extraordinary thunderstorms, how the king of Aragon cut out a bishop's tongue, canonizations, and elections of abbots. The wish to put new knowledge to work also showed when in the 1100s an increasing number of marginal notes were added to older chronicles.

The chronicle as a storehouse of historical knowledge was only a short distance from the histories included in the contemporary encyclopedic works. In Honorius Augustodunensis' *Image of the World*, history became embedded in a mass of data, particularly on geography and chronology. A century later the masterpiece of the encyclopedic genre came from a Dominican who understood the need for a compendium of knowledge, if only to furnish *exempla* for preaching. Vincent of Beauvais' *Mirror of the World* (c. 1250)—produced with the help of a staff of assistants—was a massive work with parts on doctrine, nature, and history. The historical section told of the past from Creation to 1244, even including a history of learning and a chapter on historians of the past. But one did not read the *Mirror,* one consulted it and did so often and widely. The ideal of the chronicle as a narrative was replaced here by the ideal of the encyclopedia as a handy reference work. A less elaborate work, the *Chronicle of Popes and Emperors,* by Vincent's contemporary and fellow Dominican Martinus Polonus (Martin of Troppau) served many a scholar as a handbook.

In another group of chronicles the wish to serve either edification, teaching, or preaching became most prominent. This aim marked such personal works as Guido of Pisa's *Various Histories,* Fra Salimbene's *Chronicle* of the years from 1168 to 1304 with its unstructured observations on almost everything, and James of Vitry's scholarly *Eastern History* and *Western History* (early 1200s), where good information tolerably well presented offered material for preaching, teaching good morals, setting up worthwhile examples, and defending the faith. Even more directly aimed at the general public and widely used by preachers preparing sermons was a certain kind of quasi-encyclopedic work, usually called *Flowers of History*. These digest histories were compendia of items gleaned from various chronicles, "highlights of history" works which quite often had a strong regional flavor and never failed to offer the reader information together with plenty of stories and moral *exempla.* The practical utility of the scholarly and popular historical handbooks explains why so many of their authors were friars; these clergymen understood well the needs of the teacher and preacher in the new setting.

The wish to encompass all knowledge of the past should have stimulated the writing of world chronicles, and if we take only numbers as the yardstick, it did. We know of about forty significant world chronicles which were variously called chronicle, historical mirror, compendium, *breviarium, summa historiarum,* catalogue, *mare historiarum,* or *memoriale historiarum.* But if we consider substance and organizational structure, these chronicles manifest serious problems. A fourteenth-century English chronicle, the *Polychronicon,* by the Benedictine monk Ranulph Higden testified clearly to the precarious status of the contemporary world chronicle.

In his introduction Higden showed how aware chroniclers were of the need to bring the increasingly substantial knowledge about the past under the control of some order or scheme, in accordance of course, with the Christian faith. His contribution was an inventory of eight sets of auxiliary knowledge needed for the full understanding of history:

1. Description of locations of events
2. Two *status rerum* (human straying from a reconciliation with God)
3. The three ages (before the Law, under the Law, in grace)
4. The four world empires (Assyria, Persia, Greece, Rome)
5. The five world religions (nature worship, idolatry, Judaism, Christianity, Islam)
6. The six world ages
7. The seven types of history-makers: ruler, soldier, judge, cleric, politician, merchant, monk (each with typical personality traits and modes of actions)
8. The eight ways of counting years: three of them Jewish (beginning either in January, March, or May), three Greek (Troy, Olympiad, Alexander), one Roman (Rome's founding), and one Christian (Incarnation).

But that quasi-systematic framework did not really influence Higden's work. Like other contemporary chroniclers, he wrote (still in Latin) a chronicle which demonstrated the divine design, asserted the moral purpose of historical works, borrowed freely from earlier world chronicles, put some accent on the distant and sacred past, and dealt extensively with the English past. All in all, he failed to produce more than a compendium. Nevertheless, already in 1387, the work was translated into English by John Trevisa and became so popular that not only was it continued by others but the pioneering English printer, William Caxton, chose the *Polychronicon* as one of the first books he would publish. Apparently the *Polychronicon's* blend of religious zeal, factual knowledge, good stories, and extensive coverage of British history was a fortunate one. Evidently, the best that chroniclers could do in a given situation was to be encyclopedic, to instruct, to narrate, and to still use the *series temporum* as the sole means of organization.

*The multifaceted historiography of a great war.* The so-called Hundred Years' War between England and France really was a series of campaigns interrupted by long lulls and ending in 1453 with France and England cutting centuries-old ties. Despite the profound consequences for the destinies of the two countries, the war was not treated in any history of note, rather it was mirrored in chronicles, biographies, reflective pieces, and quasi-chivalric histories.

Monastic historiography, fading rapidly in scope, substance, and vigor, contributed little to the record of the Hundred Years' War. Only Thomas Walsingham's *Greater Chronicle* (now lost) achieved distinction as a continuation of Matthew Paris's work to 1420. Segments of it appeared separately as *English History* (1272-1422), *Chronicle of England* (1328-1388), and the *Annals of Henry IV* (1399-1406). Walsingham's *Chronicle* was not innovative in form, style, or selection of events. Its only remarkable feature was the author's exceptional enthusiasm for the Roman classics, an omen of things to come.

Biography benefited since the war created many heroes and one heroine. Among English kings Henry V received most attention. One of his biographies became important not for what it told but for how it told the story. The Italian humanist Tito Livio Frulovisi wrote the biography in a manner that foreshadowed the Italian humanist influence on history writing. Thomas Elmham's *Liber Metricus* was less of a historiographical marker but more informative. It also told Henry V's story in rhyme, which conformed to the still influential *chansons de geste,* made it easy to recite, and pleased those who listened to it. The Italian poetess Christine de Pisan praised the French king, Charles V, who had ousted the English from the French territories they had seized. Charles VI, the king living for years in mental darkness, found an exact reporter of his reign in the archbishop of Rheims, Jean Juvénal des Ursins. In the end, two persons who served French kings, Bertrand du Guesclin and Joan of Arc, received considerably more attention.

Those who suffered from the war were inclined to write a more reflective sort of history. An unknown author wrote *A Parisian Journal* as a moving protest against the nobles and the wealthy who were all alike in their disregard for the welfare of the common man. Some years after the war had ended, Thomas Basin, the son of a rich merchant family, became a scholar and a bishop whose exile by Louis XI sharpened both his sense of justice and his perception. The war gave him occasion to puzzle over the respective roles of God and human beings. He ended up seeing history as a grand human drama for which God still devised the plot but in which mankind played a fairly independent role. Should historians concern themselves with the divine plot? "For myself, I shall be content with a true account of events and leave to people who think they are able to do so the task of discussing the secret workings of divinity."[9] Deeply influenced by classical works, Basin affirmed Divine Providence only perfunctorily while he tried to explain the war in human terms alone.

Good accounts of various phases of the Hundred Years' War appeared in the works by chroniclers who were Burgundian either by birth or through patronage: Jean le Bel, Jean Froissart, Olivier de la Marche, Georges Chastellain, and Enguerrand de Monstrelet. They all focused their attention on Western Europe and offered a thorough and sympathetic treatment of Burgundian history. All of them served in one way or another the ducal family; Chastellain and de la Marche did so as official historiographers of the dukes of Burgundy.

In the late fourteenth and early fifteenth centuries the realm of the Burgundian dukes had become the last refuge of the life of chivalry, and the chroniclers were sufficiently enamored by that life to describe it fully and to shape their purpose in writing history accordingly. "In order that the honourable enterprises, noble adventures and deeds of arms which took place during the wars waged by France and England should be fittingly related and preserved for posterity, so that brave men would be inspired thereby to follow such examples, I wish to place on record these matters of great renown."[10]

Aristocrats were pleased, and the dukes of Burgundy loved to have their historians read the narratives to them. In these stories with their joyous affirmation of the mundane, the traditional Christian elements of historiography vanished. On occasion Chastellain spoke of the transitoriness of human life. Froissart, a cleric, managed a few phrases about Fortune and how the world "rolls on." It was as if the society, which had stabilized around old forms, sought in its histories reassurances of stability above all and wanted to forget about change. Although towns and townspeople were decisive features of the Burgundian realm, since their economic productivity made the whole chivalric revival possible, their role in the chronicles remained that of a backdrop. At that, they still fared better than the peasants. The Jacquerie, the French peasant rising of 1358, was described as an act of "mad dogs," and a subsequent English peasant rebellion led Froissart to point out the grave danger to the social order when the rebellious peasants claimed that "they were men formed in the image of their masters, and they were treated as animals. This was a thing they could no longer endure, wishing rather to be all one and the same."[11] Without God's intervention "the mischief would have spread until every community had been destroyed and Holy Church afterwards and all wealthy people throughout the land."[12] The Burgundian chroniclers treated the great war as a glorious tournament and were equally oblivious to the sacred dimension of life and to the changes in the social structure they themselves naively noted.

*Towns acquire a past.* Great changes, a philosopher once said, come on doves' feet, and from A.D. 1000 on, in just such a way, a change had been transforming the European physical and cultural landscape. Towns were growing into denser and denser patterns, particularly in Lombardy, Tuscany, northwestern France, Flanders, the Low Countries, and eastern Catalonia. At first these cities remained integral parts of the old political entities. Then slowly, and often in bitter struggles, they acquired varying degrees of autonomy. Hence, the stories of cities were told first in the historical accounts of the established powers with whom the towns collided—in the *gesta* of bishops or in the stories of rulers and nobles. Before long, however, the new urban way of life, that had its own rhythm and image of the world, prompted some burghers to write about the past, and when they did they mirrored the different world of the burgher.

Early city chronicles were little more than lists of officeholders and actions of public bodies with some random notes on events added. With increasing pride in a town's accomplishments and an ever clearer awareness of a special urban way of life came the enrichment of the chronicles. Not everywhere, one must hasten to say, did the city chronicle flourish. The French cities remained historiographically barren, and we do not know why. But while Paris stood mute on her past, London found many narrators of its story.

During the thirteenth century, for example, a town official, most likely the alderman Arnold Fitz Thedmar, compiled the *Chronicle of the Mayors and Sheriffs of London.* He spoke of elections and appointments to town offices, of rules, laws, and regulations, and conjured up a small world in which commerce prevailed with its concerns about weights, markets, measures, fishermen's nets, and lawsuits. By the fourteenth century the Chronicles of London, a collective name for a welter of such records, showed the urban chronicle come of age. Mayors and sheriffs received at least as much attention as kings, and crimes and prices were on par with many national events.

For the early periods of English history many chroniclers accepted the *Brut,* a translation and adaptation of a French narrative, that traced the English past to Troy and Brutus. It was a vastly popular text and, together with the London Chronicles and the *Polychronicon,* dominated the view of the English past around 1400.

German town-dwellers celebrated their cities in a multitude of chronicles, with the *Great Annals of Cologne* being the most highly regarded. On occasion urban historiography was captivated by the vision of a universal Christendom. It tempted Hartmann Schedel in the late 1400s to expand his Nuremberg chronicle into an ambitious world chronicle.

One of the richest chronicle traditions was built in Italian cities, particularly in Florence, where in the late 1200s and early 1300s Dino Compagni, Ricordano Malispini, and Giovanni Villani wrote substantial chronicles. Villani's *Florentine Chronicles,* the most famous of them, still began with a biblical event—not the Creation but the building of the Tower of Babel. But after a brief account of the sacred story, the chronicle quickly turned to early Florentine history and its traditional items—the city's foundation by Caesar, its destruction by the Ostrogoths, and its rebuilding by Charlemagne. The Florentine destiny remained always close to that of Rome, the mother city. Overarching the Florentine theme in the artless account, which stitched together items from earlier chronicles, was Villani's constant affirmation of Divine Providence and of the instability of the temporal world caused by sin. Indeed, Giovanni Villani used the Christian sin-and-punishment cycle as the motor of change. When reporting the fires that devastated much of the city in the past, Giovanni saw them as a "judgment of God forasmuch as the city was corrupted by heresy... [and] through the vice of licentiousness and gluttony," and "some of them [the victorious Florentines] were very ungrateful towards God and full of other wicked sins."[13] When Giovanni warned of epidemics, thunderstorms, starvation, and general destruction, he became a new Orosius calling for virtue and repentance so that these calamities might be avoided. Just as strong a passion, however, was reserved for Florence, the *patria*. It made Giovanni view wars, empire, and grand politics from a Florentine perspective and elevate to considerable importance descriptions of the city's families, quarters, fires, administrative and constitutional changes, and routine, including even road-paving.

Giovanni's brother, Matteo, who continued the work, was a survivor of the Black Death of 1347–50. Not surprisingly, he stressed even more strongly the moral nature of history: the Flood had wiped out a sinful world (except Noah and his household and animals) and the Black Death had visited God's punishment on the contemporary world. Yet he also spoke of a capricious Fortune and of comets affecting human fate—both came to be popular concepts during the following centuries.

After 1250 the chroniclers could have looked with some bafflement at the problems they encountered in their work, but such a reflection was far from their minds. The problems that in retrospect befell historiography at that time must have appeared to them as manifestations of richness. While we see a struggle with an overwhelming volume of material, an inability to master the more complex world with the universal schemes of old, a loss of the monastic world as the nurturing soil, and the emergence of the world of the burgher, chroniclers could just as well have pointed to the chronicle's amazing capacity for adaptation: there were chronicles presenting encyclopedic knowledge, others gratifying local (including urban) and regional interests; and again others serving as devotional texts and source-books for preachers. Indeed, they were right in not sensing a "crisis of the chronicle," because up to the 1400s the traditional view of history did not change. God's Providence still supplied order and meaning even when chronicles became well-nigh amorphous. Only as the wrenching experiences of the next four centuries weakened the medieval Christian view of human destiny would new historiographical interpretations appear and medieval historiography gradually disintegrate.

# ·11·

# Two Turning Points
# The Renaissance and the Reformation

Life defies the rules of good drama: great changes do not occur within short time-spans. The erosion and eventual disintegration of the medieval historiographical model took place over four hundred years. No one scholar or innovation was responsible. Rather, the doubts that surfaced because of responses to new circumstances gradually eroded the traditional view on how past, present, and future were connected, much as the ceaseless lapping of waves erodes a coastline.

Between 1350 and the early 1700s decisive changes occurred that have led modern historians to select various persons or years in that period as the beginning of, or the transition to, the modern age. Such designations have produced sharp controversies over the exact character of this period of Western Civilization because, on the one hand, many elements of the traditional world view persisted yet, on the other hand, vast changes redrew the image of that world. In the age of discovery the world became global; scholars and philosophers conjured up new visions of nature and the cosmos; the works of classical antiquity were recovered, critically assessed, and adulated to an unprecedented degree; over a thousand years of a united Latin Christendom ended; and the state, emerging as the basic framework for peoples' lives, provoked discussions of statecraft, collective identity, customs, and laws.

Contemporary historians perceived these changes one by one. At first they could not conceive of any overall view of history divorced from the medieval Christian one and simply accommodated each change and its accompanying insights to the time-proven model of medieval Christian historiography. Eventually though, by the eighteenth century such step-by-step adaptations had yielded to a new approach, one that sought meaning on the grand scale in the flow of events from past to present to future.

## The Italian Renaissance Historians

The Italian Renaissance, with its particularly bewildering mixture of the old and the new, has long been the subject of ardent controversy among historiographers: how does one categorize Renaissance historiography? Chronicles in the old style continued to be written well beyond 1350. But in some historical accounts of the cities of northern Italy and Tuscany with full or de facto sovereignty, the chronicler's typical combination of civic pride and desire to show God's design was replaced by a new emphasis on civic pride and ancient historiographical models. During the 1400s city republics were pleased to assert their confidence in an ancient mode; the courts of Milan and Naples, as well as the papal Curia, saw classical learning as a boon to good administration and prestige. The advocates of that remarkable revival of ancient learning were the humanists, who, as they discovered, edited, interpreted, taught, and praised the classical texts, revered a pagan culture with a world view differing sharply from the Christian one. Yet the humanists muted the shock of confrontation by asserting a gradual unfolding of the "pious philosophy" up to Christ. The ancient thinkers had been as wise as one could be without the true faith. Such an affirmation of continuity softened the impact of the classical pagan culture, enabled Renaissance scholars to obtain sponsors for the humanist cause, and quietly infused a considerable dose of innovation into Western thought.

Chronologically, Italian Renaissance historiography is best discussed in two parts: first, the quattrocento histories written when the Italian states were prosperous, secure, and dynamic, and, second, the histories written after 1499 when Italy suffered sixty years of warfare as the battlefield of the European powers. Topically, one must address the humanists' tentativeness about universal history and their decisive innovations, which only gradually were seen to have a revolutionary character.

*Humanist history before the Calamità of 1499.* Humanist historiography fused enthusiasm for ancient models with pride in the contemporary *patria,* the city-state. Its prototype was created by one of the three Florentine chancellor-historians, Leonardo Bruni, after Florence's 1402 victory in her life-and-death struggle with Duke Giangaleazzo Visconti of Milan. The spirit of civic humanism pervaded Bruni's *History of the Florentine People*, with its collective hero, the Florentines, and a clear story, the rise to power of Florence. Bruni ascribed Florence's success to her republican liberty, from which flowed virtue, beauty of style, courage, industriousness, and strength. Liberty's decline, as the Roman Empire and the subsequent thousand-year lapse into darkness demonstrated, would destroy all that virtue and greatness. This assertion of a link between the republican city-state, the moral strength of its citizenry, and the state's prosperity enabled Bruni to shape his narrative into a unified composition. So rigorous was his trimming of the broad medieval manner of telling about the past that one could rightfully draw a parallel to Thucydides' opposition to the discursive Herodotean historiography.

Bruni also followed his classical models when he divided his works into books, inserted dramatic set speeches, wrote an elegant classical Latin, made a whole people the central figure, told mainly about affairs of state, and reaffirmed the civic use of history. The emphasis on politics enabled Bruni to maintain the traditional view that the individual's psyche produced the true causes of change in the world. The usual year-by-year format of the chroniclers also remained but was interrupted often by topical sections. New standards of accuracy, which discredited founding myths that could not be substantiated by credible written authorities, made him check source against source instead of simply stringing together borrowed segments and led him to deemphasize direct divine intervention as the cause of particular events. All of that, combined with great eloquence, turned Bruni's work into a model humanist history, albeit one hard to match, as the works of subsequent chancellor-historians Poggio Bracciolini and Bartolomeo Scala showed.

Humanist historiography came later and less triumphantly to the republics of Genoa and Venice. Both city-states had a rich chronicle tradition: Genoa with one reaching back to its twelfth-century statesman and chronicler Caffaro but eventually declining together with that state's fortune; and Venice with one also dating back many years and culminating in the work of Giovanni Villani's contemporary, Andrea Dandolo. Indeed, the leaders of the venerable Republic of Venice felt little need to reshape the Venetian past in the humanist manner. For a long time the chronicle tradition persisted, giving Venice a Trojan origin and a founding date of March 23, 421. When the Trojan origin became suspect to the humanist Bernardo Giustiniani, he maintained civic pride by finding a "golden age" during the sixth century. Even Marcantonio Coccio (known as Sabellico), who appreciated ancient learning, wrote in the 1470s a Venetian history that was humanist more in form than in substance. By depicting Venice as the new Rome and as the guardian of law, justice, and freedom, as well as by not doubting the Venetian traditions, Sabellico pleased his Venetian readers.

*Historians,* signori, *and popes.* A link between humanist scholars, who admired the Roman heritage, and rulers, who scorned republican aspirations, seems unlikely. Then one remembers that the Roman heritage included the Roman Empire, that a good case could be made for the benefits of princely rule, and also that the humanists were technicians whose literary and scholarly skills could and did serve many causes. Thus, Milan became a good place for humanist court historians. Both the Visconti and Sforza rulers understood well the advantage of the new learning as a buttress to their rule. A contemporary of Bruni, Andrea Biglia, already wrote a Milanese history in the humanist manner which, however, remained unknown for four centuries. Well known were Pier Candido Decembrio's biographies of the last Visconti duke, Filippo Maria Visconti, and the first Sforza duke, Francesco; both alternated flattery with good observations. But it was on the eve of Sforza rule, late in the fifteenth century, that Milanese humanist historiography showed itself at its best. Although both Giorgio Merula and Tristano Calco made the proper admiring noises about Duke

Lodovico de Moro, they also produced well-organized and well-written histories devoid of most of the unsubstantiated tales that had filled the chronicles.

No artificial buttressing of their ancestry could help the Aragonese kings of Naples, who were strangers to Naples. Those humanists imported by the "culture-conscious" kings to write on the Neapolitan past, had no real ties to Naples and produced mediocre histories. Even the best known of these histories lacked distinction, including Lorenzo Valla's *History of Ferdinand I of Aragon,* with its biographical, often gossipy narrative. Only its *proemium,* a statement of the ideals and techniques of humanist history, hinted at Valla's excellence and novel views. Decades later, Giovanni Pontano wrote an account of a few years in the life of King Ferdinand I of Naples. In his treatise, the *Actius* (ca. 1500), he betrayed thoroughly traditional views on historiography.

The historiographical fate of the city of Rome was even worse, because municipal history suffered from the city's past and present cosmopolitanism. Its overlords, the popes, never felt themselves part of the Roman communal entity so that the humanists they attracted felt no kinship to the city either. Humanist historiography in Rome fastened on the personalities of the popes, the greatness of Rome, and Italian consciousness.

One scholar, Bartolomeo Sacchi, better known as Platina, narrated the *Lives of the Popes.* The commissioned work was well-informed, often frank, sometimes critical, and vastly popular—partly because people have always craved information on the lives of the prominent and partly because Protestants used it, in Robert Barnes's translation, as proof of the medieval church's corruption. Another scholar, Flavio Biondo, showed how living in Rome tended to evoke thoughts transcending the purely local scope. He loved the grandeur and universality of ancient Rome but in his *Decades* put to rest all thoughts of an eternal ancient Rome. He agreed with many previous historians, such as Isidore of Seville, when he spoke of the decline of the Roman Empire during the Germanic migration *inclinatio Romani Imperii,* and affirmed the subsequent political reality, the world of kingdoms. At that point, just like that world of kingdoms itself, Biondo's account lost a unifying theme—except that of the Christian church— and accordingly became diffuse and annalistic.

Biondo's love for the ancient period eventually made him turn to the remains of Rome's grandeur. He not only celebrated Rome's past greatness in his *Rome Restored* and *Triumphant Rome* but also understood the value of ruins as archaeological archives full of trustworthy information. In his *Italy Illustrated* Biondo widened his vision to a general description or chorography of fourteen Italian regions. Despite its unfashionably artless form and encyclopedic content, Biondo's type of history would outlast many humanist histories by centuries. His enthusiasm for the skilled use of nonliterary remainders of the past stimulated the rise of the antiquarian movement, which in time would enhance the scope of historiography, strengthen the importance and awareness of primary sources, and evoke in historians a sense of the wholeness of past life.

*The Italian world after the Calamità.* In 1494 a French army entered Italy and ended the Italian self-contained state system. The French returned five years later and for sixty years thereafter Italy became the battlefield of Europe, suffering grievously. Prompted by these events, Italian historiography focused initially on: "Whose fault was the French invasion?" The Florentine Bernardo Rucellai blamed the treachery of Venice, the policies of the pope and of Milan, and the lack of astuteness in the king of Naples. The Venetian historians, of course, disagreed. From Milan came only Bernardino Corio's lament about the end of an Italian Golden Age and the fall of Lodovico il Moro, and from Naples Tristano Caracciolo's description of the demise of the Neapolitan Aragonese dynasty. But the suffering and changing fortunes of states also brought forth some profound reflections on the past of Italian states and of Italy as a whole. These were guided by the desire to shed light on the present and to seek hope for the future.

In Venice history writing continued nearly serenely and certainly richly, but its important works were only superficially touched by humanist ideals, with most authors even using the Venetian idiom. The traditional form of diary writing survived (Marino Sanudo and Girolamo Priuli) next to the more pretentiously classical *commentarii* (Sanudo). In the new spirit of humanist criticism, the old tales of Venetian history were now generally downgraded, but it was less any humanist ideal than the Venetian pragmatic attitude that made historians add to their works official records such as deliberations of governing bodies, correspondence, treaties, and diplomatic reports. In the main, Venetian historians told about Venetian realpolitik with love for the republic but without flourish and substantial digressions into the world of high ideals. When men of the New Learning tried to write Venetian history, they proved none too successful. Pietro Bembo, a cardinal and the librarian as well as the official historiographer of the republic, continued Sabellico's history of Venice to 1513 in elegant Ciceronian Latin but betrayed his lack of experience in government and refused to use the wealth of official records made available to him. Bembo portrayed Venice as a state entirely given to the welfare and freedom of its citizens, and his scholarly successors agreed with him. Bernardo Giustinian spoke of Venice as the guarantor of Italy's peace, and Paolo Paruta proclaimed liberty to have been the highest value affirmed by Venice.

From 1494 to 1530, Florentine politics, with its struggle for power between Medici and republican factions, stimulated political analysts and historians to reflect on the proper form of government and the fate of states. Two men responded brilliantly to that challenge: Niccolò Machiavelli and Francesco Guicciardini. Machiavelli had served the Florentine republic politically until the Medici returned to power in 1512 and confined Machiavelli's participation in politics to writing about it. Guicciardini worked for and advised members of the Medici family until his services were no longer wanted. These two historians wrote in the vernacular, used insights gained from contemporary experiences, and abandoned the idealistic affirmation of absolute justice, republican freedom, and a benevolent order of things; these ideals, except in official statements, seemed strangely out of place in sixteenth-century Italy. Instead, both men wrote history in order to teach their contemporaries the proper political lessons. Although God was acknowledged as the first cause of all events, his will was seen as unknowable and his direct interventions as too occasional to matter. Machiavelli then went well beyond the attempt of humanist historiography to explain events by discrete actions of individuals or "collective persons" when he searched history for the laws that governed the constant changes in human affairs. Yet, he still considered Roman history the major source of lessons to be learned, as he says in his *Discourses* on Livy: "those who read my remarks may derive those advantages which should be the aim of all study of history."[1] He found one master mechanism in the interplay between human actions and *necessità* (human subjection to uncontrollable conditions and forces). Another was the insoluble conflict between limitless human cupidity and the limited possibilities for its satisfaction. Given all of that, history's lessons could be at best a call to *virtù*, the willingness to take timely action with courage, energy, and intelligence. But even the leader with *virtù* will eventually fail and be overwhelmed by conditions and forces stronger than any individual (by *necessità*). Hence Machiavelli, along with the less philosophical Guicciardini, spoke in terms of Fate or Fortune. But Guicciardini was more circumspect in his estimation of examples taken from the past of Rome and other states. "It is most fallacious to judge by examples; because unless these be in all respects parallel they are of no use, the least divergence in the circumstances giving rise to the widest possible divergence in the conclusions."[2] He preferred to observe and analyze the motives and behavior of people in more recent times. Appropriately, Guicciardini used documents as the important tool and perused them often and carefully.

Machiavelli's main historical effort was his *History of Florence,* a book with few heroes and without ringing assertions of liberty or ornate oratory. His sober style matched the efficiency of naked power it revealed. Machiavelli spoke less of individuals and more of the structure of Florentine politics, of foreign policy, and of how the waves of invasions since the Germanic migrations were successful because Italy had become corrupt and hence weak.

Guicciardini's *History of Florence* remained incomplete and was overshadowed by his *History of Italy,* a contemporary history in annalistic form. It traced admirably the welter of events, alliances, wars, and diplomatic moves that shaped Italian politics in the decades after the initial French invasions. Guicciardini focused on the actions of individuals, the reasons for the actions, and their unpredictable results. However, with God's ways seen as mysterious and with theoretical schemes foreign to Guicciardini's frame of mind, his Italian history remained a series of brilliant studies of events and of persons. It never achieved a sense of wholeness. Such histories as investigations of politics became quite rare in Florence under Medici rule. As for political themes, the condemnation of the republic as a hotbed of civil strife united such historians as Filippo de' Nerli and Benedetto Varchi.

A scholar with no strong municipal ties, Carlo Sigonio demonstrated that humanist historians could write histories with astute although not ad hoc political insights. During the mid-1500s, he first showed that one could write a readable history of Bologna without fanciful founding legends. His *History of Italy,* written with impeccable scholarship and in excellent Latin, spoke much of the love of liberty. Its message was, however, disconcerting for those who glorified the Italian past: the Lombard catastrophe had created the Kingdom of Italy and the collapse of Hohenstaufen rule had ended it; and throughout its existence it had failed to provide security and peace to its inhabitants. Contemporary Italians could be proud of their past without striving to have it restored.

*The precarious state of universal history.* As much as the events in Italy fascinated the historians, Latin Christendom's proper context was still the world—however widely or narrowly it was understood. The lack of enthusiasm of humanist historians for world histories showed when Jacopo Filippo Foresti's world chronicle dominated the field from its appearance in 1483 to the mid-sixteenth century. It was one of those encyclopedic accounts of history whose success brought edition upon edition, although many scholars scoffed at its mixture of legend and fact and its artless presentation of the past. In the 1490s Hartmann Schedel, borrowing heavily from Foresti, wrote another world chronicle, this time with the accent on his native Nuremberg. Sabellico's *Enneades* could have counteracted Foresti's work had it been a true alternative. Yet, Sabellico simply stitched together material from the Old Testament, Polybius, Roman historians, and assorted chronicles without any true order or perspective. Only in the 1550s appeared a "universal" history of genuinely novel character, Paolo Giovio's *History of His Time.* His base of knowledge was much wider, built from Giovio's own experiences, interviews, and correspondence with those who mattered, and from his extensive reading in sources and narratives. Yet, this was no longer a history *ab origine mundi* with its bond of common Creation and sacred history, but rather a complete history of Giovio's world and times, a world limited to segments of the Western world and their colonies, which, however, after 1499 had become a truly united world through the conflicts among the European powers for world domination. This smaller world was united by secular, not spiritual, forces. The acceptance of power as the historical force par excellence aligned Giovio with Machiavelli. Medieval universal chroniclers would have rejected so severe a limitation of the scope and political definition of the concept "world."

Humanists restructured the Western past through the concept of the Dark Ages. Italian humanists had rejected the notion of the *translatio imperii* with its continuity between the Roman and the medieval empires, because it gave legitimacy to the Holy Roman Empire, whose claims the citizens of Italian city-states had rebuffed in long struggles. Bracciolini termed the notion a Germanic invention. When the humanists labeled the period between the end of the ancient period and the beginning of their own time as one of intellectual and artistic darkness, they arrived at a tripartite division of Western history: (1) the Ancient Period, (2) the Dark Ages, and (3) the Renaissance, which was seen as the rebirth of the Ancient Period. They rejected any kinship with the medieval world and preserved continuity only between the ancient and their own period. This view could have served as the point of departure for an understanding and a mastery of the phenomenon of change had the humanist historians not considered themselves as restorers of ancient ways first and as innovators second. They also wrote primarily political history, for which the concept of three ages, derived from the field of learning, seemed less applicable.

Could it be that the often cited secular spirit of the Renaissance was an impediment to the writing of universal history in the Christian vein? Hardly, since grand claims of secularization fade rapidly when they are held up against the reality of Renaissance life and its historiography. True, the Renaissance historians were not enthralled by theological systems; in fact, many appeared to worship pagan classical learning. But all of them were at least nominal Christians and accepted fully the framework of Christian historiography: the Creation, Christ's central role, and the Last Judgment. Renaissance historians, inspired by the ancients, simply granted mankind a greater measure of "home rule," which in turn made them stress the importance of human deeds and motives in history. There was no viable ancient model of universal history known to them which could have replaced the Christian one, even if they had wished to use it. Having rejected the medieval model in their historiographical practice, the humanist historians simply did not write universal history of the *ab orbe condita* type; and nothing in their intellectual world made them miss it.

*From restoration to radical innovation.* What humanist historians did from Bruni's time to the mid-1500s was remarkable, but what did it mean for the development of historiography?

When the humanist historians emphasized Greek and Roman models of historical explanation they began to weaken the dominant medieval Bible-centered account of human affairs. The relationship between God and human beings remained central, albeit mostly implied, crowded out by the attention given to the causal forces of events originating in the individual psyche: reason, passion, and will. Since even collective "actors" such as the "Florentines" or "Venetians" were seen as acting like individuals, few humanist historians had any need for the analysis of institutions or other social structures. Such a view of causes fit well with the view of the purpose of history shared by ancient and medieval historians: it must serve people in their lives by teaching lessons and by offering examples of proper conduct. But for humanist historians that conduct referred less to the relationship with God—a sanctified life—and more to that with one's state—a public life. Still, these humanist views on causes and purpose left intact history's traditional link to rhetoric. Despite Valla's suggestion that history was the root and core of all learning, history's status among the disciplines remained unchanged. The accounts of the past were dealt with in grammar, rhetoric, and—for the *exempla* offered—in moral philosophy. Following long-standing rhetorical practice, humanists regarded history simply as a class of narratives based on true past events.

While tentative steps were taken here and there by historians to secure documents, even to use collections of documents, the first steps toward a different historiography were taken by Flavio Biondo. His antiquarianism implied a history with the aim of reconstructing the past instead of giving lessons. The implication also involved the use of nonliterary sources, the gaining of genuinely new information over the acceptance of "authorities," and a broadening of tools by using ancillary disciplines. Western historiography had acquired a new strain that was soon to be influential. Yet the dominance of literary sources would not fade until the late nineteenth century, when the increasing tendency to describe all of human life (the tedious everyday routine as well as the exciting exceptional occurrences) necessitated a widening of methodology. As for most humanist historians, they even strengthened the link between classical philology and historiography which proved both fruitful and firm well into the 1800s.

The humanist innovation with the most far-reaching impact was a seemingly innocuous philological activity, text criticism. The general triumph of the latter was marred only by the introduction into historical studies, as late as 1498, of a celebrated forgery: the "lost works" of Berossus and Manetho in Italian editions by Giovanni Annio da Viterbo. Yet this particular work received much less ready acceptance than it would have received only a century before. When, in order to "purify" the ancient works of learning, the humanists stripped from the ancient texts all changes and additions that later generations had introduced, they did so with a new sense of "what sounded right." They understood that all people in a given period form sentences in a characteristic manner, have a certain vocabulary, and use words in identifiable ways. One must, therefore, for example, purge from Cicero's works all terms, sentence constructions, or ideas foreign to the first century B.C. The humanists had discovered the concepts of cultural context and anachronism, although they had a limited understanding of them.

At issue was by no means always a literary text, as was shown by the brilliant piece of text criticism, *The Discourse of Lorenzo Valla on the Forgery of Constantine.* It does not matter that Valla's essay invalidated, on behalf of the Neapolitan King Alfonso I, part of the legal basis for the Papal States—the Donation of Constantine—by proving it a forgery. It mattered that text criticism could now erode or even destroy the claim to authority for a document which for centuries had been accepted despite some doubts. A single scholar could now cast doubt even on essential parts of tradition. Thus Valla investigated St. Jerome's Vulgate. Eventually the critical spirit would affect all aspects of Western culture with shattering consequences for age-old traditions. The concept of anachronism also hinted at the concept of a culture as a system, one which sees all aspects of human life at a given time and place as interconnected, whether these aspects be words, laws, or ways of dress. And the humanists' awareness of the differences between Ciceronian and medieval Latin could have suggested to them a crucial pattern in change: development. Renaissance humanists saw and realized none of these possibilities. Their perception of development remained limited to a perception of the deterioration and subsequent need for restoration of the ideal ancient learning. Inertia was not the only obstacle to the acceptance of radical change. Valla already understood that to see everything as subject to change would make history truly the central discipline but would also destroy the certainties and eternal verities which his contemporaries were in no mood to give up. It was left to thinkers of the nineteenth century to take that step.

### Humanist Revisionism Outside of Italy

The neoclassicism of the Italian humanists and their conviction that they had spearheaded a return to intellectual and aesthetic glory proved contagious elsewhere. Most other countries, however, lacked those elements which had made humanism flourish in Italy: an abundance of Roman ruins, city-states and sophisticated courts, and a sense of close connections between classical Rome and the present. When acceptance occurred, the classicism of the humanists was inevitably modified by national conditions. Such acceptance was not merely of literary and aesthetic import but became an ingredient in the slow nation-forming process. While humanist criticism corroded national-origin traditions, it enhanced the prestige of other national traditions such as those concerning a country's laws.

*The quest for German history.* German humanism, including a humanist historiography, found its major support at the imperial court and in the cities. As secretary of Frederick III, Enea Silvio Piccolomini (later Pope Pius II) resided at the court for years and exerted influence on behalf of the humanist cause. He introduced Germans to Tacitus's *Germania,* with its flattering portrait of morally pure Germans, small-unit self-government, and a purely German, non-Trojan origin.

Half a century later, around 1500, the court of Maximilian I with its curious mixture of German traditionalism, incipient national feeling, and Italian innovations was loosely connected with a circle of scholars who attempted to write German history in the humanist manner. Conrad Celtis edited Tacitus's *Germania,* discovered Roswitha of Gandersheim's epic on Otto I as a source for German history, and above all, attempted to imitate Biondo's achievements with his *Germania illustrata.* However, Celtis failed to complete the task, as did Johannes Cuspinianus (Spieshaymer). The latter's main work, the *Caesars and Emperors of the Romans* (up to Maximilian), turned out to be more erudite and dynastic than nationalistic.

Similar difficulties in reconciling humanist erudition and cosmopolitanism, dynastic preferences, and regional loyalties also beset the first survey of the German past, Wimpheling's *Epitome of German History,* Johannes Nauclerus's *Memorabilia* (a universal history), and Aventinus's *Bavarian Chronicle.* Respect for the empire and German pride made all three men insist on the old idea of a transfer of the fourth empire from Rome to the Germans. The traditional longing for noble ancestors led Aventinus to reaffirm a Trojan ancestry. Less fanciful were the *Three Books on German History* by Beatus Rhenanus, whose German sympathies were matched by his admiration for Flavio Biondo's scholarship. He produced good editions of works by Tacitus and Velleius Paterculus and even analyzed the development of the German language in his quest to find a less fanciful origin of the Germans. But his somber message and uncompromising erudition restricted his readership mostly to other scholars.

By 1520 German historiography had acquired many humanistic attributes, and the new printing presses enhanced the trend. Then the Lutheran Reformation and decades of religious controversy changed the intellectual world radically. Some humanists escaped involvement in the religious controversy by Rhenanus's route of pure scholarship. In a famous example Conrad Peutinger edited a Roman road map of the third century that Celtis had discovered. Known as the *Tabula Peutingeriana,* it became a manifestation of the new interest in what we now call the auxiliary fields: working on inscriptions, collecting manuscripts and coins, and editing sources.

Other scholars tried valiantly to preserve their dedication to critical scholarship while professing the Lutheran creed. Johann Philip of Schleiden (Sleidanus) had learned political lessons as a diplomat and his lessons as a scholar in translating Froissart's chronicle and Philippe de Commynes' memoirs into Latin. All of that helped shape his *Commentaries on the Condition of Religion and State under Emperor Charles V,* a work so impartial that his Protestant sponsors did not like it. Also, it emphasized the diplomatic and political aspects so strongly that reading the *Commentaries,* one would never guess that the Reformation controversy involved ideas, passions, and the masses. But his quasi-universal chronicle *On the Four World Empires,* with its sixty-five or so editions, made him the teacher of history to generations of German students. It was a traditional world chronicle, based on Daniel's vision of four empires, and contained enough condemnations of the popes and praise of the German emperors to suit the partisan passions of the day.

*The search for a new French history.* In the 1480s and 1490s Italian humanism inspired a small but influential group of French scholars gathered around Guillaume Fichet, a professor at the Sorbonne. One of its members, Robert Gaguin, planned but found no sponsor for a grand humanist history of France. So he produced instead a compendium on the *Origin and Deeds of the French,* which turned out to be mainly a digest of the *Grandes Chroniques,* in a style and Latin that pleased the new humanist tastes. He doubted the Trojan origin of the

French but expressed his doubt so gently that scholars still argue whether or not Gaguin intended any criticism at all. In contrast, Paolo Emilio, a humanist from Verona whom Louis XII had entrusted with writing a history of the French, lacked Gaguin's reverence for the French tradition and found many suspicious stories in the *Grandes Chroniques,* including those claiming a Trojan origin for the French. His *On the Deeds of the French* (to 1488) influenced French historiography through its novel viewpoints and its artful Latin. Yet the next important step in French historiography occurred, unexpectedly, in the field of law.

The battle over the true church tradition was raging in all of Europe when in France another tradition came under attack: the centuries-old version of Roman law. Ever since the Emperor Justinian had ordered the sifting of the huge and chaotic mass of Roman laws that resulted in a systematic corpus of Roman laws, the Christian world had had in its possession the *Corpus juris civilis.* Of its four parts, the second, the *Digest* or *Pandects,* became the primary law book. Throughout the medieval period the *Corpus* had been held in awe as the body of absolute and perfect law. Medieval legal scholars had maintained that all the difficulties they encountered in applying the code to their lives were simply due to an imperfect understanding of Roman law; and since it was hardly proper to change so perfect a law in accord with new situations, one wrote glosses and commentaries ostensibly to understand the unchanging law in a new light.

The chain of glossators was broken when the humanists applied their new text criticism to Roman law. As humanists saw it, Justinian's compilers, under the leadership of Tribonian, had taken "pure" Roman law and distorted it by introducing language and concepts of their own sixth-century world. Humanists raised the battle cry: "Back beyond Tribonian!" Back, in short, to the "pure" Roman law by means of restoring the "pure" Latin texts. That was the spirit which had moved Maffeo Vegio in his word analysis of the *Digest,* Pomponio Leto in his institutional studies, Pietro Crinito in his attempts at restoring Roman law, and Angelo Poliziano in his paleographical studies of the Florentine copy of the *Digest.* Theirs was the first assault on the assertion that the *Corpus juris civilis* represented Roman law in its definitive form. The awareness of change and a sense for anachronism—the powerful forces loosed by text criticism— were about to bring a historical perspective to law.

The Italian critics found an early French partisan in Guillaume Budé. His *Annotations on the Pandects* belonged to the annotation literature that reached from Valla to Erasmus and questioned the traditional texts of authoritative works. Tribonian was seen as an illiterate, a butcher of texts. The great Italian glossators Bartolo of Sassoferato and Franciscus Accursius deluded themselves when they thought that all they did was to interpret Roman law, whereas they really altered its meanings with their amplifications, explanations, and conclusions. Budé still adhered to the "back to the pure Roman law" ideal although he sometimes hinted at a true historicizing of the law—the view that the law changes, together with its society. As an enthusiast of the classics, who had also written a pioneering work on Roman coinage, he was unable to abandon the ancient period as the ideal one.

The humanist method of restoring the "pure" Roman law through textual criticism came to be known eventually as the *mos gallicus juris docendi* (French method of teaching law) while the phrase *mos italicus* (Italian method) referred to the medieval glossators' approach. The French method of teaching law gained new strength from the work of an Italian, Andrea Alciati. He taught for only four years at the University of Bourges, where students were attracted by his expositions directly from the texts and not from glosses or other interpretations. That Alciati returned to Italy in 1532 had to do with his unpopular defense of the papacy and his derision of the French, who glorified their institutions by classicizing them. He left behind a legal tradition that at first glance appeared to be no more than a restoration of Roman law but that actually had begun to erode the position of Roman law as the one perfect law of timeless validity. Such a change made it easier for future French legists to consider the study of medieval customary law worthwhile and thus understand that developments occur in the field of law as they do in all of human life—that law, too, had a history.

*The cautious revisionism of English historiography.* In the late 1400s and early 1500s Italian humanist learning came to England. Yet the English chronicle, which had just transferred its production from the monastic scriptorium to the residences of the nobility and the homes of burghers in the cities, was not at all the worse for it. The popularity of the London Chronicles, the *Polychronicon,* and the *Brut* remained high. In particular, the London Chronicles evoke the image of a broad stream of chronicles with countless tributaries; after 1500 Richard Arnold's *Chronicle* and Robert Fabyan's *New Chronicles of England and of France* appeared. They were no masterworks but helped assure that the chronicle tradition remained strong for many more years.

In 1501 the Italian humanist, Polydore Vergil, came to England as a papal collector of the Peter's Pence and stayed on for nearly fifty years. Vergil sought to advance his own and the young Tudor cause by composing a well-written and sympathetic history in the humanist manner. Although Vergil's work, published in 1534, fit the day's humanist fashion and pleased its Tudor patrons, it disturbed the English because he downgraded, mainly by deliberate neglect, the fantastic tales about the early Britons, including the stories of the Trojan origin and King Arthur. Also, Vergil's *English History* began with the Roman period, and a Rome-centered view was offensive to well-entrenched tradition and English pride, particularly in a period of intensifying conflict with the Church of Rome. Still, the work remained for decades the prominent English history.

About 1513 Thomas More wrote his *History of Richard III,* the first English historical work carrying the marks of humanist historiography: emulation of

Roman historians; an elegant Latin; brilliantly constructed speeches; a conscious attempt to compose the narrative rather than to narrate events year by year; a stress on human characteristics and motives and a reaffirmation of history's teaching role. The work, with its lesson on the destructiveness of tyrannical rule, was much admired when from 1543 it was published in various, frequently poor, editions.

Thus the humanist seed was scattered. A more complete inventory would show that many humanists served patrons in regions from the Atlantic into Eastern Europe, producing influential humanist historiographical enclaves in the midst of chronicle territories.

### The Collapse of Spiritual Unity

*Searching the past for the "pure" church.* The Italian humanists had tried to restore the "pure" classical heritage by removing layer upon layer of accretions deposited by the "Dark Ages." Such an endeavor held no fascination for Martin Luther, who viewed the classical achievements as products of feeble human reason, devoid of spiritual purpose. But Luther engaged in his own work of restoration when he called for a return to the "pure" holy Christian church, that of Christ and his apostles. He and other reformers, laboring to remove the "corrupt" layers of tradition accumulated over centuries, realized the need for historical studies that would help to reestablish the pure and timeless faith and church. Such an attitude, of course, would deny the legitimacy of development in history.

Philip Melanchthon, Luther's friend and a systematic theologian, soon grasped that the key battle between Roman Catholicism and Protestantism would be fought over the validity of church tradition, and he saw to it that history, as the mighty weapon in that struggle, was given a prominent place in the new Protestant universities at Marburg an der Lahn, Königsberg, and Jena. He himself lectured on history. It also helped that Johann Carion published a world chronicle from a Lutheran perspective and had great success with this *Chronica.* Melanchthon reworked parts of that chronicle into a useful textbook, but left to his son-in-law Casper Peucer both the completion of the task and the continuation of the text. By then, the originally brief German-language chronicle had grown into a four-volume Latin world chronicle. As it grew in length, it emphasized the fateful distinction, drawn from Luther's teaching, between sacred history (depicting God's design for human redemption, the *Heilsorder*) and human or profane history (God's design for an orderly human life on earth, the *Erhaltungsorder*). The distinction represented another attempt to resolve the problem facing Christian theologians and historians of how to relate temporal institutions and events to the divine design for universal redemption. The new definition of that relationship had sharp repercussions. In an unexpected parallel to humanist historiography, Peucer's edition of Melanchthon's chronicle made a sharp distinction between the two orders, the sacred and the profane. Protestant historiography thus came to a fork in the road leading to two entirely separate histories: one ecclesiastical, telling the story of Christ's church, and one mundane, concerned with the state as God's instrument. Although God still linked the two, this link was deemphasized with every passing century.

After the Lutheran reform movement had matured into an institutional church, a group of Lutheran scholars under the leadership of Matthias Flacius Illyricus (Vlach from Istria) set out on a systematic exploration of the Christian church's past. The resulting *Magdeburg Centuries* (1559–74) were to document the Lutheran assertions of a step-by-step corruption of the teachings of Christ and of the simple early church by the Roman hierarchy. That theme had already been set forth by two Englishmen. Robert Barnes ascribed all guilt to the popes, whom he appropriately vilified. Luther cherished Barnes's *Lives of the Roman Pontiffs*, which simply magnified all papal weaknesses described in Platina's *Lives of the Popes* and in other works. John Bale, a more systematic church historian, blamed the whole "Roman Church" for the evil that befell the faith in the past. He eventually assisted the writers of the *Magdeburg Centuries*.

The *Magdeburg Centuries* traced in thirteen volumes the development of the church until 1300, hailing all dissenters and condemning those who supposedly contributed to the continuous corruption of the church—particularly the popes, who were denounced as the Anti-Christ. When Flacius found no convenient points of division for the volumes, he decided to have each volume treat one century and thereby pioneered one of the most durable concepts in Western historiography. Each volume, or century, had chapters dealing with standard topics: the propagation of the church, the fate of the church, doctrines, heresies, rites and ceremonies, governance of the church, councils, lives of bishops and theologians, heresies, martyrs, miracles, Jewish affairs, other religions, and political matters. While the work was not pleasingly written, its massive scholarship provided Protestant preachers and scholars with a vast collection of data.

Because it threatened the concept of an ongoing tradition, Catholics could hardly let the Lutheran interpretation of the church's past go unchallenged. First Onofrio Panvinio, the highly esteemed antiquarian and editor of an updated version of Platina's *Lives of the Popes*, set to work but died before he could accomplish anything. Then, in 1571, a papal commission selected another Oratorian, Caesar Baronius, to write the Catholic counterpart to the *Magdeburg Centuries*. Baronius's *Ecclesiastical Annals* (with the first volume published in 1588) attempted to demonstrate above all that it was wrong to reject the medieval developments in the church, since the postapostolic changes were not man-made innovations but clarifications, interpretations, and special applications of Christ's teachings undertaken with the guidance of the Holy Spirit. The emphasis on continuity made it fitting that Baronius, although he cherished humanist learning, chose the old-fashioned annalistic form. But Baronius's critical spirit was thoroughly up-to-date with its careful evaluation of sources and expurgation of undocumented traditions. The *Annals* were even popular, as the many editions show. So serious, so pious, so concerned with accuracy, and so generous in the use of documents was Baronius that his work not only buttressed the faith of Catholics but on occasion provided information even to Protestant scholars.

Still, the *Ecclesiastical Annals* were a Roman Catholic compendium and Baronius had erred a number of times. His work received a Protestant answer from Isaac Casaubon, an outstanding Calvinist scholar of languages, who pointed out errors in Baronius's Greek, Hebrew, and Latin and inferred from them that the whole text of the *Ecclesiastical Annals* was unreliable. The *Exercitationes in Baronium,* Casaubon's answer, took eight hundred pages to refute Baronius's first volume alone and remained a fragment. With Casaubon ended the attempts to win the battle over the proper church tradition by using history. Important as the ecclesiastical histories were, they ignored the involvement of the masses in the controversy. If history were to remain instrumental in the Reformation period, it needed to appeal to a wider public.

The battle over the proper tradition took on a unique shape in the gradual emergence of the Anglican church. From the beginning of this church, its articles of faith, its constitution, and its practices were debated and decided in the context of English society with its currents and cross-currents. Early Protestants like William Tyndale considered the Bible the only authority and the apostolic church the only proper model. The medieval centuries demonstrated the "great decline," a period in which the "visible" church degenerated through the "great conspiracy" of the papacy. However, the Anglican church strove for a greater continuity, first by extending the period of the "ideal" apostolic church by about 600 years, and then by stressing the distinction between the church as the mystical body of Christ, removed from all change and doubt and subject only to the few great turning points in sacred history, and the visible church, existing in specific societies and states. The visible church, being a part of the world, changed only in its nonessential aspects (the *adiaphora*). In this sense Richard Hooker defined the Anglican church as a historical institution, occupying a middle ground between Roman Catholicism and Protestantism.

Celebrating the Elizabethan religious settlement was a work with an accent on antiquities and scholarly method, the *De antiquitate Britannicae ecclesiae* (1572), compiled by a battery of scholars led by the learned archbishop of Canterbury, Matthew Parker. They had rescued large amounts of source material from being destroyed, collected it in the official residence of the archbishop, and systematically edited and used it. Parker had set out to serve the Christian faith and ended up praising its English version:

because neither my health nor my quiet would suffer me to be a common preacher, yet I thought it not unfit for me to be otherwise occupied in some points of religion; for my meaning was, by this my poor collection thus caused to be printed . . . to note at what time Augustine my first predecessor came into this land, what religion he brought in with him, and how it continued, how it was fortified and increased, which by most of my predecessors may appear, as I could gather of such rare and written authors that came to my hands, until the days of King Henry the VIIth, when the religion began to grow better, and more agreeable to the Gospel.[3]

English pride was not badly served either, as Parker and his associates became interested in the early Anglo-Saxon language and in editing Saxon sources and medieval English chronicles.

*On martyrs and councils.* Discussions of essentials and *adiaphora* and lengthy, scholarly church histories did not move the masses. Hence, it seems surprising that the most popular historical work concerning the church in England was John Foxe's *Acts and Monuments of These Latter and Perilous Days,* an English version of the original Latin work. The people called it simply the *Book of Martyrs,* although in its final form the work constituted a full-fledged ecclesiastical history. Foxe demonstrated that the new English Protestant church was no sudden or accidental occurrence but had its own continuity if Wycliff and the Lollards were taken as the medieval supports for a bridge leading back to the "pure" apostolic church. But such ecclesiastical history would not have stirred the masses had it not been for Foxe's martyrology. For centuries the stories of the early martyrs had inspired Christians. Now, both Protestants and Catholics found the same inspiration in the lives of their contemporary martyrs. In the 1500s Jean Crespin had issued a history of the "new" martyrs, "victims of the Anti-Christ"—that is, of the Roman Catholic church—and Baronius had countered with a *Roman Martyrology.* But Foxe's *Book of Martyrs* gripped more readers than all other such works. A true history for the masses, it was selective, partisan, and highly effective.

While martyrs received their share of attention, one of the more important religious settlements of the sixteenth century, the Council of Trent, suffered historiographical neglect for many years. Its first major historical account came from the Venetian Paolo Sarpi, a reform-minded, ascetic member of the Servite order. When his *History of the Council of Trent* appeared in 1619, it bore the traces of Sarpi's training and life experience. Humanist historiography had impressed on him the centrality of politics, a view strengthened by his love of the Venetian *patria* and by his deep resentment of the political use of papal power. Thus, he depicted the council essentially as a power struggle even in matters of theology. The importance of the council for the *historia sacra,* or simply its religious significance, could never be ascertained from the blow-by-blow account that Sarpi distilled from the documents available to him. In its fact-laden way it reflected the preferences of the age, which had come to interpret religious controversies politically. Only many years later did the Jesuit Sforza Pallavicino attempt to refute Sarpi's interpretation in his *Story of the Council of Trent* (1656-57). He could not counteract completely Sarpi's influence, since Sarpi appealed to Protestants, who liked his basically derogatory attitude, and to the growing number of skeptics among intellectuals, who cherished church history as exposé.

# ·12·

# The Continuing Modification of Traditional Historiography

## The Blending of Theoretical and Patriotic Answers

Historiography, still under humanist influence throughout the 1500s, became involved in and colored by the various national developments. In Italy it showed, up to 1559, the traces of the great upheavals and afterwards the marks of tranquility. In France, the turmoil of the civil wars of the second half of the sixteenth century projected the search for the proper past into the debate on national salvation. That led historians and historically minded scholars to concern themselves with Frankish customary law, feudalism, and the question of French identity (German, Roman, or Celtic). Elizabethan England, more tranquil and sure of itself, produced histories of many kinds: most characteristic of them were the antiquarian works. In the vein of Varro and Biondo some scholars explored the antiquities of England. But even that endeavor touched on questions of national identity and politics, particularly in the studies of Anglo-Saxon laws. Indeed, the nineteenth-century debate between Romanists and Germanists in England, France, and Germany can be traced to the 1500s. And antiquaries and legal historians can at least partially be credited with history's later concerns with sources, archives, and institutions.

*The struggle for the proper French past.* After 1560, what with campaign following campaign for the French, humanist historians would have had ample opportunity to practice their favorite genre: political and military history. Yet the best such histories were written by Italians—for example, by Enrico Caterino Davila, an Italian sympathizer of the queen-mother Catherine de' Medici. He observed events closely and documented his account carefully. But even he was more interested in revealing large-scale shifts in political power than in narrating the numerous events. He shared that interest with a group of the most influential French scholars: lawyers and teachers of law whose attention was focused less on individuals and their actions than on such collective forces as laws and customs. After 1550, when the battle against the *mos italicus* had been won, they pushed the historical study of law into new directions. Many of them were at one time or another connected with the University of Bourges—Charles Dumoulin, François le Douaren, François Hotman, François Baudouin, and Jacques Cujas. Others were legal experts at the royal court and at the courts of law. These *robins* (those garbed in the *robe longue*) spearheaded the new exploration of the French past.

The early proponents of the *mos gallicus* had still wished to reestablish the "pure" Roman law as a universal model. That appreciation changed when some of the legists became Protestants and extended their dislike of the Roman Catholic church to everything Roman. François Hotman considered all Roman influences on the French as corrupt. Not only was the *Corpus juris civilis* an unreliable jumble of republican and imperial Roman laws, but when Roman law had been imposed on the Franks it had suppressed the Frankish law that had best fit Frankish society. Roman law, Hotman held, was not an ideal, universal code but simply the law of the Roman people. Hesitantly, Hotman had taken one small step toward the historical interpretation of law by tying together changes in law and society. Unfortunately, however, he stepped back when he simply replaced Roman law with a new "proper" and timeless model, Frankish law. Nevertheless, Hotman's approach led to an exploration of Frankish law and in due course to a new attitude towards the Middle Ages which the humanists had so despised. When legal scholars studied that period, they puzzled over the origin of feudalism and objected to a Romanist interpretation for that development too. Dumoulin showed that the Roman law knew no fiefs, and Hotman spelled out directly their German origin.

And there was the troublesome question of what kind of people the French were. For centuries the Trojan origin of the Franks, suggested by "Fredegar," had given pride and self-confidence to the French. So eminent a scholar as Gaguin, who most likely doubted the Trojan connection, deferred to it nevertheless. Paolo Emilio, an Italian humanist with the irreverence of the new criticism and without a vested interest in a Trojan ancestry for the French, pronounced the Franks to be Germans. Beatus Rhenanus eventually proved Emilio's assumption right. Hotman, a Protestant of German origin, was eager to substitute the German-origin thesis for the Trojan and Roman theses and bluntly labeled the Trojan tradition "fables and stories to please." Although all evidence pointed to the German origin of the Franks, it was not popular with the French and the emphasis soon shifted from a Franco-German to a Franco-Gallic origin. Guillaume Postel had reemphasized the importance of the Celtic Gauls for early French history. They were, he thought, a people directly linked to the Israelites through Gomar, one of Noah's grandsons. Baudouin even labeled the Franks as Gauls who had lived east of the Rhine. Later, some scholars with an antiquarian bent became skeptical about such pronouncements. Etienne Pasquier, himself most likely convinced of the validity of the Germanic position, escaped a decision by labeling the whole issue of origins unimportant. Who could tell now what had happened in the misty past?

In their discussions of French law, the legists had assumed law to be the supreme force in shaping the body politic, and in their researches on law they had learned to appreciate the value of history. François Baudouin declared flatly that he had become aware that law books resulted from history and that whatsoever was remarkable in history evolved from books of law. He also realized that, as the areas of historical interest changed, so did the historian's sources of knowledge. If history dealt not with battles, heroes, or moral *exempla* but with the slowly changing law and social institutions, the story of the past could no longer be reconstructed by simply accepting the authority of former historians and their accounts; after all, most historians of the past had ignored the institutional structure of society. The new gates to the past were the primary sources *(primi autores)*, which now were esteemed, critically assessed, and searched for bias. They would be the new authorities prevailing in cases of doubt, overruling even centuries-old traditions.

King Francis II entrusted Jean du Tillet with the reorganization of the royal archives, thus starting a trend toward systematic archival collections. By the 1560s scholars still used archives rarely, because the collections were usually poorly organized and because access to them was not routinely granted, often being given only on the basis of partisanship. After all, even legal antiquarians did not always produce works for mere scholarly contemplation. Thus Jean du Tillet and Pierre Pithou, another keeper of the royal archives, lent their legal, antiquarian, and historical skills to the support of their monarch. Such a connection of law, history, and service to France was typical for the members of an erudite circle that included, besides Pithou, Claude de Fauchet, Louis le Caron, Antoine Loisel, and Etienne Pasquier. The latter wrote the monumental *Recherches de la France*, describing in ten books France's political, judicial, and financial institutions, its church, language, and general past. Only de Thou's *History of His Own Time* achieved a comparable recognition. These scholars did not allow their Gallic sympathies to conflict with their methodology, for which truth in history writing was guaranteed by eyewitness reports (the old authority) and by critically examined and verified documents (the new authority).

*English historiography: tradition, pride, and tranquility.* Love for the chronicle continued in England through the 1500s. A number of scholars even tried to satisfy popular tastes for a national history by writing chronicles. Edward Hall pleased Protestant and Tudor sympathizers with his *Union of the Two Noble and Illustrious Families of Lancaster and York*. Then Thomas Lanquet and Thomas Cooper abbreviated a number of chronicles into one compact account, *An Epitome of Chronicles* (1549). It ushered in a boom in short histories. The printer Richard Grafton, who had continued Hall's work, included too much material from Creation onward in his own *Chronicle at Large* and failed in the market. Finally Raphael Holinshed and some coauthors pleased their contemporaries with *The Chronicles of England, Scotland, and Ireland*. It provided a rich and appealing mixture of material taken from many chronicles, legends, Polydore Vergil, and Matthew Parker's extraordinary collection of chronicles and documents, and remained a treasure house of information for a long time.

John Stow, a tailor by profession but a scholar by vocation, compiled the *Summary of English Chronicles* (1565), particularly those of Hardyng, Fabyan, and Hall, and updated it from time to time. The share of his own contributions increased with every edition. By 1592 his attempt to provide an English history had grown into the *Annales of England*. Stow never abandoned his intention to write a really new history of England, but he failed to produce one. Then, in 1603, the Elizabethan era came to a close and with it faded the age of the chronicle.

The wave of translations and printed editions of ancient historians enhanced the new historical awareness sweeping over England and the continent. Henry Savile's translation and edition of Tacitus and Philemon Holland's Livy, Suetonius, and Ammianus Marcellinus editions were among the best-known examples. By 1600 others included Thomas Nicholls's Thucydides, Thomas North's Plutarch, Thomas Lodge's Josephus, and Thomas Heywood's Sallust. Yet, though classical historians were widely read, English historical records were not ignored. Savile loved the classical historians, but he also worked on the chronicles of William of Malmesbury, Richard Howden, and Henry of Huntingdon. Indeed, the editing and publishing of English historical accounts went on at a quick pace.

During the Elizabethan age, with its peculiar mixture of tradition, innovation, and national pride, the discovery of the English past proceeded briskly but not necessarily predictably. English scholars focused on their love of aniquities, which they had imbibed from the works of ancient writers and also from the Italian antiquarian literature from Biondo to Onofrio Panvinio. Antiquarian history prospered in England after 1570 because it allowed scholars to satisfy their curiosity about the past, their desire to acknowledge the new standards of precision, their quest for demonstrating the proud history of towns, regions and the nation, their demand that history depict all of life, and, one may suspect, their predilection for empirical data.

Preliminary work for the antiquarian period of English historiography had been done during Henry VIII's reign. When Henry VIII dissolved the monasteries, the threat of destruction of many records prompted historians to salvage whatever they could. John Bale gathered as many manuscripts as he could, only to lose them again when he himself became an exile. His plan of a depository for every shire, a mixture of museum, archive, and library, failed, too. Then in the 1570s, antiquarianism began in earnest. While historians influenced by humanist ideals told of individuals and their actions in narratives, antiquarians studied the remains of collective life. For centuries, the narrative and antiquarian approaches were rarely combined.

Still, in Henry VIII's reign, John Leland drew up a visionary plan for English scholars to inventory all references to British place names in classical literature and in later English works and to ascertain the actual locations referred to. Eventually inscriptions and objects such as coins, tombs, and ruins were added as research topics. On the basis of these new data and already available accounts, a chorography—that is, a description and mapping of England—was to be accomplished, to be followed by a county-by-county history of England. While Leland supplied little more than the plan and a set of notes, he had sketched out an ambitious program for English antiquarians.

Two protégés of Lord William Cecil Burghley, who competed with Matthew Parker for the services of historically inclined scholars, began to translate Leland's plan into reality. However, Laurence Nowell and his student William Lambarde produced, once more, only notes. Lambarde's mass of notes was published in 1730 as the *Topographical and Historical Dictionary of England*. Lambarde himself completed one true antiquarian county history, *A Perambulation of Kent* (1576), a remarkable and readable account of cities, ports, religious institutions, schools, legal rights, and customs of that shire. It influenced John Stow's the *Survey of London* (1599), the first English town history that was built not only on chronicles but also on public records and antiquities. It contained a history of London and a full description of past London life, including the water supply, fire-fighting procedures, welfare, garbage disposal, and drainage. The disparaging remark about "lay chronigraphers that write of nothing but of Mayors and Sheriffs and the dere yere, and the great frost,"[1] could not be turned against him; the world of the London burgher had found in him its historian. That his history presented no synthesis but consisted of a large number of discrete facts (without assertions about Brutus and the Trojans) did not disturb his contemporaries. William Camden wrote a chorography of Roman Britain by the use of the Antonine Itinerary, a kind of Roman-road book: by locating Roman remains; by himself traveling on many of the old roads; by interviewing knowledgeable people and consulting public records; and by inspecting locations. Although at first glance Camden's *Britannia* (editions from 1586 to 1606) appeared to be little more than a list of place names and Roman remains, it provided the basis for histories of specific localities and enhanced England's and Camden's prestige among Continental scholars. Some of these scholars were in contact with Camden, such as the geographer Abraham Ortelius and the antiquarian De Thou. Yet, the *Britannia* did not hold readers spellbound and thus never became popular, despite Philemon Holland's good English translation of the Latin text.

Antiquarians inevitably touched upon the troublesome problem of English ancestry. Historians of the Tudor period still affirmed the Trojans and the British heroes in England's distant past. Polydore Vergil, who had rediscovered Gildas's work, doubted the traditional versions of early English history but could not dissuade the English. Antiquarians may well have doubted the traditional accounts of early English history but they discarded neither Noah's descendants nor the British Arthur nor Brutus, the great-grandson of Aeneas. National pride upheld the stories of a biblical, Trojan, or British origin. Camden made light of the Trojan origin and celebrated the Roman phase of the early English past in his *Britannia*. However, to the rising English national consciousness with its strong Protestant component, the Romans were "foreigners." Now was the time the Anglo-Saxon tradition, which would eventually prevail, gathered its early advocates. Parker traced the English church's story back into the Anglo-Saxon period, other scholars became interested in the Anglo-Saxon language, and Nowell and Lambarde were intrigued by the history of Anglo-Saxon law. In 1568, Lambarde published the texts of old Anglo-Saxon laws *(Archaionomia)*, and from this time began in earnest the fascination with the common law and the unique English institution, Parliament. The legal continuity seemed so convincing that it gave rise to the idea of the common law's immemorial antiquity and of Parliament as a part of a mythical ancient constitution. For decades the attempts to interpret contemporary law and Parliament in those terms overshadowed thoughts of a development in law and politics that contemporary studies suggested.

History clearly was popular in the Elizabethan age. English readers could study military histories, learn political lessons and proper conduct from historical handbooks, indulge in nostalgia through chronicles, get spiritual uplift and material for the defense of Anglicanism from histories, catch a glimpse of the New World, learn from the topographical accounts of antiquarians about early English life, and even be entertained, taught, and inspired by historical plays, of which Shakespeare's dramas were the most famous.

While members of the gentry fervently searched the past under the banner of genealogy and heraldry, the scholars devoted to antiquarianism worked individually and cooperatively on mapping the English past. Their common interests led some of them to join forces in the Society of Antiquaries (1586). For about twenty-one years they met first in Derby House, the home of the College of Heralds, and then in Sir Robert Cotton's home. They were generally men of means and high social status, except for John Stow, the tailor, and a few others. Membership required that one did historical research either individually or collectively. Most of this research centered on English law, customs, and institutions. As for the methods of "doing history," the scholars knew the accomplishments of humanists but had to work out much of their methodology, because they usually dealt with nonliterary primary sources. Few English historians, with the notable exceptions of Thomas Blundeville and Francis Bacon, were theoreticians in the Continental mold. It therefore mattered little that Giacomo Aconcio, one of the Italian *ars historica* theoreticians, arrived in 1559 as an exile in England. Neither did it help that Thomas Blundeville made a brave attempt to push the Italian *ars historica* controversy onto the English scene with translations of two Italian tracts and his own work. When in the early 1600s Francis Bacon dealt with history, his considerations transcended the limits of the *ars rhetorica* debate and encompassed the broader concerns of the theory of knowledge.

As for the sixteenth-century English antiquaries they were content to explore the past, find and describe its remainders, and leave it at that. They felt no need for synthesis or interpretation.

## Universal History: A Troubled Tradition

After 1500, the very core of Christian universal history in the manner of Eusebius and Jerome, marked by the subordination of all histories to sacred history, was increasingly threatened. While certain bothersome chronological problems were amenable to technical solutions, the discovery of the global world and its many peoples was another matter. Christian historians had mastered similar problems when they had helped integrate the Germans into the Roman world and during the Middle Ages had played a significant role in interpreting the enlargement of Latin Christendom eastwards. Yet the global world posed problems of greater scope and profundity. Those who decided simply to separate sacred from mundane history experienced even more severe difficulties in finding a proper way to write universal history. Searching for the principle of unity, they tried geography, cycles, comparative analysis of nations, and even unity as an ideal for the future. Only the progress theoreticians of the 1700s ended the period of experimentation for secular historians. Christian universal historiography would have to continue to search.

*Chronology revisited.* Accordingly, ever since Africanus and Eusebius, time as the space for human redemption had been of great concern; one which by the late 1500s had brought forth at least fifty different dating schemes—known as world eras (the time elapsed since Creation or Adam or Abraham). Such variations resulted from the use of different Old Testament versions and counting methods. In 1583, and in the new spirit of precision, consistency, and documentation, the learned Joseph Justus Scaliger tried to end the confusion by his *Restoration of Chronology* and later by his *Thesaurus of Dates*. Using the newest insights from mathematics and astronomy, he placed Creation at about 4713 B.C. In the end his discovery that the chronology of Giovanni Annio of Viterbo was useless had a greater impact because it helped destroy the influence of Annio's Pseudo-Berossus (a forgery which had wrought much mischief since 1498). Half a century after Scaliger's death, Archbishop James Ussher produced his own "definitive" compendium. According to his *Annals of the Old and New Testament*, Creation occurred on Sunday, October 23, 4004 B.C.; Adam was created on the following Friday. Neither Scaliger nor Ussher convinced their contemporaries, and the confusion of world eras continued. The problem was never really resolved; it simply faded away together with the world eras themselves under the impact of a simpler chronological system.

The Jesuit Dionysius Petavius (Petain) had attempted to date events prior to Christ's birth according to Olympiads, world eras, and the "since the founding of Rome" scheme before he suggested, in 1627, the counting of all years by Incarnation years, which meant counting the years before Christ's birth backwards. Petavius most likely knew of the earlier experiments with the B.C. scheme by Bede, Marianus Scotus, Lambert of Saint-Omer, and, more recently, the Carthusian Werner Rolevinck, Filippo Foresti di Bergamo, and Johann Coelestinus Laziardus. Petavius gave the B.C. scheme needed publicity in an era ready for simplification, and by 1650 the B.C. system had achieved well-nigh universal application in the West. Since it still hinged the counting of years on a Christian frame of history, even Protestants found the scheme acceptable.

*The New World challenges traditional world history.* In 1519 King Charles of Spain became Emperor Charles V of the Holy Roman Empire. Universal history writers, such as Gonzalo Fernándes de Oviedo, still understood the term "empire" in its traditional Mediterranean-European connotation and spoke of Charles as an emperor in direct line from Caesar. But the very same Spain also felt the repercussions of the explorations and discoveries of her sailors and the conquests of her soldiers in the Americas. Just three years after Charles gained the imperial title, Magellan's voyage proved the world to be a globe, inhabited by diverse peoples of whom Eusebius and later universal chroniclers had known nothing.

In the 1590s Juan de Mariana still argued that the world could stay unified through a Spanish world empire—an answer so flattering to Spanish pride that it led to continuations of Mariana's voluminous *About the King and the Royal Institution* well into the 1700s, when Spanish power had all but disappeared. The concept of a Spanish universal monarchy easily captivated those who had participated in the conquest of America. It had inspired Gonzalo Fernández de Oviedo, who in his *General and Natural History of the Indies* (about 1530) had marveled at the features of the New World he had observed; years later, Francisco López de Gómara, who composed a *General History of the Indies* on the basis of considerably less personal experience, used the same concept. Yet López de Gómara understood more clearly what had happened when he called the discovery of America the greatest event since Creation and considered the Indian question a serious challenge to traditional historical interpretations.

In traditional universal histories the family of nations had had both a stable membership and a known ancestral home in the Middle East. But how did the strange inhabitants of the Americas or East Indies fit into that scheme? And fit they had to, because otherwise, universal history would in the past not have been universal and in the present and future would be impossible.

In the early stages of the ethnic confrontation, Peter Martyr of Anghiera, an Italian humanist, could still muse that these "naive," nearly naked creatures must be inhabitants of the Golden Age who had escaped corruption because their area long ago had been separated from the Western world. Theoreticians could cling to so comfortable an integration of the Indian past into Western universal history, although even Peter could hardly have put much stock in it. Missionaries and colonial administrators certainly could not, since they soon found out that the Indian mind was not a *tabula rasa* but filled with traditions. Oviedo had already been aware of the rich Indian tradition. Administrators and missionaries studied these Indian traditions about the past in order to be able to combat "errors" and "superstitions." Although such work suffered from the inherent prejudices of literate Christian Westerners toward pagan, oral traditions, some parts of the Indian traditions were collected and eventually found their way into Western historical writing. Thus, when Pedro Cieza de Leon used Inca traditions for his *Chronicle of Peru*, the work profited from its Indian component, although he produced little more than a chronicle of rulers.

Historians gained new insights from the ongoing debate between Bartolomé de Las Casas and Juan Ginés de Sepúlveda over the proper treatment of the Indians. In its course de Las Casas proposed in his *History of the Indies* that the discoveries in the New World did not contradict Christian universal history but actually fulfilled it. For centuries the unity of mankind had merely been foreshadowed; now it was becoming a reality through universal conversion. Hence, de Las Casas pleaded that the Indians were humans whose souls must be saved. Sepúlveda spoke out against such a providential integration of the Indians into Christian universal history. In that history the growth of the Spanish world monarchy was most important and the Indians, never fully human, were irrelevant. The dispute drew in many more scholars but remained mainly in the judicial-theological area.

In the late 1500s the Jesuit José de Acosta suggested a new approach for integrating the Indians into Christian universal history. Years earlier Sebastian Münster had shown that Asia and America were separated by only a narrow stretch of sea, called by the Italian cosmographer Zaltieri the straits of Anian. Now Acosta spoke of an Indian migration from Asia to America. In their new home the Indians had become highly developed barbarians who never reached the level of the civilized West. Such a transfer theory helped contemporaries explain the Indian presence in America while preserving the single origin of mankind in the Near East.

*The fragmentation of universal history.* The Spaniards, with their imperial ambitions, could quite readily support the Christian universal history in its late ancient and medieval forms. In other nations universal history was under siege. Its biblical segment, which alone made local and regional histories into more than sectional histories, had suffered increasing neglect in the late medieval chronicles and had been expelled from humanist histories with their overriding love for ancient models and love of *patria*. When the geographical discoveries piled problem upon problem and when even the Reformation failed to invigorate the writing of universal history, the unity of the sacred and the profane—however tentatively it had been established—began to fade, and with it faded traditional universal history. The attack on it nevertheless continued relentlessly.

In France, Jean Bodin opened his *Method for the Easy Understanding of History* with a programmatic statement:

> Of History, that is, the true narration of things, there are three kinds: Human, natural, and divine. The first concerns man; the second, nature; the third, the father of nature. One depicts the acts of man while leading his life in the midst of society. The second reveals causes hidden in nature and explains their development from earliest beginnings. The last records the strength and power of Almighty God and of the immortal souls, set apart from all else.[2]

Each of these histories had its own purpose and delivered knowledge of a different degree of certainty. Divine history was based on faith and yielded firm pronouncements. Natural history dealt with the inevitable, had to be studied with logic, and yielded knowledge of a slightly less secure kind. Human history produced only probable knowledge but taught man prudence, and was, despite its limitations, the most useful kind.

In the German area, Luther's distinction between God's *Erhaltungsorder*, the order of things which governed the world until the fulfillment of time, and God's *Heilsplan*, the divine plan of salvation for mankind, was by now well on its way to forming the basis for two distinct histories: one secular and the other ecclesiastical. In fact, the German clergy became concerned that teachers in the liberal arts were slighting ecclesiastical history. Thus, beginning in 1650, chairs for ecclesiastical history were established at Protestant universities, and soon afterwards compendia of ecclesiastical history appeared as guides for students. But the isolation of ecclesiastical history from other aspects of the past led to a "flattening out" of sacred history into the history of the church as an institution. Soon, influenced by an increasing rationalism, the ecclesiastical histories shifted from the simple piety of early ones to a critical, dispassionate review of the church's past, as in Gottfried Arnold's *Unparteiische Kirchen-und-Ketzergeschichte* (1699) and J. L. von Mosheim's scholarly *Institutes of Church History* (1726). Only in England, with her satisfactory accommodation between state and church (save during the Puritan interlude), did historians still write church histories which shied away from a sharp separation of the human and the sacred. Gilbert Burnet's *History of the Reformation of the Church of England* stirred the old fires with its view of the Reformation as the search for the pure church. But, in the early 1700s, John Strype's *Annals of the Reformation and Establishment of Religion*, in which documentation and information replaced passionate judgment and sacred history became institutional history, revealed already a more "continental" temper.

When sacred history became simply ecclesiastical history, it surrendered its claim to be the focal point for all of human history. It had never been easy to relate the grand plan of God in sacred history with events after Christ. Now even the attempt to do so was abandoned by most historians. In the late 1500s, Reiner Reineccius already spoke of separate political, ecclesiastical, and scholarly (intellectual) histories, sharply curtailing the religious aspect of the past. In France, Reineccius's contemporary, Nicholas Vignier, took the ultimate step, in his *Bibliothèque historiale*, by asserting that secular history had absorbed religion as just another category of human life.

*A secular scheme for ordering history.* It now was only a question of time until the traditional ordering schemes for world history would be replaced with one more attuned to the tendency to grant mundane affairs their own order. The most immediate victim was the long-cherished Four Empire scheme that was derived from the Book of Daniel. In the sixteenth century many German historians still took great pride in viewing the Holy Roman Empire as the fourth and last of the empires. But the old problem of how to adjust the rigid scheme to the changing world became more acute with the discovery of new regions and peoples. However, Jean Bodin's severe criticism of the German version of the scheme was not so much prompted by any new geographical or ethnographic knowledge as by his French patriotism: "Since it was explained in this way by Germans, I judge it was written for the glory of their name and empire, for it is altogether strange to the interpretation of Daniel."[3] The Daniel scheme had to be abandoned because it did not fit the times, Bodin could also have said, and because it became irrelevant to an increasingly secular-minded historiography. German historians deeply resented Bodin's attack and the controversy went on well into the 1700s. But in the meantime a new scheme to organize the past had begun to capture the imaginations of historians.

Petrarch had implied that the past had three periods: Rome, then darkness, and then renovation. Other humanists discerned the light of learning, then darkness, and then the return of the light. Throughout the 1500s and 1600s, these three ages were known, but scholars spoke no longer of a period of darkness but of "moyen age" (Pierre Pithou), "middle time" (William Camden), or most commonly of a *media tempestas* or a *medium aevium*. But it was a textbook writer, not a visionary or a theoretician, who finally organized Western history according to the new concept of the three stages. Just prior to 1700 Christopher Cellarius published his *Universal History Divided into an Ancient, Medieval, and New Period*. Probably neither he nor his students grasped the full impact of the change: the universal history in the manner of Eusebius and Jerome had ended; Christian history had become a mere aspect of general history; biblical history appeared as just one feature of ancient history; and the continuity between the three periods was ended.

*Forces and units in a mundane world history.* A world was gradually emerging in which God's direct governance (the first cause) was not denied but was seen as rare and in which a welter of second causes needed attention if one wanted to explain the many interlocking events of that world. Some French historians of the late 1500s and early 1600s understood that historians had to go beyond ferreting out facts and venture into new types of interpretation because, as they saw it, the essence of a work of history was the knowledge of the motives and true causes of all facts and happenings.

In the manner of the ancient Greeks, Bodin found some of the second causes in the different human temperaments and in institutions; he attributed the differences in these things to three shaping forces: specific fluid balances in the body, climates, and geographical settings. But Bodin also numbered the stars and planets among the second causes.

Some historians found the number of causes to be enormous; after all, every human and natural phenomenon could become a cause at one time or another. Nicholas Vignier struggled bravely to put it all together in his *Bibliothèque historiale* (1587) but failed to find any focus for his account. Consequently, the book's mass of material benumbed the reader, demonstrating that if the world of causes remained confusing so would be the historical account. In their search for order some French historians came close to the concept of civilization as an organizing principle, but they never grasped it. They did not even know the word and rather used terms like "state," "empire," or "society" interchangeably. Louis Le Roy engaged in some functional analysis of civilizations when he studied the function of priests in various societies and found that in each priests administered the most important knowledge—the sacred wisdom and the ritual—and derived their power from it. Italian humanists would have been interested in—although hardly pleased by—Le Roy's historicizing of human languages. What for them had been at the core of a civilized life now became just another aspect of human life, sharing the fate of its society.

In order to explain cultural differences and the change of customs in time, Le Roy designed a cultural version of the empire scheme with virtue (conceived here as civilized existence) being transferred from the Assyrians to the Medes, to the Persians, to the Greeks, to the Romans, and to the European countries. However, there was no hint that a succeeding civilization was of either a better or a lesser quality than the previous one. Some had talked of a Golden Age in the beginning of mankind, from which mankind had steadily declined, but Bodin ridiculed this as the illusion "of men carried out of port into the open sea—they think the houses and the towns are departing from them; thus they think that delight, gentle conduct, and justice have flown to the heavens and deserted the earth."[4] The Golden Age idea simply did not stand up under close scrutiny, which showed that in that early period the Great Flood had ravaged the world, giants had revolted against heaven, Hercules, one of its heroes, had been the "greatest of the pirates," and men had lived scattered like beasts in the fields and the woods. In comparison, Bodin found his own age refined, although there was no suggestion of a continuous progress, not even of a continuous development, when Bodin rated "the moderns" over the "ancients." He simply compared two periods many centuries apart.

Divorced from sacred history, world history appeared more and more as a maze of nations, empires, or societies (today we would call them "civilizations" or "cultures"). In their quest for continuity and order in a world of change, the French historians acquired a vigorous interest in the well-known cyclical pattern of things. Pasquier did little more than describe how empires rise by force of arms, acquire somewhat later "letters" (intellectual achievements), and then decline. Le Roy proceeded to an explanation that had been a favorite with ancient historians: civilization brings about an internal "disease"—that is, originally hardy people became effeminate through the life of luxury that results from increasing power and possessions. The people who formerly lived simply, suffered patiently, and were skilled in warfare, subsequently grow spoiled and soft. Eventually they fall victim to hardier conquerors. History told the story of the rise and fall of such civilizations.

Even historiography was soon looked at with a sketchy understanding of development. Reflecting on past history writing, Henri Voisin, sieur de La Popelinière saw not simply a long line of authorities who pronounced eternal verities but historians who expressed views on the past appropriate to the intellectual temper of their own periods. In the early stages of civilization the past was commemorated in spontaneously created songs, dances, and symbols. La Popelinière cited not only Greek and Roman but also American Indian examples. That "natural" stage was followed by one of poetic or epic history. When the degree of rational reflection increased, prose history writing appeared, recording events in chronological order. Finally, Herodotus created history in the "modern" form. La Popelinière indicated that his generation of scholars would take the next step with the creation of a new type of history, the "general" history, one at the same time universal and comparative.


*The elusive unity of the human past.* Medieval universal histories had been able to affirm the unity of human history by virtue of the Genesis account of early human history. Without it world histories began with histories of unconnected and diverse nations lacking a common origin. Adam and Eve proved hard to replace as the unitary origin of the human race.

While many scholars still affirmed the Genesis account, speaking at least of a postdiluvial migration of people in many directions, Bodin boldly declared that the unity of mankind was not at all a phenomenon of the past but of the future. He suggested as unifying forces the increasing connection of the regions of the world by trade, the widely shared idea of a human commonwealth *(respublica mundana)*, and the law of nations *(ius gentium)*. For an overall pattern of development Bodin relied on an updated version of the old *Vaticinium Eliae*: 2,000 years of southern predominance (Egyptians and Mesopotamians) characterized by religion and wisdom; 2,000 years of Greek and Roman hegemony, with city-states, colonial expansion, and laws; 2,000 years of northern predominance characterized by wars and technology. Yet, after having formu-

lated the scheme, which implied a unitary human history, Bodin simply dropped
it.

In 1666 the Dutchman Georg Horn(ius) tried his wits on the unity-of-
mankind problem by combining the new ethnographic and geographical knowledge with the traditional biblical view. His *Noah's Ark* was the first universal
history covering the recently discovered peoples and areas. It was based on the
proposition that, while the Flood had destroyed mankind's original unity, the
age of discoveries initiated the ingathering of all people and thus the restoration
of mankind's unity. But Hornius's ambitious attempt floundered because he
lacked sufficient knowledge of the past of the many new peoples—his diligent
use of reports from missionaries to China notwithstanding.

Another attempt at a new unitary history came from the French Oratorian
Isaac de la Peyrère, a one time Calvinist and librarian for the Prince of Condé.
For him the Book of Genesis had two distinct parts: an early narrative describing the creation of the world and (implicitly) all the peoples and a later story
which focused on the Jews and their destiny as the chosen people (the story of
Adam and Eve, the Fall, and the Flood). The first part was truly universal in
nature. The second, containing the biblical history of the Jews, was universal
only in the sense that it prepared for a universal event: Christ's coming. The story
of the ancient Jews was not identical with the early history of mankind, because
it could not explain the appearance of nonbiblical people in the age of discovery. The idea that mankind had a pre-Adamite origin may have been an
ingenious one but it denied the universal validity of the dogma of original sin
by restricting it to Jews; thus, it destroyed the structure of the traditional
Eusebian univeral history. While La Peyrère endured some censure, the world for
the most part ignored him.

It is misleading, however, to talk mainly of innovative schemes. Traditional
universal histories, which fused the new and the old, were still being written and
commanded a wide reading public, as two famous examples, about a half a
century apart, illustrate. In the early 1600s Sir Walter Raleigh spent long years
in the Tower of London because of his anti-Spanish attitudes and actions, and
he used them to write his *History of the World*. It demonstrated that even a man
who had seen the New World, advocated a new English imperialism, founded the
first English settlement in North America, applauded both Copernicus and Gali-
leo, and knew much about the new sciences, geography, and astronomy could
still hold thoroughly traditional views on the past.

His *History* balanced carefully the contributions of God (the first cause) and
of mundane forces (second causes). God retained his supremacy, but Raleigh
acknowledged the increasing importance of human actions in lieu of God's direct
governance. He saw that second or mundane causes were no more than "instruments, conduits and pipes, which carry and displace what they have received
from the head and fountain of the universal," and he deplored the fact that "all
histories do give us information of human counsels and events as far forth as the

knowledge and faith of the writers can afford, but of God's will, which all things are ordered, they speak only at random, and many times falsely."[5]

But historians ignored second causes at their peril in dealing with the past beyond biblical times since these causes alone helped uncover the patterns for past events, and by knowing them accurately one had a guide on the hazardous journey into the present and future. "We may gather out of history a policy no less wise than eternal, by the comparison and application of other men's fore-passed miseries with our own like errors and ill deservings."[6] The patterns discerned in second causes were actually God's way to implement his will in the world. Historians could investigate human experience without the fear of contradicting God, since the result would merely "illustrate and made good in human reason those things which [biblical] authority alone, without further circumstance, ought to have confirmed in every man's belief."[7] Without God's will shaping it, the order created by second causes would be little more than the one of well-arranged accidents.

After six more decades of constant erosion of the traditional image of the past, the bishop of Meaux, Jacques Bénigne Bossuet, tried to demonstrate that Christian universal history still had validity. As the educator of the Dauphin, Bossuet wrote for the young prince a *Discourse on Universal History*, published in 1681.

At first glance the *Discourse* offered well-known features: the many thousands of years since Creation, Christ's birth as the central point, seven world ages, ecclesiastical and political narratives, and the Last Judgment ending it all. But Bossuet proceeded to revive, after many centuries of neglect, Augustine's view of a dualism between the City of God and the City of the World and to use it alone as the basis for his world history. His work intended, as the subtitle said, to explain the progress of religion and the vicissitudes of empires. As empires, kings, and battles came and went, the City of God enlarged its realm on earth. However, Bossuet, contradicting Augustine, demonstrated a spiritual progress throughout the ages. Even evil forces unwittingly contributed to it; thus when Roman emperors persecuted the Christians they really strengthened the church. Confident about the dominance of the sacred, Bossuet did not hesitate to deal with a multitude of second causes. His was a brilliant effort at updating traditional universal history, although he told the story only up to Charlemagne. No less than two hundred editions and adaptations appeared, although the book was soon overshadowed by new and critically important developments in historiography.

## Historians, the New Politics, and New Perceptions of the World

The period stretching from the mid-1500s to the early 1700s constituted the last phase in the piecemeal modification of the traditional historiographical model. In the case of political historiography, still the strongest of history's genres, its uses differed little from those in previous centuries, except that in France the analysis of institutions brought new insights and that some authorities came to distrust the tendency of history writing to open the arcane act of governing to improper observers. Much more important was the beginning of the struggle, still going on today, for history's place in the house of learning. While Aristotle had separated history from philosophy as the mere study of the contingent and particular, some of those who now redefined the world and the methods for its study wished to deny history any value in comparison to philosophy and the new world of science. Such a challenge inevitably brought about considerable adjustments in historiography.

*Historians and politics in France and England.* The wars and revolutions which ravaged Europe from the late 1500s to the late 1600s raised questions about the proper order of the body politic. What once had seemed an organically ordered entity, arranged in a stable hierarchy, now became the subject of theoretical treatises and even the target of revolutionary action.

Bodin's *Method for the Easy Comprehension of History* was written in preparation for his great work on politics, *The Republic*. The profound crisis gripping France between 1550 and 1600 made concerns with proper narration and individuals secondary to the description and analysis of social institutions, customs, and laws. Only that and a comparative history of societies seemed capable of providing the needed answers. Theologians, philosophers, and lawyers also argued over the proper form and power of the state, but while a few of them used history as a quarry for their arguments, most of them preferred ahistorical legal discussions. On their part, historians had no difficulties with the debate because history's link with politics had been firm ever since Thucydides.

Bodin and other *politiques* contributed their share to the restoration of a strong France. Then, after the Bourbon monarchs gained control, discussions of political theory lost fervor as well as favor. Historians once more preferred to write elegant histories of France which narrated, glorified, celebrated, but did not question. None was better at it and became more popular for it than François Eudes de Mézeray, the royal historiographer. But even he, who kept so many of the rhetorical features, such as speeches, witticisms, and an elegant style, showed in his *History of France* that new lessons could not be ignored. He paid careful attention to the new criticisms and the discovery of institutional history. The same held true for a work by another royal historiographer, Gabriel Daniel's *History of France*. It, however, adulated the king to a much higher degree than Mézeray's work, a fitting practice for the period of Louis XIV.

After the death of Elizabeth I, English events presented historians with an abundance of material for reflections on politics, what with the Civil War, the Commonwealth, Cromwell's Protectorate, the Restoration, and finally the constitutional settlement of 1688. But for many years English historians did not engage much in discussions on power and the state since—as Raleigh had put it earlier—"whosoever, in writing a modern history, shall follow the truth too near its heels, it may happily strike out his teeth."[8] Isaac Dorislaus, the first holder of Cambridge's Greville chair of history, found out that lectures on Tacitus with "inappropriate" commentaries brought silencing. In fact, the turbulent events of this period produced not even good narratives, with one exception. Edward Hyde, Lord Clarendon, who held high office but once and was exiled twice, created out of that experience a *History of the Rebellions and Civil Wars*. It was finished in 1671 but published only in 1702-4. The author knew the affairs of state, had access to important private documents, and was free of official historiography's obligations. The reading public loved his work, because in it history writing remained focused on personalities and events, all of them vividly described, and impersonal institutions played only a minor role.

*Italian historiography and its muted controversies.* After 1559, in the tranquil Italy of principalities, Florentine historiography lost its vigor. For a brief period historians still reflected on the recent struggles between Medici and republican partisans, but gradually such Florentine historians as Jacopo Nardi and Jacopo Pitti wrote histories with a longer time-range, until Scipione Ammirato summed it all up in a multivolume set, full of facts, laid out not for easy reading but for reference. With the grand dukes as patrons, some historians led comfortable lives, and historiography was characterized either by Livian narrative history or by antiquarian history. Together, the two approaches depicted the totality of life, whether the subject was laws, rituals, buildings, or social relationships. In the main, the concerns of public policy, once the source of great vigor, yielded to those of the private or municipal life.

Neither was the Italy of princely rule and the Counter-Reformation a good host to the contemporary European debate on the nature of the state. Scholarly tradition and a measure of caution pushed that discussion into the arena of rhetoric, where it emerged as the controversy over whether Tacitus or Livy should be the model for historians. The Tacitists were in general anticlerical, opposed to the Catholic church as it had been shaped by the Council of Trent, and sympathetic to lay authority. They considered Tacitus the model for deciphering the arcane art of politics.

Tacitus had slipped into contemporary thought gradually when Machiavelli used him slightly, Bodin and Francesco Patrizi praised him, and Justus Lipsius, beginning in the 1570s, made him well known. Authorities, however, distrusted Tacitists even when these scholars, unlike François Hotman, downplayed the power of early tribal councils to limit the king's power or, unlike Paolo Sarpi and Arrigo Davila, did not consider Tacitus as the precursor of a new "realistic" politics.

Those who opposed the Tacitists formed an even more vaguely defined group. Most of them cherished the Ciceronian notion that history could teach the individual valuable lessons and foster virtue. They chose Livy as their model.

Livy had supported both the Roman tradition and the new authority of Augustus, much as the anti-Tacitists generally supported the traditional powers—the Roman Curia, Spain, and the new intellectual and religious order of Trent. Their strength rested less on their famous representatives than on the dozens of now nameless scholars who propounded traditional views in books and discourses. The most effective anti-Tacitist center was the Jesuits' Collegio Romano. One of its famous scholars, Famiano Strada, condemned Tacitus's description of Roman politics, which blamed the improper motives and machinations of those in power for undermining the respect of subjects for governmental authority and tradition. Livy, with his love of stability, tradition, and religion, was seen as a better model for historians. Agostino Mascardi's *Ars historica* of 1636 codified that attitude.

In the end it was not the Jesuits' distrust of Tacitus which mattered but rather their distrust of history as the story of the merely contingent. The Jesuit *Ratio Studiorum* of 1559, the binding curriculum for the numerous and influential Jesuit schools, assigned history no significant role at all. In a Christian version of the Aristotelian view of history's limited usefulness, the Jesuits gave preference to philosophy, philology, and theology as disciplines centered on the timeless and essential features of faith, and to logic and dialectic as approaches to truth. Historians in Catholic Europe continued to write histories, but they—like those in Protestant countries—were not equal in status to theologians and, later, legal scholars.

*The Italian* ars historica *debate.* A group of sixteenth-century Italian scholars, often referred to as the *trattatisti*, asked direct questions about the nature and goals of history writing. The modern lack of appreciation for their work stems from the fact that the *trattatisti* chose to argue the case of history within the traditional confines. Within these limits, where the influence of rhetoric, with its rules for how and what to question, was still strong, history had a clear identity and a theoretical basis that was sufficiently sophisticated to be an *ars*, or "art," a term best understood here as an accepted intellectual discipline with its own methodology.

The *ars historica* scholars were, to a degree unusual for historians, professors: Sperone Speroni, Francesco Robortello, Francesco Patrizi, and Alessandro Sardi. Others held public office, such as Giovanni Viperano (a bishop, a historian, and a legal advisor to King Philip II of Spain) and Uberto Foglietta (a lawyer at the Roman Curia and at the court of Savoy). Of Dionigi Atanagi we know only that he was a free-lance poet and poor. These men argued fervently for an *ars historica* with close links to the *ars rhetorica* in the manner of Aulus Gellius and Cicero, but Western intellectual development turned their effort into a splendid "last hurrah" of rhetorical historiography and left them among the forgotten losers.

Few of these scholars would have disagreed with Viperano's dictum that "to write history means to narrate human events in a wise and attractive form; it is a task as difficult and laborious for the historian as it is useful and pleasant for the reader."[9] But why should it be written in the first place? "Because it taught moral examples," said some; "the truth," said others; none discerned any friction between the two aims. Since any unread truth was ineffective as a lesson, the historian must aim to teach and to delight *(docere et delectare)*. There was nothing to fear from a concern with *elocutio*—that is, colorful word devices, elegant figures of speech, and dramatic exposition—as long as the historian distinguished carefully between facts and rhetorical "additions," such as speeches, and between effective presentation and partisanship. A history which gracelessly enumerated events *(narratio nuda)* was a horror, not because it bored people but because it had no effect. A historical work packed with facts served only to satisfy idle curiosity, but this was the type of history that was gaining favor, and not only among antiquaries.

When the *trattatisti* dealt with the problem of *electio*—in modern parlance the way to select properly the important data from among the infinite number of past events—they frankly admitted that one could never be quite sure of one's selection; this was an admission that provided just the right argument to those seventeenth-century scholars who attacked history for its supposed inability to yield certain knowledge. These critics could point, for example, to Foglietta's statement that the writing of history was an ongoing process and that therefore historical narratives were never *verum* (true) but at best *verax* (truthful). Patrizi, a Platonist for whom truth was the supreme aim of history, not just a subsidiary one, reminded those troubled by the subjective element in the selection process that the only absolute truth available to mankind was the message of Holy Scripture. And Atanagi argued that history's lessons were sufficiently true to relieve every generation of the need to redesign anew the rules of communal life, true enough to instruct the present by the past, to strengthen religion as the foundation of human civilization, and to free human beings from the fear of change.

History was so potent an instrument for enlightening humans on the affairs of the world that some *trattatisti* thought it suitable for only a few. Viperano would have barred youths from access to historical accounts because they lacked the wisdom and maturity necessary for such grave matters. Speroni went even further and would have closed all history books to the "people," since such books contained too much analysis of the working of the state. Knowledge of that kind would disturb the obedience of subjects. Only historians and leaders of communities should be permitted to read history books.

In line with the humanist idea of the relative autonomy of human affairs, the *trattatisti* never doubted that human events have order and that, except in those cases where God or fortune intervened, human actions were shaped by motives and situations. Would a knowledge of human motives, then, explain history? Patrizi thought so and set out—as many have done since then—to catalogue all possible human motives; he filled the seventh and the eighth of his

*Dialogues* with just such a list. He, like later compilers, found the list useless in explaining why specific human events occurred and why they turned out the way they did. But in his pursuit of patterns of explanation Patrizi encountered the cycle. It had been revived for all to see when Machiavelli had echoed Polybius's talk of a cycle of government. While some *trattatisti* spoke vaguely of the eternal repetition of similar events, Patrizi talked directly about a cultural cycle when he related an old Egyptian and Greek myth, which told how the world had so far been destroyed and "reborn" twice. The first destruction was wrought by war, famine, pestilence, earthquakes, floods, and fires and was followed by a thousand years of chaos, after which God recreated the world. When God had finished his reconstruction, the world moved—by its own dynamics—toward another destruction, and so on.

The *trattatisti* also pointed with pride to the long line of distinguished historians and their lists of historians even conveyed a sense of development in historiography. Atanagi, for example, noticed a decline in the historical art during the Middle Ages. Patrizi even understood that history writing was influenced intimately by the society in which it occurred, and Viperano proceeded to a critical assessment of some of past historiography. The pride in past achievements and the *trattatisti*'s sincere affection for history were reflected in Atanagi's resolute statement: "It seems to us that our life without you [history] would not only be poor and of a much diminished scale, but that, while we might still be alive, we might just as well be dead."[10]

The *trattatisti* had done well by the cause of traditional rhetorical historiography, but the imminent changes in the very structure of learning would outdate their views completely. Historians, who were soon to be forced to counter entirely new ideas on the world and its structure, would find in the *ars historica* armory an insufficient supply of intellectual arms.

*History and the radical redefinitions of methods and truth.* By the seventeenth century the *ars historica* discussions in the vein of the *trattatisti* had lost their relevance. The intellectual changes occurring and looming ahead were too radical to be contained within traditional confines. One essential force pushing for change originated in the seemingly conservative world of humanist thought. Humanists had exalted the ancient models as timeless guides but had at the same time evoked a sense of the transient nature of all human creations. Thus, on the basis of the accumulation of knowledge and the confidence derived therefrom, contemporaries eventually began to view the ancient models, too, as the products of just another, although brilliant, phase of human history. In the Battle of the Ancients and Moderns in Western literature, for example, the main arguments were that contemporary works surpassed the ancient ones because the Christian faith gave them nobler subjects and because contemporaries, having come later in human history than the Greeks and the Romans, simply had more knowledge. With growing doubts about the validity of the ancient models and with the fading of scholasticism, interpretations of the world became numerous, limited in scope, and devoid of a generally accepted authority. The confusion of views produced Pyrrhonism, a radical skepticism named after the ancient philosopher Pyrrho of Elis, which despaired of the human ability to gain any certain knowledge either through reason or the senses. Pierre Bayle tried to rescue the possibility of knowledge through the aggregation of "facts," and earlier in the 1600s, Francis Bacon and René Descartes had made more ambitious attempts to rebuild the house of knowledge. Although each of these three men ascribed a different role to history, all of them still saw the world in God's hands. Within that world, however, human phenomena represented a network of forces and bodies whose functioning did not involve God at every step. God planned, created, and governed the world and its events in a general way, but he gave much home rule to human beings. That opened the workings of the autonomous world to exploration and explanation.

For Bacon the quest for truth was no mere endeavor of curiosity; it held the promise of improving the condition of the world, even of restoring it to the condition it had been in before Adam's Fall. He advocated studying the world by the inductive method. This involved the observation of phenomena, including typical and atypical instances of every event, and then the compilation of insights in order to make possible generalizations. The "experimental philosophy," with its exclusion of speculation and system building, was quite compatible with the spirit and some of the practice of historiography. Indeed, Bacon had a well-defined place for history in his structure of knowledge (see fig. 12.1).

Figure 12.1

Bacon's Structure of Knowledge

| Functions of the mind | Correlated subjects | |
|---|---|---|
| reason | philosophy | natural history<br>memorials, annalistic narratives |
| imagination | poesy | civil history*<br>perfect histories { of time: chronicles / of persons: biographies / of single actions: narratives |
| memory | history | antiquities—physical remainders<br>    etymology, genealogy<br><br>*includes political, literary, and ecclesiastical history |

History clearly had the limited purpose of bringing together the "factual" material which could be used by philosophers and poets for formulating general insights and lessons. In a thoroughly traditional manner Bacon also kept the writing of history separate from the search for its sources (memorials and antiquities). That explains why his *History of the Reign of King Henry VII* did not employ his empiricism, which a search for sources could have partially satisfied. Instead it remained a compilation of existing accounts, refashioned in the humanist manner.

Some intellectual kinship with Bacon's views existed in the ideas propounded by Pierre Bayle late in the seventeenth century. However, his empiricism was considerably more radical than Bacon's. It centered on "facts," which Bayle viewed not as the building stones to be fitted into an edifice of generalizations by the method of induction but, rather, as the truth itself. In history "facts" put next to "facts," not subordinated to each other by induction or deduction, portrayed in their sheer aggregation the human past. Bayle demonstrated the illusions and errors of other ways of historiography, with their overall plans and meanings, in his *Historical and Critical Dictionary*. Such a view, however, ran counter to the developments of the subsequent two centuries that stressed interpretations of the whole. Only the disenchantment with overall historical explanation in the twentieth century created a favorable climate for a revival of Bayle's ideas, as in the neopositivist views of history.

Historiography was much less compatible with the views of Bacon's younger contemporary, René Descartes, who anchored his sense of certainty in human consciousness: "I think, therefore I am." That thinking "I," a part of the world of the mind, confronted the world of moving, extended bodies. In intellectual inquiries the two worlds encountered each other as the inquiring subject and the investigated object. Such inquiries would yield trustworthy knowledge and certainty if they proceeded from self-evident axioms by way of deductive reasoning and the mathematical method. That process of inquiry fitted the "real" world of abstract substances and causes but not the everyday world of smells, sounds, colors, love, and hate—the very world that historians investigated and found full of phenomena unique, unpredictable, and impervious to such deduction. Instead of using logic and mathematics, which proceeded from a few self-evident principles to more and more detailed insights, historians needed to observe and to interpret.

For such impurity historians were exiled to the fringes of the Cartesian world: to the wasteland of recording trivia and of chronicling the follies of man before Descartes. Like Aristotle before him, Descartes expelled history from the hall of philosophy, the place of proper truth and truth-seeking. In effect, he also severed history's connection with the newly emerging scientific disciplines, which found the mathematical method congenial. What then were historians to do in a Cartesian age?

*The erudite answer.* Most historians went their accustomed ways unaware of the problems that the new intellectual developments posed. Fortunately, historians without planning to do so, had been formulating over many decades a partial answer to those who doubted the truth of history. The main elements of this answer were derived from Italian humanist historiography (a rigorously critical attitude toward texts and undocumented traditions), French legal history (the importance of primary sources), and antiquarianism (the widening of the repertoire of sources to physical remains, the enlargement of subject matter to institutions and nonpolitical matters, and the cultivation of the ancillary disciplines). The use of at least some of these elements characterized a type of history best called erudite history. The cause of erudite historians is best served if not too much is claimed for them, such as their being protoscientific historians. They demonstrated that since 1400 history had overcome some important strictures of traditional historiography by relying on primary sources, by widening the scope of these sources, and by critically assessing them. When they then kept interpretation to a minimum, the erudite historians could think that they had made historiography impervious to its contemporary critics.

Shortly after 1600 two scholars, who had excelled in antiquarian studies, published their last works: the Frenchman Jacques-Auguste de Thou's *History of His Time* and the Englishman William Camden's *Annals of England in the Reign of Elizabeth*. Both books were contemporary histories, the last segments of which were withheld from publication until after the death of their authors. English historiography of the early 1600s still existed at the border shared by antiquarianism and erudite history. Sir Robert Cotton went on quietly collecting books, manuscripts, documents. Yet when he not only lent research materials to scholars but also engaged in politics he eventually paid the price of other politically active historians—imprisonment. Controversy also was the fate of John Selden, to whom Cotton's material was available. Selden, who had absorbed most of the available historical knowledge together with a knowledge of Hebrew, Arabic, and Persian, put all of it to good purpose in his *History of Tithes*. There he described, with the support of meticulous research, the practice of tithing throughout the centuries as if it were a neutral topic and not one that touched on a vital nerve in the English church. An equally learned man, Sir Henry Spelman, treated other sensitive issues in his various tracts, especially in his *History and Fate of Sacrilege*. Posthumously published, the work decried the dissolution of the monasteries by Henry VIII, an attitude contrary to the prevailing one.

More typically for erudite history, most of Selden's and Spelman's works evoked little controversy even though they revised time-honored traditions when they made readers aware that the Norman Conquest in 1066 had brought a distinct change in law and, by implication, in society. Although the two scholars spoke strictly in terms of how specific features had changed and not of a system-wide change, they came close to defining a feudal period in the English past. That made it possible, later, for others to gain a clear sense of development and an appreciation of the Middle Ages. Erudite history, however, became neglected in the decades of turmoil, until the constitutional settlement of 1688 reinvigorated erudition, a revival manifested by the works of Thomas Hearne and signaled above all by Thomas Madox's *The History and Antiquities of the Exchequer* (1711).

On the Continent a group of erudites chose a surprising topic for a critical historical investigation—the life stories of saints. Such biographies were numerous and, although often contradictory or imaginary in detail, had become, through centuries of pious reading, precious to believers. Now the Bollandists, a line of Jesuit scholars that was to span four centuries, undertook the task of purging these biographies of fanciful elements to make them immune to modern criticism. A young Jesuit professor, Herbert Rosweyde, decided to collect all the source material for each saint, to assess it critically, and then to write well-documented lives of all the saints. The calendar was to guide the sequence of work, beginning with the saints associated with January 1 and ending with those of December 31. After Rosweyde's death in 1629, John Bolland continued the project, gained the necessary material support, and secured the assistance of two excellent scholars, Godefroid Henskens and Daniel van Papenbroek. Thus began the *Acta Sanctorum*, a collective historical endeavor of unexcelled continuity, intensity, and thoroughness.

After 1670, scholars from the Benedictine congregation of St. Maur also tried to blend piety and the new criticism. Unlike the Bollandists, the Maurists had only a loose work-program centering on a new history of the Benedictine order, the stories of Benedictine saints, and critical editions of some medieval works. Actually, the brilliant Maurists who served the cause of erudition went well beyond that program. Luc D'Achery collected a substantial library and sponsored talented Maurists, among them Jean Mabillon. The latter edited with D'Achery the *Acts of the Benedictine Saints* and published documents, collections, and a liturgical history. But most important of all for historiography, Mabillon published his *De re diplomatica* (1681). This was a handbook that contained a summary of his methods of assessing medieval sources—including the internal and external criticisms of documents—and an analysis of and guide to Latin paleography. It became the trusted guide of scholars for nearly two hundred years.

The Maurists' link to the eighteenth century was Bernard de Montfaucon, who created the science of Greek paleography, edited works by Greek church fathers, and pioneered in archaeological studies. He and other French scholars were favored by a situation which saw Louis XIV's France internally peaceful and the church, secure in its position, sympathetic to intensive and prolonged critical scholarly studies. The harvest was rich. Aside from the Maurists' work, Sebastien Le Nain de Tillemont brought forth an *Ecclesiastical History of the*

*First Six Centuries* and then a corresponding *History of the Roman Emperors*. Etienne Baluze, a fervent Gallican, edited documents from the Frankish kingdom and wrote a history of the Avignon popes. Sieur Du Cange (Charles du Fresne) compiled handbooks for the study of medieval Latin and Greek that proved invaluable to historians.

## The Origin and Early Forms of American History

At a far distance from contemporary historiographical developments, the earliest histories of the new English settlements in North America were written in two dissimilar manners: one according to the biblical view of human destiny and the other as secular reporting of a collective venture in economics and politics. In the years up to 1776 the two views gradually lost their distinctiveness and yielded to the historiography of regions and colonies, with only a very few signs of a perception of a new nation on the eastern shores of the North American continent. Those who after 1600 crossed the Atlantic from England, whether they sought a more prosperous life or a safe refuge from religious persecution, carried with them a Protestant historical view of the cosmos, the ways of the English, and traditional memories of the English past. But the impact of the New World immediately began to erode that continuity as the American colonials developed their own identity. The early historical accounts by colonists showed how, with the exception of political developments, the history of England became less and less important to American settlers. They rather told about life in the strange, often harsh land and dangers from the Indians. On those matters the early historians of Virginia and New England agreed, but they differed sharply in their central aims: the Virginia histories stressed greater material well-being whereas those in New England focused on God's glory.

Virginia, the oldest of the colonies, got an early history in John Smith's *A True Relation* (1608) and later one in his *General History of Virginia, New England, and the Summer Isles* (1624). John Smith, adventurer, ex-Turkish slave, explorer, captain, and the leader who helped Jamestown survive, told the story of the settlers around Jamestown; he described how they lived, governed themselves, and worked and, in later editions, related the story of Pocahontas. Smith generally remained truthful, although, in order to encourage more English migration to Virginia, he sometimes dulled the edge of the harsh life there. Nature, so formidable a contestant, was painted as magnificent and benign.

In the northeast nature posed an even more severe challenge to a group of English Puritan Separatists—the Pilgrims—who in 1620 sailed into Massachusetts Bay and established the settlement of Plymouth. They were convinced that theirs was a sacred experience and that faith enabled them to endure severe hardships. They had despaired of life in England under Charles I and Archbishop Laud, an England they saw as doomed for her deviation from the "Lord's Path." In the new land the Pilgrims set about the work of building a new Zion (or Canaan). It would be a center of redemption, where God carried on his work. Thus, although the settlement was new, it acquired immediately a long history, one reaching back into biblical times and in which the settlers had a precise role: they were to defend the Christian faith against spiritual corruption. The Pilgrims would have agreed with John Winthrop, a Puritan outside their ranks: "Men shall say of succeeding plantations, 'the Lord make it likely that of *New England*.' For wee must consider that wee shall be as a citty upon a hill. The eies of all people are upon us."[11]

Early in the Puritan period, when William Bradford and Edward Winslow of the Plymouth community wrote their accounts of the past, they intended their narratives of the bitter struggle for survival to be read as more than adventure stories for the curious and the survival itself as more than a fortunate turn of events. Bradford's *History of Plymouth Plantation* (1646) and Winslow's *Journal of the English Plantations at Plymouth* (1622) were both records produced by governors of the colony who had intimate knowledge of the whole story: the Mayflower Compact, the terrible first winter, the explorations, settlement, crop raising, fishing, fur trading, and dealings with the Indians. All of that was bound together by the sense of historical continuity originating in the Pilgrims' faith. Divine Providence linked the brief story of a group of forlorn settlers in a wilderness with the similar story of God-fearing settlers in the time of Ancient Israel. But in Bradford's account one senses a sad awareness that the purity of the original settlement was threatened by the many newcomers, who viewed things differently from the first settlers.

The same view of history as firmly guided by God shaped the historical works of Puritans who settled in the wider Massachusetts Bay area: John Winthrop (*Journal*, 1630-49), Edward Johnson *(The Wonder-Working Providence of Zion's Saviour in New England, 1628-51)*, William Hubbard *(General History of New England to 1630)*, and Cotton Mather *(Magnalia Christi Americana)*. They described not so much the original venture but the fate of the community led by the "saints" (those believers who demonstrated their status under God's saving grace): its society, government, and daily life, the important trade relationships, the Indians, and, of course—the basis for their lives—its theology. Their accounts already reflect the settled life, in which the routine was only occasionally interrupted by the extraordinary, such as the presence of the "heretics" Roger Williams and Anne Hutchinson. Just as Bradford had already sensed the threat to Plymouth Plantation, Cotton Mather was aware of the increasing need to defend the special Puritan character of Massachusetts. In Hubbard's work, although it was intended as a defense of conservative Puritanism, the signs of weakening became clearly visible. He made no claims for New England as God's protectorate and gave no credence to special "providences" in Puritan history.

As year followed year, the settlements stabilized and each colony acquired a distinctiveness, including its own characteristic past. That consciousness now joined other incentives for producing histories: pride in one's area, people, and wealth; the desire to document a colony's rights and privileges in commerce or politics; and the wish to emulate the fashionable works of European rationalism and erudition. The original histories of sacred history and adventure were becoming outdated.

In Queen Anne's time Virginia's past was retold in a new form by Robert Beverley. Significantly, Beverley's *History of Virginia* (1705) owed its origin to the irritation he experienced when he read the manuscript of J. Oldmixon's *History of the British Empire in America* (1708) for its publisher. Its factual errors could be corrected but not Oldmixon's basic attitude of viewing the colonies as mere appendages to the mother country. Beverley's work demonstrated Virginia's loyalty to the crown, but its critical attitude toward English colonial administration also made visible the differing perspectives of the English and the English colonists.

William Byrd II, a prominent planter with an impressive library of four thousand volumes—the largest in the colonies—showed the same growing colonial self-esteem when he wrote on aspects of Virginia's past. And when William Stith, an Oxford-educated clergyman and past college president, wrote his history of Virginia (publ. 1747), he mentioned many times how the liberty of Virginians had been successfully defended against the royal governors as the representatives of the Crown. Stith also professed the erudite ideals of his European contemporaries in his wish "to give a plain and exact History of our Country, ever regarding Truth as the first requisite and principal Virtue in an Historian, and relating nothing without a sufficient Warrant and Authority."[12] Indeed, his account meticulously included so many small matters that it bored the reader and sold poorly. As a result, Stith did not carry his story beyond 1624.

New England had had its advocates among historians in Cotton Mather and, partially, in William Hubbard. In the 1700s, that area continued to be the subject of historical accounts, which now used more and more documentation. One historian tried to combine his zeal on New England's behalf with the new scientific spirit. Thomas Prince's *Chronological History of New England* (1736) strove for precision when he chose as his chronological guides the works by J. J. Scaliger and Archbishop Ussher. Prince's account, which spanned the time from the sixth day after Creation to the year 1633, told little that was new but could serve as a complete annals of New England. In encyclopedic fashion he mentioned anything of possible importance, including land grants, changes in ministers, events of church and public life, and "providences." Unfortunately, the work's merits were defeated by its tedium. It did signal, however, a radical change in perspective. The proclamation of the New Zion had been replaced by a narrative which affirmed Newton's mechanistic universe.

Prince said New England and meant most of the time Massachusetts, a fact resented by other New Englanders who wished to portray their own colony's past, apart from the past of its famous neighbor. But time was running out on colonial historiography. John Callender's Rhode Island history, with its plea to recognize that state as a religious creation, and Samuel Smith's New Jersey history were not yet touched by the growing tensions which led to the events of 1776, although Smith had already protested furiously against unjust taxation. Thomas Hutchinson told in the first volume of his history the story of Massachusetts, with full credit given to the early settlers whose religious vision, he, the Tory, did not share but respected. The author, the last English civil governor of Massachusetts, had to write the remaining volumes of his history in exile.

Another historiographical step was taken when, a quarter-century before the American Revolution, the first history appeared which conceived, though vaguely, the colonies as an entity. William Douglass, a petulant and quarrelsome Boston physician, wrote *Summary View, Historical and Political, of the British Settlements in North America* (1747-50). A curious book, it described, on the one hand, the American settlements in the broad context of the history of colonization since the Ancient Greeks and, on the other hand, relied on a schematic handbook style which put historical accounts of each colony side by side.

All along, the role of American Indians in colonial histories was neither primary nor clear. The theoretical image of Indians as people still in a state of nature yielded soon to one shaped by observation and experience. Early histories carried mostly descriptive accounts, often emphasizing Indian cruelty. Recorded failures to convert them led to interpretations which saw Indians as justly doomed for rejecting Christianity. The most realistic attempt at Indian history came from Cadwallader Colden, a physician and lieutenant-governor of New York, who tried to teach his contemporaries a lesson with his *History of the Five Indian Nations...* (1750). If the provincials thought of more than holding the present territory—and Colden clearly wished them to expand—the Iroquois were a key. They could be a strong weapon in the Anglo-French struggle for empire. A quarter of a century later, James Adair wrote a history of the Indians of the South still in the old manner, as children of nature and descendants of one of Israel's lost tribes.

# ·13·

# The Eighteenth-Century Quest
# for a New Historiography

### The Reassessment of Historical Order and Truth

In the 1700s the French public still read and enjoyed the thoroughly traditional histories by Francois Eudes de Mézeray, René Aubert de Vertot, and Gabriel Daniel, and the English public cherished the works by Sir Richard Baker and John Hughes, the work by the latter in White Kennett's version. The readers, who undoubtedly marveled at the informal and pleasant way one could by then write about the past, were scarcely aware that over the last three hundred years what had once been a unified and systematic Christian view of the past, present, and future had gradually disintegrated. The impact of the authority-shattering humanist text criticism, the encounters with the many pagan classical works, the radical revision of the image of the world in the geographical discoveries, the shaking of church authority and of faith during the Reformation, the new philosophical and scientific views of the world had done their work. In contemporary histories the Old Testament was doubted as accurate history, direct divine intervention was relegated to rare occasions, Divine Providence was reduced to a vague concept, ecclesiastical history was divorced from secular history, and the milestones of sacred history—Creation, Christ's life and death, and the expectation of the Last Judgment—were used less and less as markers in world histories by historians who increasingly preferred the theologically neutral scheme of ancient, medieval, and modern periods.

Some historians were about to assume no less of a task than to give meaning to the multitude of mundane events whose significance hitherto had been provided by Divine Providence. The patterns of progress or cycles of life they suggested became key features of the eighteenth century. And in their shadows grew yet another view of historical continuity; one that became a major theme of the nineteenth century: historicism. But even such universal historical themes as progress and the cycle were suggested by these philosophical historians in the context of national states and were modified by it—a fate shared by the discipline that seemed immune to it, erudite history.

Eighteenth-century England experienced the least need to change historical interpretations; this was the result in large part of the absence of serious social or constitutional problems under the Hanover dynasty. Writers did discuss—mostly approvingly—the importance of the Glorious Revolution of 1688 in English political history. Even David Hume, who as an empirical philosopher brought radical insights to bear on the problem of certainty and truth, used only a generally acceptable version of those views in his historical works. In the characteristic spirit of gradualism, William Robertson and Edward Gibbon combined French influence, erudition, and traditional narrative history into a new, important, and attractive type of history writing—all of it without fundamentally altering the role of history in English society.

Radically new interpretations came from the French *philosophes*, who felt keenly the discrepancy between their views and those of their society, one ruled by the Bourbon dynasty and deeply influenced by the Roman Catholic church. Against the Old Regime and all it stood for they pitted a whole array of new world-views. Some scholars saw the human universe as a mere mechanical system, repetitive and not much different from nature. The majority, however, spoke of rational individuals operating in a world where natural laws endowed and safeguarded individual rights. History showed no less than the transformation of a potentially rational mankind to an actually rational mankind—in other words, the story of progress. The view acted as a powerful leaven in the existing French society of privilege, caste, and absolutism.

The progress theory made considerable inroads into the German area, but there it would have needed for complete success the radical opposition of the *philosophes* to the established order. The German social and political situation was relatively sedate, and most historically inclined scholars fitted into it not as *literati* but as professors at universities. Also, many of the German historians taught history as members of law faculties, where caution and erudition were praised more than radical innovation. The resultant historical thought was characterized by a wealth of new ideas shaped into a less systematic form than the French progress theory. Yet in this amorphous variety can be discerned some common themes, views, and directions. Then, in the late 1700s and early 1800s, these were formed into systematic theories under the impact of the French Revolution and the Napoleonic wars by scholars who pursued the logical consequences of the intellectual innovations of the 1700s. Until that time the spectrum of historical interpretation remained wide. At one end of this spectrum stood a group of historians at the University of Göttingen who, merging German erudition, English empiricism, and French rationalism, developed attitudes and methods which were to become most influential in the creation of the nineteenth-century historical science.

On the other end could be found the theologian Johann Gottfried Herder's more theoretical response to the quest for a new order in history. He came close to creating a theory of history modeled after the patterns of organic life, including the life cycle. It would become as influential an interpretation of the link between past, present, and future as the progress theory. As for the cyclical model, it would stay on, too. After all, it had been espoused before Herder by Giambattista Vico, Jean-Jacques Rousseau (who had formulated a history of human decline), and even by some *philosophes.*

### New Views on Historical Truth

*The erudite concept of truth.* Erudite historians relied on a broad methodological base, the result of an expanding historical practice rather than of a conscious design. They maintained that truth resulted from the creative and rigorous application of their methods. In that manner and despite its lack of a systematic epistemological foundation, erudite history proved itself successful in a century with a distinct philosophical bent. It succeeded beyond expectations when it became a main ingredient of the new nineteenth-century historical science.

The French erudites remained dominant. The Maurists began the *Rerum Gallicarum et Franciscarum Scriptores,* later known as M. Bouquet's *Recueil des historiens des Gaules et de la France* (1737–86), which covered the sources of French history up to 1328. The endeavor even survived the French Revolution and was finished under the guidance of Dom Brial and under the sponsorship of the Institut de France. The Maurists E. Martène and U. Durand edited another collection of documents and texts (1724). Other eighteenth-century Maurists amplified the methodological apparatus with numerous editions of the chronological handbook *L 'Art de vérifier les dates.* Claude Robert's *Gallia Christiana* (1626; enlarged version by other Maurists, 1656), was a sophisticated accomplishment in a whole genre of inventory-type ecclesiastical histories. English antiquarianism had prompted Francis Godwin's catalogue of English bishops; Gallicanism had encouraged a similar work by Jean Cheny; and love of Italy and the church inspired Ferdinando Ughelli's impressive and influential *Italia Sacra* (1643–62).

Ughelli's contemporary, the Irish-born Franciscan Lucas Wadding, then residing in Rome, had produced an erudite study of the Franciscan order which combined glorification of the order with scholarship. Then in the eighteenth century Italian erudite history was stimulated beyond all precedent by a new appreciation of the "barbarous age," or the *Mezzi Tempi.* A profusion of antiquarian works, document collections, local histories, and ecclesiastical histories appeared—all of them permeated by the spirit of erudition, that is, history understood as a critical enterprise. The Italian erudite tradition culminated in Ludovico Antonio Muratori. Between 1723 and 1751 he produced in the quiet ducal seat of Modena the *Rerum Italicarum scriptores,* that is, editions of Italian historical documents and works; he critically edited, introduced, and annotated the *Antiquitates Italiae Medii Aevii,* a collection of documents and essays; and he produced the *Annali d'Italia,* containing a documentary account of Italian history. Their mixture of erudition and pride in the Italian past made these works exemplary for the best that erudition could deliver. A great many similar works appeared in Spain, Austria, and Scandinavia; however, none of them came too close to their model in learning and fame.

In the Protestant German area erudite history linked up with thriving legal studies during the 1600s. The latter were able to answer some baffling questions posed by the peculiar German constitutional arrangement between a shadowy imperial structure and the reality of princely, quasi-sovereign territorial states. While some German legal scholars, influenced by the contemporary natural-law theories, used history merely as a collection of *exempla* for proving a priori concepts, others took history more seriously when they explored the political and legal aspects of past German life. Those German professors began to appreciate the historical perspective on law developed by French legists of the 1500s. Hermann Conring's *About the Origin of German Law* (1643) demonstrated the resultant character of these legal historical studies: rationalist, cautious, precise, taking strict account of documents, and affirming continuity. Even Samuel Pufendorf, the theorist of natural law, recognized that law was at least partially a human creation. In the end the works of these legal historians proved more important to the further development of historiography than did contemporary attempts to edit and publish German sources.

Erudite historians served historiography in another way. When after 1650 learned societies sprang up all over Europe, historians found their place in most of them because erudite history had given them a claim to citizenship in the *mundus scientificum*. Historians participated in the French Academy, the Academie des Inscriptions, the Lincei, the Accademia della Crusca, the Royal Society of London, the new Society of Antiquaries, and in many similar associations. These societies fostered enthusiasm for learning and also stressed the utilitarian aspect of knowledge, its ability to enhance human mastery of the world. History could offer advice on how to manage public affairs. Only when some societies eventually embraced the ideal of "pure" science was history found lacking in proper credentials.

These scholarly associations constituted a world apart from the world of daily life, and historical works produced for learned societies usually found few readers beyond the membership. Rousseau's widely acclaimed essay on the negative effect of civilization was definitely an exception. Most of the works were technically well-done essays on local history, genealogy, and legal questions, or on topics issued as themes for competitions. The Academy of Munich listed as proper activities for historians the collection and edition of sources, work in chronology, genealogy, and constitutional history, the weeding out of fables, and finding the true histories of monasteries and of rights and privileges of cities. And, of course, the quality of work done varied from society to society and from member to member.

At first glance historians also did well at the universities, where they were employed on the faculties of liberal arts (teaching classical and universal history in the context of eloquence), of theology (teaching church history) and of law (lecturing on legal and political history). But with few exceptions they did not engage in the formulation of new interpretations of the past or in the erudite cultivation of sources. In academic institutions students were taught the products but not the "doing" of history. Universities aimed to produce good servants of the state and the church, and to that purpose history contributed useful knowledge as well as practical and moral lessons. Thus, while the historical aspect of human life was known and taught, history as an attempt to explain human existence was yet to be born. Hence the absence of a teaching subject called, simply, history and of research as a necessary ingredient of the study of history.

In this connection developments at the University of Göttingen took on special significance. The close connection of history with law had been building since the French legists of the sixteenth century and, by the 1700s, was institutionally manifested at other universities, such as the University of Edinburgh. But the link between law and history understood in terms of erudition, always the natural bridge between the two disciplines, assumed a special quality at Göttingen. Its full implications will be spelled out later; a few examples must suffice here. At Göttingen historical scholars still cultivated sources and published them, as did August Ludwig von Schlözer, who translated sources, including the Russian *Chronicle of Nestor*. Johann Christoph Gatterer worked out a sophisticated methodology. But there erudition also transcended its boundaries and produced histories that integrated critical source studies with narrative history, for example, Johann Mascov's famous works on German history. That step made these professors the true pioneers of nineteenth-century German historical science.

*A new historical concept of truth.* In 1725, Giambattista Vico, a Neapolitan professor of rhetoric who was hoping for a better-paid chair in law, published the first edition of his *New Science*. This work gave to historians not new methods but a full-fledged theory of history, including proper methods of truthfinding. He denied the Cartesian assumption that reason alone—employing philosophy, mathematics, and physics—yielded essential truth and that phenomena not accessible to those disciplines, such as the subject matter of history, were simply of no consequence. He also rejected the contemporary preference for the study of nature and its methods, based as it was on the assumption that nature was more accessible to understanding than human affairs. It was altogether wrong to concentrate on "the study of the world of nature, which, since God made it, He alone knows; and that they [the philosophers] should have neglected the study of the world of nations, or civil world, which since men had made it, men could come to know."[1] The *factum* (what man creates) was the *verum* (the true); or, in other words, human beings understood more profoundly that which they have made *(factum)* than that which they simply confront (divinely created nature). Human history was inherently understandable because all human beings experienced the hopes, fears, efforts, deeds, and wishes which entered into human events; they forever remained "outsiders" to nature, though.

What had been seen as a fixed human nature throughout time and was still affirmed by many contemporaries was really made and remade in the course of human events; and historians could understand the changes. At the core of Vico's work stood the assertion that large-scale changes in the collective frame of mind were the great events in cultural history. He demonstrated, for example, how such large-scale collective changes made one age speak through epics and myths while another produced rational discourses. Viewed in that perspective, mathematics was no timeless instrument to grasp timeless truth but just another time-bound ingredient of various world views. In an ultimate reversal the historian could understand mathematics and its role but the mathematician could not grasp history.

The lessons of Vico on the truth value of history were direct but took a long time to be acknowledged by historians. The philosophy of Vico's older contemporary, Gottfried Wilhelm Leibniz, dealt only indirectly with the practice of history but it affected views on history. Leibniz's fundamental view of the world as a system of self-contained monads, which developed in preestablished harmony, in and by itself hardly offered much assistance to German historians. Its implications, however, were important. The world developed constantly and with an aim towards completeness and beauty. With God as the world's entelechy, religion, although within rational bounds, became once more a force in human life to be affirmed and not rejected. The supposition that every monad, unique as it was, reflected the whole universe suggested a dialectical relationship between part and whole. That relationship would serve as a basis for the refusal to see the general (or universal) as separable from or superior to the individual aspect of life and for the insistence on viewing the general and the individual as co-joined in every phenomenon. From there a clear line led to the assertion that historical study must concentrate on the actual and unique event or person. One must, for example, not study "war" but must strive to understand specific wars. Each war, indeed every historical phenomenon, represented a complex and unique conjunction of forces. Hence the result of a historical inquiry can never be general laws, only a description and explanation of individual persons and events. The complex interaction of the general or typical with the individual or specific also made the retracing of human history into more than a search for simple cause-and-effect relationships. A "one cause—one effect" pattern was rarely encountered in human life.

All of these implications took nearly a century to exert their full impact on historiography. When Leibniz himself wrote history, he stayed within rather traditional bounds. For him the main issue in history's theory and methodology was still the accurate and critical study of sources rather than theories of interpretations. After all, "in mathematics one must depend on reason, in nature on experiments, in laws divine and human on authority, and in history on witnesses."[2] Such an approach appealed to the Göttingen professors of law and history. Still, they and Johann Gottfried Herder groped their way toward and perceived— as yet hazily—a soon-to-be-prominent historical method of interpretation; the *anschauende Erkenntnis* (the intuitive grasping of insights), later called *Verstehen* (understanding). Even in its vague eighteenth-century version it was meant to go beyond the mere accumulation of facts by erudites and to be a counterweight to the simple cause-effect schemes gleaned from the developing sciences as well as to the rationalist approaches of the philosophes. The intuitive approach aimed to comprehend the complex intertwining of forces as dynamic wholes and also at making explanations possible which denied neither the value of individuality nor the world of the spirit with its free decisions, customs, values, ideas, and little mechanical predictability. In that connection the German scholars encountered the "understanding" of which Vico had spoken earlier. By the late 1700s, they had put in place some basic concepts of an emerging school of thought: historicism.

### New Grand Interpretations: Progress in History

Few interpretations of history have captivated the minds of the multitude to the extent that the theory of progress has. Its central message declared that "the whole human race, through alternate periods of rest and unrest, of weal and woe, goes on advancing, although at a slow pace, towards greater perfection."[3] Past, present, and future were once more linked in a development with a common direction; this time not toward a spiritual goal but toward human betterment in this world. And it was this hope which proved to be the powerful persuader. Actually, with the exception of the Marquis de Condorcet's *Sketch for a Historical Picture of the Progress of the Human Mind* (1793–94), no one work proclaimed and explained the concept of progress. Rather progress was proposed, debated, and praised in many works, and belief in it became sustained less by an agreed-upon theory than by a broadly shared expectation.

*History as the emancipation of mankind.* The progress view had a firm support in the conviction of many eighteenth-century intellectuals that mankind had matured sufficiently to take its destiny into its own hands. God created the universe, set the orderly system of causes in motion, and from then it moved in Newtonian orderliness by itself. With the world rationally ordered and beneficent in essence, everything destructive in it was declared to be "unnatural" and remediable. Similarly, human beings were seen as basically good and not as inherently sinful. In turn, human goodness was firmly anchored in human ra-

tionality; both qualities were extant even in the distant past, when strong
passions and instincts together with the forces of the environment had suppressed
them temporarily. On that basis some philosophes proceeded to demonstrate the
story of human progress, that is, the gradual liberation of rationality from
bondage throughout the centuries and the civilizing of mankind resulting from
it. The unity of mankind's destiny was no longer vouchsafed by the common
descent from Adam and Eve but by the presence of reason in its every member,
and its development bore no longer the marks of Divine Providence but those of
the emancipation of rationality from error and superstition.

The philosophes had to reconcile the immense diversity of the world's
peoples with their view of a uniform and unchanging human nature. In taking on
that task they relied on the new concept of culture or civilization which had
eluded the sixteenth-century legists and historians when they had confronted
the diversity of peoples and customs. The philosophes could draw on the insights
proposed by the so-called *Histoire raisonnée*. Between 1660 and 1720, its
representatives had stressed the idea that sets of customs needed to be studied
and then compared with each other. When François de Fénelon had exhorted
historians to study the change of customs in time he very nearly had formulated
the charge Voltaire took up. In his *Essay on the Manners, Customs, and the
Spirit of Nations* (1754), Voltaire formulated the cultural interpretation of
history precisely and elegantly. After sympathetically treating the Chinese,
Indian, Persian, and Islamic civilizations, he nevertheless held fast to a universal
human progress, thereby affirming, for him, the obvious contemporary superiority of the West. These historians found the solution to the problem of the diversity of cultures in the concept of the uneven development of uniform human
nature. Westerners differed from the Chinese, Africans, or Indians not intrinsically but solely because of the greater progress of their rationality; the lag was
caused by the irrational forces still gripping the other societies, above all by oppressive religions, laws, and customs. The same held true for the differences
within Western societies where rationality increased first in the minds of a few
with the masses lagging temporarily behind. And if, as Voltaire and some others
maintained, the majority of people might never become fully rational in thought
and behavior, those who were fully civilized could design good laws and offer
good government for the masses. As a result, all people would partake in rationality's ultimate blessing—happiness.

By necessity, the price of the new historical order, with its progress and
perfect future, was a lack of appreciation of the very diversity which originally
had fascinated the philosophes. In his *Essay* Voltaire discussed the past views
and habits of various peoples sympathetically but still at a far distance from our
present understanding of civilizations or cultures. When, after 1770, the term
"civilization" did appear, it referred to a style of life with refined tastes and
manners, presumably brought about by the increase of rationality. Our present
contention that all civilizations or cultures constitute equally valid ways of life

would have been scoffed at by Voltaire and other *philosophes.* True happiness could not come to people with "uncivilized" views and customs but only to those with a rational mode of life.

The assertion of progress also devalued the earlier stages of the Western world, which were at best periods of human childhood, at worst periods of folly and superstition. That very attitude showed in the philosophes' laments about the Middle Ages. To them these centuries, dominated by the Christian religion, constituted a regrettable interruption of the liberation of reason which the ancients had gotten underway.

> The kings without any authority, the nobles without any constraint, the peoples enslaved, the countryside covered with fortresses and ceaselessly ravaged, wars kindled between city and city, village and village, penetrating, so to speak, the whole mass of the kingdoms; all commerce and all communications cut off; the towns inhabited by poor artisans enjoying no leisure; the only leisure which some men still enjoy lost in the idleness of a nobility scattered here and there in their castles who do nothing but engage in battles which are useless to the fatherland; the grossest ignorance extending over all nations and all occupations! An unhappy picture—but one which was only too true of Europe for several centuries![4]

And while Turgot and Montesquieu considered the medieval church's enhancement of learning at least one redeeming feature, most others condemned institutional religion as superstition and considered medieval history excellent proof for Condorcet's judgment that history was "man's confession" of past superstitions and fanaticisms.

Those more ardent about progress than the somewhat skeptical Voltaire were revolutionaries in historical interpretation. For centuries the past as tradition had guided human actions in the present and human hopes for the future. Now, in a total reversal, the expectations for the future governed the life of the present and the evaluation of the past.

*Propellants and patterns of progress.* As the philosophes saw it, progress fought against nearly impossible odds. Throughout the centuries the forces of darkness, error, and vice had held a tight grip on mankind. Reason managed to assert itself against such odds, Turgot argued, because the blindly surging human passions led to superstitions and errors, and the unhappiness they produced in turn stimulated the progress of rationality. But now that reason had become strong, errors and superstitions were no longer needed as stimuli and hence must be combated vigorously. Condorcet proclaimed his time to be the historic turning point precisely because the main weapon against error had been found: "Having long been engaged in pondering the means of improving man's fate, I have not been able to avoid the conclusion that there is actually only one such means: the speeding of the progress of enlightenment."[5] The human mastery of the social realm would follow the already highly advanced mastery of nature much as the advance of the moral (social) sciences followed that of the natural sciences. For Condorcet the liberation of mankind from the "tyrannies" of nature and irrational social authority was inevitable, because rationality once set on its victorious course asserted itself against all obstacles. When human beings had begun to order chaotic sensations into comprehensive thought, they had initiated the progress of the mind. This progress would culminate in the final Tenth Epoch when the "social art" would triumph over everything standing in the way of social harmony. History, besides being the human confession of past errors, also spurred hope for such a future when it told of the ideal state of affairs to come.

> How welcome to the philosopher is this picture of the human race, freed
> from all its chains, released from the domination of chance and from that
> of the enemies of its progress, advancing with a firm and sure step in the
> path of truth, virtue, and happiness! How this spectacle consoles him for the
> errors, crimes, and injustices that still defile the earth, of which he is often
> the victim! It is in the contemplation of this picture that he finds the reward
> for his efforts on behalf of the progress of reason and the defense of liberty.[6]

In all of that, the philosophes ascribed an ambiguous role to the natural and social environments. On the one hand reason had its own liberating dynamics while on the other hand environmental stimuli played a significant role in human progress. Thus, Condorcet and Turgot agreed that the improvement in the means of communication had helped the growth of knowledge by provoking more and more innovations. Condorcet even granted that, in the late stages of progress, liberty, equality, secular and enlightened government, property, and peace were necessary for further progress, although, quite clearly, such a social environment presupposed rational people as its shapers. In general however, the influence of the physical environment became weaker the stronger human rationality grew; that held true despite the age's fascination with the shaping force of climate. Montesquieu had elaborated on the role of climate, and Turgot mused that large-scale climatic changes might have caused past changes in government.

According to Condorcet the march of history had slowed down at times but could never aim anywhere else but "forward." Those writing before him had not been so sure. Turgot admitted temporary delays in human progress and gave it a spiral-like path towards the desired goal. "Empires rise and fall; laws and forms of government succeed one another; the arts and the sciences are in turn discovered and perfected, in turn retarded and accelerated in their progress; and they are passed on from country to country."[7] Emile Deschamps envisioned steep rises alternating with plateaus, evoking the image of steps in a huge staircase. Others tempered their optimism more severely when they pointed out the unpredictability of life, where a single battle could truly change the course of events. Condillac and D'Alembert spoke of peaks of civilized existence alternating with plainly barbaric periods: "Barbarism lasts for centuries and seems to be our natural condition, while reason and good taste are destined to pass away."[8] Voltaire, whose own rationalism never persuaded him that all people would ever behave rationally, pointed to mankind's up-and-down development: the civilized Ancient period, the barbaric Middle Ages, the recovery of civilization in the Renaissance followed by a quick rebarbarization in the Reformation, and another recovery in the French civilization of Louis XIV's period. Inevitable progress was by no means an item of faith for every philosophe.

*History's role.* While philosophes spoke of progress in terms of advances in human learning and morality, most of them were also convinced that any increase in rationality would be matched by a commensurate increase in happiness. In Condorcet's Tenth Epoch of history the conditions for happiness—peace, justice, flourishing commerce, and equality between peoples and nations—resulted from the triumph of reason as manifested in an ever-increasing knowledge, cooperative scholarship, and education. And what could history contribute to so favorable a development besides being "man's confession" of errors?

The philosophes did not study the past just in order to understand it on its own terms. They mustered little sympathy for the erudites, with their love for the patient exploration of past experience through documents and without didactic purpose. Montesquieu called them "compilers who have little to say" and Voltaire told them that not everything happening was worth knowing. History must teach the progressive enlightenment of mankind, and through it become one of the instruments of progress. In his *Age of Louis XIV* Voltaire spoke of history's cleansing property, since the "history of human stupidity" could bring people to recognize and acknowledge past errors. Thus in his own otherwise quite traditional *History of Charles XII* life should teach kings "how much a peaceful and happy rule is superior to so much glory."[9] Even the story of the Middle Ages could teach readers, when it shocked them with those "errors and superstitions" which Voltaire and others found so painful to report. But texts with such lessons would only be useful if people read them willingly, even eagerly, and so the philosophes strove for eloquence and elegance in their writing. Voltaire succeeded better than others and fame became his reward, although he rarely was as original a thinker as other philosophes. Actually an Englishman best expressed the attitude of the philosophes toward history, when he quoted Dionysius of Halicarnassus: "History is philosophy teaching by examples."[10]

*Dissent from progress.* When eighteenth-century scholars rejected the orthodox Christian views on the course of history they did not simply affirm random change. Their new order for the world acquired continuity through progress. But there were philosophes who rejected the optimistic view of development. Jean-Jacques Rousseau regretted the increase in rationality, achieved in isolation from all other human faculties, particularly emotion. A long time ago, in the state of nature, reason, passion, and emotion were of a whole and even the instinct of self-preservation strengthened natural cooperation and morality. Then, in a sort of Fall of Man, things changed. Property, hierarchy, and self-love appeared and worked to the detriment of concern for others. The human being acquired an external aspect, a false, deceptive, pretentious, and hence evil wish to impress others, and this aspect was alienated from the internal aspect, the true self. Culture was the product and producer of that alienation, one ever more enhanced by the development of reason in isolation from other parts of the psyche. With culture thus rooted in vice rather than in virtue, the story of mankind was the story of decadence.

The materialists among the philosophes simply had no use for history, with or without progress. Human beings were merely complex animals, governed by the desire to gratify their needs in order to find happiness. At all times human life was the same story of need and gratification and attraction and repulsion. In such a mechanistic world the advance of science, history included, was irrelevant to human happiness. The world of La Mettrie, Holbach, and Helvetius knew only a chain of causation, not free will, providence, God, progress, or immortality. History could teach no useful lessons about such a world of nature to human beings bound by nature's dictates.

From an entirely different viewpoint, the Scot David Hume rejected all talk about a benevolent universe and progress. He insisted that all the order we observe around us—causality, for example—was really a habit of the human mind rather than an expression of an order inherent in phenomena. Hence neither the presuppositions of science nor the metaphysics of reason can be accepted as reflecting reality. Historical viewpoints, the progress view included, also were private matters. Hume wanted historians to rely on a cautious empiricism without grand schemes, although he himself asserted the highly theoretical concept of an unchanging human nature. The doubters and opponents of progress had their followers, but Condorcet's optimism lured the majority. The message of progress evoked enthusiasm and hope. Behind the ups and downs of empires, states, wars, and nations, there was the steady advance of the natural and moral sciences. These sciences would defeat the twin evils: ignorance and the caprice of will. In Condorcet's Tenth Epoch, beginning in the late 1700s, public schools, social mathematics (for calculating the consequences of actions), and the "social art" (social science) would guarantee the infinite perfection of the human condition, with happiness as the automatic result. With Christian universal history in disarray, the West had acquired in the progress theory a new and viable synthesis of past, present, and future.

### New Grand Interpretations: The Cyclical Pattern

*Giambattista Vico: God and the cultural cycle.* When in the early 1700s Giambattista Vico formulated his grand cyclical vision of history, he based it on his anti-Cartesian view of human beings as not purely rational and as members of groups, not as isolated individuals. Since, as was already shown, Vico denied that the natural sciences could explain human phenomena, he set out to create a "new science" which could shed light on the developments in collective life. It turned into an investigation of the whole human past in terms of the life cycles of nations. All of these cycles followed one unvarying pattern, the *storia eterna ideale*, with three successive stages: the eras of gods, of heroes, and of men. Vico considered that basic pattern to have been designed by Divine Providence.

Vico, a devout and traditional Christian, preserved an essential part of Christian historiography when he treated the Old Testament's story, until the end of the Flood, as an accurate narrative. But from the time of the descendants of Noah on, a different human history began that no longer was identical with Jewish history. In the two hundred years after the Flood, human beings lost the facility for human speech, lacked all social institutions, wandered around as "horrible, stupid brutes," and gratified their drives without inhibitions and shame, until events occurred which launched them into a civilized life.

Vico's "brutes" did not suddenly conclude a social contract, as some contemporary natural-law theoreticians supposed, but created civilization gradually. As the earth dried up, excessive evaporation led to fierce thunderstorms. Their frightful thunderclaps brought to early people experiences of terror, fear, and particularly sexual shame, which prompted the brutes to reflect upon the world; as they did, they began to tame their impulses. When they buried their dead, regulated sex, and introduced formal worship, they took the first steps toward providing for a time span longer than the immediate present and created the basis for the three fundamental social institutions of burial, marriage, and religion. On these three pillars human society (we would say civilization) was built.

In the first stage of human civilization, the age of gods, the stern rules and rites were seen by people as directly ordained by the gods; a necessary conviction because divine authority alone could impose a new order. In a decisive interpretation, Vico saw that new order not only shaping the social institutions but the total collective consciousness. The natural social bonds, particularly the family, epic poetry, myths as explanations, authority resting in the heads of families, divinely sanctioned law, piety, and even a basic cruelty were no mere accidental collection of characteristics but necessary expressions of the new order. And so it was with the stages and heroes and of men. Each of them had its own structure, its own collective consciousness—its cultural climate, so to speak—which colored laws, politics, marriage, religion, poetry, in short, all human actions and institutions (see fig. 13.1). Vico had discovered the concept of culture as a systematic whole. All of that did not suggest to Vico an autonomous human world with self-regulating mechanisms but rather order and design due to Divine Providence; in biblical times the workings of that providence could be observed directly but now that it worked more subtly, by directing human feelings, passions, and reason, it needed to be studied indirectly through its manifestations.

**Figure 13.1**
**Vico's Three Stages of Civilization**

| | Age of | | |
|---|---|---|---|
| | 1. Gods | 2. Heroes | 3. Men |
| General Character | prehistoric primitive culture = period of infancy | beginning of civil/political state = period of youth | society structured according to reason and with justice for all= mature rational stage |
| Crucial social form | family (natural bonds) | state (politics) | commonwealth (voluntary civic duty) |
| Explanation of change | actions of divine, supernatural beings; all nature animated by spirits; characteristic attitudes are awe, reverence before supreme powers | actions of semidivine heroes; introduction of civilizing measures; lawgivers and founders of cities | actions of ordinary human beings who discover their powers; doubt of previous myths and heroes; the past is reinterpreted to be more palatable to logic and reason |
| Language | poetic, metaphorical; poets shape minds | military speech; "heroic blazonings" | logical, rational concepts; age of prose; philosophical-scientific character; vernacular languages |
| Records | age of myth; oral narratives concerning the nature of gods and their relations with man | age of bards; poets relate deeds of heroes | tell of exploits of even ordinary people |
| Politics | theocratic (ruler is voice of God); aristocracies of fathers (sovereign family kings) | heroic/aristocratic; those most powerful govern, still by divine right | people as source of power; democratic government, equal rights; nevertheless monarchy |
| Human nature | fierce, cruel | militant | modest, benign, reasonable |
| Law | divine origins | law of force but still controlled by religion; only force keeps force within bounds | human (dictated by reason) open process of law-making; no longer aura of secrecy |
| Customs | religious, pious | choleric and punctilious | dutiful (sense of civil duty) |

Vico valued each of the three stages equally. Those enamored by progress would value the third, the humanistic stage, as the highest and assume that it would last forever; not so Vico. As a flower begins its decay in the midst of its glorious bloom so do human societies decline in the age of men. Decadence sets in when human rational powers are strongest, justice reaches the greatest number of people, civic duty substitutes for mere obedience to law, humans feel free and strong, logic prevails in reasoning and prose in literature, science explains nature, and equal rights sustain democracies. In a paradoxical way human achievements defeat themselves. The age of men brings urbanization and with it the "disease of the cities" with its symptoms: an excessive individualism which leads to "the custom of each man thinking only of his own private interests and [in which people] have reached the extreme of delicacy or, better, of pride, in which like wild animals they bristle and lash out at the slightest displeasure."[11] A kind of thought is cultivated which erodes society's existing foundations (piety, acceptance of authority, and faith) without providing any new support for them. It all leads to a lack of civic sense and eventually to civil unrest. There follows, then, either a conquest by more cohesive people or an absolute monarch or a sinking deeper and deeper into a new barbarism. The fact that these people on the decline had once learned how to reflect makes the new barbarism only more vicious than the original one. The people will live "like wild beasts in a deep solitude of spirit and will; scarcely any two beings will be able to agree, since each follows his own pleasure or caprice."[12]

Could any society escape the cycle? Only if it accepted a halt to its own development, as in the case of the American Indians with the coming of the white man, of the Carthaginians with their destruction by the Romans, and of a few other societies which were barred from development altogether by an unfavorable climate. Otherwise the completion of the *corso* was relentless, to be followed after a few hundred years by a new beginning, the *ricorso*.

*The cycle and the* philosophes. The concept of a cultural cycle even occupied a modest niche in the edifice of the French Enlightenment. It was gleaned from ancient works and from organic life and was never systematically elaborated in the manner of Vico. It also never matched the popularity of the progress interpretation of history, missing as it did the promise of permanent rationality and happiness. Turgot, for example, was not perturbed by the coming and going of empires because, as he saw it, that fact did not impede the progress of knowledge and rationality. In comparison, the advocates of a cyclical theory sounded outright melancholy.

> There is a cycle determined for all moral things as for all natural phenomena— a cycle of birth, growth, maturity, decline, and death. So it is with the days from morning to evening, with the years in their solar revolution, with the life of man from cradle to grave, and with the course of states from their foundation to their demise.[13]

Progress was indeed a part of human life, but it was neither inevitable nor permanent.

> The fate which rules the world wills that everything should pass away. The happiest state of an individual or a nation has its limits. Everything carries within itself a hidden germ of destruction.[14]

> Almost all the nations of the world travel this circle: they begin with being barbarians; then they become conquerors and well-ordered nations; this order permits them to grow, and they become refined: refinement enfeebles them, and they return to barbarism.[15]

And as if the progress theoreticians had said enough about the time of prosperity, eighteenth-century proponents of the cyclical view talked less about the upward phase of the cycle but more about its downswing. The fall of Rome, already a feature in some works since the Renaissance, came now to be the center piece of the cyclical theories. Montesquieu, who investigated the various influences that shaped a state, found the reasons for the decline of Rome in internal forces, excessive luxury, and the failure to adjust the republican legal system to the needs of an empire. The empirical Montesquieu shunned ideas of universal progress as unwarranted by historical evidence and even connected the fate of learning with that of political power; they rose and fell together. Most other French proponents of the cyclical view also singled out luxury, with its corrosion of vigor and morals, as the culprit. A few philosophes blamed the foes of reason—the emotions, superstitions, and human passions—for the decline of societies. As for the possibility of escaping the cultural cycle—there was none. In connection with the political fate of nations Montesquieu observed that "however perfect [a government] may appear in theory, in practice and in the hands of men it will always be subject to revolutions and vicissitudes. Finally, as long as it is men that govern men, even the best government will destroy itself."[16] Little help could be gained from intensive studies of past cycles since the observable external forces, the Abbé Dubos thought, were just the particular agents of a destruction that was predestined. Montesquieu, who made an extensive analysis of the human past, had to admit that the array of possible reasons for a civilization's decay was simply as wide as life itself. The basic forces will remain unknown. The French adherents of the cyclical view found history to resemble a kaleidoscope with ever-new configurations of the same materials; or as one of them expressed it: "In the morning both man and plant appear and in the evening they are no more. Everything disappears and is replaced; but nothing perishes."[17]

# ·14·

# Three National Responses

## The British Blend of Erudition, Elegance, and Empiricism

Much has been made of the French influence, particularly that of Voltaire, on English and Scottish thought. But British historians filtered its rationalism carefully so that it blended well with their other concerns: a commonsense empiricism, a preference for the gradual change of institutions to radical changes patterned after abstract schemes, an appreciation for the critical use of sources, and a love of good writing. Nothing in eighteenth-century England and Scotland jarred those attitudes. Historiography remained a national craft in the best sense of the word.

*Progress in the English mode.* Hope for the future was present but not as the assertion of abstract schemes of progress. David Hume was typical when he based his hope on the English-style liberty affirmed by the constitutional solution following the Glorious Revolution of 1688. Opposed to speculative interpretations of the course of history and seeing only endless change in the many discrete events of human life, he suggested in his *History of England* (1763) that the Whigs were wrong in their assertion of an ancient constitution whose guarantee of liberty simply was affirmed over and over again, and also in the more recent belief in liberty as a gift of nature and reason. The seventeenth-century Stuarts could not have violated an ancient constitution because there never had been one. To the empirically minded Hume, the English way of life had been shaped by many influences, often accidentally and never according to a plan. Thus, history only showed how an unchanging human nature was shaped variously under the impact of specific conditions. Such an empirical attitude, including the recognition of royal prerogatives as well as a divorce of religious from secular affairs, would secure the English constitution better than tradition. This mixture of ahistorical thought with a sense of development yielded a surprisingly good history. Hume was praised by Edward Gibbon as the "Tacitus of Scotland," and his *History* dominated the field until that of Thomas B. Macaulay found greater favor. Its innovative organization of the material according to reigns of English kings and the exact citing of material taken from sources remained lasting features.

Another Scot, William Robertson, was still willing to affirm progress in history. But as a devout Presbyterian who could easily share the philosophes' tendency to speak in universal terms, he still avowed a divine plan for history. "Sacred" history dealt with the plan directly when it drew aside "that veil which covers the councils of the Almighty," leaving civil history free to explore the "revolutions of human affairs."[1] In these affairs God worked indirectly, often using wars, follies, cruelty and other surprising means to effect his ends. Since Robertson had no doubt that God's goal coincided with that of the philosophes in the refinement of the human race, he, too, could condemn the Middle Ages. Medieval features such as the Crusades, were, however, not follies because they were religious but because they manifested Christianity in an outdated form. Even more recent events, particularly the European wars of Charles V's time showed a rational plan behind events. These wars fostered human progress since "it was during his [Charles V's] administration that the powers of Europe were formed into a one great political system," in short a balance of power.[2]

Robertson's success (achieved against Hume's advice not to write on topics which were dry, barren, and without charm) was significant because it was gained without relenting on the use of sources. History of great erudition could be written eloquently. Even his later concern with comparative history of cultures did not reduce his popularity. In his *History of America,* he extended his empathy even to the "primitive" people, the American Indians, and wished them to be a part of every world history. His empathy for other periods and people led Robertson into comparative history when he searched for and found similarities between the old Germans and the American Indians. After all, an ancient "tribe of savages on the banks of the Danube must be very much like a tribe on the plains of the Mississippi River."[3]

*An English view of decadence.* Edward Gibbon's six-volume *Decline and Fall of the Roman Empire* was published in the years between the American Revolution and the French Revolution. Fulfilling an ideal Gibbon shared with his age, the work was "very well received by men of letters, men of the world, and even by fine feathered Ladies."[4] Gibbon succeeded in fusing erudition and its admirable products with eloquence and elegance of style. Most readers, however, agreed with Gibbon's preference for the first three volumes, on Rome's history until A.D. 476, to those whose subject matter were the "barbarians" and the second Rome in the East, the Byzantine Empire.

Gibbon asked why Rome declined but gave his answer in an intricate narrative rather than through a simple formula for the growth and decay of human institutions. The contrast between the glorious Rome of Augustus and the

shadowy Rome of Augustulus (the puppet ruler who disappeared in A.D. 476)
distressed him personally, since he admired the Roman Empire at its peak: "If
a man were called to fix the period in the history of the world during which the
condition of the human race was most happy and prosperous, he would, without hesitation, name that which elapsed from the death of Domitian to the
accession of Commodus."[5] Why then did so great a state fall so low? Gibbon
who disdained theories, pieced his evidence together step by step:

> The rise of a city, which swelled into an empire, may deserve, as a singular
> prodigy, the reflection of a philosophic mind. But the decline of Rome was
> the natural and inevitable effect of immoderate greatness. Prosperity
> ripened the principle of decay; the causes of destruction multiplied with the
> extent of conquest; and as soon as time or accident had removed the arti-
> ficial supports, the stupendous fabric yielded to the pressure of its own
> weight. The story of its ruin is simple and obvious; and instead of enquiring
> why the Roman Empire was destroyed, we should rather be surprised that
> it had subsisted so long. The victorious legions, who, in distant wars ac-
> quired the vices of strangers and mercenaries, first oppressed the freedom of
> the republic, and afterwards violated the majesty of the Purple. The emper-
> ors, anxious for their personal safety and the public peace, were reduced to
> the base expedient of corrupting the discipline which rendered them alike
> formidable to their sovereign and to the enemy; the vigour of the military
> government was relaxed, and finally dissolved, by the partial institutions of
> Constantine; and the Roman world was overwhelmed by a deluge of Bar-
> barians.[6]

Added to that must be Gibbon's conviction that Christianity's otherworldliness,
with its celibacy and pacifism, subverted Roman strength; an indictment inhabitants of the late Roman Empire had never failed to spell out.

Gibbon shared with Montesquieu the idea of a central virtue at the core of
each type of state, a virtue which, when eroded, leads to collapse; he also
believed in the connection (going back to Bruni) of liberty with creativity and
vitality. Gibbon followed these precepts into the smallest details of late Roman
history, not quite researching but carefully consulting good secondary sources.
While his topic helped to push aside all simplistic theories of progress, Gibbon
himself had vague notions that every age increased the wealth, happiness, and
even virtues of the human race. Thus the fall of Byzantium in 1453 finished the
story of Rome but was accompanied by the promise of a renewed Western culture.

## Enlightenment Historiography in a German Key

The German word for Enlightenment, *Aufklärung*, recalls the distinctiveness
of the eighteenth-century German intellectual and literary world, strong French
rationalist influences notwithstanding. In the same way as the French term,

*Aufklärung* does not refer to a uniform school of thought but to a broad range of shared ideas and themes. Among the scholars of the *Aufklärung* a group of Göttingen professors and the philosopher Immanuel Kant exerted a special influence on historiography.

*A sense of complexity.* The French proponents of progress were transfixed by rationality's upward development throughout the centuries as the force which pushed mankind across the obstacles posed by ignorance, passions, and superstitions towards a great future. In contrast, the *Aufklärer* viewed and treated reason not as an isolated force but in the context of the total human personality; there reason joined emotions and passions, both of which were acknowledged as positive forces and not simply as obstacles to rationality. After all, most great deeds in history would have remained undone except for passions. And against those French philosophes who held that human beings were integral parts of nature—seen functioning as a mechanical system with iron-clad necessity— the *Aufklärer* held out for a world in which nature did not encompass everything. In the human realm acts of free will merged with the impulses from the world of necessity to produce a complexity inaccessible to simple explanations. That view owed much to Immanuel Kant, whose works influenced German historiography during the *Aufklärung* by his views on history and, a century later, when fervent attempts were made to gain for history a theoretical base independent of that of the natural sciences, by his epistemology.

Kant stayed closer than most German scholars to the French view of history as an emancipation of reason. He envisaged it as a progress toward the still remote triumph of the highest good, manifested by universal peace, a rational religion, and freedom under law, when the moral would become natural; it was also the maturation of human reason to a point where it could explicate itself and actively support progress. Yet, even after the maturation of reason progress would still result from a complex interplay between the world of human freedom and that of nature, the realm of necessity. Human beings needed to associate with others, and they tried to build freely and consciously a harmonious society, while at the same time they were subject to the natural desire to satisfy their selfish goals. Paradoxically that natural desire also drove human beings to sociability and in the process limited itself. Kant called the phenomenon the "social insociability" and thought it enhanced the development toward a better society. "All cultures, art, which adorns mankind, and the finest social order, are the fruits of insociability, which is forced by itself to discipline itself."[7] In this case the world of nature, that is, of necessity, unwittingly enhanced the world of freedom, not smoothly or automatically but always accompanied by a struggle with no foregone conclusion.

*Historical views of law and state.* The *Aufklärung* historians respected the accomplishments of their French and English counterparts.

History is no longer just the biographies of kings, exact chronological notes of war, battles, and changes in rule, or reports of alliances and revolutions. This was the preference of almost all the *Anno Domini* men in the Middle Ages. And we Germans continued to write history in this poverty-stricken manner as recently as fifty years ago, until we were awakened by the better models of the French and the English.[8]

Nevertheless German historians differed particularly with their French counterparts on almost anything else connected with the writing of history. The Göttingen professor Johann Christoph Gatterer described how seventeenth-century French historians had searched for critically edited source material only to have their eighteenth-century successors concern themselves more with a beautiful style and theories than with patient research. Hence "the appreciation for well-researched histories and collections was furthered for a much longer time in Germany and England than in France."[9] For speculating about the past without proper consultation of sources, German scholars labeled the philosophes historiographical dilettantes, although their own work resembled only in a rough way what today would be called historical research. The philosophes, in turn, considered the German professors pedants whose works lacked both vision and a proper appreciation for rationality's central role.

A good number of *Aufklärung* historians came to the love of detail, attention to sources, and preference for a narrow range of interpretation by way of their employment on a law faculty. That fact linked history to legal studies, which, since 1600, had taken an increasingly prominent place at the Protestant German universities of Jena, Strassburg, Helmstedt, Halle, and, finally, Göttingen. Earlier, German legal scholars had found the historical approach useful for explaining the varieties of what many of them thought to be an unchanging, unitary natural law. But now the Göttingen scholars enhanced the role of history in legal studies to such a degree that they became the pioneers of the full-fledged historical interpretation of law that followed in the 1800s.

The Göttingen scholars also historicized the study of politics. They studied states as they actually existed and not as abstractions. At first they produced purely descriptive treatises, often merely compendia of data; this was an enterprise referred to as *Statistik*—the description of the state—and from it the endeavor of statistics branched off when numerical data became more and more highly regarded. But these scholars stayed neither with the static description of states nor with the abstract discussion of ideal form of states. They were more in tune with Montesquieu and his empirical approach. Montesquieu had singled out climate as one of the shapers of societies, cultures, religions, laws, customs, morals, and ideas. The German legal historians added the total geographical setting and, later in the century, also stressed the economic and social configurations of a state. In doing this, they pushed history to the threshold of nineteenth-century *Staatengeschichte:* a history of states which dealt with states as unique and constantly developing conjunctions of forces. Among these forces the historians and political theorists discerned—albeit hazily—the *Volk*, a concept which soon would play a major role in European thought, particularly Romantic thought. Once more the accent was on the fullness of life, as states were dealt with as living and unique phenomena rather than as *exempla* of timeless categories and definitions. If they were studied, they must be studied historically; abstract theories would not suffice. It was in this form that the history and theory of states was transmitted by Arnold von Heeren to the nineteenth century.

In all their studies the Göttingen legal-historical scholars conscientiously used sources and the insights of auxiliary disciplines. As time went on, the need to check on their scholarly procedures and to convey them to others, particularly students, led the scholars to construct elements of a historical methodology. Johann David Köhler did so in the introduction to one of his works, while Johann Christoph Gatterer discussed systematically his approaches to history, sources, and auxiliary disciplines. Gatterer, who came close to formulating a comprehensive theory of history, also attempted to introduce students to original work by means of a seminar, which however survived only briefly. In the light of their methodological interests, it seems only fitting that these two men were the first Göttingen professors to be named simply professors of history, not professors of history and law. It was especially Gatterer's ideas on historical explanation, his respect for sources and his attempts to publish them, and his seminar that proved seminal.

*A different universal history.* The *Aufklärung* historians, too, ventured into that ultimate test of historical views, universal history. They did so prompted not by the French celebration of progress but by their own demand for putting things in the widest context possible and by their Christian faith. With regard to the latter they rejected the view that religion was a deplorable source of errors and superstitions and an impediment to progress, one that had to be abandoned or at least reduced to the minimal scope of a rationally acceptable Deism. The German historians had a more positive attitude towards religion in accord with the better relationship between lay powers and the church in their areas. The innovative work of some eighteenth-century theologians and ecclesiastical historians, some of them teaching at Göttingen, also helped. The biblical scholars Johann August Ernesti and Johann David Michaelis and the theologian Johann Salomo Semler indicated in their work a solution to the deeply troubling contradiction between the absolute, timeless, and unchanging claims of the Christian faith and the by then obvious fact that change had penetrated even the area of religion. They distinguished the spirit of the Christian religion, based on Revelation and remaining stable forever, from its external manifestations, which changed throughout time and thus were historical. Hence, Semler claimed that Luther's attempt to restore the "pure" and presumably unchanging church was futile, since the development of religious forms cannot be denied. The philosophes also were wrong in concluding from some dying religious forms that human development would eventually phase out religion itself. Religion was not just a convenient tool of a fearful, barbarian, and not yet rational mankind; it was and always would be a basic element of human life. Such a view made it possible to historicize segments of Christian history while still maintaining the absolute validity of the core, the basic tenets of the faith, in a form which even reason could affirm.

The acceptance of God and of a cosmos governed by Divine Providence freed the *Aufklärung* historians of the need to find a meaning in the past independent from God and inherent in the secular world. Rejecting the French concept of rationality as a quasi-metaphysical force, they also rejected history as the story of rationality ascending through time to ever greater perfection. Instead, they discerned in the past changes in small steps, multifaceted, and without any aim save the Last Judgment. The lack of an immanent development directed at an ultimate mundane aim focused the attention of German historians on the process of change itself and fostered a more profound appreciation of each age. In studying a past age the *Aufklärung's* historians not only looked for the degree of rationality it had obtained, but they treated it as a unique and hence unrepeatable phenomenon. While philosophes, for example, had praised the Renaissance as the revival of clàssical rationality, the *Aufklärer* considered it a futile attempt to revive a past period in an all together different situation. The historical process was irreversible. It knew no cumulative liberation of reason that made later periods superior to earlier ones; all periods must be judged of equal value. The German historians (and philologists) practiced this egalitarian view of past ages when they lavished attention on the early history of Western people.

In his *Summary of Russian History* (1769) August L. Schlözer searched for access to the early years when humans did not write and came upon the idea of using early poetry. Under the impact of Johann J. Bodmer's work, epic poetry had come to be valued more and more highly by some German historians. Bodmer no longer viewed these epics as flights of the childish imagination of savages but interpreted them as appropriate expressions of how early people viewed the past. The audience of the Greek bards cherished and understood the Homeric epics because these works expressed their perception of the past. Bodmer even stipulated that every culture had its "Homeric age," one in which poetry served as the memory of great events. The same view of history could be used in showing how the writings of Dante sprang from the collective experience of the Guelph and Ghibelline struggle, and how *Paradise Lost* by Milton was stimulated by the Puritan struggle. In a related development Johann Mascov stressed in his *History of Germany* the correspondence between medieval German life and customary law, a fact which led him to value both. It is not difficult to discern traces of fateful concepts in all of this: the uniqueness of each people, the *Volk* as an organic unity of people, and the equality of the ages. Such concepts soon

emerged in clearly articulated form in a famous local history and in Johann
Gottfried Herder's philosophy of history.

*Articulating* Volk, *intuitive knowledge, and* Humanität. While many read
Voltaire's works, few noticed Justus Möser's *History of Osnabrück.* What could
it possibly teach those who did not live in that small German town? Yet as the
work lovingly traced Osnabrück's history, it became prototypical for much of
subsequent German historiography. It admonished the historian to understand
the unique situation existing at a given time and place and to use general terms
and insights solely to elucidate the concrete. Liberty, for example, was not seen
as an abstract force but as the accumulation of customary rights and privileges
of free people. Furthermore, Möser exhorted historians to feel with the people,
master their dialect, know their public life, and penetrate their actual thought.
One must understand the *Lokalvernunft,* which meant to appreciate all the
forces at work at a given time and place in the past and do so not by isolating
the general forces in order to analyze them separately but by comprehending
them in their full interaction. If historians had to choose an explanatory model
from among the sciences it should come from biology rather than from physics.
In biology the proper patterns prevailed; the forces of organic life dominated
over the mechanics of attraction and repulsion and the whole integrated the
individual parts.

After 1760, Johann Gottfried Herder made the Volk into the new central
unit of history. The Volk was not a man-made but an organic collective whole
which united diverse individuals through a common language, shared institutions,
the arts, and literature. Indeed the Volk's strongest unifying and formative force
as well as the best witness to its uniqueness was its language. "Has a nation anything more precious than the language of its fathers? In it dwell its entire world
of tradition, history, religion, principles of existence; its whole heart and soul."[10]
The Volk thus had a cultural base in contrast to the state which, based on
coercion and power, has in the past often been a destroyer of cultures. The celebrated Roman state destroyed first other cultures by its empire-building and
then itself by political centralization which stifled creativity. The culture which
Rome offered to other peoples in exchange for their loss of independence
proved sterile. Neither whole cultures nor cultural traits could be transferred
from one people to another. A Volk and its culture were uniquely shaped by
their very own genius.

As an organic whole, a Volk also grew, developed, and died. Such advocacy
of the organic model was well in line with the contemporary surge in the science
of biology and, perhaps knowingly, with Vico's view. As organic processes, cultural developments could neither be artificially speeded up nor halted, nor could
fundamental changes in a Volk's culture be brought about from the "outside,"
that is, through cultural diffusion. A culture's basic themes and character were
unalterably set in the early "root" period when myths and epic poetry prevailed.

The latter, Herder agreed, were not the creations of still childish minds but the mature expressions of a Volk's fundamental attitudes in a form fitting that early stage of collective life. To the scholar these myths and epic poems offered the chance to study a Volk's basic frame of mind when it was still simple and easily visible. Of course, Herder attacked those who considered the early period as one primitive in nature and worthy of only scant attention; he insisted that all periods in a Volk's life cycle were equally valuable and none represented merely a stepping stone for future stages.

What then did the whole of mankind's history add up to? Herder rejected the French notion of progress because it affirmed the superiority of European culture of the eighteenth century over other cultures and ages. This view saw human history exclusively as the augmentation of rationality, stipulated one way of life as the absolute right one, and ignored the life process, which knew not only growth but also decline and death. But he vacillated in his own answers. Because of his strict insistence on the concept of the self-contained Volk, Herder could speak only of a *Fortgang* of history, which referred to a continuous series of spontaneously emerging *Völker* without any fixed universal aim except the Last Judgment. Volk followed coequal Volk with all of it adding up to no more than endless variations on the theme of humanity. No period must therefore judge a preceding one according to present-day standards, rather each age, each culture, and each Volk carried its justification in itself. "Each age is different, and each has the center of its happiness within itself. The youth is not happier than the innocent, contented child; nor is the peaceful old man less happy than the vigorous man in the prime of life."[11] The pietist tradition helped find Herder a stable center: God, from whom each Volk was equidistant. On occasion Herder suggested some kind of theory of ages: childhood of mankind (biblical times), youth (Egypt), peak of vigor (Greece), maturity (Rome), with little choice for the Middle Ages than to mark old age, a prospect unwelcome to Herder. He changed to the image of a tree of cultures with many branches. Later in life he took a more teleological view when he hinted that Divine Providence may well direct human history towards greater *Humanität* but that this was not progress towards greater comfort and happiness—a progress which would lead only to decay—but a moral development toward a special state of civility. This divine education of mankind was the mature Herder's attempt to resolve the tension between his insistence on cultures as unique and spontaneous creations and his desire to discover order and continuity in change, an attempt which implied concessions to necessity, if not determinism.

By 1800 historiography was a sophisticated enterprise whose approaches to the past, however, remained quite separate. One group of scholars, usually allied with classical philology and increasingly with legal studies, utilized the heritage of the erudites, including the art of text edition and criticism, in order to create a picture of the past on the basis of secure evidence but limited interpretations. Antiquarians followed a parallel course, using nonliterary sources. And there were those historians who strove to discover and demonstrate the dynamics and goal of history in a world under a sovereign God who no longer interfered with the world's mechanism, whether this was viewed as progress, Vichian cycles, or the coexistence of national entities. Missing in all of that was a creative synthesis of these approaches beyond that attempted by Gibbon, Robertson, or some of the Göttingen scholars. Before the specific and highly successful synthesis by German scholars in the first half of the nineteenth century is described, the focus must shift to an emerging area of the Western world, the United States of America, and the transition of its historiography from one concerned with revolution to one characteristic of an established country. And finally the advocates of patterns of history would experience their moments of triumph. Cyclical theories would surface in moments of doubt and disenchantment while the theories of progress enjoyed the satisfaction not only of pervading the intellectual world but also of penetrating to the very quick of popular convictions.

### Recording the Birth of the American Nation

In the mid-1700s the Anglo-French struggle for empire stimulated the attention continental Europeans gave to North America; an attention so far aroused mainly by tales of a strange land, imported American plants and animals, and an interest in the exotic Indians. Still, the attention remained altogether moderate and even the momentous events of the American Revolution enhanced it only temporarily. Although the ideas of the philosophes influenced some educated colonials, the aims, ideals, and realities of the American Revolution had an English context, one foreign to continental Europeans. Even that prophet of progress, Condorcet, granted a different status to the American Revolution. It was, he thought, a less wrenching experience because Americans had no need to rebel against an intolerant church, hereditary privileges, and a feudal structure. Once the links to England were severed, Americans could exist in liberty under English law. The American voices proclaiming their Revolution to be an event of a universal historical importance were heard in Europe only faintly. The long distance between the continents, European hostility to radical republicanism, and the American preoccupation with internal affairs facilitated the relative isolation of the United States from continental Europe. As a consequence the questions raised by the American Revolution—why it had happened and how it fit into the course of human development—were mainly debated by scholars and public officials in England and the United States.

As is usual after great upheavals, the heat of conflict could be felt in the early accounts of the American Revolution. It was intense in the histories of the Revolution written by a few Loyalist officials and judges from the safety of their exile in England or Scotland. Peter Oliver condemned the break in the continuity of English development and blamed a few unprincipled demagogues— "a disgrace to Christianity" he called them—for having used some English mistakes to stir up the masses. Thomas Hutchinson, the last civil governor of the Massachusetts Bay province, was more tactful and repaid all of the vilification directed against him with a surprisingly fair account. With a good understanding of American life and good craftsmanship he portrayed the American Revolution as an uprising prompted by errors in governance. Yet Hutchinson denied that these errors justified independence or that a trend toward liberty was at work in history, as Americans argued. The Revolution was the work of rabble-rousers who had heated up "the dregs of the people" who then aroused others, although originally the general populace had not been ready for independence. Hutchinson also sensed correctly that the actual inequities in the tax system were less important than the people's perceptions of them and even the fears of future inequities to be inflicted. George Chalmers, a one-time lawyer in Maryland, blamed the Revolution on the British government's basic error of granting too many privileges and giving too much power to provincial assemblies. Excessive benevolence led to the Revolution.

The Patriots had problems with their historiography. Considerable sums of money were needed to publish in the small and poorly organized book market, and for the author there was the lack of easy access to good sources. Much like the Loyalists, they relied heavily on Edmund Burke's and James Dodsley's *Annual Register* with its accurate reports on American events. American historians described the revolutionary events convinced that the Revolution had been a legitimate revolt of English colonials for ancient rights. Hence Patriotic historians—such as David Ramsay or Mercy Otis Warren—inverted the Loyalist interpretations. Where Loyalists had seen demagogues inciting unwilling Americans, Patriots saw a few men with vision awakening their fellow citizens; where Loyalists had found the grievances being mainly those of Massachusetts and of no concern to other colonies, Patriots saw tyranny beginning in Massachusetts and spreading subsequently to all other colonies; and where Loyalists saw conspiracy brewing since the 1760s, Patriots discerned a long-time and growing awareness among colonials of fundamental differences between them and the English of the mother country. With significant consequences for America's future role and for historiography, John Adams and a few others soon perceived the Revolution as an event important for all of mankind because of the emergence of a strong new republic as a champion of liberty and a fighter against tyranny. Most Patriots would also have agreed with Benjamin Trumbull, who placed the American Revolution among the great human deeds done under God's guidance. Mercy Otis Warren pronounced American independence the starting point for world republicanism. This dichotomy between the perceptions of the American Revolution as a fight for traditional English rights and as a struggle for natural, inalienable, and universal human rights would mark American historical consciousness for a long time.

In the year of the Constitution appeared two historical accounts of the American Revolution. The Reverend William Gordon had experienced the

Revolutionary War, gotten to know many of the American leaders, and returned only in 1786 to England. Although much of his account eschews partisanship, in the end he, like other Loyalists, spoke of trickery and deception on the part of the revolutionary leaders. David Ramsay wrote the first history of the American Revolution clearly sympathetic to its cause. When he celebrated the emergence of the nation that held promise to reshape human nature, he inspired his readers and subsequent historians, among them Jedidiah Morse and Noah Webster. Their works and many more to come portrayed the Revolutionary War as the central event in which the American nation was shaped. In that nation-forming process, history had a frankly didactic purpose, that of teaching the new Republic's citizens that a republic of free citizens could only survive through the public and private virtue of these citizens—a lesson reminiscent of Leonardo Bruni and Montesquieu. Historians must help forestall failure—a United States of servile people subject to despots—by using the exhortative examples of great deeds and persons. John Adams, not a historian but concerned with history, put more trust in another buttress, the mixed constitution as celebrated by Polybius and Montesquieu.

Biographers preferred the Founding Fathers as the teachers of the new nation, and none seemed to fit that role better than George Washington. Parson Mason Locke Weems' biography of Washington (1800) knew no subtlety in transforming Washington into the hero worthy of emulation by all the people. No matter how many frowns the work caused on the faces of later, more erudite historians, Weems succeeded in shaping minds and inspiring them. Washington the national hero, not Washington the Virginian, became the personification of those virtues which the young republic wished its citizens to have: thrift, patriotism, temperance, frugality, industry, honesty, and obedience; hence the stories of hatchets, the cherry tree, and cabbage beds. The shrewd bookseller Weems had harmonized the ideals of people and the needs of a young nation in the fictional image of Washington; Weems's biography eventually became folklore. Others found a biography of Washington convenient for making comments on recent political battles. Shortly after 1800 John Marshall, Chief Justice of the Supreme Court, wrote reverently but ponderously about Washington, whom he had known and whose family gave him access to records. Yet, he did little research, copied much of the material from other books, and buried Washington's biography in general history. Marshall also tinged his discussion of general history, taxes, and individual rights with strong Federalist sympathies. His implications that the Republicans disturbed the constitutional system upset Thomas Jefferson who—without success—encouraged a number of people to write a Jeffersonian history of Washington's life and times. He ended up praising two works. In John Wood's *History of the Administration of John Adams (1802)*, which Jefferson had partially sponsored, Washington appeared as a people-loving Jeffersonian and Adams as a monarchical president. Jefferson also praised Mercy Otis Warren for her history of the Revolution. Warren had lived through the

Revolution, was related to some of the revolutionary figures, and had been close to the struggle. She loved history, observed keenly, and wrote well. Her characterizations were astute and full of patriotic fervor. Thomas Hutchinson was a villain and George III obstinate, weak, and politically wrong rather than cruel, wicked, and tyrannical. In all of that she was not deterred by John Adams's advice that "history is not the province of ladies," an opinion induced at least partially by Warren's strong Jeffersonian sympathies and her criticism of Adams's "monarchical" attitudes.

By the early 1800s many people, regardless of political convictions, agreed that history was essential in the struggle of shaping a democratic American nation, and history, conceived of as civic education, entered school curricula in force. The emphasis on the American nation as a whole also shaped the work done in the by then numerous local and regional historical societies. One strove to demonstrate the contribution of one's locality, state, or region to the national cause. A great mass of documents was collected, preserved, recorded, and published. From this ground, saturated with historical enthusiasm, rose the great American histories of the middle and later 1800s.

# ·15·

## Historians as Interpreters of
## Progress and Nation—I

In the Age of Enlightenment scholars had created, discussed, and disseminated new ideas about the order in nature, society, and history. Beginning with the 1770s, some of these ideas had inspired actions to change the social and political order of various countries. During the subsequent one hundred and fifty years, historians were called on to mediate between the demands for change and the equally strong desire to see the continuity of the past, present, and future preserved. The task proved more or less difficult depending on the national contexts. In England historiography followed a nearly serene course, disturbed more by the arrival soon after mid-century of the new critical historical science in the German manner than by large-scale shifts in society or politics. In her former North American colonies historiography, at first shaped by the momentous creation of a new nation through a revolution, told the story of the grand adventure of stretching a small nation across a vast continent. In that story the assertion of Divine Providence and progress joined with ease a commonsense empiricism about the world. Presented by careful scholars with great eloquence, these histories became popular possessions rather than scholarly curiosa.

French historiography shared the agony of French history. The radical revolutionaries, with their ardent belief in progress and with their hopes that a libertarian, rational, and perhaps even egalitarian society could be built here and now, rejected much of the French past. Only a glorified picture of the Roman republican past seemed fitting for the new society that would be constructed according to "pure" rational concepts, would know social and political equality, and would erase all traces of the Old Regime. In 1815, after the failure of both the Jacobin radical experiment and the Napoleonic Empire, the French embarked on a quest for the proper political structure for French society. Since that search clearly aimed at finding not the best political structure in the abstract but rather the one proper for French society, the answer could only be found in the French past, and historians became the guides in the search. On the other hand the French Revolution had unsettled much of Europe's social and political order, and Napoleon's ambitions and armies had done their part in the unsettling. In many areas, particularly the German, the experiences with revolutionary and Napoleonic France lessened the influence of the notion that a society need not be shaped by age-old traditions because human reason was now sufficiently developed to design a society of complete justice and happiness. In the German area, the struggle for national identity was at first aimed at reestablishing the Empire. The conservative, gradualist view which went with such nationalist aspirations offered a favorable climate of opinion for historians, who in that context created the influential German historical science.

It was not only the significant public role historians played in their societies that gave historiography great influence in the 1800s. Firmly based on a philosophy—whether that of the progress of reason or a Vichian cultural interpretation of human destiny—historiography triumphed over its old rival. Throughout the century the concept of development made the once static and eternal essences of philosophy subject to change. But there was even a greater and longer-lasting triumph. Early in the century a few German professors succeeded in synthesizing what had been separated for centuries but had been close to convergence in the decades before 1800: the tradition of text criticism of classical philology; the work with sources by the erudites and legal historians; and the concept of the nation as a unique whole in which spiritual forces bind things together and each element influences the others. Used with these elements was a methodology taken from the diverse currents that helped maintain the autonomy of the historical inquiry in relation to all other scholarly inquiries.

The acceptance of the German historical science, although often enthusiastic, was always partial because woven into the German synthesis was also a great number of contemporary metaphysical views. While these views made the new historical science of history congenial to Western societies, they also explain the controversies which engulfed it in the late 1800s when social and political changes challenged its link to the existing order and new concepts of reality eroded its philosophical buttresses.

### German Historians: The Causes of Truth and National Unity

Ironically, conservative Prussia became the sponsor of philosophers and historians who championed a thoroughly dynamic world. At the University of Berlin, that magnificent result of and symbol for the Prussian renaissance after the dismal defeat in 1806, a group of scholars proclaimed the subjugation of all life and thought to development. At "a time when we [Barthold Niebuhr and his contemporaries] were experiencing the most incredible and exceptional events, when we were reminded of many forgotten and decayed institutions by the sound of their downfall," change came to be the central concept—the world needed to be explained not in terms of eternal and essential categories but historically.[1] This audacious endeavor was favored by a fortuitous set of circumstances and the presence of a large number of creative scholars and of crucial concepts inherited from the preceding century, including the achievements of the Göttingen professors. These German scholars proceeded confidently to make the world a radically fluid one, comprehensible only through idealist philosophies and historicist approaches. Two safeguards insured stability to such a world: the acknowledgment of the state as a moral institution—as the guardian and moral educator of people—and of a metaphysical reality, whether God or World Spirit, which gave an absolute reference point for all changes. Both features fit well with the strong German nationalism of the period but certainly not with Condorcet's idea of progress and his hope for a Tenth Age of rationalism and happiness.

Set free to develop the ideas of the *Aufklärung*, some Berlin professors soon applied the idea of the dynamic whole to classical and legal studies. C. G. Heyne at Göttingen and F. A. Wolf at Halle had demonstrated how rich classical studies could be if one went beyond the critical assessment of the language of a work in isolation from its context and depicted ancient life as a whole in all its variety and change. In the Berlin of the early 1800s, Wolf's student August Böckh attempted to describe ancient Greek life, including its neglected economic aspect. In his quest to use all possible sources for the reconstruction of that life, he elevated epigraphy, the study of inscriptions, to prominence. One of Böckh's students, Otfried K. Müller, already aimed at no less than "the knowledge of man in antiquity" and portrayed how the Greek state was shaped by demographic, environmental, military, commercial, political, artistic, and intellectual forces and was constantly in flux. The financier, diplomat, and scholar Barthold Niebuhr accomplished the same transformation for Roman studies. In his *Roman History* Niebuhr explored ancient Rome critically on the basis of the sources and, going well beyond the study of isolated phenomena, demonstrated that the Roman state and Roman culture formed a whole and must be studied together. By 1830 German classical studies had overcome all preoccupation with the restoration of the proper texts of classical works in isolation from ancient life and at long last had transformed the Renaissance humanist concept of the ancient world as a static and ideal period into the modern concept of it as a stage in human development.

Göttingen's professors, particularly the philosopher of law Gustav Hugo, also had been seminal in turning German legal studies away from the study of the universal natural law to that of positive law seen as growing with the Volk it served. In the early 1800s, Karl F. von Eichhorn, a student of Hugo and later professor at Berlin, transformed the history of public law from a compilation of dynasties, rulers, and public acts into the story of the ever-changing ideals and mores of a people. Friedrich K. von Savigny traced the survival and the changes of Roman law from antiquity into the Middle Ages and showed that it, too, had had to change in conformity with life or it would have died. These ties between law, life, and Volk dated from the very beginning of all law as it developed originally from customs and only much later through judicial decisions. Not law-givers but silently operating powers instituted law. Because law changes grad-ually, imperceptibly, and always in conformity with the unique *Volksseele*, all attempts to establish codes of law patterned after a timeless natural law or to copy the successful codes of other people, such as the Napoleonic code, must fail.

*Hegel's philosophical revolution: the cosmos as history.* The scholars at Göttingen and Berlin had conjured up the image of cultures in motion. When Georg Wilhelm F. Hegel made history dictate to philosophy, he set truth itself in motion. He also reversed centuries of thinking about history as inferior to philosophy, because history could not deal with essences—with that which was permanently and most profoundly true about the world. Now, all truth was historical truth because the strict distinction between the world of the contingent and of the permanent had been obliterated *(aufgehoben)*.

At the beginning of history stood the Idea as pure thought. It was only potentiality, not yet made concrete or actual. That Idea "by which and in which all reality has its being and subsistence"[2] began a necessary process of self-realization that was to make actual what so far had been only potential. In that process all that was potential would, step by step, become actual.

When the Idea began its actualization in time and space, when it "stepped outside" of pure potentiality first as inorganic life, then as organic life, and finally as human life, it became "conscious-of-itself," that is, there was now the possibility of reflecting on the Idea and its self-realization. Hegel referred to the Idea at that particular stage of its development as the Spirit, which would rush on and on until the time when all that was potential in it would have become actual and all need for development would have ceased. Until then there neces-sarily would be tensions in the development of the Spirit since the force pushing toward the final goal of self-realization encountered constant opposition. Every time the Spirit has taken a step forward, resulting in a specific established order (the thesis), it has also created the opposing forces to that order (the antithesis). Those contradictions must be because only such constant confrontations and struggles could push the development forward in the course of which emerged ever new and always higher states of self-realization of the Spirit (the synthesis). This dialectical self-realization clearly occurred in time and involved change. "World history in general is the development of Spirit in *Time,* just as Nature is the development of the Idea in *Space.*"[3]

What has been the role of various peoples in that cosmic progress? They were either condemned by adverse climates to a "merely sensual or vegetative existence," as, for example, the Asiatic Indians, or, after having played a signifi-cant part, had sunk back into an ahistorical state, as happened to the Egyptians. The best a people could hope for was a brief moment in which their unique genius acted as the agent of the Spirit's advance. But "the accomplishment is at the same time its dissolution, and the rise of another spirit, another world-historical people, another epoch of Universal History."[4] The people whose role has ended become once more mere particulars of no consequence to the progress of the Spirit. That shooting-star existence assigned by Hegel to prominent nations has more often been discussed in relation to the heroes and heroines of history. Whether vainglory or lust for power drove Napoleon to become what he was mattered as little to Hegel as did Napoleon's eventual fate. What counted was Napoleon's work on behalf of the Spirit, even if done unwittingly. Hegel considered such a use of persons the "cunning of Reason or Spirit." For a brief moment the universal process and Napoleon's particular existence, ambitions, and accomplishments were in accord. When they parted, Napoleon was once more only a particular phenomenon of no significant universal value, one like millions of others, although better known for his brief historical role.

The state had been the key agent for the reconciliation of the universal (the process of self-realization) and the particular (everything individual). Hegel considered the state to be an ethical, civilizing institution: "the state is the Divine Idea as it exists on earth."[5] Only through it can the many with their blind self-interest be led to a level above brute existence. The state must be more than the result of a social contract between individuals; if it was no more than that, its laws would merely codify the desires of individuals and the historical mission of the state would be negated.

As the progress of freedom demonstrated, the state, like everything else, has been subject to development: "The East knew and to the present day knows only that One is free; the Greek and Roman world knew that some are free; the German world knows that All are free."[6] What will be the characteristics of the ideal state, the one coinciding in time with the full self-realization of the Spirit? In it the private interests of its citizens will be one with the common interest of the state, voluntarily and not by coercion. Hegel did not consider the contemporary Prussian state to be that ultimate ideal: it was only the best state so far. The Spirit's progress would eventually outdate it, too. No regrets were called for, since "the history of the world is none other than the progress of the consciousness of Freedom; a progress whose development according to the necessity of its nature it is our business to investigate."[7]

*The key figure: Leopold von Ranke.* Hegel's grandiose vision of the cosmos as history was not to the liking of most historians, who were accustomed to give more weight to individual phenomena and events. It failed to sway Leopold von Ranke, whom genius and the renown of his early work, *The Histories of the German and Roman Peoples* (1824), had lifted out of the obscure existence of a provincial *Gymnasialprofessor* of classical studies and into the illustrious circle of professors at the University of Berlin. Before Ranke died in 1886, ninety-one years old and widely celebrated as the "father of historical science," his intellectual gifts, his diligence, and the favorable conditions in which he was placed resulted in the creation of fifty-four volumes filled with historical and political writings.

Rarely has a phrase been so often and approvingly quoted as Ranke's declaration that he wanted not to pass judgment on the past but simply to report "*wie es eigentlich gewesen* [how it actually was] ."[8] It has been used as a symbolic description of Ranke's achievement, namely, to combine fully in his work the methodological achievements of philologists, erudites, and legal historians with substantial interpretation and traditional narrative history. In addition, Ranke innovated when he taught young historians in his seminar how to apply the proper methods in their research. Gatterer had experimented briefly with a seminar in Göttingen, yet only Ranke put the seminar into the center of the education of historians. The young historians were sent to the archives, which just at that time began to open routinely their doors to scholars. The use of these sources under sophisticated critical safeguards seemed to guarantee the objectivity of one segment of the historian's work, the establishment of facts. Actually Ranke's elaborate methodology was based on classical philology, with its maxim: check the source for trustworthiness and against its own context. For his methodological contribution Ranke has been celebrated as the pioneer of a critical historical science. He deserved that recognition also because he observed his own rules. He refused, for example, to let his own distaste for the French Revolution or for the papacy sway his findings.

But the many who have perceived Ranke as a quasi-positivist have overlooked or have chosen to overlook his second level of inquiry, and, in connection with it, the metaphysical segment of Ranke's world, which provided the base for his methodology. For the Lutheran Ranke, the "holy hieroglyphe"— God with his plan and his will—stood behind all phenomena of the past. A study of human events will yield the truth only if historians concern themselves with "humanity as it is, comprehensible or inexplicable, the life of the individual, of generations, or nations, and at times the hand of God above them."[9] Influenced by Kant and Wilhelm von Humboldt, Ranke found the link between the mundane and the metaphysical realms in ideas, those eternal forces which manifest themselves partially and temporarily in the phenomena of this world.

Much like Humboldt, Ranke argued that the finding of facts through critical research was not to be followed by induction leading to more and more general and hence abstract concepts but by a process appropriate to the spiritual realm that governed all. Ranke spoke of *Ahnen,* an intuitive cognition directed at grasping the ideas which shaped phenomena and events. Besides being keys to understanding, ideas also provided an absolute moral structure and a yardstick for assessing (but not judging) the multitude of periods, nations, and individuals.

Herder had still exalted the Volk, as a cultural unit, over the state as a product of coercion. He, unlike Ranke, had not witnessed how the power of the sword and of diplomacy had reshaped Europe. Neither had he experienced the trust Ranke's generation put in the Prussian state, that had been so essential in the defeat of Napoleon. Ranke had no difficulty in finding a proper place for the state in his spiritual cosmos. The states were spiritual entities *(Gedanken Gottes)* with the purpose of civilizing mankind and therefore they must be the central concern of the historian. Each of them represented a unique configuration of law, politics, and customs and was no mere stepping stone for the march of progress, whether of mankind or of Hegel's Spirit. Still, the variety of states did not testify simply to a maze of clashing interests and powers but to an ultimate unity in God. Thus Ranke stressed in all his works that the modern European states were different manifestations of the divine will, mediated through the universal idea of the state, and, specifically, that they grew from the fusion of the Germanic and Roman peoples. Hence when Ranke admonished historians to keep in mind the primacy of foreign policy he was not exalting power politics but wished to stress the importance of the coexistence of states for a civilized human life. With such a view of the state and with most students making pilgrimages to state archives in search of state documents, Rankean history became primarily political history. Most of Ranke's own works contain primarily narratives of war, diplomacy, and the deeds of statesmen, although he could draw masterly portraits even of the heroes of faith and intellect.

The universal core of Ranke's views explains why Ranke, in his eighties, tried fervently to conclude his work with a complete world history. He died after completing eight volumes. It probably saved him much disappointment because even Germany had grown less receptive to his interpretation of the past. Historians had abandoned Herder's cosmopolitanism as well as Ranke's grand vision of a community of European power under God in favor of the narrower view of nations purely politically conceived. Being properly appreciated continued to be Ranke's problem, even after his death. Those who have honored him have rarely referred to the universality of his historical vision but have appreciated only the Ranke of the new methodology. This, too, had to be diminished in scope of order to celebrate Ranke as the hero of "scientific historiography." Ranke the Christian and idealist soon came to be out of season.

*The liberal German historians.* Among German scholars the attraction of "pure" scholarship coupled with a moderate conservatism found many adherents but for decades this attraction had to compete with the pull of two other concerns: national unity and constitutional government. Until 1848 the two concerns were still linked, but the failure of the 1848 revolutions gave priority to the cause of national unity. German liberalism suffered from the fact that the conquering Napoleonic armies had dampened much of the ardor for French revolutionary ideals; it also suffered because German philosophy had lacked even in the eighteenth century strong advocates of the individual whose rights were anchored in natural law. The atomistic social thinking had yielded to seeing the individual as part of an integral whole, in particular the state, in which personal freedom was realized in public service.

Only in the southwestern German regions did the aim of constitutional government retain substantial strength. In that area close to France the eighteenth-century German cosmopolitanism was still alive and the 1830 French revolution with its limited popular representation was welcome. Friedrich C. Schlosser and Karl von Rotteck, both teaching history and politics, considered the French situations in 1789, 1814, and 1830 to have been examples worthy of imitation. A testimony to that spirit, Schlosser's incomplete *Universal History of the German People,* stood on many German bookshelves until its popularity faded rapidly in the 1850s. With its condemnation of despots (including even the venerated Alexander the Great), of empires, and of autocratic priests, it conveyed a moderately liberal view. Actually, Schlosser had a vague vision of liberalism as a civilized, urbane way of life. The fate of his student, Georg G. Gervinus, symbolized what happened after 1848 to well-intentioned liberals who were in favor of constitutional government but in a generally unsympathetic society. Gervinus had been one of the famous "Göttingen Seven": seven professors, who in 1837 protested the unilateral abrogation of the *Staatsgrundgesetz* (a quasi-constitution) by the Hanoverian king and as a result lost their positions. His subsequent fervent work on behalf of German constitutionalism collapsed together with the Revolution of 1848. While other German historians began now to drift into the camp of "unity under Prussian rule first," Gervinus wrote a *History of the Nineteenth Century* as a prophecy of things to come: the progress of human freedom was inevitable and would end in the emancipation of the Fourth Estate, the industrial workers. Gervinus was charged with high treason by the political authorities and accused by strict Rankeans of dilettantism for not using proper critical methods. In 1867 he stopped writing out of disgust and despair over the successes of Bismarck, which the populace and even some liberals greeted with enthusiasm. Ten years later, Treitschke's *German History in the Nineteenth Century,* which was more in line with realpolitik, military victory, and nationalism, drowned out Gervinus's voice completely.

*German unity and the so-called Prussian school.* Friedrich Dahlmann, Heinrich von Sybel, and Gustav Droysen had been Gervinus's comrades in conviction and action until German liberalism's failure in 1848 made them invest their hope for constitutional rule and German unity in the king of Prussia. Dahlmann participated actively in politics for a few more years and then limited himself to teaching. In his lectures, based on his histories of the English Revolution of 1688 and of the French Revolution, as well as on his *Politik,* he spelled out his ideals: that all politics was shaped by the actually existing people and situations and therefore can only be studied historically; that the future must be kept from becoming a triumph for either despots or the masses; and that the German national development must be resolved by unification and recourse to a constitution, as the only guarantee against the destruction of all tradition by the forces of revolution. In the 1850s, Sybel similarly warned Germans against

Jacobin infatuations in his *History of the Period of Revolution*. On the basis of vast documentary studies, which conformed well to all Rankean ideals, the work portrayed the French Revolution as a disaster even for the masses whom it supposedly was serving. In addition, the volatility of the masses that was shown during the Revolution should caution one not to entrust the welfare of the state to the general populace. When in the 1850s Droysen began his multivolume *History of Prussian Politics*, he was less concerned with the Fourth Estate than with the hope he and others placed in Prussia for German unification. He maintained that ever since the 1500s the Hohenzollern acted in the interest of German unity, a thesis which appeared less precarious than it actually was only because Droysen used mainly Prussian documents.

The empire of 1871 fulfilled partially the hopes held by many of the Germans ever since the old empire had ended under pressure from Napoleon in 1806. The empire was *kleindeutsch;* it excluded the Austrians, who then lived in a multinational empire of their own. But the *kleindeutsch* synthesis of past and present offered no clear expectations for the future. With their national aspirations fulfilled, German historians could have all asked Sybel's question: what was there left to expect from life and for a historian to strive after? Sybel himself worried about any further democratization in the German Empire and sided with Bismarck during the latter's confrontations with the Catholic church and the Social Democrats. Liberal in his own way, Sybel celebrated in his *The Founding of the German Empire by William I* the new empire not only as the triumph of the Prussian state but also as a step in the emancipation of mankind. Nevertheless, like the less fortunate Gervinus, Sybel and other liberal *kleindeutsch* historians were gently pushed into the background by Heinrich von Treitschke, the spokesman of Germany as one of the Great Powers. Treitschke, enamored of political engagement, scolded earlier historians for having earnestly striven to combine the politics of unification with their dedication to Rankean historiography. Ranke himself had disdained any such combination although he never condemned those who tried. The pro-Prussian historians, often referred to as the Prussian school, actually had managed to stay at a safe distance from sheer propaganda. Even Heinrich von Sybel, who confessed that he was four-sevenths a professor and three-sevenths a politician, struggled in all his work to adhere to the Rankean code of research. But when these German historians had shrunk Ranke's historical context from the universality of mankind to that of the German destiny and replaced trust in Divine Providence with the affirmation that in history success indicated value, they had unwittingly prepared the field for Treitschke, to whom the concepts of Divine Providence, exactitude in learning, and the ethical purpose of the state were not only foreign but objects of contempt. As Ranke's successor from 1874 on, he kept students spellbound by his lectures (although he himself was deaf) and influenced others through his political action and works.

The ideals of scholarship and the demand to be involved in German politics posed complex problems of reconciliation for some German historians, for whom Theodor Mommsen can be emblematic. After the failure of the revolutions of 1848, the young Mommsen published a multivolume *Roman History* and then entered Prussian politics, indirectly by way of the *Prussian Yearbooks* and, in 1861, directly as a founder of the Progressive party. In his *Roman History* politics and history blended well. His critical spirit even excelled that of Niebuhr; indeed, he criticized the famous Romanist for being too speculative. Yet, while the researcher Mommsen came close to being an ardent believer in "facts," the citizen Mommsen harbored passionate political commitments. It was, he said, "the worst of all mistakes to suspend being a citizen, so as not to compromise one's scholarly work."[10] The *Roman History* reflected arduous and brilliant research, but it also taught how a flourishing state needed a balance between the assertions of power and of law and between the needs of unity and of freedom. When patrician arrogance and plebeian lust for material gain disturbed that balance, Rome perished. In Caesar, Rome found its last statesman who temporarily reestablished the balance. After him came the empire, a state based on power alone; one which Mommsen never found attractive enough to describe in a narrative.

For only a few years Mommsen supported Bismarck in the struggles for German unification. Then the absence of incentives for citizen participation in the era of imperial and bureaucratic realpolitik turned him into a liberal gadfly. Depressed by German politics and stymied in his continuation of the *Roman History* by the lost political ideals and by methodological problems, Mommsen worked feverishly on scholarly projects which augmented the sources for the cultural history he favored over the purely political narrative: studies in numismatics, classical philology, and, above all, Roman epigraphy. The monumental *Corpus inscriptionum Latinarum* compensated historiography in full for the volumes on imperial Roman history he never wrote.

Bismarck felt indebted to those historians whose lives and works helped shape the Second Empire. But as for the criterion of enduring usefulness, the works that still count are not those connected directly either with liberal or national causes. Dahlmann's claim to fame has rested on the scholarly handbook of German historical sources which began as a bibliography for his students, grew under the editorship of George Waitz, and has remained an essential tool up to its present edition. Compared with it, Dahlmann's respectable *History of Denmark* has remained obscure. Sybel is remembered as the editor of many publications of Prussian documents, founder of the German Historical Institute in Rome, and initiator of the famous *Historische Zeitschrift* (1859). The latter was the first journal through which the new "scientific" historiography in the Rankean manner spoke to the scholarly community. "This periodical should above all, be a scientific one. Its first task should, therefore, be to represent the true method of historical research and to point out the deviations therefrom."[11] That commitment was joined to another: "We, therefore, wish to deal preferably with such material and such relationships in the material which still have a vital link with present-day life."[12] Yet, the *Historische Zeitschrift,* with all its initial pro-Prussian tendencies, remained true to the Rankean critical ideals.

Droysen's early works on ancient history and on the Wars of Liberation against Napoleon have long been eclipsed but not his *Encyclopaedia and Methodology of History,* often called briefly *Grundriss der Historik,* or simply *Historik.* Forgotten for many decades, it achieved some prominence when modern historians began their analysis of what they were doing and why. It formed the best and most complete statement on German nineteenth-century historiographical theory; the one which Ranke never wrote and one—as will be seen—which served as the first line of defense against advocates of a historiography patterned after the natural sciences. Put against all of that, Treitschke, the historiographer of Prussia since 1886, does not fare well. He, whose temper and deafness prevented the seminar-type exchange of ideas, had remained a historian of activism. His *German History in the Nineteenth Century* aimed "simply at narrating and judging," leaving out all scholarly apparatus. And while it showed traces of Treitschke's impressively wide interests its message of power as the essence of the state, of the superiority of the political over the social, of war as heroic, and of an excessive pride in Germany adhered too much to the mood of the contemporary period. When the future with its doubts and problems arrived, Treitschke's work had little to offer and it faded from the ongoing discourse, while historical scholarship in the Rankean manner continued to exert a profound influence around the world.

### France: Historians, the Nation, and Liberty

In 1815, after twenty-five years of turmoil, France was left a nation united and safe in her existence but without a clear identity. The calls for *liberté, egalité,* and *fraternité* had grown much fainter but the question remained whether these ideals had been best realized in the Girondists' limited monarchy, the Jacobins' republic, or Napoleon's Empire, and to what degree and in which form they should be asserted now. Although the Bourbons, once more in power, simply tried to ignore the immediate past, the problem of the proper model for France's society did not fade away. For nearly sixty years France shaped and re-shaped her body politic in a search for that proper form, and historians were her most prominent guides in that endeavor. That role turned out to be as powerful an incentive for writing history as the quest for national unity had been for German historians.

*Advocates of tradition and continuity.* After 1815, the Catholic church, in contrast to secular institutions, offered a continuity undamaged by revolutionary ideals or changes. It never had rejected the Old France or viewed the Revolution as a fulfillment of France's destiny. On the contrary, shortly after the Reign of Terror had ended, one of the church's advocates, Joseph de Maistre, defined the French Revolution not just as a conspiracy by an evil few but as a consequence of collective sin, a view which made revolutionary ideals unworthy of shaping French development in the future. The Catholic view of the past was presented much more elaborately by François René de Chateaubriand in his *The Genius of Christianity* (1802). The past knew only one truly revolutionary event, when the modern age was created "at the foot of the Cross" and the human condition changed completely. All human attempts to change conditions radically and quickly had to fail because they were based on the dream of human control over forces which were unknown, forces subject only to Divine Providence. The French past illustrated how the true, the gradually changing, and the lawful always prevailed over all sudden and violent changes. Hence, the church, a stable, essential, and moral force, offered a more reliable basis for France's future than the untested ideas of rationalists and revolutionaries.

Chateaubriand rejected the idea of a secular progress. Indeed the cultivation of rationality in isolation from emotion and imagination was not only of no social benefit, it destroyed a civilization by eroding age-old tradition. Rather than resembling a staircase leading up to the present, the past showed a sequence of equally valid periods. Chateaubriand particularly wished to rescue the reputation of the France of chivalry. That appreciation fit well into the Restoration period's sense for the French past. It was then that a whole period, the Middle Ages, was rescued from the derision of rationalists. There was also the desire no longer to skip over centuries of the French past and celebrate the Roman Republic and its heroes as idols of the Revolution. Now it made sense to do what Joseph F. Michaud did: go to the archives and spend years in studying and writing about the *History of the Crusades,* those endeavors considered sheer folly by the philosophes. With the renewed affirmation of God's Providence obviating the need to find an order immanent in human events, J. F. Michaud and Prosper de Barante, in his *History of the Dukes of Burgundy, 1364–1477,* could without embarrassment follow the precept of the *ecole narrative:* "write to tell, not to judge." Historians of that school painted grand and colorful pictures, rich in detail and drama. History became a tableau of magnificent evocations of the past, but they stood side by side, lacking any sense of development. The French narrative historians drifted with the broad current, which also pushed along Sir Walter Scott, Prosper Merimée, and countless Romantics.

The age was too agitated by the wish to find and secure the proper French form of social and political organization to be satisfied by the historical portraits of the *ecole narrative.* The contemporary intellectual climate and the sense for development engendered by the Revolution were detrimental to history as a series of portraits. Instead a new stage began in the old quest for clarifying the French identity; one as old as Fredegar's tale of the Trojan origin of the Franks.

Fittingly, the early attempt by Augustin Thierry not only favored the Gauls as true ancestors but also provided a dynamic explanatory scheme for France's development throughout the ages. He found it while preparing his *History of the Conquest of England by the Normans* (1825). "One day when ... I had attentively read over some chapters of Hume, I was struck with an idea which seemed to me a ray of light; and exclaimed, as I closed the book, 'All this dates from a conquest; there is a conquest underneath.'"[13] A people conquers a people and the repercussions shape history. In England the resistance to the Normans explained almost everything, including the "guerrillas anglo-saxonnes" after 1066, the deeds of Robin Hood, and the murder of Thomas à Becket, whose fight for church sovereignty was really a deed on behalf of the Anglo-Saxons. Eventually the conquered won out with the triumph of the middle class. In a similar manner, the Germanic migrations in early French history brought conquest, domination by the Germanic element in the Carolingian period, and finally a liberation of France by the Gallo-Romans. At first, in France, it was a straight conflict between the "race of conquerors" and the "race of the conquered." Later that conflict became a more subtle social struggle, and Thierry's definitions of the two "races" grew a bit hazier. He continued to speak out, however, for the "conquered," who once were "our forefathers—the Gallo-Romans," ensconced in the towns, and who later were identified with the Third Estate, which included simply "la masse de non-nobles." Thierry's view of history as an ongoing struggle between two unevenly powerful groups, proceeding relentlessly along a predetermined course and toward a known end, impressed no less a man than Karl Marx.

Subsequently the search for the true spirit of France went forward once more along lines that some sixteenth-century legists had suggested and that the Abbé Dubos had reenforced in the eighteenth century. In his *History of the Gauls*, Augustin Thierry's brother Amédée championed the thesis of France's Celtic origin, which in the 1850s became a favorite view. Henri Martin's popular volumes on the *History of France* celebrated the Celtic spirit of France, while Michelet credited the Celtic element with contributing the love of equality to the French spirit. Only Gallic France was truly unique, because she was genuinely free of Germanic ties. At that point, however, the search for the unique French character still remained at a safe distance from chauvinistic cravings since it satisfied mainly the Romantic need for national selfassertion rather than any desire to belittle other people. Thus, the leading liberal historian, François Guizot, respected the Germans and liked the English; he celebrated the French as cultural leaders but considered them to be a racial mix between Celts, Romans, and Germans.

The Romantic quest for a French history based on the supposition of a unique French spirit—one transcending all partisan divisions—culminated in the works of Jules Michelet. After he produced a short textbook on the *History of the Modern World*, he earned the chance to enter into academic institutions of rank, particularly the Collège de France, and to become, through Guizot's sponsorship, head of the historical section of the National Archives.

Vico and, to a lesser degree, Herder influenced the young Michelet. He translated and abridged, some would say paraphrased, Vico's *New Science*. Coming, like Vico, from the world of the Catholic faith with its essences and stability, Michelet, too, felt the need to come to terms with change. Vico could accept history as the tale of the rise and fall of cultures because he believed in God's Providence. Michelet, lacking Vico's trust in Divine Providence, found a mere sequence of cultures depressing and instead depicted the line of successive cultures as an ascending spiral whose aim he later defined as ever-fuller human liberty.

From his eighteenth-century mentors, Michelet gained an understanding for the concept of Volk, and an enhanced appreciation of the central role of language and of myth. But he proceeded beyond such understanding to a radical affirmation of the cosmos as an organic whole. Nature, France, the people, and individuals were one in essence and development. Hence he could speak of himself as France, and speak of history as rousing the dead. The same cosmic spirit obliterated the divisions of time and pervaded his work through the documents to which he as archivist had easy access and which he cherished. He viewed the archives as "catacombs of manuscripts, this wonderful necropolis of national monuments," and the documents as "not papers, but lives of men, of provinces, and of nations."[14] Attempts to explain the development of the French spirit and nation as the work of abstract forces or physical conditions were, of course, futile. Michelet also rejected all explanations of history on the basis of race or conflict (Thierry), laws of stages (Vico), and environmental determinism. The spirit of a people unfolded spontaneously, except that throughout time the different spirits of peoples have contributed to the general growth of human freedom. Now, in the mid-1800s France had become the principal agent of freedom, a role formerly played by the Germans, and had to pay a corresponding price.

> Frenchmen of all conditions, of all classes, remember one thing: you have but one sure friend on this earth—France. In the eyes of the still subsisting coalition of aristocracies, it will ever be a crime that, fifty years ago, you attempted to give the world freedom.... Be assured, France will never bear any but one name in the mind of Europe; that inexpiable name, which is also its true and eternal one—The Revolution.[15]

The French nation, with its unique spirit, dedicated to freedom and the Cross, was the central figure in Michelet's *History of France*. In *The People* (1846) the spirit of France was celebrated once more. All social differences and tensions were resolved in the community of the French, which for Michelet reached beyond the limits of the bourgeoisie to include the peasants and the workers. "One people! one country! one France!...Never, I pray you, let us become two nations."[16]

But by then the Cross, one of the two elements which Michelet had discerned in the French spirit, had suffered in the historian's esteem. A bitter conflict with the Jesuits over the control of education made Michelet reconsider the role of Christianity. He brought to bear on the church his judgment on institutions: the assertion that life created the institutional forms but only the creative drive of life itself has lasted undiminished throughout the centuries. Each historical phenomenon, be it feudalism or the order born of revolutions, drew its strength initially from the people's intuitive knowledge of life's needs. But, as time went on, institutions lapsed into a formalized routine, maintained themselves by bureaucracies, and decayed in the process. The Catholic church, which he now bitterly resented, had lost its "pure vigor" with Louis XIV. The French Revolution also fell into the hands of those who calculated, reasoned, and stripped life of emotion—the villain here was Robespierre. The desire for freedom remained the only visible and uncorrupted manifestation of life's all-pervasive creative force, and the historian must grasp that desire above all. This notion helped him to justify subjective visions of periods and of people as substitutes for documented studies. "Guizot analyses, Thierry narrates, I resurrect," he said and strove to recall the past "from the dead" in vivid and picturesque word paintings, brilliantly colored and pointillist in detail. Consequently, in the last volumes of the *History of France,* history became simpler. Love and hatred had clear objects. The Middle Ages and their clerical culture lost all their brilliance and were replaced by the Renaissance as the period full of light. The great lesson appeared clearer than ever: what life and its agent, the people, create, the evil elites of power and calculation corrupt. The center of French history must be "the people," however vaguely defined they were by Michelet.

*Historians as champions of liberty.* Michelet's French nation as a mystical whole inspired many but offered little advice on how to solve France's gravest internal problem: how much influence should the ideals of the French Revolution be granted in the shaping of the French society and state? The Bourbons, once restored, defined narrow limits of realization and tolerated no advocacy beyond them. That provoked a battle for French public opinion. The advocates of widening popular representation used the editorial rooms of newspapers and the lecture halls of universities as their bastions and history as their main weapon. The opposition to the Bourbons couched its advocacy of a moderate realization of the revolutionary ideals in a discussion of the role of the French Revolution in French history. De Maistre and Chateaubriand had stressed the Revolution's Jacobin phase, with its Reign of Terror, in order to prove that the continuity of French development had been broken in the 1790s and the French Revolution therefore stood "outside" of French history.

In the 1820s François Mignet and Adolphe Thiers contradicted such negative assessments by basing their interpretation on what would eventually become a liberal dogma: the French Revolution took place in the course of the inevitable development of freedom, which, by implication, would reach its apogee in the rule of the Third Estate. Its moderate phase (1789-93) stood well within the French tradition and, by implication, should be continued in a constitutional monarchy. Its radical phase was brought about by the needs of war. Thiers added to that another assurance for the necessary triumph of moderation. He used the mechanical analogy of pressure (oppression) and counterpressure (the demand for justice) to explain why revolutions have occurred and why after a while they all lose strength. When concessions have been wrenched from the old ruling group, some social strata, now satisfied, desert the revolutionary cause and the counterpressure weakens. He explained the Jacobin period as one of the greatest counterpressure without condoning it. In any case, history showed how peaks of revolutionary violence have never lasted because every society must offer order as well as justice and liberty to its citizens. As Thiers saw it, the Jacobins, like other advocates of democracy, asserted only liberty and thus brought, and will always bring, chaos.

In 1820, Augustin Thierry had demonstrated not only the prominence of conflict but also how the idea of liberty had all along been a part of the French tradition, akin to the true French spirit, and the winning cause. He credited the Gallo-Romans with upholding the ideal of liberty and located the birthplace of institutionalized liberty in the towns of the Middle Ages. Liberty's historical agent and hence the true carrier of the national interest had been the Third Estate, which in the Revolution's moderate phase had finally received full recognition and, by implication, should receive such recognition again.

The liberal view of the past also found historians such as Jean-Charles-Léonard Simonde de Sismondi who went beyond the Romantic notion that the cause of liberty was rooted in a specific *Volksgeist*. Although Jacobin regimes in Geneva had forced the Simonde family into first an English and then an Italian exile, Charles Simonde, better known as Sismondi, always dreamed of republics in which all citizens would share the rights and duties of government. But—and most of the contemporary liberals would agree with him on that—he cautiously hedged: "let power remain with those who comprehend its objects," that is, with those who are educated and propertied.[17] *A History of the Italian Republics of the Middle Ages* (1807-14) celebrated that type of liberty. Wherever liberty had been cherished in the past there had been virtue, and its result was a glorious civilization. "The Italian cities ... enjoyed for three centuries the protection and progressive improvement of their municipal constitutions. These three centuries, [1100-1400] with reference to the rest of Europe, are utterly barbarous."[18] Florence prospered as a republic with citizens and decayed as a Medici fiefdom with subjects. Simonde became so enthusiastic about the Italian role in the history of freedom that he "discovered" an Italian branch of his family and added Sismondi to his name. The high pitch of excitement on behalf of liberty could not be maintained in his later *History of the French*. His nineteen-volume work lacked lustre. It was soon overshadowed by Guizot's and Michelet's histories much as Sismondi's cosmopolitan image of the beneficial rule of communal republics proved no match for the union of liberty and the French spirit.

From 1820 until well into the 1840s these and other French historians transformed French history into the ultimate weapon for the defense of liberty. To call them propagandists would be to misrepresent them, for that term erases the faintly drawn but firm line which separates earnest conviction from propaganda, that deliberate misuse of the past. Guizot, in whose *History of Civilization in France* (1830) Divine Providence guided the course of liberty, would have either not understood the reproach or become angry. For him, the view of French history that depicted the shifting of power from clergy to aristocrats to kings, and finally to the middle class (bourgeoisie), was simply the true reflection of the grand scheme of history. God designed it and humans made it reality. "Men do not make the whole of history; it has laws of higher origin; but, in history, men are unrestricted agents who produce its results..."; "taking the history of France in its totality in all its phases, the Third Estate has been the most active and the most decisive element in French civilization."[19] The Third Estate was superbly fitted to dominate since it was open to all those who were educated, who were able to discuss things rationally, and who were willing to do their duty. That was what Guizot had found in his research, what he believed, and what he proclaimed out of conviction—not for narrow and temporary partisan purposes.

In the gradual transfer of power to the middle class, the Jacobin phase, frightening as it was, represented a mere sideshow; the logic of events—and Guizot's Calvinist background showed in his sense of destiny more than in his austere and aloof behavior—tolerated no long-range deviation from the grand scheme of things, which prescribed a peaceful, gradual progression to the *juste milieu*. That proper state of affairs was the constitutional monarchy based on the power of the middle class. There could be no development beyond the constitutional monarchy, since beyond it lay only the rule of the Fourth Estate, which for French liberals amounted to mob rule. In 1848 Guizot lost his position of prime minister by a revolution which had been signaled all through the 1840s. The kingship of Louis Philippe proved as temporary as the identification of his limited constitutional monarchy with the apogee of freedom and of the Third Estate. The monster of republicanism and democracy, as Guizot called it, had come back to life.

In liberal histories the constant advancement of liberty was prescribed by the "logic of events." Liberty provided the moving force in human events and its fulfillment represented the aim of all development. In a period of longing for a constitutional government with measured popular participation, such a "logic of events" provided a rich source of hope for eventual victory. That it also constituted a deterministic view of the past escaped its advocates but not Chateaubriand, who criticized liberal history as a "fatalistic school of thought" which deprived human life of drama and—even worse—of its moral dimension. If all that happened was necessary or at least advantageous for the cause of liberty, then the Reign of Terror with its thousands of victims could be condemned no more than the medieval plague, another inevitable event. There was for Chateaubriand a contradiction in viewing liberty at the same time as a source of historical necessity and as the greatest moral force.

*The Bonapartist phenomenon.* All along Napoleon Bonaparte had posed a delicate problem of interpretation for French historians. Had he destroyed or saved the ideals and institutions of the French Revolution? During his rule few touched the question. Those who did found two alternatives to choose from: a stoic acceptance of revolutions and all of their consequences, as demonstrated by François E. de Toulengeon, who resigned himself to the fact that "revolutions are the political crises as inevitable in the moral order of societies as are the physical revolutions in the material order of the universe";[20] or praise of Napoleon as a constructive force, as voiced by Jean C. D. de Lacretelle, who maintained his positive attitude even under the Bourbons, shifting his emphasis to Napoleon's role in securing France against a return of the Terror.

Through his memoirs, Napoleon I proved a capable spokesman on behalf of his cause. In the France of the 1820s, where many were either bored by or hostile to the Bourbons, the Napoleonic period took on pleasing colors. Even Thiers, in his *History of the French Revolution,* showed sympathy for Napoleon's reach for power in the coup d'etat of November 8, 1799.

The Napoleonic problem became more than one of historical interpretation when Napoleon's nephew, Louis Napoleon Bonaparte, wrote his *The Napoleonic Ideas* not as a commemoration but as a call for a new Napoleonic France. Paradoxically, the 1840s saw one critical assessment of the Napoleonic period from the same Lacretelle who earlier had been its advocate but in old age had changed his mind. Yet one critical book was no match for the surge in post-Napoleonic sentiment caused by the bloody days of June 1848, when workers tried to gain justice but, in the eyes of those who preferred moderate parliamentary reforms, seemed to threaten the lawful order and the existing social structure. By December 1851 France was governed by Napoleon III.

Napoleon III had a strong sense of his historical role as the savior of French society and of his status as a historical figure, and he wrote history accordingly. In 1865 his *History of Julius Caesar* appeared, full of implied analogies. Thiers' twenty-volume *History of the Consulate and the Empire,* published between 1845 and 1862, represented the most respectable sympathetic assessment of the Napoleonic period. It portrayed Napoleon as a force of order who stabilized the achievements of the French Revolution. But that judgment, Thiers argued, referred to the Napoleon of 1802, a sage, and not the Napoleon of 1812, a madman. Thiers used documents, prior works, and eyewitness reports, painted brilliant scenes in detail, and kept matter-of-factly to the truth as he perceived it. That explains why after an initial short imprisonment and exile, Thiers could live as a celebrated national historian in the Empire, and become the first president of the Republic following Napoleon III's downfall.

Napoleon III turned Edgar Quinet into a disillusioned exile, who now called for an abandonment of the liberal thesis on history. Throughout the centuries France had not followed a path towards liberty. France had been liberal in ideas but servile in practice. Liberal historians had been blinded by their stipulation of a necessary development towards liberty and when they had seen in everything a good purpose had forgotten the moral dimension of history. The French revolutions of 1789 and 1848 were not shining examples of how liberty asserted itself because in each case the people had betrayed liberty. Having abandoned the vision of France as the agent of liberty, Quinet transferred that role to the United States of America.

*Visions and Warnings.* For some the Bonapartist controversy was a mere surface phenomenon of the political order dominated by the middle class. They remembered that the revolutionary clamor had not only been for liberty but also for equality and pointed out that one of the major social groups of the developing industrial society, the workers, remained outside of the existing political structure. Their study of the past and present yielded new prognostications as to where the future development would carry France and other countries. In his London exile during Napoleon III's reign, Louis Blanc expressed his compassion for the laborers and foresaw the doom of the monarchy and bourgeois dominance. His historical works portrayed the French Revolution's Reign of Terror as no aberration but a necessary defensive action on behalf of a revolutionary regime threatened by outside armies, the compromise of Girondists, and skeptics like Danton. Louis Blanc's appeal for a reconciliation between bourgeoisie and proletariat went unheard. It was not in season yet; after all even Karl Marx failed in 1848 to rouse people with his *Communist Manifesto.*

Liberty and equality also interested an eminent analyst of political structures who found a disquieting relationship between the two ideals. Alexis de Tocqueville had toured Jacksonian America and had been fascinated by that strange democratic world. But could America and the Americans teach any lesson to other countries—a society with seemingly unlimited space, a sense of mission, the absence of a feudal past, and a people who were egalitarian, self-reliant, and egotistic, although still good citizens? They could, de Tocqueville thought, because all democracies share basic structural features. He urged that democracy be understood as an all-pervasive way of life and not merely as a political form of organization. By such a definition America was a democracy but not ancient Athens. Yet exactly because democracy was more than a political form it possessed a complex inner dynamic. On the one hand it releases enormous creative energies and provides for great social mobility; on the other hand its egalitarian spirit erodes all institutions and social mobility, as well as all associations that are now perceived as restraints to individual fulfillment but so far have sheltered the individual from the central power of the state. Gradually the individual becomes isolated; he exists in a vacuum of values and seeks stability in the conformity enforced by a mass society. Thus the relentless quest for individual liberty will lead paradoxically to an excessive egalitarianism which will destroy liberty understood as the space in which the individual can operate freely. By implication de Tocqueville defined the possible destination of a democratic Western civilization: totalitarianism. A more promising direction pointed toward a democracy which did not deify the masses and egalitarianism and instead preserved a variety of institutions and associations vis-à-vis the central state, safeguarded the strength of religion, and tamed all destructive passions by a constitution. Hence one must be aware that revolutions posed less of a danger to democracies, indeed to any social order, than the slow and gradual developments which sap the strength of societies. De Tocqueville showed how, in the interest of the centralization of power, the structure of the Old Regime had been eroded by a slow and steady destruction of its multiple centers of power to such a degree that the French Revolution could easily destroy the shell that remained.

# Historians as Interpreters of
# Progress and Nation—II

## English Historiography in the Age of Revolution

During the second half of the eighteenth century English historiography carried the marks of Hume, Robertson, and Gibbon. A craft in the best sense of the word, it also was an instrument of public life, never far from the great political concerns and always cognizant of its role of educating those who participated in public life. Hence, when France experienced her revolutionary turmoil, the experience had an immediate effect on English historical thought, although written assessments in a thoughtful and systematic manner came relatively late.

*The gradualist thesis under stress.* The American Revolution cost the English dearly in possessions and imperial pride, but it nevertheless had less influence on English historiography than the French Revolution because it did not involve social reconstruction. Even after 1783 Americans respected the English tradition and in many ways continued in it; the French, however, attempted to reconstruct their society according to abstract ideals, went through the Reign of Terror, and finally supported the imperial aspirations of Napoleon. The French Revolution contradicted the English ideal of a gradual social development on the basis of the great social and political compromise of 1688, which had just had its centenary celebrations, and the third threatened English security, influence, and power. Amid the many voices of concern, hatred, and fear raised when the events of the early Revolution became known, Edmund Burke's *Reflections on the Revolution in France* sounded already in 1790 the basic theme of English postrevolutionary historiography. A good society was shaped by tradition according to the wisdom of the ages. Attempts to use weak human reason and will in place of this wisdom could only result in anarchy, which could not be remedied once tradition was destroyed. History, of course, emerged in Burke's view as the supreme instructor of a people. Soon the Burkean prophecy seemed borne out by the Reign of Terror and by the end of the radical revolutionary dream in Napoleon's rule—in the English view a return of despotism. The ensuing years of war returned old-style politics and diplomacy to the center of interest and with them also the familiar diplomatic and military history.

By the time of the restoration of the Bourbons in 1815, distance in time had facilitated a reassessment of the French revolutionary events. Documents and memoirs hostile to the Revolution, once credulously accepted, were now sifted more critically by writers such as J. Adolphus. In general, the Burkean theme was revised rather than rejected, when it was conceded that in its early stages the French Revolution had made no complete break with the past. From 1789 to 1792 only remedies for inequities had been brought about and only the Jacobins cut the thread of the proper gradual French development. That was the message in the essays and lectures by William Smyth of Cambridge, the first academician to deal with the Revolution. But in subtle ways the Revolution and the issues it raised had already penetrated academe in the field of ancient history.

*The social issues and ancient history.* Political controversy intruded into classical studies because around 1800 the English, although they still looked upon these studies as fields of scholarship, also regarded them as a splendid tool for educating gentlemen in public affairs. Thus, the *History of Greece* by John Gillies expressed the proper sentiments against the weaknesses of both republics and despots and hailed the limited monarchy which the Gauls never knew and the English were proud to have. That was in 1786 when the Old Regime, Louis XVI, and Marie Antoinette still seemed secure. William Mitford's *History of Greece*, bore already marks of the revolutionary events in France. Mitford, a high Tory, rejected the usually favored democratic Athens as a model, treated Philip of Macedonia with sympathy, and attacked all demagogues.

After 1815, with England once more secure, the tranquility of routine returned to classical studies, with the next shocks originating not in the minds of revolutionaries but in those of innovative German scholars like Wolf, Böckh, Müller, Niebuhr, and Creuzer. In Oxford and Cambridge, especially in the circles around Professors Hare and Thirlwall, echoed the German call for a reconstruction of the total ancient life-context instead of the isolated text only. Also, language came to be understood as the expression of the very spirit of a nation— a witness to the nation's inner forces. Thus the vernacular languages could no longer be considered inferior to the supposedly perfect classical Latin and Greek. In time, as will be seen, that view would also transform the Anglo-Saxon studies begun by Sharon Turner into the sophisticated studies of Anglo-Saxon language and life by John Mitchell Kemble. From classical philology Thomas Arnold built a bridge to the Germanized historical studies of William Stubbs and Edward Augustus Freeman. With the gradual transformation of philology in the new German manner, the historicizing of the English intellectual world had begun; a transformation with definite limits. For example, much of English classical philology—even Grote's *History of Greece* (1846–56), a stellar scholarly achievement—preserved the didactic link between classical studies and public affairs. In a period when the question of suffrage extension moved the English, Grote, a liberal Whig member of Parliament, wrote with sympathy on Athenian democracy and reconfirmed the long-standing negative assessment of anything Greek dating from Alexander the Great.

*The triumph of the gradualist thesis.* In 1830 the July Revolution in France gave a jolt to the English conviction that gradual development had finally triumphed in France. And it happened at a time when the great reform discussions were intensifying in England. Even the Reform Bill of 1832 did not alleviate the doubts about the idea that revolutionary thrust could be deflected by timely reform. Soon after, Sir Archibald Alison argued in his influential *History of Europe from the French Revolution to the Restoration of the Bourbons* that even the slightest concession could set in motion an uncontrollable democratic revolution that would threaten all tradition. Both Alison and John Croker, who argued the same case in his *Essays,* already documented their studies well and adhered to some of the new critical standards. But their doctrine of an inevitable development toward democracy, triggered by reforms, suffered neglect when relative tranquility returned to English public life. The Whigs, gradualists at heart, pointed out that even the revolutionary year 1848 had passed without significant disturbances in England. The optimism of the period found its unrivaled spokesman in Thomas B. Macaulay. In his *History of England from the Accession of James II* (1849–61) he demonstrated that mid-nineteenth-century England was no accidental creation but the result of centuries of development. In the case of England, change had never contradicted continuity and, by implication, never would.

Macaulay's *History* represented a peak in a peculiarly English historiographical development shaped by a remarkable sense of separateness and pride. From the 1600s, elements of what Herbert Butterfield called the Whig interpretation of history had appeared, which in its broadest sense asserted that English history offered an especially felicitous reconciliation of past, present, and future and that the English were wise enough to bring about the feat of venerating the past without binding too closely either the present or the future in the process. In its earliest form that interpretation asserted an ancient constitution anchored in free Germanic institutions and confirmed by the Glorious Revolution of 1688. In the nineteenth century Macaulay and others stressed the Magna Carta as the onset of the march to liberty in English history. And Macaulay shaped this and other elements (Turner's Anglo-Saxonism, Burke's traditionalism and Hallam's constitution of liberty) with a general conviction of progress into a rousing message for the people of Victorian England.

Macaulay was well equipped for what the English wished historians to do: educate the public through history. Trained in law, he had served England in Parliament, in the Cabinet, and as a member of the supreme council of India.

From the publication of his first essay, his style captivated the public as did his good sense of the past and firm Whiggish convictions. When composing his *History*, one of the most famous and successful historical books ever written, he labored hard to ascertain the facts about the past but worked just as hard to write elegantly and lucidly. After all, facts were "the mere dross of history," and those who "miserably neglect the art of narration" should remember "that histories of great empires, written by men of great ability, lie unread on the shelves of ostentatious libraries."[1] Macaulay wished to produce something "which shall for a few days supersede the last fashionable novel on the tables of young ladies" and succeeded in doing so. In an age when few books sold in large numbers his *History* sold in the hundreds of thousands, was translated into eleven languages, and was actually read, not merely displayed on bookshelves.

Yet, Macaulay's fame diminished with the same speed at which it had gathered. One reason for this was that he wrote just before new critical standards of historical scholarship reached England from the Continent. Once these standards began to shape the writing of English history, historians called Macaulay's assessment of sources unsophisticated and his characterizations of persons and events facile. More important, his judgments were based on his conviction that English society at mid-nineteenth century could supply all standards of measurement. When, soon after 1862, even the English world proved to be more complex than liberals had suspected, Macaulay's *History* lost its power to convince. His world had been one without mysteries or unsolvable problems. Had not English development been unfailingly towards fuller liberty, greater self-government, and higher civilization? With the plot known, and with no fundamental change to come in the additional scenes, the good and the evil and the heroes and villains in the English drama could all be easily ascertained. Macaulay, sure of his judgment, made such identifications and told the world about them. His *History* suited

> the majority of Englishmen, by its virile directness, its honest clearness, its bold definiteness. Macaulay is never afraid; he never shirks, he never dissembles or cloaks; he never says "perhaps"; or "maybe," nor "the facts are obscure," nor "authorities differ".... To be sure, there is danger in that brilliant rhetoric. The glow of declamation disdains the sickly hue of circumspection.... But ... men go to the window when a fire engine gallops through the street; a gentler summons might not fetch them. There is something of martial music about Macaulay's prose. There is that in it which excites a man. It belongs to a great advocate, not to blindfolded Justice holding her cautious scales and doling out "ifs," "buts," "howevers," as she balances probabilities with all the diffidence of Doubt.[2]

History had yielded its meaning to Macaulay and he pronounced it. The calculating, unheroic, sober, and "peering-around-the-corner" middle class would safeguard England's welfare forever. *The History of England* traced that class's march to victory and in the process painted a broad picture of the English past.

Indeed, Macaulay had pointed an accusing finger at the history of mere state-craft and war as he spoke out in favor of a history dealing with the whole life of the nation. His execution did not match his ideal and the book's intended scope proved too large; Macaulay's early death left it a fragment, reaching only from 1685 to 1702.

*Other views of the past.* The theme of the gradual realization of liberty in England fit the English conditions well. English society had not recently been divided by a ditch filled with blood—Chateaubriand's characterization of France—and had no need to pick up the pieces of a broken tradition. That fact relieved English historians of much of the need for the Romantic concept of the nation as the unit transcending all social divisions, grievances, and resentments. But while the British lacked exact counterparts to Michelet and the German nationalist historians they, too, were fascinated by the question of national identity and the Romantic answer to it.

In the 1760s James Macpherson published what he claimed to be translations of two epics and several poems by the third-century Gaelic poet Ossian. The ensuing controversy over the authenticity of Ossian and his works stimulated much interest in the early history of the British Isles; it came at a time when Rousseau and Herder were calling for an appreciation of early mankind. Sharon Turner, whose studies of the Norse language assisted scholars interested in early English history, complained as an Englishman that "We roam the most distant oceans to explore the manners of uncultivated savages, and even the philosopher reads, with interest, every description of their customs and transactions. Why should he [an Englishman] then despise the first state and the improving progress of his Saxon ancestors?"[3]

Turner himself published a *History of the Anglo-Saxons,* in which the Germans, while not flawless, were vigorous and certainly worthy of being acknowledged as the English ancestors. In 1815, *Beowulf* was published and during the 1810s and 1820s the historical novels of Sir Walter Scott enthralled the public. The novels caught the spirit of the Middle Ages through the empathy of the author and, brilliantly written, aroused curiosity about that period; this fascination opened a whole historical period to the British imagination. The first rescue of the Middle Ages from obscurity was attempted in 1818 by Henry Hallam with his *View on the State of Europe during the Middle Ages.* His willingness to study the Middle Ages was the more remarkable for the fact that he did not write out of any Romantic enthusiasm; he did not even like the period. As he studied state after state between the time of King Clovis and 1494 he formed some harsh judgments on whole sections of the Middle Ages. "Many considerable periods of time, especially before the twelfth century, may justly be deemed so barren of events worthy of remembrance, that a single sentence or paragraph is often sufficient to give the character of entire generations, and of long dynasties of obscure Kings."[4] Still, Hallam's work opened the door to further medieval studies. It helped that Hallam wrote not just about battles and kings but mostly about institutions and even about language, literature, and the church. His contention, formulated more precisely in his *Constitutional History,* was that the English government had always been or was meant to be a constitutionally limited monarchy (the ancient constitution concept); this thrust medieval history into the midst of contemporary political debates and was a marvelous assurance against it being once more forgotten.

*The issue of the Fourth Estate—the "people."* Only eight years after Macaulay's death, his assumption of permanence for mid-century English society proved an illusion. In 1867 the suffrage had to be widened again, a signal of things to come. Not only could calls for democracy no longer be satisfied by a limited election-reform, the freedoms granted by a liberal order would also not let harsh working conditions for laborers go unchallenged for long. Some Tories had already been working for laws to ameliorate these conditions in the framework of a laissez-faire economy. But as for changes in the direction of democracy, Whigs and Tories alike agreed that social reforms were meant to safeguard tradition and to prevent the unleashing of the destructive forces of democracy.

Thomas Carlyle, a Scot of humble origin who struggled to follow the mandate of Sir Walter Scott and Macaulay that one must reconstruct life in its fullness, saw things differently. At times he became distraught over the paucity of sources available even to the most ardent Rankean or Niebuhrian seeker of sources. While from such a slim base no binding lessons or philosophy of history could be derived, patient observers could perceive the fullness of life and deepen their awareness of God. In that sense history was an appeal to the innermost qualities of human beings as well as a witness to a divine plan.

At a far distance from traditional English historiography with its cautious empiricism and persistent gradualism, Carlyle asserted a metaphysical interpretation of the course of human life in time. History was a drama of that divine justice which is asserted in great upheavals and forgotten in centuries of quietude. In the turbulent times life triumphs over all schemes of thought that in quiescent periods fossilize the products of bygone creativity. Thus, the English idea of gradual reform to prevent revolutionary eruptions was doomed to fail just as the decadent French elite had failed to preserve an encrusted social order, albeit one more repressive. There were two forces of innovation that erupted into history from time to time, the people and the great men (heroes).

Carlyle did not romanticize the people, despite their historical role, but he insisted that history must show the inward life and spiritual condition of people; above all it must be "filled by living men, with color in their cheeks, with passions in their stomachs, and the idioms, features and vitalities of very men."[5] Such an obligation to depict the fullness of human life will lead historians away from tales of kings, "Senate-houses," or "King's Antechambers"; after all,

Which was the greatest innovator, which was the more important personage in man's history, he who first led armies over the Alps, and gained the victories of Cannae and Thrasymene; or the nameless boor who first hammered out for himself an iron spade? When the oak-tree is felled, the whole forest echoes with it; but a hundred acorns are planted silently by some unnoticed breeze. Battles and war-tumults, which for the time dim every ear, and with joy or terror intoxicate every heart, pass away like tavern-brawls.[6]

In his *The French Revolution,* which after its publication in 1837 made him famous, Carlyle did not trace constitutions, rights, or laws but listened to the heartbeat of life. The Revolution was no struggle over constitutional arrangements but an act of justice—divinely willed—in favor of millions of poor people: one of those infrequent eruptions by which life created forms and social orders only to have them preserved well beyond the point where they agreed with public wishes and collective habits. Then the creative anarchy, ever-present in people, would once more break forth in revolutions and destroy the moribund institutions, until the rampant forces were tamed, just as the French Revolution ended in the Napoleonic order. Given the English solution, with its preference for gradual change, would the English society ever become one of those "vast Solecisms," moribund and ready to collapse? Carlyle stated clearly that it already was just that.

In the end, Carlyle did not entrust the cause of Life, the Spirit, or the Divine Idea to the people. He could not overlook that the people were unregenerate sinners and that over long stretches the people had not been creators or actors but a gray, dull mass. The true hope sprang from the Great Men, the true kings by divine right.

> For, as I take it, Universal History, the history of what man has accomplished in this world, is at bottom the History of the Great Men who have worked here. They were the leaders of men, these great ones; the modelers, patterns, and in a wide sense creators, of whatsoever the general mass of men contrived to do as to attain.[7]

In his books on Cromwell and Frederick the Great Carlyle showed these great men to be the brilliant manifestations of life's spiritual core, the texts of historical revelation. If "History is the essence of innumerable biographies," then the biographies of the heroes, be they warriors, rulers, artists, or prophets, yielded more of that essence.[8] Once more, the institutions were secondary, since the heroes more often destroyed than recognized them.

Carlyle's record as a historian is mixed. He had widened the meaning of the term "people" beyond the narrow image of the Fourth Estate waiting to enter or destroy the established societies. His ideas, rooted in metaphysics, did not fit in well with the logic of the English historical argument. The Fourth Estate, on the other hand, found its inspiration not in being the manifestation of Carlyle's Spirit of Life but in the wish to vote and bring about a more decent life for its members; a goal for which Carlyle himself had little sympathy. In this limited sense he had been a precursor of a broad social history. Yet his Great Men theory, celebrated by some, would eventually be outdated as a contradiction of that very same social history. As a historical scholar Carlyle found no favor with those who were influenced to a higher degree than Carlyle by the German critical school and thought of themselves as "scientific" historians. They accused Carlyle of not having heeded his own advice that the two pinions of history were stern accuracy in inquiry and bold imagination in interpretation. The critics, among them Stubbs, Freeman, and Green, saw only the Romantic who talked of the Spirit, painted vivid pictures, and spoke in ecstatic terms. His researches for *The French Revolution* had had too narrow a base and thus no number of foot-notes could earn him the label "scientific."

*History as Rankean science.* William Stubbs and Edward Freeman paralleled the work of the English classical scholars when they transformed English histor-iography according to the highly successful and esteemed German model. They instituted history as an academic discipline in the new sense, one that wished for a national education not through well-told stories about the past or from fixed lessons gleaned from the past but through a mastery of the development of the English nation by means of vigorous studies of the sources. But the two men did not merely transplant the procedures of Ranke's seminar to England; they worked out an English version of the German views on God, nature, Volk, and universal history. From it rose the peculiar Germanist interpretation of English history, best discussed later in the context of institutional history.

### Historians and the Building of the American Nation

In 1783, the Treaty of Paris acknowledged the existence of the American nation. Four years later, the U.S. Constitution provided the legal and political framework for a national life. But it was during the following century that the American nation in the modern sense was built. Soon after 1789 historians had done their share. The nation was celebrated in histories of the American Revolu-tion and its heroes, and in the now nationally oriented local and regional his-tories. By the early 1800s histories of such limited scope proved inadequate to portray properly the large-scale drama which was unfolding. In the span of a century the United States, originally sparsely populated, predominantly rural, and located along the Atlantic seaboard, expanded thousands of miles to the south, west, and southwest, engulfed a vast continent, drew in millions of immi-grants and assimilated them, preserved its democratic government originally designed for a much smaller state, fought wars, grew into a formidable industrial power, became urban in character, and finally maintained the Union and ended slavery in the ferocious Civil War. In the nineteenth century the American national experience had epic character and brought forth appropriately epic histories by five major historians: George Bancroft, Francis Parkman, William

Prescott, John Motley, and, less successful in gaining popular renown, Richard Hildreth. All but Hildreth were New Englanders, imbued with the sense of tradition of that region, highly literate, Harvard-educated, and possessed by a missionary commitment to what they considered "the higher purpose" of their country.

*Providence, progress, and America's past.* Bancroft exerted by far the greatest influence with his *History of the United States.* His life prepared Bancroft admirably for his role as America's most influential nineteenth-century historian. He was a scion of an old New England family with a deep sense of tradition who grew up in an area immensely proud of its past. He wrote well and had learned the new historical methods at Göttingen and Berlin from von Heeren, Eichhorn, and Böckh. He learned about his country's concerns, aspirations and strength through his experience in public affairs as a Democratic politician in Massachusetts, secretary of the navy, ambassador to England, sometime advisor to President Andrew Johnson, and ambassador to Berlin, where he became acquainted with Bismarck and witnessed the great European events between 1867-73. Longevity, too, favored him; born four years after Washington's Farewell Address, he lived until 1891. The writing of his *History* alone spanned so many years—the first volume appeared in 1834 and the twelfth in 1882—that tastes and moods changed during its composition. In preparing the Centenary Edition (1876) Bancroft felt compelled to tone down his original enthusiastic style by "slaughtering adjectives." But his *History* remained, in Guizot's phrase, *très démocratique;* Ranke judged it "the best history from a democratic view"; and Carlyle characterized it as containing "much light and no shade."

For Bancroft the American Revolution was no sudden struggle of colonists who wished to shed the fetters of the mother country but a crucial way station in the development that had begun with the first English settlement in North America. Divine Providence had ordained the emergence of the United States in the course of human progress, an event to which the colonial experience was the prelude: "A Nation was already planted in New England; a commonwealth was ripened."[9] In turn, the creation of the United States was not the ultimate achievement. The new nation would act as the pioneer of a *novus ordo seclorum,* a new order of the ages. America was not to be just another nation but would exist "for the advancement of the principles of everlasting peace and universal brotherhood. A new plebeian democracy took its place by the side of the proudest empire."[10] The "ages of servitude" and "inequality" would end. With so lofty a theme, heroes, too, were representations of greater forces. They were magnificent manifestations of national character.

Bancroft considered the love of liberty the prime desire of all human beings. Hence he had no doubt that Americans acted as one in the 1770s and 1780s, and would do so forever. What divided them did not match in importance or intensity their love of liberty. The specific American form of liberty had an

Anglo-Saxon origin. Virginians were "Anglo-Saxons in the woods again," and the New Englanders carried on the tradition of Germanic liberty in their character-istic institutions. That "Vital principle of Teutonic liberty lies in the immemorial usage of the meeting of all the people with the equal rights of each qualified in-habitant to give counsel and to vote on public affairs."[11]

The process of severing the tie between England and her American colonies began imperceptibly with the French and Indian War. After Protestant England had triumphed over Catholic France, matters drifted inexorably toward the decisive conflict. "The change which Divine Wisdom ordained, and which no human policy or force could hold back, proceeded as majestically as the laws of being." While liberty had all along revealed itself at least to a few of the wise, "in America it was the breath of life to the people." Americans "heard the glad tidings [of liberty] which promised the political regeneration of the world." Their ideals and convictions were proclaimed to the world in the Declaration of Independence, "the confession of faith of the rising empire" and "the announce-ment of birth of a people."[12] And where there were blemishes on the American record, such as slavery, Bancroft demonstrated how they had originated outside of the American realm and were continued as useful evils.

Bancroft presented his story of the American past with enthusiasm, told it in a lively narrative, and, in comparison with most contemporary historians, did careful research. What made the esteem for his work eventually fade was the fact that from the 1880s on Bancroft's nationalistic enthusiasm encountered histor-ians possessed of a more critical, reflective mood. For some time the public still read and cherished Bancroft's *History* for its drama and color. The new type of historians, however, with their enthusiasm for the methods and theories of science, a more complex vision of America, and a distrust of large-scale interpre-tations, honored him as a great historian at the same time as they discounted the value of his *History*.

*Doubts without an echo.* Decades before the so-called "scientific" American historians criticized Bancroft, Richard Hildreth put an altogether different account of the American past against Bancroft's work or, to be precise, against its first three volumes. Hildreth's work, the first American history reaching to 1821, was shaped not by the idealist but by the utilitarian philosophy; it knew no nation as historical actor and recognized no divinely ordained progress. That made Hildreth's history an instrument of analysis, not a voice for national inspiration, and his life one of disappointments.

> Of centennial sermons and Fourth-of-July orations, whether professedly
> such or in the guise of history, there are more than enough. It is due to our
> fathers and ourselves, it is due to truth and philosophy, to present for once,
> on the historic stage, the founders of our American nation unbedaubed with
> patriotic rouge, wrapped up in no fur-spun cloaks of excuses and apology ...
> often rude, hard, narrow, superstitious, and mistaken, but always earnest,

downright, manly and sincere. The result of their labors is eulogy enough; their best apology is to tell their story exactly as it was.[13]

Hildreth depicted not an American people united by an American spirit but a nation of social groups, each following its materialistic interests. Landowners opposed shareholders, entrepreneurs opposed workers, as in general the working people confronted aristocratic elites. Even the writers of the Constitution were partially guided by such interests. The public was unwilling to accept such a past. New Englanders did not appreciate his calling the Puritans religious enthusiasts dominated by superstition. Southerners rejected Hildreth for his criticism of slavery. If one thought, as Bancroft did, of a general progress towards liberty in America one hardly appreciated Hildreth saying that

> This is not a true representation of the case. If in certain parts of the
> American Union, the experiment of Democracy be steadily and quietly pur-
> sued, and at length become predominant, in certain other parts of the coun-
> try it is quite overshadowed, and is reduced to creep pale and sickly on the
> ground, by another experiment, less important, to wit, the experiment of
> Despotism.[14]

It did not help that his inductive history deprived his *History* of any guiding themes or lessons, and his cool, dry style found no favor with readers who had the choice of reading Bancroft. Hildreth had anticipated the age of realism in America and failed.

*History as drama.* The other three narrative historians, Francis Parkman, William Prescott, and John Lothrop Motley, held much in common: a New England origin, Harvard associations, a gift for writing well, and the fact that their fascination with the American past did not lead them to write histories of the United States but of topics more or less related to it. Parkman and Prescott also shared a handicap: severely impaired sight.

Despite the sneers of those who denied that a Harvard man could have a true understanding of the West and the frontiers, Parkman left to posterity a lucid and fascinating account of the land and those who explored it, of the Indians, and of the struggle between England and France for the control of the continent. All of that was grand adventure and Parkman treated it as such: the world of the forest and the deeds of venturesome men dominated his work. On occasion the events transcend their narrow frame. The *History of the Conspiracy of Pontiac* (1851) described people and their actions at a point where "the American forest and the American Indian...received their final doom."[15] Parkman's many volumes on France and England in North America were varia-tions on a grand theme: France, representing the Old Regime, absolutism, and Rome, struggled against England, standing for liberty and Protestantism. But these forces did not obscure the deeds of brave individuals. Thus while Parkman disliked Catholic doctrine and its representative, France, he admired the Jesuit explorers. Even the final battle between the two great forces came down to one between two brilliant generals, Wolfe and Montcalm. Parkman's sympathy was joined to a lawyer's desire for accuracy. Nearly blind, he retraced many of the routes of the French Jesuits, visited battlefields, studied hundreds of documents, talked with settlers, and lived among Indians—all in order to capture life's fullness.

Spain, with her past grandeur and power, interested nineteenth-century Americans, who in their drive to greatness still had to consider Spain and did so with the suspicion they reserved for "tyrannical" states. She evoked a special interest in William Prescott because of his association with George Ticknor, professor of French and Spanish at Harvard, who had brought together a considerable collection of Spanish material. When Prescott, a gentleman of means, searched to find a lifework task he decided to write a *History of the Reign of Ferdinand and Isabella,* an account of Spain's birth. After its favorable reception Prescott proceeded to write on the conquests of Mexico and Peru and on Philip II. While Prescott disdained absolutism and Catholicism, he managed to see the Spanish past through Spanish eyes, and his American readers forgave him the lack of the customary disdainful view of Spain because his books held their interest.

Spain figured as the grand adversary in three works on Dutch history by John Motley, another Boston Brahmin. He had learned his historical craftsmanship in Göttingen and Berlin, possessed the literary aspirations and skills of other New England historians, and knew Europe from his prolonged diplomatic service there. His message was once more that history was progressing unalterably toward liberty for all. Indeed, without the story of progress, he found history a contemptible enterprise. In his best-known work, *The Rise of the Dutch Republic,* he depicted the Dutch war for independence as a historical parallel to the American Revolutionary War. The hero, Protestant William of Orange, fought the oppressor, Catholic Philip II, much the same as Washington later battled George III. And like other contemporary historians he hoped that his works would influence the public. "If ten people in the world hate despotism a little more and love civil and religious liberty a little better in consequence of what I have written, I shall be satisfied."[16]

These, then, were the histories people read most often from among the rich assortment of historical works available. Despite the label of "literary" historian which now stigmatizes Bancroft, Parkman, Prescott, and Motley, their works were based on sincere scholarly efforts, although their methods have seemed outdated to later historians. Readers liked it that these historians kept at a fair distance from pedantry and made the narrative flow in the manner of dramas and novels. They appreciated the appropriately chosen language. Prescott had expressly worried about a democratic style, marked by a choice of simple words, juxtaposing it to English aristocratic eloquence and the complex German scholarly language.

The service the literary historians rendered their nation compared well with that offered by contemporary European historians to their countries. From the works of these historians a young and vibrant nation drew new inspiration, pride, and even plain enjoyment as readers watched liberty emerge through the ages, democracy establish its historic bulwark in the United States, and the once great Spain decline. And when Bancroft, Parkman, Prescott, and Motley yielded their places to a new generation of historians, more skeptical and with stricter methodologies, that generation was helped immeasurably by the public interest literary historians had created for historical works.

*The persistence of "national" history.* Bancroft lived long enough to notice not only the continuing popularity of his works but also the gradual changes in the United States after the Civil War. That war had clearly been a turning point in American life and was becoming a new focus for historical interest. Bancroftian "national" historians had to accommodate it in their scheme of history, in which, so far, the Revolutionary War and its period had been the crucial American experience. It was not Bancroft, whose works never reached beyond the period of the Revolution, but the national historians of the later 1800s who formulated the proper response. For them the preservation of the Union in the first truly modern war, with all its horrors, was one more testimony to the providential course America steered; a conviction even shared by those national historians who counted themselves among the new "scientific" historians. Although on that basis it was still possible to speak of the good side versus the evil side—those who supported the Union and rejected slavery and those whose preferences were for the Confederacy and slavery—the question "Why such a catastrophic war?" still needed an answer. The debate which ensued has not ceased yet. In it the ideas of the national historians on nation, progress, and liberty were not immediately questioned, but the ever closer scrutiny to which the politics and events of the Civil War period were subjected soon put in doubt the Romantic notion of the American nation as a harmonious whole. Competing interests, ideals, and groups became all too visible.

In the immediate aftermath of the Civil War there ensued—as is usual in such cases—a war-guilt debate. The question raised was not so much "Why did it happen?" but "Whose fault was it?" The highly partisan historiographical scene resounded quickly with recriminations. Southerners accused the North of ignorance about Southern life, of being motivated by fanaticism and an unrealistic ideal of equality, and of disregarding the South's legitimate grievances. Northerners spoke of a slave-power conspiracy in Congress and in the executive branch prior to the war and deplored all the preceding compromises on slavery as futile and evil. Southerners denied above all that slavery had constituted the main issue; the issue really was states' rights versus federal power, specifically the right to secede. Northern writers insisted on the centrality of the slavery issue and saw the Civil War as an "irrepressible conflict" between freedom and slavery.

As the years went by, the bitterness faded bit by bit and the transformation of the Civil War into an event in national history began. In the 1870s, books and magazines presented accounts from writers of both the North and the South. Gradually those who praised persons, groups, and regiments, whether on the losing or the winning side, referred to the national framework. A further reduction of partisanship came from the ideal of "scientific" historiography. But while the heat of the debate lessened and some conspiracy theories and the worst epithets were dropped, the discussion of the Civil War remained firmly linked to moral issues and judgments. Hermann von Holst found no contradiction between his German critical training, which made him appreciate sources like newspapers and congressional records, and his speaking of the immorality of slavery, of the need of decaying societies to yield to vigorous, better ones, and of the "logic of morality" in history. James Schouler replaced the term "conspiracy" with the less sinister word "rebellion" and held that differing ideas and circumstances led to the war rather than conspiracies of individuals. Stern antislavery moral judgments could even be combined with sympathies for some Southerners, as James Ford Rhodes demonstrated. These historians saw no contradiction between their scientific aspirations and their moral stance because they, in the Bancroftian manner, still identified the goals of the Union with the goals of history. Hence a pro-Union view was simply the true view. That made it possible for them to make concessions to the other side, such as expressing admiration for General Lee and condemning certain aspects of Reconstruction.

### Historiography's "Golden Age"

Historiography reached its peak of prominence when a few powerful currents combined forces. The philosophes had thrust a comprehensive interpretation of history into the midst of public discussions. At the same time the historians of the German *Aufklärung*, somewhat less concerned with charting a common course for humanity, articulated an intricate body of methods designed to make possible accurate knowledge and an "understanding" of past periods. Then the American and French revolutions introduced fundamental and rapid changes into Western culture. As the quest for knowing the meaning of the multitude of often puzzling events grew, people relied on historians to find explanations for the many changes as well as the assurance of continuity and stability in the midst of change. Some historians searched past centuries for the origin, development, and nature of liberty. Others were captivated by the Romantic concept of the nation as the spiritual unity of a people and attempted to trace a nation's course through the ages. In either case historians often left the quiet of the scholar's study to become counselors of rulers, guides for political parties, and articulators of the *Volksgeist*. Even those who remained simply scholars contributed to the enhancement of history's prominence by their contributions to a historical science. Historians did not quite replace the philosophers and theologians but in many ways they surpassed them in influence, as the educated became used to calling on historiography to interpret human life, or at least to aid in approaching most problems historically.

*Historians as public figures.* One could have thought that the ancient period had returned, as history writing and public service once more were frequently linked. In France, Thiers and Guizot served King Louis Philippe as minister and prime minister while the famous poet Alphonse M. C. Lamartine planned his *History of the Girondists,* conceived as history but executed as a novel, to discredit the monarchy of Louis Philippe. He briefly became a prominent figure in the Revolution of 1848. Most other French historians had ties to one or the other of the political groups, and Thiers and Mignet began their careers as journalists in order to influence public opinion. Conversely, historians suffered for their commitment through dismissals from archival and academic positions when the political power-constellation shifted (for example, Mignet and Michelet) and through exile (Quinet and Thiers). Few perservered as well as Thiers, who in old age became the first president of the Third Republic.

Bismarck considered some German historians essential figures in the creation of the German Empire of 1871. Their public commitment, however, differed from that of their French colleagues. In the 1830s, Ranke did edit the *Historische Politische Zeitschrift,* to plead the cause of the unique German *Volksgeist* and of a moderate conservatism with the educated public, and Gervinus edited a liberal periodical. But such journalistic ventures were rare for German historians, and equally so was Ranke's role as occasional advisor to two kings, Friedrich Wilhelm of Prussia and Maximilian II of Bavaria. It mattered much that most German historians were professors at public universities. Despite considerable academic freedom, the stake of historians in the existing order and the aspirations of their state made cooperation between the existing powers and historians more characteristic for German historiography than acts of opposition. The outstanding example of the latter occurred in the 1830s when seven professors, including Dahlmann and Gervinus, protested against the Hanoverian king's revocation of the constitution. Later, after the publication of his *History of the Nineteenth Century,* Gervinus was tried for treason, while Dahlman, who had joined the unsuccessful Frankfurt Parliament of 1848, hoping for a German liberal and national reconstruction, associated himself with the so-called Prussian school of historiography, which favored a German Empire under Prussian leadership. On behalf of that cause many historians spoke well and effectively.

In England the liaison between history writing and public life had always been firm but had rarely been closer than in Macaulay's case. He was a fortunate man since his sympathies, mode of work, and experiences all were in harmony with the prevailing Whig political philosophy. "Being in tune" with the prevailing spirit of one's nation was also characteristic of the American historians of the pre–Civil War period, although, with the exception of Bancroft, they had little direct involvement in public life. Macaulay and the narrative American historians were not professors who wrote mainly for a small circle of scholars. They wished for their often many-volumed works to reach the "people" and therefore strove for eloquence and dealt with issues which concerned the public. The "people," of course, meant the lay public which through public education was growing steadily. Guizot thought that readers or listeners "required light, and life together, [and] they wished to be illumined and excited, instructed, and amused."[17] Notwithstanding the subsequent disapproval by the so-called "scientific" historians of such "literary" history, nineteenth-century historians could not write in any other way if they wished to reach their goals.

Even Ranke, never intent on promoting a cause, strove for a narrative with dramatic highlights, sharp characterization of persons, and a steady flow. He succeeded as a writer but not as a lecturer. His lecture audiences, except during the 1830s, were small. In that respect he stood in sharp contrast to Heinrich Treitschke, whom the Berlin University faculty picked to succeed Ranke precisely in order to link history and public life more directly or, in other words, "to do justice to those circles of students who seek instruction in history for other purposes than to dedicate themselves exclusively to the study of history and historical research."[18] Treitschke fulfilled this hope, and his work became an enthusiastic affirmation of the German nation and its past from the perspective of its new standing in Europe.

*The German historical science.* Ranke had already instilled the code of *wie es eigentlich gewesen* in dozens of young historians when Macaulay still celebrated English liberty in his works and Guizot wrote a work which originated in "the paternal pleasures of telling my grandchildren the history of France."[19] German historiography had rushed ahead of the rest of European historiography in methodological sophistication. Only in the 1860s would the mediation of Gabriel Monod facilitate the transfer of German methods to France, while the German mode of "doing history" influenced the idiosyncratic English development through the so-called Oxford and Cambridge schools of historiography and American historiography through the numerous Americans who studied at German universities. The German historical seminars were the training ground for the missionaries of *Geschichtswissenschaft* and the German historical works were its missionary tracts.

Yet the view of German historical science as simply the culmination of the critical historiography that began with Renaissance humanism—a sort of saturated erudition—cannot explain the great controversies over that historical science in the late nineteenth century, conflicts which were more philosophical than methodological in nature. The issue was the idealist ingredient in that science which interpreted historical phenomena in terms of God or his mediators, the ideas, and saw the world of persons and institutions as marked by uniqueness and development. Nineteenth-century rulers and governments found such a historical interpretation, with its clear negation of abstract ideals and radical change, congenial. On the other hand the idealist basis made the Rankean historical science vulnerable to attack once another philosophical base was chosen.

Up to the 1880s, a supreme confidence stilled all doubts. History no longer was the servant of any other discipline; it had come into its own, complete with ancillary disciplines and a methodology. The latter revealed both its promise and its limits. The desire to reconstruct accurately and fully all of past life tended to widen the scope of sources continuously, with the new science of epigraphy supplying the prominent example. Niebuhr had pioneered the use of inscriptions in Roman history. Böckh had done the same for Greek inscriptions, while Theodor Mommsen enhanced the knowledge of Roman inscriptions. The demand that every historical work be based on the critical use of documents, a procedure Ranke did not originate but made mandatory, led students into the archives, where they promptly learned much about politics, diplomacy, law, and a few social phenomena. Many of the sources for economic history, intellectual, artistic, and religious history, however, could not be encountered in the state archives and this circumstance combined with the preoccupation of the age with politics in the grand style worked to the detriment of these fields. Also, when the historians emerged from the archives many of them found the apparatus of scholarship and the mind set of the erudite scholars formidable obstacles to achieving eloquence. While gifted historians still succeeded in exciting their readers, pedantry crept into historical works.

One period of the past gained especially from the new scholarship. With archives full of medieval documents and with the age filled with Romantic notions of *Volksgeist*, German historians began to bring to light the Middle Ages when, as they thought, the German spirit had manifested itself in a brilliant empire. On their part, some French historians searched the Middle Ages for the traces of liberty, the growth of the Third Estate, and the role of kings, while the English retained their strong interest in the classical age and gave intermittent attention to the medieval period. English historians were fascinated by the Anglo-Saxons and the Middle Ages particularly in the context of exploring the seemingly constant struggle between crown and parliament. In all countries a strong desire grew to rescue the remains of the nation's past by collecting, editing, and publishing source materials (see fig. 16.1). This Romantic-nationalist dedication to the past produced brilliant text editions. Students were trained to judge and use sources in historical seminars and special institutes such as the *École des Chartes*, which Guizot had furthered, and the *Oesterreichisches Institut für Geschichtsforschung*. In these circumstances medieval studies flourished, achieving results that have altered our ideas about Western history profoundly.

Amidst the celebration of the successes of the new critical history nobody noticed that historiography had arrived at one of its turning points. The view of historical knowledge as cumulative, with scholars contributing their small share to

Figure 16.1
The Great Source Collections of the Nineteenth Century

| German Area | France | England |
|---|---|---|
| *Monumenta Germaniae Historica* | Continuation of: *Gallia Christiana* | *Chronicles and Memorials of Great Britain and Ireland during the Middle Ages* (=Rolls Series) |
| Initiator: Baron Karl von Stein in 1819. | Initiators: Maurists to 1816, then Institut de France/Académie des inscriptions et des belles lettres. | Editors: H. Petrie suggested the idea and lobbied for it. Collected *Monumenta Historica Britannica* (1848) (extracts from pre-1066 sources). |
| Editors: Phase I–G. H. Pertz, J. F. Böhmer, G. Waitz, L. Bethmann, W. Wattenbach, R. Köpke, P. Jaffé. Phase II–G. Waitz, T. Mommsen, W. Sickel, W. von Giesebrecht, W. Wattenbach, E. Dümmler. | Editor: B. Haréau (1816–65). | Next publications of administrative records by series of Record and State Papers Commissions beginning in 1838. Public Records Office established 1838 under Master of the Rolls (M.R.). |
| Range: A.D. 500–1500. | *Recueil des historiens des Gaules et de la France* | |
| | Initiators: Maurists to French Revolution, then Académie des inscriptions et des belles lettres. | 1857: beginning of Rolls Series Proper |
| *Regesta* (of various emperors) from 1831 on: J. F. Böhmer, later J. Ficker (published from remaining documents and his own *Acta imperii selecta*). | Editor: Dom Brial. | Initiators/editors: T. Hardy, F. Palgrave, J. S. Brewer, J. Stevenson, J. Romilly (M.R.); later, especially, W. Stubbs. |
| Range: 928–1399. | *Collections des documents inédits sur l'histoire de France* | |
| *Fontes Rerum Germanicarum* | Initiators: F. Guizot (1830s) and Société de l'histoire de France whose members included A. Thiers, F. Mignet, F. Fauriel, P. de Barante, L. Delisle. | |
| Initiators/editors from 1843 on: J. F. Böhmer; P. Jaffé | | |
| Range: Middle Ages. | | |

it, excluded historians whose methods had not been "fully developed." All histories created prior to the early 1800s had become tainted and they all had to be "done over again" in the proper manner. They offered at best source material that could be consulted for bits of information but had to be rejected as valid history. As a consequence, one not perceived by the German historical scholars and their allies, the value and authority of all older historiographical models and all histories based on them began to vanish. Paradoxically, *Geschichtswissenschaft* had the same corrosive effect on traditional historiography as did the advocacy of the exclusive use of the natural science model for the explanation of human phenomena.

*Historical scholarship in a young nation.* The enthusiasm for history shown by nineteenth-century Americans equalled that shown by Europeans. The two continents differed considerably, however, in their historiographical endeavors. Americans, too, had their publications of sources but these were not sustained by monarchical or princely subsidies and by a strong contingent of historical scholars drawn from the academic community. Instead the historical societies formed by states, regions, and localities assumed the task of collecting, preserving, and publishing source materials. Such a society began in Massachusetts as early as 1791, and by 1860 there existed over one hundred such societies. A few scholarly entrepreneurs also did their share in preserving the documentary heritage of the nation, such as Jared Sparks, who published forty-seven volumes of sources, including the writings of Washington.

Prominent among those who formed and sustained the historical societies were lawyers, clergymen, doctors, teachers, and gentlemen of means. They shared an immense pride in the new nation and its steady development. The nation's past as well as its future destiny were clear to them: God's Providence had created the United States as the defender of the ideal of liberty in the ongoing struggle between the forces of liberty and its opponents. The remains of the American past were the witnesses to that struggle and needed to be preserved so that they could teach and inspire future generations. In publishing these sources editors needed therefore to be accurate but also sympathetic. The strict critical editorial standards of contemporary German historiography had no measurable influence on American editors of documents. Sparks for example, still corrected George Washington's grammar, spelling, and sentence structure because such editing seemed to do no harm to accuracy and enhanced the didactic and inspirational use of the documents.

From about 1870 on the new standards of critical-text editions and interpretations were taught in graduate programs in history at universities. Up to that time history had had a strong position in high schools but a precarious status on the college level. Since 1643, when Harvard College began to offer a *Historia Civis,* some occasional teaching of history as a separate subject occurred. In the

1830s, for example, Jared Sparks lectured on the American Revolution at Harvard and in the 1850s history appeared at the University of Michigan. Academic history grew from then on. Thus, throughout most of the nineteenth century, history was not a professional endeavor of academicians, although it had a clear didactic purpose: whether the subject matter was American, ancient, or world history, the historian was to provide information and educate democratic citizens.

# ·17·

## A First Prefatory Note to Modern Historiography (1860–1914)

The historiography of the years between 1870 and 1914 could best be compared to a section of ocean whose tranquil surface was increasingly disturbed by the effects of swift and turbulent undercurrents. On the surface the Golden Age of historiography continued to the First World War. The discipline of history was well represented at the universities, the historical approach pervaded other disciplines, and the still largely unbroken tradition helped maintain a confident historical sense.

A constant stream of works on political, military and diplomatic history poured forth, reflecting and affirming the preoccupations of the world of nation-states. That type of historical writing fit with the contemporary historical science and also served well the European power system that was temporarily at an equilibrium. Germany and Italy had achieved national unity, France had settled on the republican form of government, the United States had become one nation free of slavery, and England continued on a steady course as a world power. All of them were exuberantly expansionist, and seemed to have gained access to perennial power, to be able to assure an ever-increasing well-being for more and more of their citizens, and to have reached a stable compromise between tradition and innovation. Yet four broad forces—science, industrialization, the emancipation of the masses, and the emergence of a global world—were already reshaping contemporary life. Historiography was affected because, since the 1700s, it increasingly undertook the ambitious task of reconstructing the past without any aid from existing traditions. That, by necessity, involved historians in formulating their own philosophical explanations of the world's order and the methods of finding that order. Thus, the proliferation of philosophical explanations of the world had a marked impact on historiography. The latter had exchanged the limits put on it by tradition for an unlimited freedom of explanation; it proved a complex, often troublesome, exchange.

*The pull of the sciences.* By 1880 the sciences enjoyed immense prestige. Many scholars were enthusiastic about the image of a nonmysterious world without essences and spiritual entities and about the scientific method as a way to certain and timeless truth. The public was impressed by science's off-spring, technology, with its promises of more food, products, health, comfort, and mobility. Not surprisingly, scholars in all fields, including history, felt impelled to emulate so successful an endeavor and transfer its views and methods from the inquiry into nature to the inquiry into human phenomena. Historians soon found that historiography could not simply be made to conform to the natural science model by undergoing a few adaptations here and there. They would have to accept not only the research methods but also the basic views of the world of the sciences. The emulation of strict scientific empiricism would exact a high price by dislodging from dominance the unique phenomena and their idiosyncratic contexts and putting in their place general and predictable phenomena or forces. Historians would have to abandon indeterminism in favor of determinism. This explains why in the six decades prior to 1914 an increasingly fierce battle raged between those who were ready to make the change—Auguste Comte, Henry Buckle, Hippolyte Taine, Karl Lamprecht, and some American historians—and those who opposed historiography's absorption into a unified science. Among the latter were the large majority of historians who found the methods of history that had been developed earlier in the nineteenth century fully adequate to insure the scientific standing of history. They, as George M. Trevelyan put it bluntly, considered the idea of history becoming a science harmful if not grotesque.

In the 1880s, even German scholars grew aware of a precarious situation in the German historical science that had been brought about when Ranke's successors had discarded the philosophical and theological elements the master had used in his synthesis. But Ranke's system had gained its persuasive power from the correspondence between form, methods, and the perceived order of the world—stable, divinely ordered, and with ideas as mediators between the transcendent and the mundane. The scholars also understood that historians under the obligation to reconstruct the past but having left only the modern version of erudition and the narrative form, to master the task could no longer avoid speculating on the nature of the world, particularly on its human phenomena. While in the ancient and medieval periods history's limited purpose required only a methodology equally limited in sophistication, the ambitious ideal of reconstructing the past independent of and often against traditional views of the historian's society now demanded an elaborate methodological and epistemological apparatus. Historians who truly stripped themselves of all traditional views (seen as prejudices) had to reconstruct the world from scratch on the basis of sources and a philosophical explanation of the world as a substitute for tradition. But the resulting multitude of views would threaten the truth value of history and that in turn prompted an agonizing struggle to ward off the specter of relativism. Positivist historians, who were sure of the world's nature and the methods for its study, had, of course, no such problems.

Positivist historians, relying on a "scientific" explanation of the world that drew on Ranke as well as Newton, Comte, and Darwin, saw the problem simply as one of using appropriately scientific methods in their research. They took an ambivalent stand on the existing traditions. Mostly employed by public institutions, they left unsaid, often unthought, that science knew neither a fatherland nor cultural preferences. They also continued to adhere to or even affirm national traditions and the progress view of the Enlightenment period.

*The industrial age discovers the "real force" in history.* The age of the machine had begun for many Western countries centuries ago. But in the second half of the nineteenth century industrialization proceeded at a staggering pace and triggered changes vast in number and scope. Factories and cities grew in tandem, destination points of a migration from the countryside that dwarfed the famous Germanic migrations. These migrants saw the industrial cornucopia as a promise of betterment for all. The hardships and sufferings caused by long and hard work at low pay were real enough, but so were improvements and a hope for a steadily growing affluence in which even the masses would share. By mid-century economic activities were perceived as sufficiently important for a few German historians to create economic history, although they held fast to the view that economic forces were only one component in a field of forces. Their restraint was shattered by Karl Marx, who, inspired by Hegel, built a historical theory on a grand scale. Critics pointed out that with its strict determinism and its prediction of a "historyless" ideal end stage, the theory was destructive to the existing social order, to empirical research, and to a truly historical view of the world. By the late 1800s a process of revision and interpretation began in an attempt to adjust Marx's historical theory to the fullness of life.

As for non-Marxist economic studies, they took a completely ahistorical turn when in the late 1800s economics began its spectacular rise as a science based on the assumption of a pure *homo oeconomicus,* timeless mechanisms, and the isolation of the economic sphere from all other human phenomena. Economic history as a field remained weakened by the defections of Marxists and the new economists, but a general assertion of economic forces as dominant pervaded not a few subsequent historical works, particularly some by historians of the American "New History" school.

*The masses at the gates of historiography.* The industrial workers of Europe found in Marxism a rallying point, but their march to equality was enhanced by their sheer numbers, improving education, and concentration in the urban areas, as well as by the willingness of some societies to ameliorate hardships. When the age of the masses began, somewhere in the late 1800s, historians were hardly prepared for it. So far, peasants and workers had gotten little attention in historical works. Theirs had been an anonymous presence marked by no more than the routine cycles of birth, growth, work, marriage, reproduction, illness, and death. Intermittently the "common" people had revolted or had been victims of catastrophes and on those occasions had received brief mention. Even when nineteenth-

century historians spoke of "the people," they usually referred to distinct collectives, the nations, who found their proper acknowledgement in national histories.
Their access to the story of "the common people" was blocked by the types of
sources they consulted—diplomatic, political, and military records. Undoubtedly most historians also were among the supporters of the existing order in
Western societies prior to 1914 and were suspicious of the masses. Thus institutional histories dealt with the development of social roles, rules, and customs that
held society together. Only Marxists celebrated industrial workers as the great
antithesis to capitalist societies that in the end would transform those societies.
However, orthodox Marxism, too, defined the common people as a group with
given characteristics. The empirical study of the masses took only tentative steps
in the decades prior to 1914. John Green's celebrated *History of the English
People* did no more than replace political and military history with cultural
history. It was in the United States, during the Progressive period, that the first
democratically oriented historiography appeared in the works of the "New History" school.

*The triumphant West and its world histories.* The world had been known to
be a globe since 1522, but only by the late 1800s did the global world become a
part of everyday life. Accordingly the need to write world history should have
grown more and more urgent. It did not. In fact, as long as the flags of Western
countries still flew over vast expanses of the globe, those areas remained essentially appendages to Europe and therefore the past of Africa and Asia was mainly
treated in the context of colonial and imperial histories. For Marxists, world
history was simply a generalized Western experience with its perceived development proceeding toward the eternal socialist-communist stage. Christian scholars
were severely handicapped because theological higher criticism and empirical
archaeology put essential parts of their traditional universal history into doubt.
Those who wished for world histories based on new images of human life and the
world were not successful either. Darwinians provided little more than a general
suggestion of evolution as the developmental model for world history. The view
of human beings as purely biological entities yielded the basis for racial histories,
and the concept of the "survival of the fittest" served other historians as the
justification of imperial ventures. That left a few scholars who simply studied
civilizations comparatively while putting aside the question of a truly unitary
world history. In sum, at its peak of world dominance, Western culture betrayed
little firm grasp or keen analysis of world history together with much uncertainty,
doubt, and confusion. Some historians would take that as a reflection of an
insufficiently developed data base while others were moved to describe decay.

# ·18·

# History and the Quest
# for a Uniform Science

### Comte's Call to Arms and the Response

*Comte's vision.* Condorcet had looked forward to a future filled with peace, harmony, and happiness that would arrive once superstitions and outdated habits had been expelled from the human world. In the 1830s Auguste Comte, eager to bring about the new order, redefined the course of history and replaced Condorcet's vision with a systematic theory. He did so as a man who in his early years had rejected family, monarchy, and God, and had exchanged for them the social reformist ideals of Claude Henri de Saint-Simon.

Comte proclaimed the great change to come in his *Course of Positive Philosophy*. He spoke in terms of mankind, although he, like many others at that time, really referred to the European West because of the "peculiar capacity of European countries to serve as the theatre of the preponderant evolution of humanity."[1] This evolution must be the central subject of history, not individual nations and their particular *Volksgeist* or their politics and battles, and not the individual which "is, properly speaking, at bottom, no more than an abstraction."[2]

The evolution of humanity was propelled by the evolution of the collective human mind, which followed a three-stage pattern, an idea already suggested in a less precise way by Turgot and Saint-Simon. Comte's excitement stemmed from his belief that mankind's mental development, having already passed through the two preceding stages, was in his time at the threshold of the third and final stage (see fig. 18.1). In it would come the perfect realization of all potentialities of the human mind and hence a radically different society, politics, and culture. In that age the sciences would organize human life according to the laws governing phenomena, laws that had been established, in the positivist vein, through generalizing from sensory experience. Even the investigation of social phenomena would now be entrusted to a positivist social science, sociology, whose insights in turn would help to safeguard social harmony and stability. Later, Comte became less sure of that and even promoted his own "religion of humanity" to fill the void left by the vanished traditional beliefs and habits.

272

Figure 18.1
Comte's Three Stages of History

| | The theological era | The metaphysical era | The positive era |
|---|---|---|---|
| | ← Time → | | |
| What causes the changes in the collective mind? | Internal development due to incoherence of elements (e.g., fetishism, polytheism, monotheism. | Internal development due to incoherence of elements (e.g., never succeeds in bringing egotisms under control of mind). | Total coherence of elements—no further development. |
| | 1st discontinuity | 2d discontinuity | 3d discontinuity |
| When did the stage begin and end? | | | |
| | The origin of the world | Luther (opened break for deism and atheism) | French Revolution and the industrial movement        has no end |
| How are events explained? | by God's will | by natural laws | by positive philosophy which rejects absolutes and essences and aims to ascertain the laws governing the relationship between phenomena (e.g., laws of succession, variance). |
| The encompassing nature of the change. | All thought, emotive forces, sciences go through these stages. | | Thus all intellectual endeavors must become positive sciences, including thought about human phenomena: see Comte's new sociology. |

273

Few of Comte's contemporaries were impressed by his visionary scheme for all of history and no historians were. They preferred their own methods of investigation and could see no task left to them in the third age with its lack of any development in time. Comte, who had read little history, in turn criticized contemporary historians for producing "the shapeless heap of facts improperly called history."[3] Historians had not yet understood that "historical appreciation has no other purpose than to show the reality and the fecundity of the theory of social development which we have already established."[4] The variety of past human experience, which historians had been so fond of, did not interest Comte. One must confine one's analysis "to the development of the most advanced peoples, and the scrupulous avoidance of every digression to other centres of civilization, whose evolution has so far been, for some cause or other, arrested at a more imperfect stage."[5] Great individuals, the maze of events, and less-developed nations, all were not the stuff of proper history, which can "only be a history without names of men, even without names of peoples."[6] Such a history will concentrate on the development of the collective human mind, the moving force for the progress of mankind.

*H. T. Buckle's response.* Comte did bequeath to posterity not only his vision of a three-step progress but also a philosophy fitting the positive stage—positivism. It demanded that all knowledge be based on directly observed phenomena and that all scientific endeavors aim at finding the general laws governing phenomena. Since only sensory experience counted, the whole structure of idealist philosophy collapsed; god, ideas, uniqueness, *Ahnen* (empathetic intuition), and all. Only the positivist approach could yield knowledge reliable enough as a guide for the reshaping of human life; hence observing, searching for regularities, generalizing from research results, and forming laws must be the tasks of all scientific disciplines. Once-mighty philosophy was no longer expected to deliver knowledge but needed simply to see that the methods and approaches used in the search for knowledge were proper. As the positivists saw it, historiography as practiced in the late 1800s was definitely out of step with progress. Not only was its subject matter, past events, impossible to reconcile with the principle of direct observation, historians compounded the problem by not striving after general insights and laws. Unless historians wished to be relegated to playing a trivial role, they had better become positivist in spirit and practice—somehow.

In 1856 and 1861 Henry Thomas Buckle published two volumes of a history in Comte's spirit. His *History of Civilization in England,* left incomplete, became an exhortation for historians to stop writing political annals and to devote their energy to "tracing the progress of science, of literature, of the fine arts, of useful inventions and . . . of the manners and comforts of the people."[7] Equally important, they must discard the view that "in the affairs of men there is something mysterious and providential which makes them impervious to our investigations, and which will always hide from us their future course."[8] Instead historians must emulate the natural scientists and strive to find fixed laws, in this case those governing human life. They can succeed because human actions are not guided by metaphysical forces or otherwise distinguished from the phenomena of nature but "are merely the result of a collision between internal and external phenomena."[9] The latter can be scientifically analyzed, especially the four which shape civilization: climate, food, soil and the general aspect of nature.

Buckle shared with Comte the inconsistency of affirming positivist methods in combination with a speculative pan-psychic overall development that did not satisfy positivist criteria of truth-finding. He did, however, make a valiant effort to explain why the scientific age came to Europe rather than to other areas. The reason was Europe's peculiar climate, soil, and configuration. Once the European mind was able to devise laws for natural occurrences, that mind could also use them to master human destiny, and progress became assured. Historians must now fall in step with progress and become positivist in outlook, that is, abandon the historiography of description and moral lessons for one patterned after the successful natural sciences. If they did not, they would be ignored. While British historians were not impressed, except for William Edward Lecky, and, later, John Bagnell Bury, Buckle's ideas found enthusiastic supporters among the American "scientific' historians.

*The French positivist historians.* In his own country Comte evoked a variety of responses. The French counterpart to H. T. Buckle was Hippolyte Taine. For him, a skeptic since youth, who pleaded for the sciences to fill the void created by the demise of metaphysics, the past held no mystery. It could be wholly explained if one ascertained empirically, first, facts and more facts and then established the precise relationships between these facts or groups of facts. He admired the German historians for their critical approach, which, as he saw it, produced such facts. But unlike the Germans, Taine rejected all transcendence and the notion of unique phenomena and wished to proceed beyond the accumulation of facts to broad generalizations, even laws. To do this, he borrowed models and concepts from zoology, physiology, and the budding science of psychology. But although he sometimes spoke of history as "mechanics applied to psychology," mathematics and physics, with their characteristic measurable relationships, did not influence his work much. Taine wished less to quantify and measure than to demonstrate as precisely as possible how a people's "soul" was shaped by the milieu (geographical conditions) and by race (a vague biological concept). Compared to these two forces, the moment (the temporarily effective circumstances) lagged in importance. Of course, the term "soul" shared nothing with the Christian concept of the same name. It connoted no more than a compound of physiological and psychological characteristics, just as Taine viewed moral concepts, for example, justice, as peculiar cumulations of psychological elements. Nothing reached beyond the confines of nature. As for general laws, Taine found none.

Other responses to Comte were more vaguely positivist, such as the one by Numa Denys Fustel de Coulanges, whose "positivism of the document" had no intention of finding general laws in history. As a young scholar he had compared Greek and Roman cities in *The Ancient City* (1864) and had ventured bravely into generalizations on the development and impact of religion. But he became convinced that France was best served by history if it remained a science of facts and banned all generalizations, metaphysics, and patriotism—notwithstanding the wave of patriotism in 1870–71. In his *History of the Political Institutions of Ancient France* he argued that what was not in the documents did not exist, since for reconstruction of the past, if

> one may hope to succeed in the matter, it can only be by a patient study of the writings and documents that each age has left of itself. No other means exists which allows our spirit to detach itself sufficiently from present preoccupations and to escape sufficiently from every kind of predilection or prejudice in order to be able to imagine with some exactness the life of men of former times.[10]

Bias could not sway Fustel de Coulanges, who was determined neither "to praise nor to disparage the ancient institutions of France. I intend solely to describe them and to indicate their development."[11] Thus he could tell his students that when he lectured it was not he who spoke to them but history itself.

Coulanges's model of a "scientific" history was close to that of a group of scholar-politicians whose desire to emulate the German example had been increased markedly by the shock of the 1870–71 defeat. They aimed at wresting dominance from the amateurs or *littérateurs* who gave stirring lectures at the Collège de France and the Sorbonne—institutions that held no classes, gave no examinations, conducted no seminars, in short, offered no academic training in the modern sense. The excellent École Normale Supérieure had that academic routine, but history there was shaped by literary and classical ideals. The would-be reformers of history along German lines had already entered the educational establishment when, in 1868, Victor Duruy, Napoleon III's minister of public instruction, initiated the École Pratique des Hautes Études. One of its four sections was devoted to history and philology. Soon it was populated by German-trained scholars who set about to teach history in seminars as a craft with its own methods. A historical journal appeared (the *Revue historique* in 1876), archives were organized and opened, document collections were published, and monographs on specialized topics appeared. Although Ernest Lavisse complained that too many highly specialized monographs were being produced, for the time being the spirit of France and that of science seemed to have been united in the study of the past.

This movement had its monument in an influential handbook of methodology: *An Introduction to the Study of History* (1898) by Charles V. Langlois and Charles Seignobos. In it documents were celebrated as the only remaining embodiments of and access to past reality. As document joined document, so fact joined fact, eventually permitting some generalizations. But the two authors disagreed on the possible and desirable degree of generalization in history. Langlois, trained in the École des Chartes, practiced an asceticism of truth which stressed the analysis of documents and fact-finding, followed by severely limited generalizing. In a book on methods published only three years after the *Introduction,* Seignobos ventured much further into generalizations. He had the satisfaction, by that time, of seeing that current opinion was running in his direction.

The Germanist model for the French historical science had always evoked opposition because of the marks made on it by German idealism and because of its German origin. Such latent opposition assisted Emile Durkheim's endeavor to rescue Comte's sociology from obscurity and to build it into the new science of man with a French origin. Central to it was the existence of "social facts" as phenomena in their own right rather than as mere products of actions by individuals. Such facts must be ascertained and examined for those large-scale ordering forces that really matter in society (the *idées directrices*). All of that entailed putting causal analysis over description and narration, the general over the unique and individual, the directly observable present over the unobservable past, and the mastery of society over contemplation. Durkheim, who respected the historian's creative imagination, did not write off historiography completely but left it with only the auxiliary role of finding, cleansing, and presenting the raw material for the generalizations of sociologists. Historians were quick to reject such a role, one that made them mere suppliers of facts. Charles Langlois affirmed an independent historical science with its accent on the unique and the individual. Others, including Langlois's one-time collaborator, Seignobos, tried to "conquer" the new social science by making the historical approach its prevailing methodology. After all, every phenomenon studied by sociology was already a past phenomenon; strictly speaking there was no present which could be analyzed.

From this conflict resulted two quite different approaches to the study of human phenomena, each of them issuing a claim for being "scientific." At the turn of the century the philosopher Henri Berr tried to build a bridge between them but stayed himself safely ensconced on the historical side. He chose as his starting point the perennial human craving for synthesis, that is, the desire to arrive at the most complete picture of the past in order properly to explain it. Such generalizations could come neither from the legions of specialized monographs nor from old-style philosophies of history. In a time where "scientific" was the watchword, an acceptable synthesis could be accomplished only by empirically minded historians. With all their empirical methods sociologists could not do it because they analyzed only the social aspect of human life. Those who agreed with Berr's call for a synthetic history found support in his Center for

Synthetic History and the *Revue de Synthèse Historique* (1900), which became an international journal for the synthesis of knowledge. A massive hundred-volume history of the evolution of mankind by a group of scholars was to support the same aim. Berr's guiding principles in these endeavors foreshadowed those of the later *Annales* scholars: cooperation of scholars from many disciplines; a belief in a science of history that would proceed beyond the careful gathering of facts to a synthesis; the assumption that reality is ordered, permitting laws but not determinism, which for Berr was a "new impersonal God"; the rejection of Great Men as the decisive historical agents in favor of *homme même* (the anonymous human); and abandonment of the excessive concern with individual motivation that had led to a superficial, event-oriented history *(histoire historisante)*.

## The German and English Responses to Positivist Challenges

*Droysen's answer to Buckle and Ranke.* Even in his younger years, when he wrote ancient history, Johann Gustav Droysen dealt with theoretical problems. His innovative interpretation of Greek history from the death of Alexander the Great to the Roman conquest as "Hellenism" serves as an example. The fascination with theory persisted, notwithstanding his Prussian and national commitments, and it led him to the insight that "there is no scientific discipline that has such a long distance to go before it will be theoretically justified, delimited, and structured, as history has."[12] Beginning in 1857 he gave his lectures on the "Historik" (a methodology of history) for twenty-five years, and published their text.

Droysen had become keenly aware of the advances, successes, and increasing prestige of the natural sciences. He also grasped their radical challenge to the views on human life and the world held by the German historians. Therefore, Droysen had relished the task of reviewing, in the *Historische Zeitschrift*, Buckle's recently published work.[13] Yet he was far from a noble knight fending off attacks on a Rankean Grail. Nearly alone among contemporary German historians Droysen investigated the theoretical structure of Ranke's historical school and found it wanting. He denied the Rankean notion of what historians do: secure the remains of the past, mostly documents; assess them critically; and then synthezise through *Ahnen* the parts into a whole that reflects a transcendent reality. Such a view saw historians standing completely aloof from ongoing life and recreating in utmost methodological purity what was taken to be objective past reality. That view emphasized the antiquarian endeavor over the work of interpretation. Then, when historians after Ranke deemphasized the transcendent, they were left with no more than their critical method as theory.

Droysen perceived the historian's work as creative throughout. Abandoning the transcendent element (God and the ideas) he saw all historical work as resulting from the encounter of historians, whose own lives were shaped by elements of the past (the very conventions, institutions, customs, and modes of thought of their own society, together with the physical remains of the past —documents, monuments, etc.). From such encounters came a creative and critically controlled recreation of the past, clearly from the standpoint of the present. A reconstruction that assumed a static past, testified to by remains (*Überreste*), was possible neither by Ranke's method nor by the positivists'. Where Rankeans had sought through critical and objective research to give an accurate glimpse at past and present reality (a reality at bottom transcendent in nature), the positivists tried to explain the world by methods which forced them to see nature, intellect, and morality as features of a uniformly structured world. In his critique of H. T. Buckle's work, Droysen objected to the transformation of the family, the state, and the nation into natural phenomena, thereby depriving them of their moral quality and purpose. It was as fallacious to submerge morality in nature as it was to link it to the transcendent. Instead, the ethical constituted a separate and higher sphere of life, and historians of the family, nations, law, politics, economics, thought, and the arts had to understand that. Neither the world nor the methods for its exploration should be forced into Buckle's positivist mold of uniformity.

*The Lamprecht controversy.* In 1878 the well-known scientist Du Bois-Reymond called on German historians to acknowledge the laws worked out by the natural sciences as their guiding principles. Chemists, physicists, and biologists were now engaging in history writing. They puzzled above all about the root cause of historical change and found it variously in the degree of energy use, soil exhaustion, and racial mixtures. These amateur historians annoyed the professionals, but it was the fellow historian Karl Lamprecht who, beginning in 1891, caused a furious controversy with his *German History,* a twelve-volume work full of challenges to the philosophical and methodological foundations of contemporary German historiography.

Lamprecht rejected Ranke's approach to history because it left no room for causality in the positivist sense. Ideas were transcendent forces not subject to causality, and hence everything they shaped remained singular and unique. In Lamprecht's view such a history affirmed the irrational, was condemned to describe individual phenomena, and therefore knew no cumulative advance in what it studied. Against it he put a historiography concentrating on collective phenomena (at least typical phenomena), affirming the immanent and natural character of phenomena, and using a positivist, that is, empirical approach to explanation.

Lamprecht himself stipulated psychological forces as the basic forces in all of history. But they derived from the collective psyche of every nation and not from the idiosyncratic forces of individual psyches. German history was no less than an analysis of the manifestations of the changes in the German *Volksseele* throughout the centuries. History must become collective psychology. Only then would historians find, first, the key to German developments and, later, through comparative history, the key to the patterns, forces, and laws that have governed the development of all nations. Of course, such a history could no longer be merely political and military history but would deal with all aspects of human culture.

Lamprecht found supporters among those historians who themselves dealt with collective phenomena; the economic and social historians Gustav Schmoller and Werner Sombart and the historian of cultures Kurt Breysig. But most of Lamprecht's colleagues, particularly Georg von Below and Friedrich Meinecke, spoke out quickly and forcefully against his approach. This rejection stemmed mainly from a profound philosophical disagreement and to a lesser extent from political considerations, inertia, or professional jealousy. Most German historians agreed with Lamprecht's critics, continued to write history in the traditional manner, and were not receptive to theoretical experimentation. Lamprecht found a more sympathetic audience at the 1904 St. Louis Exhibition, where some of the American historians considered his scientific aspirations to be in line with theirs, although there, too, his influence remained insignificant.

*Redefining historicism.* Droysen's modification of the German historical science and the Lamprecht controversy signaled a wider crisis of German historicism. While the two challenges were defused by either being ignored or defeated, the world of the late 1800s grew increasingly hostile to the intellectual structure of the Rankean school. The triumphant natural sciences and their philosophical advocate, positivism, made metaphysical systems crumble in their search for a nonmetaphysical truth. The industrial revolution's repercussions put in question the traditional social and political order, and German Realpolitik rejected Ranke's idealist concept of the state. In addition, German historiography suffered from a paradox of its own creation. Throughout the early part of the century historians had persuaded scholars to approach all problems historically, and they themselves had won for historiography great achievements and prestige. But the prevailing historicism obligated historians to interpret each period in its own terms in order to let past-mindedness prevail over present-mindedness, and to preserve the uniqueness of individuals and groups. The result was an image of the human world marked by spontaneous changes and a ceaseless flux. In the early 1800s this celebration of change had been counterbalanced by an assertion of a timeless and absolute meaning to all changes through either God and his Providence or the "World Spirit" in motion or even the nation romantically conceived. But those anchors lost their hold not only because of outside challenges but also because many German historians neglected or were unwilling to retain the religious or idealist basis of early nineteenth-century historiography. So thoroughly a Rankean historian as Georg Waitz distrusted all philosophical speculation. Historians must not reason beyond the document; they must be critics, not interpreters. Droysen already understood that such a stance reduced the theoretical base of post-Rankean historiography to a methodology, a positivism of the document. The truth it delivered seemed trustworthy because the basic assumptions underlying it were not explored. These attitudes were enshrined in the standard methodological handbook of the time, Ernst Bernheim's *Lehrbuch der historischen Methode* (1889), although the author was a bit more courageous in the range of sources and the scope of interpretations he allowed. The Ranke renaissance of the years around 1900, in which Max Lenz and Erich Marcks were prominent, also shied away from debating the troubling theoretical issues. The works of this time reaffirmed Ranke's critical methods, the concept of a great-power balance, and the assertion of the primacy of foreign affairs, while little was made of Ranke's religious and theological presuppositions. In the end it was philosophers and a social scientist who went about sorting out the theoretical problems of history.

The task was clear but most difficult. Change and continuity in human phenomena needed to be reconciled in such a manner that a generally valid historical truth could be found at the same time as one asserted: the uniqueness of individuals and their separateness from nature or an all-encompassing matter; a constant flux, encompassing everything including historians and their findings; the inappropriateness of generalizations and laws; and a historiography free of metaphysics.

The first systematic attempts to create a new theory of history came between 1883 and 1910 from Wilhelm Dilthey and Wilhelm Windelband. Although Dilthey respected the achievements of the sciences, he rejected the attempts to see the world of human phenomena as an analogue to the world of atoms and mechanical forces and to separate strictly the subject and object in all research. He found in the human realm elements which were absent in nature: intentions, purposes, and ends, as well as the actions guided by them. But these elements with suspiciously metaphysical names were for Dilthey not metaphysical at all. They could not be links to or ciphers of a hidden reality, because Dilthey's human world was self-contained, with no gates left open for God or a World Spirit to enter. Thus when Dilthey spoke of *Geist,* the word came closer to the English word "mind" than to "spirit."

Both nature and human phenomena, including the world of the spirit, were aspects of life, which encompassed everything in its dynamic whole. Successive phenomena were linked together because the present was "filled with pasts and pregnant with the future," and contemporary phenomena influenced each other. In this context of interconnectedness historians dealt with the actions of human beings and their results. Those historians would always fail who simply observed, counted, measured, found regularities, and consequently wished to formulate laws. Their methods fit the natural world of necessity but not the human world of freedom and they could not grasp the complex process in which intentions, purposes, or ends shaped human actions. That process was accessible only through understanding *(Verstehen),* which entailed entering through empathy into the motives and intentions of those who have acted in the past. Historians could do so by using the visible manifestations of the human mind such as the existing states, works of art, religions, and languages. For example, an analysis of a Gothic cathedral as a cultural "document" must become a re-experience of the motives and ideas that prompted and shaped its creation. A historian who looks at the past only from the "outside" (in the positivist manner) will grasp little. "We *explain* nature, we *understand* the human world, which is the world of the mind."[14] Hence Dilthey classified history among the *Geisteswissenschaften*, a term best understood as referring to all those scholarly disciplines which deal with the world so far as it is a creation of the mind in freedom.

There emerged the view of a restless life hurrying on and on. "Every given state of affairs in the infinite series precipitates a change because the needs which release the existing energies into activity can never be satisfied and the hunger for all kinds of satisfactions can never be satiated."[15] Each period structured the exuberant variety of vital expressions by relatively stable interpretations of the world *(Weltanschauungen)*. But they had no permanence, as new world views were forever pushing aside old ones. Histories, as interpretations of the past, suffered the same fate, depriving historical truth of a firm base, too. Such relativism troubled Dilthey, who had set out to write a critique of historical reason as a counterpart to Immanuel Kant's *Critique of Pure Reason*. He had hoped to find for historical knowledge what Kant had found for the knowledge of phenomena: timeless categories of understanding. They alone could give a firm anchor to historical knowledge. But he found none which fit the world as he had defined it. He could not take refuge in the conviction of Herder and Ranke that, although whole epochs have disappeared into the gray mist of the past, they were all equally valuable because they were all equidistant from God. Dilthey, who had banned absolutes from his system, even generalizations of all sorts, was left with everlasting, aimless change and hence also with the radical relativity of all historical insights. Dilthey had defined history as a science in a nonpositivist way—at a price. At times he shielded himself from the full impact of his relativism, with its potential for nihilism, by a vague personal belief that life had been achieving "higher and higher" levels and at other times by the conviction that "the historical awareness of the finitude of all historical phenomena, of every human or social situation, the consciousness of the relativity of every sort of belief is the final step towards the liberation of man."[16]

The specter of relativism continued to haunt German scholars. The philosopher Wilhelm Windelband observed how positivists restricted philosophy to being a guardian of the proper methods of scientific enterprises and historicists reduced it to the history of philosophy. When he rebuilt the system of the sciences in the face of the psychological and relativistic (including the new historicist) theories of truth, Windelband found that history, like philosophy, needed a new axiological structure in order to have the possibility of arriving at binding truth. Kant's fixed categories for understanding natural phenomena fascinated Windelband. Just like Dilthey, he searched for such categories in historiography and found them in values. With historical truth once more possible, history's standing among the sciences could be clarified. The reality confronting human beings could be studied in two ways: by the nomothetic approach aiming at general insights (typical for the *Naturwissenschaften*—natural sciences) and by the idiographic approach attempting to understand the unique, individual event (typical for the *Geisteswissenschaften*—humanities). The idiographic approach could still make use of the nomothetic approach as an auxiliary tool without surrendering to its generalizing aim. The discussion on the proper theoretical structure of history and the social sciences filled the decades prior to 1914. At issue remained the search for an anchor point to which historical truth could be secured—the absolute point of reference. Max Weber considered such an attempt futile. Western empiricism and reflection had developed doubt to the point where any affirmation of absolutes had become impossible. Modern Westerners were condemned to remain strangers in a world from which they had removed all mysteries and absolutes. From now on they could grasp only aspects and never the whole human situation. A modern intellectual must accept that uncomfortable if not frightful situation. Could order be found by scholars, particularly historians, in a world which never would reveal its inner workings?

Historians must not even try to formulate grand systems of explanation for the past but be content with studying segments of it. Also, when historians talked of states, nations, societies, Protestantism, Capitalism, and the like, they must always remember that these terms connoted hypothetical concepts which were constructed by scholars as tools for analysis but do not refer to real entities outside of the historian's mind. Only individuals and their actions exist, and therefore the historian and the social scientist must analyze the motives, purposes, and results of individual actions. For that analysis of causal connections Weber suggested his best-known contribution to methodology: the "ideal type." An "ideal type" was not a compound of characteristics of an actually existing entity (for example, "capitalism") but a construct of characteristics put together experimentally by the historian, who then tried to match it with past individual actions. In that process it proved either a fruitful tool of explanation or not, but in either case the "ideal type" disappeared once its analytical role had been played: if successful it "lived on" in the insights it had fostered—segments of order established by the historian in the maze of the past—and if unsuccessful it was discarded.

The social sciences, including history, could do no more for us. They explained small areas of reality when they showed how actions have occurred, demonstrated the values guiding them, and pointed out both the actual and the possible consequences of certain actions. But on occasion Weber himself violated his own injunctions against affirming any large-scale order immanent in reality and abandoned his stoic and detached attitude toward the mysterious world. He betrayed a deep concern over the relentless drift towards a world administered by vast bureaucracies which in the interest of efficiency sponsored impersonal and rational production and administration. Such substantial comments on the future hinting at objective general developments contrast sharply with his methodology, which was based on a totally individualistic interpretation of society. With Weber, historians had been separated completely from the world of values they investigated. They were totally detached observers who objectively created islands of explained actions in a landscape of total obscurity. Theory and practice had been separated as the price for keeping the human world distinct from the natural one and for still claiming a modicum of adherence to "scientific" precepts.

*The genteel English debate.* Ever since science had appeared as a new view of the world it had had its supporters in England, where it proved congenial to the empirical strain in English culture. Yet in the late 1800s and early 1900s English scholars did not rush to transform history into a science in the positivist image, indeed, did not even seriously discuss that possibility. History continued to serve society, which successfully maintained its world-power status and was gradually becoming more democratic, by continuing to be the educator of the public person—the politician, the lawyer, or simply the gentleman. Histories offered political and moral lessons or simply well-written narratives for general education and delectation. Neither deliberate detachment from the world for objectivity's sake nor striving for universal laws in the manner of the natural sciences were prized.

Historians sympathetic to "scientific" history found its German, post-Rankean version entirely sufficient. It made English history more accurate without radically altering its nature. William Stubbs still wrote with sympathy on English topics but now did so on the basis of "verified facts." Samuel Rawson Gardiner called for the "pure past," which could be useful to the present but was not colored by it. Lord Acton, whose Roman Catholicism had driven him to Munich for his studies, learned there the German historical methodology firsthand. Ranke's call for historians to show "how it actually had been" reappeared in Acton's advice to the collaborators on the *Cambridge Modern History:*

> Contributors will understand that we are established, not under the
> Meridian of Greenwich, but in Long. 30° W.; that our Waterloo must be
> one that satisfies French and English, Germans and Dutch alike; that
> nobody can tell, without examining the lists of authors, where the Bishop
> of Oxford laid down the pen, and whether Fairbairn or Gasquet,
> Libermann or Harrison took it up.[17]

Yet the same Lord Acton never tired of warning that historiography must not be treated as the mere collection of facts and of pointing out the moral purpose of history, which happened also to be testimony to the religious dimension of life. And though he recognized the strength of evil, particularly in the tendency of power to corrupt men, he considered the progress of human liberty to be the true story of history.

Then in 1903, John Bagnall Bury spoke on "The Science of History" in his famous inaugural address as Regius Professor at Cambridge. He celebrated the scientific character of the German critical school, affirmed the positivist call for generalization in history, and condemned history as a literary genre and moral teacher. When he ended by saying that history was "simply a science, no less and no more" he had become for some a prophet of positivism in historiography. That certainly was too grand a claim, but in the early 1900s Bury was the only English participant in the fervent Western discussion on the nature of history.

A prophet Bury could not be, because he was torn between his wish for large-scale generalization, even general laws, and the lesson he had learned as a practicing ancient historian about the severe limits to such generalizations. He ended up affirming the possibility of uniformities, causes, and even laws in history, yet denying these generalizations any binding quality or predictive power. Even that halfhearted determinism applied only to matters of large scale, such as whole cultures or economic forces, and not to individuals or small-scale events. There the historian encountered the seemingly accidental, the contingent, as for example when "the shape of Cleopatra's nose" influenced Caesar's life. Bury sought to neutralize the threat which the contingent posed to a generalizing history by seeing it not as accidental but as the sudden intersection of some causal chains (each of them entirely explainable, as for example those of Caesar's and Cleopatra's personal developments). The word "accidental" must be stricken from the historical vocabulary.

But Bury also understood that even critically sifted facts piled one on the other did not constitute history. The historian must interpret the past, an activity which will always bring forth views varying from individual to individual and from period to period. Bury hoped to rescue history as a science from the clear threat of relativism by affirming the concept of progress, in which it may be said that views on history, "like the serpents of the Egyptian enchanters," are "perpetually swallowed up by those of the more potent magicians of the next generation; but—apart from the fact that they contribute themselves to the power of the enchantment which overcomes them—it is also true that though they may lose their relative value, they abide as milestones of human progress."[18] At some distant time the truth would emerge.

Few English historians discovered a taste for history perceived in the positivist vein or developed any taste for discussions of theory and methodology. Comte's, Buckle's, and Bury's precepts collided with the still vigorous English historical tradition. The fundamental point of contention was not so much any one item—such as the quest for laws—but positivist historiography's interest in a "general," even "basic," human history with all that that entailed. English historiography was intricately interwoven with the English fabric of life in all its views: on what human beings were, on how they behaved, and on their purposes in studying history. When William Stubbs introduced the German historical science—when he submitted to the "dark industry" of research, Hume would have said—he found less resistance. That type of historical science still allowed

Lord Acton to philosophize about history as the story of freedom and Sir John Seeley to treat history as lessons in statesmanship. On the whole, however, most English historians sided with Charles Oman, the outstanding military historian and an admirer of William Stubbs, who asserted in a typical manner that historical methods were best learned by reading works of the masters of historiography, that scientific historiography was impossible, and that the well-educated amateur was still the best historian. The English public agreed. The *Cambridge Modern History,* with Lord Acton as editor and famous historians as contributors, never could rival in sales the *History of England* (1926) by George M. Trevelyan. The latter defended the English tradition of history writing as a craft. With a wit and charm which would have pleased his great-uncle T. B. Macaulay, he confessed a lack of faith in history perceived as science. History would never have any causal laws or direct utility, such as "to invent the steam engine, or light a town, or cure cancer." Causal laws could not be the primary concern of historians, who wish as keenly to know what Caesar did as why he did it. "In short, the value of history is not scientific. Its true value is educational"; this was a purpose best served by narrative history.[19] Here Trevelyan also took on those contemporary historians, trained by a "Germanising hierarchy," who saw history not as a "story," "evangel," or a means to educating people, but as a "science": "they have so much neglected what is after all the principal craft of the historian—the art of narrative."[20]

In the realm of history the term "science" had a limited reference.

> There are three distinct functions of history, that we may call the scientific, the imaginative or speculative, and the literary. First comes what we may call the scientific if we confine the word to this narrow but vital function, the day-labour that every historian must well and truly perform if he is to be a serious member of his profession—the accumulation of facts and the sifting of evidence.[21]

The view of history as a science "no less and no more" was an illusion and a dangerous one at that. The older Bury surprised quite a few when he, too, lost hope in the eventual "scientific" redemption of historical truth. He resigned himself to the impossibility of a "scientific" history. "I do not think that freedom from bias is possible, and I do not think it is desirable. Whoever writes completely free from bias will produce a colourless and dull work."[22]

### The Peculiar American Synthesis

By the mid-nineteenth century history had achieved a strong position in American life, with the nation and its historians seeming to be as one. On the surface little changed in that relationship until late in the century, when the public and the historians became fascinated with, perhaps even awed by, science, although few people knew what exactly they meant by the term. This new fascination produced, among other things, a large number of scientific associations, and in 1884 the historians followed the trend by founding the American Historical Association. Among its forty-one founders were some German-educated, academic historians, including Herbert Baxter Adams. These historians were full of enthusiasm for a "scientific history" in the German manner and demanded a vigorous training of young historians in the search for and critical use of sources. Such a training would eventually create a split between the old-style amateur historians and the new-style professional historians. But for quite a few years they coexisted in the association just as history as a research endeavor coexisted with history's perceived civic duty to educate the democratic citizen and guard American ideals. History's continued commitment to civic education and Herbert B. Adams's skilled lobbying even persuaded Congress to give a charter to the American Historical Association. Adams, although considering himself a "scientific" historian, still stressed the public role of history.

*The great divorce.* For a while the marriage of amateur and professional historians worked. The association's presidents, members, and readers of papers at meetings came from both groups, with professional historians being mostly university professors. But the association had signaled its eventual course when it made Leopold von Ranke its first and only honorary member. Year by year the disdain for "literary" or "romantic" history and consequently for amateur historians grew, and the nonacademic historians steadily lost influence. In 1895 the *American Historical Review* was founded by the most ardent "scientific" historians; twenty years later it became the association's official publication. When in 1907 J. Franklin Jameson, a leader of the "scientific" historians, became president of the American Historical Association, the transformation of the association into an organization of academic historians neared completion. The amateur historians withdrew, no longer feeling at ease or welcome.

The great divorce prompted the establishment of the Mississippi Valley Historical Association in 1907 as a countervailing action. At that time it had as its purpose to foster cooperation between academic historians and local and state historians. The latter resented being pushed rudely aside by the new professional historians after long service in collecting, guarding, and publishing sources as well as rallying public interest to history.

But the strength of the academic historians grew rapidly as history flourished at colleges and universities, particularly in the new graduate programs. In 1857 the University of Michigan named Andrew D. White as its first professor of history, and he introduced aspects of the training he had received in Germany. From 1876 on Herbert B. Adams made systematic use of seminars in the training of historians at John Hopkins. His students formed the vanguard of Jameson's "noble army of Doctors" that propagated the idea of history in the new mode. Soon their monographs dominated historical publication. That professionalization of history writing is well illustrated by the comparison of two cooperative works on American history. Justin Winsor's eight-volume *Narrative and Critical History of America* (1884–89) had thirty-four authors two of whom were academic historians, while in Albert Bushnell Hart's *American Nation* series (1904–7) twenty-one academically trained historians were among the twenty-four authors.

With an excellent library system, accessible and rich archives, good publication chances, and a firm base at the universities, history seemed secure, if not triumphant. The implications of the divorce from the amateur historians and, at least to a degree, from history with a direct public purpose bothered only a few professional historians. Why worry about any isolation of historians from the broader American life when more and more professors taught more and more history to more and more students? Already in 1909 the American Historical Association had about 2,700 member. Only a few of those concerned with history criticized professional history's exclusive reliance on academics, its concentration on monographs by specialists for specialists, and its disdain for a manner of writing which pleased the public. Among these was Theodore Roosevelt, who spoke out bluntly against professional historians, whom he credited with "the excellent revolt against superficiality" but who had also become so enamored of detailed research that they "did much real harm in preventing the development of students who might have a large grasp of what history should really be."[23] In years to come Roosevelt's concern would prove appropriate for the strain of American historiography based on the conviction that earnest research presented in careful but often dull monographs could have the same public impact as "literary" history or that the public role of history could be dispensed with entirely in favor of a pure historical science. For the time being, however, professional historians had no need for concern about any contradiction between the public purpose and the science of history because the discipline of history flourished. It also would soon become clear that American attitudes toward the nature and theory of history constantly blurred the line between the public purpose and the strictly scientific purpose of historiography, theoretical statements to the contrary. The "New History" of the Progressive Period would demonstrate that blending of the two aims.

*Vagueness in lieu of conflict.* From the 1880s on continental European historians had been asking "What is history?" and had searched for a proper philosophical foundation to their discipline. American historians pondered also, but their question was more often "What was history to do?" They agreed that history ought to be a science but were as unclear as many of their contemporaries about the meaning of the term "science." For most of them "scientific" referred to the German *Geschichtswissenschaft* with its reverence for written sources, strict evidence, text criticism, archives, and seminars. Many of the influential early American professors of history had studied in Germany, respected the level of scientific studies there, and showed their sympathies in most of their professional work. Yet, with all their admiration for German historical science, American historians neither accepted the religious and philosophical foundations of Ranke's work—by then neglected even in Germany—nor were they as fond as Ranke had been of considering every event and phenomenon of the past as unique and requiring a special intuitive act for its comprehension. The American intellectual tradition, pervaded not only by German historicism but by concepts of natural law and progress, offered insufficient support to exclusive claims for concepts like uniqueness, individuality, and spontaneity. While accepting them in some measure, American historians did not share the fear of their German contemporaries that the generalizing approach might destroy the integrity of history as a discipline. Instead, they were fully expecting that laws explaining the past would be forthcoming once historians had gathered enough facts. For the present, however, most historians agreed with George Burton Adam's counsel of patience:

> At the very beginning of all conquest of the unknown lies the fact, established and classified to the fullest extent possible at the moment. To lay such foundations, to furnish such materials for later builders, may be a modest ambition, but it is my firm belief that in our field of history, for a long time to come, the man who devotes himself to such labors, who is content with this preliminary work, will make a more useful and a more permanent contribution to the final science, or philosophy of history, than will he who yields to the allurements of speculation and endeavors to discover in the present stage of our knowledge the forces that control society, or to formulate the laws of their action.[24]

That view agreed with the nonspeculative attitudes of post-Rankean historians, except that it did not preclude "speculations" or "laws" for future historians when the time was right. Such an attitude kept American historiography open to the influx of some quite un-Rankean ideas: those of Comte, Buckle, and Darwin. Already about 1860, Buckle's history fascinated a few scholars by its talk of a history in the manner of the natural sciences. The scientist-turned-historian John William Draper tried his hand at an intellectual history of Europe, filled with the philosophes' contempt for the early ages of superstition and with pride in the progress of rationality. Darwin inspired many more historians. For Charles Francis Adams, Darwin had replaced the cosmogony of Moses with the theory of evolution, and his brother Henry proclaimed:

> Those of us who read Buckle's first volume when it appeared in 1857, and almost immediately afterwards, in 1859, read the *Origin of Species* and felt the violent impulse which Darwin gave to the study of natural laws, never doubted that historians would follow until they had exhausted every possible hypothesis to create a science of history.[25]

But despite the young Henry Adams's brash assertion that "should history ever become a true science, it must expect to establish its laws," American historians never discovered or even searched the past seriously for the great laws governing human affairs.[26] Fascination with them lingered on in an abstract sort of way for a few decades, but American historiography settled for monographs with more modest interpretations.

The peculiar theoretical structure of American historiography explains why the United States never experienced a Lamprecht controversy, a *Methodenstreit*, or any of the other European theoretical controversies, although the same contesting schools of thought were present in America. In the 1890s and early 1900s, American historians were in no mood for a grand theoretical dispute. They were building their discipline into a powerful and respected force, and many of them were ready to be the proponents and educators of the coming reform era. Why should one struggle to clarify the phrase "scientific history" when, even ill-defined, it inspired historians and gave the aura of modernity to history? Thus it came to be that American "scientific history" could accommodate German critical historical scholarship, Comtean positivism, Darwinian evolutionism, and traditional faith in progress. Contradictions between these theoretical elements did not matter much because the "New Historians," just emerging in the early 1900s, worried less about a systematic structure of historical knowledge and, instead, viewed history as a tool for building a new society in the Progressive spirit. Historiography used as a tool had no need to be theoretically impeccable.

# ·19·

# The Discovery of Economic Dynamics

## An Economic Perspective on the Past

Human beings always have had to work to survive or to enjoy the world. They just as persistently have disagreed among themselves as to whose back should be bent over the fields of toil and how the fruits of labor should be divided. Early reflections on economic matters from Hammurabi to Aristotle to Thomas Aquinas centered not on the mechanisms of economic activities but on their moral aspects, such as equity in prices and wages. Then, after 1300, with the commercial revolution in its initial stages, the analysis of economic matters was gradually detached from moral considerations; calculations of cost and profit grew more precise; greed, avarice, and selfishness became pardonable attitudes (since they were socially useful); and machines enhanced production. Finally, those who studied economic matters began, however vaguely, to view the diverse economic activities as components of self-contained systems with their own typical interrelationships between wages, prices, production, consumption, and trade that must be explored without constant recourse to moral questions. The first theoreticians of that kind, the mercantilists of the seventeenth and eighteenth centuries, stipulated as the highest goal of all economic activity the maximum wealth of a state, as measured in precious-metal possession. They deduced from this assumption a whole system of appropriate economic policies, which were based on consciously formulated generalizations, thought to be valid for all states, on the beneficial effects of positive trade balances, manufacturing, colonies, and protectionism. Still, since the mercantilists always dealt with a specific country, they remained aware of the unique conditions of each country, including its past. They were succeeded by the physiocrats, who accepted the eighteenth-century concept of a timeless nature order and equated a country's economy with a circulatory system. In their system agricultural and to a lesser degree mining products flowed into the economy, were modified along the way into consumable products, while money as compensation flowed back to the original producers to complete the cycle. This circulation system constituted the natural (that is, ideal) order of any economy. The history of past economic conditions held no value beyond giving examples of how the economic circulation worked or did not work depending on the degree to which the positive man-made order adhered to the ideal natural order. The physiocratic view of the economy as a self-contained system governed by universal and timeless mechanisms influenced Adam Smith in his *Inquiry into the Nature and Causes of the Wealth of Nations (1776)*. He and the classical economists of the nineteenth century were fascinated by the "pure" economic order regulated by supply and demand. Were the market's "invisible hand" to be given free play, mankind would use capital, labor, and land most efficiently in a global division of labor and experience constant improvement in economic matters—Adam Smith's economic version of progress. Once more, little was left to history but to serve as a supplier of examples of how deviation from the natural order led to failure.

Classical economic theory penetrated the Continent and found adherents: Jean-Baptiste Say in France and Johann H. von Thünen in Germany. But in the German area it encountered a hostile intellectual climate and, in the mid-1800s, evoked the first systematic reflections on economic matters in a historical vein, the so-called Old School of economic history. Its representatives opposed the classical economic model in which isolated individuals acted solely according to selfish and unchanging economic motives which were divorced from religion, ethics, and politics—a view simplistic enough to permit timeless generalizations, even laws. The German opposition was strengthened by strong Romantic notions of the collective as the indispensable framework of individuals. For the German economic historians the goal of economic activities was not the greatest possible gratification of the desires of isolated individuals but the welfare of the whole Volk (nation). Even a vast accumulation of individual wealth did not necessarily constitute collective prosperity. Hence the proper study of the economic aspect of human life cannot be the analysis of timeless and universal mechanisms involving the selfish, isolated individual but that of the given situation in terms of the economic activities and institutions of a specific nation throughout history. Accordingly most of the Old School's economic history was descriptive. When its scholars proceeded to generalize, they did so on a problem close to their interest: economic development. Friedrich List had first recognized the industrial lag of the German area as the central problem and advocated "educational" tariffs as a remedy for it. He highlighted the new view that the English industrialization was no unique phenomenon but a typical stage of all national economics. The search for such stages in Western economic developments led Wilhelm Roscher to suggest a succession of typical economics: a hunting and fishing economy; livestock breeding; agriculture; a mix of agriculture and crafts; and finally a mix of agriculture, crafts, and commerce. Bruno Hildebrand saw a progress from a barter economy to a money economy to a credit economy. For him and Roscher these laws of economic development were valid for all nations. Karl Knies, however, doubted that these types transcended the unique national framework and granted transnational comparisons only the status of analogies.

## Karl Marx: Paneconomic Historiography

In the rapidly industrializing West it was virtually inevitable that the increasingly keen and broadly shared interest in economic concerns would be translated into an economic interpretation of human life. But when Karl Marx made such an interpretation he was motivated not by the general fascination with, even admiration for, industry and its undoubted benefits but by a critical awareness of its shadowy side, the industrial laborer's sorrow, heartbreak, sweat, and toil in the emergent industrial society of the mid-nineteenth century. Equally important, Marx's mind had been shaped by the Hegelian system of thought. It pushed him (and his friend Friedrich Engels) beyond the writing of critical tracts on what he saw as injustices and induced him to create a theory based on economic forces, a grand theory which would not only explain all of history but also deliver the tools for eventual human redemption from all injustice; his was a new type of prophetic history for a Kingdom of God without God.

Marx's world was a world of matter, of which the human world was merely the most complex segment. Neither God nor progress nor the absolute idea nor any other metaphysical entity could explain that world; they all were mere creations of the human imagination. In order to explain human phenomena properly, one must study how people make a living, what goods they produce, and how they do it. Marx called these arrangements of productive forces the mode of production. It shaped every aspect of human life, governed every change, and was itself not influenced by anything outside of itself, as it supplied its own driving force.

Each mode of production shaped a set of corresponding productive relationships between human beings, such as who owns what and how much property, specifically the means of production. Thus whenever the modes of production have changed, the productive relationships have changed, too, since they were wholly governed by the former. "In acquiring new productive forces men change their mode of production, and in changing their mode of production, their manner of gaining a living, they change all their social relations. The handmill gives you society with the feudal lord; the steam mill a society with the industrial capitalist."[1] Throughout history changes in the productive relationships have lagged behind those in the productive forces because the people with a vested interest in the existing relationships always have resisted these inevitable changes. When the lag between the new mode of production and the "old" productive relationships became too great, violent adjustments occurred. In the end any resistance to adjusting all aspects of society to the development of the productive forces must fail, since no aspect of life could ever be independent from its economic base.

Marx was especially eager to accuse of harboring illusions those who have viewed religion, ideas, art, or philosophy as dynamic forces which could bring about change, instead of seeing that these phenomena were mere reflections of productive relationships, had no value in and by themselves, and had no strength to change anything. They constituted a superstructure with no dynamics or strength other than that which they derived form their economic base. Although Marx never clarified exactly how the superstructure and the basic mode of production were linked, all Marxist thought relied on that crucial relationship of dependence.

Art, philosophy, political ideas, and religion, once they were defined as mere reflections of existing modes of production and their concomitant productive relationships, were by necessity tied closely to those people who uphold the status quo—those who own the means of production and are called by Marx the exploiters or the ruling class. Indeed, the whole superstructure represents a vast instrument of oppression directed against those who are struggling to change the productive relationships in accordance with the dictates of history, that is, to bring about changes in the mode of production. Looked at in this way the state is not an ethical educator—the idealist view—or an arbiter in the interest of law and order—the liberal view—but the tool by which the exploiters hold the exploited in check. And religion refers not to a metaphysical reality but to mere illusions created and perpetuated in the interest of keeping the exploited servile; religion, for Marx, was the opiate of the people.

The changes originating the mode of production, although not influenced by any external force, were nevertheless not a matter of chance but followed inescapable patterns. Once a mode of production had been established, it completed its course, that is, it continued until all its productive potential was exhausted. However, in the course of that development, every mode of production evoked forces antagonistic to itself. These were better tools or productive arrangements, which from a certain point on outdated the old mode of productions, as, for example, when the windmill prepared the way for and eventually was replaced by the steammill. These changes brought about corresponding changes, first in the productive relationships and then in the superstructure. History is "a continual movement of growth in productive forces, of destruction in the social forces, of formation of ideas; there is nothing immutable but the abstraction of the movement—*mors immortalis*"[2]—until, that is, Marx should have added, the ideal state of affairs is created.

Individual human beings were the agents of change, but they neither originated it nor determined its course nor set its ultimate aim. They had no choice but to implement the changes prescribed by the "logic of economic development." The actions of individuals were needed most for adjusting the productive relationships to the new modes of production, an endeavor that could not be completed without conflict because of the antagonistic economic interests present in every society. This concept of an inevitable struggle within every established order, since every mode of production and the society based on it produced its own contradiction, owed much to Hegel's dialectic. But while in Hegelianism idea contested idea, in Marx's dialectical materialism social class fought social class. Every mode of production created such classes, which were groups whose members held comparable positions in the productive relationships. Marx discerned in his time, among others, the classes of large landowners, quasi-feudal lords, free farmers, tenant farmers, merchants, and laborers. But in the class struggle of every age all classes lined up on two warring sides: one affirming and the other negating the existing order. Victory always went to those representing the next, higher form of production. So far, according to Marx, there have been four periods, each with its own characteristic mode of production (see fig. 19.1).

In 1848, Marx and Engels foresaw the imminent collapse of capitalism and proclaimed their convictions in the *Communist Manifesto;* although disappointed in that hope, they continued to present their arguments in many subsequent works. The modern class struggle was rooted in the fact that although laborers had become the only productive force they reaped a minimum of rewards and had no proper place in capitalistic society. Their production enriched fewer and fewer capitalists, in whose hands larger and larger amounts of capital accumulated and who now confronted a vast, powerless, and impoverished proletariat. Soon Socialism (and later communism) would be established either through a peaceful transition or by violent revolution. While Marx remained ambivalent on that issue, he spelled out what the new society would accomplish: "appropriation of the means of production, their subjection to the associated working class, therefore the abrogation of wage-labor, of capital, and of their reciprocal relations."[3] This time, Marx thought, the reorganization of productive relationships would bring about a new order without inner contradictions. The common ownership of all means of production would bar the forming of social classes and establish a perpetual, stable, and perfect harmony between the mode of production (assumed to stay forever that of an industrial economy), productive relationships, and the superstructure.

Without an ongoing class struggle—since there would be no exploiters and exploited—that part of the superstructure which so far had supplied the tools of oppression would disappear. The new society of cooperating individuals would need no state apparatus to administer production and consumption. In the ultimate restraintless society goods would be dispensed on the basis of needs declared by individuals—"from everyone according to his ability, to everyone according to his need."[4] With the happiness of all people assured, religion would lose its usefulness and simply fade away.

Could not individuals, out of greed or simple selfishness, violate the order of the perfect society? Not according to Marx, who did not recognize the individual

Figure 19.1
The Four Historical Modes of Production (Karl Marx)

| TIME | 1 Primitive Communism (Asiatic mode) | 2 Ancient Slavery | 3 Medieval Feudalism | 4 Capitalism | 5 (Yet to come) Socialism/Communism |
|---|---|---|---|---|---|
| **DIRECT CHARACTERISTICS** | No private property in means of production | *The first great change* → | Private property in means of production | | *The second great change* → No private property in means of production |
| **ATTENDANT CIRCUMSTANCES** | —communal property<br>—society organized in "gens" (large family groups)<br>—upper stage of barbarism, dawn of civilization<br>—cooperative order | —based on slavery<br>—manufacture<br>—rise of merchant class<br>—dissolution of communal ties; stigma on labor | —small handicraft and farming mode of production<br>—manor and guild<br>—gradually money economy erodes order | —discoveries and impact of cities/industry/capital-economy, with wage earners (labor a commodity); from it great antagonism between capitalist and proletariat | —the the stage which harbors no contradictions within itself and hence will last forever |

as a unit independent of the collective fabric. Individuals represent no more than points of intersection of social relations. Once these relations would reflect the new social reality, a reality that would logically exclude greed and selfishness, individuals must then automatically demonstrate a "new being," too. Only cooperative behavior could occur in the new society.

Old history, with its tales of wars, dynasties, treaties, and economic exploitation, would end. For a while historians could rewrite in the Marxist manner the story of the past prior to the great change. In the new age historians would have little to do except record technological progress, production increases, contentment, and happiness. While generations would come and go, true historical process itself would have ended and the goal of history would be reached. History, defined by Marx at one time as the "theory of the conditions for the emancipation of the proletariat," would have served its purpose. Humans would be eternally free, peaceful, and happy; or, expressed in other terms, human alienation would be ended and the passage of time would have lost its decisive importance.

## Economic History after Marx

*Adjusting Marx.* History professors paid little attention to Marx's interpretation of history, and only a few scholars in other fields took up Marxist theory to expound on it or criticize it. Eugen Böhm-Bawerk engaged Marxists in an ardent controversy over their crucial contention that goods have value to the degree labor has been used to produce them. He maintained the marginalist view that psychological mechanisms in the buyer determine value; this was a view that would prevail in Western economics and that was destined to discredit Marx's labor theory of value, on which rested much of the Marxist claim that laborers were the only producers, as well as Marx's vision of capitalism's demise. Much of what Max Weber wrote also challenged Marx's social thought and historical views, such as Weber's insistence on capitalism's origin in complex human relationships and ideas, including the ethical scheme of Protestantism, and, above all, on value-guided actions by individuals as the true shapers of events in history.

On the other hand a large group of laborers and their sympathizers among intellectuals considered the concepts of surplus value, class, class struggle, exploitation, and accumulation of capital to be the long-sought explanations of the laborer's problems in Western society. These groups transformed Marx's theory of society and history into an action program for socialist parties. While the multitude was content simply to be inspired by Marxism, some sympathetic yet more cautious intellectuals kept checking and rechecking the accuracy of Marxist theory out of scholarly habit and also to make it perform even better in the arena of political life. Soon a tension arose, one yet to be relieved, between Marxism as an action program for mass movements and Marxism as a theory for scholars.

The first called for a devout, unquestioning belief in Marxist tenets, indeed in his whole system of thought including the unqualified promise of an end to the history of toil and struggle with the collapse of capitalism. The Marxist scholars, on the other hand, needed some critical distance between themselves and Marxist theory for testing the Marxist theses. The first view sponsored an orthodox Marxism, the second—at least in a few Marxists—a more empirical Marxism.

In 1899 Eduard Bernstein called for some empirical adjustment in the orthodox Marxist theory of history because capitalism had turned out to be more adaptive and imaginative than expected. In many industrial countries credit provisions, cartels, and trusts modified the business cycle, trade unions helped blunt social conflict through social reforms, and parliamentary governments gave increasing influence to the proletariat. All of that tended to postpone the penultimate conflict of classes and therefore to put in doubt the tenet of the imminent and inevitable collapse of capitalism. Bernstein advocated dropping the Marxist concept of a sudden apocalyptic end to capitalism in favor of an evolution toward socialism by way of constant social reform. He confessed that "to me that which is generally called the ultimate aim of socialism is nothing, but the movement is everything."[5] Hints of such gradualism also appeared in Jean Jaures's work, with its doubts about rigid economic determinism.

Bernstein's ideas brought angry rebuttals and the label of "revisionist" from the advocates of literal adherence to Marxist tenets. As for Marxist theory, Bernstein put in doubt what Engels had said: "Just as Darwin discovered the law of development of organic nature, so Marx discovered the law of development of human history."[6] Marxism became, instead of the ultimate statement on social development, the instrument for social reform. As for Marxist political practice, doubts about capitalism's collapse as an actual, inevitable, and imminent event eroded the hope of the masses for their emancipation. Confronted with problems and ambiguities, orthodox Marxists, rather than change Marx's (and Engels's) system, engaged in extensive studies in order to clarify "what Marx had really meant." Whenever they deviated from Marx's words it was seen as an interpretation, not as a change. Their central historical tenet remained the collapse of capitalism, that grand event which would end the long era of human prehistory and begin a truly human history. Karl Kautsky essentially reaffirmed Marx's views; Rosa Luxemburg reiterated the need for resolution as an inspiration to the proletariat; Rudolf Hilferding stressed need for political action over reliance on an automatic collapse; the Austrian Marxists produced sophisticated studies but in the end supported Kautsky; and Georgi Plekhanov affirmed Marx's doctrine of a necessary historical development so faithfully that he even advocated the building of a capitalist-industrial Russia before any changes toward Socialism were introduced.

*Economic history and its problems.* The impact of Marxism marked even the works of the non-Marxist New School of economic history in Germany, particularly those of its chief scholar, Gustav Schmoller. At first sight the work of the New School resembled closely that of the Old School, with the same preferences for studying economic institutions and development rather than timeless market processes and for treating the more distant past rather than the recent one. But also evident were a greater sophistication in research and in Schmoller's case, a clear intent to use economic history for coping with Germany's social policy dilemma: how could one satisfy the demands of the working class for a more equitable treatment and thus reduce the attractiveness of Marxism? Schmoller's eventual suggestions on social policy grew out of his study of economic history in which he considered the state, not the market or the class, as the key entity. Economic and social policy must treat the human being not as a theoretical *homo oeconomicus,* an abstract, isolated individual, or as a member of an economic class, but as a citizen of a nation. Accordingly, economic policy must be guided by insights gained from national history, not from theoretical models. Economic history demonstrated that questions of ethics and justice must figure in political economy (as Schmoller still called economics) with the same prominence as markets and economic motives. In the case of Germany, her social and economic problems could only be solved by a national effort under the traditional leadership of the Hohenzollern dynasty. Intending to help implement that solution, Schmoller and a few others founded the Verein für Sozialpolitik (1872) and —despite being derided as *Kathedersozialisten* (mere academic socialists)— persuaded Bismarck to institute the earliest social programs of any industrial nation, including health and pension insurance.

That, however, was the last hour of prominence for the New School. In the 1880s Schmoller became embroiled in a *Methodenstreit,* an ardent discussion over the proper method for economic studies. Schmoller's historical approach collided with the "pure" theory of the neoclassicist Carl Menger: the one emphasized the historically concrete, the other the abstract; the one relied on price history, the other on price theory; the one spoke of actual past economic behavior, the other of typical economic behavior; the one stressed lessons gained from descriptive history, the other worked with theoretical models applicable everywhere and at any time. Like most discussions of methods, this *Methodenstreit* was really a far-reaching dispute over the structure of reality, in this case of economic reality. It did not bring about the divorce of economic theory from economic history, it only made visible a separation that had already developed. The gap widened when Menger's followers opened the doors of economics even wider to psychology and mathematics as they emphasized microeconomics, the study of the economic behavior of firms, industries, and private households, with its short-run perspectives and its emphasis on price theory. Little remained of the analysis of long-range economic change or attempts to find historical economic types. Now economists preferred to theorize on the timeless and typical processes of the market and thereby moved ever closer to the ideals of the ahistorical natural sciences.

*The United States—once more a special case.* Late nineteenth-century America, in the process of being rapidly transformed from a rural into an urban industrialized society, also showed a heightened awareness of economic matters. It helped that in the 1880s economic history became an acceptable endeavor in England. In that decade William Cunningham, William J. Ashley, J. E. Thorold Rogers, and Arnold Toynbee published important works on English economic history and the subject began to be taught at academic institutions. Although direct German influence was tenuous, the English economic historians worked within a similar framework of ideas, including the interdependence between the economic and other aspects of human life, the state as an important instrument of economic and social reform, economic development seen as evolution, and the centrality of economic change. But no *Methodenstreit* rocked English economic history; an empirical attitude characterized economic theoreticians and historians alike. Such cooperation also dominated the second meeting of the American Historical Association (1885), at which the American Economic Association was founded; for some years the two societies lived in a symbiotic relationship and economic history enjoyed a modest boom. In the early 1900s Harvard called on W. J. Ashley to teach economic history there and the Carnegie Foundation planned an economic history of the United States. Economic matters also interested the New Historians of the early 1900s who wished to widen the scope of history beyond the political area.

In the early 1900s some American New Historians, who searched for what they considered the "real" forces shaping society, focused their attention on the economic aspect of life. A few of them even acknowledged a debt to Marx's theory, but the grand philosophical scope of that theory fit poorly with American pragmatic activism. Edwin R. A. Seligman, an admirer of Marx, stated the moderate stance on Marxism well:

> As a philosophical doctrine of universal validity, the theory of "historical materialism" can no longer be successfully defended.
> But in the narrower sense of the economic interpretation of history—in the sense, namely, that the economic factor has been of the utmost importance in history, and that the historical factor must be reckoned with in economics—the theory has been, and still is, of considerable significance.[7]

In the spirit of "realism," Seligman also conceded that "it [Marx's theory] has taught us to search below the surface," that surface where Seligman thought all political and diplomatic history remained.[8]

But in the United States, too, those who took up the cause of an economic interpretation of the past remained outside the mainstream of theoretical economics. Just as in Europe, in the United States economic theory and history had separated. The original union of the American Historical Association and the American Economic Association had been dissolved when economists began to prefer to study and deal in timeless patterns rather than the maze of contingent phenomena of economic history. Thorstein Veblen tried to stop this drifting apart. He attacked the picture of the economic world drawn by the neoclassicist economists, one of whom, J. B. Clark, had been his teacher. Veblen denied that it was possible to understand the economy of a country by viewing it abstractly as a system of forces in equilibrium, one in which people were seen as always calculating rationally and one which was unaffected by complex social changes. The abstract model of the economic sphere was kept artificially simple by a deliberate isolation from the real-life situation. Through his own analysis Veblen discovered such typical phenomena as the curtailment of productivity by the wasteful practices of a leisure class, artificial restraints introduced by established business itself, and irrational behavior by consumers, for example, their proclivity to ape others and to waste their money on conspicuous consumption. Most influential turned out to be Veblen's view on the overall development of the American economy. It was governed by the conflict between industry— producing "real" values, being based on workmanship, and serving the interest of common people; and business—satisfying mere acquisitiveness, creating pecuniary values only, and conspiring to keep the status quo. Veblen expected the conflict to end in the collapse of capitalism.

Despite their eagerness for social reform, the New Historians did not rush to study economic history. From Veblen's and Marx's works they took primarily the concept of social conflict fueled by economic motives. That concept inspired Charles Beard, whose social activism was stimulated by his Quaker background, a visit to turn-of-the-century Chicago, the social sciences, and an admiration for Fabian socialism. In 1913, he applied the economic interpretation of the past to a well-known topic in American history. *An Economic Interpretation of the Constitution of the United States* challenged the traditional view that the Constitution resulted from a wise blend of theory and experience, a balance between affirmation and restraint of liberty, and a grasp of past and present wisdom—as if the whole people in their desire for liberty and order had created the Constitution. Beard rejected all such talk about idealism, wisdom, and providence, be it that of God or of the progress of liberty. It was based on illusions that an industrial society must expunge before true democracy could be established. The economic interpretation of history alone offered the proper historical understanding for guiding the democratization of society. Its basic tenet taught us that

> different degrees and kinds of property inevitably exist in modern society;
> party doctrines and "principals" originate in the sentiments and views
> which the possession of various kinds of property creates in the minds of
> the possessors; class and group divisions based on property lie at the
> basis of modern government; and politics and constitutional law are
> inevitably a reflex of these contending interests.[9]

The Constitution bore the marks of just such a conflict, which in American society was fought between "a popular party based on paper money and agrarian interests, and a conservative party centered in the towns and resting on financial, mercantile, and personal property interests generally."[10] The Founding Fathers represented specific property interests, those of the owners of liquid capital, who had no sympathy for the small landowners and the "property-less mass." If political genius guided the drafting of the basic law of the Republic, it had at least an influential constant companion in economic interests. From that perspective the Constitution was a conservative measure which tamed the spirit of the American Revolution, which Beard perceived as a radical social upheaval. The suspicion that economic motives, the true dominant forces, were hidden behind lofty ideals—often deliberately—would be a prominent feature of Progressive history and its successors. It also would make conflict the key explanatory concept in some variants of social history.

# ·20·

# Historians Encounter the Masses

## Jubilant and Dark Visions

Throughout the nineteenth century there was much talk of "the people," but the term had many meanings. Yet not even those who used it in a seemingly all-inclusive way—like the Romantics with their vision of Volk—meant to bridge the gap which in reality separated a substantial group from full participation in Western society: the members of the Fourth Estate, mainly the less educated and propertyless laborers. Many of those who spoke of "the people" were either insensitive to the exclusion or found it a proper one. Early in the century, with industrialization not yet fully developed, it was easy to affirm the concept of the people as a whole and to ignore social divisions. Thus, Ranke wrote histories of *Völker,* in the sense of nations. Michelet stayed close to that meaning, too, when he praised the people whom he loved and who in turn inspired him.

> I then shut the books, and placed myself among the people to the best of my power; the lonely writer plunged again into the crowd, listened to their noise, noted their words. They were perfectly the same people, changed only in outward appearance; my memory did not deceive me. I went about, therefore, consulting men, listening to their account of their own condition, and gathering from their lips, what is not always to be found in the most brilliant writers, the words of common sense.[1]

In the people were the noblest features of French history: the faculty of devotion and the power of sacrifice. The "people, these paupers really so rich," possessed heroism.[2] They were France. Thomas Carlyle, just as fascinated by the people as Michelet, tilted more distinctly towards the common people, "the nameless multitude." A bit abstractly he spoke of his awe of them. "Great is the combined voice of men; the utterance of their instincts which are truer than their thoughts: it is the greatest a man encounters, among the sounds and shadows which make up this World of Time."[3] Although Carlyle wished for historians to treat real human beings "with colour in their cheeks, with passions in their stomachs, and the idioms, features, and vitalities of very men,"[4] the common people he praised, at least in his earlier works, still were not the people who revolted or demanded their just share through radical reforms; rather there remained an intimate bond between them and their society. Such visions of harmony could not last because in the 1800s the members of the Fourth Estate were taking seriously the call for equality and were in no mood to equate contemporary conditions with social harmony. They eventually disappointed Carlyle by, as he saw it, being obsessed with wrong, mostly material goals. The rise of the Fourth Estate to recognition and power would change the perception of "the people" in historiography.

*The past and dark visions of the future.* Carlyle's "cloudcapt, fire-breathing Spectre of Democracy"[5] conveys well the sense of unease, even alarm, caused by the onrush of democracy throughout European societies. That sense spurred philosophers and historians to attempts to ascertain the status of their period in Western development. While the majority of intellectuals remained full of hope in the positive forces of science and progress in the midst of a profound shift in the Western world, a small group of scholars comprehended the vast potential of such a shattering of tradition. Jacob Burckhardt spoke for those who had visions of catastrophic consequences while Friedrich Nietzsche celebrated the chance to revolutionize human life.

Burckhardt preferred to analyze the great transitional periods of the past (that of Constantine the Great and the Renaissance) which he perceived as akin to his own times. On the basis of what he learned about cultural dissolution and through his own critical observation of life he pointed to some contemporary hopes as follies: the trust in Bismarck's Germany, the philosophy of progress, or the trend toward an egalitarian society. Particularly the latter was now—after 1870—beginning to show its corrosive effects and reveal its frightful ultimate results. As ever new attempts would have to be made to achieve equality among people who by nature were unequal, traditions, laws, and values would be destroyed as roadblocks on the way to absolute equality until, finally, social stability would disappear. In order to restore that stability and achieve ultimate equality people would call upon socialism with its ever-increasing regimentation and centralization; this was a perfect situation for the emergence of despots—the terrible simplifiers—who offered order to a world without true legitimacy and tradition. In such a new society tradition and with it history would be replaced as society's guides by fickle public opinion and quickly changing fashions of thought.

Of the three perennial stabilizing forces in human affairs, the state was developing according to wrong models and religion had been weakened beyond efficacy. Only culture offered contemporaries a spiritual refuge in a period of increasing debasement of all values, and thus he preferred cultural history, which reached beyond the confines of politics, diplomacy, and war into those of thought, art, and literature. Burckhardt, who otherwise rejected all speculative interpretations of history, found in culture a quasi-metaphysical force: it inspired all creativity, was perennial and universal, and offered hope to those anxious about the age of the masses.

Burckhardt's educated contemporaries shared his conviction that what is now called "high culture" was central to Western civilization. For the past hundred years that conviction has maintained a vigorous branch of historiography—intellectual history. Its basic contention has been that the motive force of history, at least for those of its aspects that mattered, was ideas, a force that no longer was connected to a transcendent entity in the mode of idealist philosophy but constituted simply the creative and shaping element in human life. With that view intellectual history has stood as a strong bulwark against all types of determinism, although it has never formed a rigidly cohesive school. Outstanding representatives have reached from Burckhardt to Dilthey, J. Huizinga, and Ortega y Gasset, and its primary American voice has been the *Journal of the History of Ideas*. It has faced its greatest challenge in recent years when culture was redefined as a natural dimension of human life, one which included everything done and thought by everybody, and was heavily determined by social and natural environmental forces. Ideas came to be seen not as shapers of phenomena but as shaped by phenomena.

Burckhardt's refuge in cultural history was rejected by Friedrich W. Nietzsche. He agreed with Burckhardt that the emancipation of the masses was the last blow to a Western tradition that had been eroding for centuries; indeed, ever since Copernicus, Western man seemed to have got upon an inclined plane, and "he is now rolling faster and faster away from the center—whither? Into nothingness?"[6] Nihilism threatened, and with it a "herd existence" under despotisms which were necessary consequences once the rootless masses of modern industrial society had destroyed the traditional ties holding Western societies together. As individuals would become increasingly isolated from each other, an ever more powerful state would be needed to keep things together. Year by year, hope for cultural vitality would grow more faint as industrial work wasted the nervous energy of the populace, the barbarism of specialization stupified those who thought, the sciences destroyed old values without offering new ones, and philosophy and religion retained too little strength to help. Nietzsche himself hoped for the creative Higher Man to rescue the world from nihilism, while the masses could do little more than be the soil from which these individuals would rise.

These fears of and opposition to the emancipation of the masses stood as a formidable obstacle in the way of creating a new history which incorporated the past of all the people. The Marxist version of a people's history strengthened the resistance to such a history even more. Enthusiasm for a democratically oriented history also was lessened by a technical problem. In past centuries the common people had led a shadowy life and the few traces they had left were nearly invisible in those sources contemporary scholars were accustomed to study. Only occasionally an outstanding commoner, a revolt, or a great feast found mention in documents while the life cycles of the multitude ran their course without direct references to them. These difficulties were felt not so much by those who talked about "the people" or "the masses" as entities but by those who wished to employ empirical methods for assessing the actual life and importance of the common people. The problem showed plainly in the work often considered—with some justification—as the first English attempt to write social history, John R. Green's *Short History of the English People.*

Green, an Oxford-trained clergyman, who for years had ministered to the poor people in a London district, was enchanted by the common people. His sympathy showed in his work, the first complete and concise English history, which after 1874 became a best-seller. His sympathies with the common people as well as his conviction that social and religious development were fundamentally more important than politics persuaded him to leave behind "drum and trumpet" history. Accordingly he discarded the usual organization of English history by dynasties in favor of sketching a period-by-period image of English culture. But Green did not really write a history of the common people, although he showed his sympathy for them wherever he could. In his work the term "people" still referred to the nation as a whole and little was said about the actual life of the masses. At best, Green's work was a gentle hint of the social history to come. The democratization of historiography was still quite a few years away. Most historians were unconvinced by Michelet's outcry:

> Often, in these days, the rise and progress of the people are compared to the invasion of the Barbarians. The expression pleases me; I accept it. Barbarians! Yes, that is to say, full of new, living, regenerating sap. Barbarians, that is, travellers marching toward the Rome of the future, going on slowly, doubtless; each generation advancing a little, halting in death; but others march forward all the same.[7]

Throughout the 1800s social history remained institutional history and dealt with the people as a nation—as a whole. The questions that were raised concerned not social tensions and conflicts but the source of national identity, unity, and destiny. The earliest attempt at matching historiography and the democratic spirit came in turn-of-the-century America, which had recently acquired both continental scope and industrial stature and where a call went forth for a democratic history: the so-called New History.

## Social History as Institutional History

While some of those who lived in the late 1800s and early 1900s noticed the rise in social tensions, most people celebrated the period's stability and steady progress and were proud of the achievements of their respective nations. That pride led historians to search for national roots and to analyze the development of national identities. As their objects of study they selected the institutions of their nations. Understood as the durable relationships between members of a society, these institutions, whether they were constitutions, laws, economic organizations, or voluntary associations, appealed to the temper of the turn-of-the-century West since they reconciled change and continuity in a manner that did not threaten stability. As long as scholars did not notice that these institutions were most often interpreted as expressions of a *Volksgeist* (the spirit of a nation), conceived of in an idealist manner, they could even see these studies as compatible with the most influential contemporary model of genetic development, Darwin's evolutionary concept, and thus align institutional history with "scientific" history. A stronger link was that between these new institutional histories and much earlier institutional studies by scholars of the 1500s and 1600s. The concern of these scholars with national identity returned in nineteenth-century France, England, and Germany in the form of the controversy between Romanists and Germanists.

*The European versions.* In the German area feudalism and the medieval empire was at issue. The numerous and influential German medievalists, with Georg Waitz as their leader, produced a massive body of works on these topics which demonstrated among other things that feudalism, thought to have been a common and crucial shaper of medieval societies, was a primarily Frankish and hence German institution. However, Fustel de Coulanges, as painstaking a scholar as any German, found that the Frankish invasion had little impact on Romanized Gaul and her institutions and culture. Feudalism developed from the Roman clientele system. Fustel knew that such findings would please his French compatriots, dispirited by the defeat in 1870–71, but neither he nor his German counterparts were motivated by mere partisanship.

The nineteenth-century debate over the role of the medieval German empire —the Holy Roman Empire of the German nation as it came to be called— involved some historians of the Prussian school, most prominently Heinrich von Sybel, and a few Austrian scholars, notably Julius Ficker. The empire had long been a source of pride for German-speaking people because through it German history had been linked to the universal Christian faith and the idea of a universal empire. But in the decade of nationalist struggles prior to the unification in 1871, those historians who sided with the Prussian Hohenzollern found fault with the medieval empire. It drew Germans into Italian politics, costly controversies with the papacy, and futile quests for universal rule. What could be more detrimental to a national sense of dignity, they argued, than the excommunicated emperor, Henry IV, standing in 1077 as a penitent sinner for days outside of a castle at Canossa in order to obtain absolution from the pope? "Going to Canossa" acquired a sinister ring unless one saw in the affair—as nationalists eventually did—a masterful piece of political deception. According to von Sybel, the preoccupation with the empire prevented for too long the development of a genuine national German state. Ficker disagreed, as an Austrian with no Hohenzollern sympathies, as a Catholic with an empathy for universality, and as a scholar who rejected judgments on medieval institutions made on the basis of present controversies. Waitz regretted the whole debate and scolded both camps: "But I am firm in my opinion that these questions have nothing to do with any estimation of the old empire, and that one must strive always and everywhere that historiography should not be misled by the temper and wishes of the present."[8]

English history had for a long time been something akin to institutional history what with the concepts of an ancient constitution and the implications of the Whig interpretation of English history. Institutions had also been at the center of the long-standing quest for a clarification of the identity of the English nation. In the 1800s the two themes once more became tightly interwoven in new institutional histories.

Once more the Anglo-Saxons had more champions than the Celts among scholars; they reached from Archbishop Parker in the Reformation period to Sharon Turner and John Mitchell Kemble in the 1800s. Kemble was one of those amateurs who in fact were learned men. A student of Jakob Grimm, he edited *Beowulf*, lectured on Anglo-Saxon language and literature, compiled the *Codex diplomaticus aevi Saxonici*, and summarized his knowledge in *The Saxons in England* (1849). Kemble used a wide range of sources so as to understand fully all facets of Anglo-Saxon life. He emerged with the conviction that the very roots of English political life were the customs of the early Anglo-Saxon peasant society with its assemblies of free people—an organically growing society in which free people could exist. Such Germanist preferences were contradicted by Sir Francis Palgrave, a lawyer and researcher of the Norman period in English life. Setting out to correct Thierry's work, he ended up as a proponent of a Romanist interpretation of English institutions; for him, central royal power characterized English history since early British times.

Beginning in the 1860s, two celebrated Oxford historians buttressed the Germanist thesis: William Stubbs, a brilliant scholar in the Rankean tradition who produced the best editions in the Rolls Series of documents and texts as well as a monumental *Constitutional History,* and Edward Augustus Freeman, who wrote a *History of the Norman Conquest of England.* The two men differed in many ways but both of them wrote works well within the long-established range of political and constitutional history, although they rejected the usual "highlights in the development of liberty" approach. Instead, they suggested in the German vein that English history was the realization of the English national spirit: a gradual unfolding from its core, which was the Anglo-Saxon institutions with their fortuitous blending of free individuals and the collective. Hence the Norman invasion was for Freeman only a superficial interruption of a powerful process. The cradle of English freedom and greatness remained the Germanic village. But both historians did not in Ranke's manner perceive a universal historical dimension to English history, not even to the extent of permitting a comparative institutional history.

Although neither Stubbs nor Freeman founded a "school"—Stubbs left the university to become bishop of Oxford and Freeman simply hated teaching—the Germanist thesis survived through the efforts of Paul Vinogradoff and, especially, John R. Green's popular *Short History of the English People.* Sir Frederic Seebohm, a banker-historian, who revived the Romanist interpretation in his *The English Village Community* (1883), did much less harm to the Germanist thesis than did the anti-German passions aroused by World War I. Those also failed who wished to dislodge the Whig interpretation and Germanist thesis and to see English history in different contexts. James Anthony Froude suggested, as Carlyle had, that change was discontinuous and did not occur simply within the confines of constitutional arrangements. Sir John Seeley's concern, the empire, could be more easily linked to contemporary political reality. Yet English political life still kept on favoring, above all, the Whig interpretation with its Germanist preferences.

The Germanist thesis also colored the debate over English law, in which Sir Henry Maine battled against those who upheld a timeless natural law and also against those who saw the origin of law in the command of the sovereign. Against them, Maine influenced by Savigny, advanced the historical interpretation that saw all law develop in the context of the whole society. In his works on ancient law, the comparative analysis of village communities in Europe and India, and the history of institutions, Maine demonstrated the relationship between legal and societal changes. The Germanist thesis, never directly espoused, seeped in wherever an opening occurred. A moderate version of the thesis received a more pronounced recognition in Frederick D. Maitland and F. Pollock's *History of English Law of 1272* (1895). But here, too, the main concern was not the Germanist thesis but the historical nature of English law; indeed the work proved to be the high point of the historical interpretation of law in England.

*The American versions.* American historians, like their European counterparts, came upon institutional history through national pride and the desire to establish their nation's identity. George Bancroft and other "literary" historians spoke of the nation's birth, rise, and mission much as if the nation were a whole; a people of one mind and one purpose enjoying a unity that was natural to some, mystical to others. That view accorded well with one aspect of nineteenth-century American life: the people went about building a new nation with vigor, enthusiasm, and national pride despite constant political conflict. The sense of unity even survived the Civil War, that bloodiest of all internal conflicts. Indeed, in the end, that war strengthened national unity by abolishing the divisive institution of slavery.

But an erosion of the quasi-natural sense of unity and wholeness began nevertheless. Like many European countries, the United States became increasingly urbanized with a population that became less and less homogeneous in ethnic composition through large-scale immigration. The rapid economic development brought about an economic and social complexity visible in sharp conflicts of interest-groups—farmers, railroad owners, bankers, merchants, industrial entrepreneurs, and laborers. How long could the concept of the nation as a seamless whole survive before being replaced by a new interpretation of the nation as a complex network of distinct units and their sometimes troubled relationships?

Yet about 1900 the assertion of nationhood still thrived, particularly when the American republic asserted its power in Latin America, Hawaii, and the Spanish Empire. Naval and not social history fascinated those who carried out or applauded the new expansionism. They listened to Alfred Thayer Mahan when he spoke of the importance of seapower. The strength of America's navy would determine whether the Atlantic and Pacific oceans would be barriers to or avenues for America's commerce and the extension of her influence. From *The Influence of Sea Power upon History* Americans learned that between 1660 and 1815 the British Empire had been built on naval superiority. Mahan had always thought that historians should not merely accumulate facts but give guidance to "way-faring man." Now he taught his fellow citizens the lesson he had learned from history, that of the interdependence of trade, great-power status, and naval supremacy.

The concept of the nation as a historical person was also kept alive by historians with an enthusiasm for the old Manifest Destiny, although in some of their works the term "nation" assumed a more down-to-earth connotation. Theodore Roosevelt's *The Winning of the West* (1905) presented an exuberant account of the great westward movement of the nation. And who accomplished it?

> The Americans began their work of western conquest as separate and
> individual people, at the moment when they sprang into national life. It
> has been their great work ever since. All other questions save those of the
> preservation of the Union itself and the emancipation of the blacks have
> been of subordinate importance when compared with the great questions
> of how . . . they [the people] were to subjugate that part of their
> continent lying between the eastern mountains and the Pacific.[9]

But it was neither the nation as a mysterious whole nor Parkman's fascinating heroes who accomplished the mastery of the continent but the common people, first the "Indian fighters, treaty-makers, and wilderness-wanderers" and then "the settlers." Such singling out of the common people would soon become the mark of American history. Before that happened, however, the "national" historians took two other turns in defining the American past.

The new university-bred historians of the 1880s and 1890s, with their "scientific" aspirations, were bent on subjecting national history to a more rigorous analysis. They distrusted contemporary historiography with its declamatory character and its assertion of progress without theoretical proofs. The growth of the nation must be traced as it had occurred, step-by-step, through the examination of documents according to the new canon. In the 1880s American historians could find no better guide for their endeavor than the precepts of the European institutionalists in history and political science. Institutional history satisfied the American sense of nationhood and, to some degree, even the contemporary enthusiasm for history as a science, particularly for history as an example of Darwin's evolutionism. Change, even the bitter conflicts in contemporary American society, could be acknowledged without hesitation because America's supposedly inevitable "upward bound" direction made all change beneficial while the stable American institutions guaranteed continuity.

When they looked for the origins of American institutions, many of the American institutionalists accepted the findings of Sir Henry Maine and Edward A. Freeman concerning the Germanic ancestry of liberty and democracy. They stipulated that the English settlers had transferred the institutions of liberty to the new world.

> The science of Biology no longer favors the theory of spontaneous generation. Wherever organic life occurs, there must have been some seed for that life. History should not be content with describing effects when it can explain causes. It is just as improbable that free local institutions should spring up without a germ along American shores as that English wheat should have grown here without planting. Town institutions were propagated in New England by old English and Germanic ideas brought by Pilgrims and Puritans.[10]

From the 1880s on, students heard this Germanist thesis propounded by their professors, among them Herbert Baxter Adams, Henry Adams (whose title was Professor of Institutional History), John W. Burgess, and Albert Bushnell Hart. Through the work of such men all of American history, not just the colonial period, became firmly anchored in the many centuries of Anglo-Saxon history.

The more seriously the call for a "scientific" history was taken and the more critical historical analysis became, the less well the simple Germanist thesis worked as an explanation. Institutions similar in name and appearance to English counterparts turned out to serve different purposes in American society. In addition, such a transfer theory of institutions left dissatisfied those who stressed the uniqueness of American society over the continuity of English tradition in American history. In the late 1800s and early 1900s that objection took a radical turn with Frederick Turner and the New Historians. It was at about the same time that institutionalists abandoned the Germanist thesis in favor of the views of the so-called imperial school.

American society and its institutions, imperial historians argued, were not born in the Teutonic forests but were shaped within the matrix of the British Empire. Historians wishing to understand the early American past need not travel back to the Germanic village but could rely on comparative studies between two sets of institutions much closer together in time: those of the British Empire and those of the British colonies in the New World. Such studies demonstrated how the mother country and her colonies had gradually drifted apart. That fact was crucial for understanding the separation during the American Revolution. From 1887 on Herbert L. Osgood suggested to fellow historians the new interpretation which demonstrated the gradual separation of the American colonies from their English mother country despite the substantial remaining similarities between the institutions of the two societies. His student, George Louis Beer, described the shaping influence of British economic policies on early American history. In Beer's perspective the collision of colonial economic interests and imperial mercantilist interests was a more important triggering mechanism for the American Revolution than all the wishes to be freed of English tyranny.

Osgood's contemporary, Charles McLean Andrews, produced the most mature statement of the imperial school on American colonial history and was its leader for a generation. His central theme was the gradual but dramatic divergence of American society from British society—the one becoming individualistic, democratic, and flexible; the other remaining aristocratic and relatively static. That basic structural shift turned frictions into incidents and, finally, incidents into a successful revolution. His first major statement in 1912, *The Colonial Period*, still had the effect of novelty, while the *Colonial Background of the American Revolution*, coming in the 1920s, was already located in the period of the school's declining influence. His third work on the colonial period appeared in the 1930s, when many historians were hostile to the imperial school and its emphasis on heritage, continuous development, and measured change. By the 1930s the New or Progressive Historians had been at work for two decades accenting abrupt change, even stressing conflict over continuity. In their portrayal, the American Revolution appeared not as the end point of a gradual development but as a radical break. Other historians, enamored of recent American history, disliked the built-in limitations of the imperial view. The further away from the colonial period an era of American history was located the less the imperial historians could contribute to its explanation.

Institutional history even made its mark on Civil War historiography, in which discontinuity and disruption seemed predestined to dominate. Institutionalists searched for and found much continuity. They emphasized that the Union had been preserved, many institutions had remained stable, and all radical experimentation had failed. Radicalism of the Northern and Southern varieties had foundered on the rock of stable American institutions. Such was the approach to the problem of Reconstruction by William A. Dunning and his school, which included Ulrich B. Phillips. These views were pleasing to Southerners and to a generation tired of controversy. Eager to show continuity and disliking radical changes, the Dunning school was not bothered by the unresolved problem of civil rights for black Americans.

By its very nature, constitutional history proved to be the hardiest remnant of institutional historiography. There, historians such as Andrew C. McLaughlin and, later, Edward S. Corwin traced the gradual shaping of many institutions by the nation's supreme legal forum and in turn analyzed the layers of "legal sediments" which American life had deposited over the years in the American Constitution.

### The American "New History": Call for a Democratic History

After the Civil War, American society had experienced an explosive growth in industries and cities, the arrival of millions of new immigrants, and new problems in the rural sector. What was the just social order for that new society with its many interest-groups and their aspirations, each of them claiming fuller rights to life, liberty, and the pursuit of happiness, and how could it be established? Few people talked in such abstract terms but specific controversies occurred in great numbers. Since the 1880s, American life had been full of discontent as the Populists called on government to protect the many against the few possessing power and wealth. But even though their program did include some demands by urban laborers, the Populists were essentially a rural group and they failed. In the early 1900s, however, the failure of Populism was atoned by Progressivism, the broad reform movement with an urban accent. It saw as its task the reconciliation of democratic ideals with the political, social, and economic realities of the new urban and industrialized America.

*Turner's revision of American history.* Scientific history claimed to be the response to the call for a New History appropriate for the modern period. But calls advocating a different New History were heard in the 1890s. Among them, those of Karl Lamprecht in Germany and Henri Berr in France have been much more appreciated than that by Frederick Jackson Turner in the United States. While in Turner's appeal for historiographical modernization, published as "The Significance of History" in 1892, his methodological approach remained generally in line with the prevailing positivism of contemporary American historiography, his ideas on the substance of history were remarkably innovative. Historiography must become life-encompassing rather than being dedicated to affairs of politics and state, deal with all the people and not just elites, explain history in terms of the structural forces "behind" the institutions, recognize the pervasiveness of change, and have world history as its ultimate reference. His limited interest in theory made Turner develop his reformist ideas in his works on American history rather than in additional theoretical essays. These works focused on the process that transformed the many different groups of immigrants into a democratic nation. In accounting for the process Turner stressed the central role of space and its settlement; a geographical orientation that paralleled but was not caused by contemporary European developments (Friedrich Ratzel and Vidal de la Blache).

His first attempt at a geographical interpretation of American history, presented as "The Significance of the Frontier" at the 1893 meeting of the American

Historical Association at the Chicago Columbian Exposition, came at a fortunate moment. America was rapidly evolving into a large, industrialized nation and embarked on a democratic experiment on a grander scale. Americans were enamored of technology, conscious of being pioneers in democracy, science, industry, and general progress, and ready to reject too close a linking of their past to that of England or continental Europe.

However, at the time Americans also were deeply concerned about the repercussions of the closing of the frontier. Turner's acknowledgement that a whole period of American history had come to a close could have contributed to that anxiety, but his frontier thesis allowed for a great deal of optimism because of what it said about the American character and the origin of American democracy.

The thesis spoke of an American nation that was unique in character and development because it had been shaped less by cross-Atlantic links than the dramatic conquest of a vast continent. It refuted the Germanist thesis which Turner's teachers had propounded. The frontier thesis became America's declaration of historiographical independence from Europe.

Turner, a native of Wisconsin, studied the settling of the American continent and concluded that American history must not be viewed from the Atlantic coast since the "real lines of American development, the forces dominating our character, are to be studied in the history of westward expansion." The vast, empty continent offered free land aplenty, but the price of its mastery was a life of self-reliance, simplicity, and practicality, as well as some coarseness and cupidity. And "this ever-retreating frontier of free land is the key to American development," because the American "forest clearings have been the seed plots of American character" and of American-style democracy.[11] That democracy "was born of no theorist's dream" but was "shaped in ceaseless struggle with the environment."[12]

In his thesis Turner partially answered his own call for a history shaped by structural forces other than individual persons and events, celebrated change, acknowledged the role of economic forces, and gave the "common" people a decisive importance. The latter he described with special eloquence. "But history has its tragedy as well, which tells of the degraded tillers of the soil, toiling that others might dream, the slavery that render possible the 'glory that was Greece,' the serfdom into which decayed the 'grandeur that was Rome'—these as well demanded their annals."[13]

Yet the frontier thesis gave to the agrarian past the dominant role in the shaping of the American character, nation, and democracy. Turner would find it impossible to deduce from his thesis a satisfactory historical interpretation for a strongly progressive and future-oriented nation. He had romanticized the frontier, limited to one aspect the much broader American mobility, and overlooked the fact that, except for the dynamic of the settlement process, his geographical interpretation of American history had a pronounced static quality.

From 1895, Turner's work carried the mark of the section as the key concept. The new approach was exemplified by his only book-length work, *The Rise of the New West, 1819–1829*. The sections were units shaped by a complex mixture of geographical, economic, and social influences. The people of a certain section shared distinctive life experiences and specific interests over the span of generations. Thus Americans carried the marks of the sections which shaped them, and the American past could not be understood if one ignored the sectional rivalries between East, West, and South.

In the sectional interpretation American history (with the exception of the Civil War) appeared as a sequence of successful compromises between regions. Even Congress was seen as "an assembly of geographical envoys." Critics argued that Turner's insistence on the centrality of the sectional interpretation was flawed because the ever denser network of communications was diminishing its value. At best it could serve as one interpretive scheme for pre-industrial America. Turner spent his remaining years composing a sectionalist-oriented American history for the period between 1830 and 1850. He hoped that the "Big Book," as he called it, would be persuasive enough to convince his critics also. But the work remained unfinished and was completed by co-workers (*The Significance of Sectionalism*, 1932).

Turner's work on behalf of a New History remained unappreciated in comparison to similar efforts by Europeans. He had issued and partially answered the call for a structural history, the inclusion of the broad masses into history, and a greater emphasis on the economic aspect of history. Yet even at home his influence would soon be overtaken by another group of New Historians—The Progressive historians—who were perceived as being more in tune with industrialized and urbanized America. It also helped that the prominent Progressive historians published considerably more than Turner, who was hampered by his inability to complete book-length manuscripts. The Progressive historians gave Turner credit for having appreciated the economic aspect of history (albeit not the economic interpretation of history). They, who affirmed progress as the key historical pattern and saw it accomplished through social conflict, found some sympathy for Turner's early agreement on that point. Thus, at one time Turner had hinted at a contest between the "capitalist" and the "democratic pioneer" from the earliest colonial days, but he found class conflict not as congenial— perhaps not as genuinely American—as his concept of sectional conflict and did not pursue it. But all of that proved a fragile link from the Progressive historians to a historian whose work was far afield from theirs in historical interpretation and activist aims.

*Truth as servant of action.* Many Progressive ideals and the ensuing changes originated in the scholarly world, where a decisive shift in outlook had occurred. The belief in history as progress remained as strong as ever but it underwent a metamorphosis. Up to that point its driving force had been providential (God) or at least metaphysical (reason). Now progress was seen as resulting from human actions increasingly informed by rational planning and considered to be more effective because of it. Specifically, at the turn of the century, it was thought necessary not only to expose the divergence between democratic ideals and the realities in American life but to remedy it. Indeed, there was present a pervasive suspicion that traditional ideals were used to hide the selfish interests of those in power and thus to mask the "real" forces at work in society. In the new scheme of preferences experimentation ranked above tradition, the "real" above the "ideal," change above stability, assertion of conflict in the interest of democracy above its deliberate reduction, and the recognition of separate constituencies above the ideal of a harmonious nation. Such a new attitude came easily to the new American intelligentsia, whose members were no longer drawn mainly from well-established families but from the middle classes, and whose actions and thoughts were not so much guided by tradition as by a vision for the future: the promise of American life was to be fulfilled in a truly democratic American society pervaded by a spirit of equality and rationalism.

Little of American life remained untouched once some of the long-standing American traditions were questioned. Trust in universal, eternal, and benevolent forces was replaced by faith in the efficacy and benevolence of rational human actions aimed at social reforms and planned by intellectuals. Traditions impressed the new activists as irrational, mere impediments to progress; and adherence to them was considered empty formalism. Roscoe Pound, Louis Brandeis, and Oliver Wendell Holmes proclaimed law to be a means of social reconstruction. John Dewey denied the absolute validity of philosophical concepts and made them into instruments for the mastery of life. Thorstein Veblen called for an activist economics in order to achieve an economic democracy with a just distribution of wealth. These activities were joined by proponents of the New History who expected their discipline to find its proper place in the new American enlightenment as soon as it would analyze the past in a "scientific" manner rather than narrating it or using it for entertainment. There already were, to their minds, substantial hopes for a "scientific" history.

> She [the muse of history] had already come to recognize that she was ill-prepared for her undertakings and had begun to spend her mornings in the library, collating manuscripts and making out lists of variant readings. She aspired to do even more and began to talk of raising her chaotic mass of information to the rank of science.[14]

Once the insights of such a history could be used as tools for social and political action, the "historiography for reform" would have arrived. In 1912, James Harvey Robinson chose Edward Eggleston's phrase the "New History" as the title of his manifesto and it became the name of the new school of historical writing. Actually that school may be most accurately described as the initial phase of American Progressive historiography.

For those New Historians who would become the Progressive historians, James H. Robinson, Charles A. Beard, and Carl L. Becker, the need for social, political, and economic reforms held the first priority and hence historians must be advocates for and sponsors of them. Such service to the present and the future had its price, for it forced historians to be present-minded, even to the point of having as their "ever conscious aim to enable the reader to catch up with his own times; to read intelligently the foreign news in the morning paper."[15] Mere erudition smacked of contemplation and hence led to a nonuseful history. Representatives of the New History accepted with no regret the fact that the strong emphasis on recent history downgraded the regard for works dealing with the remoter past. These periods, particularly the European Middle Ages, were simply not as relevant, yielding at best examples of how things should not be.

*Some implications.* As partial compensation for the loss in the time-span covered, the New History offered an account of the past that was, in Turner's words, the biography of society in all its departments. This kind of history would be a democratic history because it would lift the masses out of undeserved obscurity; it would be an activist history because it would grasp the "real" forces governing history and then teach people how to use them. Since the search for the "real" forces must go beyond the limits of political history, the New Historians called for an alliance of history with sociology and economics. How else could one study all aspects of society? But the call found scant response among historians and social scientists. Ironically, just when Robinson and Beard admonished historians to see the social scientists as their comrades-in-arms, the sociologists and economists were moving away from the evolutionary model, which had tied them loosely to history, toward ahistorical approaches. The social scientists now expected experimentation and present-day observations to yield the laws they wished to find. The bridge between historians and social scientists was never built. The New Historians had to construct their social history by themselves.

The failure to cooperate occurred despite the fact that the two groups shared many attitudes and approaches, including an incipient environmental determinism. Bancroft had thought of the ideas of progress and liberty as autonomous forces, lodged and fostered in human minds and hearts. But the advocates of the Germanist thesis had already treated the idea of liberty less as a universal human endowment than as a product of the Germanic village, forest, and spirit. Turner had credited the frontier with creating the American spirit and character. One need only set Edward Eggleston's *Transit of Civilization* (1901), describing the flow of ideas from Europe to America, against Turner's view to perceive the difference between the traditional and the new interpretations of what ideas represent—here a quasi-autonomy of ideas, there a dependence of ideas on the environment. The New Historians, who counted themselves among the pioneers of a new democratic society, were quite willing to consider ideas, at least to a high degree, as products of the social environment. They expected, therefore, that a truly democratic society, once established, would foster proper ideas, namely those close to rationalism and science and far away from superstition, error, oppression, and even religion.

But what were those "real" forces in the human environment that governed the ideas and actions of human beings? In the early 1900s, as was seen above, economic motivations fascinated a number of scholars. To some American historians it seemed obvious that after all the emphasis on the power of ideas and ideals and of American society as an organic and homogeneous whole one should turn to a more "realistic" approach and speak of economic self-interest and conflict. Typical for the distrust of traditional views and the desire to expose the "true" motives of "real" life was Charles Beard's already mentioned *An Economic Interpretation of the Constitution.*

The directions and themes of the New History were well set when the United States was drawn into World War I and for a time foreign policy overshadowed domestic policy. A few years after the war's end, Americans once more turned inward, opening the way for further development of the New History, which after 1912 is best referred to as the Progressive school of historiography.

# ·21·

# The Problem of World History

*The new task.* The first half of the nineteenth century, a time of faith in the oneness of human destiny, in the purposefulness of the world's order, and in the human ability to know, brought forth the most ambitious systems of world history. Hegel's philosophy of history traced the whole course of the World Spirit itself—an impersonal God fashioned by idealist philosophy—from total alienation from itself to complete unity with itself. Ranke, who looked askance at history as philosophy, was confident that the European state system and its overseas dependencies were part of God's plan guaranteeing meaning, order, and continuity. The French, engaged in an agonizing struggle for their own proper political institutions, envisioned world history as the march of liberty towards its triumph under the leadership of the *Tiers Etat*. Indeed, Michelet maintained that one needed to study world history in order to understand France. Since 1789, the French nation was making its unique contribution to human destiny because, in Guizot's words, it had become *la nation chef*, liberty's main agent. Bancroft spoke in a similar vein of the United States. In these cases the Volk or nation of Herder's concept had changed from being the subject of cultural cycles to acting as the agent of progress.

But as the nineteenth century ran its course the currents of intellectual development shifted. The advances of the natural sciences supported the progress view of history and the increasing challenge to the existing social order by the Fourth Estate gave strength to the Marxist interpretation of history. The idealist and Christian framework for history suffered greatly in structural strength for reasons August Schlözer had uncannily foreseen in the eighteenth century. He perceived clearly the need for an integral view of history: "one can know every single street of a big city, but without a plan or a view from an elevated point, one will not have a feeling for the whole."[1] With God and God's Providence having been the final and immediate cause for all events, "universal history has so far been only a mass of data necessary for the theologian in his biblical studies and the philologist for his explanation for the Greek and Roman writers and remains;

it was nothing but an auxiliary science." It would now need to be replaced by world history, which "is a systematic compilation of factual statements, by means of which the present changed condition of the earth and mankind can be causally understood."[2]

*A task not performed.* Schlözer's new world history as a synthesis of facts was not forthcoming in the five decades prior to 1914. From the ruins of Hegel's philosophy of history had risen the Marxist interpretation of history, speculative in manner, and not a truly empirical world history. The Christian framework that for centuries had served to uphold a universal view of history had not received a refurbishing since Bossuet's attempt to up-date the periodization in ages. Now the empirical mood of late nineteenth-century thought made such a restoration of Christian world history even less likely. In fact, theological higher criticism and modern archaeology even shed doubt on Israel's ancestral role for mankind. The Old Testament became for many scholars one among many Near Eastern records, and while it would later be shown to be remarkably accurate, contemporaries held it in low esteem as history.

Jesus of Nazareth as the Christ and hence the central historical figure fared little better. Hegel's Spirit had no need for a God incarnate, and to the so-called Hegelian Left God became a mere projection of human imagination or, in the case of Marx, a tool of oppression. But even contemporary Christian theologians tried to interpret Jesus' life and role either in an ahistorical way or in a manner which deprived them of true significance for universal history. In Germany many Protestant theologians deemphasized the historical Jesus and tried to detach Christian faith from any need to affirm the historicity of the New Testament events when they transformed that faith into a timeless spiritual experience of individuals. In Catholic France, Ernest Renan made Jesus the Christ into Jesus the brilliant, charming man and moral teacher, who was eventually caught up in the messianic mood of his era. With Jesus reduced to either a personal Christ-myth, implying a rejection of a sacred history, or a brilliant wandering rabbi, the traditional links between universal history and the Christian faith were severed. The heritage of Eusebius, medieval chroniclers, and Bossuet appeared finally to have faded.

However, in this hour of its opportunity scientific history in the positivist sense proved unable to replace the idealistic and Christian world histories—at least immediately. Underlying its very assumptions was Comte's speculative scheme for progress with its three stages in the development of the collective human mind. According to that scheme, all decisive change in human development had ceased when the positive stage was reached in the nineteenth century. Now historians were to study the past in order to find the general laws operative in human behavior. They would not only explain past events but also help manage human affairs. As for the past events themselves, they were mere raw material in the search for such laws. The world history that mattered—the ascent to the positive stage—had already been written by Comte. The story of the third stage would be only the tale of increasing mastery of human life through science. Thus, whenever empirical historians wished to explore an ongoing world history, they had first to reject Comte's claim for the triad of ages in the interest of positivism itself. Henri Berr did so at the turn of the century when he attempted to grasp the evolution of mankind. One hundred separate volumes, filled with empirical studies, would, like the interlocking parts of a giant picture-puzzle, allow a general overview. But although Berr wished to penetrate beyond the facts he did not think much of general historical laws—a substitute God, he called them. As was seen, Marx's theoretical system, too, experienced the fate of Comte's Triad. The call for empiricism (understood in positivist terms) could not be combined with adherence to large-scale interpretations of history, including systematic world histories, with their inevitably speculative elements.

Darwin's influence on world-history writing showed the same pattern. The sociologist Herbert Spencer accomplished the "authoritative" interpretation of the course of human development as evolution. Nevertheless, his system itself fell to empirical criticism. In historical work Darwin's evolution appeared mostly as a scientific support for the assertion that progress marked the course of human events. A few special concepts, particularly the struggle for survival and survival of the fittest, saw some broad applications. The only truly biological interpretation of world history came in the race theories. Already in the eighteenth century, the term "race" had been used widely in a nonbiological and vague connotation. Then in the 1850s, still prior to Darwin, Count Gobineau had argued in his *Essay on the Inequality of Races* that mankind constituted a reservoir of groups whose "blood" ranged from inferior to superior. In Western culture the superior strains had by now been exhausted and cultural decay was inevitable. On the other hand social Darwinists brought a sort of optimism to racial theory when they attributed the success of the "European race" to being the fittest of all and saw it continuing in the future. In those two forms the racial interpretation of the past found adherents, although the term "race" remained largely undefined.

*Progress and doubts.* By far the greatest number of people equated the concept of evolution with the interpretation of world history as human progress, bringing to that already dominant view additional strength. At a safe distance from biologism and positivist empiricism, Lord Acton, in 1898, restated superbly the view of universal history based on human progress:

> By Universal History I understand that which is distinct from the combined history of all countries, which is not a rope of sand, but a continuous development, and is not a burden on the memory, but an illumination of the soul. It moves in a succession to which the nations are subsidiary. Their story will be told, not for their own sake, but in reference and subordination to a higher series, according to the time and degree in which they contribute to the common fortunes of mankind.[3]

But even in the contemplation of world history undercurrents of doubt were already surfacing on occasion. It was indicative for the presence of grave doubts about progress, both of distrust of the new industrial mass society, that an American wrote *The Law of Civilization and Decay*. In that work Brooks Adams proclaimed that the West had reached its end state. The "economic mind," governed by greed and fond of accelerated innovation as well as of ruthless efficiency, had finally prevailed over the "imaginative mind" that had marked the attitudes of peasants, warriors, saints, and thinkers. In the stable situation around 1900 the book caused few ripples; that was also true of the ominous prophecies of dark developments to come by critics from de Tocqueville to Jacob Burckhardt and of Nietzsche's prediction of the advance of nihilism as the penultimate product of the rationalist-technological civilization.

# ·22·

# Historiography between Two World Wars (1918–39)

## The Twentieth-Century Context

When in 1914 soldiers marched among masses of jubilant onlookers on their way to the battles of the First World War, many of them were aware that they might die, but not that a whole way of life would be buried with them. The marchers led the world into decades of monumental changes in how life was led and thought about. Many of the developments, already underway in Western culture since the late nineteenth century, were vastly energized and accelerated after 1918: advances in the sciences and technology, making the masses benefactors of the production of goods and means of communication; the political, social, and economic emancipation of so far neglected groups; and the progress of globalization. Prior to 1914, many people had viewed these developments, visible in their early impact, as validation of an optimistic, strongly progressive assessment of the future. Expectations had been high for an unbroken amelioration of the human condition.

But events in the twentieth century showed the ambivalence of these seemingly beneficial processes. First, science and technology's increasing understanding of and control over natural forces led to substantial improvements in human life, but also would provide the tools for new types of warfare, genocides, and weapons of mass destruction.

Second, the masses did become the benefactors when the ideal of equality was approximated to a higher degree in the situation of women, minorities, and other marginalized groups. But this humanitarian development was counterbalanced by the misuse of mass movements for experiments in building new societies that ruthlessly enforced limited visions on what the human being should be. The results were dictatorships of previously unthinkable brutality. In liberal democratic societies the excesses of mass consumption, mass media, and mass production made their own far less destructive but still negative impact on human life and nature.

Third, until 1945, globalization increased but was still marked by the presence of vast colonial empires. Nevertheless, what used to be a Western-centered world gradually developed into a truly global world of states. The mobilization of many parts of the globe for World War I was still in accord with the existing colonial world order, although its longtime implications would be contrary to it. Signs of things to come were, in retrospect, clearly visible. Beginning in anthropology, the study of cultures developed as an alternative to a state-centered approach to history. The anthropological approach to cultures could be linked to the preferences for context and uniqueness in historicism. On their parts, Oswald Spengler and Arnold Toynbee revived the long-standing model of cultural cycles—rise, peak, and decadence—in their approaches to world history. The revived cyclical model would become a keen competitor for the progressive view in the twentieth century. But only after 1945 did globalization become a major feature in Western thought, and specifically in historiography.

## Challenges to Historians

The increasing disenchantment with aspects of the modern world also shaped historiographical developments. The impact was not uniform but varied according to specific national and cultural contexts. To this transformational process, historiography contributed its own developmental trends that became intertwined with those of life in ways far beyond simple dependency. In the aftermath of enormous shocks emanating from the great human drama played out in the first four decades of the twentieth century, historians faced the now especially difficult challenge of how to connect the past with a sharply different present, and with the new expectations for the future in the construction of the historical nexus. In many Western nations, sudden and extraordinary changes called into question the sense of, but not the need for, continuity. There, historians found it hard to discern the intertwining of continuity and change that were normal for human life in a context where change seemed to be absolutely triumphant.

By 1918, history found itself firmly established as a discipline in the Western system of knowledge. Historians were aware of the need for adequate and complex rules governing their inquiries (methodology) as well as for a set of basic views on the dynamics and structure of both the world and the human condition. As they have at all times, most historians in the early twentieth century worked within the confines of mainstream historiography that has never been shaped by just one grand dominant theory neatly followed by another, but rather by a composite of elements from old and new approaches and methods. The remainders of past historical thought and practice had themselves once been innovative approaches to the understanding and explanation of the past human condition. After their possibilities had been explored and their excessive claims to sole validity had faded, elements of them augmented and modified the basis of mainstream historiography. As new theories were suggested, the process of adjustment repeated itself. Therefore, history's theoretical base has never been organized systematically, but craft-like by cumulating insights. At the cost of theoretical purity, historical thought and practice acquired a high degree of adaptability.

From the 1880s, historians agreed that historical methodology should be "scientific," although disagreements developed over the exact meaning of the term. That demand met with a mainstream historiography guided by widely shared methodological elements, sometimes reaching back to ancient times: the critical use of sources to establish facts, proper restraint in the construction of the account of the past, and the obligation of historians to strive for objectivity. Reshaping these elements in the "scientific" mode became the primary task. In it, two large-scale approaches would figure prominently.

*Historicism.* As the century progressed, the divergence widened on what was meant by the phrase scientific approach. On one side stood the perspective known best as historicism. This rose to prominence in conjunction with the German *Geschichtswissenschaft* (historical science). The word *Wissenschaft* differed in its connotations from that of the English word science, with its close association with the natural sciences. *Wissenschaft* referred to an inquiry after truth that was conducted according to strict and agreed-upon rules, and in the proper inquisitive spirit of objectivity. Historicism's earliest important representatives, Johann Gottfried von Herder and Leopold von Ranke, were followed in the 1880s by Wilhelm Dilthey and the neo-Rankeans. Historicist tenets strongly influenced historiography well into the twentieth century. At historicism's core stood the affirmation of an obtainable authoritative truth about the past. Access to it was afforded by the critical study of sources conducted in optimal detachment from the contexts of the present (objectivity). That held true despite the insight that historians themselves were seen as being immersed in the flux of life. Indeed, this very immersion gave historians the ability to understand (*Verstehen*) the human ways of coping with a world in which each phenomenon was unique and not just a variation of something general. Empathetic understanding arguably yielded a sufficiently approximate reconstruction of the past. Historians therefore no longer needed to apply the generalizing methods of the natural sciences, but could instead rely on empathetic understanding of the specific contexts of life, each unique in itself. Such a perspective was well suited to seeing the individual as the important historical agent. All phenomena of past life had to be grasped in terms of unique entities (such as persons, cultures, or nations), and as results of their actions (events). Some historians even stressed the organic becoming of all entities. In any case, all phenomena—be they individuals, events, nations, or cultures—existed in a web of meanings (*Sinnzusammenhang*); the unfolding of which, however, had no universal aim (*telos*). The world was not the necessary result shaped by and expressive of grand general structures and forces, and therefore it could not be explained in terms of abstract interconnections. No large generalizations, and no laws, were possible. Each context carried its own unique meaning. Hence, the writing of history must not aim at reporting cause and effect sequences, but must produce narratives.

Truth in history inhered in individual contexts. Therefore historicists rejected the use of standards derived from other contexts. They especially objected to those large-scale teleological meanings that marked the progress view, including the schemes of Hegel or Marx. These patterns negated the truths to be learned from unique smaller contexts. Historians were left with a multitude of contexts unconnected with each other. For early historicists, such as Herder, Ranke, and others, God was still the unifying force of the multiple contexts, preventing a relativism of perspectives. Yet by the late 1800s, transcendent entities were no longer tolerated in what was now the historical science. In their absence, the unifying force came to be an immanent, generalized life force (as in the philosophy of vitalism) that nevertheless preserved a degree of uniqueness since it fostered spontaneity. Mostly, the idea of a universal energizing, and hence pan-explanatory, force was dropped altogether. This trend strengthened the relativist inclinations inherent in historicism. As a result, relativism became an acute issue.

*Precursors of an empirical social history.* Since the mid-1800s, some historians had begun to look at the world in different ways. They used the term scientific in the manner of natural scientists as they championed various degrees of empiricism, the centrality of general and large-scale structures and forces, cause and effect chains, and laws of history. These historians delved into aspects of life not readily dealt with by historicist inquiries; economic and social histories were favored in all their aspects. Eventually, the state had to yield its prominence to civil society. The prewar calls for a New History attuned to the social sciences still reverberated. Responses to them did reinforce the ideal of a history relying on methods that could grasp the phenomena beyond the individual and included generalizations, perhaps even laws. These new historians argued that history could, in that way, more readily encompass all aspects of life. Hope was strong that such a history—a new social history—could be more useful to modern life. Social strife and the Great Depression tended to enhance interest in the new perspective on history, but after 1918 opportunities to develop new ways to deal with history were too few and the resistance to innovation too strong.

The pioneering scholars of the *Annales* worked for most of the years preceding 1939 in Strasbourg, not in Paris, the intellectual center of France. In Germany, the failure of Lamprecht's social and cultural history, as well as general suspicions of Marxist influence in both of these types of history, reduced social history to a strongly ethnically accented *Volksgeschichte*. Only in America did a version of social history—American Progressive History—obtain a position of prestige. Its success was due to the powerful presence of the affirmation of progress in the American sense of history. The expectation of a steadily increasing rationality inspired confidence in the future. Economic history, subject to less prejudice against it, prospered modestly. Yet the period of prominence for social history, attuned to the scientific spirit, came only after 1960.

Major and fateful exceptions to the mainstream's development were the historiographies of two official ideologies that rejected much of the Western tradition and its views on history. Communism tolerated only a paneconomic interpretation of history, while fascism offered little more than a quasi-biological and voluntarist reductionism. It can be cogently argued that their simplistic views of history misguided many of their actions, with catastrophic consequences.

## Historicism: From Dominance to Crisis

*Historicism's prominent role.* The period of peace expected after 1918 turned out to be short and politically turbulent. Defeat caused bitterness and victory disappointment. In the 1920s, the great gap between postwar hopes and expectations—even outright illusions—and life's realities in a reorganized political world put obstacles in the way of a proper adjustment of historiography. In Europe old political entities were dissolved and new ones constructed, often without the consent of substantial segments of the population. Resentments, even hatreds, were kindled and rekindled with tragic consequences. In the end, most European nations ended up impoverished. The hardships of the Great Depression of the 1930s added their measure to an already difficult situation.

Historians encountered corresponding difficulties when they attempted to build new historical nexuses in various national contexts. The reassessment of what constituted a true and usable national history, in light of the decisive upheavals of the immediate past, proved the key problem. The attendant social, political, and cultural implications made dealing with the issues of continuity and change a public affair. To historians in the academy, who by then had gained the authoritative voice on historical matters in most European countries, fell the task of reassessment done in terms of the prevailing mainstream historiography. That continuity was assured by the fact that prewar historians still held the key positions in academe. It also mattered that the organization of the historical enterprise—such as the institutions, the education of historians, and the standards of enforcements—showed a good deal of continuity. With continuity came a strong position for historicism. Hence, it was relevant that historicism came to be troubled by an acute crisis caused, as was seen before, by its inherent relativism.

*The scope of the crisis.* Three problems did pose special difficulties for historicists: the uncertain status of general pronouncements about individual and unique phenomena, the danger of subjectivity in all matters of truth, and the moral neutrality fostered by the purely contextual nature of all values. The first problem inhibited the development of different types of history. The second settled historicism with an uninhibited relativism. The third deprived historicism of a more than contextual truth when confronted with the grand ideologies—a severe handicap in circumstances that demanded moral choices. The issue of truth about the past and its moral implications became an issue in the 1920s and 1930s, particularly in Germany.

Beginning with Dilthey, German scholars had striven to establish history at a safe distance from both the natural sciences and metaphysical entities such as God or the Spirit. They retained, however, the idealist conviction that the autonomy of history as a discipline called for the unique individual, group, or event to remain at the center of historiography. The price of abjuring generalizations and of ignoring forces on a larger scale was the denial of any overall development in history and the loss of an objectively ordered world which could be understood in its totality. While all of that disturbed few people in the tranquil atmosphere of pre-1914 Germany, the horrors of World War I reduced the willingness to be satisfied with Dilthey's "despite-it-all" optimism, and Weber's stoic acceptance of a world as basically incomprehensible could not hide the problem. Thus, the search for a concept of an ordered world and the adequate methods of understanding it continued, always on guard against positivist certainties as well as their opposite, the relativist denial of the possibility of a binding truth.

A few German scholars were willing to follow historical relativism to its radical conclusion. In the midst of World War I, Theodor Lessing drew the last consequence of a human world without intrinsic order when he pronounced history to be no science at all but a creative act which gave meaning to meaningless life. All views of the past were myths created by people who wished to engender faith and hope in the future. The idea of a scientific history was just another such myth since only the realm of nature yielded truth which could be expressed in firm propositions or even in numbers. Others attacked the last vestiges of a rational cognition which Max Weber had preserved. Karl Mannheim viewed even the rational processes not as autonomous but as shaped by economic, social, and political conditions, making even scientific theories into ideologies, while Erich Rothacker knew only the logic of life, unique with each individuality and with no universal validity.

But in the period after 1918, with its profound political and cultural changes and uncertainties, most historians were now disturbed by a question Dilthey had once asked only rhetorically: did not the view of all religious and philosophical ideas as changing and subjective lead inevitably to an "anarchy of convictions"? Despite historicism's relativistic inclinations, German historicist historians still discerned in the multitude of individual perspectives the presence of eternal verities of the good and the true. But Ernst Troeltsch found such aestheticism no match for the prevailing relativism. He rather hoped that a synthesis of traditional European values could provide a firm basis for living and for writing history with a solid order. In 1932, one year before Hitler came to power, Karl Heussi published his *The Crisis of Historicism.* The reconciliation of the general with the individual as well as of change with continuity had failed. In practice relativistic historicism failed, too, as it found no real answer to Hitler's totalitarian state. Friedrich Meinecke ventured a subtle protest. His book on historicism tried to redefine German history and character in the image of the neoclassical ideal of *Humanität* that German thinkers had cherished in the period between 1750 and 1890, although he must have known that giving such prominence to one age and its views violated the "no age was superior to any other" doctrine of historicism.

*Croce's assertive historicism.* During the 1920s and 1930s the German defenders of history's truth value could have turned to Benedetto Croce for some assistance. He, too, wished to defend history against those who would convert it into a science; indeed he ended up with an endorsement of history as the all-embracing view of the world. Whether he overcame the relativism that bothered the German historicists so much depended on one's acceptance or rejection of Croce's view of human life as onrushing, ever-creative process. In it stood the historian as a full participant—necessarily so as a human being—who still could be impartial through scholarly discipline but not objective in the sense of having no views on the world. The latter attitude produced historians "who shut themselves up within the four walls of their private affections and private economic life, cease to be interested in what has happened and in what is happening in the great world, and they recognize no other history but that of their limited anxieties."[1]

That made all history contemporary history, because the present was no mere point in time from which historians could look back at a finished past. Rather, the present and the past were linked inextricably—the past existed in present reality. Historians, therefore, had to redefine their task: it was not the collection and critical assessment of sources as facts on which to build an interpretation (the Rankean approach) or even general laws (the positivist approach) but the incorporation into the present of a living past. That task would produce histories narrative in character, reflecting the uniqueness of specific historical contexts, empathetic in spirit, thus obviating the need to judge in terms of good and evil. Such histories would demonstrate how at every instant human achievements were accomplished only to be overcome by doubts about them. Problems were reborn and "solved" again by new achievements, and so life proceeded. In Croce's understanding life and history were one—the one incomprehensible without the other. Records, sources, events were meaningless outside of life and without historical reflection life would make no sense. Thus, embedded in a consistent philosophical scheme, Croce's historicism forestalled those serious doubts of German historicists and with its affirmative spirit appealed to two American historians, Carl Becker and Charles Beard.

*A joyous relativism.* American historians, notwithstanding the influence of German historical science, did not share the German agony over history's access to truth. They remained convinced that scientific history would eventually bring reliable and valid results. This confidence rested on their rejection of the German doubts that reality could be grasped in a subject-order separation conducted according to strict methodological rules. The conviction that reality could be represented "as it was" in historical accounts even marked Progressive history when its dynamic principle, progress, was seen not as a construct but as a "fact." Indeed, objectivity was defined as viewing history in terms of progress. Therefore, James H. Robinson saw no conflict between the ideals of a scientific history with timeless insights and the view of history as a tool for action. He emphasized "the fact that history should not be regarded as a stationary subject which can only progress by refinishing its methods and accumulating, criticizing, and assimilating new material, but that it is bound to alter its ideas and aims with the general progress of society and of the social sciences."[2] Robinson and the Progressive historians considered such a relativity harmless since they trusted that each subsequent stage would be more rational and democratic and therefore each subsequent historical truth would be more accurate. Hence the ideal of objectivity did not prescribe a deliberate and contemplative standing back for assessing matters but involved the affirmation of that view which was in accord with progress. That historical insights will forever be invalidated when the period which produced them passes did not matter since both the period and the insights will have helped to bring about something better. Thus, relativism that had caused epistemological agony to European historians sounded a joyful note in the United States because it demonstrated that progress proceeded unimpeded. Harry Elmer Barnes celebrated the vanishing of the traditional concept of truth as a great victory over pietism, obscurantism, and political fetishism.

Only a few American historians, among them Carl L. Becker and Charles Beard, engaged in a more serious discussion of historical objectivity and truth. Both men realized that World War I, the New Physics, and the Great Depression had shaken faith in progress as an inevitable aspect of reality and thus had destroyed the easy connection between progress and objectivity. Progress, so far considered to be the structural force in historical reality, now became a construct either by society or by individual historians. Becker, who once had believed it possible to capture the real past, had begun in 1910 to become skeptical about that possibility. After all, the historian

> cannot deal directly with this event itself, since the event itself has disappeared. What he can deal with directly is a statement about the event. . . . There is thus a distinction of capital importance to be made: the distinction between the ephemeral event which disappears, and the affirmation about the event which persists. For all practical purposes it is this affirmation about the event that constitutes for us the historical fact.[3]

History as depiction of the actual past was an illusion.

Becker put a cheerful face on his skepticism. All historical interpretations with a long range were declared to be neither true nor false but only more or less useful. They were myths, that is, with no foundations in rational arguments or procedures. Historians had to "tend" the prevailing myths (Everyman's historical interpretations), especially casting them into more attractive—that is, more useful—forms. In "Everyman His Own Historian" he set forth the theoretical framework for his view, and in *The Heavenly City of the Eighteenth Century Philosophers* he demonstrated the transformation of one myth (Christianity) into another (rationalism of the Enlightenment).

Charles Beard remained affirmative and optimistic even when he, too, said good-bye to the ideal of objectivity in his essay entitled "That Noble Dream." Beard denied that the past could be grasped as an external object, that historians could face it with impartiality, that the multitude of events had any inner structure, and that the past could be intellectually conquered by man. The subject matter of history is so charged with values that historians themselves cannot avoid making judgments when they select and arrange facts for their accounts. And while "it is almost a confession of inexpiable sin to admit in academic circles that one is not a man of science working in a scientific manner with things open to deterministic and inexorable treatment," one must do so and "face boldly . . . the wreck of matter and the crush of worlds."[4] It was also the wreck of Beard's once strong conviction that history should be a science in the positivist mold.

But if a historical view was only the product of a specific period, class, group, nation, race, or region, a view to be devoured by change, what then was truth and what was the meaning of history? Beard thought that historians had a choice among three views: "History is chaos and every attempt to interpret it otherwise is an illusion. History moves around in a kind of cycle. History moves in a line, straight or spiral, and in some direction."[5] Neither objectivity nor positivistic science could assist historians in making their choices. Of course, "the historian may seek to escape these issues by silence or by a confession of avoidance or he may face them boldly, aware of the intellectual and moral perils inherent in any decision—in his act of faith."[6] Beard's own act of faith affirmed that history had a direction; it aimed at fulfilling the American dream of a just and democratic society—in Beard's interpretation a society of a planned and collectivist nature. Everything in the past must be judged against this. It was this reaffirmation of progress towards an "absolute good"—now entirely dependent on human choices—that made American historiographical relativism so bearable. When the New Historians or Progressive historians spoke in a relativist vein they could do so with joy and optimism because in the end progress—either self-propelled or resulting from human actions—provided a sense of security and truth.

In fact, Beard never practiced his relativism consistently. His works of the 1930s on behalf of the reform of American society were argued in a sturdily positivist manner, including a progress considered to be part of the actual structure of reality. Then, in the ideological struggles after 1936, both Beard and Becker veered away from a genuinely relativistic interpretation of history, which could give little support to the defense of liberal democracy. They found new certainties in the American tradition (Becker) and in the unique American civilization (Beard). But neither man had enough time left to work out the implications of his new stance. Progressive history's relativist phase was brief and did not lead to a thorough epistemological debate in American historiography. Only a few scholars, notably Maurice Mandelbaum, subjected the theoretical foundation of American historical relativism to a substantial critical review.

### Historians and the War Guilt Debate

The debate about the proper historical thought and practice, significant as it was, was largely confined to the academic world. Another debate, not at all unrelated to the first one, was conducted in the public sphere. Historicist historians found the debate after the First World War on the responsibility for that war quite congenial to their views since its focus on diplomats, statesmen, and military commanders affirmed the individual as the historical agent. A wealth of archival material provided source material for analyzing decisions and actions. Yet forces that went beyond the scope of the individual, be they social, economic, technological, or geopolitical, remained invisible.

Historians became engaged in the peacemaking process, but even more so in the subsequent debate on the so-called war guilt question. Which power or group of powers led the world into war? Historians in many countries lent their skills to what they thought was a good cause. National mindsets prevailed in the accounts of the road to war, and the fault lines of the war were preserved. German, Austrian, French, and English historians engaged in editing and publishing documents designed to justify their government's actions in 1914. Archives were made accessible earlier than usual for that purpose. George Gooch, Harold W. Temperley, and James W. Headlam-Morley's *British Documents on the Origin of the War* presented the British view. Emile Bourgeois and Georges Pages's *Origines et la responsibilité de la grand guerre* (1921) did the same for the French cause.

Yet a few voices critical of the simple condemnation of Germany could soon be heard. In England, such a revision was suggested by Harold Nicolson and the older Gooch. In France, it came more indirectly from the works of Pierre Renouvin and Henri Hauser, who each saw the war in a wider perspective, thereby making the war guilt question itself a more complex one.

The German response did not differ in the kind of historiography produced, but was especially bitter as it came in the context of military defeat, the collapse of the monarchical state, and the deep resentment of the conditions of the Versailles peace treaty. Especially relevant was article 231 that forced Germany to state that it was the sole responsible party for the war. Counterarguments came from the *Zentralstelle für Erforschung der Kriegsursachen* (Center for research on the causes of the war). But the most substantial debate on the issue of the war occurred in the context of the discussion about the new German identity. In it, the main result of the war was at stake: the democratic German state (the *Weimar Republik*).

The United States was spared a strident war guilt debate as the origin of the war could not possibly be found in American actions. The debate focused on the circumstances of and justification for the American intervention. There, too, it was conducted in the historicist vein, stressing diplomatic, political, and military history. Many of the historians who engaged in the debate had actively supported the war effort through the National Board of Historical Service (among them James T. Shotwell and Albert B. Hart), and a few had participated in the peace-making process. But, after 1925, some studies were critical of attributing the guilt solely to Germany. Among them were those by Harry Elmer Barnes's *The Genesis of the World War* (1927), Sidney Fay's *Origins of the World War* (1929), and Bernadotte Schmitt's *The Coming of the War, 1914* (1930). In them, objections were voiced to the narrow framework of the debate. Economic, social, and cultural considerations came into play in works by C. J. H. Hayes, Parker T. Moon, Preston Slosson, and Edward R. Turner. For all of them, the prewar debate—roughly described as the one between isolationists and interventionists—provided the central theme of the American version of the war guilt debate.

Two other countries escaped the war guilt debate for other reasons. In Italy, the course of events left only four years between the end of the war and the seizure of power by the Fascists under Mussolini. Being among the victors, the issue of war guilt was of lesser importance than Italy's unhappiness with the gains from the war. And the Soviet Union, setting out to construct an entirely new state for an envisioned new era of humanity, considered the world of the past as part of the vanishing and totally flawed old order. Marxist orthodoxy offered an explanation for wars in the capitalist world that made specific war guilt questions irrelevant.

# ·23·

# History Writing in Liberal Democracies (1918–39)

## American Historiography after the "Great War"

With its position strengthened by the war, the U.S. returned in life and historiography to the stance of an only slightly modified isolationism. The interest in the outside world led to a flourishing of diplomatic history. In it, internal conflicts played a secondary role and the nation as a collective actor returned, transcending the conflicts between interest groups. The sense of an American mission on behalf of democracy inspired Samuel Flagg Bemis to set America's uniqueness and goodness against the tired and corrupt European societies. But America's increasing isolationism soon dimmed history's "outward" look, and American historiography retained only the tentative but fruitful beginnings of Latin American and Asian histories. However, the link to Europe was strengthened, visible in the growth of Western Civilization courses.

Many historians had supported the war effort through service in the armed services, membership on the National Board of Historical Service, or assistance in propaganda efforts. After the war, the majority of them returned to their professional routine in a country that in the 1920s strove for "normalization." Institutional historians, for example, still retained influence. Charles MacLean Andrew's last work appeared in the late 1930s and his student Lawrence H. Gipson finished a broadly conceived work on the British Empire as recently as 1970. But historiography saw the flourishing of one variety of social history, American Progressive History.

Social history was gathering strength in a country where democratic roots went deep. In the 1870s Green's enormously popular *History of the British People* had influenced Moses Coit Tyler's histories of American literature. Later, James Schouler wrote about the life of the colonists in 1776 and John Bach McMaster related in his *History of the People of the United States* how Americans had dressed, entertained themselves, worked, distinguished good and evil, and built a humane society. McMaster barely kept his mass of material together by means of a central theme: how love of liberty and peace had produced the most prosperous society yet. Theodore Roosevelt acknowledged the common people's role in settling the content; and while Frederick Jackson Turner never wrote a history of the American people, they were nevertheless the true subject of most of his work.

### American Progressive History

*The Progressive historians.* In the early 1900s, James Harvey Robinson, Charles A. Beard, and Carl L. Becker began to construct the New History that eventually came to be known as Progressive history. It reached its greatest prominence in the 1920s, entered a period of epistemological turmoil in a brief (previously discussed) relativistic period, went through a difficult adjustment period in the 1940s, and faded after 1945. Robinson, Beard, and Becker were midwesterners who in their youth had acquired a spirit of revolt against what they considered traditionalism: Protestantism and the laissez-faire approach to economics and government. Philosophically they became part of the pragmatic revolt. Historically, the Progressive historians joined the movement toward a New History that aimed to replace the predominant political history, emphasizing elites, with a history focused on large-scale structural forces, particularly the "people." But since the Progressive historians wished historiography to serve above all the reform of the United States, they modified their historiographical revisionism and still granted a substantial role to progressive political leaders and a new elite of reform-minded intellectuals. In the interest of decisive reform, historiography must become the weapon in the emancipation of American society from an outdated tradition. Objectivity now demanded that historians write history in the light of the new insights—that is, in a progressive vein. Social scientists were to be allies in the great cultural battle, although in reality the connection to them remained one of an ad hoc conceptual cooperation.

Progressive historians were confident of success because they considered progress toward ever greater rationality as the pattern inherent in the evolution of humankind. Nevertheless, that quasi-natural process still needed the support of historians, who therefore must abandon the contemplation of eternal verities or of distant periods for a pragmatic analysis of the more recent past. American life's "real" structure and forces must be dug out from underneath layers of outdated concepts which were kept in place by those who wished to preserve the status quo. Once the people would know about the "real" forces at work, the conspiracy by special interests aimed at hiding these true forces could be ended. Abstractions like providence, nation, and democracy had evoked a false sense of continuity between past, present, and future and had helped to preserve injustice. True continuity in the American past was provided by the long struggle of the people against those who conspired to keep them from their proper place. Progressive historiography, proud to be "scientific," had from its beginning the character of a didactic and moral endeavor. In it, the course of history tended toward an ideal society perceived as rational, cooperative, and at least partially planned. In a series of works on the Constitution, the Supreme Court, and Jeffersonianism, Charles Beard tried to show the "real" forces at work in the American past. Carl Becker denied that the American Revolution constituted primarily a fight for home rule and argued that it was in equal measure an internal conflict over who should rule at home. Becker and Beard had sketched the Progressive model of the revolutionary period. It depicted the Revolution as a struggle of the people against England and against their own oligarchs of power and wealth. The Constitution became a conservative counterrevolution that deprived the people of their proper place in American society. Then, in the 1920s, Charles Beard's *The Rise of American Civilization* not only portrayed Americans as a vigorous and democratic people but made their continuing struggle against property interests, particularly big business, the main theme of the American past.

*Progressive history and ideas.* The world of ideas and the flourishing field of intellectual history proved to be a difficult problem for Progressive historians. On the one hand, these historians were fond of the "realism" of the economic or other environmental interpretations and distrusted ideas as movers of history. They rejected the concept of a *Zeitgeist* molding the thought and actions of a period and the use of intellectual history as a refuge from naturalism and materialism in the manner of German historians and Jacob Burckhardt. They also refused to continue Tyler's type of intellectual history in which historical events were primarily caused by ideas and past ages were compared favorably with an overly materialistic present. On the other hand, the Progressive historians's very cause rested on an idea: the idea of progress, in which reason was central to the fate of the nation and mankind. Therefore these historians liked the evolutionary intellectual histories of Buckle, Lecky, and Eggleston, which hailed reason's steady emancipation from superstitions and errors. Robinson proclaimed that thought properly applied assured the pinnacle of progress: "the abolition of poverty and disease and war, the promotion of happy and rational lives."[1] That view could be combined easily with the concepts of progress and of history as a tool of democratic emancipation.

Progressive historians seldom reflected on these tensions in their historiographical model: progress was an exception in the world of ideas because its value did not derive from being a mere instrument but from being the essence of history itself. Only in Progressive history's relativistic phase did progress lose its privileged position. Until then, ideas were either right and powerful or wrong and weak depending on how they related to the future ideal society. The wrong ideas asserted the status quo in the interest of selfish groups, tended to veil the true situation, and impeded progress. These wrong ideas would lose strength once historians enlightened the people on the selfish economic or sectional interests at work, and they would eventually disappear altogether in the future rational, planned, and just society. In that society the economic and environmental forces and the ideas would coincide in substance and aim. They were contradictory only in periods with an unjust social order.

In his *Main Currents of American Thought* (1927–30) Vernon Parrington linked ideas, particularly in literary expressions, firmly to the social milieu. Literary form and content became objects of sociological and not "formal literary" criticism since now the social situation of the writer determined everything. Accordingly, literary standards and convictions were discounted as prescriptions sponsored for selfish reasons by those in power, and the contemplative study of literature yielded to the study of intellectual history as a form of social activism. In that perspective writers were either heroes, if considered democratic, or villains, if viewed as either unenlightened or as conscious supporters of the establishment. Poems and novels were viewed not as aesthetic expressions but as remainders of earlier social battles. Literary and intellectual history became a report on the perennial dualism of democratic versus antidemocratic forces which has varied throughout the past only in the specifics of the contestants and issues. About a quarter of a century later, Merle Curti presented *The Growth of American Thought,* a work more subtly argued than Parrington's, with a wider scope and more knowledgeable, yet still in the Progressive spirit, wishing to be not simply "a history of American thought but a social history of American thought, and to some extent a socio-economic history of American thought."[2] Its general optimism regarding the egalitarian trend, the progress of science, and the growth of individualism was only slightly tempered in later editions by the fears, anxieties, and questions of the atomic age. Indeed, the ideal of progress, no longer a self-evident truth, had now become an instrument to "guide men through a new era to a new maturity."[3]

*The problem of the Civil War.* When they approached the problem of the Civil War, Progressive historians, who prided themselves on their realism, retained their strong predilection for interpreting the American past as a continuous social conflict and for viewing that conflict in economic terms. The most typical and influential formulation of the mixed economic-sectional approach was that of Charles Beard. For him the central consequence of the Civil War was not the abolition of slavery but the enhancement of the Second American Revolution, which enabled industrial and business interests to dominate the United States. But the view that the Civil War was an irrepressible conflict, prompted by the collision of large-scale economic forces, fit poorly with the Progressive historians' faith in the shaping of human life by effective and rational actions and with their implicit moral attitudes. In later life, Beard himself deliberately put some distance between himself and economic determinism.

The Beardian interpretation enthralled many. A number of scholars, however, found it unacceptable. Some scholars, such as Owsley and Vann Woodward, criticized Beard's opposition of a strictly agrarian South to the industrial and commercial North and East. Others revolted directly against the economic determinism in Beard's view and its acceptance by many Progressive historians. They did not share the Progressive view that even bloody events with questionable results were points on a line leading toward the consummation of justice and happiness. These scholars were more impressed by contemporary condemnations of America's entry into World War I as a folly or at least as an unnecessary step caused by emotion-guided policies and a skillful manipulation of mass opinion. These revisionist historians pleaded that statesmanship could have prevented the Civil War, which was brought about by cheap politicians, and they rallied around James G. Randall's catchphrase, "A blundering generation." The Civil War was caused by delusions, mischievious propaganda, bogus leadership, emotionalism, and fanaticism; in short, by the absence of calm reason and statesmanship. The Civil War was, wrote Avery Craven, "a work of politicians and pious cranks." The war was neither necessary for national unity nor the inevitable collision of economic forces; it was a needless and repressible conflict. Implicitly the revisionists, most of whom were Southerners, rejected all thought of a moral superiority of the North. Owsley called the abolitionists wild-eyed propagandists and Charles Ramsdell argued that slavery would have receded anyhow. Both sides lacked patience, statesmanship, and understanding, if anything the North more so than the South.

The revisionists flourished only briefly. They went against empirical findings and cherished tradition when they denied the role of ideas as shapers of mass attitudes, overlooked the importance of slavery as a moral and economic issue, underestimated the proper role of emotions, highlighted in the low caliber of democratic politics (at least in 1850), trusted in the South to set its own house straight, and were as amoral as Beard's determinism. Their view also contradicted the national mood after World War II with its pride in victory in a "necessary" war. Non-Beardian Progressive historians saw the whole democratic process impugned, and the new generation of so-called Consensus historians had too much respect for ideas and ideals to have them labeled as illusions or delusions.

## Other Social Histories

*A forgotten conflict.* It is surprising that the Progressive historians, who were so keenly attuned to conflicts in American society, virtually ignored the racial conflict, until one realizes that they chose modes of explanation not conducive to highlighting the race question. When they dealt with the Civil War they used the Beardian model, stressing sectional and economic conflicts, and in that light the race conflict was of minor consequence. The issue came closest to being joined in the histories of Reconstruction, since there the status of black Americans in society was at the heart of the matter. With Progressive historians treating racial problems as secondary problems, discussions of the matter produced answers that separated historians along regional, political, and philosophical lines. Early in the period James F. Rhodes and the scholars of the William A. Dunning school had blamed the failure of Reconstruction on a blundering North and the excesses of black Republicans. Dunning understood the crucial importance of the race question but his conclusions were guided by the racial superiority views of most of his contemporaries.

> This was that the ultimate root of the trouble in the South had been, not the institution of slavery, but the coexistence in one society of two races so distinct in characteristics as to render coalescence impossible; that slavery had been a *modus vivendi* through which social life was possible; and that, after its disappearance, its place must be taken by some set of conditions, which, if more humane and beneficient in accidents, must in essence express the same fact of racial inequality.[4]

Along similar lines, Ulrich B. Phillips explained that slavery had been democracy's way to cope with the presence of an "inferior race" in its midst. Progressive historians did not contradict these findings; they simply did not deal with the crucial issue of discrimination against black Americans. When they took up the issue of the post-Civil War South they adhered to the model of economic determinism. Beard had seen Reconstruction as an endeavor to secure the economic victory of Northern capitalists, and in Howard K. Beale's view Reconstruction could not help black Americans since Radical Republicans instituted all its measures in their own economic interest. Fascinated by economic interpretations and not contradicting the theory of the inferiority of black Americans, Progressive historians could indeed easily overlook the crucial racial issue. But by discussing the issues of emancipation, democracy, justice, conflict, and the common people, Progressive historians encouraged indirectly some pioneering works on black American history by black Americans. It mattered here that America's educational progress between 1865 and 1900 was producing an ever larger group of literate black Americans. Gradually black American history left the purely inspirational vein, which had still marked James W. C. Pennington's *A Textbook of the Origin and History of the Colored People* (1841) and instead patterned itself after the emerging historical science. In 1883, George Washington Williams published a *History of the Negro Race in America from 1619 to 1880* in which he stressed primary and secondary sources and his own objectivity.

> Not as a blind panegyrist of my race, nor as a partisan apologist but from a love for "the truth of history" I have striven to record the truth, the whole truth, and nothing but the truth. I have not striven to revive sectional animosities or race prejudices. . . . My whole aim has been to write a thoroughly trustworthy history; and what I have written, if it were not other merit, is reliable.[5]

With Williams ended the line of black American historians whose theological training had taught them respect for texts and whose religious faith gave their work its moral and providential elements. W. E. Burghardt DuBois, Harvard- and German-educated, followed the thoroughly secular ideal of "scientific" history. He shared the contemporary view that history's course aimed at a steady increase in rationality which, the young DuBois thought, would automatically alleviate all social problems, including the race problem. The black American cause and scientific historical scholarship could thus live in smooth cooperation.

> I was going to study the facts, and all facts, concerning the American Negro and his plight, and by measurement and comparison and research, work up to any valid generalization which I could. I entered this primarily with the utilitarian object of reform and uplift; but nevertheless, I wanted to do the work with scientific accuracy.[6]

Later DuBois lost the conviction that as people became more educated their enhanced rationality would cause them to abandon racial prejudice. His contemporary, Carter G. Woodson, a Harvard Ph.D., avoided the sequence of high hopes and eventual disenchantment when he proceeded in a more pragmatic manner. His life's work yielded the Association for the Study of Negro Life and History (1915), the *Journal of Negro History* (1915), a publishing house dedicated to bringing out works on Negro history and life, and finally, many works on Negro history. Woodson intended to rebut in a scholarly manner the assumption of the racial inferiority of black Americans on which much of the work by scholars of the Dunning-Phillips school rested.

DuBois and Woodson, each in his way, combatted the entrenched views on the inferiority of black Americans and on their "proper social place" which from the late 1800s until well into the 1930s pervaded American society and histories. The new black American history wished to enlighten American society on the race issue as well as to build a black identity. "If a race has no history, if it has no worthwhile tradition, it becomes a negligible factor in the thought of the world, and it stands in danger of being exterminated."[7]

In the midst of the Depression and at a time of enthusiasm for the economic interpretation of history, especially its Marxist version, and disappointed by the lack of social change through persuasion, W. E. B. DuBois published *Black Reconstruction*. DuBois, who earlier had hoped that increasing rationality would automatically bring about racial equality, now put his hopes in the economic and social development Marx had predicted. If one looked at the Southern past in this manner, the race issue became a force detrimental to the economic-social development of the South. The strength of the Southern proletariat was sapped when white labor deserted black labor and made common cause with white business. Once proletarian solidarity had been shattered, there could be no social change. L. D. Reddick took up a similar cause when he spoke out against the liberal ideal of solving the racial dilemma through political and legal reforms and advocated outright social and economic reconstruction. Then the bombs fell on Pearl Harbor, ushering in World War II and a subsequent age of vast social change.

*Toward an encompassing social history.* Arthur Schlesinger, Sr., brought social history to academe with his courses on American society. In them the masses, the Great Many, were the driving force of history while the elite, the Great Men, were merely their agents. But when he and Dixon Ryan Fox edited the *History of American Life* series they did not think of social history exclusively in Beard's categories of classes and social conflict. Many aspects of social history, for example, the role of women and of immigration, as well as much of the common people's life, was beyond the grasp of Beard's "the people versus the business interests" theme. The two editors aimed at social history with a broad scope: a panorama of American life. Its main theme was not "the people in politics" but the people with their common concerns for food, jobs, health, entertainment, joys, and sufferings. That gave to the volumes in the series and to the works that followed in this vein as richness in color and detail but deprived them of drama and a clear focus. "American life" proved to be too diffuse as a unifying concept. Unity of description and development was more easily accomplished in the many specialized studies issuing forth from social historians, who dealt with urban problems, ethnic groups, immigrants, and religious constituencies. These studies, Oscar Handlin's *The Uprooted* for example, demonstrated clearly a wholly un-Beardian complexity in the common people, with their varied backgrounds and adjustment processes. But the conflict theory continued to enjoy much success. Its dualism between the masses and business interests took on various forms and terminologies and was applied to various eras of the American past. The Jacksonian period offered particularly good opportunities and was viewed as a time when capitalists of all kinds confronted the masses, who were agrarian and inspired by the frontier spirit.

*Turner's fading New History.* The frontier thesis still had offered Turner the opportunities to answer his own call for giving prominence in history to the common people. But after 1908, as already noted, Turner's work in terms of sections highlighted the people in a much more indirect manner, aborting Turner's career as a pioneer of social history. But not all of sectional historiography was a celebration of the views of Turner and the Progressives. New England's historiography clashed especially hard with Turner's environmentalism and the Progressives' disdain for the Puritans. While Bancroft had considered the Puritans outright pioneers of liberty, the Progressive historians viewed them as bigots an adherents of an outdated theocracy and considered their religious ideals to be disguises for economic motives. Thus, for James Truslow Adams and Vernon L. Parrington the Puritans were not forerunners of great things to come but an obstacle to them. Abhorrence of reductionism and presentism, a great pride in New England's traditions, objections to environmental determinism, and a more sympathetic and careful analysis led Samuel Eliot Morison, Kenneth Murdock, and Perry Miller to reject the progressive image of Puritans.

The South, with its distinct way of life, offered many opportunities for sectional historians, although the events of the Civil War and of Reconstruction attracted the greatest attention. The William A. Dunning school remained dominant in that field and its proponents, who included Philip A. Bruce, Ulrich B. Phillips, and Walter L. Fleming, brought forth a large number of studies on the South as a section. That vigorous tradition of Southern studies reached well into the 1970s, from William E. Dodd to Frank Owsley and to C. Vann Woodward.

During the 1930s sectional histories, particularly on Western history, suffered a decline as the country searched for national and not local or regional remedies for its problems. The advocates of the New Deal shared the Progressive historians' perceived need for a new social order fitting industrial America. In this regard Turner's talk of frontier virtues, such as freedom of opportunity and self-reliance, was less helpful and appreciated; indeed, it went counter to the new ideals of social cooperation. Marxists even blamed Turner for letting sectionalism crowd out the concept of class struggle. The attitudes of some sectional historians changed when they analyzed the past of various regions in minute detail, and the empirical evidence ran counter to Turner's frontier thesis.

Frontier life lost its simplicity and glamour when its "impurities" showed, for example, in T. P. Abernethy's study of early Tennessee. In other words the saga of the West lost its exaggerated sense of drama and Turner's thesis its neat pattern. In Walter P. Webb's *The Great Plains* the arid Western country fashioned a way of life different from that shaped by the Eastern tree-rich areas. For Webb, there was more than one type of frontier, and he already was ambivalent regarding the exploitation of the land. Herbert E. Bolton showed the inapplicability of the Turner thesis to the Far Western area. By the 1940s Ray A. Billington and others began a conscious modification and reinterpretation of the frontier thesis. The changing American scene also was eroding much of the fascination with the frontier. America's status as a world power fostered other interests and views. After 1945, when advances in technology made sophisticated communication and transportation technology available at relative low cost, sectionalism faded significantly in American life and subsequently as a theoretical construct. It was characteristic that in 1950 Henry Nash Smith's *Virgin Land* explored images of the West and not the West itself, implying that the frontier concept may well have been more myth than substance.

## England: Historiography in a Fading Empire

England, victorious and still of imperial stature, saw the routine of life returning gradually. In that context, English historians experienced few stimuli to change their ways of studying and writing history. The long-standing emphasis on remarkable persons and their actions found its support in a historicism that had been well adjusted to both the strong English empiricism and the priority given to liberty. All of that was supported by an abundant confidence in England's perceived unique development, one marked by gradual and beneficial social change. Its line led from the Magna Charta (1215) to the Glorious Revolution (1688), and to the present in a series of social reforms. The affirmation of this process and the assertion of a special English gift for liberal democracy formed the core of the Whig interpretation of history. George Trevelyan's *History of England* (1926) epitomized that view of England's destiny.

The philosophical base of English historiography also remained stable. The two sets of principles that had governed English historiography—idealism (and the connected historicism) and pragmatism—were still prominent. But after 1918 the notion of a quasi-organic state, an important feature in idealism, fell victim to the objection to Germany's excessive statism. However, the historicist approach to research and interpretation still prevailed. And so did the view that history involved the motives and actions of individuals, interactions by unique entities, and multiple meanings. Historians must reconstruct the thoughts and actions of those who "made" history. A special predilection for biographies fit that view admirably.

The number of those who doubted a beneficent overall historical process and politics as a rational process remained small. The most effective criticisms of the Whig theory came from two dissenters. In 1929, Sir Lewis B. Namier published *The Structure of Politics of the Accession of George III* in an attempt to demonstrate that the self-interests of individuals and groups, material circumstances, and struggles for power—but no special *telos*—governed historical events. And in 1931, Herbert Butterfield's *The Whig Interpretation of History* declared both the maintenance and discernment of a rigorous straight-line history to be beyond human capacity.

Even the realization of a social history that dealt with large-scale forces and structures came in an English version. Although a strong empiricism governed English social and economic history, the ethical aspect was hardly ever absent. The latter was emphasized in the writings on workers' lives by Barbara and John Lawrence and Le Breton Hammond, as well as in Richard H. Tawney's writings on the conflict between capitalism and traditional society.

### French Historians: The Revolutionary Tradition and a New Vision of the Past

*The sustaining image of the Revolution.* Despite the hard-won victory, the French republic of the 1920s and '30s remained rather volatile, politically and socially. In that situation, the country and its historians found inspiration and continuity in the memory of the French Revolution. The envisioned nature of that event was of key importance since it still had a determinative influence on France's understanding of her present and future. Hence it was significant that mainstream historiography's image of the French Revolution remained firmly within the boundaries set by Alphonse Aulard. Although not a trained historian, Aulard did "translate" Michelet and Taine's visionary images of the French Revolution into the shape of "scientific" history. According to it, the Revolution was an event that conquered and buttressed the proper place for the Third Estate, although external circumstances led to the radical excesses in the Jacobin period. The Revolution triumphed over all subsequent attempts to reinstall less democratic social and political systems. The Revolution proved invincible because it was attuned to the inherent destiny of humankind, indeed it represented one of the great civilizing events in history. This line of reasoning set forth in Aulard's *Histoire politique de la Révolution francaise* (1901) still served as the pattern of reference for most historians as well as for the officially sanctioned republican interpretation. Two socialist historians, Albert Mathiez and Georges Lefebvre, diverged significantly from that view. Mathiez tried to rescue the radical revolutionary phase and its leader, Robespierre, from the condemnation of the prevailing historiography. The Jacobin period was no longer the result of contingent events but part of the Revolution's logic. Lefebvre brought the multitude of rural dwellers into the considerations of historians. In the process, he also pioneered studies in mass psychology (*La Grande Peur de 1789* [1924]). That aspect of his work became important for the early *Annalistes* who otherwise would pay little attention to the Revolution. A starkly contrary image of the Revolution emerged in the writings of some conservative critics of the French Revolution who rejected revolutions as inherently detrimental developments.

French historiography remained, for the time being, in a traditionalist framework. However, to this framework, since the 1880s, methods and findings from sociology and psychology had been added with the intent to make history more encompassing in methods and content. Georges Lefebvre's works, with their interwoven social and economic historical elements, testified to that. Politics acquired a range larger than it had heretofore, as economic elements entered and statistical and other quantitative methods saw use in analysis. Social psychological approaches assessed the actions and thoughts of masses. Histories of the French Revolution benefited from the concomitant use of wider sources (Philippe Sagnac and Jean Robiquet).

*The beginnings of the* Annales *School.* The *Annales* school had its roots in what Henri Berr, in the 1890s, sensed as a malaise caused by historiography's perceived inadequacy for the modern age. That age seemed to call for a science-like discipline that would favor generalizations over the relating of individual events and lives, encompass all of life, not just the affairs and men of state, and explain or give meaning without recourse to transcendent philosophical or theological elements. Henri Berr's founding of the *Revue de synthèse historique* began the quest for a New History in France that took issue with the prevailing academic history. The latter accented political history and rested on the theoretical precepts of Charles V. Langlois and Charles Seignobos's *Introduction to the Study of History*. Berr would eventually be superseded as pioneer of a New History by Lucien Febvre and Marc Bloch, who after World War I taught at the University of Strasbourg until both received calls to Paris (Febvre to the College de France, 1933; Bloch to the Sorbonne, 1936). In 1929 they founded the journal *Annales d'histoire économique et sociale,* which became the rallying point for reform-minded historians. Bloch and Febvre rejected what would be called the *histoire événementielle*—event-oriented history—because its narrative with a primarily political content failed to grasp the fullness of human reality and thereby endangered the position of history among the disciplines studying human life. The public would see here "a handful of antiquarians who for the sake of a macabre love unwrap the dead gods; the sociologists, economists, publicists: the only inquirers into life."[8] Febvre also knew what needed to be done: "History must cease to appear as a sleeping necropolis haunted solely by shadowy schemes."[9] The labor for a total history required a wide repertoire of interests and methods. Historians must invite their "comrades and brothers" in the social sciences to work together in the proper spirit: "Down with all barriers and labels!"[10] Once the disciplines worked together, all scholars would soon acknowledge the importance of time—that the study of human life must be historical. History, when emphasizing the general structures of life, would once more stand at the core of all inquiry, one richer and broader than ever before.

The much wider scope, complex content, and varied structure of the total history necessitated a new methodology. There the maxim had to be: "Man cannot be carved into slices. He is a whole. One must not divide all of history—here the events, there the beliefs."[11] Yet despite their unabashed revisionism, Febvre and Bloch were not particularly active in the field of the theory of history. While a member of the French resistance, Marc Bloch did write a book on the historian's craft. Even under these trying circumstances he remained cool, rational, and much less fiery than Febvre, whose passionate nature never quite fit the theoretical mold and who offered the opinion that "generally speaking . . . it is not a good thing for the historian to reflect too much upon history. All the time he does so his work is held up. And the philosopher (whose job in fact it is) folds his arms. That makes two men not working."[12] But Bloch's book impressed him as practical. "Is the book a system of history? Not a bit of it. Does it consist of pseudo-philosophical reflections on history? No. Does it correct false or obsolete concepts? You might say so. The book is above all a critical review of wrong ways of thinking and practicing history."[13] In the end, there would be a considerable theoretical ingredient in *Annales* historiography, but few books on theory. In his *The Historian's Craft* Bloch realized the theoretically complex task the *Annalistes* would face when he argued that historians must go beyond written or oral documents, which told only of the intentions of individuals, to a wide array of sources, which would enable historians to understand past social facts, such as institutions.

Even before 1945, the works of Febvre and Bloch sounded many of the themes of the later *Annales* schools. Febvre demonstrated an approach to total history in his *Philippe II et la Franche-Comté* (1911), the value of the geographical accent in his *La terre et l'evolution humaine* (1922), and the importance of psychological explanations in *Un destin, Martin Luther* (1928) and *The Problem of Unbelief in the Sixteenth Century* (1942). Bloch explored the medieval belief in the healing power of the royal touch in the case of scrofula (*Les rois thaumaturges;* 1924), but above all he dealt in a comparative and structural manner with feudalism (*La société féodale;* 1939–40). His works would have a considerable impact on French medieval studies, particularly through Georges Duby.

All along there had been preparatory steps taken in related areas: Henri Sée in comparative economic history, the Belgian Henri Pirenne in medieval economic history, and Gaston Roupnel in geography. French scholars had been sympathetic to quantitative economic history since the early 1900s, when quantifiable data were abundant there, numerical relationships seemed to fit economic processes particularly well, and the discipline of economics traveled more and more along the mathematical route. French scholars have been sympathetic to quantitative economic history ever since the first quarter of this century, when François Simiand began to study long- and medium-range economic developments quantitatively. Simiand's long series of price and wage data were prototypical for the later French approaches, as were C.-Ernest Labrousse's attempts in the 1930s to shed new light on the coming of the French Revolution by his inquiry into price developments and economic crises in the eighteenth century.

# ·24·

# Historiography and the Grand Ideologies

## Italian Fascism and Historiography (1922–43)

In the four years between the end of the war and the Fascist coup in 1922, Italian historians hardly had time to reflect anew on the past. The historical endeavor showed a strong historicist influence in methods and approaches (partially due to Benedetto Croce's prominence), but also displayed a noteworthy openness to the social sciences. The predominant theme was still the Risorgimento and its success or failure in creating a unified Italy as well as a liberal order. That held true, although to a more limited degree, even after 1922. Other strong fields were the histories of the regions and those periods of national pride—ancient Rome and the Renaissance.

Social science influences (often combined with Marxist approaches) were quite visible in Italian historical practice. In Gaetano Salvemini's works on the Renaissance, the idea of class struggle had a prominent place. Early in his career, Giacchino Volpe drew on some Marxist concepts. But while Salvemini became an exile, Volpe developed into a protagonist of Italian imperialism and fascism. Yet even under fascism, again within ideological limits, Italian historiography continued to be shaped by historicist, positivist, social scientific, and legal patterns.

A new political order came to Italy in 1922. It was not the egalitarian state of emancipated individuals, which the progress theoreticians of all kinds had foreseen, but a totalitarian state demanding complete subservience and sacrifice from its citizens. In return it offered stability and a sense of belonging which many of those not used to democratic politics felt were lacking in the state of free and isolated individuals.

Fascism, as Benito Mussolini and his movement demonstrated, made the historian's task both easy and difficult. It was difficult for historians to accommodate the crucial fascist assertion that the leader's will represented the incarnation of the national will and purpose. That will and its aims were timeless, with

347

only its specific manifestations changing, and left to historians only as recitation of various expressions of the national will, which was without a true development. Quite a few historians had political and moral objections to such assertions. It was easy for historians to agree with Fascism's glorification of the nation's power and greatness and to highlight those periods of the Italian past that told of empire, war, victory, and national enthusiasm, especially the periods of the Roman Empire and the Risorgimento. These emphases, along with the fascist preference for political history and the narrative form and the fascination with great personalities, were not innovations but long-standing features of Italian, indeed, of European historiography. Actually, even those historians who dissented from fascist views adhered to traditional historiography; they retained the traditional forms but shifted accents and interpretations away from fascist preferences. Croce did so in his histories of Naples, the baroque age, and nineteenth-century Europe. In them he proclaimed his faith in liberty and progress; a liberty, however, not seen in liberal and democratic terms but conceived of as general human creativity. Delio Cantimori defended the power of ideas, particularly those of heretics. Federico Chabod dealt with those contradictions between power and ethics that fascism denied, and Adolfo Omodeo celebrated quietly the ideals of liberalism and republicanism. Antonio Gramsci, on the other hand, who espoused a Marxist interpretation of the Italian past, paid for it with the loss of his liberty and life. The persistence of a nonfascist bloc of scholars writing traditional historiography and a lack of a systematic fascist view on the past prevented the identification of traditional historiography with the fascist period. Thus the years after 1944 brought the excision of fascist ideas but no call for a new beginning in Italian historiography.

### German Historians in the Weimar Republic and Hitler's *Reich*

*The debate about the appropriate past.* German historians had slightly more than a decade to create a historiography appropriate for the new liberal-democratic republic. They had to accomplish that in the wake of the overthrow of the monarchy, in a country full of violent conflicts, a fervent nationalism fueled by the military defeat with its subsequent "stab in the back" legend, and resentments against the peace treaty. Mainstream historians went on with their work in their special fields, producing accounts of excellent scholarship in the general historicist vein. But many of them, directly or indirectly, joined in the grand debate on the new balance between change and continuity in German history. More specifically, how could one construct a socially useful and scholarly persuasive nexus between the past and the present after so profound a rupture? What historical nexus could offer acceptable expectations, even hopes for the future? Would historians heed the timeless admonition that "German historiography must open its eyes and look at the world as it really is, not how a parochial isolation and arrogant self-esteem wish it to be"?[1]

The general debate on how much continuity or change should be acknowledged in the new German history was closely linked to the historians' attitudes toward the new Weimar Republic. Some historians saw no possibility for a new nexus between the past and the expectations for the future and argued for strict continuity, thus rejecting the new republic (Johannes Haller, Georg von Below, and Adalbert Wahl). They were of the school of thought that saw the German state as a historically grown entity with its own order, in which Western liberal ideas were foreign elements. Many more historians found sufficiently strong reasons in the German past for accepting the Weimar Republic as the legitimate present and future. The most famous of them was Friedrich Meinecke, who was led into the republican camp by reason, and not the heart (*Vernunftrepublikaner*). That issue also concerned Hermann Oncken, who had ventured into the then unusual studies of political parties and socialism. Yet as a strong nationalist he continued to publish anti-French works. Hans Rothfels supported the republic, despite strong sympathies for the *Kaiserreich* and praise for Prussian qualities such as loyalty to the state, sense of duty, and willingness to serve the state. He was one of the Königsberg scholars who conducted studies of ethnicity (albeit with a clear German bias). A similar path led Otto Hintze into the republican camp. He had conducted innovative administrative studies in imperial Germany, using methods that transcended the boundaries of historicism. His student, Fritz Hartung, an eminent constitutional historian, proposed a mixed republican-monarchical state as a guarantee of continuity. Other well-known moderates who adjusted themselves to the republic were Hans Delbrück (military history), Ernst Troeltsch (intellectual history), and Hans Herzfeld. Again others affirmed the republic but regretted the absence of radical social reforms. Veit Valentin wrote a history of the German national assembly of 1848–49, whose failure he attributed to the missing voices of the true advocates of a liberal order. Arthur Rosenberg regretted the rejection of the postwar soldiers and workers' councils in favor of the republic as a moderate compromise.

A whole group of younger historians favored the Weimar Republic but had their careers in Germany cut short in and after 1933. Eckart Kehr's case was especially noted because he criticized the primacy of foreign policy in history, and accented the important connections between military, business, and politics in the prewar German naval armament effort that contributed to the enmity with England.

The defeat of Lamprecht's attempts to lift cultural and social history to prominence still reverberated in German historiography. Only a small group of historians at the University of Königsberg (now Kaliningrad)—including Hans Rothfels, Werner Conze, and Theodor Schieder—engaged in a ethnically accented social history. Its openness to sociology (Hans Freyer, G. Ipsen) was unusual. After 1933, the emphasis on the *Volk* and on the German eastward expansion made it easy to adjust that history to the Third Reich's preferences. Cultural history remained a history of ideas, and great personalities were still the decision makers. Few scholars continue the work of the New German Economic History founded by Schmoller.

*Historiography in Hitler's Germany.* With Hitler's accession to power in 1933, the debate over the Weimar Republic ceased. That republic was officially rejected. The continuity and nature of German history was now traced to historical events, persons, and periods more akin to the ideology of Hitler's Third Reich.

*Hitler and the historians.* German National Socialist historiography, like that of Italian fascism, glorified the leadership principle, the nation, and power. It acquired a greater complexity, however, through its racism, particularly its virulent anti-Semitism, a conscious attempt to create a strictly ideological history, and a stronger push to have official views dominate. Still, Hitler's Germany never had an agreed-upon view of the German past. The *Gleichschaltung* (the official attempt to develop uniformity) only partially succeeded in historiography since too many agencies vied for dominance and academic institutions retained a strong voice. In the departments of history academic routine proceeded as before and the German *Geschichtswissenschaft,* with its text criticism, objectivity, *Verstehen,* and seminars, while not liked by radicals, remained acceptable. The most profound change came with the ouster of professors who were Jews or were ideologically suspect. Through these purges German academic life lost some of its finest scholars. However, there was a successful *Gleichschaltung* of sorts because many historians shared the National Socialist affirmations of a strong pan-Germanism, the central role of power in life, and the view of the state as a collective whole which must be served. They also shared Hitler's antipathy toward socialism and communism. Only much later did historians understand that to add loyalty to Hitler to those attitudes was not only a morally flawed course of action but a self-destructive one.

In 1935, National Socialism achieved one victory in German historiography by conquering the publishing bastions outside academe. The steering commission of the *Monumenta Germaniae historica* became part of a *Reichsinstitut für ältere Geschichte,* modern historiography came under the aegis of the *Reichsinstitut für Geschichte des neuen Deutschlands* led by Walter Frank, and Meinecke was forced to yield the editorship of the *Historische Zeitschrift* to Karl Alexander von Müller. A few years later, the war curtailed all publishing. The outlines of what German historiography would have been after a victory by Hitler were nevertheless discernible. It would have been primarily political history with a heavy accent on heroes, battles, and victories. The country's Germanic origin would have been stressed and Prussia's contributions to building the modern Germany would have been made central. To a high degree historiography would have been a veneration of the proper ancestors and German heroes. It is doubtful that the Holy Roman Empire of the German nation would have fared well, tainted as it was by its Christian mission and faith and its connection with the papacy and Italy. Only the desire to see a continuity in the German Reich could have prevented its complete condemnation.

The Germanic ancestry would have been used as the link to the second major ingredient of a National Socialist historiography: racism. Some academic historians supported racism; most prominent among those who did were Alexander von Müller and Ernst Krieck. Müller established a section on the "Jewish problem" in the *Historische Zeitschrift,* and Krieck spoke about Germans in terms of racial superiority. Those were the two themes of racial historiography: the existence of superior and inferior races and the definition of Jews as the most inferior race. National Socialists could draw for their racial theories of history on a variety of nineteenth-century ideas—those of Count Gobineau, of A. Pictet and his celebration of the Indo-Europeans or Aryans as the basic racial stock of Western culture, and of the Social Darwinists and their talk of the "European race" as the "fittest" of all races. In the 1920 and 1930s, Hitler and his movement expounded an ill-defined but rabid racism, which declared the tall, blond, blue-eyed North German types to be superior people, although the term Aryan was left standing as a wider description of the superior race. National Socialists soon knew a whole gradation of good (Germanic), worse (Slavic), degenerate (French), and worst races (Jews). A few National Socialist propagandists and textbook writers busied themselves with demonstrating the beneficial effects of the presence of Aryan, especially Nordic, types in various cultures, even in ancient Egyptian culture, and the detrimental effects of any non-Aryan, especially Jewish, influence on German history. The execution of these studies was inevitably crude and without any theoretical rigor or substantial evidence.

A significant counterweight to these developments was provided by the second German historiographical establishment, that of the émigrés. A sizable number of historians who left, or had to leave, Hitler's Germany settled in England and the United States. Among them were Ernst Kantorowicz (symbolic interpretations), Erwin Panofsky (art history), Ernst Gombrich, Hajo Holborn, and Hans Rosenberg. Many advanced to influential professorships and continued to work along their accustomed lines of interpretation. American historiography profited from their work through the strong impetus they gave to intellectual history (their *Ideengeschichte*). In a sense they preserved German *Geschichtswissenschaft* in its purest form. But since they wrote their works in English and only a very few of them returned to Germany after the war, their influence on German historiography remained modest.

### The Soviet Union: The Imagined Future as the Guide for History

Ever since Marx's death the disputes over "what Marx really meant" have been intense. Some Marxists have quarreled bitterly over purely theoretical issues; after all the ideas of Marx and Engels had changed as their system of explanation evolved. But most disputes were triggered when the Marxist interpretation of human life confronted actual life situations. In scholarly terms that meant the need to reconcile empirical evidence with Marxist theory and the recognition that Marxist theory, too, was subject to the critical scholarly code. But the fiercest disputes have arisen when mass movements used Marxist ideas as tools in the business of life. To the masses of industrial workers Marxism offered a guide in the political struggle and a source of inspiration, hope, and faith, with its promise of a coming age of plenty, nonexploitation, and happiness. Hence the Marxist vision of history formed an integral part of many socialist party programs and became subject to the disputes involving them. These disputes took on a new coloration after 1917, when an orthodox Marxism became the official view of the Soviet Union.

*The tensions in the Marxist philosophy of history.* The exposition of the Marxist interpretation of history in an earlier chapter was deliberately didactic, that is, it aimed at simplicity and clarity. It avoided pointing out the complexities and internal tensions in Marx's views, thereby also reflecting Marx's own confidence that he had brought to congruence reality and theory. But even if that had been true at Marx's time, life went on changing and brought about or revealed ever-new internal friction in Marx's system. The most serious source of friction had, however, been there from the beginning: Marx's twofold intellectual heritage. On the one hand, the speculative elements inherited from Hegel (even if the latter's philosophy had been, in Marx's expression, turned on its head) postulated a timelessly true structure for historical development. On the other hand, the young Marx had observed the actual conditions of factory workers, that is, he had gained empirical insights. In its widest sense, the discussion on and about the Marxist philosophy of history has been over which role each of these two elements should play in the ongoing adjustment of that philosophy to changing conditions.

In the Soviet Union and its dependent states the discussion was short-circuited by excluding empirical modifications of the basic historical interpretation, although in Soviet historiography the influence of the Russian past and Soviet experience actually became all-pervasive. In the Western world the strong critical and empirical traditions and the entirely different social and political developments brought adaptive changes that reached deep into Marxist historical thought, even to the point of interpreting Marxism only as a method.

*Marxist historiography as state ideology.* At the beginning of the new Marxist state stood a paradox. In 1917, disintegrating Czarist Russia offered to the revolutionary Marxism of Lenin a chance for success. Yet there was irony in the fact that the Russian Revolution, one of the most important Western revolutions, proclaimed itself to be Marxist in aims and character but happened in violation of Marxist historical logic. Russia, with an underdeveloped industry and a relatively small industrial proletariat, was decades away from an advanced capitalism. Lenin rectified that contradiction between theory and reality when he replaced Marx's scheme for historical development with a theory of revolutionary action in which a disciplined cadre overthrew a still weak capitalism, in the interest of the proletariat, because the mass of workers did not have a clear enough class consciousness to be relied upon. The historical agent, the Communist party, would retain dictatorial power in the new state until (as they hoped in those heady days of postwar ferment) communism was firmly entrenched in the whole world. Lenin's stress on revolutionary action was a break with the Marxist insistence on the inescapable necessity of historical development and could have provided a point of departure for further discussion of Marxist historiography in the Soviet Union. It was not to be.

Imperial Russian historiography had in general paralleled that of contemporary Western Europe. The state was the focus of attention in the histories of Russia by N. M. Karamzin during the 1820s, S. M. Solovyev in the mid-1880s, and V. O. Klyuchevsky at the turn of the century. With Solovyev, a student of Ranke, began the dominance of the German historical science that was challenged only in the early 1900s by Plekhanov's rigid Marxist mold for history. During the 1920s historians in the Soviet Union continued to teach and write history as members of social science faculties. Gradually history even recovered a measure of its former prominence through the works of Mikhail N. Pokrovsky. His *Russian History* (1920) pleased Lenin because it stressed Marx's schematic elements: broad generalizations, the clear identification of historical periods with Marx's mode of production, a strict economic determinism, the downgrading of the individual's role, and even the deemphasis of Russian history in favor of an internationalist outlook. Its unsophisticated approach also made Pokrovsky's *Russsian History* an effective instrument of indoctrination. Pokrovsky did not object to such a use since he considered history the most political of all the social sciences.

The situation changed radically when the Soviet Union entered a decade of political turmoil in the late 1920s. Stalin's suppression of his internal opponents, the First Five-Year Plan with its merciless economic demands, and an increased sense of isolation from the world led to an end of the latitudinarian attitudes and to ever tighter limits of the permissible for historians. Gradually the suspect old bourgeois historians with their attachment to neutral scholarship were replaced by younger historians with proletarian backgrounds and an ideological enthusiasm without critical checks. The proper historical interpretation was defined more and more narrowly and deviations from it were seen not as merely erroneous but as subversive. In October 1931, Stalin himself intervened in a historiographical dispute over the history of Bolshevism and set the themes for future historiographical work: the concept of Bolshevism was fixed and not discussible; the Russian Revolution was the prototype of all coming revolutions; and history was no longer to be dedicated to critical analysis but to affirming established ideological tenets.

Soon after Stalin's attack Pokrovsky died and a few years later Soviet histo-

riography took a sharp turn away from Pokrovsky's historical views. His strict
Marxist schematism contradicted the newly emerging interpretations which were
more inclined towards enhancing the importance of individual actions and the
Soviet state. Lenin and Stalin's actions were declared to have been decisive to
the course of human events. There also grew the awareness that all the talk of
objective conditions governing everything and of the "withering away" of political institutions once exploitation had disappeared were detrimental to the building of the socialist state. Pokrovsky's views were declared to have been aberrations and the relationship between objective conditions and superstructure was
redefined by Stalin himself. In the new socialist state

> the part played by so-called objective conditions has been reduced to a
> minimum; whereas the part played by our organizations and their leaders
> has become decisive, exceptional. What does this mean? It means that
> from now on nine-tenths of the responsibility for the failures and defects
> in our work rests, not on "objective" conditions, but on ourselves, and on
> ourselves alone.[2]

That meant the abandonment of a strict historical determinism. The Soviet
Union emerged as a creation of the will and skill of revolutionary leaders as
much as it did of the logic of human events.

Pokrovsky's approach posed another problem. He had completely subjugated Russian history to the Marxist scheme of development. Soviet citizens had
only one assurance of continuity in their collective life: they had to see themselves as participants in the gradual, worldwide development toward a Communist society. But in that grand global scheme the Russian past had no more and
no less a status than any other past. Hence, Pokrovsky had not hesitated to offend Russian nationalism by admitting the crucial role of the Vikings in the
founding of the first Russian state, by granting the conquering Mongols equal
cultural status to the Russians, and by calling the Russian Empire a prison for
nationalities. But Stalin, who insisted on the leading role of the Soviet Union in
the development of world communism, once again wished to foster patriotism in
the Soviet Union. The continuity of Russian history became an important support for social cohesion. Historians continued to be concerned with when exactly
the periods of feudalism, capitalism, and socialism had begun and when they had
ended or how many modes of production Marx and Engels had stipulated (three
or four such modes). But they also spoke in slavophile terms about the Soviet
Union's leadership role, patriotism, and love of the homeland. Historical figures
and picturesque descriptions of past Russian personages and events overshadowed abstract schemes. The basic periodization of Western history, too, reverted
to the traditional triad: ancient, medieval, and modern. In addition, controversies
once hotly debated by scholars now were settled in accordance with the party
line. It was simply stipulated, for example, that feudalism existed in Russia from
the ninth to the nineteenth centuries. The Second World War, subsequently called
the Great Patriotic War, fortified the supremacy of national history over the

Marxist global outlook, except that Marxist-Leninism still envisaged a Communist world to be brought about by virtue of a strong Soviet Union. That formula served to resolve the apparent contradiction between the patriotic Soviet view and the Marxist internationalist view of the past—between the reality of the world and Marx's stipulated structure of historical development.

# ·25·

# American Historiography after 1945

### New Realities and Traditional Horizons

In the aftermath of the Second World War, the war guilt debate among historians turned out to be rather unlike the one after 1918. The guilty party was clearly Hitler and his regime. Yet the shock emanating from recent events would prove to be too great for so simple an answer. Millions of people had been killed, wounded, or disabled, dislocated from their homes, murdered in genocides, or starved to death. As time went by, historical inquiries into the greatest human catastrophe known to date would reach farther and deeper. But even the magnitude of the shocks experienced did not instantly transform the writing of history. Until the mid-1960s, the national versions of Western historiography were aimed primarily at the restoration of continuity after the great rupture. That meant a return to ways in which national history had linked the past and the present with the expectations for the future.

*The historicist mainstream.* There were, of course, sharp differences between the democratic nations and the ideologically rigidly controlled communist areas (the Soviet Union and Eastern European states). For two decades after 1945, mainstream historiography in the liberal and social democratic Western world seemed rather unchanged in its theoretical base, including approaches, methods, and many of its themes. Strongly influenced by historicism (perceived here in the widest sense), historiography retained its methodology: a document-centered inquiry and corresponding methods. The emphasis on objectivity and cautious interpretations added the needed restraints on subjectivism. Such a historiography, with its emphasis on unique entities, supported the tendency of people to think about history in terms of their national contexts. That held true even in light of the increasing interconnection of the world by modern means of communications. Although influences, particularly innovative ones, would travel much faster and more easily, national contexts still screened, blocked, or transformed ideas offered in the transfers. And, with the exception of America, the concept of progress as a pattern of overall development found a reluctant acceptance—also in line with historicist thought.

Nevertheless, some adjustments became necessary, since the enormity of what had happened could hardly be ignored. In Germany, historicism's relativism yielded much ground to a new ethical awareness in historiography. In France, the reaffirmation of the traditional Revolution-centered political history experienced the ideological pulls of the Cold War. American historiography witnessed the surprising demise of Progressive history as ill suited to the new society with world power status. Yet for about two decades after 1945, mainstream history in the liberal and social democratic Western world remained in its existing confines.

From the late 1960s, a number of innovative perspectives in historiography challenged the status quo. Of them, social history and cultural history would be most prominent. These two broad currents encompassed a wide array of historical theories and practices.

*The prominence of social history.* The great variety of social histories and their subdisciplines were products of the wish to transform history into a "scientific" discipline in the mode of the social sciences. August Comte's philosophy of positivism, Henry Buckle's science of history, Henri Berr's Synthetic History, and the New History proponents had tried to decipher life by analyzing social structures and forces. That goal inspired two differently accented social histories. One used history as an instrument for the advocacy of social and political changes. The American New Left history and the German *Historische Sozialwissenschaft* would be two, albeit quite different, examples. A second type of social history emphasized its scientific ambitions although its findings were put to pragmatic uses. The French *Annales* group represented an intentionally apolitical, if not antipolitical, history. A wide range of social historians wished for history to encompass all of life. All along, there was Marxist history as a special kind of social history with openly political intentions.

*Postmodernism and the New Cultural History.* Beginning in the 1970s, talk of an end to modernity and fierce criticism of the progress view of history came to be major themes among some historians. Postmodernism began to challenge history. Its energy and enthusiasm derived from a profound disenchantment with what modernity had wrought in the twentieth century, and a hope for a much better—if not perfect—human condition. Postmodernity would constitute no less than the end stage in the development of the human condition.

The most important consequence of postmodernist theories for historiography would be the increasing prominence of a new type of cultural history. That history was perceived to be best attuned to the prevalent postmodernist views of the world. All of these developments, rather than forming a uniform intellectual current, have manifested themselves in national variations.

*The new global scope.* Modernization and two world wars strengthened the making of a truly global world. Historiography had known attempts at world histories even in ancient times, but in the twentieth century these attempts acquired an increasingly global reach. In a decisive change world history lost its imperialist perspective. The complex world of newly independent nations with greatly varying cultures posed a formidable task for understanding, knowing, and telling history. These problems showed in the variety of overall explanatory concepts used for world history: the progress view with a steadily "upward" development (including economic development theories), sequence of culture models, and anthropologically conceived histories.

## Historiographical Repercussions of America's New Status

*The debate about America's entry into the war.* After 1945, the most decisive development for the U.S. was its ascendancy to world power status. Not surprisingly then, the debate about the war turned out to be a continuation of the long-standing debate on isolation versus intervention. While the attack on Pearl Harbor made the choice between war and peace for the United States of America, some historians focused attention on the possible policy choices and decisions in the prewar years. Revisionist historians, including Charles A. Beard, Harry E. Barnes, and Charles C. Tansill, suggested a conspiracy in favor of going to war by the decision to arm and support England. President Roosevelt was seen as a master of deceit, who pursued a purposefully aggressive policy against Germany and Japan, and then sold out Eastern Europe to Stalin. The bitterness of the debate stemmed from the insight that the policy of isolation was losing its one-time dominant influence in an America becoming increasingly integrated into the global world.

*Coming to terms with world power status.* At the end of World War II, America found itself propelled out of a still relatively strong isolation into intricate involvement with an increasingly global world. The special ties to Europe and its traditions weakened gradually as Asia assumed a greater importance for the United States. During the following decades, these trends would be reflected both in the teaching and research of history.

The status of world power had come to the country after an internal social and economic settlement in the New Deal and an external effort in a momentous war. The latter had built a strong social solidarity and a vigorous economy. In addition, the country had been spared the destruction that forced European nations for two decades into a difficult rebuilding process. The victory in war and the new world power position could be interpreted as a vindication of the American progressive sense of history. Nevertheless, historiography turned out to be one of the areas in which expectations for a simple unbroken continuity of developments were disappointed.

In 1945, Arthur Schlesinger, Jr., published his highly praised study *The Age of Jackson.* It seemed to augur well for a resumption of Progressive historiography in postwar America; instead it turned out to be a monument to a school of thought which had reached its zenith years before. Progressive historians found the America of the late 1940s and 1950s not too hospitable to their historiography. World War II could not be blamed on the machinations of businessmen, and it had reemphasized national unity over internal conflict. That awareness of unity was further strengthened by the pride in America's new world-power status and the anxieties of the Cold War. Even Progressives responded favorably to the call for an American mission on behalf of democracy in the world. The Progressive dualism of business or vested interests against the people also seemed out of place in twenty years of growing prosperity. On the other hand, progress had become less self-evident in the course of human affairs in a century of total war, large-scale genocide, and potential nuclear war. Finally, the masses of detailed research produced by academic historians were not kind to broad interpretative generalizations. The half-century of Progressive historiography had ended. In the two decades after 1945—rather placid ones for American society—cultural criticism came from scholars who revised or even rejected long dominant tenets in favor of a greater complexity of interpretation, called counter-Progressive by Gene Wise and Critical Liberals here. Another group reflected more directly the self-confident and powerful United States. The Consensus historians discovered and depicted the nation as an operative whole, shaped not by abstract designs but by collective ideals and shared life experience.

*Critical Liberal historiography.* The reassessment of Progressive historiography began in intellectual and cultural history where Progressive historians had always placed the accent on economic motives and on dualistic societal conflict. But in postwar America, with its new awareness of the complexity of human existence, the simple Beardian dualism was out of place. So was the labeling of ideas as evil when they were seen as defenses of vested interests, and as good if they were in favor of "the people." Once historians saw ideas in their total relationship to life, things were no longer that simple. In his second volume on New England's history, Perry Miller reaffirmed the mind, a term referring to all of conscious experience, as the core of human life. But he also discovered that, when ideas were translated into guiding forces for the life of the people, there existed a surprisingly uncertain relationship between the intent governing the application of an idea and the results it produced. Miller's findings were broadly shared. The anomalies besetting the neat and simple Progressive scheme went well beyond those Miller had demonstrated in the Puritan past. Intent and result gaped widely in more recent experience with its discrepancies between the ideals of the Russian Revolution and Stalin's despotism, the hopes of progress and modern totalitarian states, and the praise of the common people and their widespread assent to evil.

Critical Liberal historians tried to master the new complexity of reality by interjecting a layer of myths, images, and symbols between actual reality and human experience. Human actions and discourses were dominated by that layer. Henry Nash Smith had worked with myths in his *Virgin Land* (1950). Richard W. B. Lewis constructed a whole theory of American culture by stipulating as its central myth or image the American Adam and by viewing the culture as a dialogue on that myth. Of course, a culture seen in terms of myth and dialogue did not move along the straight line of progress but followed an unpredictable zigzag course. The unexpected turns in history were for scholars of the myth, symbol, or image school signals of discrepancies between perception and reality and meant that the myth or image used needed to be refined or replaced. Here the Progressive truth in mastering the world was translated into a search for proper myths or changes. These scholars pronounced the end of American innocence that had inspired Progressive history, above all the end of truth in an unerring development toward an ever-improving democracy through rational action. Differing with the image-symbol-myth school, the theologian turned historian Reinhold Niebuhr found the concept of irony to be the answer to the paradox that the best human intentions can bring about horrible consequences. The reason was not the insufficiency of the image but the very evil in human beings that Christians had talked about for centuries. The long-standing European doubts about a direct grasp of reality and the countermeasure of mental constructs had now arrived in American historiography. The task of Critical Liberal historians was not to lead people in a fight against all foes of full democracy but in a necessary move from innocence to wisdom.

The certainties of Progressive historiography were gone. Bancroft's view of the infallible people and the Progressive's conviction of the goodness of the common people had turned out to be equally unrealistic. The failure of those views doomed the Progressive prediction that, once the conspiracies of vested interests had been foiled and the institutions were in the hands of the people, a "good" world would arrive and persist. Power was not just evil in the hands of vested interests, it could be dangerous even in those of the people. While these new interpretive models of the past seemed to some scholars to fit better in an increasingly complex world, they offered no concrete plan of action for social reforms, no prophecy of a better future, and no sense of urgency that now was the time to act.

> The liberal society analyst is destined in two ways to be a less pleasing scholar than the Progressive: he finds national weaknesses and he can offer no absolute assurance on the basis of the past that they will be

remedied. He tends to criticize and then shrug his shoulders, which is no way to become popular, especially in an age like our own.[1]

"And in any other one, too," one would add. New Left historians would soon storm against what they perceived as academic apathy and elitism.

*The so-called Consensus historiography.* The new American position in the world, the memories of national unity in World War II, the pressures of the Cold War, and the confidence of most Americans that they now could participate in a rapidly growing prosperity brought about a change in the national mood favorable to the emergence of the so-called Consensus view of American history. Underlying this view was the conviction that beneath all the conflicts and competing forces in American society there has persisted a fundamental unity of experiences, ideals, and purposes. One could argue that even Progressive historians, with all their talk about conflict, had asserted such a unity. Did not all those who argued with each other in the past and the present over the proper American way of life believe in democracy, progress, and even some form of capitalism? Reform, not complete change, had been the goal of the Progressives. Hence the so-called Consensus school can be better understood as a shifting of emphasis: tradition, seen as a common core of ideas and experiences and supportive of the concept of the nation as a whole, now ranked as a shaping force above and ahead of the vision of an ideal democracy which was prepared by necessary and continuous conflicts between competing interests and groups.

Already in the 1920s Ralph Gabriel had searched for the fundamental beliefs and ideas that had sustained American society from its beginning. Twenty years later he pointed out that the modern "principles of dependence on reason, of individual freedom, of individual honesty and responsibility, and of mutual cooperation," were the sober twentieth-century expressions for the philosophical concepts about democracy of the eighteenth century.[2] The latter concepts, in turn, were rooted in the religious ideals of an even earlier America, and, actually, religion itself remained a major unifying force. Gabriel had no doubt that continuity and consensus marked American culture. In 1944, even Charles and Mary Beard made a quasi-consensus contribution with *The American Spirit,* in which the dualism of business interests and the people faded in favor of something akin to a unifying American collective spirit. In the 1950s Louis Hartz argued more concretely, if somewhat regretfully, that at the heart of American thought has been and seemingly will be the general acceptance of John Locke's views of the state and government as creations by the people in the interest of liberty and security. These views have not only been held in theory but have effectively shaped all of American political life. Richard Hofstadter demonstrated the common ideological matrices of individualism and capitalism for American life and thought. Another group of historians, including Clinton Rossiter, Daniel Boorstin, and David Potter, did not attribute the national consensus so much to shared ideas as to the shared life-experience of generations of Americans. It formed the unalterable bond holding together even those with most discordant interests and views. Boorstin stated the case for the "unity through life experience" most forcefully, when he began his work *The Americans: Colonial Experience* (1958) with these words:

> America began as a sobering experience. The colonies were a disproving group for utopias. In the following chapters we will illustrate how dreams made in Europe—the dreams of the zionist, the perfectionist, the philanthropist, and the transplanter—were dissipated or transformed by the American reality. A new civilization was being born less out of plans and purposes than out of the unsettlement which the New World brought to the ways of the Old.[3]

Clinton Rossiter pointed out that by 1776 American society was already shaped into so distinctive a unit that independence was not a call to but a recognition of nationhood. In his *People of Plenty* (1954), David Potter analyzed the importance of material wealth and progress to America's identity. From the perspective of these historians American development no longer resembled a constant improvement on the way to a glorious future but a sequence of variations on constant themes.

In that general spirit a body of important works was created. The American Revolution ceased to be a radical but aborted social revolution. Instead, it was seen as the struggle for independence with little impact on the social order. It largely confirmed and secured the rights the colonists had already achieved. According to Edmund S. Morgan Americans of the revolutionary period, although less solidly united than Bancroft had maintained, were nevertheless agreed on such rights as property, liberty, and equality. Louis Hartz pointed out that a radical social revolution could not occur where there was no entrenched feudal ancien régime, and in Clinton Rossiter's view the revolution was de facto finished before it started since no real transformation was needed. A study of the colonists by Carl Bridenbaugh found them not to have been radical revolutionaries but troubled Englishmen with anxieties and hopes over the prospect of separation. Robert E. Brown's detailed studies of popular political participation in colonial and revolutionary Massachusetts revealed no large group of disenfranchised people who would have needed a radical revolution. All of these authors at least implied that the colonists were united and had reached, prior to 1776, some sort of American consensus on their way of life and thought. The denial of a radical revolution also rendered invalid the Beardian concept of the Constitution as a counterrevolution by men of property. On that point, recent studies also have tended to discredit the Beardian dualism with its implied dominance of economic motives. Quantitative studies, for example, have dissolved Beard's two opposing blocs into many and varied interest groups. Bernard Bailyn's study of the role of ideas in the Revolution upheld the event as a radical one but rejected the view of ideas as mere functions of economic and social forces. The relatively simple Beardian paradigm of the American Revolution had become untenable and, freed from it, studies in colonial and revolutionary history showed a new vigor. Similar reassessments occurred in other periods of the American past, too.

The new sense of national purpose and the appreciation of the unique genesis of the American nation once more enhanced the awareness of how different America was from Europe. Turner and the Progressive historians had stressed that difference. Nevertheless Beard and others had used the European theoretical schemes of economic determinism and class conflict in a modified form. Consensus historians insisted more adamantly on the uniqueness of the American experience and society. While Europe's class conflicts have been caused by remainders of an undemocratic past, the social dynamics of the United States have been fuelled solely by the quest for a proper realization of the shared ideals embedded in the American tradition or by its own societal tensions and resolutions. Accordingly, the analysis of the American past must eschew philosophies and concepts which do not fit the American experience. Nor did it make any sense to try to export the American model of life; assertions of its uniqueness deal a blow, in historical theory, to comparative studies.

## Historiography as Call for Reform

*The New Left historians.* Beginning in the 1960s, a series of changes affected the American position in the world, the structure of American society, and the American perspective on the past: the gradual turning of the Cold War into detente, the non-Western world's assumption of a more active role, Europe's lessening dependence on America, the Vietnam War, the civil rights struggle on behalf of black Americans, and finally the various Watergate-related events. Throughout that period of turmoil the social fabric strained under great stress and demands grew louder and more insistent for a radically new society and a commensurate rewriting of American history. The New Left historians, also known as Revisionists or Radical Historians, attacked the established order and its views on the past, including Progressive history.

Walter La Feber challenged the whole of diplomatic history when he stipulated that the United States never pursued any other goal in foreign policy than an "open door" for American capitalists. In that spirit New Left historians revised the prevailing views on the Cold War. They denied that the Soviet Union's postwar behavior was aggressive and motivated by a desire for a Communist conquest of the world. The Soviet Union was simply concerned with her security when she built a *cordon sanitaire* of satellite nations on her western frontiers, while the United States was driven by a wish to build a capitalist world with an "open door" for American products and investments. Hence, only the Soviet Union needed to feel threatened during the late 1940s and the 1950s. American policies, on the other hand, were at best blunders or, even more likely, devious.

A good many of the New Left historians were students of or influenced by William A. Williams, whose works set the tone for the general reinterpretation of the American past by the New Left. According to Williams the abundance of free land made it unnecessary for Americans to tackle the job of building a nation of social harmony and justice. When free land ran out in the 1890s exploitative policies simply turned outward in various imperialistic ventures. This choice of expansion over necessary social reforms constituted the "Great Evasion." Williams, who called for policies with an inward look, explained America's outward thrust as capitalism's need to gain new markets. Once more, American foreign policy was seen as dominated by a radical "open door" demand for American investment and goods. Yet despite the Marxist ring of that assertion Williams saw no historical "law" prescribing such expansionism. He and other New Left historians, although they borrowed heavily from Marx, have generally been unwilling to accept Marx's systematic framework.

During the late 1960s, at the peak of the social unrest, when it seemed to some that American society was about to enter a revolutionary period, a group of New Left historians, disenchanted by what they considered the ineffective moderation of Progressive historians, set out to create a Radical History as an instrument of total social transformation. They did so through a radicalization of Progressive themes and goals. Beard and his many followers had not hesitated to treat ideas as tools for building a just, democratic, and rational society. But with all their talk of economic motivation determining the shape of ideas, Progressive historians also had maintained—somewhat paradoxically—that some ideas had autonomous and overriding power: progress, the rationality of the world, and the goodness of human beings. And Progressive historians had affirmed all along methodological rigor and the efficacy of intellectual discourse. The New Left historians removed all optimistic hedging and moderation from the basic Progressive position.

Those among the New Left who strove with special fervor for a complete social change worried no longer about a balance between history's scientific status and its social emancipatory role. They transformed history into a "consciousness-raising activity" on behalf of the social revolution, which had replaced Progressive reform as the ultimate aim. New Left historians bemoaned the discrepancy between the vigor with which Progressive historians for decades had debunked elements of the American tradition and the cautious Progressive aim of measured reform. If American history was indeed a grand battle between those with property and those without it, then historians must work for fundamental change and not for compromise. Since the future American society would differ radically from the American past, continuity would be broken and it made little sense for historians to be reconcilers of the past, present, and future, whether by maintaining traditional views or by proclaiming the continuity of reform from Populism to Progressivism to the New Deal. Historiography as a contemplative or reformist enterprise must be replaced by revolutionary historiography on behalf of all disadvantaged groups, a historiography that will educate everybody concerning the erroneous ways of the past and help identify and destroy harmful institutional remnants in the present. Historians must join those who wished to free American society from elitism, particularly from the "Puritan morality," broadly seen as self-restraint in sex, consumption, and the building of individual wealth, and from the "Protestant outlook," particularly the work ethic with its sense of vocation and individual achievement. Both were considered buttresses for the "establishment," which had built a society of injustice, dominated by WASPs, exploiters, racists, and agrarian values.

In the American histories written by New Left historians heroes turned into dark figures, losers became heroes, the American Revolution was a stunted social revolution, the Constitution emerged as an iniquitous basic law, the pioneer appeared as a looter and killer, the Civil War failed to bring a new society, Reconstruction was a noble failure, the Progressive Era was really a triumph of conservatism, the New Deal deferred and betrayed true populism, and the two World Wars were adventures promoted by economic interests. All the talk of an age of American innocence was nonsense. The debunking of American business, which Progressives had begun, now reached its peak, when the role of pure evil fell to the business interests. Consensus historiography appeared as history written on behalf of the "establishment" that perpetuated exactly those "myths" which needed to be destroyed in the interest of perfect justice. Historians must completely abandon all pride in the American past since only then will people see the basic injustices in American society. It did not matter that such a radical change of institutions and associated values would obliterate much of the American tradition, since once the crusts of error, particularly economic exploitation and racism, would be broken the proper and good order, though never clearly defined, would emerge.

Yet the vast social changes of the 1960s and 1970s have only partially worked in favor of and pleased the New Left. The phenomenal growth of individualism, skepticism, and relativism in that period ran counter not only to the affirmation of American tradition but also to the revolutionary spirit and action which required dedication to the group and absolute faith in an authoritatively defined order. The New Left itself showed the mark of the new American mood in its lack of an organizational hierarchy and of clearly and systematically formulated goals. The unity of the New Left historians did not go beyond their criticisms and revolutionary appeals. Their historical works remained a spur to radical social action, an analysis of the revolutionary situation, and a revealer of social injustices but did not define the future. Among them were Gabriel Kolko, Christopher Lasch, Jesse Lemisch, Walter LaFeber, Staughton Lynd, and Howard Zinn. New Left historians also opposed most of America's outward projections as political and economic imperialism. They therefore condemned assertions of American power in the world, be it in the Cold War, Vietnam War, or Latin American affairs.

Marxist historians accused New Left historians of a superficial neoidealism, because the latter relied for the realization of their goals on appeals to individuals. The Marxist historians maintained that only Marx's theory yielded the proper historical perspective and basis for the restructuring of society. On their part, New Left historians hesitated to accept the strict economic determinism of Marx's theory of history because, although they stressed the economic interpretation of human life, they also celebrated individualism in all its forms and manifestations. Their revolution and the new order were expected to result from individual actions and to be in the interest of individuals. The New Left historians ended up rejecting the established historiography's discipline of evidence in the interest of history as a tool of social revolution and the Marxist discipline of a strict theory of history in the interest of individualism.

*Historians and the civil rights struggle.* Beginning in the mid-1960s, two longstanding movements of emancipation began to prevail over social inertia and outright resistance—those of African Americans and women. The ideal of equality, part of American revolutionary heritage, was to be actively sought by these groups and, soon after, by others less prominent.

After 1945, the tension between the actuality of Afro-American life and the ideals of America became starkly visible when the war had been defined as one for democracy and against fascist racism. Gunnar Myrdal's *The American Dilemma* (1944) had helped to put the focus on race relations. And so did the twentieth-century large-scale African American migration northward, which changed the race problem from a seemingly regional issue to a national one.

In 1947, John Hope Franklin's *From Slavery to Freedom* began a new phase in Afro-American historiography. A series of books focused on slavery with the intent to have the image of victimization and suffering replace the Dunning-Phillips view of Afro-American life in the antebellum South. The activist aspect of the new historiography was a plea for remedy and equality in the present. In the 1950s, well-known works in that spirit came from Kenneth M. Stampp, Stanley M. Elkins, and C. Vann Woodward. Carl Degler began the integration of Afro-American history into mainstream American history. From the beginning, there existed a tension between the goals to demonstrate the harmful effects of slavery and the one to show a viable and creative Afro-American culture. In the civil rights struggles of the 1960s and early 1970s, the primary focus in the literature of slavery shifted from victimhood to the slaves' resistance to oppression—be it by superficial adjustment, daily quiet resistance, or open revolts. The Black Power movement tried to reserve Afro-American history writing for black historians, raised doubts about its integration into the broader American history, and emphasized black pride in African culture (Sterling Stuckey). Yet by then, Afro-American history was already becoming a vast field of study with a rich scholarship and open to all kinds of scholars. Influential works on the consequences of slavery for blacks and whites, as well as on the continuity of black consciousness, came from Eugene Genovese, James Blassingame, Eric Foner, and Georg Rawick. Controversy resulted from Robert Fogel and Stanley Engerman's *Time on the Cross: The Economics of American Negro Slavery* (1974), which attempted to assess the quality of the slaves' lives in purely economic terms, refraining from all ethical judgments. By the 1980s, Afro-American history had achieved the status of an important segment of American history—highly visible in textbooks, conference contributions, publications, and discussions. The range of publications reached well beyond the traditional topics of slavery and the rural South as exemplified by histories of the pan-African movement (books on Marcus Garvey) and controversial Afrocentric interpretations (for example, the concept of the Black Athena). Inevitably, as black or Afro-American history has grown in stature and volume, it also has come to reflect increasingly the wider issues of American life, among them those of the women's movement. In the widening civil rights struggle, Native Americans strove for the recognition of pre-Columbian America and Americans, as well as their sufferings during the post-Columbian settling of the continent.

*From women's history to gender studies.* At the beginning of women's history stood the "recovery of memory"—that is, remedying the absence of women from historical accounts. This compensatory history discovered and celebrated outstanding women of the past ("women worthies") in the interest of historical accuracy and as a call to emancipatory action. With the success of that endeavor came the insight that, in line with modern trends toward an all-encompassing history, women's history would have to deal not only with outstanding persons but with the multitude of women of different races, classes, nations, and religions. The academic field of women's studies, well established since the 1970s, focused on that wider concept of women (Nancy Cott, Linda Kerber, Gerda Lerner, Kathryn K. Sklar, Carroll Smith-Rosenberg, Joan W. Scott, Barbara Welter). Conceptual schemes in that phase of women's history included the "cult of true womanhood" and "domesticity," both seen as cultural, male-oriented models for defining (and thereby limiting) women and their roles. Some critics pointed to the initially strong focus on middle-class women and the loss to direct action brought about by transforming women's history into an academic discipline. A broader criticism referred to the tension connected with the attempt to integrate women's history into modern social history—the tension between the claim to be an important separate endeavor and the aim to demonstrate the commonality of all human experience. It produced calls for widening women's history to gender studies (Joan W. Scott), which explored not so much the role of women but the more encompassing element of gender in history. The trend has been to detach all biological determination from the definition of women and view male/female differences primarily, if not completely, as constructions—in the past, by dominant men. That approach, it has been hoped, would integrate women's history more effectively into the whole of historiography and make it a more useful instrument in the struggle for women's emancipation.

By the 1980s, American history had developed into an encompassing enterprise with a still strong empiricist bent. While influences from abroad were stronger than before, especially from the *Annales* group, American history kept its own profile. Its interdisciplinary character was strengthened when ties to sociology, economics, and political science were added to those with anthropology, demography, and social psychology. The democratization of society came to be reflected in "histories from below," for which oral history was both an important tool and symbol.

# ·26·

# History in the Scientific Mode

In contrast to the social historians with a reformist or pragmatic purpose, other historians maintained a more clearly theoretical stance. While in the 1970s the influence of the *Annales* group was felt, American historians put their own stamp on a social history in the scientific mode. One of its characteristics was a empiricism with a strong quantitative bent.

## History in the Language of Numbers

It should not be surprising that an age uncertain about historical truth eventually discovered the promises of clarity and certainty inherent in quantification, although one must caution against the view that quantification's rise in history was sudden. While our age is predisposed to hope that the logic of numbers will overcome the seeming illogicality of life, that hope has a venerable ancestry. Ancient philosophers, such as Pythagoras and Plato, and the religious gnostics had relied on numbers as accesses to the mysteries of life. Without such grand aspirations, historians have, ever since Herodotus, quantified some of their statements in a rudimentary manner much as most people do: "when historians cite 'typical' newspaper editorials and the beliefs of 'representative men,' or when they use terms such as 'significant,' 'widespread,' 'growing,' 'intense,' in effect they are making quantitative statements."[1] Yet, it is also true that quantification by today's quantitative historians goes considerably further in vigor, scope, and sophistication.

Both the modern state, in the interest of centralized power, and modern business, in the interest of efficiency, favored the development of quantification. In the process of administering, planning, measuring, and tabulating, they left behind mountains of records which promised rich insights to historians. But there also emerged new expectations for quantification. By 1850 some historians who responded to the positivist quest for generalizations, even scientific laws, had become appreciative of the quantitative approach. H. T. Buckle looked for the fixed and universal laws of the human world and expected much help in the search from statistics, which he praised as the "branch of knowledge, which though still in its infancy, has already thrown more light on the study of human nature than all the sciences together."[2] Clearly, he expected that numbers could help reveal, to a degree not possible otherwise, the ways in which humankind developed. They served no longer as in the early modes of quantification, merely as shorthand expressions or passive indicators. Properly arranged and interpreted numbers and numerical relationships could tell historians things they had not known before. In this case quantification as a way of expression would then be replaced by quantification as a source of new insights.

*The favorite fields.* Not surprisingly, quantification acquired an especially strong position in economic history. Early on, Febvre and Bloch, the founders of the *Annales* school, were already calling for a total history, which would emphasize social and economic phenomena, a type of history especially well suited to the quantitative approach. Thus when, after 1945, the *Annales* group triumphed, quantification was assured a proper place in French historiography. Simiand's and Labrousse's quantitative approach was used as serial history, most prominently by Pierre Chaunu. In it one feature of the world was chosen, quantified for many points in time and place, and then studied in long time-sequences. These series of numerical data reaching over long periods, whether on prices, wages, or population figures, were to yield insights into long-term patterns and trends (*conjonctures*). Perhaps it was thought that many such series would eventually "add up" to a system, a hope not yet borne out. That approach, gleaned from the old positivist pattern of "from observations to generalizations to a scientific law," was challenged by the cliometricians, who infused mathematical models into historical research.

The American New Economic history, the most prominent advocacy group for cliometrics, took its clues from modern systems theory and econometrics, both of which view reality as a system whose parts are linked to each other in a measurable pattern. Thus changes in one area affect the whole system. Economic reality with so strict a pattern of interdependence makes it possible to construct mathematical models, match them against data, and subsequently assess the models' performance—all of this in quantitative form. As will be seen in a subsequent section, even the highly technical works of economic cliometricians can spark emotional discussions.

Quantification penetrated the traditional field of political history, too, when the age of democratization had shifted scholarly interest away from prominent individuals to the masses of people and when population developments received increased attention. Groups were more accessible to quantitative research, as has been demonstrated by the long series of works on American election returns. In many cases their results confirmed and in others they revised long-held views;

for example, the conventional view of the Jacksonian period as a decisive turning point came to be doubted. Again, other studies tried to shed light on problems in social history: which groups formed the elites, owned property, won lawsuits, married whom and at what age, supported or opposed governments, could and did move upward in society, made revolutions, had more or less influence, and on and on ad infinitum. While the variety was endless, two periods received special attention—the early modern period because of its role as the cradle of industrialization and the French Revolution as the shaper of modern Europe.

After 1945, the needs of social history helped transform simple population statistics into the full-fledged and sophisticated discipline of demography. Earlier, a few historians had done some work in estimating population figures, usually on the basis of tax records. Now, demographic inquiry became systematic and was taken up by many more scholars, among others those in the Institute National d'Études Demographiques (Paris), some *Annalistes,* and members of the Cambridge Group for Population and Social Structure. New methods were devised and new sources of data located for studies over long periods. The most detailed and revolutionary results came through the "reconstitution of family" technique used by Louis Henry, Michel Fleury, and E. A. Wrigley, where all information relating to families were recorded on "reconstitution" forms. With data from parish records, sometimes stretching over centuries, one could then compile exact rates of marriages, fertility, and mortality. The results were enlightening but the problems encountered were formidable. Records were seldom rich enough. Data-gathering took such an inordinate amount of time that the scope of research projects and with it data interpretation remained narrow. A multitude of such projects will have to be carried out until an accurate picture of the whole can emerge and the data in such publications as the *Histoire générale de la population mondiale* will need less constant revising than now.

The chores of quantitative history—data collecting, storing, and processing—have been made less formidable by the advent of special machines, especially the computer. The use of computers facilitated the work of quantitative historians, but cost and time considerations encouraged collective efforts, particularly in the field of data collecting and storing. That in turn enhanced the institutionalization of quantitative history. The *Annales* group had its Sixth Section of the École Pratique des Hautes Études. Americans chose voluntary association: in 1963 the American Historical Association established a Committee on Quantitative Data; a year later the Inter-University Consortium for Political Research (University of Michigan) was founded; and finally in 1967 the *Historical Methods Newsletter* appeared.

Today the computer has made a clear imprint on historiography. Its main advantage is its large memory and the quick retrieval of data from it, as well as its facility for doing complicated computations speedily and accurately. Still, the large-scale computer research projects take many years of work by research teams and consume vast financial resources in the preparation of the data base.

Examples are the study of the French censuses of conscripts from 1819 to 1930 (Le Roy Ladurie), D. Herlihy's analysis of the 1427 Florentine *Catasto* (an early income and property tax), and a number of American census studies.

*One approach among others.* By now quantitative history has joined the mainstream of historiography. Scholarly battles will always be fought over where the proper borders of quantification are to be drawn. Quantification, like all emerging scholarly enterprises, has had its enthusiasts who have claimed too much for it. For them *the* solution to all puzzles of history had been found. Those a bit less visionary simply expected that within two decades or so a significant segment of American historians would use quantification as their primary tool. Opponents have rejected the claims by quantifiers to undistorted objectivity and have pointed out how not even the quantitative historian escaped the need for personal choices. The latter entered into the initial hypotheses which researchers needed in order to structure their data-collecting and interpreting. These hypotheses were not results of research but a matter of choice. Many opponents have been most alarmed by what radical quantifiers assumed about the human realm. Where does the preoccupation with quantifiable general insights, trends, and forces leave the singularity of a situation or the specific and unique event? While acknowledging the scholarly spirit and the contributions of quantitative historians, Arthur Schlesinger, Jr., expressed the fundamental problem with quantification: "As a humanist, I am bound to reply to that that almost all important questions are important precisely because they are not susceptible to quantitative answers."[3]

When the smoke clears and the noise abates after scholarly battles outright winners and losers are usually rare. In the present uneasy truce the debate goes on and so does quantitative work. The value of quantification within clear limits has been conceded and most quantifiers are now satisfied with narrower claims. In this perspective quantification represents a further refinement of the already sophisticated historical methodology, serving, according to William O. Aydelotte, primarily as "a means of verifying general statements" in history. Quantification also has shown that it does best in analyzing areas of human life where human beings act in ways that are prompted by observable and clearly definable circumstances or by a few easily isolated motives, and do so in large numbers. Many historians, however, doubt that the area of purely habitual behavior or behavior resulting from simple internal or external stimuli is large. On their part quantitative historians could point out that modern society has enlarged precisely that area and that the increasing rationalization of government in modern times offers great masses of quantitative material. The objection that quantitative methods are of small use for earlier periods with little material to work with has some justification although it has been defused partially by innovators who have devised new quantitative accesses to the past such as exploration of neglected legal archives, extensive scouting, and a more sophisticated analysis of population data, lists of officeholders, and conscription lists.

## Reshaping Economic History

Interest in economic matters was kept high by the turbulent prosperity of the 1920s, the Great Depression of the 1930s, the rebuilding of the economic machinery of parts of Europe after 1945, the problems of economic development in the Third World, and the affluent 1960s and 1970s when the gross national product finally became the index of collective happiness. Why then did economic history play so small a role? Slowness to adjust on the part of historians was a less important factor than the contemporary conviction that economic well-being could best be assured by economics interpreted as technology. In the Soviet Union economic history had theoretically ended with the arrival of the ultimate mode of production and its corresponding Communist society. The new and permanent society needed only economic technology. In the West, neoclassicists, John Maynard Keynes and the Keynesians, the monetarists, and other theoreticians studied every economy as a self-contained system whose working was determined by universal and timelessly valid forces and patterns. Its analysis must proceed mathematically, be based on data with a short range in time, and be concerned essentially with remedying any disturbance in the equilibrium and with the desirable growth of the gross national product. The historical perspective held little attraction since, in the absence of trust in genetic explanations, the forces at work in any but the recent period of the past were considered irrelevant for the present-day situation. Also, due to the lack of sufficient data most past economic activities could not be studied exactly enough for the formulation of valid generalizations and laws. The historical perspective found its main refuge in the analysis of economic change, such as the study of business cycles, and in the quasi-biographical studies of entrepreneurs.

*Traditional approaches with new accents.* Made homeless in economics, economic historians went their own way, pursuing their interests and practicing their trade in a quiet corner of academic history. While theoretical economists were successful in persuading influential persons that their insights could help substantially in mastering the complexity of the industrial economy, economic historians for their part continued along the lines laid out by the pioneers of the late 1800s and early 1900s. But many of them withdrew more deeply into their studies and dropped their concern for social activism, reduced the scope of their analysis from general economic evolution to short- and medium-range changes, became less concerned with interrelationships between various institutions, and did fewer comparative studies.

After 1918 traditional studies of economic institutions in medieval history came from disciples of Karl von Inama-Sternegg's Austrian school, among them Alfons Dopsch. The latter tried to shed light on landholding patterns, manorialism, serfdom, and the village. In economic development, still perceived as a sequence of clearly defined stages, two transitional periods held a special fascination for Continental scholars. One was the transition from *Naturwirtschaft,* an agrarian economy with the barter system, to *Geldwirtschaft,* a commercial economy based on money, capital, and entrepreneurs. The other transition, the one from the ancient to the medieval period, was studied by the famous Belgian economic historian, Henri Pirenne, who made a good case for a continuity between the ancient and early medieval economies. Not the German migrations but the Saracen conquests broke that continuity, a fact which made Carolingian Europe the beginning of a new historical period.

In England and the United States, in works of traditional, scrupulous scholarship, the old guard of economic history (M. M. Postan, J. H. Clapham, J. U. Nef, T. C. Cochran, and F. C. Lane) dominated the scene until about 1960. In the United States pride in the role of American business in the building of the Republic led to the flourishing of business history. At the turn of the century Edwin F. Gay of Harvard University wrote and taught an institutional version of this history. From it came, after 1918, both Norman S. B. Gras's business history, emphasizing entrepreneurship and how it functioned in the American context, and Arthur H. Cole's entrepreneurial history, which embedded business even more securely in the wider framework of American life.

Institutional theories of economics continued in many ways the ideas and concerns of traditional English and German economic historians and of Veblen. But the institutionalists, who gave considerably more weight to historical approaches than to timeless, universal, and "pure market" models of the economy, neither turned their backs completely on the prevailing economic theory nor accepted Veblen's vision of a collapse of capitalism. From John R. Commons to John K. Galbraith, they were heavily involved in redefining capitalism, whether as "reasonable capitalism" or lately as "guided capitalism."

Some of the concerns and ideas of institutional economists penetrated into the New History and its continuation, Progressive History. None had a greater impact than Veblen's dichotomy that divided industry and common people from business. It thrived in the 1920s when economic history was drawn into the public discussion of America's role in World War I and the issue was reduced to the simplistic question of whether munition makers and Eastern bankers had tricked their country into getting involved in the war for their own selfish purposes. Charles and Mary Beard's popular *The Rise of American Civilization* argued in general for the prominence of economic forces in human life and gave the thesis of a conflict between American society (the people) and business a place of honor. Even the Civil War's importance lay not in the demise of slavery but in being an important phase in the Second American Revolution in which the capitalists, laborers, and farmers of the North and West defeated the planters of the agrarian South. The war's outcome gave the dominant role in the United States ultimately to business. The many subsequent studies of the Civil War in the economic vein by no means all adhered to that master scheme. Even historians of an economic bent produced more thorough and comparative analyses of Northern and Southern prosperity, distribution of wealth, and labor systems. Charles Beard himself emphasized in his later years that he always spoke of economic motives and influences, never of economic determinism. Yet prior to the 1930s he spoke so forcefully and with so few qualifications that his many partisans thought they had a mandate for a rigid economic interpretation, a view which the economic struggles of the Depression era reinforced. The series of studies in economic history in the Beardian spirit faded only in the late 1940s.

French economic history, like so much of French history, had as a prime focus the Revolution. In the years after 1871 the Third Republic's quasi-official interpretation of the French Revolution had emerged. It portrayed the Revolution as the decisive step in the coming to power of the Third Estate, the social group which constituted the main buttress of the Republic. According to Alphonse Aulard that process of emancipation conformed to the logic of history, despite such "unfortunate aberrations" as the Rule of Terror, Napoleon, and the repressive regimes between 1815 and 1830 and from 1848 to 1871. Not everybody agreed. Taine considered the whole Revolution misguided since it affirmed radical change patterned after abstract ideals. Instead, the French should have resolved their social issues through gradual changes in the English manner. But the most severe challenge to the consensus view of the French Revolution came from those who engaged in the economic interpretation of the past. For that interpretation it did not suffice that one spoke, like Taine, of the poverty of the peasants, unless one gave that fact sufficient weight. Marx and the Marxists finally shifted the accent decisively from politics to economics. In the early 1900s Jean Jaurès held that the French Revolution was the first necessary adjustment of social and political institutions to the new industrial mode of production. The rule by the aristocracy had become anachronistic and that by the bourgeoisie appropriate. The laboring class had failed to gain from that Revolution because class consciousness among workers had still been weak. Therefore the identity of the exploiting class had changed but not that of the exploited class. This simple orthodox Marxist scheme did not endure for long. Closer scrutiny showed significant differences within social groups, which weakened the class argument. George Lefebvre urged scholars to take into account the many levels of income and property instead of using a simple scheme that pitted the poor against the wealthy, that is, two large, uniform classes against each other. C.-Ernest Labrousse's careful attribution of dominant causal roles to the economic recession of 1778–89, troubled state finances, and high bread prices impressed many, although critics ascribed to them only a triggering role. The orthodox Marxist view of the French Revolution acquired new critics, when, under the influence of psychology, studies of mass behavior, like Lefebvre's *The Great Fear,* modified purely economic interpretations. In recent studies, the sansculottes were shown to have had more the character of a temporary alliance between diverse groups than that of a real class. A whole group of scholars, among them Alfred Cobban, continued to demonstrate in their works how complex a phenomenon and how distant from simple schemes the French Revolution actually was.

Explanations based on economic determinism have fared ill not only in studies of the French Revolution. Since 1945, the *Annales* scholars have produced sophisticated economic interpretations but have held fast to the ideal of a total history with no one dominant force. Their economic histories have been portraits of the economic life in certain periods, unattached to any grand scheme of development. Rather than look for fixed schemata the *Annales* scholars have widened the base on which economic history is built by seeking out new sources, such as administrative records and documents in private and legal archives. Their wish to mirror the actual and not the intended life—fulfilled well in Georges Duby's *Rural Economy and Country Life in the Medieval West* (1962)—made them go far beyond the traditional study of official rules, regulations, and charters. That led them away from the typology of German economic history as well as from the rigid Marxist schemes and toward detailed studies of past economic life. This attitude was shared particularly by scholars who have studied the economic history of early modern Europe with its price revolution, commercial development, and rise of capitalism.

*The cliometricians.* During the years following 1945, when the spirit of technology triumphed not only in industry but also in intellectual endeavors, economic history experienced attempts to bring it "in line with the age." Of this spirit was born the New Economic History, which in essence wished to make economic history a science in the natural science manner. No longer were economic historians to describe or explain particular phenomena; instead they must deal with categories of events involving aggregates and group behavior. All analysis must be quantitative and have as its model not the messy world of experience with its multitude of interrelated phenomena but a manageable, systematic world. The key tool of analysis were econometric models which tested and expressed economic phenomena in mathematical form. In order to do this successfully, scholars dealt with models containing relatively few variables.

The best-known examples of their methodological repertoire have been the so-called counterfactual hypotheses. Robert W. Fogel tested a widely accepted thesis when he asked whether the railroads were really the central feature in American development. He designed a model of the nineteenth-century United States without railroads and found that America's development would not have changed much since alternative methods of transportation would have taken over. Fogel's work has remained the standard example for the "counterfactual conditional concept" which establishes and measures what could have happened in order to understand what did happen. Nevertheless many historians have remained skeptical. If important features of the past did not matter all that much, where did that leave causal necessity? In the specific case, would every aspect of American life really have stayed the same without railroads? Could one ever "cut out" the railroads and their impact in so "clean" a manner from the American context?

Cliometricians also tackled a more controversial issue: slavery as an economic institution in the antebellum South. They asked whether it indeed was, as most historians have maintained, moribund, unprofitable, inefficient in labor use, a drag on the South, and a producer of a harsh life. First John R. Meyer and Alfred H. Conrad, and then Robert W. Fogel and Stanley L. Engerman in their *Time on the Cross* (1974), said no, although they personally found slavery abhorrent. Particularly the latter work led to extensive discussions of the theoretical foundations, and the possibilities as well as limitations, of cliometrics. Critics have not only questioned the reliability and selection of the data but, often overlooking the qualifying subtitle of Fogel and Engerman's book, *The Economics of American Negro Slavery,* also have asked to what degree statistical correlations, equations, and adherence to strictly theoretical concepts and a "pure" economic reality could ever encompass human reality, especially its moral aspect. Although the authors would state that the latter consideration was outside of the economic realm, the wider question remains unanswered of whether the New Economic History, with its narrow theoretical base, would ever be able to create a synthetic interpretation of even economic reality. The theoretical world in which market forces and totally rational human beings operate without friction is located at a long distance from the actual world in which societal rules and customs as well as complex human motivations interfere heavily in economic phenomena.

Reservations along that line have accounted for a reluctance by historians, including those of the French *Annales* group, to accept the cliometric model. The *Annales* ideal of a total history did not fit well with the ideals of a cliometric approach, and *Annales* scholars, especially Pierre Chaunu, preferred the model of "serial history" and the ascertaining of trends (*conjonctures*). This approach continues the French tradition begun by François Simiand in the 1920s and 1930s, one in which quantification of economic data is ancillary and not primary. Once many series have been constructed it may well be possible to construct a total model. Only a few French economic historians have joined the New Economic Historians.

*A return to stages of economic development.* In recent years a significant rapprochement between economic theory and history has occurred in the studies of economic development. After 1945 the Western economies had startled everyone by their robust growth. Marxists pondered the reasons for this growth, given the expected demise of capitalism, while others linked democracy causally with

Figure 26.1
Rostow's Typical Stages

| 1 | 2 | 3 | 4 | 5 | 6 |
|---|---|---|---|---|---|
| Traditional society and economy | Transitional society and economy | Take-off stage | Mature society | Stage of mass consumption | Beyond mass consumption |

the efficiency, productivity, and ability to grow of a free-enterprise economy. But an even more intense debate on economic development was spurred by the contrast between the industrialized nations on the one side and a large number of "stagnant" economies around the world. The question arose whether and how all economies of the world could or would reach the economic maturity of the West, the Soviet Union, and Japan. These discussions redirected attention to the problem of long-range economic development, a problem which by its very nature is historical. It has been assumed generally that the process of industrialization formed a universal pattern that would be repeated by every nation. In the 1960s the search for that pattern intensified and, since even a highly abstract universal model needed to be based or tested on a vast body of historical data, the historical dimension of the whole endeavor was undeniable. Indeed the concept of stages in economic development, embedded in nineteenth-century German economic history and in Marx, experienced a revival. One spoke of stages, transitional periods, and dynamic forces. With the Marxist model still prominent, Walter W. Rostow suggested an alternative with a capitalist perspective, a six-stage model (see fig. 26.1).

Critics have questioned various elements of Rostow's theory. Yet, in the process they, too, had to deal with the historical dimension of economic activities and have thereby done their share in invigorating economic history. The latter had already derived much strength from the rise to prominence of social history which—as will be seen—incorporated a keen interest in how people earned their living and how economic power relationships shaped society.

## Growing Dissent: Narrativism

*Positivism reinvigorated.* In the 1920s and 1930s, Comtean positivism regained new strength in philosophy as neo- or logical positivism. Then it was agreed that philosophy must drop all aspirations to gain substantial insights into objective reality, leaving that task to the sciences, and instead become the arbiter of which methods, concepts, language, and propositions were proper for scientific endeavors; this agreement paralleled a shift of emphasis in history from substantive to analytical concerns. In historical studies, the shift appeared as one from "speculative" philosophies of history that found historical truth and explanation by looking for and finding the ultimate causes or patterns governing events, to "analytical" or "critical" philosophies of history that scrutinized not the meaning of history but the ways of "doing history." In other terms, since these philosophers distrusted the authority of interpretative schemes (whether of progress, Divine Providence, cycles, or something else) they wished to anchor history in a method of truth-finding and a language which would guarantee the truth of historical accounts.

Initially, the cause of history looked endangered when early neopositivists recognized only statements based on direct observation as having the status of hypotheses, and those not accessible at all to proper verification were declared meaningless. Such demands were hardly reassuring for history's existence as a discipline. Yet in the end neopositivists were willing to concede the existence of the past and the feasibility of historical work, although in the 1930s A. J. Ayer wondered "whether we have sufficient ground for accepting any statement at all about the past, whether we are even justified in our belief that there has been a past."[4]

Karl Popper and Carl Hempel have been the most prominent advocates of the assimilationist view. Popper has argued that in a proper science the selection of what to study and the methods of study are both prescribed by the logic of that science. They therefore can be tested for congruence. In history, however, "outside" forces intruded into the selection of the subject matter; in other words, interpretations intruded in the very formulation of the account and all one could hope for was consistency with the original assumption. The very nature of historiography, a concern with particular events, made all of that unavoidable. Viewed that way history stayed a second-rank science. It could progress upward, to a truly "scientific" status, if the statements on particulars could be made to conform with general scientific findings and forms. Hempel went furthest in that direction when, in 1942, he put the issue of causal explanation into the center of the discussions on historical theory. If one assumed that human beings and nature were parts of a uniform reality, historical theory, too, would have to conform to the hypothetic-deductive model, better known as the Covering Law theory of history. Historians must go beyond describing individual events and link types of events causally to other types of events. Hempel asserted that

> historical explanation too, aims at showing that the event in question was not a "matter of chance," but was to be expected in view of certain antecedent or simultaneous conditions. The expectation referred to is not prophecy or divination, but rational scientific anticipation which rests on the assumption of general laws.[5]

Thus when historians wished to explain an event they had to do so by describing the initial conditions (singular statements) and by deducing from one or more universal laws the central statement on why things happened in a certain way.

These laws would be absolute. A given set of conditions always would produce the same effects. There would be, for example, one law governing population migrations, whether of Germans, Magyars, Normans, or Dust Bowl farmers.

Hempel came soon to recognize that not all explanations could be based on deductions from universal laws allowing no exceptions. Induction and probability were admitted into explanations. Hempel began speaking of "explanation sketches" as valid, temporary substitutes for explanations by deduction and covering laws. While neopositivist and analytical approaches to the theory of history faded away, positivism in a much less vigorous fashion would flourish in the increasingly dominant form of scientific historiography—the varieties of social or structural history. All of them built on the positivist assumption that historians were able to grasp objectively the life-shaping structures and forces and to explain their workings causally.

*The return of the narrative.* The opposition to the newly strengthened positivism came from a traditional but recently neglected strain of historiography: the narrative. In the late 1890s, historians deliberately stressed historiography's separation from literature when they limited the role of linguistic and rhetorical structures in historical accounts to being, at best, suppliers of aesthetic forms, irrelevant to the substance of a scientific history. Since the 1960s, in a reversal, narrativists challenged scientific historiography's ideals and practices as well as its identification with modernity. They denied causal explanation its dominant position and argued for an approach more reflective of the contingency of life. The autonomy of history was to be safeguarded by crediting the narrative not only with describing the past but also with offering a proper ordering scheme for the seemingly seamless flow of life. The endeavor proved more complex than expected. At issue were the exact links of the narrative to reality, especially whether or to what degree the narrative was a reflection of reality or a construction.

In the early stages of the ensuing debate some narrativists tried to establish the autonomy of history with a still strong emphasis on explanation. Croce's English sympathizer, Robin G. Collingwood, defined the subject matter of history in a manner which has as its premise the autonomous position of both historical theory and human life. Collingwood denied the positivist claim that historians could study the past from the "outside" with the methods of the natural sciences, because that approach could not grasp the very force shaping history: rational actions by individuals. Even the influences of the physical world were only factors in historical events when they were translated by human reflections into motives. "All history is the history of thought: and when an historian says that a man is in a certain situation this is the same as saying that he thinks he is in this situation. The hard facts of the situation, which it is so important for him to face, are the hard facts of the way in which he conceives the situation."[6] It therefore was the task of historians to account for past human actions by studying the thought processes which preceded them and to do so directly from the sources. In order to understand why Caesar or Napoleon acted in the ways they did, historians must reconstruct their definitions of a given situation, intentions, and decisions. No other way to the understanding of the past is available. General propositions or laws could never cover adequately the complexities of the human mind—that which others have called free will—and therefore could not explain the basically indeterminate individual events.

An autonomist position closer to the usual practice of most historians was put forth by Collingwood's contemporary, Michael Oakeshott. He agreed with Collingwood in seeing history's task as dealing with individual details and feared that the acceptance of the explanatory model of the natural sciences would mean that "History is dismissed."[7] Oakeshott called instead for the complete account of change on the basis of detailed sources. As item was fitted to item in a dense web, an accounting of change in order to explain change needed no recourse to generalizations. Neither moral judgments, practical lessons, nor the singling out of some causes as especially important were proper in that context. Among the many historians who have been in accord with Oakeshott simply by their way of "doing history" Herbert Butterfield and G. R. Elton have been those most interested in theoretical clarifications. Elton's work has sternly held to a Rankean discipline of the document that has yielded narrative history with occasional analytical passages. The unity of the narrative was preserved by political history with its sequence of datable events. All of that was at a safe distance from philosophical interpretations and generalizations, especially laws.

Others who straddled philosophy and narrativism dealt more extensively with the complexity of the narrative's relation to explanation. William Dray pointed to the purely theoretical character of the covering-law model, since no such tightly constructed laws have been forthcoming. In any case historians did not aim at laws but at accounting for particular events. They have searched for the sufficient and not the necessary conditions and have described them. Dray suggested a "continuing series" model, which accounted for an event by breaking it down into a true series of connected subevents. He also replaced Hempel's model of causation with one relying on the reconstruction of the rational calculations by individuals before they acted. Once one knew with reasonable certainty what agents thought, how they interpreted the situation, and what potential consequences they saw, explanation was achieved.

William Gallie put "history as a narrative" more directly into the center of the historical enterprise. Detractors have overlooked that only the imaginative intelligence at work in the narrative could produce a sense of the whole and thus could shed light on the past. Properly done, that is on the basis of adequate and critically examined evidence, the historical narrative is self-explanatory and does not need large-scale generalizations on laws. That view paralleled an earlier suggestion by William Walsh on the validity of a narrative built on sufficient research—the "significant narrative." "If the narrative has now been made consistent, plausible, and in accordance with all the evidence, if it is the best narrative that we can get, then the explanation that helped us to get to it is the best explanation as yet available."[8] Walsh, too, saw the narrative explanatory method as a genuine species, separate from the natural science model. It fit with his method of colligating, "the procedure of explaining an event by tracing its intrinsic relations to other events and locating it in its historical context."[9]

These and other narrativists did not doubt an accessible objective reality. In the vein of Dilthey, who based his philosophy of history on the basic pretheoretical experience of life (*Erlebnis*), Paul Ricoeur spoke of the inescapable temporality of life (pre-figured time), and David Carr pointed to the fundamental existential experience. For early narrativists the order of reality still supplied a basic order to the narrative. Yet since the 1970s, a tendency has gathered strength to minimize the shaping force of reality and to give dominance to the element of rhetorical construction. Indeed, life was treated as formless in itself because its order was inaccessible to human beings. The narrative came to be seen as pure construction, one that could not be authenticated as an accurate representation of past life. Much of narrativism would merge into the postmodernism of the late 1900s.

### Psychohistory: Promise and Problems

Psychohistorians were not the first to discover that the inner world of human beings helped shape events. Historians, beginning with the ancient writers, had all along been aware of the psyche's importance whenever they spoke of a human nature with perennial motives, sketched biographical or character portraits, or analyzed human behavior under tyrants. Nevertheless psychohistory is a thoroughly modern endeavor which owes its present status to the quest for a science of human behavior, to the strong individualism in contemporary Western culture, and to the inclination to view order as originating at least to a high degree in the mind of the observer rather than being a feature of the observed world. In such a view psychological forces assume overwhelming importance because they in a sense create the "outside" reality and its order.

*The concept of a collective psyche.* From 1750 to 1900, when scholars still asserted the reality of entities beyond the scope of individuals, the patterns of and developments in human affairs were often ascribed to the working of a collective psyche. Every change in that psyche affected every aspect of the life of a group or period; so it was with Vico's three stages of the collective psyche, Herder's primordial formation of human groups and their developments, and Comte's three stages of the collective human mind. Other historians spoke more vaguely of a national character and its role in the shaping of events. The early empirical psychologist Wilhelm Wundt still wished to create a science of the *Volksseele* (that is, the collective psyche), and in the last decade of the nineteenth century Karl Lamprecht tried to write German history as a reflection of the German *Volksseele*'s transformations. Lamprecht failed to convince other historians, but a mutant of the idea of a *Volksseele* intruded into French historiography as the concept of a period's mentality, especially as *mentalité* or *sensibilité* in Febvre's work. However, that *mentalité* was no longer a mysterious entity but simply a convenient way to describe the conceptual range within which a period's scholars stayed, to which most people conformed, and against which a few innovators usually revolted. Those who revolted successfully reshaped the collective mentality. The exploration of mentalities as the task of historians found sturdy defenders among the *Annales* group, eventually even among scholars of the psychoanalytical school who at first had found the concept of *mentalité* too rationalistic an interpretation.

*The dominance of the psychoanalytical approach.* From 1880 to 1914 challenges to the concept of a collective psyche were plentiful. Wilhelm Dilthey stipulated that historians did not deal with objective reality, including a collective psyche, but only with the perceptions individuals of one group and one period shared about reality. In such a world, constituted through interpretation, the past consisted of a sequence of world views (*Weltanschauungen*), that is, patterns of understanding shared by specific people at certain periods. The historian's task had come to be the comprehension of the various world views constructed by human consciousness with its mixture of reason, emotions, and will. In practice, Dilthey's history was intellectual history perceived as the internal drama of creative individuals. On their part, positivists of all kinds, too, rejected the collective psyche because it was unobservable. They liked John B. Watson's behaviorism better for basing explanation ahistorically on the exclusive observation of present and overt behavior.

By far the most influential revision of the psychological approach to history was suggested by Sigmund Freud, who in the 1880s set out to explore the causes of certain types of behavior, and ended up with large-scale explanations of the human experience. Roughly speaking, there were two phases to Freud's work. In the major part of his work Freud dealt mostly with individual psychology, particularly the processes in which the personality is formed. The older Freud became more and more interested in society, social institutions, and civilization.

Few American historians used the Freudian mode of explanation until after 1945, when the sturdy American faith in progress and rationalism had been jolted by the realities of totalitarian regimes. Shocked by the barbarism of those regimes, historians discovered that the code of objectivity did not allow them to condemn these regimes, and that modern definitions of human beings did not permit the use of the term *evil*. In this situation a number of historians found useful the psychoanalytical recasting of "evil" as "abnormal" or "psychotic." The value judgment contained in these terms were less visible and in, any case, more in tune with the modern temper. Psychohistory's rise was furthered when many famous European Freudians settled in America as exiles. In 1957, William Langer appealed to historians to plumb the depths of the human psyche in the interest of fuller historical explanations.

> There is, however, still ample scope for penetration in depth, and I personally have no doubt that the "newest history" will be more intensive and less extensive. I refer more specifically to the urgently needed deepening of our historical understanding through exploitation of the concepts and findings of modern psychology.[10]

American psychohistorians, by far the largest such group, have relied heavily on Freudian individual psychology. Central to this view was the individual as the main agent, who, however, no longer was the celebrated rational being but the scarred battlefield of contesting internal forces. The fundamental force in the universe was the libido, a rushing, unorganized, and irresistible energy that was manifested in every individual as the sexual drive. This aspect of the human personality (called the id) knew in and by itself no limits or constraints, only the drive toward gratification which to Freud meant freedom. Limitations of the biological id were imposed from the "outside" by cultural, that is, nonbiological forces in order to assure the existence of groups. These agencies, particularly the family, shaped the socialized aspect of human beings (the *super ego*). Each human being experienced a fundamental conflict between the drive for unlimited sexual gratification and the collective restraints. Its outcome was foreordained, because the unrestrained id had to be tamed in the interest of the group and of civilization. That unavoidable struggle produced the unique self (the ego) with its two layers: the visible one, seemingly adjusted to collective expectations, and the hidden one, the subconscious, filled with repressed sexual impulses or sublimated ones (impulses turned towards acceptable aims). Constant conflict was inevitable and so was damage to the individual psyche, which manifested itself in "irrational" and "abnormal" behavior. The conflict which occurred during early childhood in the family was the crucial one, with its enforcement of sexual restraint and its oedipal conflict, that is, the son's love of his mother and his jealousy of his father, and the daughter's love of her father and jealousy of her mother.

American psychohistorians have so far held fast to this view of the formation of personality and have used it to explain all collective phenomena. That has given all collective phenomena the purely negative connotation of being inhibitors of drive gratification and the root of infantile emotional disturbances which grow into an adult's problems. The view precluded relationships between individuals and their world other than those of conflict or reluctant accommodation. That all left psychohistorians little choice but to write psychobiographies and to accept a new version of the Great Men theory—the great individuals were to be shown as they "really" were. In 1910 Freud wrote on Leonardo da Vinci, and later William C. Bullitt, with some cooperation from Sigmund Freud, conducted a posthumous analysis of Woodrow Wilson, thereby creating the prototypes for psychoanalytical history. Then the authors assumed that Wilson's flawed psyche shaped all of his actions, including those guiding American politics between 1912 and 1920.

Such an approach maintained a radical reductionism, viewing even the fate of nations and of civilization in terms of the psychoanalytic patterns of personality development. In its simplest form the approach contended that leaders of groups made their collectives prosper if they themselves had a smooth personality formation or caused the group to suffer by their unreconciled maladjustments. Freud had set an example for this approach in his *Moses and Monotheism,* where he had traced the relationship between Moses and the fate of the Jews. Psychobiographies of Hitler have tried to account for the horrors of German totalitarianism. Once more, childhood experiences have figured as the direct causes of later successes and ultimate failure.

*The search for a larger scope.* Freud's individual psychology has dominated psychohistory, although his later theories on the collective life have all along offered insights more directly relevant to history. Already in 1907 he had dealt with the basic conflict between the pleasure-carrying instinct and renunciation-demanding civilization. Was the price of Western civilization's solution too high? The constant production of neuroses by civilization's repressive demands and acts made Freud skeptical of history as a source of hope; still that "is what they are all demanding—the wildest revolutionaries no less passionately than the most virtuous believers."[11] It struck Freud that, looking at human cultural development, "one is bound to come to the conclusion that the whole effort is not worth the trouble, and that the outcome of it can only be a state of affairs which the individual will be unable to tolerate."[12]

Freud's pessimism increased when he eventually admitted the presence of a powerful force of nonsexual origin: the death instinct (*Thanatos*), manifested by aggression. It was the great destroyer of civilizations as the counterforce to eros, which permeated society as the binding force. History carried the marks of the great dichotomy:

> But man's natural aggressive instinct, the hostility of each against all and all against each, opposes this programme of civilization. This aggressive instinct is the derivative and the main representative of the death instinct which we have found alongside of Eros and which shares world-dominion with it. And now, I think, the meaning of the evolution of civilization is no longer obscured to us. It must present the struggle between Eros and Death, between the instinct of life and the instinct of destruction, as it works itself out in the human species. This struggle is what all life essentially consists of, and the struggle for life of the human species.[13]

Yet even in their later attempts to transcend Freud's id/ego/super ego psychology, American psychohistorians, with such exceptions as Norman O. Brown, have not had recourse to the thought of the older Freud. Its strong pessimism may well have been a potent deterrent. Rather, they have extended the range of some of Freud's concepts in individual psychology in order to give a more positive role to the social and cultural context. In Erik Erikson's *Young Man Luther* (1959) Luther's search for identity was an infinitely more complex process than the id-super ego collision with its mechanisms of repression and the Oedipus complex. And the outcome of Luther's search for his identity was not only a "new Luther" but also the Reformation, which brought about a new psychic climate in Western religion wherein "inward" religiosity prevailed over "outward."

*The status of psychohistory as a discipline.* In the late 1960s psychohistory, somewhat freed from the narrow limits of orthodox Freudian theory, gained adherents and recognition. It acquired academic courses, journals—*The Journal of Psychohistory,* for example—and vaguely defined schools of thought, but it still remains in a precarious state due to its slim and troublesome theoretical base. Historians have remained cool toward a psychoanalytically oriented psychohistory because the link between evidence and interpretation in psychohistory was too often unconvincing. Psychohistorians have insisted that what a source says must be searched for its "real meaning," which lies in the world hidden behind observable reality, in short, the subconscious world. Historians have complained that such a procedure threatened to submerge the clarity and precision of historical research in the quagmire of the subconscious. There has also been a reluctance to yield to the exclusive assertion of one explanatory model, particularly one that involved the obliteration of the rational human being by a psychosexual determinism.

Many psychohistorians wished for psychohistory to become a scientific endeavor and labored to strip Freudianism of its metapsychological, even metaphysical, basis. The id became an aspect of individual personality only and no longer was a manifestation of sexuality in Freud's quasi-cosmic terms. They also toned down Freud's pessimism in accordance with contemporary hopes for a "better world." As a result such concepts as "complex," "repression," or "compensation" no longer constituted parts of an all-encompassing world view—a Freudian cosmology—but became technical terms of limited scope. Thus, when American historians used such psychohistorical terms as a "paranoid style" of politics, "status revolutions," or "social-psychological" tensions, but failed to give these terms a systematic framework, they did not contribute much of substance. On his part, Peter Gay has tried to narrow the gap separating psychohistory from mainstream history by blunting excessive psychoanalytical interpretations and making them more fruitful for dealing with collective phenomena. But, clearly, psychology has not yet fulfilled Sir Lewis Namier's hope that it would become to history what mathematics has been to the sciences.

# ·27·

# Transformations in English
# and French Historiography

## Voices in the War Guilt Debate

English historians unhesitatingly identified Germany as the instigator of the Second World War. But questions were raised on the role of the Treaty of Versailles—its burden on Germany, the many compromises with the French hard line, and the constitution of the League of Nations as a club of victors. Another important topic turned out to be Neville Chamberlain's appeasement policies and their role in England's lack of preparedness.

In French historiography the shock of military defeat in 1940 triggered inquiries into the history of the Fifth Republic, particularly its weaknesses. There, too, the war guilt issue evoked little debate. Questions were raised about some missed opportunities for peace (Raymond Aron), but far more attention was given to the weak democratic institutions in the interwar years and the lacking will to pursue the war after it had started. A few years before his execution for being a member of the resistance movement, the well-known historian Marc Bloch had agreed with such criticism. Even more controversial proved to be historical studies of the Vichy government (1940–45). At issue were its legitimacy, actions, and the degree of collaboration of French citizens with it. A committee on the war and liberation spoke the official word on that chapter of French history.

## History Writing in Post-imperial England

Developments were quite intricate in England, where a social revolution and England's altered standing in the world provided new contexts. After four centuries of empire construction and preservation, England became once more a state at the periphery of Europe, although the connection with the wider world remained strong. Remarkable world historians served as one confirmation. Another was the fact that the history of the Empire continued to supply fascinating personages and events for genres of historiography, such as memoirs and biographies. The image of a gradual and steady development of an increasingly democratic England also continued. The Cold War helped political history retain its strong position. All of that buttressed traditional historiography. Its features were still intact: intellectual excitement, eloquence, and an empiricism which saw the world as open, filled with unique phenomena, and accessible to conscientious research. In that vein George Kitson Clark and Geoffrey Elton have labored with Rankean caution in building historical works scrupulously on evidence, rejecting *engagé* history; Hugh Trevor-Roper has demonstrated the wide range and power of the historical imagination; and A. J. P. Taylor has shown how traditional research can yield innovative, in not idiosyncratic, interpretations.

The turn to the welfare state in 1945 could be persuasively linked to changes in historiography. The new universities brought about a change in the composition of the student body and faculty. The latter, feeling less obligated to tradition, would prove to be venturesome in the thinking and writing of history. D. H. Carr's *What is History?* (1961) could be considered as a symbol for change, the most important of which was the turn to a new social history. Its faces would be many. While influenced by both the *Annales* group and Marxism, English social history retained much of the tradition of a proven empiricism. That social history focused on the lives of the elite as well as everyday life, with its habits, joys, and sufferings of the anonymous masses (Asa Briggs, Harold J. Perkin, J. H. Plumb, and Lawrence Stone). *Annales* influences, particularly through the journal *Past and Present*, were favored by the shared empirical emphasis. An excellent example came in demography, particularly Peter Laslett and the Cambridge Group for the History of Population and Social Structure. Another source of influence were the works by a well-known group of British Marxists (E. P. Thompson, Eric Hobsbawm, and others). American social history was the source of inspiration for some quantitative historians, especially those interested in the analysis of election results (Frank O'Gorman, John A. Philipps). Yet even at the high tide of social history, English historiography never neglected the traditional topics, dealt in customary ways: the Norman invasion, parliamentary development, the Civil War and the Stuarts, the Glorious Revolution of 1688, industrialization, and reform.

### Traditional and New French Historical Perspectives

*History in the French republican tradition.* France's victory in 1945 was overshadowed by memories of the military defeat in 1940. French historiography participated in the soul-searching with critical inquiries into the shortcomings of the Third Republic, the disastrous military campaign in 1940, and the Vichy period. The history of coping with such memories did eventually lose out to one full of vigor and innovative ideas (the *Annales* group). But mainstream history retained remarkable strength and continuity, particularly so in the historiography of the defining event of the French Republic: the French Revolution.

That traditional area of history, with its intimate links to the public sphere, flourished but remained within remarkably steady confines. The liberal-democratic perspective, firmly set in its outlines by Aulard, continued to dominate as its influence was reinforced by many publications, particularly influential textbooks. But in the years of dominance by the French Left (1945 to 1980s) the Jacobin period was reevaluated. Far from being a purely contingent event—an unfortunate result of external threats—that period was seen as part of the logic of history. The emancipation of the bourgeoisie was to be succeeded by that of the proletariat, although that sequence was temporarily foiled in 1794. For Albert Soboul (with a sympathetic glimpse at the Soviet Union) even the terror was in accord with that logic. George Lefebvre exerted much influence as the head of the Institut d'Histoire de la Révolution française and by his continuing attempts to widen the scope of historical inquiry.

Important non-French historians were instrumental in revising that image of the French Revolution. Robert Palmer and his coauthor, Jacques Godechot, integrated that revolution into a wider Atlantic one (American and French) in which the bourgeoisie confronted the privileges of the nobility and monarchy. More importantly, scholars, such as Alfred Cobban, insisted on detailed studies in archives, unencumbered by grand perspectives. The revolution that emerged from these studies was one marked by great local and regional differences, a more prevalent contingency, and a surprising degree of continuity.

Quite influential proved a "revisionist" venture by two *Annalistes*, Francois Furet and Denis Richter. They labeled the prevailing image of the Revolution as an apologia for an endeavor that had mostly failed to realize its program of individual freedom and equality. The liberal revolution did not provide a legal status for an opposition, and thus the Jacobin one proved chaotic and harmful. No guiding scheme inhered in the events of 1789 and thereafter; instead, much chaos prevailed, but so did once more a surprising degree of continuity through the prerevolutionary years. Much emphasis was placed on studying symbols and language, in preference to dealing with the "real" (concrete) forces and structures as previous theories had done.

As a result of the work of the various critics, empiricists, and revisionists, the celebrations of the French Revolution's bicentennial occurred when, at least in academic history, the grand vision of a historical cataclysmic event with universal implications had dissolved into a multitude of developments with lesser scope.

*The* Annales *Group triumphant.* In the victorious, post-1945 France, much traditional historiography was still written in the historicist manner and the French republican tradition. With fine scholars, such as Roland Mousnier at the Sorbonne, and control of the *Revue historique,* traditional historiography's influence was still considerable. But the bitter memory of defeat also created a resentment of the "old" France and an openness for innovation that benefited the *Annales* school. Febvre became the marshal of the *Annaliste* forces. With a keen sense for organizational politics he built the institutional foundation for the *Annales* dominance: the Sixth Section of the Ecole Pratique des Hautes Etudes. The journal, now named *Annales: Economies, Sociétés, Civilisations,* resumed publication. The historiographical revolution transformed the *Annales* school from an outside group into the French historical establishment. Although much teamwork occurred in the new research institutes on projects with a vast scope, the outstanding achievements of the school were the work of innovative individuals.

While the key message of the *Annales* school spelled out no grand scheme, it still was influenced by a strong contemporary French philosophical and literary movement: structuralism. Its operative form in the 1960s went back to the linguistics of Ferdinand de Saussure which viewed language as a system manifested in the minds of individuals. Its study required no journeys into the past—diachronic studies—but only the analysis of existing language systems, that is, synchronic studies. The meaning of any part of the language and the changes it undergoes could be understood by finding the part's position in the arrangement of all the parts of the language. That whole was in no way a living or mysterious entity referring to a transcendent meaning but a chosen arrangement; one permutation of the parts out of many possible arrangements. It represented the code that governed the thought and actions of the group. Nobody knew why that code was chosen out of many. Kant still thought that his categories for the understanding of phenomena formed a code valid for all human beings. But then he lived in the world of Newton's physics with its certainties that have long been abandoned. Yet it still was true that the code preceded its manifestations; people did not choose their codes freely. Or as the French structuralists, influenced by semiology and its interpretation of life as communication, also have stated it: the code preceded the message.

Lévi-Strauss transferred the structuralist theorems into the discipline that in recent years has acquired a special relationship with history: anthropology. For him the social life of a group was shaped by exchanges governed by the special code of the group; it in turn was linked to the universal code for all human life, which was anchored in a common human nature (see fig. 27.1).

In this scheme human beings disappeared as acting, deciding, and decisive individuals. All research was now directed toward finding the invisible, impersonal, and timeless structures—the keys to human behavior. The structure of the human world as well as the aim of research had become ahistorical. The search for the invisible structures could be best conducted by analyzing their present specific manifestations without recourse to the mostly incomplete records of the past. There was no harm in rejecting the past since structuralists rejected genetic explanations, that is, they denied that the past manifestations of the structures have shaped those of the present. All changes occurred according to the system's

Figure 27.1
The Structuralist View of Culture

| 1 | 2 | 3 |
|---|---|---|
| The univeral code: timeless, stable, independent of human will and consciousness, visible in the invariant elements of all specific codes. | Specific codes of groups: variants of the universal code governing human behavior.<br><br>actual hierarchy of codes | The codes become visible in specific relationships of actual participants; they are time-bound and changing. |

→

research direction

←

| find universl code | find specific codes | study the visible manifestations |
|---|---|---|

own transformational rules. Hence the human condition must no longer be studied diachronically, that is, by acknowledging the importance of succession in time. Historical studies would be replaced by synchronic analysis in the present.

It can be said that the *Annales* historians did find in their affirmation of varying rhythms of change a more fruitful solution to the perennial problem of reconciling change and continuity than the structuralists had achieved with their intrinsically static solution where change remained a negligible surface phenomenon, perhaps a bit of an annoyance.

The lack of a grand scheme or agreement on one definition of the nature of the historical world granted *Annales* scholars much latitude in choosing methods and interpretations. They absorbed historiographical innovations rather than yielding to them. One common thrust, however, pervaded all of *Annales* history: the search for a life-encompassing history that recognized large-scale but rationally explicable structures. Its scholars proceeded under the aegis of causality, comparison, and quantification.

It has been argued that, in the broadest sense, the *Annales* scholars have desired to create a *humanisme historique,* a humanism which acknowledged the impact of large-scale forces on human life while respecting the role of the individual. Yet, in its eagerness to reject traditional historiography, *Annaliste* historiography has in practice tended to neglect the individual. Its type of social and economic history, with its strong collectivist and environmental emphasis, has consistently put the concept of order above that of a deciding and acting individual.

Fernand Braudel would come closest to an overall explanatory scheme for total history. In 1956, he had inherited Febvre's leading institutional positions and added to them that in the new Maison des Sciences de l'Homme. As a scholar he established his preeminent status with *The Mediterranean World in the Age of Philip II* (1949; 2d ed., 1966), in which he intended to show all of the region's life in a given period. For that purpose Braudel did make a major and innovative effort to discover and use integrative structures. His appreciation for such structures was stimulated by the human geography of Vidal de la Blache and the early structuralism (1940s) of Gaston Roupnel. Braudel's structures derived from the central fact that everything in the world changed but did so according to three different rhythms. Land, sea, climate, and vegetation change so slowly that they appear to us as immobile—the quality of the *longue durée* (the long duration). *Annaliste* scholars have become particularly fascinated by these quasi-stable elements, perhaps because many of them have studied the early modern period with its "long slow, immobile, hard, dense, geological rhythm of traditional society."[1] And a more rapid rhythm of change characterizes the phenomena with a cyclical aspect (*lentement rythmés*). Some cycles run their course within a human lifetime, many transcend it. *Annaliste* historians have most frequently studied the cycles governing the economic and demographic aspects of life. They have come more and more to refer to those kinds of changes as *conjonctures,* connoting cyclical patterns or trends in prices, landholdings, population movements, and the like. Finally there is life's episodic aspect, typical of political history with its individual actions and rapid change, which had been stressed by *histoire événementielle* at the cost of a "deeper" understanding. Whatever names *Annales* historians have given to these three types of changes—Jacques le Goff, for example, calls them immobile, more mobile, and highly mobile structures—historians have found the concept of interlocking rhythms to be a valuable conceptual framework. The nuanced understanding of the temporal structure of life proved a potent answer to any ahistorical structuralism.

Braudel's love for geography inspired but did not dominate a number of works that also answered the call for a total history with a regional scope. In them the geographical accent was joined by one on demographic analysis. Demography was bound to be prominent in the *Annales* school because it too presented *conjonctures.* A new concern among the general populace over the increase in the world population also helped. Jean Meuvret's pioneering work was noticed and demography developed into a sophisticated discipline. Louis Henry's family reconstitutions and a series on "Demography and Societies" sponsored by the Sixth Section testified to it. Among regional histories of the new type, Pierre Goubert's *Beauvais et le Beauvaisis* (1958) stood out.

Braudel's second major work, *Civilisation materielle et capitalisme* (1967), was only loosely structured according to the rhythms of change. It presented a mass of interesting and useful data, but had little dynamic or systematic structure. One could argue that it was one of the stimuli for the emergence of microhistory or the history of the structure of everyday life (the title of the English translation of Braudel's work).

Attention to economic structures was facilitated by important work done on the economic interpretation of history in the 1930s by François Simiand and

Ernest Labrousse. Both were concerned with long-range developments. Simiand found in them a rhythmic change from an expansive A phase to a contractive B phase. Labrousse linked price developments and social upheavals in France. In his investigations of the economic developments preceding the French Revolution he used the analytical tool of the multiplier effect (newly found by John Maynard Keynes) on the French economy. A strong quantitative emphasis marked the early works of *Annaliste* scholars, among them those of Emmanuel Le Roy Ladurie. For Braudel the economic development patterns were the important *conjonctures.* In many ways the massive study by Pierre and Huguette Chaunu on *Seville and the Atlantic* (1955–60) represented the synthesis of many of these approaches (serial history).

Of considerable import has been the reaffirmation of the role of consciousness through the affirmation of psychological structures. With large-scale structures preferred, the psychology of individuals was judged insufficient for explaining social phenomena. Febvre, who had been impressed by Levy-Bruhl's study of the "primitive mentality," explored the psychological phenomena in their collective manifestations. The key concept *"mentalité"* referred to mental structures that defined an array of thoughts and concepts available to a group at a certain time, delimiting the possibilities of what could be thought and understood in a culture at a certain time. After 1950, a whole series of studies appeared that was based on variations of the concept of *mentalité:* Gabriel Le Bras's studies of the religious mind; Jacques Le Goff's analyses of the concepts of time and purgatory in the context of the medieval church; Robert Mandrou's work on the *Bibliothèque Bleue* (a popular series of chapbooks); and Philippe Aries, a scholar with an affinity for but not belonging to the *Annales* group, with works on the perceptions of childhood and death. Related to these works were the quantitative studies of books; of literacy, as well as of the literary tradition (François Furet, Adeline Daumard, and Jacques Ozouf); and of the cultural imagination (Roger Chartier).

A major shortcoming in *Annaliste* historiography, one contradicting its ideal of a total history, was the much too radical diminution of the role of all things political. This neglect of studies of power and power relationships stemmed from resentment of the former dominance of political history and from distrust of politics with its unavoidably strong accent on human volition. Marxist historians have been the sharpest critics of such an illusory world, one lacking the phenomenon of power and a clear goal for its development. Although never completely absent from *Annaliste* writing, the political aspect has found increased attention in works by the medievalist Philippe Wolff, who attempted to integrate politics into the functional network of society, and Bernard Guenée, who ventured forth with a history of the state. Loosely associated with that criticism was one aimed at the nearly exclusive concentration of studies in the early modern period.

One must concede that, after 1970, the use of the phrase *"Annales* school" is at best a didactic device, because the creative imagination of its scholars has in fact dissolved any semblance of cohesion. The grand synthesis, made so difficult in a total history, did not come about, and was exchanged for a vast panorama of past human life. One scholar typified that development of the *Annales* school: Emmanuel Le Roy Ladurie. Brilliant and productive, he pursued total history singlehandedly in books on the peasants of Languedoc (with a geographic, economic, and demographic accent), the history of climate (a comparative historical geography), a history of the Carneval in Romans (an exploration of the symbolic meaning and actual importance of customs with a limited use of the *mentalité* concept and a return of the narrative), and the story of Montaillou (a microhistory of a heretical village).

While French historiography has assumed a definite social science cast, it has in its great works refused to yield to a view of the human being as imprisoned by external conditions. True, the proper balance between the individual on one side and collective as well as natural forces on the other continues to be precarious and the danger of encasing the individual in structures of overwhelming power is still there. Yet there are indications in the changing form of important *Annaliste* works—a definite turn to a quasi-narrative presentation—that individuals are being elevated just a bit from their lowly status; at the least that history as a craft still survives in France. It is characteristic that only some gifted individuals and not the cooperatives of busy scholars have produced works that have excited the imagination and told much that had been unknown about the past.

The diversity of the *Annales* school was mirrored in the multivarious influence it had on historiographies in other countries. Few national historiographies did not show *Annaliste* marks.

# ·28·

# Marxist Historiography in the Soviet Union and Western Democracies

### The Problems and the End of the Soviet Union's Marxism

After 1945, historiography in the Soviet Union continued on its well-established, officially regulated path. Then, in March 1953, Stalin died and the Soviet Union entered two decades in which, broadly speaking, a period of slightly loosened controls was followed by a time of even tighter ones. But by the late 1980s, the whole system of state control began to unravel, ushering in a chaotic transition phase.

*The struggle for a flexible Marxism.* Soon after Stalin's death, some historians set out to regain a degree of autonomy for the study of history (Anna M. Pankratova and Eduard N. Burdzalov). They succeeded to an unexpected degree in freeing some areas of studies from the tight ideological control of the state. In the sixties, discussions of theoretical and methodological issues took on a long-absent scope, vigor, and critical rigor at the cost of party "guidance." In broad terms the debate concerned two problematic areas. The first focused on the scheme of historical periods fundamental to the understanding of history in the Marxism sponsored by the Soviet Union. Its centerpiece was the rigid master scheme: feudalism, capitalism, and communism. The lengthy debates on the time limits of each of the stages had eventually been ended by decree. The new discussions could not avoid the issues of determinism, contingency, and—as it was called euphemistically—alternatives. A special risk and obstacle to a thorough debate was represented by the "personality cult" that gave one individual, Stalin, the key historical role. Traditionalists (Alexandr I. Danilov) fought against the reformers who emphasized flexibility rather than rigidity. Another group of reformers took up the issues of methods used in history writing. Its members found their forum for debate in the section on methodology headed by Mikhail Gefter. They discussed such ideologically touchy topics as facts, laws, and objectivity, all with implications for the highly deterministic official version of Marxism and its base, historical materialism. Some of these historians also were active in the New Direction movement centered in the ideologically most tightly controlled field, the history of the Soviet Union. The latter's centerpiece was the history of the October Revolution, including the events leading up to it and the internal developments afterwards. This was a highly sensitive topic, since the official version of that history formed the very foundation of the Communist Party's legitimacy. That included such issues as what stage in capitalism's development prevailed at the time of the October Revolution, and where the Soviet Union stood in the master pattern of development from feudalism, to socialism, to communism. The space for discussion remained rigorously restricted in the case of these and other hot-button issues.

The years between 1954 and 1972 did see an uneasy coexistence of history as a tool of the Party's rule, and history with a modicum of autonomy from central guidance. However, in the new era of intolerance following the Soviet Union's repression of the Czech experiment with democratic socialism (1968), the limits of tolerance were drawn much more tightly. The primary institutions of historical studies (Moscow State University, the sections of the Academy of Sciences on General and on Soviet History) saw personnel changes. The methodology section was dissolved. Soviet historiography became dormant, and remained so until the Glasnost and Perestroika period (1986–1990) initiated by Mikhail Gorbachev. With greater freedom, the search for an unexpurgated account of the Communist years became intense. Writings that previously had to be secretly published and circulated (*Samizdat*) were now openly available. The truth about the Communist regime and Stalin's brutality were revealed. The Soviet Union's orthodox Marxism began to fade rapidly.

*The search for a new Russian history.* After the end of the Communist regime, historians, together with all Russians, faced the key problem how to account for the continuity of Russian history in the aftermath of a regime dominant for seven decades but now rejected. Put in simple terms, the Communist period was set aside. The legitimacy of the new Russian state and its identity were linked to the Russian Empire. Many works explored the pre-1917 past and found much to praise. Individuals that had fought for liberal reforms prior to 1917 (Sergei Y. Witte and Peter A. Stolypin); an aristocracy now viewed as guardians of a sense of duty, ethics, and culture; and the imperial family as source of legitimacy and (with Nicholas II) as victims—all of these became elements of a new Russian history. As the routine of the new society settled in, a historiography emerged that was open to Western models. Yet a substantial part of the new history writing was firmly anchored in a long-standing tradition: a tendency now often referred to as Russianism. The rather awkward term refers to an emphasis on the absolute uniqueness of the Russian people, Russian spirit (which puts the collective over the individual), Russian culture, and Russian history. That stipulation has been especially central to the so-called culturology. Set apart from the social and cultural sciences, culturology viewed Russia as a unique entity in a world of other unique entities—a radical negation of the Hegelian-Marxist world history as unified process with rigidly defined stages and a deep bow to historicism.

## Marxist Historical Theory in the West

*The dilemma of Marxist historical theory.* After World War II the Soviet Union's brand of Leninist Marxism became the official ideology of the "people's democracies" in Eastern Europe, and there, too, its interpretation was no longer a question of scholarly debate. The situation was vastly more complex in the non-Communist West where only the Communist parties adhered to Marxist-Leninism and where socialists and social democrats were more impressed by the adaptability of capitalist societies and appreciated democratic political forms. They usually interpreted the Marxist theory of historical development in Bernstein's terms of continual reform and in line with actual political experience. After 1945, Marxists in capitalist societies found the growing gross national product and the comforts it bestowed on the masses a formidable obstacle to attempts at radical social change and a contradiction to Marx's prediction of accelerating mass poverty in late capitalism.

Actually, two powerful forces had challenged the foundations of Marxist theory already before 1945. The strong individualism that shaped Western life and thought and the empiricist current with its strict interpretation of what counted as evidence were inimical to the Marxist emphasis on collectives, uni-causality, and a grand historical scheme, as well as to the Marxist claim to absolute truth. Finally, if, as Marxists always maintained, all historical development was necessary and not accidental, the autocratic and totalitarian regime in the Soviet Union raised doubts about Marx's prediction of a beneficent final stage.

The intent to give Marxism a looser form in order to fit it to the temper of Western thought and enable it to absorb insights from other schools of thought inspired a group of German scholars. They were associated with the *Institut für Sozialforschung,* founded in 1923 in Frankfurt am Main. Friedrich Pollock, Max Horkheimer, and Felix Weil were among those who wished to reestablish Marxism as an active force at a distance from "vulgar Marxism," as they called orthodox Marxism.

Holding firmly to individualism and democratic ideals, to the gradual integration of the proletariat into the main stream, and to the intellectual climate of spontaneity, they rejected Marx's rigid historical theory. The Frankfurt scholars wished to reconquer openness and dynamism for Marxism by emphasizing its dialectical and critical components. Thought was neither the shaper of grand theories to behold forever (the fallacy of pure theory practiced by conventional philosophy) nor the result of shaping external forces or conditions (economic ones in Marx and *völkisch* ones in fascism). True thought resulted from the dialectical interaction between theory and praxis. Or as a more recent Critical school scholar, Jürgen Habermas, has put it: Marx's theory is to be understood as the catalytic agent for the very societal life-context that it analyzes; and it analyzes that context as an integral whole with a view to its possible *Aufhebung* (that is, its overcoming). In short, Marxist thought must always be informed by life as it exists at a given time, in order to be able to shape that life by its insights. That view forced these scholars to abandon two crucial orthodox Marxist tenets: the assertion that all noneconomic features of life were determined by the prevailing economic structure; and a rigid, preset scheme of historical development.

In the 1930s, shocked by Stalin's rule, the Frankfurt scholars became less interested in restoring Hegel's dialectic to Marxism and began to draw heavily on Freudian psychology for an enrichment of Marxist thought. The subsequent Anglo-Saxon exile of most of the Frankfurt scholars (by then referred to as the Critical school) brought a critical analysis of Western culture, the *Dialectic of Enlightenment* (English, 1972). Adorno and Horkheimer decried contemporary Western culture as the Enlightenment gone wrong. Mass society—communist and capitalist alike—mistook conformity for equality, hindered the creative life, deprived human beings of true sensibility, and turned reason into a mere instrument of calculation. Indeed, Horkheimer and Adorno came to equate the development of the sciences and scientific modes of thought with a steadily increasing and excessive domination of nature. Eventually that drive to dominate also affected the social sphere and led to an ever harsher dominance of one group over others. Viewed in this perspective modern totalitarianism was not an aberration but the logical result of the West's development. Hence, the prospects for the future were dim.

The historical approach has been essential to the Critical school because its adherents analyzed each problem dialectically, a procedure which by necessity involved past developments, present conditions, and future resolutions. Jürgen Habermas has pointed out the problems connected with realizing the ideal of a unity of thought and praxis. But he also stressed the need for redefining the relationship between thought and the world of action, since the assertion by orthodox Marxists that the truth is a closed system, including a rigid scheme of historical development, can too easily be converted into the justification of totalitarian systems.

Many reform-minded Marxists in the non-communist West looked back to the "young," more empirically inclined Marx, who spoke much of the worker's alienation from his own potential, his society, and the products of his work. That facilitated the adaptation of Marxism to the modern concern with alienation. But since in the West alienation has been understood either psychologically or existentially, in any case as an individual problem, the "adapted" Marxism has deemphasized the role of a necessary historical development that had led to Stalin's totalitarianism. On their part orthodox Marxists had long been suspicious of the young Marx and therefore had always labeled his works as immature and mere stepping stones to his later mature system. Speaking for their parties or states, they found assurance and guidance in an ironclad law of historical development with its unvarying scheme of class struggle and its predetermined, clearly discernible final goal. Belief in such a law could help maintain revolutionary discipline, hope, and loyalty among the masses and an existing Communist order. Hence the law of history could not and must not be contradicted.

The dilemma remained. "If all that exists is subject to dialectical 'law,' how can man be exempted? And if man is not excepted, how can we speak of his freedom and creativity?"[1] In the Anglo-Saxon world, never a fertile ground for speculative systems, the strict Marxist interpretation of history on the basis of economic determinism convinced few scholars. Marxism as the supplier of various analytical models for historical studies was a different matter. Understood in this way Marxist historical thought has been used by historians like Eric J. Hobsbawm, Edward P. Thompson, and Christopher Hill. They all wished for a more flexible Marxism, although each of them struggled in his way with the rigidly hierarchical Marxist link between the economic basis and the cultural superstructure. The aim was to create a viable alternative to the dominant structural-functional models in the social sciences. The structural-functionalists have viewed the societies as systems which need to be maintained in a stable condition by neutralizing changes (regarded as "dysfunctions"), an interpretation the Marxist historians have considered false because of its being ahistorical. The Marxists have stressed that the internal contradictions present in all social systems had the positive function of being the motor of change. And where social scientists have seen a continual side-by-side existence of equally valuable cultures, Marxist historians have discerned a progress in the human emancipation from nature. In their attempts to give a historical nature to the Anglo-Saxon social sciences, Marxist historians have sacrificed the reductive clarity of the rigid Marxist scheme in which the economic base prescribed a certain superstructure and all of history moved inevitably toward an ideal, everlasting society. For them Marxist historical thought has become partially valid, changing constantly in form and accent, and offering only partial truth rather than a complete blueprint for past, present, and future. They could all subscribe to Georg Lukács's dictum on orthodox Marxism:

> Let us assume for the sake of argument that recent research had disproved once for all every one of Marx's individual theses. Even if this were to be proved, every serious "orthodox" Marxist would still be able to accept all such modern findings without reservation and hence dismiss all of Marx's theses in toto, without having to renounce his orthodoxy for a single moment. Orthodox Marxism therefore does not imply uncritical acceptance of the results of Marx's investigations. It is not the "belief" in this or that thesis, nor the exegesis of a "sacred" book. On the contrary, orthodoxy refers exclusively to method.[2]

The collapse of the Marxist regimes in Eastern Europe and the Soviet Union has clearly negated the claim of Marxist theory to offering the valid grand scheme of history. Its overly simplified interpretations of the human condition proved to be no match for life's true complexity. Whether or to which degree scholars will have recourse to it for specific insights or methods is yet to be seen.

# ·29·

# Historiography in the Aftermath of Fascism

## Historical Perspectives in Postwar Italy

The first Fascist country, Italy, entered World War II late and switched sides to join the Allies in 1943. Hence the postwar debates were not primarily about the war guilt question, but on how fascism gained power. Historians came closest to a war guilt debate in dealing with Mussolini's imperialistic foreign policy. In it, the alliance with Germany in 1938 (the Axis) came to play a significant role. All in all, post-fascist Italy's return to liberal parliamentary politics proved to be less complicated than Germany's. A brief revolutionary "cleansing" period had removed from public life the most crucial features and personalities of fascism.

Italian historiography also experienced fewer problems in reestablishing the continuity between past and present. That held true despite large-scale changes in the economic and social structures. Continuity also marked historical practice and its theoretical base. While Benedetto Croce's influence was diminished, he had found able successors, among them Adolfo Omodeo. But, as it had before, historicism coexisted with elements of social science—oriented and Marxist history. With the exception of the latter, continuity had not been radically broken even under the Fascist regime. After 1945, one reminder of the break was the fact that few of the exiles returned, most notably the well-known Arnaldo Momigliano and Franco Venturi.

Confronting the twenty-one-year Fascist period, historians asked why Italian liberalism had yielded power so meekly in 1922. Among the frequently cited reasons were dissatisfaction with the Italian rewards in the peace treaties, fear of communism, and socialism's perceived insufficient nationalism. To that Luigi Salvatorelli and Giovanni Mira added the impoverishment of the middle class (*Storia d'Italia nel periodo fascisto*, 1956). Marxist scholars cited Italian society's structural problems. The general inquiry also extended into the Risorgimento as the crucial period of modern Italian history. Did Cavour's solution prevail too completely over the populist ideals of Garibaldi? Delio Cantimoro and Marxist historians, especially Antonio Gramsci, would regret the absence of a Jacobin (radical) period in the Risorgimento. They also pointed to Italy's insufficient modernization. In contrast, Rosario Romano pointed out the detrimental effect such a radical phase would have had. Others, like Gaetano Salvemini, rejected the proposition of a weak liberalism altogether.

In the lively discussion on the nature of fascism, Croce suggested that fascism had no Italian roots but was a foreign ideological import. Those in agreement stressed fascism's connection to international socialism and syndicalism. But Renzo De Felice saw fascism as a nationalist, Italian movement that only through its dictatorship resulted in discontinuity. Fascism also lacked a systematic ideology beyond the idea of a corporate economic order, the nationalist glorification of Ancient Rome and the Renaissance, imperialism, and the celebration of the Great Individual—especially of the leader Mussolini. Hence the term fascism should not be extended to Hitler's movement. Indeed, De Felice and Federico Chabod saw Mussolini's pact with Hitler (1938, the Axis) as the fatal turning point in his career. Being against Italian interests, it destroyed the loose consensus supporting Mussolini.

After these topics concerning the nation receded in importance in the 1970s, Italian historiography opened itself widely to the contemporary currents in historical theory. Italian historians contributed significantly to developments in social and cultural history.

### History for and of a New Germany

*The historiographical mastery of the German catastrophe.* In Germany the postwar historiographical debate occurred in a country that was judged by some to have arrived at the zero hour in its history. Cities lay in ruins, industries were destroyed, people were starving, and the status of Germany had become a point of contention. For about two decades, German historians engaged in the mastery of the past (*Vergangenheitsbewältigung*). The task was no less than to find continuity in a country that recently had experienced changes at the very basis of its national identity, and do so without denying the enormous evil committed.

Historiographically, the issue was one of continuity and discontinuity: had the Nazi regime been a singular aberration, or the culmination of a long development? Historians inside and outside of Germany were drawn into the debate. Of the aberration views, the most popular one attributed all guilt to Hitler. Surprisingly, in this light, the first Hitler biography of substantial historical value appeared only in 1973 (Joachim Fest). In contrast, the focus rested on continuity in the view that all past German development had been on a course destined for catastrophe. However, the most widely accepted view located a misdirection of German development either away from the Western Enlightenment or, in 1848, away from liberalism. German historiography had contributed to this development by its affirmation of historicism, its narrow national aspirations, and its attraction to power. The *Sonderweg* (separate way) thesis offered a clear direction for the rebuilding of the shattered German state on a democratic basis by overcoming the break in continuity.

At first, a moderate revisionism prevailed. In it, the German tradition was found only partially at fault in the matter of Hitler. German society and attitudes were seen as particularly susceptible to the steady accumulation of power in the state and to the consequences of modernity's rejection of tradition: the destruction of values and the isolation of the individual. Hitler made clever use of all of these circumstances and was favored by the popular resentments and fears of revolution after World War I. Thus, the German version of the demonic streak (discerned in all societies) could be unleashed (Gerhard Ritter's *Dämonie der Macht;* 1948). Post-1945 historians agreed here with the few German historians of the 1920s who had warned against the transformation of Ranke's state as a moral institution into the *Machtstaat* (a state governed primarily by power considerations; Friedrich Meinecke). That change had to be condemned but not the whole German tradition. Nazism was an aberration, a discontinuity not rooted in German society and its institutions. Gerhard Ritter, Hans Rothfels, and Hans Herzfeld called for a much stronger moral component in German historiography, but not for its large-scale revision.

In the late 1940s and early '50s, attempts were made to rescue some continuity by differentiating between worthy and unworthy elements in the German tradition. Prominent figures in the attempt were Friedrich Meinecke and Gerhard Ritter. Meinecke pointed to the unresolved social questions, particularly the integration of the working class. In general, blame fell on Prussian militarism and the Prussian solution to German unity in 1871. Gerhard Ritter spoke out for renewing history writing as a moral force. He did not doubt that this could be achieved by rescuing the positive elements of the German tradition. For it, he still saw in historicism—methodology, worldview, and all—a fitting instrument once it was adjusted according to the experiences of the immediate past.

The *Vergangenheitsbewältigung* continued in many different forms. The role of the post—World War I disappointments with the defeat and the Versailles Peace Treaty were key because they helped the rise of Hitler to power. Noting them, but not justifying the actions of Hitler with them, brought some balance to the issue (Hans Rothfels). Such a view served as a counterweight against those who pronounced verdicts of total German guilt (A. P. J. Taylor), or those pleading Germany's total innocence (David L. Hoggan). But coping with the immediate past took less the form of a discussion of war guilt, and more of a struggle for a new historical nexus between past, present, and the expectations for the future. This discussion preserved continuity without denying the enormity of what happened in the years between 1933 and 1945. In the context of that debate the turn to social history would occur.

The absence of a significant war guilt debate had as its reason the general agreement on Hitler and his regime's clear fault. The centrality of Hitler as the key agent of history gave whatever debate there was a marked historicist tinge. But the main attention soon shifted to Hitler's *Reich* as a system. There, questions concerning political, social, and economic structures entered, providing a spur to new developments in historical research and writing with social and cultural focuses.

In that connection, the question of what accounted for the turn away from liberal democracy in 1933 evoked much debate. One group of historians focused on the weaknesses of the Weimar Republic as a contributing element. Constitutional features, the electoral system, and the ideological party structure were cited. The role of anti-Semitism received increasing attention (Martin Broszat, Hans Rothfels). Other scholars saw German liberalism handicapped in a state that had a tradition of relying on power and foreign policy for maintaining itself in an exposed central location (Ludwig Dehio).

*New types of history.* In the context of the general ferment and upheaval of the 1960s, challenges were mounted to traditional views of the German past. Fritz Fischer's *Griff nach der Weltmacht* (1964) saw Hitler's military and foreign policies not as exceptional but as standing in a long tradition of expansionism. While his work was hardly pathbreaking in historical theory, it nevertheless created an opening through which more radical revisions could pour. Particularly so, since at that time a whole generations of scholars came into their own who sympathized with innovative developments. A German social history was emerging. Some of its basic features would be: the ranking of large-scale structural forces as historical causes over individual actions; the downgrading of biographies unless the individual lives were integrated into the social, economic, and political structures; the abandonment of the primacy of the political aspect of life; and the preference for viewing the state no longer as an organic whole (in terms of *Volk*) but as an institution within which conflicts were resolved.

Reform-minded historians began to work in terms of social or structural history. They were in general agreement with the *Annales* schools on history's duty to go beyond the faithful description of unique events and persons and to search for the larger forces which account for the dynamics of societies. But the German historians developed their views primarily within the German intellectual tradition.

After 1945, *Volksgeschichte* lost its key concept: *Volk*. For centuries it had been a respectable word, until the Third Reich misused the term—a misuse with horrible consequences. Thus, the budding German social history became *Strukturgeschichte*. The controversy over the exact connection between the two forms of social history has not subsided even in recent years, although no direct link can be drawn. In their different ways, Werner Conze, Theodor Schieder, Otto Hintze, and Otto Brunner provided the main works of *Strukturgeschichte* (structural history). The horizon of the new social history was implied by the term society. Absorbing influences from sociology (Hans Freyer), generalizations were part of *Strukturgeschichte* although its themes were never far from national history. Structures were categories that helped to describe the web of connections in society. They remained suspended uneasily between real forces and typological means. Their historicist heritage also was not quite in step with the search for a social history with reformist intentions. In *Strukturgeschichte* the economic, political, and social forces were interwoven as they fluctuated in influence, defying any hierarchical structure, in particular reductionism. Accordingly, activist engagement was not promoted.

Such distance of theory from practice was avoided in social histories with emancipatory intent. In many of them, the German *Sonderweg* in life and historiography was the result of the maladjustment between advanced economic developments and traditional social and political institutions. The theme of the stalled social and political evolution would be a major one for historians of the democratic Left.

Most prominent of the new varieties of social history was the *Historische Sozialwissenschaft* (Hans-Ulrich Wehler, Jürgen Kocka). Keenly theory conscious but eschewing grand theoretical schemes, it has combined many strains of historical methods and interpretations (particularly those of Max Weber and Marx). In characteristic contrast to the deliberate neglect of the political aspect by many scholars of the *Annales* school, the long-standing German concern with the state as a coordinating institution has made for an integration of political aspects of life into the new German social history. Also, the influence of the so-called Weber renaissance has given new strength to the mental or conceptual structures never absent from most of German historiography. As history remained dependent on *Verstehen* for the study of values or mental structures as important features, social history, too, was to a substantial degree *Begriffsgeschichte* (conceptual history). That feature contributed to the relative weakness of quantitative historiography, even after 1945.

Other historians have not shared the enthusiasm for a strong social science orientation. Those of the Critical School found patterns worth emulating in the views of Theodor Adorno and Max Horkheimer, who had returned to Germany after 1945, with a message directed against all interpretive schemes built on excessive rationality (scientific, progressive, or otherwise). Such schemes dulled the emancipatory edge of historiography, as they ignored the element of a grand alienation in Western civilization. Overcoming the latter required constant critical assessments of that which exists—a liberation from all myths.

Then, from the 1970s, two countercurrents to German social history made themselves felt. The first derived its strength from the growing distance from 1945 and its historiographical legacy. The historiographical focus shifted from coming to terms with the legacy of Hitler's regime to issues connected with the emergence of a new German republic now clearly set apart from the recent past. Historical works reflected the building of the new German republic and its fitting historical nexus—the connection between the past, present, and expectations for the future. In them, a widened conventional historiography was employed. Historicist elements appeared in the histories in biographical form (of Konrad Adenauer and Karl Schumacher). New assessments of past statesmen yielded insights and helpful orientation (Bismarck biographies). The narrow confines in which German history had been viewed were widened to include the Europe and Atlantic community. Nationally accented and neohistoricist historians strove for a more balanced view of the *Kaiserreich* (Thomas Nipperdey); stressed broad cultural differences in the development of Germany from that of other countries, rather than just one *Sonderweg;* and pointed to the historical consequences of Germany's central location in Europe. These historians, each in his own way, argued for viewing the German catastrophe not as the necessary outcome of past developments and decisions. What they considered to be a realistic historicism was preferred to a well-intentioned, structural, and partially determinist view.

The *Historikerstreit* (literally: quarrel among historians) was related to these historiographical revisions. It originated in a reevaluation of the horrendous events between 1933 and 1945. The central issue was the degree of uniqueness of Nazism, especially the Holocaust. The facts and intrinsic evilness of the events were not in question; their origin and position in modernity was. Some historians (Ernst Nolte, Michael Stürmer, Andreas Hillgruber, and Klaus Hildebrand) interpreted Nazism as a reaction to and imitation of Bolshevism, with both movements sponsored by modernity's destruction of traditions. Critics, prominent among them Jürgen Habermas, attacked such views as an attempt to deprive the Holocaust of its unique horror and permanent cleansing effect on German society (*Verdrängungsversuch*).

An alternative social history, *Alltagsgeschichte* (history of everyday life), aimed to replace the grand concepts that give structure to the *Historische Sozialwissenschaft* and the *Annales* with empirical description of relationships, attitudes, and actions of the common people. That earned them much criticism for romanticizing the people and contributing to the deficit in historical theory that H-U. Wehler, Jürgen Kocka, Reinhart Koselleck, and Jörn Rüsen had deplored for decades. Yet *Alltagsgeschichte* did engage indirectly in theory when its historians spoke of oppression, sought assistance from the anthropology of Clifford Geertz ("thick description"), and advocated the "de-centering" of history, that is, the negation of all unilinear developments, such as progress. Pioneers for the new perspective have been Alf Lüdtke Lutz Niethammer, and Hans Medick.

In the German Democratic Republic, the elaborate institutional apparatus for the study of history (academy, institutes, and universities) was centrally controlled by the communist leadership. Research was conducted along prescribed *Schwerpunkte* (official themes) selected for their support of the ideological struggle and intended to construct a German history along Marxist-Leninist lines. Limited openings for a less ideological historiography presented themselves in ancient and medieval history and in social history (Jürgen Kuczynski). In the 1970s a marked turn to German nationalism occurred. After the fall of the communist regime little has remained of the once favored historiography and of the institutional structure.

# ·30·

# World History Between Vision and Reality

Since 1918 the products of historical scholarship have become increasingly sophisticated and numerous, but the problem of how to write world history has remained unresolved. The need to find a solution, however, has grown more urgent with each of the many steps taken toward a truly global world. In the absence of a generally accepted conceptual scheme which could provide the framework of unity, those attempting to write world history have so far used three approaches: the multiple cultures model, in which all cultures are subject to the same developmental pattern; the progress models now on a global scale; and the world system model.

### The Multiple Cultures Model

Since the ancient period, this model has been intermittently the preferred way to discern patterns and meanings in the course of history. Its reliance on a universal cyclical developmental pattern for the many separate collective entities made it in recent centuries a readily available antiprogressive historical interpretation. Its pattern roughly mimicking the organic life cycle also gave the model some claim at empiricism.

*Spengler: sensation and substance.* In 1918, the most sensational attempt to break new ground in writing world history came with Oswald Spengler's *The Decline of the West.* Actually many of its elements had been known prior to World War I: its philosophical ideas derived from Goethe's organicism, Schopenhauer's pessimism, Nietzsche's vitalism; its theme of decadence had been voiced by Jacob Burckhardt, who feared the consequences of a radical egalitarianism, by Count Gobineau, who predicted Western civilization's decay for racial reasons, and by Vilfredo Pareto, who pictured world history as the graveyard of those elites whose fate determined the rise and fall of societies; while its destruction of the Eurocentric view had been advocated earlier by Kurt Breysig, whose students were introduced to cross-cultural comparative history and were admonished by a sign in his seminar room that "here no one must speak of progress." Spengler contributed creative imagination and a prophetic language. He found many people in the West receptive, disillusioned by the horrors of modern war, and in the case of the Germans bitter over their defeat. Their mood made them accept a world history without hope and good news, one which in Spengler's view signified a revolution in historiography: the traditional Eurocentric world history was replaced by one without any center at all.

Spengler presented world history as the story of "high" cultures, of which so far there have been eight: Indian, Babylonian, Chinese, Egyptian, Arabic, Mexican, Classical, and Western. High cultures were those among the many cultures that, because of their special dynamics, brought forth outstanding achievements. The other cultures as well as the high cultures, after their creative careers had ended, existed in a static, "historyless" state. That assertion was based on viewing every high culture as an organic entity with a life cycle of a determined length and with no purpose beyond its unfolding.

> A culture is born in the moment when a great soul awakens out of the proto-spirituality of ever-childish humanity, and detaches itself—a form from the formless, a bounded and mortal thing from the boundless and enduring. It blooms on the soil of an exactly definable landscape, to which plant-wise it remains bound. It dies when this soul has actualized the full sum of its possibilities in the shape of peoples, languages, dogmas, arts, states, sciences, and reverts into the proto-soul.[1]

This soul also gave a culture its basic, unique, and unchanging attitudes towards life. Cultural diffusion could cause only minor superficial modifications in cultures.

The reading public was fascinated by Spengler's general pattern for the cultural life cycle of high cultures (see fig. 30.1).

The dreaded decadence could not be avoided because cultures were organic entities whose vitality peaked and then declined. Spengler termed the declining phase of high cultures the Age of Civilization, when "at last, in the grey dawn of Civilization, the fire in the Soul dies down."[2] Tradition loses its effectiveness, vitality and creativity are fading, the megalopolis depopulates the countryside and corrupts the morality and civic-mindedness of the city-dwellers, the "arts and crafts" of religious cults and a secondary religiosity replace genuine religious faith, and Caesars rule militaristic states and initiate imperialist ventures.

*Toynbee's two models.* The publication of Spengler's work nearly caused the English historian Arnold Toynbee to give up his own plan to trace the fate of the world's cultures until a closer look convinced him that Spengler's approach was not his at all. Both men did deal with similar collectives—Spengler called them cultures and Toynbee civilizations—and viewed world history as a se-

Figure 30.1

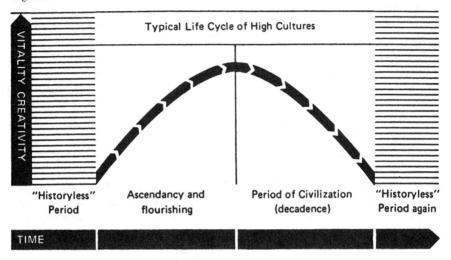

quence of these entities. Yet Toynbee had no taste for "souls" of cultures, uniform cultural life spans, and organicist parallels. Civilizations, rather than representing the unfolding of unique souls, were the results of the dialectic relationship between the challenge of the environment and the response to it by a group of human beings. The appropriateness and creativity of the response determined whether one of the world's noteworthy civilizations was born or not. Once launched, such a civilization followed a typical course (see fig. 30.2).

With painstaking care and much erudition Toynbee identified, analyzed, and described more than twenty civilizations, making his *Study of History* (1934–39) universal in scope. But, after years of study, Toynbee found history as an endless sequence of civilizations a sterile concept. In his seventh volume he dropped civilization as the basic structural element of human life and substituted religion for it. The religions of mankind provided the soil from which civilizations grew, not the other way around. The religions also could transcend civilizations and thus permitted patterns and meaning reaching beyond a single transitory civilization. Indeed, history as the vision of God at work in the world even allowed for progress. Toynbee's progress referred to the world proceeding toward the fusion of the great religions, perhaps even to a world civilization and peace.

## Progress and Westernization

*Progress theories.* For centuries, Christian and secular progress interpretations of human history have defined the unity of world history and given direction to historical phenomena through, respectively, divine providence and the in-

Figure 30.2
Toynbee's Scheme of Civilizations

|  | Period of Growth | Time of Troubles | Universal State | Interregnum (end) |
|---|---|---|---|---|
| (time line) |  | | | ⟶ |
| challenge evokes: | response by creative minority with the masses following ("mimesis") | the creative minority becomes the dominant minority | internal strife ends; peace, stability, prosperity; no classes left | internal proletariat (creative group excluded from influence) together with external proletariat (foes with greater vitality and creativity) destroys state |
| | increasing control over environment yields human self-determination; the period of classes | failure to develop further leads to idolization of existing institutions

turbulent transition | | |

exorable march of rationality. Both interpretations clearly indicated an "upward" development and thus disturbed the egalitarian schemes of cultures constructed by social scientists. For the latter, culture was simply a fact; every group had one. A group needed to achieve no special level of rationality to "have a culture"; no culture was superior to any other and one stage of a culture did not constitute progress beyond the preceding stages. In this egalitarian and ahistorical perspective a culture was a functional structural system used in the process of adjusting to given conditions. Yet the social sciences proudly carry the term "science" in their name. That implies a claim that the scientific—that is, modern Western—way of reflecting on social phenomena has a higher truth value than other ways. All in all, the phenomenon of the sciences has given the diffusion of Western culture a distinctly nonegalitarian and developmental character.

Historians confronted the very problem of accounting for the West's position among other cultures when they wished to explain the centuries of Western dominance and expansion. Did either objectivity or respect for the sensitivities of the new non-Western nations obligate history to neglect the fact of Western culture's at least temporary superior dynamics? Believers in progress among historians claimed that Western culture has unified the world and have praised Western influence on other cultures by pointing to the advances in hygiene, education, science, self government, and individualism. Herbert Butterfield credited Western influence with the eventual global triumph of personalism, even if Westernization itself would fail ultimately. But other scholars have rejected any positive evaluation of Western influence on non-Western cultures as a violation of the concept of equally valid cultures. Some even characterized world histories containing such an appraisal as born of a will to power and conquest, in short, as ill-disguised forces of Western imperialism.

The unresolved problem of how to evaluate the ongoing Westernization of the world has bedeviled all scholarly attempts to write world history. Whenever historians have dropped Westernization as the integrating theme for their world histories they have been left with side-by-side arrangements of cultures. Many authors did just that when they simply lined up the past of nations and cultures in consecutive chapters and let the bookbinder accomplish the synthesis with glue, bindery tape, and cardboard. Actually, most works on world history since 1945 have been less evasive on the process of Westernization. The ambitious works of many volumes—often cooperative endeavors—have to different degrees and in various ways affirmed the unifying force of Westernization. The latter's impact has drawn enthusiastic affirmation as well as sharp criticism. Most of the recent ambitious multivolume world histories have retained a positive emphasis on Westernization without affirming Eurocentrism (the *Propyläen Weltgeschichte, Historia Mundi,* and UNESCO's *History of Mankind*).

After 1945, different views have emerged of the development of scientific-technological Western culture. Under the impact of the human catastrophes of the 1930s and '40s, some scholars have spoken of an "end of history" and a subsequent postmodern age with antiprogressive characteristics. For Roderick Seidenberg, Arnold Gehlen, and Hendrik de Man, that end of history was the product of an out-of-control rationality, Western culture has exhausted its creative potential and is entering a stage of utter stability. In this static and soon-to-be-global stage, changes would happen only within a limited range. The increasingly "frozen" conditions (characterized as crystallization and petrification) would make anachronisms of all concepts linked to a rational, free, and creative subject. Ironically, modernity—the most dynamic period—was moving toward entropy. That postmodern stage offered no escape since all past forces of change will have been neutralized: collective agents (Marx's proletariat), the arts, and critical thought. It also would know no overall meaning or unitary development. While this vision of the postmodern world has found little resonance in the main body of historiography, it has led Marxist scholars to reinterpret the stages of capitalism, search for new change agents, and rediscover history's dialectic (Fredric Jameson). Much later, and in an optimistic postmodernist vein, Francis Fukuyama saw in the victory of modernity's liberal democracy and the market economy signals for the "end of history."

*New attempts at a Christian world history.* Some scholars have considered the French eighteenth-century progress view of history, proclaimed enthusiastically after 1800, to be a secularized version of the Christian universal history (Carl L. Becker). But by 1800 that universal history, in the form as it had been practiced from Eusebius to Bossuet, had already lost most of its influence. Nineteenth-century biblical criticism led many Christian scholars to consider the Old Testament's story of the genetic unity of humankind and the events described in the New Testament as only symbolically, not historically, true. Also, much of modern theology has been disinterested or even hostile to attempts at constructing a new Christian historiography. Thus some Protestant theologians have interpreted Christian faith as an occurrence in the consciousness of individuals without visible connection to collective events. They and other theologians have rejected the concept of a *Heilsgeschichte* that is a history in which God's plan and acts of will are realized and hence become visible. Such detachment from all historical development was rejected by other Christian scholars, especially by those who found the fusion of Christian faith and the progress theory proper and promising. The fusion was most often accomplished by identifying contemporary calls for social justice and reform with the expectation of the future kingdom of God. That promise of a kingdom of God on earth has persisted from the American Social Gospel movement of the early 1900s, with its sketchy theoretical base, to Gustavo Guiterrez's full-fledged theory of liberation of the 1960s in which the fate of Christianity and that of the Third World liberation movements became linked. These and other scholars spoke much of how the Jewish-Christian heritage freed believers from the domination of nature and how through Jesus Christ human beings could not only free themselves of sin but also learn to cooperate in attaining a "higher stage" of existence. Thus, Teilhard de Chardin defined salvation as no more and no less than reaching the highest complexity in human consciousness. All of these views attuned Christian historiography to the hopes evoked by the progressive interpretations of history.

Such fusions of secular progress theories and Christian theology seemed inappropriate to other scholars. After looking at the man-made catastrophes of the twentieth century, Karl Löwith concluded that far from yielding any sense of order and meaning world history was more likely an antithesis to Christian faith. Many others, under the influence of Karl Barth's theology, which since the 1920s has brought Christians to reaffirm the "otherness" of God, the independence of the Christian tenets of faith from secular theories, and the relevance of sin and eschatology, rejected any accommodation of Christian faith to the progress view of history. Obviously, the so-called new orthodox Protestants saw no reason for rushing into historiography but they nevertheless did find a spokesman on history in Reinhold Niebuhr. He, who once had combined faith in progress and in Christ, knew that it was difficult to speak of the past in Christian terms to people for whom most biblical occurrences were at best either myths or symbols, who insisted on the intrinsic goodness rather than on the sinfulness of human beings, and who firmly believed in secular progress. Niebuhr demonstrated to them that increases in control over nature, in rationality, and in personal freedom had not produced the happiness and well-being the theoreticians of progress had envisaged: history showed that evil was more than a cultural lag between the growth of ethical behavior and of rationality and that even the best ideals could produce evil results. History testified not to the march of progress but to the futility of a life of immanence and denial of the sacred. On the other hand, although God and the sacred worked in this world, they were not of it. All attempts to identify the sacred with secular institutions, nations, or movements have failed, often at great cost. In an Augustinian manner Niebuhr warned that history was creative but not redemptive.

In contrast, the period after 1945 has seen what is known as evangelical interpretations of history. There the emphasis rested on the past, interpreted strictly in biblical terms, and the future envisioned in various versions of millenarianism. The accent was on a future of hope and the emphasis once more on a universal history strictly interpreted in terms of biblical prophecy.

At a distance from such theological and philosophical considerations on historical interpretation Herbert Butterfield wrestled with the problem of how to integrate the critical historical science, which he practiced, and the Christian faith, which he affirmed. The historian, he thought, must recognize three perspectives for viewing historical events: as results of individual decisions and actions, as products of large-scale processes, and as expressions of Divine Providence. A modern Christian historiography acknowledged the proper claims of each of these perspectives. World history, too, can and must be written with that awareness.

## World System Theories

The multiple cultures models with their mechanism of rise and fall, and the progress scheme—be it of the triumphal or the "end of history" variety—have both been system theories. After 1945, some world system theories have emerged with affinities to the two models, but also with significant variations from them. They stipulated a multitude of collectives that in the course of history, through dynamic forces, became intertwined to form an interdependent system, albeit not necessarily through the Westernization scheme. Thus, the philosopher Karl Jaspers stipulated the so-called Axis period (800 B.C. to 200 B.C.) as the phenomenon which gave unity to human history, at least during the centuries preceding modernity. During it the common spiritual foundation of mankind was constructed by Confucius, Lao-tse, and other philosophers in China: the Upanishads, Buddhism, and philosophy in India; Zarathustra in Iran; the Hebrew prophets in Palestine; and Homer, the philosophers and tragedians in Greece. But the commonality built on spiritual principles has been replaced in the modern period by the new network of communications (alas, a Western contribution again).

> Despite all conflict and division, the fact that the world is now a single unit
> of communications gives rise to a growing drive toward political unification,
> either by force in a despotic world-empire or through mutual agreement in a
> world order based on the rule of law.
> It is possible to claim that there has been no world history until now,
> but only an aggregate of local histories.[3]

More recent theories tried to shun metahistorical explanations in favor of empirically ascertained processes. They aspired to trace a global development by means of methods, approaches, and conceptual frameworks already available to historians. That was true for the emphasis on economic development, as has already been described. Development theories have looked at history from an economic or sociological perspective because they were formulated to cope with the fact that an industrialized and economically wealthy United States and Europe faced their antithesis in the so-called Third World societies. The gap between the two areas suggested to theoreticians of economic development that scholars should accept the European and American industrialization as the prototypical model, study it, find its inner workings, and then apply these findings to the economic and social policies of underdeveloped countries. World history seemed to exhaust itself in the repetition of the development of the industrialized West in the many new states of the non-Western world. What mattered most was that traditional societies were developing into modern societies. "Tradition" served as a catchall, the antithesis of modernity, connoting a lack of education, social mobility, social equality, secularization, division of labor and roles, industry, and technology. Once a traditional society accepted any modern feature it triggered a process that forced it to revise itself completely, because all societies were seen as systems of interrelated parts. It would be difficult not to see how closely this new world historical scheme resembled the old progress theory's pattern: from barbarism to civilization. The end result would be a completely "modernized" world—a Westernization of global proportions, although that term is avoided in favor of less offensive ones: industrialization and development.

In opposition to the economic development theory, the so-called dependency theory viewed negatively the growing together of the world since the age of discovery and the subsequent colonization. In particular, Latin American scholars interpreted the process as the creation of a core of highly developed commercial and industrial states at the cost of peripheral economically dependent states that were destined for perpetual poverty and exploitation (André Gunther Frank). Immanuel Wallerstein produced a systematic version of the dependency theory by using elements of other interpretive systems, including Marxism.

An entirely different approach has been taken by William H. McNeill in his *Rise of the West* (1963) and subsequent works. The world grew together through the cumulative effects of cultural interactions (the diffusion of successful adaptations). That process of growth also weakened national traditions and caused unavoidable but in the end beneficial collective psychological dislocations. World history as a continuous adjustment process has now arrived at a point where, in order to avoid a catastrophe, another adjustment must be made: the establishment of a world government relying on a vast bureaucracy, strong military power, and a dedicated corps of technicians and administrators. Historians must supply to this endeavor a world history that transcends the histories of special groups in a global mythistory (a mixture of empirical and mythological elements) that would identify with the past triumphs and tribulations of all of humanity.

An even greater rigor concerning empirical findings and rejection of metahistorical elements marked studies of specific global forces of expansive quality. Smaller collective units could not confine them. Among these forces have been the exchange of goods and services (Jeremy Bentley, Philip Curtin); and, on a wider scope, studies of cultural influences in general, migrations, the diffusion of techniques and ideas, social revolutions, economic features, and natural phenomena such as diseases and life forms (Alfred W. Crosby, William McNeill). Many of them were assisted by the expansion of states and empires. These studies have contributed to the writing of world history with a more life-encompassing scope and a distinctly empirical tone. They demonstrate in detail the working of the globalization process although, in and by themselves, they do not hold a ready promise of a synthetic world history.

# ·31·

# Recent Historiography: Fundamental Challenges and Their Aftermath

Some historians have considered the tracing of historiography's course from Clio to cliometrics a nostalgic endeavor, akin to idle rummaging among dusty period pieces. They have been trying to restructure and redefine history without looking back beyond the recent decades, seemingly unaware that by doing so they were denying the fruitfulness of the very historical approach they had set out to defend. The difficulties encountered in tracing historiography's course render such neglect explainable but not justifiable. More accurately and substantially than anything else, the story of historiography can help define the task facing historiography today, demonstrate the essential role of the historian, and dispel any present doubts about history's utility and viability.

## The Maturation of the New History

*The issue of historiography's full modernity.* Over the centuries, history's existence as a significant independent endeavor has appeared occasionally to be endangered by certain developments in human life, or by the temporarily overwhelming influence of other intellectual endeavors. The years since the late 1800s have produced two such periods of uncertainty for historians. One of them was located in the decades on either side of 1900. At that time, some historians (later counted among the New Historians) worried about the future of history. History's response to modernity seemed to them inadequate in comparison to that of the new social sciences just then beginning their ascent to prominence. The concern persisted despite the fact that the criticized mainstream history had secured history a place among the disciplines in the new realm of scientific knowledge and, with it, in academe. In the end, the worries of these scholars proved unfounded. The twentieth century posed severe challenges to historians, with its dizzying heights of achievements and abysmal depths of horror and brutality. Yet historiography responded with significant and innovative adjustments, albeit with some delays.

417

The New Historians had assigned themselves the task of reshaping main-stream history fully in the image of modernity. But during the decades after 1918, their desired new scientific history, conceived as social history, made slight progress. Only after 1945 did the extreme shocks of two world wars, the Great Depression, the horrors of atrocious authoritarian ideologies (fascism and communism), genocides, and brutalities and sufferings on a scale previously unimaginable provide an intellectual climate for remarkable historiographical in-novation.

Yet, even then, there was an initial delay. Change had run its rampant course. Now, for about two decades after 1945, mainstream history in Europe and America was marked by the desire for stability in the aftermath of the im-mense upheavals. Experience has shown that life does not tolerate the domi-nance of either change or continuity for any considerable length of time. But the emphasis on continuity took different shapes in specific national contexts. The most prominent examples were the German quest for a newly mastered past, the French reconsolidation of their revolutionary heritage, the English adjustment to the loss of Empire and social reform, the radical reorientation of the United States toward involvement in a global world as well as a consensus interpreta-tion of the American past, and the reassertion of an orthodox Marxism in the Soviet Union. All of that favored the prevailing historical thought and practice, albeit not without a good measure of adjustments, mainly in the spirit of empiri-cism.

Then, between the mid-1960s and 1990, a plethora of innovations in histor-ical thought and practice poured forth, the most important of which was the rise to prominence of social history. Traditional mainstream historiography main-tained its strong position, with neither its practices nor its ideas abandoned in their entirety; but its vulnerabilities, visible already in the days of historicist dominance, were now readily used against it. The relativism of historicism—of practical importance as ethical certainty in the midst of ideological struggles—compared unfavorably with the claims to an empirically ascertainable truth by social history. The view of the individual as the key agent of history was seen to stand in the way of studying with appropriate methods and approaches the phe-nomena of a mass society. However, after adjustments, mainstream history re-tained sufficient claims on truth to remain an effective historical approach. With the individual's role now carefully delimited, a wealth of methods and ap-proaches critically reassessed, and the importance of the state stripped of ex-treme nationalist colors, these elements survived radical reform attempts. Thus, the rise of social history led not to a total reconstruction of historical thought and practice, but to a large-scale widening of historiography's scope, methods, and approaches to inquiry. However, there were areas of life that were pushed tem-porarily out of the range of attention in some types of social history. Political, diplomatic, and military history almost vanished in the early phase of the *An-*

*nales* group. The state was seen as one of a number of subphenomena in society. The events it shaped were considered ephemera in comparison to the grand social forces and structures. Accordingly, the young Le Roy Ladurie and some American social historians saw the essence of a new history in rigorous quantification. Qualitative aspects receded into the background. Later on, social historians would put phenomena of the private sphere (such as childhood, marriage, and burial) into the center of their work. Interestingly, the basic worldviews varied greatly among well-known social historians, such as Fernand Braudel's new humanism, Lucien Febvre's skepticism toward progress, and the generally social and liberal democratic convictions of key proponents of the German *Historische Sozialwissenschaft*.

By the 1980s, social history had grown into a far-flung and powerful endeavor of admirable creative force. Wide segments of human life had been opened to inquiry and found to be worthy of such attention. Corresponding methodological innovations enriched the historian's instrumental repertory. In that new history had also been established a new continuity in stipulated grand forces and structures. Also, with some notable exceptions (such as Lucien Febvre) social historians had affirmed, to different degrees, the concept of progress either as a humanizing development or as a process of rationalization (in the sense of Max Weber's *Rationalisierungsprozess* as the constant augmentation of the rational in human life). In doing so, social history was well in tune with the spirit of modernity. But together with social history, all of historiography had become more encompassing of life. The broadening of its content found its parallels in the areas of methods, perspectives, and approaches used. These developments reaffirmed history's vitality.

*A powerful opposition.* Yet, by 1980, very unexpectedly, began the second of the twentieth-century's periods of uncertainty about the historical endeavor. There were signs of an exhaustion of creative energy in social history, as has been typical in the trajectory of theories of history. At the same time, scholars haunted by the horrors of the twentieth century criticized modernity's faith in reason and progress as illusory, if not dangerous. All types of historiography experienced a formidable challenge by those who discerned no less than the emergence of a totally new age: postmodernity. These scholars either deprived progress of its promise of a perfect end stage, or found it to be an inherently pernicious concept. The lever of the predicted change from modernity to postmodernity would be a radical redefinition of the dimension of time as it pertained to the human condition. That involved the relationship between continuity and change, as well as the typical historical nexus between past, present, and expectations for the future. As a result, the human condition would not only be far removed from the hopes and optimism engendered by the idea of progress, but also from the whole previous human experience.

## History and Two Visions of Postmodernity

After 1945, the long-standing criticisms of specific features of modernity were joined by criticisms that represented an outright rejection of modernity, including the progressive view of history. The nearly incomprehensible catastrophes of the twentieth century provided a clear rationale for the new attitude. Talk increased of a postmodern age with appropriately postmodern ways of life and thought that could avoid the vicissitudes of modernity, if not of all of history. The opposition to modernity manifested itself in two chronologically and substantially different critical currents. From 1945 to the mid-1960s, a group of scholars did not reject modernity's key historical concept—progress—but reinterpreted it in a pessimistic manner. In the 1980s, they were succeeded by a much more influential group, whose members saw the human catastrophes of the past decades not as deviations from but as revelations of the true nature of modernity. Both groups of postmodernists suggested radically different versions of the human condition, each of them with severe implications for historiography.

*The early postmodernists and their static postmodernity.* The group of postmodernists active in the first two decades after World War II abandoned notions of the end of progress in the Marquis de Condorcet's terms of progress: an ultimate era of peace, happiness, freedom, and virtue. In doing so they paralleled the thought of a mid-nineteenth-century French polymath, A. A. Cournot, who had spotted the supreme irony at work in progress: reason guided history toward a perfectly rational world which, when established, would due to its perfection know only the continuity of an ever same routine. The irony of history made progress, dominated by relentless change, into the march *vers fixité*. Cournot spelled out the price of that end stage. Human life would resemble life in a beehive—perfectly organized but lacking any freedom. In the 1930s, Alexandre Kojeve had projected a Hegelian development toward a postmodernity that he, too, viewed as no longer deserving of being called human.

In the works of the post-1945 postmodernists, that end stage—postmodernity with a human life radically restricted in scope—remained the main theme in a number of variations. For Hendryk de Man, mass-production, mass-consumption mass media and the transformation of all creativity into mere technique will lead to a monotonous life. According to Bertrand de Jouvenel, the lure of the promise of complete material security will bring about the Great Protectorate (the state that takes care of everything at the price of freedom). Arthur Gehlen foresaw a petrified society in which the natural instincts have been replaced by minute organization. Roderick Seidenberg envisioned postmodernity's society of organization as the triumph of the perfect social machine. In each case, the dynamics of progress had ended in a sort of entropy.

In a popular and optimistic version of the same theme, Francis Fukuyama's

*The End of History and the Last Man* (1992) projected a more optimistic post-modern life in triumphant liberal democracy. In this postmodernity, life would be kept within safe but not oppressive boundaries. The two decisive and conflicting desires for recognition—one for superiority, the other for equality—have been transformed into a creative tension by liberal-democratic institutions. Change had been limited but not suppressed.

The message was clear. The ultimate goal of progress had been misunderstood because the irony of history had not been grasped. If human development were to end in a state of perfection, then the human condition would be by definition a static one. Modern developments must therefore not automatically be understood as harbingers of all that is good, but ironically as deceptive builders of a life strictly limited in dimensions for the sake of the perennial continuity of routine.

Progress's claim to universal validity for its view on the course of history rested partially on empirically verifiable improvements in human life, but primarily on the extreme simplification of the historical dynamic: all changes wrought by reason over time would result in the moral and material perfection of human life. Change energized by increasing rationality was perceived to have only temporary and not intrinsically bad consequences. Human development will end in a totally static, and by definition infinite, state of perfection. Postmodernists accepted such a turn in the human condition, except that their end stage did not conform to the usual joyous expectations of the advocates of progress. In the ultimate irony, however different their projected end stages were, these postmodernists accepted the radical reductionism inherent in traditional progress views: the perfection of the end stage is made possible by reducing the two basic temporal experiences (change and continuity) arbitrarily into one. This early group of postmodernists saw the ultimate stage marked by the triumph of continuity. In it, change, if any, would be negligible.

Historians were not disturbed by what in theory posed a grave threat to their endeavor, but to them appeared to be speculative philosophy. On the positive side, these postmodernists used methods and approaches to scholarly inquiry that were empirical in the manner of the social sciences, some of which had proved useful in reconstructing the past's reality. But historians could not have been pleased by the role assigned to them in postmodernity (except for Fukuyama), one reduced to writing annals that recorded an unchanging narrow routine. Historians could have pointed out that millennia of human existence have shown the two temporal experiences (change and continuity) to comprise the unalterable full time dimension of the human condition. Theories could not change that reality.

*The later postmodernists and their postmodernity of total flux.* Beginning in the 1970s, another radical criticism of modernity gained increasing currency, primarily through the work of French scholars, among them Michel Foucault,

Jacques Derrida, and Jean-François Lyotard. The new group of postmodernists, also disillusioned and shocked by the great human catastrophes of the twentieth century, again foresaw an age in which a new outlook on and way of life would exclude the crucial causes for the vicissitudes of history. Its basic proposition maintained that all assertions of universality and permanence present in theory and life were dangerous illusions. They too easily led to claims of absolute truth or knowledge which, when wedded to sufficient power, have caused immense human catastrophes. Such a tie-in could be avoided if the world were seen as being in a state of complete, directionless, and endless flux. In terms of historical theory, the dual human experience of time had to be redefined. This group of postmodernists resolved the perennial and crucial tension between continuity and change by declaring change to be the sole temporal reality. Continuity acquired the nature of a temporary human construct. In such a world of flux, truth could no longer be declared to be absolute. All notions and features of efficacious continuity—such as thinking in terms of the "natural," "essential," or "inherent"—had to be abandoned. Interpretations of individuals, texts, and truth with such qualities had to be "decentered," that is, to be deprived of such anchors of stability. Only then could diversity, multiplicity, heterogeneity, and utter flexibility be made to prevail over artificial homogeneity.

*The "linguistic turn" and historical practice.* While the earlier postmodernists had affirmed objective and permanent forces and patterns to be at work in human life and history, the new postmodernists did not. They were best characterized as poststructuralist. French structuralists in the vein of Claude Levy-Strauss had still acknowledged the presence of permanent codes or even a universal code behind the myriad phenomena of the world. For their rejection of such elements of fixity, these postmodernists had recourse to a broad intellectual current that since the early 1900s has swept language into the center of thought—the so-called linguistic turn. In the early 1900s, the pioneering Ferdinand de Saussure had reinterpreted language from being the passive image of reality to an active self-regulating network of signifiers (words) and signifieds (their objects or ideas). Meanings resulted strictly from relationships within the language system. Decades later, Roland Barthes translated that into a more radical view, in which all meaning and truth were freely created constructs (poststructuralism). Historical accounts had no more claim to truth than any other texts. The whole scholarly apparatus that intended to assure accuracy in the relation between historical accounts and past reality produced not an image of that reality at all but only a "reality effect." Poststructuralist influence on history, most importantly through Michel Foucault and Jacques Derrida, aimed at ending a period of thought in Western culture in which the consciousness of the rational and world-shaping subject had been at the center. That subject was now itself seen as being shaped and defined by the linguistic network in which it was embedded. As a linguistic construct, its identity lacked all permanent features.

Hence derived the talk of the death of the subject and its correlate, the end of history (Foucault).

By the 1980s, poststructuralist concepts had gained a strong presence in historical theory. With the past as it had been lived (actual reality) declared to be veiled completely and available only in what had been traditionally called secondary sources (stories of the past), truth, research, objectivity, facts, and meaning were redefined. All historical accounts were seen as constructs written in reference to earlier texts (other constructs). Texts referred to texts, never to anything outside of them. Beset by internal tensions and contradictions between their textual elements, texts were fragile and incapable of making more than tentative truth claims. Research, no longer an attempt to reconstruct the actual past, became the self-reflexive reading of other texts. In the analysis of historical accounts authors and readers would be equals. No text could lay claim to superiority over other texts based on a special kinship to or profound insights into past reality. As for historical accounts, objectivity now was replaced by stringent self-reflexivity (critical self-examination on the part of the authors).

*The dynamics of postmodernity and history's role.* The need to fit the multi-faceted tension between change and continuity in human existence into the dimensions of the linguistic world brought its transformation into the opposition of affirmation and exclusion. Michel Foucault—less closely tied to linguistic theory—stressed the aspect of hegemony in his view of history as a sequence of periods constituted by different discourses. Dominant discourses created collective identities through the exclusion of other discourses. Historical changes (those in prevailing discourses) were not brought about by thinking and acting subjects but occurred in the manner of geological shifts. Thus, instead of delving into the world of individuals, historians needed to become archaeologists of linguistic structures of power and oppression encrusted in writings and institutions.

Derrida relied on the central concept of différance (his own term) that referred to the fact that for everything affirmed, there is the "other" that differs from it and is excluded from being present in favor of the affirmed. But, although absent, the "other" is nevertheless present as being "deferred," thus, still "real." Text analysis involved deconstruction that, among other aims, ascertained presences and absences (that which was left out of the given text) as well as linkages to other texts.

In all of that, historical accounts had no special position, they were texts like all others. They, too, needed to dispense with the connection between text and objective reality (the non-linguistic "referent") as the source of all illegitimate claims to authority; substitute the endless creation of meanings for the accumulation of knowledge; reject all truth claims hinging on now rejected permanent features of the human condition; deny the existence of the rational and efficacious role of the autonomous individual; and dispense with authoritative meta-historical schemes of history (metanarratives, following Jean-François Lyotard's usage). Special objections were raised to the progress view of history (the modern metanarrative) because of its dominance and subversion of other narratives. For its affirmation of progress, Western culture was condemned as Eurocentric and hegemonic. In an ironic side effect, poststructuralist postmodernists did affirm their own metahistory when they spoke of an "end of history" in postmodernity. Such an end implied a two-phase human development with starkly different human conditions, of which the later was by far superior to the earlier one.

The debate about these theoretical propositions became fierce. Critics concentrated on the postmodernist stipulation of the absolute inaccessibility of past reality. They found that stipulation (often referred to as non-referentiality) impossible to prove even according to the logic of postmodernism. As the basis for historical accounts it remained fruitless. Opponents could point to the absence of historical accounts that fully conformed to postmodernist theory. Proponents of a linguistically and/or literary accented (narrativist) view of history produced a large number of theoretical works that tried to come to terms with the stipulation of non-referentiality (Hayden White, Hans Kellner, and F. R. Ankersmit). Yet aside from attempts to view historical accounts as narratives with special safeguards, poststructuralist postmodernists did not demonstrate how they could establish a historical practice reflective of and useful to life. These difficulties had their deepest root in the recourse to another theoretical oversimplification in mastering life's complexity. Like the earlier postmodernists, the poststructuralist postmodernists engaged in a radical reduction of the temporal human experience to only one component. This time it was change. The second component, continuity, was declared to be a dangerous illusion—the cause of the vicissitudes in the past and an obstacle to the proper affirmation of the world in complete flux, marked by perfect flexibility and a total lack of harmful elements of stability.

Although poststructuralist postmodernists could not realize their grand vision of a complete revision of historical thought and practice, they did make valuable contributions to both. Language will never again be seen as a purely passive element in historical practice. Its role was far more important than contributing style to an account. Linked to that was an enhanced status of the narrative. Historians also will be much more aware of the full implications (even ethical ones) of the choice of methods. That choice was no mere technical matter as it determined what was seen and dealt with. And while good historians have never made claims of absolute truth for their works, postmodernists have strengthened the warnings against overly broad truth claims. And as postmodernists have explored the issue of inclusion and exclusion, they have contributed to an awareness of the need to safeguard heterogeneity. Such marks on mainstream history will be lasting.

In one largely unnoticed way, both versions of postmodernism have made an important contribution to historical thought. When they gave dominance to either change or continuity, they focused attention on the role of time in life and its history. The shift of focus was most salutary, although its full implications have not yet been explored.

## The New Cultural History

In the last decade of the twentieth century, by far the most important influence of poststructuralist postmodernism on historiography showed in the revival of cultural history as the New Cultural History. By then, the genre of cultural history had a venerable history. While elements of cultural history could be traced to the ancient period, its modern version dates from the late 1700s. Johann Gottfried Herder stipulated collectives that had affinities with the modern concept of culture. Early nineteenth-century historicism, influenced by Herder and shaped by Wilhelm von Humboldt and Leopold von Ranke, stressed the culturally defined uniqueness of collective entities. The most influential representative of modern cultural history was Jacob Burckhardt with his work on the civilization of the Italian Renaissance. Decades later, Johann Huizinga's book on the fading of the Middle Ages added significantly to the tradition. In those works of cultural history, understood as *Geistesgeschichte* (a history primarily shaped by immaterial forces), art, music and thought were taken as the central manifestations of a people or period's spirit. The more brilliant the cultural achievements were, the closer they led critical observers to a culture's core. In short, these cultural historians attempted to decode culture by finding patterns, themes, forms, ideas, and ideals presumed to be representative of the collective network of meaning. Huizinga added patterns of feeling and mood. All of these historians learned to value the world of symbols and symbolic interpretation. Symbols were such powerful keys to understanding because they had a dual nature: they represented meanings and at the same time were part of them.

Cultural history gained ground despite the presence of competitors: a still strong Marxism and social history, and a weakened intellectual history. In the strongly empirical social history, cultural phenomena had been seen as shaped, even determined, by social and economic conditions. In the Marxist view, culture was primarily a means to facilitate oppression by exploiting classes. As a superstructure it was entirely dependent on the economic structure. For Antonio Gramsci, culture offered an effective way to assert hegemony. Advocates of ideas as decisive forces found strength in the history of ideas that for four decades exerted a powerful influence (Arthur Lovejoy). Even Charles and Mary Beard, primarily economic interpreters of history, relied on the powerful American spirit for American culture's strength when confronted with the task of defending America against fascism. Later, Perry Miller's book on the Puritans represented cultural history as intellectual history.

Matters changed considerably in the 1960s. History's "anthropological turn" would demand significant changes in historical theory and practice. History and anthropology had been close to each other before. In the late 1800s, evolutionary anthropologists, who understood human development in terms of progress, affirmed the historical mode of thinking. But in the first half of the twentieth century, anthropologists began to think and work in terms of timeless structures and functions. Cultural phenomena were interpreted as answers to common human needs and were best studied by social science methods. Decades later, in the 1970s, a humanistic wave engulfed anthropology. Clifford Geertz (influenced by Max Weber) began to speak of culture as a network of meanings. Symbols became the operative terms in the making of "reality." Rites, rituals, and festivities were manifestations of meanings that gave order to life. They could affirm the social hierarchy, thereby strengthening the status and power of the ruler, but also voice protests against the existing order. Even events of a routine nature came to be seen as symbolic acts, often manifesting hidden opposition or repression. In this new view of culture, "thick description" offered the key to deciphering all human actions by discerning the many layers of meanings conveyed in them. The aim of such an inquiry would never be to find lasting, stable structures and forces, or even laws. Instead, an informal logic displaying the unique patterns of life would become visible.

In an important confluence, the poststructuralist postmodernist mode of thought and the new anthropological approach joined forces to exert a strong influence on the "doing of history." There were even suggestions to incorporate history into a newly formed field of cultural anthropology. Yet the actual result, the new cultural history, was a rather amorphous endeavor that got its coherence mainly from some postmodernist themes. The central one was the stipulation of the world being in constant flux. Change was the permanent and proper state of the world, while continuity and stability were at best temporarily successful attempts in counteracting change. Such attempts were illusory because they assumed an effective equality between change and continuity. Truth as the continuity of knowledge based on the observation of reality was seen as the key illusion. Its only sources were narratives or, more generally, texts.

In the postmodernist vein, the new cultural historians voiced objections against the reliance on "essences," "natures," or other stable qualities in the definition of entities ("wholes"). No group, state, or culture must be seen as possessing fixed or even long-term stable features. Such a constitution of collectives led to the exclusion of outsiders (the other). In the interest of a culture's homogeneity the ideal of heterogeneity was diminished. Even the word *people*, or the phrases *popular culture* and *popular religion*, assumed improperly the homogeneity of these groups or phenomena. The use of the term *human* had the same effect, as it suppressed important differences among human beings (for example, between female and male). Indeed, the vast complex of identity designations was to be distrusted altogether since every definition of identity indicated a degree of stability and brought with it detrimental exclusions. In this vein, some historians have been resisting the temptation to see our views of the human body as true reflection of a "natural" entity. They have instead treated these views as deliberate constructs.

In two decades of creative excitement, cultural history tried to encompass the totality of life. But after a period of innovative vigor, cultural history's creative energy began to wane. The fullness and reality of life, larger than the scope of any theory, was reasserting itself. There, too, the quest for nonreferentiality remained unfulfilled. Traces of that were clearly visible. In the often and rightly praised cultural narratives by Emmanuel Le Roy Ladurie, Robert Darnton, and Natalie Davies, the nonconstructed elements in the human condition were clearly present and important. They constituted anchors for the narratives that limited the range for constructing narratives. Indeed, they have proved to be a defense against a pure subjectivism. The poststructuralist postmodernists had been correct in their assertion that referentiality, naively and excessively employed, posed dangers in theory and in life. But the advocacy of nonreferentiality—history as pure construction—carried its own ethical and cognitive problems that were no less dangerous. Still, cultural history did contribute its share to the twentieth-century enlargement of the scope of historical thought and practice, primarily through its thorough exploration of the concept of culture, the recovery of some autonomy for the role of meanings, and an enhanced sensitivity for the unique and heterogeneous.

## Prospects

Twentieth-century historiography has added new and dramatic chapters to the long story of history writing, a testimony to the undiminished vitality of the historical endeavor. Whatever works of history will be created in the twenty-first century, they will be shaped by the unpredictable configurations of life. History will remain the integral part of the human condition it has been throughout the centuries. That link between the writing of history and life will continue to be forged by the centrality of time to both of them. And, as the history of historiography demonstrates, the role of time in history is not limited to providing the chronological organization to historical accounts. Time emerges as more than a quasi space in which events happen. It is a decisive part of the dynamics of life and hence of its history. Putting it into abstract terms, human coping with life involves attempts to balance two key temporal experiences: relentless change with elements of continuity—opposites, but mutually interdependent aspects of time. Away from the realm of grand abstractions, individuals and collectives experience the struggle in the midst of life as the striving for an acceptable nexus between past, present, and expectations for the future. This historical nexus with its dynamic tension between the views of the past (effective as the counsel of experience), the expectations for the future (part experience, part creative imagination), and the actions and decisions taken in the present under the influence of both, has been—and will continue to be—at the core of human life. Historical accounts show the observer how life's irrepressible changes have met with both actual and constructed continuities in the human condition. In and to all these undertakings, the history of historiography serves as an essential guide.

The proper understanding of the dynamic role of time yields a new perspective to the longstanding discussion about history's usefulness for human life. Indeed, one of history's most enduring qualities has been the trust placed in its capacity to be helpful in mastering life.

Among the most frequently suggested uses of history have been to serve as guardian of collective memories, teacher of "lessons," producer of scientific insights, and source of entertainment. But history's usefulness also has clear limits. George M. Trevelyan warned that history should not pose as a technology because "it has no practical utility like physical science. No one can by a knowledge of history, however profound, invent the steam-engine, or light a town, or cure cancer, or make wheat grow near the artic circle."[1] The fruitful insights gleaned from the study of many historical accounts have proven to be neither technical instructions nor ready prescriptions for application. Their complexity has been enhanced as they were revised, augmented, and simply changed in accord with the experiences of later years. Much continuity meets with constantly changing specific contexts.

At this point, where even the promise of "lessons" from history seem to be put in doubt by relentless change, the history of historiography can bring some assurances, albeit no simple ones. It relates the story of many nexuses that shaped life for a while, were adjusted to the limits inherent in nexuses, and eventually replaced. Such insights seem to yield a mere story of futility—one drab, even senseless. Yet these "failed" nexuses stand not merely as silent, burned-out ruins, but also as testimony to splendid human achievements. They were hard-won ways to make sense of life in a pragmatic and theoretical form. The "failures" resulted not from remediable technical flaws. They originated in two features of every nexus: the always-limited knowledge of the past (with it, limits in the experience guiding the expectations for the future), and the imperfect match between the future as expected and the future as realized. Over the centuries, the writers of history have narrowed the gaps considerably, but because of the dynamics of life itself they could not close the gaps. Indeed, the limits to the knowledge and understanding of the past at any given time, and similar limits on the expectations for the future, have caused all nexuses to remain open-ended. Lacking finality, they eventually fade away when the future become actual stands at a greater and greater distance from the expected one.

Many attempts have been made to design nexuses that would end in final closure in theory and life. Time would never be able to erode that new timeless context of life or the theoretical foundation (the final nexus) on which it rested. In the twentieth century, attempts at final closure included (among others) some " scientific" historians who relied on special (ultimate) methods and approaches, orthodox Marxists convinced that a few crucial insights into the economic development sufficed, and progressive historians who observed a clear ascendancy of rationality that would lead necessarily to perfection. Even the phenomenon of postmodernism has its roots in the issue of closing the gap. The early group of postmodernists relied on the forces of modernity that ironically would bring about a human life of unchanging routine within narrow limits. The permanent identity of past and future would render nexus construction superfluous. In such a life historical thought and study would be of little use.

The later group of postmodernists affirmed the open-ended gap when they identified change as the only valid temporal experience. Therefore the gap could not, indeed must not, ever be closed. Such closure brings the danger of the link between claims to absolute truth and absolute power based on it. As the price for the avoidance of closure these postmodernists denied to the second temporal experience, continuity, any efficacy beyond reproducing ephemeral constructs. They had no substantial link to the reality of life—a reality that was seen as completely inaccessible. The dangerous effects of truth claims based on the authority of past experience (assertions of continuity) would be avoided. Yet the lack of a foundation for historical accounts in past reality left in doubt the exact standing of these accounts in the realm of knowledge.

The ideal of a "final" and "perfect" history might have some usefulness as a spur to achieve the best possible explanations and understandings of the past. But as the history of historiography demonstrates, claims to have achieved finality inevitably turn out to be illusions. Even a quest driven by certainty about the aim yields too easily to simplistic means to get there and claims that one got there. On the other hand, the absence of timelessness and perfection from historiography does not make the endeavor to write history a useless enterprise. Each historical account, resulting from a skilled and serious effort, contributes a deposit of knowledge about how life was led and perceived. The history of historiography as the cumulative record of these efforts demonstrates history's eminent usefulness for the conduct of and inquiry into life. In its unmatched panorama, stretching across millennia, become visible the potentialities and limits of the human condition. From such insights derive counsels of caution and inspirations for creative action and hope. As such, history emerges as a superb guide for the time-bound aspects of the human condition.

In the early part of another millennium, historians face the perennial problems encountered in the writing of history. They enjoy the advantage that, by overcoming many challenges, their predecessors have made history into a richer, more encompassing endeavor in substance and methods. Historians also have the history of historiography to caution them that no simplifications, regardless of their sophistication, can make the writing of history's fundamental theoretical problems disappear. These problems reflect the complexity of the human condition. That complexity will even increase in the multicultural world of truly global scope. In the intensely comparative historiography of the future elements of commonality in the human condition will play key roles. Among them, the perennial human attempts to establish a proper balance between change (the re-lentless sequence of new contexts) and continuity (the attempt to secure stability over time) should receive much attention. In this as it has in past situations, the bond between history, time, and life has established the history of historiography as the unique record of the ways in which human beings have tried to master the temporality of human life. A temporality that has allotted to human beings the roles of emigrants from the past, inhabitants of the present, and immigrants into the future.

# ·NOTES·

### Introduction

1. T. Carlyle, "On History," in *Works of Thomas Carlyle,* 5 vols. (reprint, New York, 1969), 2:83.

### Chapter 1

1. Homer *Iliad* 1. 1–2. Trans. and ed. Richmond Lattimore.
2. Ibid., 1. 5.
3. Ibid., 6. 146–51.
4. Thucydides *The Peloponnesian Wars* 2. 2. Trans. Benjamin Jowett.

### Chapter 2

1. Thucydides *The Peloponnesian Wars* 1. 1.
2. Hecataeus *Genealogies,* in Felix Jacoby, ed., *Fragmente griechischer Historiker* (Leiden, 1957) 1:1a; p. 1.
3. Herodotus *The Histories* 1. 32. Trans. Aubrey de Selincourt.
4. Ibid., 7. 10.
5. Ibid., 7. 9.
6. Thucydides *The Peloponnesian Wars* 1. 23.
7. Ibid., 5. 89.
8. Ibid., 1. 22.
9. Herodotus *The Histories* 1. 1.
10. Ibid., 2. 147.
11. Ibid., 7. 185–86.
12. Ibid., 7. 138–39.
13. Thucydides *The Peloponnesian Wars* 1. 21.
14. Herodotus *The Histories* 1. 1.
15. Thucydides *The Peloponnesian Wars* 1. 22.
16. Xenophon *Anabasis* 3. 4, in *The Greek Historians,* ed. F. R. B. Godolphin, 2 vols. (New York, 1942), 2:289.

### Chapter 3

1. *The Geography of Strabo* 15. 1. 28. Trans. H. L. Jones.

2. Flavius Arrianus *Anabasis of Alexander* 1. Preface. Trans. E. I. Robson.
3. Aristotle *Poetics* 11:1451b. Trans. G. F. Else (Ann Arbor, 1967), p. 33.
4. Polybius *The Histories* 29. 12. Trans. E. S. Shuckburgh.
5. Ibid., 2. 56.
6. Ibid., 12. 11.

## Chapter 4

1. Polybius *The Histories* 6. 6–9.
2. Ibid., 15. 20.
3. Ibid., 1. 4.
4. Ibid., 3. 20.
5. Ibid., 1. 1.

## Chapter 5

1. Sallust, *The Jugurthine War and the Conspiracy of Catiline,* trans. and intro. S. A. Handford (Harmondsworth, Middlesex, 1963), *The Conspiracy of Catiline* 10. 1–6, p. 181.
2. Ibid., 2. 8–9, p. 176.
3. Ibid., *The Jugurthine War* 1. 1–2, p. 35.
4. Cornelius Nepos 16, 1. 1, in *Justin, Cornelius Nepos, and Eutropius.* Trans. J. S. Watson (London, 1910), p. 305.
5. Ibid., 1. 1. *Praefatio,* p. 384.
6. Cicero *De oratore* 2. 15. 62. Trans. E. W. Sutton.
7. Cicero *Epistulae ad familiares* 5. 12. 3. Trans. W. G. Williams.
8. Cicero *De oratore* 2. 36.

## Chapter 6

1. Diodorus Siculus *The Library of History* 1. 1. 1. Trans. C. H. Oldfather.
2. Ibid., 1. 7. 1.
3. Ibid., 1. 8. 1–2.
4. Dionysius of Halicarnassus *The Roman Antiquites* 1. 1. 2. Trans. E. Cary.
5. Ibid., 1. 2. 1.
6. Ibid., 1. 4. 2.
7. Ibid., 1. 5. 1.
8. Livy *The Early History of Rome,* bks. 1–4, 1. 19. 4–5. Trans. and intro. de Selincourt (Baltimore, 1960), p. 38.
9. Vergil *Aeneid* 1. 278. Trans. F. O. Copley.
10. Tacitus *Annals* 4. 34. Trans. A. J. Church and W. J. Brodribb.
11. Velleius Paterculus *Compendium of Roman History; Res Gestae Divi Augusti* 1. 17. 7. Trans. F. W. Shipley.
12. Tacitus *Annals* 1. 2.
13. Ibid., 4. 32.
14. Tacitus *Histories* 1. 3. Trans. A. J. Church and W. J. Brodribb.
15. Tacitus *Annals* 14. 12.
16. Flavius Josephus *Jewish Antiquities* 1. 27. Trans. H. St. J. Thackeray.
17. Ibid., 1. 14.
18. Appian of Alexandria *Roman History* 1. 1. Trans. Horace White.
19. Ibid., Preface. 7.

20. *The Age of Alexander: Nine Greek Lives by Plutarch.* Trans. Ian Scott-Kilvert, introd. G. T. Griffith (Harmondsworth, 1973), p. 252.

21. Flavius Arrianus *Anabasis of Alexander* 1. 12. 4.

22. Ibid., 1. Preface.

23. Ibid., 7. 4–5.

24. Lucianus of Samosata *How to Write History* 6. Trans. K. Kilburn.

25. Ibid., 7.

26. Ibid., 5.

27. Ammianus Marcellinus *Res Gestae* 14. 6. 4. Trans. J. C. Rolfe.

28. Ibid., 26. 1. 1.

Chapter 7

1. Justin the Martyr, 2 *Apologia* 10.8, in E. J. Goodspeed, ed. *Die ältesten Apologeten* (Göttingen, 1915), p. 86.

2. Mark 13:10.

3. Origenes, *Contra Celsum* 8. 69. Trans. H. Chadwick (Cambridge, 1965), p. 505.

4. Daniel 2:32–34.

5. Ibid., 35–36.

6. Ibid., 38–41.

7. Augustine, *The City of God,* 14, 28. Trans. M. Dods (New York, 1950), p. 477.

8. *The Babylonian Talmud.* ed. I. Epstein, 2 vols. (New York, 1939), 1:47.

9. Paulus Orosius, *The Seven Books against the Pagans,* 1 (Prologue). Trans. R. J. Deferrari (Washington, D.C., 1964), p. 4.

10. Ibid., p. 5.

11. Cassiodorus Senator, *The Letters of Cassiodorus,* trans. and ed. T. Hodgkins (London, 1886) 9, 25, p. 412.

12. Isidore of Seville, *History of the Kings of the Goths, Vandals, and Suevi,* trans. G. Donini and G. B. Ford, Jr. (Leiden, 1966), pp. 30–31.

13. *The Works of Gildas,* in *Six Old English Chronicles,* trans. and ed. T. A. Giles (London, 1900), 19; p. 307.

14. Gregory of Tours, *History of the Franks,* 1 (Preface), trans. L. Thorpe (Harmondsworth, 1974), p. 67.

15. Ibid., p. 69.

16. Isidore of Seville *On Times,* 39, 42, in E. Brehaut, *An Encyclopedist of the Dark Ages* (New York, 1912), p. 183.

17. Gregory of Tours, *History* 1, 1; p. 67.

18. Isidore of Seville, *De ordine creaturarum,* MPL, 83, 939–40.

19. Cassiodorus Senator, *An Introduction to Divine and Human Readings,* trans. and intro. L. W. Jones (New York, 1966), 19, 1, p. 115.

20. Bede, *A History of the English Church and People,* trans. L. Shepley-Price (Baltimore, 1955), Preface, p. 33.

21. Cassiodorus Senator, *An Introduction,* I, 2, p. 68.

22. Bede, *A History,* 3, 7, pp. 148–49.

23. *The Fourth Book of the Chronicle of Fredegar,* trans. and introd. J. M. Wallace-Hadrill (London 1960), Prologue, p. 2.

24. Gregory of Tour, *History,* 3, 37, p. 71.

25. *Early Lives of Charlemagne,* trans. and ed. A. J. Grant (New York, 1966), p. 37.

26. Ibid., p. 38.

27. Asser, *Life of King Alfred,* trans. and intro. L. C. Jane (New York, 1966), pp. 56 and 88.

28. Thegan, *Vita Hludowici,* sec. 3 in *Quellen zur karolingischen Reichsgeschichte,* part 1, Latin with German trans. O. Abel (Dortmund, 1974), p. 216.

29. Ibid., sec. 17, p. 226.

30. Ibid., sec. 19, p. 226.

31. *Carolingian Chronicles: Royal Frankish Annals and Nithard's Histories,* trans. B. W. Scholz with Barbara Rogers (Ann Arbor, 1970), p. 37.

32. Ibid., p. 39.

33. Ibid., p. 40.

34. Ibid., p. 81.

35. Ibid., 4. 7, p. 174.

36. Paul the Deacon, *History of the Lombards,* trans. W. D. Foulke and ed. E. Peters (Philadelphia, 1974), p. 1.

37. Nennius, *History of the Britons,* trans., intro., and ed. A. W. Wade-Evans (London, 1938), 56, p. 75.

## Chapter 8

1. *Dudonis Sancti Quitini De moribus et actis primorum Normanniae ducum,* ed. M. J. Lair, 4 vols., (Caen, 1865), 3:86.

2. *Quellen zur Geschichte der sächsischen Kaiserzeit,* Latin with German trans. P. Hirsch, M. Budinger, and W. Wattenbach; newly ed. by A. Bauer and R. Rau (Darmstadt, 1971), *Widukinds Sachsengeschichte* I. 15, p. 45.

3. Ibid., 1. 20, p. 21.

4. Ibid., p. 23.

5. Thietmar of Merseburg, *Chronicon,* trans. into German and ed. Werner Trillmich (Darmstadt, 1957), 1, 14, p. 18.

6. Adam of Bremen, *History of the Archbishops of Hamburg-Bremen,* trans., annotated, intro. J. F. Tschain, (New York, 1959), 3, 2, pp. 115–16.

7. Ibid., 3, 46, p. 154.

8. *The Chronicle of Henry of Livonia,* trans. and ed. James A. Brundage (Madison, Wis., 1961), p. 27.

9. *The First Nine Books of the Danish History of Saxo Grammaticus,* trans. O. Elton, comment by F. Y. Powell (Nedeln, reprint, 1967), Preface, 1, p. 1.

10. Ibid., Preface, 3, p. 4.

11. Geoffrey of Monmouth, *Histories of the Kings of Britain,* 1, 1, trans. S. Evans, rev. C. W. Dunn, intro. G. Jones (London, 1958), p. 3.

12. Ibid., 1, 16, p. 26.

13. Ibid., 9, 11, p. 195.

14. *The Carmen de Hastingae Proelio of Guy, Bishop of Amiens,* ed. C. Morton and H. Munta (Oxford, 1972), p. 5.

15. Eadmer, *History of Recent Events in England,* trans. G. Bosanquet, intro. R. W. Southern (London, 1964), p. 143.

16. Orderic Vitalis, *The Ecclesiastical History of England and Normandy,* trans. with notes Thomas Forester, 4 vols. (London, reprint, 1953), Preface, 1:4.

17. Ibid., 2, 24, 1:130.

18. Orderic Vitalis, *The Ecclesiastical History,* 4, 2, 162, trans. and ed. H. Chibnall, 5 vols. (Oxford 1969–75), 2:191.

19. *Antapodosis,* 3, 1, in *The Works of Liudprand of Cremona,* trans. F. A. Wright (London, 1930), p. 109. For the Greeks Lamia connoted a demon devouring children.

20. Leo of Ostia, *Chronica Monasterii Casinensis,* in MG SS 7. 2. 37, p. 652.

21. *Vie de Louis le Gros par Suger*, ed. A. Molinier (Paris, 1887), Prologue, pp. 1–2.
22. *The Life of St. Louis*, in *Memoirs of the Crusade*, trans. Sir Frank Marzials (New York, 1958), p. 135.

## Chapter 9

1. *Jahrbücher von Quedlinburg*, year 998, in *Geschichtsschreiber der deutschen Vorzeit*, vols. 34–40 in one, p. 14.
2. Ibid., year 1001, p. 22.
3. *Herimani Augiensis chronicon*, in MGH SS 5, p. 74.
4. *Frutolfs und Ekkehards Chroniken und die anonyme Kaiserchronik*, Latin with German trans. F. J. Schmale and I. Schmale-Ott (Darmstadt, 1972), *Ekkehardi Chronica*, Version 1, year 1099, p. 133.
5. *Imperial Lives and Letters of the Eleventh Century*, trans. T. Mommsen and K. F. Morrison, intro. K. F. Morrison, ed. R. L. Benson (New York, 1962), Wipo, *The Deeds of Conrad II*, pp. 55–56.
6. Ibid., p. 56.
7. Ibid., anonymous, *The Life of the Emperor Henry IV*, p. 105.
8. John of Salisbury, *Memoirs of the Papal Court*, trans. annotated, and introd. M. Chibnall (London, 1956), p. 3.
9. Ibid., p. 5.
10. *Ex Rudolfi Glabri historiarum libri*, ed. G. Waitz, MGH SS 7; 4, p. 65.
11. *The Chronicle of Henry of Huntingdon*, ed. T. Forester (London, 1853), pp. xxvii.
12. Orderic Vitalis, *The Ecclesiastical History*, 7, 3, 249, trans. and ed. M. Chibnall, 5 vols. (Oxford, 1973), 4:103.
13. Ibid., 6, 2, 2, 3:215.
14. *The Chronicle of Henry of Huntingdon*, pp. xxvii.
15. Ibid.
16. Ibid., 6, entry year A.D. 1035, p. 199.
17. *Chronicon Luxoviense*, Cod. 151, fol. 93v, Bibliothèque de la Faculté de Médicine de Montpellier. Excerpt in A. D. van den Brincken *Die Lateinische Weltchronistik* (Munich, 1969), p. 164.
18. This version of the episode by Robert the Monk, *Historia Iherosolimitana*, 1–3 in *Recueil des Historiens Croisades: Historiens Occidentaux*, 8:727–730.
19. *The Chronicle of Henry of Huntingdon*, p. 227.
20. William of Malmesbury, *Chronicle of the Kings of England*, ed. J. A. Giles (London, 1847), p. 364.
21. Orderic, Vitalis, *The Ecclesiastical History*, 9, 3, 458, 5:5.
22. *Gesta Francorum et Aliorum Hierosolimitanorum*, Latin and English. Trans. and ed. R. Hill (London, 1962), 38, p. 92.
23. *Frutolf's und Ekkehards Chroniken und die Anonyme Kaiserchronik*, Latin and German, trans. F. A. Schmale and I. Schmale-Ott (Darmstadt, 1972), pp. 147–49.
24. William of Tyre, *A History of Deeds Done Beyond the Sea*, trans. and annotated E. A. Babcock and A. C. Berry (New York, 1948), 3, p. 41.
25. Odo of Deuil, *De profectione Ludovici VII in orientem*, Latin and English, trans. and ed. V. G. Berry (New York, 1948), 3, p. 41.
26. Ibid., 3, p. 45.
27. *Annales Herbipolenses*, MGH SS, 16, year 1147, p. 3.
28. William of Tyre, *A History*, 23, Preface, 2:505–6.

29. Ibid., 2:506.

30. Robert of Clari, *The Conquest of Constantinople*, trans. E. H. McNeal. (New York, 1936), p. 59.

31. Joinville and Villehardouin, *Chronicles of the Crusades*, trans. with intro. M. R. B. Shaw (Baltimore, 1963), p. 346.

## Chapter 10

1. Anselm of Havelberg, *Dialogues*, 1, i, 114, 1C, ed. G. Salet (Paris, 1966), 1, 34.

2. Ibid., I, 114, 2C; 1, i, 36.

3. Ibid., I, i, 1160A; 1, 13, 116.

4. The Revelation of John 14:6.

5. Otto of Freising, *The Two Cities*, trans. and intro. C. C. Mierow, ed., A. P. Evans and C. Knapp (New York, 1928), 2, 43, p. 205.

6. Ibid., Prologue, p. 94.

7. John of Salisbury, *Memoirs of the Papal Court*, trans. annotated, and intro. M. Chibnall (London, 1956), Prologue, p. 3.

8. Matthew Paris, *English History*, trans. J. A. Giles, 3 vols. (London, 1852–54), 1:312–13.

9. T. Basin, *Histoire de Charles VII*, ed. Charles Samoran (Paris, 1933), 1:46.

10. J. Froissart, *Chronicles*, sel., trans., and ed. by G. Brereton (Baltimore, 1968), p. 37.

11. Ibid., pp. 211–12.

12. Ibid., p. 152.

13. G. Villani, *Chroniche Fiorentine. Selections from the First Nine Books*, trans. R. Selfe and ed. P. H. Wickstead (London, 1896), 4, 30, and 5, 8, pp. 96 and 108.

## Chapter 11

1. Machiavelli, *The Discourses*, 1, Preface, in *The Prince and the Discourses* (New York, 1950), p. 105.

2. Guicciardini, *Ricordi*, ser. C, n. 117 in *Opere*, ed. E. L. Scarano (Turin, 1970), p. 762.

3. *Correspondence of Matthew Parker*, ed. John Bruce and T. Perowne (Cambridge, 1853), p. 425.

## Chapter 12

1. C. L. Kingsford, ed. *A Survey of London by John Stow*. 2 vols. (Oxford, 1908), 1:xxviii.

2. J. Bodin, *Method for the Easy Comprehension of History*, trans. B. Reynolds (New York, 1945), p. 15.

3. Ibid., pp. 291–92.

4. Ibid., p. 302.

5. Sir Walter Raleigh, *History of the World*, 6 vols. (Edinburgh, 1820), I, i, x, 1:25.

6. Ibid., Preface, 1:vi.

7. Ibid., 1, 3, 1:266.

8. Ibid., Preface, 1:lxii.

9. G. Viperano *De scribenda historia* (Antwerp, 1569), p. 9.

10. D. Atanagi, *Ragionamento della historia* (Venice, 1559), p. 78.

11. In J. P. Green, ed., *Settlements and Society: 1584–1763* (New York, 1966), p. 68.

12. W. Stith, *The History of the First Discovery and Settlement of Virginia* (New York, 1865), p. 2.

### Chapter 13

1. G. Vico, *The New Science*, trans. T. Goddard Bergin and M. H. Fisch (Ithaca, New York, 1968) no. 331, p. 96.

2. G. W. Leibniz, *Werke*, ed. O. Klopp, 10 vols. (Hanover, 1864–77), 5:368.

3. *Turgot*, trans., ed., and intro. R. L. Meek (Cambridge, 1973), p. 41.

4. Ibid., pp. 54–55.

5. J.-A.-N de Condorcet, "De l'influence de la révolution d'Amérique sur l'Europe," in *Oeuvres*, ed. O'Connor and M. F. Arago, 12 vols. (Paris, 1847–49), 8:30.

6. K. M. Baker, *Condorcet* (Chicago, 1975), p. 281.

7. *Turgot*, p. 41.

8. J. L. R. d'Alembert, *Discours préliminaire de l'Encyclopédie*, in *Oeuvres*, 5 vols. (Paris, 1821–22, reprint, 167), 1:82.

9. Voltaire, *History of Charles XII of Sweden*, trans. and abridged J. H. Brumfitt, in *The Age of Louis XIV and Other Selected Writings* (New York, 1963), p. 119.

10. H. S. J. Lord Bolingbroke, *Historical Writings*. ed. and intro. I. Kramnick (Chicago, 1972), p. 9.

11. G. Vico, *The New Science*, no. 1106, p. 424.

12. Ibid.

13. V. de Mirabeau, *L'ami des hommes, ou traité de la population* (Paris, 1883), p. 317.

14. d'Alembert, *Mémoires et Réflexions*, in *Oeuvres*, 2:132.

15. *Pensées et fragments inédits de Montesquieu*, ed. G. de Montesquieu, 2 vols. (Bordeaux, 1899–1901), 1:114.

16. *Encyclopédie*, 17 vols. (Paris, 1751–65; reprint, 1969), 7:790.

17. J. O. de la Mettrie, *Oeuvres philosophiques*, 2 vols. (Berlin, 1764), 1:278.

### Chapter 14

1. W. Robertson, *The Progress of Society in Europe*, ed. F. Gilbert (Chicago, 1972), p. xvii.

2. Ibid., p. 4.

3. W. Robertson, *History of America* (Philadelphia, 1799), 2:261.

4. *The Letters of Edward Gibbon*, ed. J. E. Norton, 3 vols. (London, 1956), 2:100.

5. E. Gibbon, *The Decline and Fall of the Roman Empire*, abridged D. M. Low (New York, 1960), p. 1.

6. Ibid., pp. 524–25.

7. I. Kant, "Idea for a Universal History," in *On History: Immanuel Kant*, ed. L. W. Beck, trans. L. W. Beck, R. E. Anchor, E. L. Fackenheim (New York, 1963), p. 17.

8. A. L. von Schlözer, *Statsgelartheit* (Göttingen, 1804), pt. 2, p. 92. Quoted in P. H. Reill, *The German Enlightenment and the Rise of Historicism* (Berkeley–Los Angeles, 1975), p. 35.

9. J. C. Gatterer, ed., *Historisches Journal* (Göttingen, 2 1773), p. 120. Quoted in Reill, *The German Enlightenment and the Rise of Historicism* (Berkeley–Los Angeles, 1975), p. 36.

10. J. G. Herder, *Sämtliche Werke*, ed. B. Suphan, 33 vols. (Berlin, 1877–1913), 17:58.
11. Ibid., 11:225.

## Chapter 15

1. B. Niebuhr, *Römische Geschichte*, 3 vols. (Berlin, 1873), Preface.
2. G. W. F. Hegel, *Philosophie der Weltgeschichte*. 4 vols. (Leipzig, 1944), 1:28.
3. G. W. F. Hegel, *Reason in History* (Indianapolis, 1953), p. 87.
4. G. W. F. Hegel, *Philosophie der Weltgeschichte*, 1:163.
5. Ibid., 1:90.
6. Ibid., 1:40.
7. Ibid.
8. L. Ranke, *Fürsten und Völker*, ed. W. Andreas (Wiesbaden, 1957), p. 4.
9. Ibid., p. 5.
10. Quoted in A. Wucher, "Theodor Mommsen," in *Deutsche Historiker*, ed. H.-U. Wehler, 5 vols. (Göttingen, 1971–72), 4:18.
11. *Historische Zeitschrift*, 1 (1859), Preface, p. iii.
12. Ibid., p. iv.
13. A. Thierry, *A History of the Conquest of England by the Normans*, 2 vols. (New York, n.d.), 1:xiii.
14. J. Michelet, *History of France*, trans. G. H. Smith, 2 vols. (New York, 1892) 1:Prefatory Note.
15. J. Michelet, *The People*, trans. G. H. Smith (New York, 1846), p. 27.
16. Ibid.
17. J.-C.-L. Sismondi, *History of the Italian Republics*, intro. W. Ferguson (New York, 1966), p. 127.
18. Ibid., p. 78.
19. F. Guizot, *History of France to 1849*, trans. R. Black, 5 vols. (New York, 1872), p. v.
20. F. E. Toulengeon, *Histoire de France depuis la révolution de 1789* (Paris, 1801), 1:vii–viii.

## Chapter 16

1. T. B. Macaulay, "History," in *The Complete Writings*, 10 vols. (Boston and New York, 1901), 1:276.
2. H. D. Sodjwick, Introduction to T. B. Macaulay, *The History of England*, 5 vols. (Boston–New York, 1901), 1:xlvi.
3. S. Turner, *History of the Anglo-Saxons*, 2 vols. (London, 1799–1805), 2:xi–xii.
4. H. Hallam, *View of the State of Europe during the Middle Ages*, 6th ed. (New York, 1858), p. iii.
5. T. Carlyle, *Selections*, ed. A. M. D. Hughes (Oxford, 1957), p. 30.
6. T. Carlyle, "On History," in *Works*, 2:86.
7. T. Carlyle, *On Heroes, Hero-Worship, and the Heroic in History* (London, 1968), p. 1.
8. T. Carlyle, "On History," in *Works*, 2:86.
9. G. Bancroft, *The History of the United States of America from the Discovery of the Continent*, ed. and abridged R. B. Nye (Chicago, 1966), p. 39.
10. Ibid.

11. Ibid., p. 45.

12. Ibid., pp. 136, 137, 205.

13. R. Hildreth, *History of the United States of America*, 3 vols. (New York, 1849), 1:iii.

14. R. Hildreth, *Despotism in America: An Inquiry* (New York, 1968), p. 8.

15. F. Parkman, *History of the Conspiracy of Pontiac*, 2 vols. (London, 1908), 1:xxxi.

16. J. L. Motley, *The Correspondence of John Lothrop Motley*, ed. G. W. Curtis, 2 vols. (New York, 1882), 2:292.

17. F. Guizot, *History of France*, 1:vi.

18. Rationale for appointment in G. Berg, *Leopold von Ranke als akademischer Lehrer* (Göttingen, 1968), pp. 50–51.

19. F. Guizot, *History of France*, p. v.

Chapter 18

1. *The Essential Comte*, ed. S. Andreski, trans. and annotated M. Clarke (New York, 1974), p. 205.

2. A. Comte, *Cours de Philosophie Positive*, ed. E. Littré, 6 vols. (Paris, 1864), 6:590.

3. *The Essential Comte*, p. 204.

4. Ibid., p. 199.

5. Ibid., p. 199.

6. Ibid., p. 203.

7. H. T. Buckle, *History of Civilization in England* (New York: London, 1934), p. 1.

8. Ibid., p. 6.

9. Ibid., p. 26.

10. N. D. Fustel de Coulanges, *Histoire des institutions politiques de l'ancienne France*, ed. C. Jullian, 6 vols. (Paris, 1891), 1:xi. Quoted in F. Stern, *Varieties of History* (New York, 1956), p. 188.

11. Ibid.

12. J. G. Droysen, *Briefwechsel*, ed. R. Hübner, 2 vols. (Berlin: Leipzig, 1979), 2:976.

13. J. G. Droysen, "Die Erhebung der Geschichte zum Rang einer Wissenschaft," *Historische Zeitschrift*, 9 (1863):1–22.

14. W. Dilthey, *Die Geistige Welt* (Leipzig: Berlin, 1924), p. 144.

15. W. Dilthey, *Pattern and Meaning in History: Thoughts on History and Society*, ed. and intro. by H. P. Rickman (New York, 1962), pp. 157–58.

16. W. Dilthey, *Gesammelte Schriften* (Leipzig, 1927), 7:290.

17. Lord Acton, *Essays in the Liberal Interpretation of History*, ed. W. H. McNeill (Chicago, 1967), p. 399.

18. J. B. Bury, "The Science of History," *Selected Essays of J. B. Bury*, ed. Harold Temperley (Cambridge, 1930), p. 18.

19. G. M. Trevelyan, *Clio, A Muse* (London, 1913), p. 143.

20. Ibid., p. 148.

21. Ibid., p. 160.

22. J. B. Bury, *Selected Essays*, pp. 70.

23. J. G. Bishop, *Theodore Roosevelt and His Times*, 2 vols. (New York, 1920), 2:139–40.

24. G. B. Adams, "History and the Philosophy of History," *American Historical Review* 14 (January, 1909):236.

25. H. Adams, "The Tendency of History," *Annual Report of the AHA for 1894*, pp. 17–18.

26. H. Adams, *History of the United States*, 9 vols. (New York, reprint 1962), 9:222.


Chapter 19

1. K. Marx and F. Engels, *The Poverty of Philosophy* (New York, 1976), p. 166.
2. Ibid.
3. K. Marx, *The Class Struggles in France (1848–1850)* (New York, 1934), p. 10.
4. K. Marx, *The Gotha Program* (New York, 1922), p. 31.
5. E. Bernstein, *Evolutionary Socialism*, trans. E. C. Harvey (New York, 1961), p. 202.
6. F. Engels, *Werke* (Berlin, 1962), 19:333.
7. E. R. A. Seligman, *The Economic Interpretation of History* (New York, 1902), pp. 159–60.
8. Ibid., p. 163.
9. C. A. Beard, *An Economic Interpretation of the Constitution*, (New York, 1913), pp. 15–16.
10. Ibid., p. 292.


Chapter 20

1. J. Michelet, *The People*, trans. G. H. Smith (New York, 1846), p. 10.
2. J. Michelet, *History of the French Revolution*, trans. by C. Cocks, ed. G. Wright (Chicago, 1967), p. 329.
3. T. Carlyle, *The French Revolution* (New York, n.d.), 1:160.
4. T. Carlyle, *Selections*, ed. A. M. D. Hughes (Oxford, 1957), p. 30.
5. T. Carlyle, *The French Revolution*, 1:18.
6. F. W. Nietzsche, "Zur Genealogie der Moral," *Werke*, 11 vols. (Goldmann edition, n.d.), 9:130.
7. J. Michelet, *The People*, p. 24.
8. G. Waitz, Review in *Göttingische Gelehrte Anzeigen* (1862, pt. 1), p. 131.
9. T. Roosevelt, *The Winning of the West*, 6 vols. (New York, 1905), 1:40–41.
10. H. B. Adams, "Germanic Origins of New England Towns," *Johns Hopkins Studies*, 1st series, 2 (Baltimore, 1888), p. 8.
11. F. J. Turner, *Frontier and Section*, ed. R. A. Billington (Englewood-Cliffs, 1961), p. 29.
12. F. J. Turner, *The Frontier in American History*, ed. R. A. Billington (New York, 1920), p. 293.
13. F. J. Turner, "The Significance of History," in *The Early Writings of Frederick Jackson Turner*, ed. F. Mood (Madison, 1938), pp. 47–48.
14. J. H. Robinson, "History," in *Lectures on Science, Technology, and Art* (New York, 1907–8), p. 14.
15. J. H. Robinson and C. A. Beard, *The Development of Modern Europe*. 2 vols. (New York, 1907–8), 1:iii.


Chapter 21

1. A Schlözer, *Weltgeschichte* (Göttingen, 1792), p. 78.
2. Ibid., pp. 3 and 4.
3. Lord Acton, *Essays*, p. 398.

## Chapter 22

1. B. Croce, *History as the Story of Liberty* (New York, 1955), p. 43.
2. J. H. Robinson, *The New History* (New York, 1912), p. 25.
3. C. L. Becker, "What Are Historical Facts?" *The Western Political Quarterly* 8, no. 3 (September 1955):330.
4. C. A. Beard, "Written History as Act of Faith," *American Historical Review* 39, no. 2 (January 1934):221–22.
5. Ibid., pp. 228–29.
6. Ibid.

## Chapter 23

1. J. H. Robinson, *The New History* (New York, 1912), p. 263.
2. M. Curti, *The Growth of American Thought*, 2nd ed. (New York, 1951), p. vi.
3. Ibid., p. 799.
4. W. A. Dunning, "The Undoing of Reconstruction," *The Atlantic Monthly* (1901), p. 449.
5. G. W. Williams, *History of the Negro Race in America from 1619 to 1880* (New York, 1883), p. vii.
6. W. E. B. DuBois, *Dusk of Dawn* (New York, 1940), p. 51.
7. C. G. Woodson, "Note on Negro History Work," *Journal of Negro History* 11 (April 1926):239.
8. M. Bloch, *Apologie pour l'histoire ou métier d'historien*, Cahiers des Annales, 3, p. 11.
9. L. Febvre, *Combats pour l'histoire* (Paris, 1953), p. 32.
10. L. Febvre, *A New Kind of History*, ed. P. Burke, trans. K. Folca (New York, 1973), p. 31.
11. L. Febvre, *Pour un histoire à part entière* (Paris, 1962), p. 852.
12. L. Febvre, quoting Peguy, *A New Kind of History*, p. 29.
13. Ibid., p. 31.

## Chapter 24

1. W. Goetz, *Historiker in meiner Zeit* (Cologne and Graz, 1957), p. 422.
2. J. Stalin, "Report to the Seventeenth Congress of the CPSU," *Problems of Leninism* (Moscow, 1940), p. 529.

## Chapter 25

1. L. Hartz, The Liberal Tradition in America (New York, n.d.), p. 32.
2. R. Gabriel, "Democracy: Retrospect and Prospect," American Journal of Sociology 48 (1942):418.
3. D. Boorstin, The Americans, The Colonial Experience (New York, 1958), p. 1.

## Chapter 26

1. L. Benson, *Toward the Scientific Study of History* (New York, 1972), p. 6.
2. H. T. Buckle, *History of Civilization in England*, 2 vols. (New York, 1892), 1:24–25.
3. A. Schlesinger, Jr., "The Humanist Looks at Empirical Statistical Research," *American Sociological Review* 27 (1962):770.
4. A. J. Ayer, *Philosophical Essays* (London, New York, 1965), p. 168.

5. C. Hempel, "The Function of General Laws in History," in *Theories of History*, ed. P. Gardiner (New York, 1939), pp. 348–49.

6. R. G. Collingwood, *The Idea of History* (Oxford, 1946), p. 317.

7. M. Oakeshott, *Experience and Its Modes* (London, 1933), p. 154.

8. W. B. Gallie, *Philosophy and the Historical Understanding* (London, 1964), p. 124.

9. W. Walsh, *An Introduction to the Philosophy of History*, rev. ed. (London, 1967), p. 59.

10. W. Langer, "The Next Assignment," *American Historical Review* 63 (October 1957–July 1958):284.

11. S. Freud, *Civilization and Its Discontents*, trans. and ed. J. Strachny (New York, 1961), p. 69.

12. Ibid.

13. Ibid.

Chapter 27

1. P. Chaunu, "L'histoire géographique," *Revue de l'enseignement supérieur*, 54/55 (1969):67.

Chapter 28

1. G. Petrović, *Marx in the Mid-Twentieth Century* (New York, 1967), p. 64.

2. G. Lukács, *History and Class Consciousness*, trans. R. Livingstone (Cambridge, Mass., 1971), p. 1.

Chapter 30

1. O. Spengler, *Today and Destiny: Excerpts from The Decline of the West of Oswald Spengler*, ed. E. F. Dakin (New York, 1940), p. 144.

2. Ibid., p. 147.

3. K. Jaspers, *The Origin and Goal of History*, trans. Michael Bullock (New Haven, 1953), p. 24.

Chapter 31

1. G. M. Trevelyan, *Clio, A Muse* (London, 1913), p. 143.

# ·ABBREVIATIONS·

| | |
|---|---|
| *AA* | *Antike und Abenland* |
| *AK* | *Archiv fur Kulturgeschichte* |
| *AHR* | *American Historical Review* |
| *CH* | *Church History* |
| *CP* | *Classical Philology* |
| *DA* | *Deutsches Archiv* |
| *He* | *Hermes* |
| *Hi* | *Historia* |
| *HJ* | *Historisches Jahrbuch* |
| *HT* | *History and Theory* |
| *Hy* | *History* |
| *HZ* | *Historische Zeitschrift* |
| *JHI* | *Journal of the History of Ideas* |
| *JRS* | *Journal of Roman Studies* |
| *MH* | *Medievalia et Humanistica* |
| *NJ* | *Neue Jahrbücher* |
| *PP* | *Past and Present* |
| *RH* | *Revue historique* |
| *S* | *Saeculum* |
| *Sp* | *Speculum* |
| *T* | *Traditio* |
| *TRHS* | *Transactions of the Royal Historical Society* |
| *WDF* | *Wege der Forschung* |
| *WG* | *Die Welt als Geschichte* |
| *ZKG* | *Zeitschrift fur Kirchengeschichte* |

# ·BIBLIOGRAPHY·

Since a comprehensive bibliography proved not feasible a selection according to clear criteria was made.

1. Only works which deal sufficiently with historiographical topics were included. Exceptions were made for a few works which contain closely related material.

2. Preference was given to important works published since 1945.

3. Editions of works by the historians discussed were not listed in the guide, since they can easily be located through bibliographic tools in academic libraries. Thus, for example, the works *by* Tacitus were not listed but books *about* Tacitus were.

4. The organization of the bibliography follows in general that of the text but is not identical with it. Convenience of use was the overriding principle.

## General Bibliographies of Historiography

Useful volumes are:

Berding, Helmut, *Bibliographie zur Geschichtstheorie* (Arbeitsbücher zur mudernen Geschichte 4), Göttingen, 1977.
*History and Theory.* Beihefte 1, 3, 7, 10, 13, and 28.
Stephens, Lester D., comp. and ed. *Historiography: A Bibliography.* Metuchen, N.J., 1975.

## Historiography—General Works

*Surveys and Books of Readings*
Barnes, H. E. *A History of Historical Writing.* Norman, Okla., 1937.
Bentley, M. *Modern Historiography. An Introduction.* London, 1999.
Bentley, M. *Companion to Historiography.* London, 1997.
Blanke, H. W. *Historiographieegeschichte als Historik.* Stuttgard-Cannstadt, 1991.

Burke, P., ed. *New Perspectives on Historical Writing*. Cambridge, Engl., 1991.

Cannadine, D. *What is History Now?* London, 2002.

Carbonell, C.-O. *Histoire et historiens*. Toulouse, 1976.

Conklin, P. K., and Stromberg, R. N. *The Heritage and Challenge of History*. New York, 1971.

Cook, A. S. *History/Writing. The Theory and Practice of History in Antiquity and Modern Times*. Cambridge, Engl., 1979.

Delbrück, H. *Geschichte der Kriegskunst im Rahmen der politischen Geschichte*. 6 vols. Berlin, 1900–1936.

Finley, M. I. *Use and Abuse of History*. New York, 1975.

Fitzsimons, M. A. *The Past Recaptured: Great Historians and the History of History*. Notre Dame, Ind., 1983.

Fogel, R. W. *Which Road to History? Two Views of History*. New Haven, 1983.

Fueter, E. *Geschichte der neueren Historiographie*. 3d ed. Berlin, 1936; reprint, 1968.

Gay, P., et al., eds. *Historians at Work*. 4 vols. New York, 1972–75.

Hay, D. *Annalists and Historians: Western Historiography from the Eighth to the Eighteenth Centuries*. London, 1977.

Hexter, J. H. *Reappraisals in History*. 2d ed. Chicago, 1979.

Higham, J. *History: Professional Scholarship in America*. Baltimore, Md., 1983.

———. *Writing American History. Essays on Modern Scholarship*. Bloomington, Ind., 1970.

Higham, J., Krieger, L., Gilbert, F. *History*. Englewood Cliffs, N.J., 1965.

Himmelfarb, G. *The New History and the Old: Critical Essays and Reappraisals*. Cambridge, Mass., 1987.

Iggers, G. G. *The German Conception of History*. Middletown, Conn., 1968.

———. *New Directions in European Historiography*, rev. ed. Middletown, Conn., 1984.

Iggers, G. G. *Historiography in the Twentieth Century: From Scientific Objectivity to the Postmodernist Challenge*. Hanover, N.H., 1997.

Kelley, D. R. *Versions of History from Antiquity to the Enlightenment*. New Haven, 1991.

Kelley, D. R. *Fortunes of History: Historical Inquiry from Herder to Huizinga*. New Haven, 2003.

Kenyon, J. *The History Men: The Historical Profession in England since the Renaissance*. London, 1983.

Kon, I. *Die Geschichtsphilosophie des 20. Jahrhunderts*. 2 vols. Berlin (East), 1964.

Koselleck, R. *Futures Past: On the Semantics of Historical Time*. Cambridge, Mass., 1985.

Kozicki, H., ed. *Western and Russian Historiography*. New York, 1993.

———, ed. *Developments in Modern Historiography*. New York, 1993.

Kraus, M., and Joyce, D. D. *The Writing of American History*. Rev. ed. Norman, Okla., 1985.

Lefebvre, G. *La Naissance de l'historiographie moderne*. Paris, 1971.

Lessing, T. *Geschichte als Sinngebung des Sinnlosen oder die Geburt der Geschichte aus dem Mythos*. Munich, 1921. Reprint Hamburg, 1962.

Loewenberg, B. J. *American History in American Thought: Christopher Columbus to Henry Adams*. New York, 1972.

Löwith, K. *Meaning of History*. Chicago, 1949.

Martin, G. *Past Futures: the Impossible Necessity of History*. Toronto, 2004.

Nash, Ronald, ed. *Ideas of History.* 2 vols. New York, 1969.

Ritter, H. *Dictionary of Concepts in History.* Westport, Conn., 1986.

Roehner, B. and T. Syme. *Pattern and Repertoire in History.* Cambridge, 2002.

Schulin, E. *Traditionskritik und Rekonstruktionsversuch. Studien zur Entwicklung von Geschichtswissenschaft und historischem Denken.* Göttingen, 1979.

Seliger, H. R. *Kirchengeschichte, Geschichtstheologie, Geschichtswissenschaft.* Düsseldorf, 1981.

Shotwell, J. T. *The History of History.* New York, 1939.

Srbik, H. Ritter von. *Geist und Geschichte vom deutschen Humanismus bis zur Gegenwart.* 2 vols. Munich, 1950–51.

Stern, Fritz, ed. *The Varieties of History.* New York, 1956.

Thompson, J. W. *A History of Historical Writing.* 2 vols. New York, 1942.

Tucker, A. *Our Knowledge of the Past: A Philosophy of Historiography.* Cambridge, Engl., 2004.

Van Tassel, D. D. *Recording America's Past.* Chicago, 1960.

*Others*

Aron, R. *Introduction to the Philosophy of History.* Boston, 1962.

Barzun, J. *Clio and the Doctors: Psychohistory, Quanto-history and History.* Chicago, 1974.

Bebbington, D. W. *Patterns in History. A Christian View.* Downers Grove, 1979.

Butterfield, Sir H. *Man on His Past.* Cambridge, 1955.

———. *The Whig Interpretation of History.* New York, 1965.

———. *The Origins of History.* New York, 1981.

Cairns, G. E. *Philosophies of History: Meeting of East and West in Cycle-Pattern Theories of History.* New York, 1962.

Carr, E. H. *What Is History?* New York, 1967.

Coleman, J. *Ancient and Medieval Memories: Studies in the Reconstruction of the Past.* Cambridge, Engl., 1992.

Dirlik, D., V. Bahl, and P. Gran. *History After the Three Worlds: Post-Eurocentric Historiography.* Lanham, Md., 2000.

Elton, G. R. *Future of the Past.* Cambridge, 1968.

Fischer, D. H. *Historians' Fallacies: Toward a Logic of Historical Thought.* New York, 1970.

Gay, P. *Style in History.* New York, 1974.

Gilbert, A. N., ed. *In Search of a Meaningful Past.* Boston, 1971.

Halperin, S. W., ed. *Essays in Modern European Historiography.* Chicago, 1970.

Hamerow, T. *Reflections on History and Historians.* Madison, Wis., 1987.

*History and the Concept of Time.* Studies in the Philosophy of History. *HT,* Beiheft 6 (1966).

Kinzig, W, V. Leppin, and G. Wartenberg, eds. *Historiography and Theologie.* Leipzig, 2004.

Kirn, P. *Das Bild des Menschen in der Geschichtsschreibung von Polybius bis Ranke.* Göttingen, 1956.

Küttler, W., Rüsen, J., and Schulin, E. *Geschichtsdiskurs.* Vol. 1: *Grundlagen der Methoden und Historiographiegeschichte.* Frankfurt a.M., 1993.

Lutz, H. and Rüsen, J. *Formen der Geschichtsschreibung.* Munich, 1982; Chicago, 2001.

Marrou, H. I. *The Meaning of History.* Trans. R. J. Olsen. Dublin, 1966.

Mazlish, B. *The Riddle of History.* New York, 1966.

Momigliano, A. *Essays in Ancient and Modern Historiography.* Oxford, 1977.

Muller, H. J. *The Uses of the Past.* New York, 1952.

Nadel, G. H., ed. *Studies in the Philosophy of History.* New York, 1960.

———. "Philosophy of History before Historicism," *HT* 3 (1964):291–315.

Nisbet, R. A. *Social Change and History: Aspects of Western Theory of Development.* New York, 1969.

Patrides, C. A. *The Grand Design of God: The Literary Form of the Christian View of History.* Toronto, 1972.

Randa, A., ed. *Mensch und Weltgeschichte.* Salzburg-Munich, 1969.

Rapoport-Albert, A., ed. *Essays in Jewish Historiography.* HT Beiheft 27 (1988).

Rüsen, J. *Zeit und Sinn. Strategien historischen Denkens.* Frankfurt a.M., 1990.

Stern, A. *Geschichtsphilosophie und Wertproblem.* Basel, 1967.

Tillinghast, P. E. *Th Specious Past.* Reading, Mass., 1972.

Tosh, J. *Pursuit of History: Aims, Methods and New Directions in the Study of Modern History.* London, 2000.

Trompf, G. W. *The Idea of Historical Recurrence in Western Thought.* Los Angeles, 1979.

Wang, Q. E. and Georg Iggers. *Turning Points in Historiography: A Cross-cultural Perspective.* Rochester, N.Y. 2002.

Wehler, H. U., ed. *Deutsche Historiker.* 9 vols. Göttingen, 1971–82.

Whitrow, C. J. *Time in History. View of Time from Prehistory to the Present.* Oxford, 1988.

Wilcox, D. F. *The Measure of Times Past: Pre-Newtonian Chronologies and the Rhetoric of Relative Time.* Chicago, 1987.

Woodward, E. L. *British Historians.* London, 1943.

## Ancient Historiography—General Works

Breebart, A. B. *Clio and Antiquity: History and Historiography of the Greek and Roman World.* Hilversum, 1987.

Burstein, S. et al. *Ancient History: Recent Work and New Directions.* Claremont, Cal., 1997.

Canfora, L. *Teoria e tecnica della storiografia classica.* Bari, 1974.

Dentan, R. C. *The Idea of History in the Ancient Near East.* New Haven, 1955.

Dodds, E. R. *The Ancient Concept of Progress.* Oxford, 1973.

Edelstein, L. *The Idea of Progress in Classical Antiquity.* Baltimore, 1967.

Finley, M. I. *Ancient History: Evidence and Models.* New York, 1986.

Fornara, C. W. *The Nature of History in Ancient Greece and Rome.* Berkeley, Calif., 1983.

Gentili, B., and C. Giovanni. *History and Biography in Ancient Thought.* Translated by David Murray and Leonard Murray. Amsterdam, 1988.

Grant, M. *The Ancient Historians.* New York, 1970.

Ishida, T. *History and Historical Writing in Ancient Israel: Studies in Biblical Historiography.* Leiden, 1999.

Lemche, N. P. *Israelites in History and Tradition.* London, 1998.

Lemche, N. P. *Historical Dictionary of Ancient Israel.* Lanham, Md, 2004.

Marincola, J. *Authority and Tradition in Ancient Historiography.* Cambridge, 1997.

Momigliano, A. *The Classical Foundations of Modern Historiography.* Berkeley, Calif., 1990.

Morley, Neville. *Ancient History: Key Themes and Approaches.* London, 2000.

Preller, H. *Geschichte der Historiographie.* Vol. 1, *Altertum.* Aalen, 1967.

Shuttleworth, K. C., ed. *Limits of Ancient Historiography: Genre and Narrative in Ancient Historical Texts.* Leiden, 1999.

Smelik, K, A. D. *Converting the Past: Studies in Ancient Israelite and Moabite Historiography.* Leiden, 1992

Strasburger, H. *Die Wesensbestimmung der Geschichte durch die antike Geschichtsschreibung.* Wiesbaden, 1966.

Usher, S. *The Historians of Greece and Rome.* London, 1969.

Van Seters, J. *In Search of History: Historiography in the Ancient World and the Origin of Biblical History.* New Haven, 1983.

Woodman, A. J. *Rhetoric in Classical Historiography.* London, 1988.

## Greek Historiography

*General*

Austin, N. *The Greek Historians.* New York, 1969.

Brown, T. S. *The Greek Historians.* Lexington, Mass., 1973.

Bury, J. B. *The Ancient Greek Historians.* New York, 1909; reprint, 1958.

De Sanctis, G. *Studi di storia della storiografia greca.* Florence, 1951.

Finley, M. I., ed. *The Greek Historians.* New York, 1959.

Fritz, K. von. *Die Griechische Geschichtsschreibung.* Vol. I (text and notes). Berlin, 1967.

Jacoby, F. *Griechische Historiker.* Stuttgart, 1956.

Luce, T. J. *The Greek Historians.* London, 1997.

Meister, K. *Griechische Geschichtsschreibung von den Anfängen bis zum Ende des Hellenismus.* Stuttgart, 1990.

Momigliano, A. *The Development of Greek Biography.* Cambridge, Mass., 1971.

———. "Greek Historiography," *HT* 17 (1978):1–20.

Romilly, J. de. *The Rise and Fall of States According to Greek Authors.* Jerome Lectures, no. 11. Ann Arbor, 1977.

Shrimpton, G. S. *History and Memory in Ancient Greece.* Montreal, 1997.

Toynbee, A. J., ed. *Greek Historical Thought.* London, 1950.

Walbank, F. W. "The Historians of Greek Sicily," *Kokalos* 14–15 (1968):476–98.

*Early Greek Historiography*

Accame, S. "La concezione del tempo nell'età omerica e arcaica," *Rivista di filologia,* n.s., 39 (1961):359–94.

Chatelet, F. *La naissance de l'histoire.* 2 vols. Paris, 1973.

Forsdyke, J. *Greece before Homer: Ancient Chronology and Mythology.* New York, 1964.

Jacoby, F. *Atthis: The Local Chronicles of Ancient Athens.* Oxford, 1949.

Latte, K. "Die Anfänge der griechischen Geschichtsschreibung." *Entretiens Hardt,* 4" *Histoire et historiens dans l'antiquité.* Geneva, 1956, pp. 3–37.

Momigliano, A. D. "Time in Ancient Historiography," *HT,* Beiheft 6 (1966), pp. 1–23.

Page, D. L. *History and the Homeric Iliad.* Berkeley, 1959.

Pearson, L. *The Local Historians of Attica.* Lancaster, Pa., 1942.

———. *Early Ionian Historians.* Oxford, 1939.

Schadewaldt, W. "Die Anfänge der Geschichtsschreibung bei den Griechen." *Die Antike* 10 (1934):144–68.

Snell, B. "Homer und die Entstehung des geschichtlichen Bewusstseins bei den Griechen." *Varia Variorum.* Munster-Cologne, 1952, pp. 2–12.

Starr, C. G. *The Awakening of the Greek Historical Spirit.* New York, 1958.

Wardman, A. E. "Myth in Greek Historiography." *Hi,* 9 (1960):403–46.

*The Era of City States*

Herodotus

"Erodoto." *Storia della Storiografia.* Numero speciale (1985).

Gould, J. *Herodotus.* London, 1989.

Hartog, F., ed. *The Mirror of Herodotus. The Representation of the Other in the Writing of History.* Berkeley, 1988.

Hunter, V. *Past and Process in Herodotus and Thucydides.* Princeton, N.J., 1982.

Lang, M. L. *Herodotean Narrative and Discourse.* Cambridge, Mass., 1984.

Lateiner, D. *The Historical Method of Herodotus.* Toronto, 1989.

Legrand, Ph.-E. *Herodote.* 2d ed. Paris, 1955.

Marg, W., ed. *Herodot. WDF,* 26. Darmstadt, 1965.

Myres, J. L. *Herodotus, Father of History.* Oxford, 1953.

Romm, J. *Herodotus.* Berkeley, Cal., 1998.

Selincourt, A. de. *The World of Herodotus.* Boston-Toronto, 1962.

Waters, K. H. *Herodotus, the Historian.* Norman, Okla., 1985.

Thucydides

Allison, J. W. *Word and Concept in Thucydides.* Atlanta, Ga.,1997.

Crane, G. *The Blinded Eye: Thucydides and the Written Word.* Lanham, Md., 1996.

Cochrane, C. N. *Thucydides and the Science of History.* Oxford, 1929; reprint, New York, 1965.

Connor, W. R. *Thucydides.* Princeton, N.J., 1984.

Cornford, F. M. *Thucydides Mythistoricus.* London, 1907; reprint, 1965.

Dover, K. J. *Thucydides.* Oxford, 1973.

Finley, J. W., Jr. *Thucydides.* Cambridge, Mass., 1942; reprint, Ann Arbor, 1963.

———. *Three Essays on Thucydides.* Cambridge, Mass., 1967.

Gomme, A. W. *A Historical Commentary on Thucydides.* 4 vols. Vol. 4 revised and edited by A. Andrewes and K. J. Dover. Oxford, 1945, 70.

Grundy, G. B. *Thucydides and the History of His Age.* 2 vols. Vol. 1, 2d ed. Oxford, 1948.

Herter, H., ed. *Thukydides. WDF,* 98. Darmstadt, 1968.

Hornblower, S. *Thucydides.* London, 1987.

Hunter, V. *Thucydides: The Artful Reporter.* Toronto, 1973.

Rawlings, H. R. *The Structure of Thucydides' History.* Princeton, N.J., 1981.
Romilly, J. de. *Thucydides and Athenian Imperialism.* Trans. P. Thody. New York-Oxford, 1963.

*Other Topics*
Anderson, J. K. *Xenophon.* New York, 1974.
Bowie, E. L. "Greeks and Their Past in the Second Sophistic." *Past and Present* 46 (1970):3–41.
Bruce, I. A. F. *An Historical Commentary on the Hellenica Oxyrhynchia.* Cambridge, 1967.
———. "Theopompus and Classical Scholarship." *HT* 9 (1970):86–109.
Champion, C. B. *Cultural Politics in Polybius's Histories.* Berkeley, Cal., 2004.
Connor, W. R. *Theopompus and Fifth Century Athens.* Washington, D.C., 1968.
Delebecque, F. *Essai sur la Vie de Xenophon.* Paris, 1957.
Dillery, J. D. *Xenophon and the History of his Times.* London, 1995.
Flower, M. I. *Theopompus of Chios: History and Rhetoric in the Fourth Century B.C.* Oxford, 1994.
Fritz, K. von. *Aristotle's Contribution to the Practice and Theory of Historiography.* Berkeley, 1958.
Gigante, M. *Le Elleniche di Ossirinco.* Rome, 1949.
Gray, V. J. *The Character of Xenophon's Hellenica.* Baltimore, 1989.
Henry, R. *Ctesias: La Perse, L'Inde: Les Sommaires de Photius.* Brussels, 1947.
———. *Greek Historical Writing: A Historiographical Essay Based on Xenophon's Hellenica.* Chicago, 1967.
Nickel, R. *Xenophon.* Darmstadt, 1979.
Shrimpton, G. S. *Theopompus the Historian.* Buffalo, N.Y., 1992.
Weil, R. *Aristote et l'Histoire.* Paris, 1960.

*The Periods of Alexander the Great and Hellenism*
Andreotti, R. "Die Weltmonarchie Alexanders des Grossen in Überlieferung und geschichtlicher Wirklichkeit" *S* 8 (1957):120–66.
Baynham, E. *Alexander the Great: The Unique History of Quintus Curtius.* Ann Arbor, 1998.
Brown, T. S. *Timaeus of Tauromenium.* Los Angeles, 1958.
———. *Onesicritus. A Study in Hellenistic Historiography.* Berkeley-Los Angeles, 1949.
Brunt, P. A. *Arrian. Selections.* 2 vols. Cambridge, Mass., 1976–83.
Cartledge, P., P. Garnsey, and F. S. Gruen. *Hellenistic Constructs: Culture, History and Historiography.* Berkeley, Cal., 1997.
Hammond, N. G. L. *Three Historians of Alexander the Great: The So-Called Vulgate Authors, Diodorus, Justin, and Curtius.* New York, 1983.
Meister, K. *Historische Kritik bei Polybios.* Wiesbaden, 1975.
Pearson, L. *The Greek Historians of the West: Timaeus and His Predecessors.* New York, 1960.
———. *The Lost Histories of Alexander the Great.* New York-Oxford, 1960.
Pedech, P. *La méthode historique de Polybe.* Paris, 1964.
Sacks, K. S. *Diodorus and the First Century.* Princeton, 1990.

Sacks, K. *Polybius on the Writing of History.* Berkeley, Calif., 1981.
Schnabel, P. *Berossos und die babylonisch-hellenistische Literatur.* Berlin, 1923; reprint, 1968.
Schwanbeck, E. A. *Megasthenes Indica.* Bonn, 1846; reprint, 1967.
Walbank, F. W. *Aratos of Sicyon.* Cambridge, 1933.
————. *A Historical Commentary on Polybius.* 2 vol. Oxford, 1957–58.

## Roman Historiography

*General*
Burck, E. "Grundzüge römischer Geschichtsauffassung und Geschichtsschreibung." *Geschichte in Wissenschaft und Unterricht* 25 (1974):1–40.
Deininger, J. *Der politische Widerstand gegen Rom in Griechenland.* Berlin, 1971.
Dorey, T. A., ed. *Latin Historians.* New York, 1966.
————. *Latin Biography.* London, 1967.
Fuchs, H. *Der geistige Widerstand gegen Rom in der antiken Welt.* 2d ed. Berlin, 1964.
Kraus, C. S., and A. J. Woodman. *Latin Historians.* Oxford, 1997.
Laistner, M. L. W. *The Greater Roman Historians.* Berkeley, 1947.
Mellor, R. *Roman Historians.* New York, 1999.
Pöschl, V., ed. *Römische Geschichtsschreibung.* WDF 90. Darmstadt, 1969.
Touloumakos, J. *Zum Geschichtsbewusstsein der Griechen in der Zeit der Römischen Herrschaft.* Göttingen, 1971.

*Legendary Rome*
Alfoldi, A. *Die Trojanischen Urahnen der Römer.* Basel, 1957.
Gabbe, E. *Dionysios and the History of Archaic Rome.* Berkeley, 1991.
Galinsky, G. K. *Aeneas, Sicily, and Rome.* Princeton, 1968.
Gelzer, M. "Der Anfang römischer Geschichtsschreibung." *Kleine Schriften,* 3 Wiesbaden, 1964, pp. 93–110.
Gjerstad, E. *Legends and Facts of Early Roman History.* Lund, 1962.
Grant, M. *Roman Myths.* New York, 1971.
Miles, G. B. *Livy: Reconstructing Early Rome.* Ithaca, 1995.
Perret, J. *Les Origines de la légende troyenne.* Paris, 1942.

*Republican Rome*
Astin, A. E. *Cato the Censor.* Oxford, 1978.
Badian, E. "The Early Historians." In *Latin Historians,* ed. T. A. Dorey. London, 1966, chap. 1.
Crake, J. E. A. "The Annals of the Pontifex Maximus." *Classical Philology* 35 (1940):375–86.
Forbe, N. W. *Cato the Censor.* Boston, 1975.
Schröder, W. A. *M. Porcius Cato: Das erste Buch des Origines.* Meisenheim, 1971.
Skutsch, O. *Studia Enniana.* London, 1968.

*The Age of Civil Strife*
Buchner, K. *Sallust.* Heidelberg, 1960.
————. *Cicero.* Heidelberg, 1964.

Earl, D. C. *The Political Thought of Sallust.* Cambridge, 1961.

Henderickson, G. L. "The Memoirs of Rutilius Rufus." *CP* 28 (1933):153–75.

Latte, K. *Sallust.* Darmstadt, 1962.

Pöschl, V., ed. *Sallust.* Darmstadt, 1970.

Syme, R. *Sallust.* Berkeley, Calif., 1964.

Ullman, R. *La Technique des discours dans Salluste, Tite-Live, et Tacite.* Oslo, 1927.

Welwei, K. W. *Römisches Geschichtsdenken in spätrepublikanischer und augusteischer Zeit.* Munich, 1967.

Zimmerer, M. *Der Annalist Qu. Claudius Quadrigarius.* Munich, 1937.

### The Principate

Barrow, R. H. *Plutarch and His Times.* Bloomington, Ind.-London, 1967.

Burck, E. *Wege Zu Livius. WDF* 132. Darmstadt, 1967.

Chaplin, J. D. *Livy's Exemplary History.* Oxford, 2000.

Dorey, T. A., ed. *Livy.* Toronto, 1971.

Gianakaris, C. J. *Plutarch.* New York, 1970.

Hellmann, F. *Livius Interpretationen.* Berlin, 1939.

Kajanto, I. *God and Fate in Livy.* Turku, Finld., 1957.

Levi, M. A. *Plutarco e il V secolo.* Milan, 1955.

Luce, T. J. *Livy: The Composition of His History.* Princeton, 1977.

Russell, D. A. *Plutarch.* London, 1973.

Stadter, P. A. *Plutarch and the Historical Tradition.* London, 1992.

Stübler, G. *Die Religiosität des Livius.* Amsterdam, 1964.

Walsh, P. G. *Livy.* Cambridge, 1961.

Wardman, A. *Plutarch's Lives.* London, 1974.

Willie, G. *Der Aufbau des Livianischen Geschichtswerks.* Amsterdam, 1973.

### The Empire

Avenarius, G. *Lukians Schrift zur Geschichtsschreibung.* Frankfurt am M., 1954.

Blockley, R. C. *The Fragmentary Classicising Historians of the Later Roman Empire: Eunapius, Olympiodorus, Priscus, and Malchus.* Liverpool, Engl., 1981.

Brugnoli, G. *Studi Suetoniani.* Lecce, 1968.

Büchner, K. *Publius Cornelius Tacitus—Die Historischen Versuche.* Stuttgart, 1963.

Croke, B., and A. M. Emmett, eds. *History and Historians in Late Antiquity.* New York, 1983.

Dorey, T. A., ed. *Tacitus.* New York, 1969.

Elliott, T. G. *Ammianus Marcellinus and Fourth Century History.* Sarasota, Fla., 1983.

Flach, D. *Tacitus in der Tradition der antiken Geschichtsschreibung.* Göttingen, 1973.

Goodyear, F. R. D. *Tacitus, Greece, and Rome.* New Surveys in the Classics, no. 4. Oxford, 1970.

Häussler, R. *Tacitus und das historische Bewusstsein.* Heidelberg, 1965.

Homeyer, H. *Lukian—Wie man Geschichte schreiben soll.* Munich, 1965.

MacCulloch, H. Y., Jr. *Narrative Cause in the Annals of Tacitus.* Koenigstein, 1984.

Martin, R. *Tacitus.* Berkeley-Los Angeles, 1981.

Millar, F. *A Study of Cassius Dio.* Oxford, 1964.

Mouchova, B. *Studie zu Kaiserbiographien Suetons.* Prague, 1968.

O'Gorman, Ellen. *Irony and Misreading in the Annals of Tacitus.* Cambridge, Engl., 2000.

Pöschl, V., ed. *Tacitus. WDF* 97. Darmstadt, 1969.

Stadter, P. A. *Arrian of Nicomedia*. Chapel Hill, N.C., 1980.

Steidle, W. *Sueton und die antike Biographie*. Munich, 1951.

Strasburger, H. "Poseidonios and the Problems of the Roman Empire." *JRS* 55 (1965):40–53.

Swain, J. B. "The Theory of the Four Monarchies: Opposition History under the Roman Empire." *CP* 35 (1940):1–21.

Syme, Sir R. *Tacitus*. 2 vols. Oxford, 1958.

———. *Ammianus and the Historia Augusta*. Oxford, 1968.

———. *The Historia Augusta*. Bonn, 1971.

Thompson, E. A. *The Historical Work of Ammianus Marcellinus*. Cambridge, 1947.

Walker, B. *The Annals of Tacitus*. Manchester, 1960.

Wallace-Hadrill, A. *Suetonius: The Scholar and His Caesars*. New Haven, 1984.

Woodman, A. J. and T. J. Luce, eds. *Tacitus and the Tacitean Tradition*. Princeton, 1993.

Woodman, A. J. *Tacitus Reviewed*. Oxford, 1998.

# Medieval Historiography

*General*

Balzani, U. *Early Chroniclers of Europe: Italy*. London, 1883.

Boehm, L. *Der wissenschaftstheoretische Ort der historia im früheren Mittelalter*. Munich, 1965.

Borst, A. *Geschichte an mittelalterlichen Universitäten*. Konstanz, 1969.

Boyce, G. C., comp. and ed. *Literature of Medieval History 1930–1975: A Supplement to Louis Paetow's A Guide to the Study of Medieval History*. 5 vols. Foreword by Paul Meyvaert. Millwoods, N.Y., and Cambridge, Mass., 1981.

Brandt, W. J. *The Shape of Medieval History*. New Haven, 1966.

Breisach, E., ed. *Classical Rhetoric and Medieval Historiography*. Kalamazoo, 1985.

Brincken, A-D. Van den. *Studien zur lateinischen Weltchronistik bis in das Zeitalter Ottos von Freising*. Dusseldorf, 1957.

———. *Die Lateinische Weltchronistik*. Munich, 1969.

Büdinger, M. *Die Universalhistorie im Mittelalter*. Vienna, 1900.

Bulst, N. and J.-P. Genet, eds. *Medieval Lives and the Historian. Studies in Medieval Prosopography*. Kalamazoo, 1986.

Caenegem, R. C. Van, and Ganshof, F. L. *Guide to the Sources of Medieval History*. New York, 1978.

Cantor, N. *Inventing the Middle Ages: The Lives, Works, and Ideas of the Great Medievalists of the Twentieth Century*. New York, 1991.

Cognasso, F. "Storiografia medievale." In *Questioni di storia medioevale*, ed. E. Rota. Milan, n.d., pp. 785–836.

Dahmus, J. *Seven Medieval Historians*. Chicago, 1981.

Damico, H. and J. R. Zavadil, eds. *Medieval Scholarship: Biographical Studies on the Formation of a Discipline*. New York, 1995.

David, D. C. "American Historiography of the Middle Ages, 1884–1934" *Speculum* 1935 (10):125–37.

Dübler, C. E. *Geschichtsschreibung im spanischen Mittelalter*. Bercelona, 1943.

Engen, J. van. "The Christian Middle Ages as an Historiographical Problem." *AHR,* 91/3 (June 1986):519–52.

Galbraith, V. H. *Historical Research in Medieval England.* London, 1951.

Given-Wilson, C. *Chronicles: The Writing of History in Medieval England.* London, 2004.

Goez, W. *Translatio Imperii. Ein Beitrag zur Geschichte des Geschichtsdenkens und der politischen Theorien im Mittelalter.* Tübingen, 1958.

Gransden, A. *Historical Writing in England, c. 550–c. 1307.* London, 1974.

Grundmann, H. *Geschichtsschreibung im Mittelalter.* Göttingen, 1965.

Guenée, B. "Histoires, Annales, Chroniques." *Annales: Economies, Sociétés, Civilisations* 28 (1972):997–1016.

———. *Histoire et Culture historique dans l'Occident médiéval.* Paris, 1980.

Haskins, C. *The Renaissance of the Twelfth Century.* Cambridge, Mass., 1927.

Hen, Y. and M. Innes, eds. *The Uses of the Past in the Early Middle Ages.* Cambridge, Engl., 2000.

Holdsworth, C., and T. P. Wiseman, eds. *The Inheritance of Historiography, 350–900.* Exeter, England, 1986.

Huizinga, J. *The Waning of the Middle Ages.* London, 1924.

Lacroix, B. *L'Historien au Moyen Age.* Montreal, 1971.

Lammers, W., ed. *Geschichtsdenken und Geschichtsbild im Mittelalter.* Darmstadt, 1965.

Löwe, H. *Von Theoderich dem Grossen zu Karl dem Grossen. Das Werden des Abendlandes im Geschichtsbild des frühen Mittelalters.* Darmstadt, 1956.

Morgan, D. O., ed. *Medieval Historical Writing in the Christian and Islamic Worlds.* London, 1982.

Oman, C. W. C. *History of the Art of War in the Middle Ages.* 2nd ed., 2 vols. New York, 1924.

Patze, H., ed. *Geschichtsschreibung und Geschichtsbewusstsein im Mittelalter,* 1987.

Scharer, A. and G. Scheibelreiter, eds. *Historiographie im frühen Mittelalter.* Vienna, 1994.

Smalley, B. *Historians in the Middle Ages.* London, 1974.

Southern, R. W. "Aspects of the European Tradition of Historical Writing." *TRHS* 20:173–96; 21:159–79; 22:159–80; 23;243–63.

Spiegel, G. M. *The Past as Text: The Theory and Practice of Medieval Historiography.* Baltimore, 1997.

Sterns, I. *The Greater Medieval Historians: An Interpretation and a Bibliography.* Lanham, Md, 1980.

*(La) storiografia altomedievale.* Settimane di studio del Centro italiano di studi sull'alto medioevo 17. Spoleto, 1970.

Stuard, S. M., ed. *Women in Medieval History and Historiography.* Philadelphia, 1987.

Van Engen, J. *The Past and the Future of Medieval Studies.* South Bend, Ind., 1994.

van Houts, E. *Memory and Gender in Medieval Europe, 900–1200.* Toronto, 1999.

Voss, J. *Das Mittelalter Im Historischen Denken Frankreichs.* Munich, 1972.

Wallace-Hadrill, J. M., ed. *The Writing of History in the Middle Ages.* Oxford, 1981.

*Early Christian Historiography*

Amari, G. *Il concetto di storia in San Agostino.* Rome, 1950.

Brincken, A-D. v.d. "Weltären." *Archiv für Kulturgeschichte.* 39 (1957):133–49.

Campenhausen, H. v. "Die Entstehung der Heilsgeschichte. Der Aufbau des christlichen Geschichtsbildes in der Theologie des ersten und zweiten Jahrhunderts." *S* 21 (1970):189–212.

Chesnut, G. F. *The First Christian Histories: Eusebius, Socrates, Sozomen, Theodoret, and Evagrius.* Paris, 1977.

Cullman, O. *Christ and Time: The Primitive Christian Conception of Time and History.* Trans. F. V. Filson. London, 1962.

Foakes-Jackson, F. J. *Eusebius Pamphili, Bishop of Caesarea in Palestine and First Christian Historian.* Cambridge, 1933.

Gamble, W. M. T. "Orosius." In P. Guilday, ed., *Church Historians.* New York, 1926.

Geis, R. G. "Das Geschichtsbild des Talmud." *S* 6 (1955):119.

Gelzer, H. *Sextus Julius Afrikanus und die byzantinische Chronographie.* 2 vols. Leipzig, 1880–98.

Goetz, H-W. *Die Geschichtstheologie des Orosius.* Darmstadt, 1980.

Guthrie, H. H., Jr. *God and History in the Old Testament.* Greenwich, Conn., 1960.

Lacroix, B. *Orose et ses idées.* Montreal, 1965.

Loewenich, W. v. *Augustin und das christliche Geschichtsdenken.* Munich, 1947.

Markus, R. A. *From Augustine to Gregory the Great: History and Christianity in the Middle Ages.* London, 1983.

Marrou, H. I. *Time and Timeliness.* Trans. by V. Nevile. New York, 1969.

Milburn, R. L. P. *Early Christian Interpretations of History.* New York, 1954.

Momigliano, A. "Pagan and Christian Historiography in the Fourth Century A.D." In *The Conflict between Paganism and Christianity in the Fourth Century.* Oxford, 1963.

Mommsen, Th. "Augustine and the Christian Idea of Progress: The Background of the City of God." *JHI* 12 (1951):346.

Mosshammer, A. *The Chronicle of Eusebius and Greek Chronographic Tradition.* Lewisburg, Pa., 1979.

Patterson, L. G. *God and History in Early Christian Thought.* New York, 1967.

Pelikan, J. *The Mystery of Continuity: Time and History, Memory and Eternity in the Thought of Saint Augustine.* Charlottesville, Va., 1986.

Ruotolo, G. *La filosofia della storia e la città di Dio.* 2d ed. Rome, 1950.

Schmidt, "Aetates mundi. Die Weltalter als Gliederungsprinzip der Geschichte." *ZKG* 67 (1956):288–317.

Wallace-Hadrill, D. S., *Eusebius of Caesarea.* London, 1960.

*The Fusion Period*

### Goths

Baar, P. A. van den. *Die kirchliche Lehre der translatio imperii Romani bis zur Mitte des 13. Jahrhunderts.* Rome, 1956.

Bassett, P. M. "The Use of History in the *Chronicon* of Isidore of Seville." *HT* 15 (1976):278–92.

Borst, A. "Das Bild der Geschichte in der Enzyklopädie Isidors von Sevilla." *DA* 22 (1966):1–62.

Diesner, H.-J. *Isidore von Sevilla und zeine Zeit.* Stuttgart, 1973.

Messmer, H. *Hispania—Idee und Gotenmythus.* Zurich, 1960.

O'Donnell, J. *Cassiodorus.* Berkeley, 1979.

### Britons and Anglo-Saxons

Bonner, G., ed. *Famulus Christi: Essays in Commemoration of the Thirteenth Century of the Birth of the Venerable Bede.* London, 1976.

Brown, G. *Bede the Venerable.* Boston, 1987.

Duckett, E. S. *Anglo-Saxon Saints and Scholars.* New York, 1947.

Hanning, R. W. *The Vision of History in Early Britain: From Gildas to Geoffrey of Monmouth.* New York-London, 1966.

Hunter, B. P. *The World of Bede.* Cambridge, Engl., 1990.

Jones, C. W. "Bede as Early Medieval Historian." *MH* 4 (1946):26–36.

———. *Saints' Lives and Chronicles in Early England.* Ithaca, N.Y., 1947.

Lapidge, M. ed. *Bede and His World. The Jarrow Lectures.* Aldershot, Engl., 1994.

Lapidge, M., and D. Dumville, eds. *Gildas: New Approaches.* Dover, N.H., 1984.

Levison, W. "Bede as Historian." *Aus rheinischer u. fränkischer Frühzeit.* Düsseldorf, 1948, pp. 347–82.

Lot, F. *Nennius et l'Historia Brittonum.* Paris, 1934.

Markus, R. A. *Bede and the Tradition of Ecclesiastical Historiography.* Jarrow on Tyne, Engl., 1975.

O'Sullivan, T. D. *The De Excidio of Gildas: Its Authenticity and Date.* Columbia Studies in the Classical Tradition, no. 7. Leiden, 1978.

Thompson, A. H., ed. *Bede, His Life, Times, and Writings.* London-Oxford, 1935; reprint, 1966.

Whitelock, D. *The Genuine Asser.* Reading, Eng., 1968.

Franks

Beumann, H. *Ideengeschichtliche Studien zu Einhard und anderen Geschichtsschreibern des früheren Mittelalters.* Darmstadt, 1962.

Gerberding, R. *The Rise of the Carolingians and the Liber Historiae Francorum.* Oxford, 1987.

Goetz, H.-W. *Translatio Imperii. Ein Beitrag zur Geschichte des Geschichtsdenkens und der politischen Theorien im Mittelalter.* Tübingen, 1958.

Krusch, B. "Die Chronicae des sogenannten Fredegar." *Neues Archiv* 7 (1882):421–516.

Löwe, H. "Regino von Prüm und das historische Weltbild der Karolingerzeit." *Rheinische Vierteljahrsblätter* 17 (1952):151–79.

Thurlemann, F. *Der historische Diskurs bei Gregory of Tours: Topoi and Wirklichkeit.* Bern, 1974.

Wehlen, W. v. *Geschichtsschreibung und Staatsauffassung im Zeitalter Ludwigs des Frommen.* Lübeck-Hamburg, 1970.

Werner, K. F. "Zur Arbeitsweise des Regino von Prüm." *Die Welt als Geschichte* 19 (1959):96–116.

*Other Topics*

Delehaye, H. *The Legends of the Saints.* Trans. D. Attwater. 4th ed. New York, 1962. First published as *Les légendes hagiographiques* in Brussels, 1905.

Goffart, W. A. *Barbarians and Romans.* Princeton, 1980.

Goffart, W. A. *The Narrators of Barbarian History (A.D. 550–800): Jordanes, Gregory of Tours, Bede, and Paul the Deacon.* Princeton N.J., 1988.

Poole, R. L. *Chronicles and Annals.* Oxford, 1926.

Wolpers, T. *Die englische Heiligenlegende des Mittelalters.* Tübingen, 1964.

## The Christian Commonwealth

*The Empire*

Bach, E. *Politische Begriffe und Gedanken sächsischer Geschichtsschreiber der Ottonen-zeit.* Osnabrück, 1948.

Beumann, H. *Widukind von Korvei. Untersuchungen zur Geschichtsschreibung und Ideengeschichte des 10. Jahrhunderts.* Weimar, 1950.

———. "Geschichtsbild und Reichsbegriff Hermanns von Reichenau." *AK* 42 (1960):37–60.

Mommsen, T. E., and Morrison, K. F. *Imperial Lives and Letters in the Eleventh Century.* New York-London, 1962.

Schieffer, Th., "Heinrich II. und Konrad II. Die Umprägung des Geschichtsbildes durch die Kirchenreform des 11. Jahrhunderts." *DA* 8 (1951):384–394.

*England*

Chibnall, M. *The World of Orderic Vitalis.* Oxford, 1984.

Fletcher, R. H. *Arthurian Material in the Chronicles, Especially Those of Great Britain and France.* Boston, 1906; reprint, New York, 1958.

Jackson, K. H. "The Arthur of History." In R. S. Loomis, ed., *Arthurian Literature in the Middle Ages: A Collaborative History.* London, 1959.

Keeler, L. *Geoffrey of Monmouth and the Late Latin Chroniclers, 1300–1500.* Berkeley-Los Angeles, 1946.

Pahler, H. *Strukturuntersuchungen zur Historia Regum Britanniae des Geoffrey of Monmouth.* Bonn, 1958.

Partner, N. F. *Serious Entertainments: The Writing of History in Twelfth-Century England.* Chicago, 1977.

Richter, H. *Englische Geschichtsschreiber des 12. Jahrhunderts.* Berlin, 1938.

Schirmer, W. F. *Die frühen Darstellungen des Arthurstoffes.* Cologne-Opladen, 1958.

Southern, R. W. *Saint Anselm and His Biographer.* Cambridge, 1963.

Tatlock, J. S. P. *The Legendary History of Britain: Geoffrey of Monmouth's Historia Regum Britanniae and Its Early Vernacular Versions.* Berkeley-Los Angeles, 1950.

Werner, K. F. "Die Legitimität der Kapetinger und die Entstehung des *Reditus regni Francorum ad stirpem Karoli.*" *Die Welt als Geschichte* 12 (1952):203–25.

Wolter, H. *Ordericus Vitalis. Ein Beitrag zur kluniazensischen Geschichtsschreibung.* Wiesbaden, 1955.

*France*

Boehm, L. "Gedanken zum Frankreich-Bewusstsein im frühen 12. Jahrhundert." *HJ* 74 (1954):681–87.

Kortüm, H.-H. *Richer von Saint-Remi: Studien zu einem Geschichtsschreiber des 10. Jahrhunderts.* Stuttgart, 1985.

Lindheim, H. v. *Rodulfus Glaber.* Leipzig, 1941.

Vogelsang, M. *Rodulfus Glaber, Studien zum Problem der cluniazensischen Geschichts-schreibung.* Diss. Munich, 1962.

*Crusades and Eastward Expansion*

Boase, T. S. R. *Kingdoms and Strongholds of the Crusaders.* London, 1971.

Edgington, S. B. and S. Lambert. *Gendering the Crusades.* New York, 2002.

Erdmann, C. *The Origins of the Idea of Crusade.* Translated by M. W. Baldwin and W. Goffart. Philadelphia, 1977. (German, 1935).

Knoch, P. *Studien zu Albert von Aachen. Der erste Kreuzzug in der deutschen Chronistik,* Stuttgart, 1966.

Larsen, S. *Saxo Grammaticus.* Copenhagen, 1925.

Madden, T. F. *New Concise History of the Crusades.* Lanham, Md., 2005.

Philipp, W. *Ansätze zum geschichtlichen und politischen Denken im Kiewer Russland.* Breslau, 1940.

Runciman, S. *The History of the Crusades.* 3 vols. Cambridge, 1951–55.

Schwinges, R. C. *Kreuzzugsideologie und Toleranz: Studien zu Wilhelm von Tyrus.* Stuttgart, 1977.

*Other Topics*

Brincken, A.-D. v. d. "Die Welt- und Inkarnationsära bei Heimo von St. Jakob. Kritik an der christlichen Zeitrechnung durch Bamberger Komputisten in der ersten Hälfte des 12. Jahrhunderts." *DA* 16 (1960):155–94.

———. "Marianus Scottus. Unter besonderer Berücksichtigung der nicht veröffentlichen Teile seiner Chronik." *DA* 17 (1961):191–238.

Kirn, P. *Aus der Frühzeit des Nationalgefühls. Studien zur deutschen und französischen Geschichte sowie zu den Nationalkämpfen auf den britischen Inseln.* Leipzig, 1943.

Landis, C., E. Gow, E. Van Meter, and D. C. Van Meter, eds. *Apocalyptic Year 1000: Religious Expectation and Social Change, 950–1059.* Oxford, 2003.

## The Period of Consolidation and Accelerating Change (1100–1400)

*General*

Baron, R. "Hugues de Saint-Victor: contribution à un nouvel examen de son oeuvre." *T* 15 (1959):223–97.

Brooke, C. *The Twelfth Century Renaissance.* London, 1969.

Chenu, M. D. "Conscience de l'histoire et théologie zu XII² siècle." *Archives d'histoire doctrinale et littéraire du Moyen Age* 21 (1954):107–33.

Cohn, N. *The Pursuit of the Millennium—Revolutionary Messianism in the Middle Ages and Its Bearing on Modern Totalitarian Movements.* London, 1957.

Damian-Grint, P. *The New Historians of the Twelfth-Century Renaissance: Inventing Vernacular Authority.* Woodbridge, U.K., 1999.

Funkenstein, Amos. *Heilsplan und natürliche Entwicklung. Formen der Gegenwartsbestimmung im Geschichtsdenken des hohen Mittalalters.* Munich, 1965.

Goetz, H.-W. *Hochmittelalterliches Geschichtsbewusstsein im Spiegel nichthistoriographischer Quellen.* Berlin, 1999.

Helbling, H. *Saeculum Humanum. Ansätze zu einem Versuch über spätmittelalterliches Geschichtsdenken.* Schriften des Istituto Italiano per gli studi storici 11. Naples, 1958.

Mierau, H. J., A. Sander-Berke, and B. Studt. *Studien zur Überlieferung der Flores temporum.* Hannover, 1996.

Palmer, J. J. N. *Froissart: Historian.* Totowa, N.J., 1981.

Patz, H., ed. *Geschichtsschreibung und Geschichtsbewusstsein im späten Mittelalter.* Sigmaringen, 1987.

Schmeidler, B. *Italienische Geschichtsschreiber des 12. und 13. Jahrhunderts. Ein Beitrag zur Kulturgeschichte.* Leipzig, 1909.

Southern, R. W. *Medieval Humanism and Other Studies.* Oxford, 1970.

———. "Aspects of the European Tradition of Historical Writing." *TRHS,* 5th ser. 20:173–96; 21:159–79; 22;159–86; 23:243–63.

Spiegel, G. M. *Romancing the Past: The Rise of the Vernacular Prose Historiography in Thirteenth-Century France.* Berkeley, Cal., 1993.

Spörl, J. *Grundformen der hochmittelalterlichen Geschichtsanchauung. Studien zum Weltbild der Geschichtsschreiber des 12. Jahrhunderts.* Munich, 1935.

Töpfer, A. *Das kommende Reich des Friedens. Zur Entwicklung chiliastischer Zukunftshoffnungen im Spätmittelalter.* Berlin, 1964.

*Theologies of History*

Benz, E. *Ecclesia Spiritualis. Kirchenidee und Geschichtstheologie der franziskanischen Reformation.* Stuttgart, 1934; reprint, Darmstadt, 1964.

Bloomfield, M. W. "Joachim of Flora: A Critical Survey of His Canon, Teachings, Sources, Biography and Influence." *T* 13 (1957):248.

Classen, P. *Gerhoch von Reichersberg.* Wiesbaden, 1960.

Fina, K. "Anselm von Havelberg. Untersuchungen zu Kirchen- und Geistesgeschichte des 12. Jahrhunderts," *Analecta Praemonstratensia* 32 (1956):69–101, 193–227; 33 (1957):5–39, 268–301; 34 (1958):13–41.

Goetz, H-W. *Das Geschichtsbild Ottos von Freising.* Cologne, 1984.

Grundmann, H. *Neue Forschungen über Joachim von Fiore.* Marburg, 1950.

Kahles, W. *Geschichte als Liturgie. Die Geschichtstheologie des Rupertus von Deutz.* Münster, 1960.

Kamlah, W. *Apokalypse und Geschichtstheologie. Die mittelalterliche Auslegung der Apokalypse vor Joachim von Fiore.* Berlin, 1935.

Koch, J. "Die Grundlagen der Geschichtsphilosophie Ottos von Freising." In Lammers, *Geschichtsdenken,* pp. 321–49.

Magrassi, M. *Teologia e storia nel pensiero di Ruperto di Deutz.* Rome, 1959.

Petry, R. C. "Three Medieval Chroniclers: Monastic Historiography and biblical Eschatology in Hugh of St. Victor, Otto of Freising, and Ordericus Vitalis." *CH* 34 (1965):282–93.

Schneider, W. A. *Geschichte und Geschichtsphilosophie bei Hugo von St. Victor.* Münster, 1933.

## The Transformation of Medieval Christian Historiography (1350–1750)

*General*

Baker, H. *The Race of Time: Three Lectures on Renaissance Historiography.* Toronto, 1967.

Buch, A. *Das Geschichtsdenken der Renaissance*. Krefeld, 1957.

Buck, A., T. Klaniczay, and S. Németh. *Geschichtsbewusstsein und Geschichtsschreibung in der Renaissance*. Budapest, 1989.

Burckhardt, J. *Die Entstehung der modernen Jahrhundertrechnung*. Göppingen, 1972.

Burke, P. *The Renaissance Sense of the Past*. New York, 1970.

Chiantella, R. *Storiografia e pensiero politico nel Rinascimento*. Turin, 1973.

Cotroneo, G. *I Trattatisti dell' "Ars Historica."* Naples, 1971.

Dickens, A. G., J. M. Tonkin, and K. Powell. *The Reformation in Historical Thought*. Cambridge, Mass., 1985.

Ferguson, W. K. *The Renaissance in Historical Thought: Five Centuries of Interpretation*. Boston, 1948.

Fryde, E. B. *Humanism and Renaissance Historiography*. London, 1983.

Grafton A. *Defenders of the Text in an Age of Science 1450–1800*. Cambridge, Mass., 1991.

Grimm, H. J. *The Reformation in Historical Thought*. Washington D.C., 1967.

Headley, J. M. *Luther's View of Church History*. New Haven, 1963.

Kaegi, W. *Grundformen der Geschichtsschreibung seit dem Mittelalter*. Utrecht, 1948.

Kessler, E. *Theoretiker Humanistischer Geschichtsschreibung*. Munich, 1971.

Klempt, A. *Die Säkularisierung der universalhistorischen Auffassung. Zum Wandel des Geschichtsdenkens im 16. und 17. Jahrhundert*. Göttingen, 1960.

Landfester, R. *Historia Magistra Vitae. Untersuchungen zur humanistischen Geschichtstheorie des 14. bis. 16. Jahrhunderts*. Geneva, 1972.

Momigliano, A. "Ancient History and the Antiquarian." *Studies in Historiography*. New York, 1966.

Mousnier, R., and Pillorget, R. "Contemporary History and Historians of the Sixteenth and Seventeenth Centuries." *Journal of Contemporary History* 3, no. 2 (April 1968):93–109.

Muhlack, U. *Geschichtswissenschaft im Humanismus und in der Aufklärung: Die Vorgeschichte des Historismus*. Munich, 1991.

Popkin, R. H. "The Pre-Adamite Theory in the Renaissance." In *Philosophy and Humanism*, ed. E. P. Mahoney. New York, 1976, pp. 50–69.

Quinones, R. J. *The Renaissance Discovery of Time*. Cambridge, Mass., 1972.

Reynolds, B. R. "Latin Historiography: A Survey, 1400–1600." In *Studies in the Renaissance, II* (1955):7–66.

Schellhase, K. D. *Tacitus in Renaissance Political Thought*. Chicago, 1976.

Seifert, A. *Cognitio historica. Die Geschichte als Namensgeberin der frühneuzeitlichen lichen Empirie*. Berlin, 1976.

Struever, N. S. *The Language of History in the Renaissance*. Princeton, 1970.

*Italy*

Baron, H. *The Crisis of the Early Italian Renaissance*. Rev. 2d ed. Princeton, 1966.

Bertelli, S. *Ribelli, libertini e ortodossi nella storiografia barocca*. Florence, 1973.

Cochrane, E. *Historians and Historiography in the Italian Renaissance*. Chicago, 1981.

Gilbert, F. *Machiavelli and Guicciardini: Politics and History in Sixteenth-Century Florence*. Princeton, N.J., 1965.

Green, L. F. *Chronicle into History: An Essay on the Interpretations of History in Florentine Fourteenth-Century Chronicles*. Cambridge, 1972.

Hay, D. *Flavio Biondo and the Middle Ages.* London, 1959.

Kessler, E. *Petrarca und die Geschichte: Geschichtsschreibung, Rhetorik, Philosophie im Übergang vom Mittelalter zur Neuzeit.* Munich, 1978.

Labalme, P. *Bernardo Giustiniani.* Rome, 1969.

McCuaig, W. *Carlo Sigonio: The Changing World of the Late Renaissance.* Princeton, N.J., 1989.

Pertusi, A. *La storiografia veneziana fino al secolo xvi. Aspetti e problemi.* Florence, 1970.

Phillips, M. *Francesco Guicciardini: The Historian's Craft.* Toronto-Buffalo, 1977.

————. "Machiavelli, Guicciardini and the Tradition of Vernacular Historiography in Florence." *American Historical Review* 84 (1979):86–105.

Pullapilly, C. K. *Caesar Baronius, Counter-Reformation Historian.* Notre Dame, Ind., 1975.

Seigel, J. E. *Rhetoric and Philosophy in Renaissance Humanism.* Princeton, N.J., 1968.

Spini, G. "Historiography: The Art of History in the Italian Counter-Reformation." In *The Late Italian Renaissance,* ed. Eric Cochrane. New York, 1970.

Ullman, B. "Leonardo Bruni and Humanistic Historiography." *Medievalia et Humanistica* 4 (1946):45–61.

Wilcox, D. *The Development of Florentine Humanist Historiography in the Fifteenth Century.* Cambridge, Mass., 1969.

Wooton, D. *Paolo Sarpi: Between Renaissance and Enlightenment.* Cambridge, Engl., 1983.

*German Area*

D'Amico, J. F. *Theory and Practice in Renaissance Textual Criticism: Beatus Rhenanus between Conjecture and History.* Berkeley, 1988.

Grafton, A. *Joseph Scaliger: A Study in Classical Scholarship.* Oxford, 1983.

Joachimsen, P. *Geschichtsauffassung und Geschichtsschreibung in Deutschland unter dem Einfluss des Humanismus.* Berlin-Leipzig, 1910.

Menke-Glücker, E. *Die Geschichtsschreibung der Reformation und der Gegenreformation.* Osterwieck, 1912.

Scherer, E. C. *Geschichte u. Kirchengeschichte an den deutschen Universitäten.* Freiburg-Br., 1927.

Strauss, G. *Historian in an Age of Crisis: Aventinus.* Cambridge, Mass., 1963.

*France*

Bouwsma, W. J. *Concordia Mundi: The Career and Thought of Guillaume Postel.* Cambridge, Mass., 1957.

Brown, J. *The Methodus Ad Facilem Historiarum Cognitionem of Jean Bodin.* Washington, D.C., 1939.

Dubois, C. G. *La Conception de l'histoire en France au 16ᵉ siècle (1560–1610).* Paris, 1977.

Franklin, J. H. *Jean Bodin and the Sixteenth Century Revolution in the Methodology of Law and History.* New York, 1963.

Gundersheimer, W. L. *The Life and Works of Louis le Roy.* Geneva, 1966.

Huppert, G. *The Idea of Perfect History. Historical Erudition and Historical Philosophy in Renaissance France.* Urbana, Ill., 1970.

Kelley, D. *Foundations of Modern Historical Scholarship. Language, Law, and History in the French Renaissance.* New York, 1970.

Kinser, S. *The Works of J.-A. de Thou.* The Hague, 1966.

Kuntz, M. L. *Guillaume Postel.* The Hague, 1981.

Reynolds, E. *Bossuet.* New York, 1963.

*England*

Brooks, C., Kelley, D., and Sharpe, K. "Debate: History, English Law, and the Renaissance." *PP* 72 (August 1976), 133–46.

Dean, L. *Tudor Theories of Historical Writing.* Ann Arbor, 1947.

Ferguson, A. B. *Clio Unbound: Perception of the Social and Cultural Past in Renaissance England.* Duke Monographs in Medieval and Renaissance Studies, no. 2, Durham, N.C., 1979.

Fox, L., ed. *English Historical Scholarship in the Sixteenth and Seventeenth Centuries.* London, 1956.

Fussner, F. S. *The Historical Revolution, English Historical Thought and Writing, 1580–1640.* London, 1962.

———. *Tudor History and the Historians.* New York, 1970.

Hay, D. *Polydore Vergil: Renaissance Historian and Man of Letters.* Oxford, 1952.

Hill, C. *Intellectual Origins of the English Civil War.* Oxford, 1965.

Kelley, D. "History, English Law, and the Renaissance." *PP* 65 (Nov. 1974):24–51.

Kingsford, C. *English Historical Literature in the Fifteenth Century.* Oxford, 1913.

Korshin, P. J., ed. *Studies in Change and Revolution. Aspects of English Intellectual History, 1640–1800.* Menston, Eng., 1972.

Levine, J. M. *Humanism and History: Origins of Modern English Historiography.* Ithaca, NY, 1987.

Macgillivray, R. *Restoration Historians and the English Civil War.* The Hague, 1974.

McKisack, M. *Medieval History in the Tudor Period.* Oxford, 1971.

Levy, F. *Tudor Historical Thought.* San Marino, Calif., 1967.

Pocock, J. *The Ancient Constitution and the Feudal Law.* Cambridge, Mass., 1957.

Preston, J. "English Ecclesiastical Historians and the Problem of Bias, 1559–1742." *JHI* 32 (1971):203–2.

Sharpe, K. M. *Sir Robert Cotton, 1586–1631: History and Politics in Early Modern England.* Oxford 1979.

Trevor-Roper, H. R. *Queen Elisabeth's First Historian: William Camden.* London, 1971.

Trimble, W. "Early Tudor Historiography, 1485–1548." *JHI* 11 (1950):30–41.

Wormald, B. H. G. *Clarendon: Politics, Historiography and Religion, 1640–1660.* Cambridge, Mass., 1951.

Woolf, D. R. *Idea of History in Early Stuart England.* Toronto, 1990.

## The Eighteenth-Century Syntheses

*General*

Anderson, M. S. *Historians and Eighteenth-Century Europe, 1715–1789.* Oxford, 1979.

Berlin, Sir I. *Vico and Herder: Two Studies in the History of Ideas.* New York, 1976.

Black, J. B. *The Art of History: A Study of Four Great Historians of the Eighteenth Century.* New York, 1926; reprint, 1965.

Bury, J. B. *The Idea of Progress. An Inquiry into Its Origin and Growth.* New York, 1932.

Corsano, A. *Bayle, Leibniz e la storia.* Naples, 1971.

Dobbek, W. J. G. *Herders Weltbild. Versuch einer Deutung.* Cologne-Vienna, 1969.

Hammer, K., and Voss, J. *Historische Forschung Im 18. Jahrhundert. Organisation, Zielsetzung, Ergebnisse.* Bonn, 1976.

Hazard, P. *The European Mind. The Critical Years, 1680–1715.* New Haven, 1953.

*L. A. Muratori storiografo. Atti del Convegno internazionale di studi muratoriani, Modena 1972.* Biblioteca dell'edizione del Carteggio di L. A. Muratori 2. Florence, 1975.

Schargo, N. *History in the Encyclopédie.* New York, 1970.

Shaffer, A. H. *The Politics of History: Writing the History of the Revolution, 1783–1815.* Chicago, 1975.

Stromberg, R. "History in the Eighteenth Century." *JHI* 12 (1951):295–305.

Trevor-Roper, H. "The Historical Philosophy of the Enlightenment." *Studies on Voltaire and the Eighteenth Century* 27 (1963):1667–87.

Voller, K. *Die Kirchengeschichtsschreibung der Aufklärung.* Tübingen, 1921.


*French Enlightenment*

Baker, K. M. *Condorcet.* Chicago, 1975.

Brumfitt, J. H. *Voltaire, Historian.* New York, 1968.

Guerci, L. *Condillac Storica: Storica e politica nel "Cours d'études pour l'instruction du Prince de Parme."* Milan, 1978.

Leffler, P. K. "The 'Histoire Raisonnée', 1660–1720: A Pre-Enlightenment Genre." *JHI* 37 (1976):219–40.

Meek, R. *Turgot on Progress, Sociology, and Economics.* Cambridge, mass., 1973.

Vyerberg, H. *Historical Pessimism in the French Enlightenment.* Cambridge, Mass., 1958.

Wade, I. *The Intellectual Origins of the French Enlightenment.* Princeton, 1971.


*The German* Aufklärung

Barnard, F. M. *Johann Gottfried von Herder on Social and Political Culture.* Cambridge, 1969.

Barnes, S. B., and Skerpan, A. A. *Historiography under the Impact of Rationalism and Revolution.* Kent, Ohio, 1952.

Baur, E. *Johann Gottfried Herder.* Stuttgart, 1960.

Bödeker, H. E., et al., eds. *Aufklärung und Geschichte.* Göttingen, 1986.

Booth, W. J. *Interpreting the World: Kant's Philosophy of History and Politics.* Toronto, 1986.

Clark, R. T., Jr. *Herder: His Life and Thought.* Berkeley, 1969.

Despland, M. *Kant on History and Religion.* Montreal-London, 1973.

Engel, J. "Die deutschen Universitäten und die Geschichtswissenschaft." *HZ* 189 (1959):1–378.

Engel-Jánosi, F. *The Growth of German Historicism.* Baltimore, 1944.

*Enlightenment Historiography: Three German Studies.* Beiheft 11. *HT* 1971.

Fürst, F. *August Ludwig von Schlözer, ein deutscher Aufklärer im 18. Jahrhundert.* Heidelberg, 1928.

Galston, W. A. *Kant and the Problem of History.* Chicago, 1975.

Hammerstein, N. *Jus und Historie.* Göttingen, 1972.

Hunger, K. *Die Bedeutung der Universität Göttingen für die Geschichtsforschung am Ausgang des 18. Jahrhunderts.* Berlin, 1933.

Knudsen, J. *Justus Möser and the German Enlightenment.* Cambridge, 1986.

Liebel, H. P. "The Enlightenment and the Rise of Historicism in German Thought." *Eighteenth-Century Studies* 4 (1970):359–85.

Meinecke, F. *Die Entstehung des Historismus.* Munich, 1965.

Paulsen, F. *Geschichte des gelehrten Unterrichts an den deutschen Schulen und Universitäten vom Ausgang des Mittelalters bis zur Gegenwart.* 2 vols., Leipzig, 1885.

Reill, P. *The German Enlightenment and the Rise of Historicism.* Berkeley, 1975.

Sheldon, W. F. *The Intellectual Development of Justus Möser: The Growth of a German Patriot.* Osnabrück, 1970.

Spitz, L. W. "Leibniz's Significance for Historiography." *JHI* 13 (June 1952):333–48.

———. "Natural Law and the Theory of History in Herder." *JHI* 16 (October 1955): 453–75.

Wells, G. A. "Herder's Determinism." *JHI* 19 (January 1958):103–13.

Yovel, Y. *Kant and the Philosophy of History.* Princeton, 1980.

*English and Scottish Historians*

Bongie, L. *David Hume: Prophet of the Counter-revolution.* Oxford, 1965.

Carnochan, W. B. *Gibbon's Solitude: The Inward World of the Historian.* Stanford, Cal., 1987.

Fuglum, P. *Edward Gibbon. His View of Life and Conceptions of History.* Oslo-Oxford, 1953.

Giarrizzo, G. *Edward Gibbon e la cultura europea del settecento.* Naples, 1954.

Gossman, L. *The Empire Unpossess'd.* Cambridge, 1981.

Hale, J. R. *The Evolution of British Historiography: From Bacon to Namier.* Cleveland, 1964.

Jordan, D. P. *Gibbon and His Roman Empire.* Chicago, 1971.

Kramnick, I. "Augustan Politics and English Historiography: The Debate on the English Past, 1730–1735." *HT* 6 (1967):33–56.

Manuel, F. E. *Isaac Newton, Historian.* Cambridge, Mass., 1963.

Norton, D. F., and Popkin, R. H. *David Hume: Philosophical Historian.* New York, 1965.

Peardon, T. *The Transition in English Historical Writing, 1760–1830.* New York, 1933; reprint, New York, 1966.

Porter, R. *Gibbon: Making History.* New York, 1988.

Swain, J. *Edward Gibbon the Historian.* New York, 1966.

Thomson, Mark A. *Some Developments in English Historiography during the Eighteenth Century.* London, 1957.

Voigt, U. *David Hume und das Problem der Geschichte.* Berlin, 1975.

Wexler, V. G. *David Hume and the History of England.* Philadelphia, 1979.

*Vico*

*The Autobiography of Giambattista Vico.* Trans. M. H. Fisch and T. G. Bergin. Ithaca, N.Y., 1944.

Berry, T. M. *The Historical Theory of Giambattista Vico.* Washington, D.C., 1949.

Burke, P. *Vico*. Oxford, Eng., 1985.
Crease, R. *Vico in English: A Bibliography of Writings by and about Vico, 1668–1744*. Atlantic Highlands, N.J., 1978.
Lilla, H. G. B. *Vico: the Making of the Anti-Modern*. Cambridge, Mass., 1993.
Pompa, L. *Vico: A Study of the New Science*. New York, 1975.
Tagliacozzo, G., and White, H. *Giambattista Vico. An International Symposium*. Baltimore, 1969.
Verene, D. P. *Vico's Science of Imagination*. Ithaca, N.Y., 1981.

## The Nineteenth Century: Progress and Nation (1790s to 1880s)

*General*
Bann, S. *The Clothing of Clio: A Study of the Representation of History in Nineteenth-Century Britain and France*. New York, 1984.
Brancato, F. *Storia e Storiografia nell' età del Romanticismo*. Palermo, 1970.
Gooch, G. P. *History and Historians in the Nineteenth Century*. London, 1913; rev. ed., 1952.
Hamilton, P. *Historicism*. London, 1996.
Hünermann, P. *Der Durchbruch des Geschichtlichen Denkens im 19. Jahrhundert*. Freiburg-Vienna, 1967.
Knowles, D. *Great Historical Enterprises: Problems in Monastic History*. Toronto-New York, 1963.
Mandelbaum, M. *History, Man, and Reason: A Study in Nineteenth-Century Thought*. Baltimore, 1971.
McClelland, C. E. *The German Historians and England. A Study in Nineteenth-Century Views*. Cambridge, 1971.
Trevor-Roper, H. R. *The Romantic Movement and the Study of History*. London, 1969.
White, H. V. *Metahistory: The Historical Imagination in Nineteenth-Century Europe*. Baltimore, 1973.


*German Area*
Blanke, H. W., and J. Rüsen, eds. *Von der Aufklärung zum Historismus: Zum Strukturwandel des historischen Denkens*. Paderborn, 1984.
Dotterweich, V. *Heinrich von Sybel: Geschichtswissenschaft in politischer Absicht (1817–1861)*. Göttingen, 1978.
Guilland, A. *Modern Germany and Her Historians*. London, 1915.
Krieger, L. *Ranke: The Meaning of History*. Chicago, 1977.
Laue, T. H. v. *Leopold Ranke, The Formative Years*. Princeton, 1950.
Mommsen, W., ed. *Leopold von Ranke und die Moderne Geschichtswissenschaft*. Stuttgart, 1988.
Southard, R. *Droysen and the Prussian School of History*. Lexington, Ky., 1995.
Spieler, K-H. *Untersuchungen zu Johann Gustav Droysens "Historik."* Berlin, 1970.
Wilkins, B. T. *Hegel's Philosophy of History*. Ithaca, N.Y., 1974.
Wucher, A. *Theodor Mommsen. Geschichtsschreibung und Politik*. 2d ed. Göttingen, 1969.
Ziolkowski, T. *Clio the Romantic Muse: Historicizing the Faculties in Germany*. Ithaca, NY, 2004.

*England*
Ben-Israel, H. *English Historians on the French Revolution.* Cambridge, 1968.
Burrow, J. W. *A Liberal Descent.* Cambridge, 1981.
Clive, J. *Macaulay: The Shaping of the Historian.* New York, 1973.
Culler, A. D. *The Victorian Mirror of History.* New Haven, 1985.
Huth, A. H. *The Life and Writings of Henry Thomas Buckle.* 2 vols. New York, 1880.
Jann, R. *The Art and Science of Victorian History.* Columbus, Ohio, 1985.
Parker, C. *The English Historical Tradition since 1850.* Edinburgh, 1990.
Wormell, D. *Sir John Seeley and the Uses of History.* New York, 1980.
Young, L. M. *Thomas Carlyle and the Art of History.* Philadelphia, 1939; reprint, 1971.

*France*
Baret-Kriegel, B. *Les historiens et la monarchie.* 4 vols. Paris, 1988.
Becher, U. A. J. *Geschichtsinteresse und historischer Diskurs: Ein Beitrag zur Geschichte der französischen Geschichtswissenschaft im 19. Jahrhundert.* Wiesbaden, 1986.
Boer, P den. *History as a Profession: The Study of History in France, 1818–1914.* Translated by Arnold J. Pomerans. Princeton, N. J., 1998.
Burton, J. K. *Napoleon and Clio: Historical Writing, Teaching, and Thinking during the First Empire.* Durham, N.C., 1979.
Campbell, S. L. *The Second Empire Revisited. A Study in French Historiography.* New Brunswick, N.J., 1978.
Clark, T. N. *Prophets and Patrons: The French University and the Emergence of the Social Sciences.* Cambridge, Mass., 1973.
Crossley, C. *Edgar Quinet, 1803–1875.* Lexington, Ky., 1983.
Hartog, F. *Le XIXe siecle et l'histoire: le cas Fustel de Coulanges.* Paris, 1988.
Herrick, J. *The Historical Thought of Fustel de Coulanges.* Washington, D.C., 1954.
Keylor, W. R. *Academy and Community: The Foundation of the French Historical Profession.* Cambridge, Mass., 1975.
Loubere, L. A. "Louis Blanc's Philosophy of History." *JHI* 17 (1956):70–88.
Mellon, S. *The Political Uses of History.* Stanford, Calif., 1958.
Mitzman, A. *Michelet, Historian: Rebirth and Romanticism in Nineteenth-Century France.* New Haven, 1990.
O'Connor, Sister M. C. *The Historical Thought of François Guizot.* Washington, D.C., 1955.
Orr, L. *Headless History: Nineteenth-Century French Historiography of the Revolution.* Ithaca, N.Y., 1990.
Smithson, R. N. *Augustin Thierry: Social and Political Consciousness in the Evolution of a Historical Method.* Geneva, 1972.
Stadler, P. *Geschichtsschreibung und historisches Denken in Frankreich, 1789–1871.* Zurich, 1958.
Walch, J. *Les Maitres de l'Histoire: Augustin Thierry, Mignet, Guizot, Thiers, Michelet, Edgar Quinet.* Paris, 1986.

*United States*
Bass, H. J., ed. *The State of American History.* Chicago, 1970.
Bellot, H. H. *American History and American Historians.* Norman, Okla., 1952.

Calcott, G. H. *History in the United States, 1800–1860; Its Practice and Purpose.* Baltimore, 1970.

Cooke, J. E. *Frederic Bancroft, Historian.* Norman, Okla., 1957.

Cruden, R. *James Ford Rhodes.* Cleveland, 1966.

Emerson, D. E. "Hildreth, Draper, and Scientific History." In *Historiography and Urbanization: Essays in American History in Honor of W. Stull Holt,* ed. E. F. Goldman. Baltimore, 1941, pp. 139–70.

Garraty, J. *Interpreting American History: Conversations with Historians.* New York, 1970.

Handlin, L. *George Bancroft: The Intellectual as Democrat.* New York, 1984.

Higby, C. P. *John Lothrop Motley.* New York, 1939.

Higham, J. *The Reconstruction of American History.* New York, 1965.

Higham, J., Krieger, L., and Gilbert, F. *History.* Englewood Cliffs, N.J., 1965.

Holt, W. S., ed. *Historical Scholarship in the United States, 1876–1901.* Baltimore, 1938.

Howe, M. A. D. *James Ford Rhodes: American Historian.* New York, 1929.

Levin, D. *History as Romantic Art.* New York, 1967.

Loewenberg, B. J. *American History in American Thought.* New York, 1972.

Nye, R. B. *George Bancroft, A Brahmin Rebel.* New York, 1944.

Pease, O. A. *Parkman's History: The Historian as a Literary Artist.* New Haven, 1953.

Vitzthum, R. C. *The American Compromise: Theme and Method in the Histories of Bancroft, Parkman, and Adams.* Norman, Okla., 1974.

Wade, M. *Francis Parkman: Heroic Historian.* New York, 1942.

## Modern Historiography: 1880 to the Present

*Surveys*

Burke, P., ed. *New Perspectives on Historical Writing.* University Park, Pa., 1991.

Iggers, G. G. *Geschichtswissenschaft im 20. Jahrhundert.* Göttingen, 1993.

Iggers, G. G., and Parker, H. T., eds. *International Handbook of Historical Studies. Contemporary Research and Theory.* Westport, Conn., 1979.

Meinecke, F. *Historism.* Translated by Anderson (rev. by H. D. Schmidt). London, 1972.

Raab, T. and Rotberg, T., eds. *The New History: The 1980s and Beyond. Studies in Interdisciplinary History.* Princeton, N. J., 1982.

Schlatter, R., ed. *Recent Views on British History: Essays on Historical Writing since 1966.* New Brunswick, N.J., 1984.

Schnadelbach, H. *Geschichtsphilosophie nach Hegel. Die Probleme des Historismus.* Freiburg im Br., 1974.

Schulz, G. *Geschichte heute: Positionen, Tendenzen und Probleme.* Göttingen, 1973.

Stone, L. *A History of the New History. The Past and Present.* Boston, 1981.


*General*

Bann, S. *The Clothing of Clio: A Study of the Representation of History in Nineteenth-Century Britain and France.* Cambridge, Engl., 1984.

Bauer, G. *Geschichtlichkeit. Wege und Irrwege eines Begriffs.* Berlin, 1963.

Commager, H. S. *The Search for a Usable Past.* New York, 1967.

Gilbert, F., and Graubard, S. R., ed. *Historical Studies Today.* New York, 1972.

Gombrich, E. H. *In Search of Cultural History.* Oxford, 1969.

Halperin, S., ed. *Some Twentieth-Century Historians.* Chicago, 1961.

Hedinger, H-W. *Subjektivität und Geschichtswissenschaft. Grundzüge einer Historik.* Berlin, 1969.

Huizinga, J. "Über eine Formveränderung der Geschichte seit der Mitte des 19. Jahrhunderts." In Huizinga, *Im Banne der Geschichte.* Zurich, 1941.

Koselleck, R. *Historia Magistra Vitae. Uber die Auflösung des Topos im Horizont neuzeitlich bewegter Geschichte.* Stuttgart, 1967.

―――. *Geschichte, Geschichten und formale Zeitstrukturen, Geschichte-Ereignis und Erzählung.* Munich, 1973.

Mandelbaum, M. *The Anatomy of Historical Knowledge.* Baltimore-London, 1977.

Murray, M. *Modern Philosophy of History: Its Origin and Destination.* The Hague, 1970.

Ortega y Gasset, J. *An Interpretation of Universal History.* Trans. Mildred Adams. New York, 1973.

Plumb, J. H. *The Death of the Past.* London, 1970.

Powicke, F. M. *Modern Historians and the Study of History.* London, 1955.

*Germany and Italy*

Berengo, M. "Italian Historical Scholarship since the Fascist Era." *Daedalus* 100 (Spring 1971):469–84.

Bourgin, G. "Histoire contemporaine d'Italie." *RH* 175 (1935):316–97.

Chickering, R. *Karl Lamprecht: A German Academic Life (1856–1915).* Atlantic Highlands, N. J., 1993.

DeFelice, R. *Mussolini il rivoluzionario.* Turin, 1965.

DeFelice, R. *Mussolini il fascista.* 2 vols. Turin, 1966–68.

DeFelice, R. *Mussolini l'Alleato.* Vol. 1., *L'Italia in guerra.* Turin, 1990.

Dorpalen, A. *German History in Marxist Perspective: The East German Approach.* Detroit, 1985.

Faulenbach, B. *Ideologie des deutschen Weges: Die deutsche Geschichte in der Historiographie zwischen Kaiserreich und Nationalsozialismus.* Munich, 1980.

Fest, J. *Hitler. A Biography.* New York, 1974.

Friedman, S. S. *The History of the Holocaust.* London, 2004.

Graus, F. "Geschichtsschreibung und Nationalsozialismus." *Vierteljahrshefte für Zeitgeschichte* 17 (1969):87–95.

*Historikerstreit. Die Dokumentation der Kontroverse um die Einzigartigkeit der nationalsozialistischen Judenvernichtung.* Munich, 1987.

Lehmann, H., and Melton, J. V. H., eds. *Pathways of Continuity: Central European Historiography from the 1930s to the 1950s.* Washington, D.C., 1994.

Maier, C. *The Unmasterable Past. History, Holocaust, and German National Identity.* Cambridge, Mass., 1988.

Salvemini, G. *The Origins of Fascism in Italy.* New York, 1973.

Schorn-Schuette, L. *Karl Lamprecht.* Göttingen, 1984.

Schulin, E., ed. *Deutsche Geschichtswissenschaft nach dem Zweiten Weltkrieg (1945–1965).* Munich, 1989.

Schulze, W. *Deutsche Geschichtswissenschaft nach 1945.* Munich, 1989.

Stone, D. ed. *The Historiography of the Holocaust.* Basingstoke, Engl., 2004.

Vierhaus, R. "Walter Frank und die Geschichtswissenschaft im nationalsozialistischen Deutschland." *HZ* (1969):207, 617–27.

Weber, W. *Priester der Klio. Historisch-sozialwissenschaftliche Studien zur Herkunft und Karriere deutscher Historiker und zur Geschichte der Geschichtswissenschaft 1899– 1970.* Frankfurt a. M., 1984.

Werner, K. F. *Das NS-Geschichtsbild und die deutsche Geschichtswissenschaft.* Stuttgart-Berlin, 1967.

Winkler, H. A. *Griff nach der Deutungsmacht: Zur Geschichte der Geschichtspolitik in Deutschland.* Göttingen, 2004.

*Modern American Historiography*

Early "Scientific" Historians

Altschuler, G. C. *Andrew D. White—Educator, Historian, Diplomat.* Ithaca, N.Y., 1979.

Cunningham, R. J. "The German Historical World of Herbert Baxter Adams: 1874–76." *Journal of American History* 68, no. 2 (1981):261–75.

Donovan, T. *Henry Adams and Brook Adams.* Norman, Okla., 1961.

Eisenstadt, A. S. *Charles McLean Andrews: A Study in American Historical Writing.* New York, 1956.

Goldman, E. F. *John Bach McMaster: American Historian.* Philadelphia, 1943.

Haines, D. "Scientific History as a Teaching Method: The Formative Years." *Journal of American History* 63 (1977):893–912.

Surveys and General Works

Ausubel, H. *Historians and Their Craft: A Study of the Presidential Addresses of the American Historical Association.* New York, 1950.

Barzun, J. *Clio and the Doctors: Psycho-History, Quanto-History, and History.* Chicago, 1974.

Billias, G. A., and Grob, G. N., eds. *American History: Retrospect and Prospect.* Riverside, N.J., 1971.

Cunliffe, M., and R. W. Winks. *Pastmasters: Some Essays on American Historians.* Westport, Conn., 1979.

Dillon, M. L. *Ulrich Bonnell Philips: Historian of the Old South.* Baton Rouge, 1985.

Fetner, G. L. *Immersed in Great Affairs: Allan Nevins and the Heroic Age of American History.* Albany, 2004.

FitzGerald, F. *America Revised. History Schoolbooks in the Twentieth Century.* Boston, 1979.

Foner, E., ed. *The New American History.* Philadelphia, 1990.

Higham, J. *Writing American History: Essays on Modern Scholarship.* Bloomington, Ind., 1970.

Kammen, M. *The Past before Us: Contemporary Historical Writing in the United States.* Ithaca, N.Y., 1980.

Novick, P. *That Noble Dream: The "Objectivity Question" and the American Profession. New York, 1988.*

Skotheim, R. A. *American Intellectual Histories and Historians.* Princeton, 1966.

Wish, H., ed. *American Historians: A Selection.* New York, 1962.

"New History," Progressive History, Consensus History, The New Left

Abelove, H., et al., eds. *Visions of History.* New York, 1983.

Billington, R. A. *The Frontier Thesis: Valid Interpretation of American History?* Chicago, 1966.

————, ed. *The Reinterpretation of Early American History.* San Marino, Calif., 1966.

————. *Frederick Jackson Turner.* New York, 1973.

Breisach, E. *American Progressive History: An Experiment in Modernization.* Chicago, 1993.

Brown, R. E. *Carl Becker on History and the American Revolution.* East Lansing, Mich., 1970.

Green, J. R. "American Radical Historians on Their Heritage." *PP,* 69 (1975):122–30.

Hofstadter, R. *The Progressive Historians.* New York, 1968.

Jacobs, W. R., ed. *The Historical World of Frederick Jackson Turner.* New Haven, 1968.

Marcell, D. W. "Charles Beard: Civilization and the Revolt against Empiricism." *American Quarterly* 21 (1969):65–86.

Siracusa, J. M. *New Left Diplomatic History and Historians: The American Revisionists.* Port Washington, N.Y., 1973.

Sternsher, B. *Consensus, Conflict, and American Historians.* Bloomington, Ind., 1975.

Strout, C. *The Pragmatic Revolt in American History: Carl Becker and Charles Beard.* New Haven, Conn., 1958.

White, M. G. *Social Thought in America: The Revolt against Formalism.* New York, 1949.

Wilkins, B. T. *Carl Becker.* Cambridge, Mass., 1961.

## History of Women and Minorities

Affeldt, W., and A. Kuhn, eds. *Frauen in der Geschichte.* Düsseldorf, 1986.

Bernal, M. *Black Athena The Afroasiatic Roots of Classical Civilization.* 2 vols. New Brunswick, N. J.,1987–91.

Duby, G. and M. Perrot, eds. *A History of Women in the West.* 5 vols. Cambridge, Mass., 1994–96.

Freedman, E. B. *Intimate Matters: A History of Sexuality in America.* New York, 1988.

Grimal, P., ed. *Historie mondiale de la femme.* Paris, 1966.

Hausen, K. ed. *Frauen suchen ihre Geschichte: Historische Studien zum 19. und 20. Jahrhundert.* Munich, 1983.

Hine, D. C. *The State of Afro-American History: Past, Present, and Future.* Baton Route, 1986.

Hufton, O. *The Prospects Before Her: A History of Women in Western Europe, 500–1800.* London 1995.

Kelly, J. W. *Women, History and Theory: Essays.* Chicago, 1984.

Lefkowitz, M. R., and Rogers, G. M. *Black Athena Revisited.* Durham, N.C., 1996.

Martin, C. *The American Indian and the Problem of History.* New York, 1987.

Meier, A., and Rudwick, E. *Black History and the Historical Profession: 1915–1980.* Urbana, Ill., 1986.

Nicholson, Linda, J. *Gender and History.* New York, 1986.

Ofen, K., et al. *Writing Women's History: International Perspectives.* Bloomington, Ind., 1991.

Partner, N., ed. *Studying Medieval Women.* Cambridge, Mass., 1993.

Quarles, B. *Black Mosaic: Essays in Afro-American History and Historiography.* Amherst, Mass. 1988.

Scott, J. W. *Gender and the Politics of History.* New York, 1988.
———. "Women's History," in P. Burke, ed. *New Perspectives in Historical Writing.* Cambridge, 1991.
Shapiro, A.-L., ed. *History and Feminist Theory.* HT, Beiheft, 31 (1991).
Smith, B. G. *Gender of History: Men, Women, and Historical Practice.* Cambridge, Mass., 1998.
Sicherman, B., et al. *Recent United States Scholarship on the History of Women.* Washington, D.C., 1980.

*The Debate on the Nature of History*

General

Fischer, D. H. *Historians' Fallacies: Toward a Logic of Historical Thought.* New York, 1970.
Goldstein, L. J. *Historical Knowing.* Austin, Texas, 1976.
Murray, M. E. *Modern Philosophy of History: Its Origin and Destination.* The Hague, 1970.
Postan, M. M. *Fact and Relevance. Essays on Historical Method.* Cambridge, 1971.
Teggart, F. J. *Prolegomena to History.* Berkeley, 1916.
———. *Theory and Processes of History.* Berkeley, 1977.
White, M. *Foundations of Historical Knowledge.* New York, 1965.

Positivist and Analytical Views

Acham, K. *Analytische Geschichtsphilosophie. Eine kritische Einführung.* Munich, 1974.
Atkinson, R. F. *Knowledge and Explanation in History: An Introduction to the Philosophy of History.* Ithaca, N.Y., 1978.
Dray, W. H. *Laws, and Explanation in History.* London, 1964.
———. *Philosophy of History.* Englewood Cliffs, N.J., 1964.
Fain, H. *Between Philosophy and History: The Resurrection of Speculative Philosophy of History within the Analytic Tradition.* Princeton, 1970.
Gallie, W. B. *Philosophy and the Historical Understanding.* 2d ed. New York, 1968.
Gardiner, P. *The Nature of Historical Explanation.* New York-Oxford, 1952.
Popper, K. R. *The Poverty of Historicism.* New York, 1964.
Walsh, W. H. *An Introduction to Philosophy of History.* 3d ed. London, 1967.

Historicist, Idealist, and Existentialist Views

Ales Bello, A. *Edmund Husserl e la storia.* Parma, 1972.
Antoni, C. *From History to Sociology: The Transition in German Historical Thinking.* Detroit, 1959.
Berlin, I. *The Hedgehog and the Fox: An Essay on Tolstoy's View of History.* New York, 1953.
———. *Historical Inevitability.* London, 1955.
Bianco, F. *Dilthey e la genesi della critica storica della ragione.* Milan, 1973.
Bulhof, I. N. *Wilhelm Dilthey.* Boston, 1980.
Carr, H. W. *The Philosophy of Benedetto Croce: The Problem of Art and History.* New York, 1969.
Engel-Janosi, F. *The Growth of German Historicism.* Baltimore, 1944.
English, J. C. "Existentialism and the Study of History." *Social Science* 41 (June 1966):153–60.

Ermarth, M. *Wilhelm Dilthey.* Chicago, 1978.

*Essays on Historicism. HT,* Beiheft 14 (1975).

Heussi, K. *Die Krise des Historismus.* Tübingen, 1932.

Hodges, H. A. *The Philosophy of Wilhelm Dilthey.* London, 1952.

Holborn, H. "Wilhelm Dilthey and the Critique of Historical Reason." *JHI* 11 (1950):93– 118.

Krausz, M., ed. *Critical Essays on the Philosophy of R. G. Collingwood.* London-New York, 1972.

Lee, D. E., and Beck, R. N. "The Meaning of 'Historicism.'" *American Historical Review* 59 (1954):568–77.

Makkreell, R. A. *Dilthey: Philosopher of Human Studies.* Princeton, 1975.

Masur, G. "Wilhelm Dilthey and the History of Ideas." *JHI* 13 (January 1952):94–107.

Meinecke, F. *Die Entstehung des Historismus.* Munich, 1936.

Miller, J. *History and Human Existence.* Berkeley, 1979.

Mink, L. O. *Mind, History, and Dialectic: The Philosophy of R. G. Collingwood.* Bloom- ington-London, 1969.

Mommsen, W. J. *The Political and Social Theory of Max Weber.* Chicago, 1989.

Munz, P. *The Shapes of Time: A New Look at the Philosophy of History.* Middletown, Conn., 1977.

Oakeshott, M. *On History.* Oxford, 1983.

Owensby, J. *Dilthey and the Narrative of History.* Ithaca, NY, 1994.

Rickman, H. P. *Wilhelm Dilthey: Pioneer of the Human Studies.* Berkeley, 1979.

Roberts, D. D. *Benedetto Croce and the Uses of Historicism.* Berkeley, Calif., 1987.

Runciman, W. G. *A Critique of Max Weber's Philosophy of Social Science.* Cambridge, 1972.

Sprigge, J. S. *Benedetto Croce, Man and Thinker.* New Haven, 1952.

The Critical Theory

Feenberg, A. *Lukács, Marx, and the Sources of Critical Theory.* Totowa, N.J., 1981.

Groh, D. *Kritische Geschichtswissenschaft in emanzipatorischer Absicht.* Stuttgart, 1973.

Jay, M. *The Dialectical Imagination: A History of the Frankfurt School and the Institute of Social Research, 1923–1950.* Boston, 1973.

McCarthy, T. *The Critical Theory of Jürgen Habermas.* Cambridge, Mass., 1978.

Tar, Z. *The Frankfurt School: The Critical Theories of Max Horkheimer and Theodor W. Adorno.* New York, 1977.

Wiggerhaus, R. *The Frankfurt School: Its History, Theories and Significance.* Translated by Michael Robinson. Cambridge, Mass., 1994.


*Economic Interpretations*

General

Engerman, S. L., and Fogel, R. W. *The Reinterpretation of American Economic History.* New York, 1971.

Fogel, R. W. "The New Economic History: Its Findings and Its Methods." *Economic His- tory Review,* ser. 2, 19, no. 3 (1966):642–56.

Fogel, R. W., and Engerman, S. *Time on the Cross: The Economics of American Negro Slavery.* 2 vols. Boston, 1974.

Gerschenkron, A. *Continuity in History and Other Essays.* Cambridge, Mass., 1968.

Hershlag, Z. Y. "Theory of the Stages of Economic Growth in Historical Perspective." *Kyklos* 22 (1969):661–90.

Kindleberger, C. P. *Historical Economics: Art of Science?* New York, 1906.

Kuczynski, J. *Zur Geschichte der Wirtschaftsgeschichtsschreibung.* Berlin, 1978.

Levy-Leboyer, M. "La ~'New Economic history'." *Annales: Economies, Sociétés, Civilisations* 24 (1969):1035–69.

McClellan, P. D. *Causal Explanation and Model Building in History, Economics, and the New Economic History.* New York, 1975.

See, H. *The Economic Interpretation of History.* New York, 1929.

Temin, P., ed. *The New Economic History.* Harmondsworth, 1972.

### The Marxist Theory of History

Adamson, W. A. *Hegemony and Revolutions. Antonio Gramsci's Political and Cultural Theory.* Berkeley, Cal., 1980.

Barber, J. *Soviet Historians in Crisis, 1928–1932.* New York, 1981.

Bober, M. M. *Karl Marx's Interpretation of History.* Cambridge, Mass., 1927; reprint, 1965.

Cohen, G. A. *Karl Marx's Theory of History. A Defence.* Oxford, 1978.

Fleischer, H. *Marxism and History.* Trans. Eric Mosbacher. London, 1973.

Gandy, R. *Marx and History.* Austin, Texas, 1979.

Geyer, D. *Klio in Moskau und die sowjetische Geschichte.* Heidelberg, 1985.

Heer, N. W. *Politics and History in the Soviet Union.* Cambridge, Mass., 1971.

Hösler, Joachim. *Die Sowjetische Geschichtswissenschaft 1953 bis 1991.* Munich, 1995.

Jameson, F. *Postmodernism or the Cultural Logic of Late Capitalism.* London, 1991.

Karkwick, R. D. *Rewriting History in Soviet Russia: The Politics of Revisionist Historiography, 1956–1974.* Basingstoke, Engl., 2001.

Kaye, H. J. *The British Marxist Historians: An Introductory Analysis.* New York, 1984.

Kolakowski, L. *Marxism and Beyond: On Historical Understanding and Individual Responsibility.* Trans. Jane Zielonko Pell. London, 1969.

Lichtheim, G., ed. *George Lukács.* New York-London, 1970.

McLennan, G. *Marxism and the Methodologies of History.* London, 1981.

Mazour, A. G. *The Writing of History in the Soviet Union.* Stanford, 1971.

Petrovic, G. *Marx in the Mid-Twentieth Century.* New York, 1967.

Pundeff, M. *History in the U.S.S.R.* Stanford, Calif., 1967.

Rader, M. *Marx's Interpretation of History.* New York, 1979.

Seiffert, H. *Marxismus und bürgerliche Wissenschaft.* Munich, 1971.

Shaw, W. H. *Marx's Theory of History.* Stanford, Calif., 1978.

Shtepa, K. *Russian Historians and the Soviet State.* New Brunswick, N.J., 1962.

### *Psychohistory*

Brown, N. O. *Life against Death: The Psychoanalytical Meaning of History.* Middletown, Conn., 1959.

Cocks, G., and Crosby, T., eds. *Psychohistory.* New Haven, 1987.

Erikson, E. H. *Young Man Luther.* New York, 1958.

Friedlander, S. *History and Psychoanalysis: An Inquiry into the Possibilities and Limits of Psychohistory.* New York-London, 1978.

Gay, P. *Freud for Historians.* New York, 1985.

Gilmore, W. J. *Psychohistorical Inquiry: A Comprehensive Research Bibliography.* New York, 1984.

Kren, G. M., and Rappoport, L. H. *Varieties of Psychohistory.* New York, 1976.

Loewenberg, P. *Decoding the Past: The Psychoanalytic Approach.* New York, 1983.

Mause, L. *Foundations of Psychohistory.* New York, 1982.

Mazlish, B. *Psychoanalysis and History.* New York, 1971.

Pomper, P. *The Structure of the Mind: Five Major Figures in Psychohistory.* New York, 1985.

Runyan, W. K. *Psychology and Historical Interpretation.* New York, 1988.

Stannard, D. E. *Shrinking History: On Freud and the Failure of Psychohistory.* New York, 1980.

Weinstein, F. *History and Theory after the Fall.* Chicago, 1990.

#### Quantitative History

Aydelotte, W. O. *Quantification in History.* Reading, Mass., 1971.

Aydelotte, W. O., Bogue, A. G., Fogel, R. W., eds. *The Dimensions of Quantitative Research in History.* Princeton, 1972.

Benson, L. *Toward the Scientific Study of History.* Philadelphia, 1972.

Kurgan, G., and Moureaux, Ph., eds. *La Quantification en histoire.* Brussels, 1973.

Lee, C. H. *The Quantitative Approach to Economic History.* New York, 1977.

*Studies in Quantitative History and the Logic of the Social Sciences. HT,* Beiheft 9 (1969).

Swierenga, R. R., ed. *Quantification in American History: Theory and Research.* New York, 1970.

#### Social and Structural History

Allegra, L., and Torre, A. *La nascità della storia sociale in Francia: Dalla Commune alle "Annales."* Turin, 1977.

Beidelman, T. O. "Lèvi-Strauss and History." *Journal of Interdisciplinary History.* 1 (1971):511–25.

Bosl, K., "Der soziologische Aspekt in der Geschichte. Wertfreie Geschichtswissenschaft und Idealtypus." *HZ* 201 (1965):613–30.

Burke, P. *The French Historical Revolution: The 'Annales' School, 1929–89.* Stanford, Calif., 1990.

Deleuze, G. *Foucault.* Paris, 1986.

Dreyfus, H. L., and Rabinow, P. *Michel Foucault: Beyond Structuralism and Hermeneutics.* 2d ed. Chicago, 1983.

Eribon, D. *Foucault.* trans. Betsy Wong. Cambridge, Mass., 1991.

Febvre, L. *A New Kind of History,* ed. Peter Burke, trans. K. Folca. London, 1973.

Fink, C. *Marc Bloch: A Life in History.* Cambridge, Eng., 1989.

Furet, F. "L'Histoire quantitative et la construction du fait historique." *Annales: Economies, Sociétés, Civilisations* 26 (1971):63–75.

Groh, D. "Strukturgeschichte als totale Geschichte." *Vierteljahresschrift für Sozial- und Wirtschaftsgeschichte* 58 (1971).

Iggers, G. G. "Die 'Annales' und ihre Kritiker. Probleme moderner französischer Sozialgeschichte." *HZ* 219 (1974):578–608.

———. *Ein anderer historischer Blick. Beispiele ostdeutscher Sozialgeschichte.* Frankfurt a. M., 1991.

Lai, C.-C. *Braudel's Historiography Reconsidered.* Dallas, Tx, 2004.

Nugent, W. *Structures of American Social History.* Bloomington, Ind., 1981.

Smart, Barry. *Michel Foucault.* London, 1985.
Stoianovich, T. *French Historical Method: The Annales Paradigm.* Ithaca-London, 1976.
Wehler, H.-U. *Geschichte als historische Sozialwissenschaft.* Frankfurt am M. 1977.

*New Perspectives, Fields, and Methods*
Berkhoffer, R. F., Jr. *A Behavioral Approach to Historical Analysis.* New York, 1969.
Burke, P. *History and Social Theory.* Ithaca, N.Y., 1992.
Dumoulin, J., and Moisi, D., eds. *The Historian between the Ethnologist and the Futurologist.* Paris-The Hague, 1973.
Frisch, M. "American Urban History as an Example of Recent Historiography." *HT* 18(3):350–77.
Furet, F. *Interpreting the French Revolution.* Cambridge, 1981.
Ginsburg, C. *Clues, Myths, and the Historical Method.* Translated by John Tedeschi and Ann C. Tedeschi. Baltimore, 1989.
Goldman, E. F., ed. *Historiography and Urbanization.* Baltimore, 1941.
Handlin, O., and Burchard, J. *The Historians and the City.* Cambridge, Mass., 1963.
Hollinger, D. A. *In the American Province: Studies in the History and Historiography of Ideas.* Bloomington, Ind., 1985.
Hollingsworth, T. H. *Historical Demography.* London, 1969.
Hunt, L., ed. *The New Cultural History.* Berkeley, Cal., 1989.
Lewis, I. M., ed. *History and Social Anthropology.* A.S.A. Monographs, no. 7. London, 1970.
Lüdtke, A., ed. *Alltagsgeschichte.* Frankfurt a. M., 1989.
McDonald, T. J. *The Historical Turn in the Human Sciences.* Ann Arbor, 1992.
Vansina, J. *Oral Tradition: A Study in Historical Methodology.* London, 1961.
Wilson, A. "The Infancy of the History of Childhood: An Appraisal of Philippe Ariès." *HT* 19 (1980):132–53.

## Narrativism, the Literary Turn, and Postmodernism

Ankersmit, F. R. *The Reality Effect in the Writing of History.* Amsterdam, 1989.
Ankersmit, F. R. and H. Kellner, eds. *A New Philosophy of History.* Chicago, 1995.
Appleby, J., L. Hunt, and M. Jacob. *Telling the Truth about History.* New York, 1994.
Berkhofer, Robert. F. *Beyond the Great Story. History as Text and Discourse.* Cambridge, Mass., 1995.
Bonnel, V. E. and L. Hunt, eds. *Beyond the Cultural Turn.* Berkeley, Cal., 1999.
Breisach, E. *On the Future of History: The Postmodernist Challenge and its Aftermath.* Chicago, 2003.
Canary, R. H., and H. Kozicki, eds. *The Writing of History: Literary Form and Historical Understanding.* Madison, Wis., 1978.
Carr, D. *Time, Narrative and History.* Bloomington, Ind., 1986.
Chartier, R. *Cultural History: Between Practices and Representations.* Translated by L. G. Cochrane. Ithaca, NY, 1988.
Clark, J. C. D. *Our Shadowed Past: Modernism, Postmodernism, and History.* Cambridge, Mass., 2004.
Danto, A. *Narration and Knowledge.* New York, 1985.

Evans, R. *In Defence of History.* New York, 1999.

Fukuyama, F. *The End of History and the Last Man.* New York, 1992.

Gossman, L. *Between History and Literature.* Cambridge, Mass., 1990.

Himmelfarb, G. *The New History and the Old: Critical Essays and Reappraisals.* Rev. ed., Cambridge, Mass., 2004.

Hoesterey, I. *Zeitgeist in Babel. The Postmodernist Controversy.* Bloomington, Ind., 1991.

Jenkins, K. *Rethinking History.* London, 2003.

Koselleck, R., and H-G. Gadamer. *Hermeneutik und Historik.* Heidelberg, 1987.

LaCapra, D. *History and Criticism.* Ithaca, N.Y., 1985.

LaCapra, D., and S. L. Kaplan, eds. *Modern European Intellectual History: Reappraisals and New Perspectives.* Ithaca, N.Y., 1982.

Levi, G. "On Microhistory." In *New Perspectives on Historical Writing,* 2nd ed., edited by Peter Burke. University Park, Penn., 2001.

Niethammer, L. *Posthistoire. Has History Come to an End?* Translated by Patrick Camiller. London, 1992.

Norris, C. *Derrida.* Cambridge, Mass., 1987.

Palmer, B. *Descent into Discourse: The Reification of Language and the Writing of Social History.* Philadelphia, 1989.

Poster, M. *Foucault, Marxism, and History.* New York, 1984.

*Reassessing Collingwood. HT.* Beiheft 29 (1990).

Shapiro, A.-L., ed. *History and Feminist Theory. HT,* Beiheft 31.

Taylor, D. S. *A Bibliography of the Publications and Manuscripts of R. G. Collingwood, with Selective Annotations. HT* Beiheft 24 (1985).

*The Representation of Historical Events. HT* Beiheft 26 (1987).

Thomas, B. *The New Historicism and Other Old-fashioned Topics.* Princeton, 1991.

Veeser, H. A., ed. *The New Historicism.* New York, 1989.

Weinsheimer, J. C. *Gadamer's Hermeneutics: A Reading of Truth and Method.* New Haven, 1985.

White, H. *Metahistory: The Historical Imagination in the Nineteenth Century Europe.* Baltimore, 1973.

White, H. *The Content of the Form: Narrative Discourse and Historical Representation.* Baltimore, 1987.

Windshuttle, K. *The Killing of History: How Literary and Social Theorists are Murdering Our Past.* New York, 1997.

## Universal and World History

*Historical and Philosophical Interpretations*

Aron, R. *Introduction à la philosophie de l'histoire.* Paris, 1938.

Brocke, B. v. *Kurt Breysig, Geschichtswissenschaft zwischen Historismus und Soziologie.* Lübeck-Hamburg, 1971.

Butterfield, H. et al. *Sir Herbert Butterfield, Cho Yun Hsu, and William H. McNeill on Chinese and World History.* Hong Kong, 1970.

Costello, P. *World Historians and Their Goals.* DeKalb, 1993.

Farrenkopf, John. *Prophet of Decline. Oswald Spengler on World History and Politics.* Baton Rouge, 2001.

Fuchs, E. and B. Stuchtey. *Across Cultural Borders: Historiography in Global Perspective.* Lanham, Md. 2002.

Green, W. A. *History, Historians, and the Dynamics of Change.* Westport, Conn., 1993.

Guha, R. *History at the Limit of World History.* New York, 2002.

Huntington, E. *Civilization and Climate.* New Haven, 1933.

Jaspers, K. *The Origin and Goal of History.* New Haven, 1953.

Kon, I. S. *Die Geschichtsphilosophie des 20. Jahrhunderts.* 2 vols. Berlin, 1964.

Lessing, T. *Geschichte als Sinngebung des Sinnlosen.* Munich, 1921.

Löwith, K. *Weltgeschichte und Heilsgeschehen. Die theologischen Voraussetzungen der Geschichtsphilosophie.* Stuttgart, 1953.

———. *Permanence and Change: Lectures on the Philosophy of History.* Cape Town, 1969.

Jung, T. *Vom Ende der Geschichte. Rekonstruktionen in kritischer Absicht.* Münster, 1989.

Ludz, P. C. *Spengler heute.* Munich, 1980.

McNeill, W. H. *Arnold J. Toynbee: A Life.* New York, 1989.

Meyerhoff, H. *The Philosophy of History in Our Time.* Garden City, N.Y., 1959.

Mommsen, W. J. *Die Geschichtswissenschaft jenseits des Historismus.* Droste, 1971.

Nolte, H.-H. *Weltsystem und Geschichte.* Göttingen, 1985.

Pomper, P., R. H. Elphick, and R. T.Vann, eds. *World History: Ideologies, Structures, and Identities.* Malden, Mass., 1998.

Riesterer, B. *Karl Löwith's View of History: A Critical Appraisal of Historicism.* The Hague, 1969.

Schnadelbach, H. *Geschichtsphilosophie nach Hegel. Die Probleme des Historismus.* Freiburg-Munich, 1974.

Stromberg, R. N. *Arnold J. Toynbee, Historian for the Age of Crisis.* Carbondale, Ill., 1972.

Stuchtey, B. and E. Fuchs, eds. *Writing World History 1800–2000.* New York, 2003.

Thompson, K. W. *Toynbee's Philosophy of History and Politics.* Baton Rouge, 1985.

Troeltsch, E. *Der Historismus und seine Probleme.* In *Gesammelte Schriften* 3, Tübingen, 1912–25.

Voegelin, E. *Order and History.* 4 vols. Baton Rouge, 1956–74.

Wallerstein, I. *The Modern World-System.* 3 vols. New York, 1974–89.

Webb, E. *Eric Voegelin: Philosopher of History.* Seattle-London, 1981.

Wehler, H.-U. *Modernisierungstheorie und Geschichte.* Göttingen, 1975.

Wells, H. G. *The New and Revised Outline of History.* Garden City, N.Y., 1931.

Winetrout, K. *Arnold Toynbee: The Ecumenical Vision.* Boston, 1975.

Wojtecki, A. W. *Vom Untergang des Abendlandes; zyklische, organische und morphologische Geschichtstheorien im 19. und 20. Jahrhundert.* Berlin, 2002.

*Christian Views*

Berkhof, H. *Christ: The Meaning of History.* Richmond, Va., 1966.

Bravo, F. *La Vision de l'histoire chez Teilhard de Chardin.* Paris, 1970.

Bultmann, R. *The Presence of Eternity: History and Eschatology.* New York, 1957.

Butterfield, H. *Christianity and History.* New York, 1950.

Daniélou, J. "The Conception of History in the Christian Tradition." *Journal of Religion* 30 (1950):171–77.

Dawson, C. *Progress and Religion: A Historical Enquiry.* New York, 1929.

―――. *The Dynamics of World History.* New York, 1956.

Faricy, R. L. *Teilhard De Chardin's Theology of the Christian in the World.* New York, 1967.

Guthrie, H. H. *God and History in the Old Testament.* Greenwich, Conn., 1970.

Gutierrez, G. *The Theology of Liberation: History, Politics, and Salvation.* New York, 1973.

Hobert, M. "History and Religion in the Thought of Herbert Butterfield." *JHI* 32 (October–December 1971):543–4.

Keyes, G. L. *Christian Faith and the Interpretation of History.* Lincoln, Neb., 1966.

Löwith, K. *Meaning in History: The Theological Implications of the Philosophy of History.* Chicago, 1950.

McIntire, C. T. *God, History, and Historians: An Anthology of Modern Christian Views of History.* New York, 1977.

―――, ed. *Writings on Christianity and History.* New York, 1979.

MacKenzie, R. *Faith and History in the Old Testament.* Minneapolis, 1963.

Marsden, G., and Roberts, F., ed. *A Christian View of History?* Grand Rapids, 1975.

Moltmann, J. *The Theology of Hope.* New York, 1967.

Niebuhr, R. *Beyond Tragedy: Essays on the Christian Interpretation of History.* New York, 1937.

―――. *Faith and History: A Comparison of Christian and Modern Views of History.* New York, 1949.

Pannenberg, W. *Theology and the Kingdom of God.* Philadelphia, 1969.

Patrides, C. A. *The Grand Design of God: The Literary Form of the Christian View of History.* London, 1972.

Reinitz, R. *Irony and Consciousness: American Historiography and Reinhold Niebuhr's Vision.* East Brunswick, N.J., 1981.

Rienstra, M. H. "Christianity and History: A Bibliographic Essay." In *A Christian View of History?,* ed. G. Marsden, F. Roberts. Grand Rapids, 1975.

Teilhard de Chardin, P. *The Phenomenon of Man.* New York, 1965.

Tillich, P. *The Interpretation of History.* New York, 1936.

Young, N. J. *History and Existential Theology: the Role of History in the Thought of Rudolf Bultmann,* Philadelphia, 1969.

# · INDEX ·

## Persons and Anonymous Works

481

# ·INDEX·

# Subjects